William Faubion's

You are cordially invited
to the

BEST CHOICES
IN
WESTERN WASHINGTON

For additional copies, write or call:
Gable & Gray, The Book Publishers
1307 West Main Street
Medford, Oregon 97501
In Oregon: 1-800-622-7753
Outside Oregon: 1-800-522-7753

Published in the U.S.A.

Gable & Gray Publishing "Best Choice Series"

SERIES # 1	Best Choices in the Rural N.Willamette Valley: 1985
SERIES # 2	Best Choices on the Oregon Coast: 1986
SERIES # 3	Best Choices on the Oregon Interstate: 1986
SERIES # 4	Best Choices in Central and Eastern Oregon: 1987
SERIES # 5	Best Choices in Portland / N. Willamette :1987
SERIES # 6	Best Choices In N.California/Bay Area: 1987
SERIES # 7	Best Choices in Northern California: 1987
SERIES # 8	Best Choices in Western Washington: 1987
SERIES # 9	Best Choices in San Diego: 1987
SERIES #10	Best Choices in Orange County: 1987
SERIES #11	Best Choices in Sacramento: 1987
SERIES #12	Best Choices along the California Coast: 1987
SERIES #13	Best Choices in Arizona: 1987
SERIES #14	Best Choices in Colorado: 1987
SERIES #15	Best Choices in Seattle: 1987
SERIES #16	Best Choices in Houston: 1987
SERIES #17	Best Choices in Dallas: 1987
SERIES #18	Best Choices in San Antonio: 1987
SERIES #19	Best Choices in Tampa: 1987
SERIES #20	Best Choices in Orlando: 1987
SERIES #21	Best Choices in Vancouver, B.C.: 1987
SERIES #22	Best Choices in Edmonton/Calgary: 1987
SERIES #23	Best Choices in Eastern Washington: 1987
SERIES #24	Best Choices in Western Oregon: 1987
SERIES #25	Best Choices in Los Angeles: 1987
SERIES #26	Best Choices in Utah: 1987
SERIES #27	Best Choices in New Mexico: 1988
SERIES #28	Best Choices in Idaho: 1988
SERIES #29	Best Choices in Kansas City: 1988
SERIES #30	Best Choices in Minneapolis/St. Paul: 1988

Copyright© 1987 by Gable & Gray, The Book Publishers
All rights reserved. No part of this book may be reproduced in any form or by an electronic means, including information storage and retrieval systems, without permission in writing from the author, except by a reviewer who may quote brief passages in a review.

Library of Congress Catalog Card Number: 87-081992
ISBN: 0-9615833-7-1   First Edition 1987

Editor	Carole Johnson
Associate Editor	Jane Picknell
Associate Editor	Joseph R. Kiefer II
Author	Eric Larson
Cover design	Laura Kay
Cover Photography	Karl Weatherly
Maps	David Ruppe
Business Manager	Debbie Winters
Bookkeeper	Vicki Nelson
Secretary	Sherrie Reynolds

FOREWARD

Discover a variety rarely found in a single state. Explore Western Washington as defined by the imposing Cascade Mountain Range. Diversity in a full range of appeal is apparent, from the newly designated Columbia Gorge National Scenic area with its basalt cliffs and forests, home to the second-largest monolith in the United States, Beacon Rock, to the only rain forests in North America, clamming on the rocky beaches, or enjoying the vistas of rugged mountains and the placid lakes found along the Olympic Peninsula. Enjoy a world of water, whether it be a ferry boat trip, kayaking the San Juan Islands, pleasure craft on the rivers, or whitewater raft the rapids, catch that salmon you've always wanted, explore the naval shipyards at Bremerton, or drive along the Hood Canal. It's all here...and more.

Western Washington, with its heritage of Scandinavian, Dutch and Norwegian communities, welcomes you to a fresh, clean environment, from the state's cosmopolitan cities of Olympia, Tacoma, Bellevue and Seattle to the towns and villages of Mukiteo, Friday Harbor or Vashon. Savor Washington's distinctive premium wines. Locally produced, rich Cabernet Sauvignon, a spicy Gewürztraminer or a resilient Riesling. Raised and bottled from the Olympic Peninsula to the Blue Mountains. It's all here...and more.

Washington, noted as the world's apple capital also brings you month's of unending winter recreation for snowmobiling, snowshoe hikes, ice fishing and the cross-country or downhill skiier. Hike the nation's longest trail, the Pacific Crest Trail. It scales Mount Adams and affords views of towering Mount Rainier and smoldering Mount St. Helens. There's more to do...more to see...more unique shops and shopowners with just the right selection of marvelous items to enhance your life. As I keep saying, "It's all here."

You'll find hundreds of recreational and cultural opportunities. Each county outlined offers individual attractions, unique experiences and a broad variety of scenic and historical contrasts. You'll find the same type of allure and diversity, which the country has, in the "Best Choice" businesses listed in this book. You'll find new places and new friends where you'll feel very comfortable. People who work hard and care very much about their products and the service delivered.

In addition to the business owners, who contributed their time and tales to this book, I would also like to thank other members of the hard working crew who helped do the work necessary to bring this book to fruition. My sincere thanks goes to William Faubion, the publisher, whose creativity, positive attitude and tenacity made this book possible. Debbie Winters who brought her extraordinary communication skills to bear in smoothing out administrative snags and was also responsible for having the foresight to bring Carole Johnson, our editor, to us.

As Managing Editor, Carole has added a polished professionalism to our editorial staff. She maintains a great sense of humor while dealing with mountains of paper and juggling time, people and resources to meet unmeetable deadlines. Carole manages by example. She is always the first person to fearlessly dive into new territory, tackling things which I hope remain a mystery to me, and coming back with a workable, understandable plan to make things better and run smoother.

Associate Editor Jane Picknell does an excellent job serving as the liaison with the business owners, gathering and deciminating information and re-editing their stories, when necessary. Her quick wit keeps everyone here on their toes; while at the same time knocking us off our feet.

Associate Editor Joseph Kiefer II is a new addition to our editorial staff, but an old hand at writing. Many of the articles within this book, if they're witty and have received written praise from the shop owners, are Joe's work.

Contributing writers, noted for their flexibility-under-fire, are: Sherry O'Sullivan, Liz Redler, Roy Scarborough, Joan Wood and Mark Roseland. An especial thanks is due Tam Moore for his contributions to the county and city introductions. Technical computer advice was given by Scott McKay and special software programming by Loren Martin.

My final thanks go to Dale Birdsell and Linda Janson for their consistently being available, on short notice, to travel through Western Washington to personally contact owners for first-hand information about their businesses. Dale, a native Washingtonian, a former Professor of Microbiology at the University of Washington, provided me with the impetus to produce the highest quality, comprehensive travel guide I was capable of engendering. Linda grew up in Latah on a wheat farm. She has a great appreciation of the outdoors and the wilderness beauty of this state. A graduate of the University of Washington; she now is a resident of Seattle area and great proponent of the theatre and nightlife offerings of the capital city. The staff was further augmented by the services of Alan Diede, James Bailey, Greg Thorson, Paul Mertz, Joe Stanavich, William Chubb, Gerald Ford and Beverly Little.

These people were the backbone of our organization and share my goal to bring you the best travel book available. I hope this book will help open up Western Washington to you and make your travels more exciting.

HOW TO USE THIS BOOK

This book is set up with the counties of Western Washington listed in alphabetical order, with each county being a chapter. Each chapter begins with an introduction highlighting that county's major highways and cities, climate and topography and a smattering of history. Following the county introductions are pieces about points of interest within the county's public lands and a list of attractions relating to such things as museums, scenic tours and state parks. Two consistently used abbreviations relating to roadways are SR, which relates to Washington state highways, and FR, which refers to national forest roads.

A profile of the major cities in each county is next, with information about the "Best Choices" of that city listed alphabetically by category and by name. The page on which each of these headings appear within each chapter is listed in the Table of Contents. The Index in the back of the book is your easy-to-use guide for finding what page each specific attraction and business is listed. If you would like to have a day adventure and good food, try one of our self-guided tours listed within or at the end of each chapter. Many of the state parks listed here include prime attractions, camping amenities and boating facilities.

DEDICATION

To Karl and Maxine Larson, my parents, whose life together in the Pacific Northwest has brought them adventure, joy, shared love, great strength and wisdom.

To them I dedicate this book, and in doing so thank them for their caring contribution to my development and that of my eight brothers and sisters: Lynn, Alan, John, Susan, Joanne, Kristine, Andrew and Karl, Jr. Collectively, my family provides me with loving support and boundless resources. With these riches I go forth with confidence and the knowledge that the future holds no obstacles that cannot be surmounted.

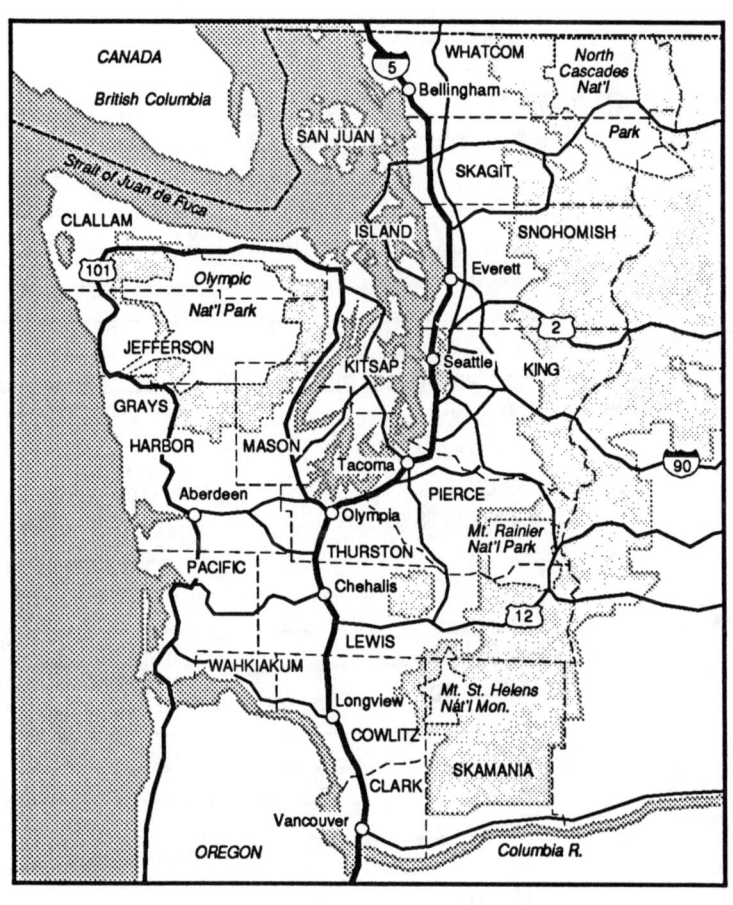

TABLE OF CONTENTS

CLALLAM COUNTY 1
  Olympic National Park 1
  Carlsborg 4
  Dungeness 4
  La Push 5
      Resort 5
  Port Angeles 5
      Art Gallery 7
      Bed and Breakfast 7
      Gift Shops 7
      Golf Course 9
      Resort 9
      Restaurants 10
  Sequim 11
      Accommodations 11
      Antiques 12
      Art Gallery 13
      Attraction 13
      Bakery 13
      Deli 14
      Farm 14
      Florist 15
      Golf 15
      Marina 16
      Restaurant 17
      Wine 18

CLARK COUNTY 20
  Battle Ground 22
  Brush Prairie 23
      Golf Course 23
  Vancouver 24

Accommodations	25
Antiques	27
Bakery	27
Craft Supplies	28
Delicatessen	28
Florist	29
Food Store	29
Gift Shop	30
Golf Course	30
Restaurant	31
Wine	32
Yacolt	33
Attraction	33
COWLITZ COUNTY	**34**
Mount Saint Helens	35
Ariel	38
Gift Shop	38
Cougar	39
Chamber of Commerce	39
Market	40
Pottery	40
Restaurant	41
Kelso	41
Accommodations	42
Antiques	43
Restaurant	43
Longview	44
Antiques	45
Art Gallery	45
Books	46
Delicatessen	46
Florist	47
Restaurant	48
GRAYS HARBOR COUNTY	**50**
Aberdeen	52
Accommodations	53

Delicatessen	54
Farm	54
Gift Shop	55
Restaurants	56
Copalis Beach	58
Art Gallery	58
Gift Shop	59
Grayland	60
Gift Shops	60
Restaurant	61
Hoquiam	62
Bed and Breakfast	63
Gift Shop	64
Moclips	65
Accommodations	65
Ocean Shores	65
Accommodations	66
Apparel	68
Art Gallery	69
Bed and Breakfast	70
Books	70
Delicatessen	71
Gift Shop	71
Restaurant	72
Travel	74
Pacific Beach	74
Accommodations	75
Point Roberts	75
Bed and Breakfast	75
Restaurant	76
Westport	76
Accommodations	77
Art Gallery	78
Bed and Breakfast	78
Bakery	79
Restaurant	80

Tours	82
ISLAND COUNTY	**84**
Coupeville	86
Accommodations	87
Freeland	89
Bed and Breakfast	89
Langley	89
Bed and Breakfast	90
Restaurant	91
Oak Harbor	92
Accommodations	93
Restaurant	94
JEFFERSON COUNTY	**95**
Port Ludlow	96
Resort	96
Port Townsend	97
Accommodations	99
Antiques	101
Apparel	101
Art Gallery	102
Bed and Breakfast	102
Delicatessen	104
Florist	104
Gift Shop	105
Ice Cream	106
Market	106
Restaurant	107
Sporting Goods	110
Tavern	111
Wine	112
KING COUNTY	**113**
Auburn	116
Bellevue	117
Accommodations	118
Antiques	121
Apparel	122

       Art Gallery 123
       Bed and Breakfast 123
       Candy 124
       Farm 125
       Florist 126
       Furniture 127
       Gift Shops 128
       Golf Course 130
       Ice Cream Parlor 131
       Kitchen Supplies 132
       Maps 133
       Nautical Equipment 134
       Party 135
       Restaurants 136
       Wine 145
Bothell 147
       Antiques 147
       Rafting 148
       Restaurant 149
       Shopping Mall 150
Burien 152
       Restaurant 153
Carnation 154
       Farm 154
       Golf Course 156
Des Moines 156
       Restaurant 157
Enumclaw 158
       Accommodations 158
       Art Gallery 159
       Gift Shop 160
       Restaurant 160
Fall City 161
       Farm 161
       Golf Course 162
Federal Way 162

- Gift Shop ... 163
- Golf ... 164
- Issaquah ... 164
  - Antiques ... 165
  - Apparel ... 166
  - Art ... 166
  - Bakeries ... 167
  - Bed and Breakfast ... 167
  - Books ... 168
  - Candy ... 169
  - Delicatessen ... 169
  - Entertainment ... 169
  - Gift Shop ... 170
  - Gym ... 171
  - Ice Cream ... 171
  - Jewelry ... 172
  - Restaurant ... 172
  - Signs ... 176
- Kent ... 176
  - Apparel ... 176
- Kirkland ... 176
  - Accommodations ... 177
  - Antiques ... 178
  - Apparel ... 179
  - Art ... 180
  - Bed and Breakfast ... 180
  - Gift Shop ... 181
  - Restaurants ... 182
  - Tours ... 184
  - Wine ... 185
- Leavenworth ... 185
  - Ski ... 185
- Maple Valley ... 186
  - Bed and Breakfast ... 186
- Mercer Island ... 186
  - Antiques ... 187

Apparel	188
Bed and Breakfast	189
Delicatessen	189
Gift Shop	190
Ski Resort	191
North Bend	191
Bakery	192
Restaurant	193
Redmond	194
Accommodations	195
Bed and Breakfast	196
Delicatessen	197
Florist	198
Furniture, Children's	198
Gift Shop	199
Glass	199
Restaurant	200
Wine	204
Renton	205
Antiques	206
Delicatessen	207
Restaurant	207
Seattle	209
Accommodations	216
Antiques	226
Art, Artists and Galleries	236
Bakeries	252
Banquets	255
Bed and Breakfast	256
Books	261
Bowling	261
Cannery	262
Candy	262
Coffee	264
Collectables	265
Delicatessen	266

- Furnishings ... 267
- Garden Center ... 269
- Gift Shops ... 270
- Glassware ... 280
- Golf Course ... 281
- Hats ... 282
- Herbs and Spices ... 283
- Ice Cream ... 283
- Jewelry ... 284
- Kitchen Supplies ... 285
- Kites ... 288
- Knitting Supplies ... 289
- Markets ... 290
- Museum ... 293
- Nautical ... 294
- Party Supplies and Costumes ... 295
- Pizza ... 296
- Restaurant ... 296
- Sailing ... 310
- Spa ... 311
- Sporting Goods ... 312
- Stationery ... 312
- Tours ... 313
- Toy Store ... 313
- Wine ... 315

Snoqualmie ... 316
- Accommodations ... 317
- Farm ... 318
- Golf ... 318
- Wine ... 319

Tukwila ... 320
- Accommodations ... 320

Vashon Island ... 321
- Accommodations ... 323
- Antiques ... 324
- Apparel ... 325

- Bed and Breakfast 325
- Bakery 326
- Gift Shop 326
- Restaurant 328
- Woodinville 329
  - Antiques 330
  - Attraction 330
  - Florist 332
  - Garden Center 333
  - Gift Shop 334
  - Jewelers 334
  - Pottery 335
  - Restaurant 336
  - Sporting Goods 339
  - Wine 341

KITSAP COUNTY 343
- Bainbridge Island 345
  - Accommodations 346
  - Restaurant 347
- Bremerton 348
  - Accommodations 349
  - Farm 351
  - Restaurant 351
- Gorst 351
  - Golf Course 352
- Port Orchard 352
  - Antiques 353
  - Art Gallery 353
  - Bed and Breakfast 353
  - Golf Course 353
  - Restaurant 354
- Poulsbo 354
  - Accommodations 355
  - Art Gallery 355
  - Gift Shops 356
  - Restaurant 357

- Textiles ... 358
- Silverdale ... 358
  - Restaurant ... 359
- Winslow ... 359
  - Delicatessen ... 360
  - Gift ... 360
  - Restaurant ... 362
  - Yarns ... 364

LEWIS COUNTY ... 365
- Centralia ... 367
  - Accommodations ... 368
  - Antiques ... 369
  - Apparel ... 369
  - Restaurant ... 370
- Chehalis ... 370
  - Bed and Breakfast ... 372
  - Apparel ... 372
  - Books ... 373
  - Country Art ... 373
  - Gift Shop ... 374
  - Glass ... 375
  - Golf Course ... 375
  - Restaurant ... 376
- Morton ... 377
  - Accommodations ... 379
  - Resort ... 379
  - Restaurant ... 380

MASON COUNTY ... 380
- Hoodsport ... 382
  - Wine ... 382
- Union ... 382
  - Accommodations & Restaurant ... 383

PACIFIC COUNTY ... 384
- Chinook ... 385
  - Restaurant ... 386
- Concrete-Birdsview ... 387

Accommodations	387
Restaurant	388
Ilwaco	388
Accommodations	390
Delicatessen	390
Florist	391
Restaurant	391
Long Beach	391
Accommodations	393
Bakery	395
Camera Supplies and Services	395
Restaurant	395
Ocean Park	396
Restaurants	396
Oysterville	396
Seaview	398
Accommodations	398
Tokeland	400
Restaurant	401
Seafood Market	402
PIERCE COUNTY	402
Mount Rainier National Park	403
Crystal Mountain	407
Resort	407
Fife	408
Restaurant	408
Gig Harbor	409
Apparel	409
Art Galleries	410
Bed and Breakfast	411
Gift Shop	412
Restaurant	413
Lakewood	413
Puyallup	414
Accommodations	415
Antiques	416

Farm	417
Restaurant	418
Steilacoom	420
Restaurant	421
Sumner	422
Golf Course	422
Tacoma	423
Accommodations	426
Antiques	429
Apparel	430
Florist	432
Gift Shop	433
Golf Course	434
Restaurant	436
Theater	444
Tours	444
SAN JUAN COUNTY	**445**
Lopez Island	448
Accommodations	449
Campsite	449
Restaurant	449
Orcas Island	450
Deer Harbor	451
Accommodations and Restaurant	451
Eastsound	451
Accommodations	452
Delicatessen	453
Resorts	453
Restaurant	455
Olga	455
Art Gallery	456
Restaurant	456
Orcas	456
Accommodations	457
Bed and Breakfast	457
San Juan Island	458

- Friday Harbor 459
    - Accommodations 460
    - Bed and Breakfast 462
    - Jewelry 464
    - Restaurant 464
    - Tours 466
- Roche Harbor 467
    - Restaurant and Accommodations 467

SKAGIT COUNTY 468
- Anacortes 470
    - Accommodations 472
    - Airline/Tour 475
    - Bed and Breakfast 476
    - Delicatessen 477
    - Museum 477
    - Restaurant 478
- Bow 479
    - Bed and Breakfast 480
    - Restaurant 480
- Burlington 482
    - Accommodations 482
- Concrete 483
    - Restaurant 483
- La Conner 483
    - Accommodations 485
    - Antiques 486
    - Art Galleries 488
    - Books 490
    - Gift Shop 491
    - Restaurant 492
    - Seafoods 495
    - Seeds 496
- Mount Vernon 496
    - Accommodations 497
    - Cheese 499
    - Gift Shop 499

Restaurant	500
Sedro-Woolley	502
Art Gallery	503
Outdoor trip-planners	503
SKAMANIA COUNTY	**504**
SNOHOMISH COUNTY	**507**
Edmonds	509
Bed and Breakfast	510
Delicatessen	511
Florist	512
Gift Shops	512
Restaurant	513
Recreational Vehicle Repair	517
Seafood	518
Textiles	519
Everett	520
Accommodations	522
Antiques	527
Attractions	527
Florist	528
Jewelry	529
Restaurant	529
Textiles	532
Woodcarver	533
Sporting Goods	534
Lakewood	534
Golf Course	535
Restaurant	535
Lynnwood	536
Accommodations	536
Restaurant	537
Marysville	537
Mukilteo	538
Restaurant	539
Snohomish	539
Bed and Breakfast	541

Antiques	541
Art Gallery	542
Gift Shop	542
Golf Course	543
Honey	544
Ice Cream parlor	545
Pottery	545
Restaurant	546
Sport	548
Tour	549
Stanwood	549
Golf Course	550
Tulalip	551
Gift Shop	551
THURSTON COUNTY	552
Olympia	554
Accommodations	556
Bed and Breakfast	557
Bakery	558
Books	559
Delicatessen	560
Gift Shops	561
Ice Cream	562
Restaurants	562
Yogurt Parlor	570
Tumwater	570
Accommodations	571
WAHKIAKUM COUNTY	573
Cathlamet	574
Bed and Breakfast	575
WHATCOM COUNTY	577
Acme	579
Bellingham	579
Accommodations	582
Antiques	584
Bed and Breakfast	587

- Bakery ... 590
- Books ... 591
- Coffees ... 592
- Florist ... 593
- Gifts ... 594
- Glassware ... 595
- Jewelry ... 596
- Kitchenware ... 597
- Pottery ... 597
- Resort ... 598
- Restaurants ... 600
- Sport ... 606
- Sailing ... 608

Birch Bay ... 610
- Candy ... 611
- Gift Shop ... 611
- Resort ... 611

Blaine ... 611
- Accommodations ... 612
- Apparel ... 613
- Bed and Breakfast ... 613
- Florist ... 614
- Gift Shop ... 614
- Resort ... 615

Deming ... 616
- Accommodations ... 616
- Restaurant ... 616
- Tavern ... 617
- Wine ... 617

Ferndale ... 618
- Bed and Breakfast ... 619

Lummi Island ... 619
- Accommodations ... 619

Lynden ... 620
- Art Gallery ... 621
- Attraction ... 621

```
            Bed and Breakfast ................................................. 622
            Bakery ................................................................. 623
            Campsite ............................................................ 624
            Gift Shop ........................................................... 625
            Restaurant ......................................................... 625
      Point Roberts ............................................................... 627
      Sumas ......................................................................... 628
            Restaurant ......................................................... 628
APPENDIX ............................................................................ 629
```

CLALLAM COUNTY

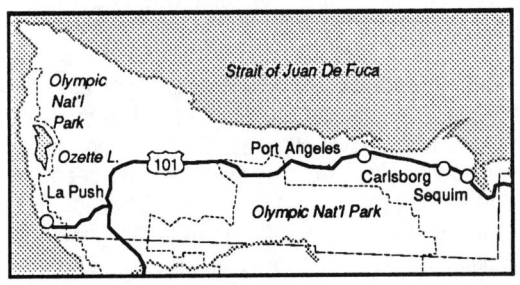

Big and sparsely settled, this north guardian of the Olympic Peninsula has the Pacific Ocean to the west, the Strait of Juan de Fuca sweeping its northern beaches and the waters of Puget Sound on the east. This is the gateway to Olympic National Park's most visited areas. The Olympic Mountains make the south county boundary and the park continues into Jefferson County.

The massive mountains of the Olympics, sculptured by ice with peaks towering over 7,000 feet above sea level, dominate the county and its economy. On the rain-drenched coast, spruce, cedar, hemlock and other trees thrive in a temperate-zone rain forest. Forks, one of the few communities on the coastal side, is always among the top annual rainfall stations in the the continental United States. Sequim, on the straits in the lee of the mountain range, has seventeen inches of rain a year and most cultivated farm land is under irrigation each summer.

Puget Sound's entrance is steeped in history, first described precisely by John Meares in 1788. The name goes back to a Greek who used the name Juan de Fuca while sailing for the Spanish in 1592. The first oral description of the straits from the Spaniards, recorded in 1596, seems to correspond to the actual geography of this great passage. Meares figured de Fuca had been there first and honored him with the name. The straits separate Vancouver Island from the continent and give the sheltered harbors of the sound a broad access to the sea without any of the perils of sand bars which mark almost every harbor on the Pacific Coast. Port Angeles, the county seat and largest community, trades on its location as a shipping point for paper and forest products milled from the fast-growing timber in nearby hills.

Olympic National Park

Snow-capped all year, the peaks of the Olympics are in the midst of a vast wilderness. Roads ring the park and surrounding national forest lands

Clallam County

which are parts of three peninsula counties, Clallam, Jefferson and Mason. Most park visitors observe the wild lands from Hurricane Ridge, a steep drive south from Port Angeles, or from Deer Park on an eighteen mile road which takes off from Highway 101 five miles east of Port Angeles. Long hikes or excursions with an outfitter and pack train are the only way to get to the interior of this rugged land.

Here is a quick run-down on the other vehicle access points to this varied park: On the west, beach and coastal corridor are reached by a long round-about road to Ozette Lake which leaves Highway 101 at Sappho. Carved by glacial scouring like Crescent Lake, Ozette is over 340 feet deep and parallels the coast line. More direct coast access is down the Soleduck River from Forks to LaPush or Rialto Beach, and down the Hoh River on Highway 101 itself which follows the Kalaloch portion of the park's coastline.

Three rainforest areas of the park, where moss drapes the conifers, all have western access points off Highway 101. From the north, **Hoh Rainforest** is reached by an eighteen mile drive east from the highway at a junction thirteen miles south of Forks. **Queets Rainforest** is almost at the highway, sixteen miles north of Lake Quinault. Above Lake Quinault on the north shore is the **Quinault Rainforest**.

On the park's east side, there is a **trailhead** at the upper end of Lake Cushman, west of Lilliwaup. Another trailhead and **campground** is up the Dosewallips River, fifteen miles west of Dosewallips State Park.

The northern entrance points in addition to **Deer Park** and **Hurricane Ridge**, are up the Elwha River Road eight miles west of Port Angeles, and from a turn-off just west of Lake Crescent which leads to a road up the headwaters of Soleduck River. A hot springs is at the campground eleven miles up that road.

Hikers should check with the National Park Service in Port Angles for snow conditions on the higher passes, since the deep snow pack often blocks some routes well into July. Late spring in the mountains also means a wildflower show into the summer months on Hurricane Ridge, the ridge above Olympic Hot Springs and in the back country. Hikers in the rainforests are cautioned that during the rainy season streams are subject to quick rises and are very cold.

Over 100 lakes are located in the park, providing fishermen a choice from little mountain pools beneath glacial cirques to trolling the depths of Lake Ozette at the coast. Washington **fishing** licenses are required in all park waters. At Lake Quinault, the fishing is regulated by Indian Reservation rules which often require special permits.

Several venerable resorts offer overnight lodging on the park's edges. Write to the **Olympic Peninsula Resort and Hotel Association,** care of Washington State Ferries, Colman Terminal, Seattle WA 98104 for the current list of facilities.

For more information, contact the **Olympic National Park,** 600 Park Avenue, Port Angeles WA 98362.

Attractions

Bogachiel State Park, six miles south of Forks on Highway 101, is on a river famous for its salmon and steelhead runs. Hikers and hunters use it as a base for trips into the forest to the east. There are forty-one campsites, none with RV hookups.

Lake Crescent, which Highway 101 runs alongside, is a popular resort area and connects by county roads to Agate Beach and a public campground at Crescent Beach. Glacial ice gouged out the lake to a depth 600-feet below sea level. Some trout taken here have topped thirty-pounds, and are a sub-species known as Beardslee trout, a land-locked steelhead.

One of the most visible examples of **reforestation** in the west can be seen west of Crescent Lake, where over 150,000 acres of timber was burned in 1907 by a fast-moving forest fire. Replanting was completed in the 1940s. The new forest is approaching age fifty in its youngest areas.

Neah Bay, headquarters for the tiny **Makah Indian Reservation,** is on Highway 112 just short of Cape Flattery, the western entrance of the straits. A side road to Ozette goes twenty miles to a resort lake which marks the start of the coastal extension of **Olympic National Park.**

Foot trails and beach connect hikers with **La Push,** the next community to the south. The first settlers in what is now Washington state landed at Neah Bay in May 1791. They left after five months and it wasn't until 1851 that whites returned, establishing a small trading post. The Makah Indian people were whale hunters and expert builders of sea-going dugout canoes.

The **Timber Museum** is in the small logging community of Forks on Highway 101. Old time logging is featured. Modern logging continues, and tours are offered at both mills and in the woods. Call Washington Women in Timber at 374-5179 for tour information.

Hoh Rainforest, south of Forks off Highway 101, is a place of Sitka spruce trees over 300-feet tall, draped with moss. Mushrooms abound in the forest. Most of the forest, part of the national park lands, is actually in Jefferson County.

For further information, contact the **Olympic Peninsula Tourism Council**, Box 303, Port Angeles WA 98362. Telephone 479-3594.

Carlsborg

Located between Highway 101 and the railroad tracks, this small community was a sawmill town from its founding in 1915 until the plant halted work in 1968. Carlsborg was named after a city of the same name in Sweden, the home town of C.J. Erickson who launched the settlement in 1915.

Dungeness

The town of Dungeness, five and one-half miles toward the straits from Sequim, was named by Capt. George Vancouver. In 1792 he titled the long sand spit after a similar place in the English Channel. Behind the spit's sandy lee are thousands of crabs of the species common from California northward, all called Dungeness crab. The spit has been a national wildlife refuge since 1915.

Attractions

Dungeness Spit has been a national wildlife refuge since 1915. Offshore are vast mud flats which confounded early sailors. A lighthouse marks the spit, and low tide exploration may yield a crab for properly-equipped beach walkers.

Nearby are the **Olympic Game Farm** on the road to Dungeness, and the **Dungeness State Salmon Hatchery** south of Sequim on a side road off Highway 101.

Offshore are vast mud flats which confounded early sailors. A **lighthouse** marks the spit, and low tide exploration may yield a crab for properly-equipped beach walkers. Nearby are the **Olympic Game Farm** on the road to Dungeness, and the **Dungeness State Salmon Hatchery** south of Sequim on a side road off Highway 101.

La Push

A narrow county road leaves Highway 101 north of Forks to follow the flood plain of the Quillayute River to La Push at the river's mouth. The name in Chinook jargon means "mouth." Indians traditionally netted salmon here, where a Coast Guard station, resorts and a small village have grown up.

Attractions

Offshore are the **Quillayute Needles,** a mass of rocks which were designated as a **National Wildlife Refuge** in 1907. The action was triggered in part by a bird census on Hunington Rock showing 40,000 Leach petrels in residence, the most populous bird colony known in Washington state.

The **Shaker Church** in LaPush was built in 1880, part of a missionary effort to the Indian people.

La Push offers a harbor for coastwise small craft. Several private parks handle recreational vehicles and tent campers.

Quileute Indian Reservation is just south of the village. Created by President Grover Cleveland in 1889, the reservation failed to resolve settler's homesteads claimed where the traditional village was located. When fur traders came, the main village was on James Island.

Resort

LA PUSH OCEAN PARK RESORT, P.O. Box 67 (fifteen miles west of Forks off U.S. 101), La Push, Washington. Motel rooms, townhouses, cottages, and cabins. Ocean views and scenic beach access. Call about steelhead and salmon fishing.

Port Angeles

This major city of the peninsula now has about 17,400 residents, most living on a bluff above the harbor and on the hillside which rises up to the foot hills of the Olympics. Mount Angeles, 6,454 feet above sea level, looks down on the port, which in turn overlooks the seventeen-mile wide straits to Canada's Vancouver Island. A regular ferry service connects Port Angles with Victoria, British Columbia on the island.

The Spanish Porto de Nuestra Senora de los Angeles, port of our Lady of Angles, was named in 1791 when Spanish ships anchored in the lee of Ediz Hook, the narrow sand spit which makes the harbor. By order of Abraham Lincoln, the town was laid out in 1862 as a federal city on five square miles to be site of government military facilities. Lincoln's order used the street plan for Cincinnati, Ohio. Coast artillery and now U.S. Coast Guard units use the military reservation. The port was summer headquarters of the U.S. Pacific Fleet from 1895 to 1935.

While much of the surrounding plateau before the mountains is dedicated to dairy farming, the town has been an industrial center for years. Pulp, paper, lumber and concrete products brought growth in the decades before World War II. At one time, local creameries bragged that the highest butter-fat production per cow in Washington could be attributed to the Clallam County milk-producers.

Attractions

Angeles Point is four miles west of town, at the entrance of the Elwha River into the straits. This is one of the land marks which cause Meares and other navigators of the 1780s to believe that Juan de Fuca had indeed entered the straits in another century. At the end of the county road you will find one of the International Boundary Monuments established by Canada and the United States in 1902. The actual boundary in the straits changes direction due north of Angeles Point.

Olympic Hot Spring, a combination of twenty-one springs at the 2,100 foot elevation in the Elwha canyon, is one of several attractions within the Olympic National Park reached from Elwha. This was once a remote resort with hotel, concrete swimming pool and mud-bath therapy. The resort closed in December 1966 and a heavy snowfall crushed most buildings.

Boulder Creek Campground operated by the park service has fifty tent sites. The road is not suitable for trailers or large recreational vehicles.

Ediz Hook is a demonstration of wave erosion at work. The lighthouse began operation in 1865. A Coast Guard station is next to it. But, in the 1970s, erosion of the western portion of the spit which connects both facilities to the mainland became so severe that engineers feared it would breach into the bay. A survey also showed that 280-feet of sand on the eastern end of the spit was lost from 1883 to 1970.

In town is an old **courthouse** still in use, and a **museum** which has next to it a log cabin built in 1887. Much of the early construction was swept away by a flood in 1863 caused when a natural dam on Valley Creek failed. A county road due south of the city leads to an overlook above the location of the landslide associated with the flood.

About one mile east of the main harbor on the shore is site of **Puget Sound Cooperative Community**. Established in 1887 as a utopian dream of George Venable Smith, the colony opened Port Angeles' first sawmill. The commune went into bankruptcy in 1889 and dissolved in 1904. A Clallam Indian burial ground is at the commune site.

For further information, contact the **Olympic Peninsula Tourism Council,** Box 303, Port Angeles WA 98362. Telephone 479-3594.

Art Gallery

THE WOODBOX AND GALLERY, 215 West First, Port Angeles, Washington. An art gallery, and a shop featuring quality ready-to-finish antique- style furniture.

Bed and Breakfast

HARBOUR HOUSE, 139 West Fourteenth at Oak Street, Port Angeles, Washington. Non-smokers welcome at this elegant Cape Cod style B&B. Some view rooms. Visa and MasterCard accepted.

THE TUDOR INN, 1108 South Oak, Port Angeles, Washington. The Inn was built in 1910. It offers lovely accommodations with views of Mount Olympus and the Strait of Juan de Fuca.

Gift Shops

ARLENE'S MADE-IN-WASHINGTON, 122 West Lamoureux, Highway 101 West and Oak Street, Port Angeles, Washington. Gifts, wines, and foods made exclusively in Washington.

BROWSERY 318
318 West 8th Street
Port Angeles, WA 98362
Tel. (206) 452-1233
Hrs: Mon. - Wed.   10:00 a.m. - 5:00 p.m.
         Thu. - Sat.   9:30 a.m. - 6:00 p.m.
Visa and MasterCard are accepted.

Partners Carmen Jarvis and Donita Henke had a furniture refinishing business before they opened their gift shop Browsery 318. They put their skills to work and renovated the old house in which the shop is located. The results are well worth the effort spent. Every room is tastefully decorated and stocked with unique and carefully selected gift items and antique furniture.

Each room has a special gift selection. The kitchen has a 1920s refrigerator and many kitchen gadgets, foods and coffees. The counter room is stocked with greeting cards, imported gift papers, decorations and delectable truffles. Upstairs is a room dedicated to men which includes numerous brass items and wooden duck decoys. Down the hall is the antique room and a children's room with toys, stuffed animals, dolls, and clothes. The bathroom is full of fragrant potpourris and colorful towels.

These are just a few of the exciting and interesting rooms at Browsery 318. Stop in and discover for yourself the multitude of unique gifts and antiques available in this charmingly renovated shop.

INSIDE STUFF AND THE LANDING RESTAURANT
101 West First Street
Port Angeles, WA 98362
Tel. (206) 457-9386
Hrs: Mon. - Sun.   10:00 a.m. - 5:30 p.m.
Visa, MasterCard, AMEX, and Discover cards are accepted.

Inside Stuff specializes in interior household accessories. When it began, it was a bed and bath shop, but the owners, a mother-daughter team, couldn't resist adding more variety. They seek to bring you unique, unusual, and unexpected gift items from which to choose. They have everything from elegant Fitz and Floyd china to stuffed rabbits that roller skate. You'll find high tech fun gifts and elegant hand blown crystal, candle holders, unique soaps, and fragrant potpourri.

Golf Course

PENINSULA GOLF CLUB
105 Lindberg Road
Port Angeles, WA 98362
Tel. (206) 457-6501
Hrs: Open dawn to dusk all year round.
Visa and MasterCard are accepted.

The Peninsula Golf Club has been a favorite of golfers for fifty-five years. It was originally a nine hole course, but was expanded to eighteen holes in 1979 with the addition of nine new holes on the west side. The course has one of the most spectacular views you'll ever enjoy while golfing. You can see all the way to Victoria, B.C. on a clear day and the Olympic Mountains form the backdrop on the south side. This is a lovely course with seventy to eighty year old maples and evergreens, some of which are more than one hundred feet tall. The newer part of the course was literally carved out of the forest.

This course offers a mixture of level and slopes to challenge you. There is a pro shop with a good selection of equipment and a clubhouse for members and their guests. A driving range, rental clubs and carts are also part of the facilities. Peninsula Golf Club offers two tournaments, one on Memorial Day and one on Labor Day, which are attended by more than 200 golfers from Washington, Oregon and Canada.

For a change of pace, take the ferry to Port Angeles and play the Peninsula Golf Club course. You can tee off by mid morning and enjoy some truly challenging golf in a spectacular setting.

Resort

LAKE CRESCENT LOG CABIN RESORT, 6540 East Beach Road, Port Angeles, Washington. On Lake Crescent in beautiful Olympic National Park, the resort is open mid-May/October. Also has a marina with boat rentals, restaurant, grocery store and gift shop.

Clallam County

A HEAVENLY ESCAPE

a.m.	The Greenery	Best breakfast	Porta/Restaurant
a.m.	Peninsula Golf	Best golf	Porta/Golf
a.m.	Olympic Hot Springs	Best swimming	Porta/Attraction
a.m.	Browsery	Best antiques	Porta/Gift
p.m.	Larson's	Best lunch	Porta/Restaurant
p.m.	Woodbox	Best art	Porta/Art
p.m.	Arlene's	Best gifts	Porta/Gift
p.m.	Inside Stuff	Best crystal	Porta/Gift
Now take yourself out to dinner. It's been a long day.			

It's true: Port Angeles is "a port of angels."

Restaurants

THE GREENERY
117 B E 1st Street
Port Angeles, WA 98362
Tel. (206) 457-4112
Hrs: Mon. - Thu.   7:00 a.m. - 10:00 p.m.
     Fri. - Sat.   7:00 a.m. - 11:00 p.m.
     Sunday   8:00 a.m. - 8:00 p.m.
Extended hours in the summer.
Visa, MasterCard accepted.

When nightly specials are determined by what comes off the fishing boat in Port Angeles, you know you are dealing with restaurant management that is fastidious. The main ingredient common to all of the dishes is attention to detail.

Dave and Marsha Reynold's attention to detail extends to preparing just the right sauces and seasonings for a bill of fare steeped in 17th century French cooking. Everything is prepared from scratch. Breakfast can be as simple as an omelette, or as lavish as a spinach and bacon souffle. Lunch features homemade pastas such as seafood fettuccini and chicken spaghetti, to special sandwiches and charbroiled burgers. All totaled, the combine lunch and breakfast menu lists 200 items. For dinner, expect hearty portions. Again, depending on what the boat brings in, you may have baked stuffed sole in mornay sauce, along with huge crab and shrimp Louies, Try the pan fried oysters or halibut Amandine, both accompanied by a Ceasar salad and French bread.

If you miss having a meal at the Greenery, you will have missed the boat on fine dining in Port Angeles.

LARSON'S, 136 East First Street, Port Angeles, Washington, California. An eclectic bill of fare here at breakfast, lunch and dinner. Visa and MasterCard accepted.

Sequim

Sequim, a farming town of about 3,100, is in what is known as the Dungeness Valley. Sequim comes from the name of an Indian village located east of here on a small inlet to the bay of the same name.

Attractions

Sequim Bay State Park is four miles east of Sequim on Highway 101. This is a developed camp for RVs and tent campers, located at the mid-point for people taking a motor-tour around the Olympic Peninsula. Tusk of mammoths have been taken from clay cliffs above the beach. There is bay-side camping and boat-launching, plus swimming beaches.

Accommodations

RED RANCH INN
820 W Washington
Sequim, WA 98382
Tel. (206) 683-4195
Hrs: Coffee   Mon.- Fri.   6:00 a.m. - 3:00 p.m.
     Dinner   Mon. - Sat. 5:00 p.m.-10:00 p.m.
              Sunday   4:00 p.m. - 9:00 p.m.
Visa, MasterCard, AMEX, Diners and Discover cards accepted.

Howdy, and welcome to the Red Ranch Inn! One of the best accommodations in Sequim, the newly remodeled western style motel has fifty rooms and suites, each with queen sized beds, color cable TV, movies, direct dial phones and some units have kitchenettes.

The coffee shop serves a full breakfast and lunch daily. The attractive dinner house is famous in the area for its prime rib dinner and salad bar, which contains over fifty items to choose from. The soups are homemade and the menu also features steaks and seafood. A specialty of the house is mesquite grill cooking, and the wine list offers a selection of local northwest wines.

The lounge is open from 3:00 p.m. until 2:00 a.m. for cocktails and relaxation. So pull off them boots, put your feet up and enjoy some western hospitality at the Red Ranch Inn!

Antiques

WOODEN HORSE ANTIQUES
323-A E Washington Street - Creamery Square
P. O. Box 1029
Sequim, WA 98382
Tel. (206) 683-9026
Hrs: Mon. - Fri.   10:00 a.m. - 4:30 p.m.
       Saturday   10:00 a.m. - 4:00 p.m.
Or by appointment, (206) 683-8498.
Visa, MasterCard, AMEX and layaway are accepted.

A continued expansion of both out of state and local estate sales give Wooden Horse Antiques a large selection of antiques and collectibles and allows for unusually modest pricing. Shelves and walls are overflowing with inventory and any specifically requested item is noted and filed to try and meet customer needs.

You'll find prints, frames, clocks, linens for all occasions, jewelry, from semi-precious stones to rhinestones, glassware and china, large and small furniture pieces, books, toys, dolls, lamps and other infinite possibilities! Recent expansion of the business has resulted in "and, Wooden Horse, too" in Creamery Square. There you'll find an even larger inventory, with glassware, oriental and military memorabilia, current antique reference books, bead knotting and jewelry repair.

Estate sale management and appraisal services are always available, so whether you've found "the treasure of the century" in Granny's attic and need help determining its value, or its function, or are looking for a treasure of your own, put Wooden Horse Antiques on the top of your list!

Art Gallery

SIRRAH COLLECTIBLES
108 W Washington
Sequim, WA 98382-2285
Tel. (206) 683-7584
Hrs: Wed. - Mon.   10:00 a.m. - 6:00 p.m.
Visa and MasterCard are accepted.

   Nationally and internationally known artists are presented at Sirrah Collectibles, which carries a variety of limited edition plates, prints and figurines. Members of the Bradford Exchange, the proprietors stock plate and print collections from Dali to Rockwell to Edna Hibel, and if a particular piece is not in the shop, an attempt to locate it for you will be made.
   The gallery was opened in 1985 so that interested collectors and potential collectors would have a place to share their interest and knowledge.
   One area in the shop of particular interest is the portion dedicated to John Wayne memorabilia. Sirrah Collectibles is one of its kind in the Sequim area, and shouldn't be missed.

Attraction

   OLYMPIC GAME FARM, 383 Ward Road, Sequim, Washington. Enjoy a drive-through tour to see a lot of wild animals, from Kodiak bears to buffalo.

Bakery

   SCARBOROUGH FAYRE, 126 East Washington, Sequim, Washington. A quaint tearoom/bakery featuring tradtional British foods, sausage rolls, and sweet pastries. Visa and MasterCard accepted.

Deli

SUNNY FARMS COUNTRY STORE
1546 Highway 101 W
Sequim, WA 98382
Tel. (206) 683-8003
Hrs: Mon. - Sun. 8:00 a.m. - 7:00 p.m.
Open all year.

Owner Roger Schmidt refers to Sunny Farms Country Store as, "a naturally good food market." His family moved to Sequim, a retirement community, in the 1970s and built the store in 1979. Roger and his wife Ellie wanted to create a store that would be filled with food stuffs of best quality for healthful living. This market carries low salt and no sugar products which are free of chemicals whenever possible.

The building that houses the store is all natural wood, open to the outdoors. It is filled with fresh fruits and vegetables, quality seafood, and poultry plus an extensive selection of cheese and bulk foods. In addition to delicious edibles carried by the store, there are garden plants, flowers, locally crafted gifts, stuffed animals, baskets and even Sunny Farms t-shirts and sweatshirts.

Roger is extremely careful about what is served in the deli. Everything is made from scratch using the highest quality ingredients. There is a good selection of salads, cheeses, meats, breads and pizzas of which they sell more than 1,000 every month! A visit to Sunny Farms Country Store is an experience well worth your time. A little country store with a lot of heart.

Farm

CEDARBROOK HERB FARM, 986 Sequim Avenue, Sequim, Washington. An herbalist's delight! Over one hundred varieties of herb plants for kitchen rockeries, teas, medicines and cooking. Closed during January and February.

Florist

SOFIE'S FLORAL AND GIFTS
Sequim Village Center Suite 1
Sequim, WA 98382
Tel. (206) 683-7949
Hrs: Mon. - Sat. 8:30 a.m. - 6:00 p.m.
All major credit cards are accepted.
Member FTD & Wire service.

Not only does Sofie's Floral offer custom designed floral arrangements with fresh or silk hand wrapped artificial flowers, but this "Best Choice" shop also carries a lovely selection of cut crystal and brassware.

A full service florist that carries the largest selection of artificial flowers on the peninsula, it has been so successful that a second shop is now open in Seattle at the corner of Second and Cherry streets.

Be prepared to walk out of the shop with an irresistible stuffed animal from a gigantic stuffed toy section! And rest assured that a floral order from Sofie's will be designed and delivered with the utmost skill and care.

Golf

DUNGENESS GOLF COURSE AND RESTAURANT
491 A Woodcook Road
Sequim, WA 98382
Tel. (206) 683-6344
Hrs: Dawn to Dusk
Visa and MasterCard accepted, excluding green fees and carts.
Call for reservations.

Dungeness Golf Course, managed by PGA Professional Ron Hagen, is a very dry golf course and excellent for winter play. Those are important features when you play golf in the Pacific Northwest. Because of Sequim's low rainfall and the unique location of Dungeness Golf Course, it offers some of the best year round golf in Western Washington. Dungeness is a championship eighteen hole course easy to walk. Streams and ponds dot the entire course.

The pro shop has a good selection of equipment and clothing and offers golf lessons, video taping, rental club, carts and a driving range. The restaurant is Tuesday through Sunday and is a full service lunch and dinner house.

Once you visit Dungeness, you will understand why people journey here from all parts of the Pacific Northwest to play this lovely and challenging course.

SUNLAND GOLF CLUB
109 Hilltop Drive
Sequim, WA 98382
Tel. (206) 683-6800
Visa and MasterCard are accepted.

A beautiful semi-private championship course, the Sunland Golf Club is open from dawn to dusk year round and closed until 9:00 a.m. on Mondays. An easy walk with individual fairways, the course features 6,000 yards for men and 5,600 yards for women.

Sunland also represents a retirement community, with condominiums and home sites located along the fairway. There is a pro shop on the premises which carries a complete line of new and used golf equipment, including Difini, David Smith and Ultra Sport.

Sunland has an active men and womens club with individual tournament and team matches, and golf lessons are available by appointment. Tuesday is couples day with parties held every last Tuesday of the month during the summer. Join in the fun....tee off at Sunland during your tour of the peninsula!

Marina

JOHN WAYNE MARINA
615 West Sequim Bay Road
Sequim, WA 98382
Tel. (206) 683-9898
Hrs: Flexible, depending on the time of year; please call.

John Wayne had a special fondness for the Sequim area. He used to sail to the area on his refurbished mine sweeper, *The Wild Goose*, whose sister ship is Jacques Cousteau's *Calypso*, and go hunting with the locals or drop into town for a bite to eat and conversation. He liked the area so much that he purchased more than one hundred acres of land, part of which included Pitship Point. John Wayne used to sit aboard *The Wild Goose* and envision a marina in those scenic, protected waters.

When the Port of Port Angeles decided to build a marina, they wanted it to be in Sequim Bay. After lengthy negotiations, John Wayne donated several waterfront acres for the marina. In order to insure the protection of the bay, the Port had to establish a program to monitor clams, replace the grass which would be displaced during the dredging process, and realign Johnson Creek, which is a spawning creek for fish. The marina was completed in 1985 and was dedicated to the memory of John Wayne.

John Wayne Marina has a supply store, convenience shop, the "True Grits" restaurant and Sequim Bay Yacht Club. There are slips available for transit use, public showers, laundry facilities, a picnic area, boat launch ramp, and public clam beach. Several charter fishing outfits are run by the marina. John Wayne's dream was completed after his death, but it's a marina he would be proud to have dedicated to him.

Restaurant

CASONI'S, Highway 101 and Carlsborg Road, Sequim, Washington. Enjoy sauté specialties, seafood, veal steak, and gourmet desserts here. Visa and MasterCard accepted.

THE OAK TABLE CAFE, Third and Bell, Sequim, Washington. Delicious breakfasts and creative lunches. No credit cards, please.

THE 3 CRABS RESTAURANT
101 Three Crabs Road
Sequim, WA 98382
Tel. (206) 683-4264
Hrs: Mon. - Thurs. 12 noon - 10:00 p.m.
　　　Fri. - Sat. 　　12 noon - 11:00 p.m.
　　　Sunday 　　　12 noon - 9:00 p.m.
Closed Christmas and Thanksgiving.
Visa, MasterCard accepted.
Reservations are recommended.

Sitting alone on the beach at Dungeness Bay, The 3 Crabs Restaurant serves excellent seafood, prepared from scratch under the strict supervision of owner Norma Marshall.

Dungeness crab is one of the more popular entrees, fresh from October through March, and the menu also features such delectables from the sea as steamed clams, homemade clam and oyster chowder, halibut, prawns, scallops, lobster and more. Steaks are also available, as are very special and tasty omelettes.

With a terrific view of the bay, the restaurant has a massive fireplace and cedar interior. During the spring and summer, the restaurant's retail store, The Crab Shack, sells fresh fish, their own special dressing, smoked salmon and halibut. Join in the tradition of many others who travel to the

Olympic Peninsula...enjoy a feast from the sea at The 3 Crabs Restaurant in Sequim!

Wine

LOST MT. WINERY
730 Lost Mt. Road
Sequim, WA 98382
Tel. (206) 683-5229
Call for an appointment.

Lost Mt. Winery sits perched on the side of Lost Mountain on forty wooded acres. The setting is serene and scenic, with the Olympic Mountains in the background. Before building his combined home and winery on Lost Mountain, owner Romeo Conca made red table wines at his home in Shelton. By the seventies he was producing over 200 gallons a year. In 1981, Romeo Conca built his new facility and now produces over 1,200 gallons per year.

Romeo's red wine blend carries the name Lost Mt. Red. He also produces quality Zinfandel Petite Sirah, Merlot and Pinot Noir. His wine is of award winning quality, although has not yet entered a competition, since they require a larger quantity of wine than he produces. People visit the winery from all over the United States. Every year there is an open house, the last week in June and the first week in July.

To reach Lost Mt. Winery, head west from of Sequim on Highway 101 across the Dungeness River. Turn south on Taylor cutoff road which becomes Lost Mt. Road after several miles. Stay on Lost Mt. Road until you reach Box 730 and the winery sign on your right. You'll enjoy the scenic route that takes you to Lost Mt. Winery and some truly outstanding wine once you arrive.

NEUHARTH WINERY
P.O. Box 1457
Still Road
Sequim, WA 98382
Tel. (206) 683-9652
Hrs: Wed. - Sun. 12:00 noon - 5:00 p.m.
Visa, MasterCard accepted.

In 1978 Maria and Eugene Neuharth began their plans for a winery in Sequim. Eugene was a retired viniculturist from the Lodi district of California and felt the clean air and mild climate of the Sequim area were ideal for producing fine dinner wines. An old dairy barn of interesting log pole construction was chosen as the site of the winery and restored. After being fitted with the proper equipment for wine producing, including European and American oak barrels, the Neuharths were ready to produce their first wines.

All the grapes used in their fine wines come from Eastern Washington and the small winery vineyard. Their first crush of grapes was in the fall of 1979, when about thirty tons of Riesling, Cabernet Sauvignon, Chenin Blanc and Zinfandel grapes were received. The juices were blended to achieve balance and the first wines released were Johannesburg Riesling, Chenin Blanc, Zinfandel and White Zinfandel. The tasting and sales cellar, a replica of old world cellars, was built in 1980. Their wines have been very well received and they enjoy a reputation of producing high quality, fine dinner wines.

Neuharth Winery now produces many different varietal wines including Merlot, Chardonnay and Cabernet which have won gold and silver medals in several regional, state, national and international competitions. You'll enjoy a visit to this charming and picturesque vineyard and will be delighted by the wonderful wines that they produce.

CLARK COUNTY

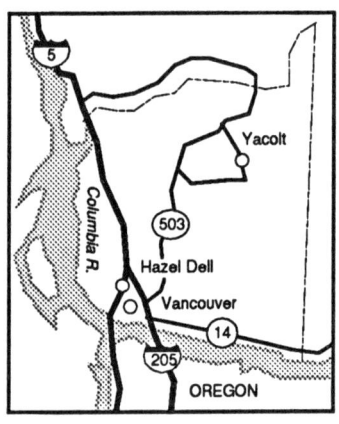

This small, 633 square mile county is on the Columbia River about 100 miles upstream from the mouth. It was here that the Hudson Bay Company set up headquarters for its regional fur trading operations. Farms and orchards which thrived in the 218-day growing season and thirty-seven inches of rainfall each year fed residents of the trading post and later became major producers of food for the growing Portland metropolitan area. An estimated 203,000 people now live in Clark County, concentrated in Vancouver, the Camas and Washougal manufacturing area upstream, and farming centers at Battleground, Ridgefield and LaCenter.

The Columbia River, which makes a major bend downstream from Vancouver, is the west and south boundary of the county. On the north, the Lewis River divides Clark from Cowlitz County. The eastern line with Skamania County is an arrow-straight map-maker's line, with one jog, through the length of the Cascade Range foot hills. The highest point in the county is only 290 feet above sea level while Vancouver's waterfront is still within tidewater on the Columbia, at eighteen inches above sea level.

Clark County was created in August 1845 by act of the Oregon Territorial Legislature. It is the oldest county in what later became the state of Washington. The name honors William Clark who camped at several spots in the county during the 1806 Lewis and Clark expedition. When Washington Territory's Legislature met in 1854, it incorrectly called this Clarke County, a mistake that went unchecked until a 1925 session of the assembly dropped the "e" and restored the proper spelling to Clark's name.

Pulp and paper manufacturing and other wood processing provide the base for a diversified economy. Crown Zellerbach, with 2,100 employees, is the county's largest manufacturer. Aluminum Company of America has an aluminum plant within the county, taking advantage of favorable "direct service industry" rates from the federal Bonneville Power Administration. In recent years, new electronics assembly plants have located in the Orchards area east of Vancouver near the I-205 Glenn Jackson Bridge over the Columbia River.

Clark County

Attractions

Pendleton Woolen Mills has a major plant in Washougal. One hour tours are offered Monday through Friday between 9:00 a.m. and 1:30 p.m. Telephone 835-2131.

Parkersville archaeological site, near Washougal, has shown Indian settlement dating back an estimated 3,000 years. Artifacts link the ancient residents to the present Indians of the river who speak the Chinook language.

Gentry's Landing, on the Columbia River between Ellsworth and Camas, Highway 14, has Indian petroglyphs of undetermined age, one of two petroglyph locations on the river. Look at the boulders right at water's edge.

Tidland Machine Company at Camas offers tours of its plant at 2363 Southeast Eighth Monday through Friday between 8:00 a.m. and 4:00 p.m. You need to call first, 834-2345.

Just off I-5 at the Ridgefield exit are **LaCenter** and **Paradise Point State Park**. LaCenter is a community bypassed by time. It was the head of navigation in the 1870s when steamboats worked the lower Lewis River, with the names of Mascot and Walker. Originally known as Timmen's Landing on whose ground the town was platted in 1875, boosters adopted LaCenter as a name, confident that as a shipping point from boat to wagon this would be the center of commerce for Clark County's farms. Drought years soon made the Lewis too shallow for navigation during summer months. The railroad gave some new economic life to the town, and the Pacific Highway came through in later for years. Now, all importance has vanished with the interstate two miles to the west. The park is a popular picnic stop for travelers who find their way off of I-5.

Ridgefield has two attractions at what was a single sawmill town on the Columbia River. Over 3,000 acres of riparian area above and below the town are part of a **National Wildlife Refuge** where beaver, otter and huge numbers of birds live. **Sinclair Arboretum**, 18816 Northwest Forty-first Avenue, Ridgefield is a fifteen acre private arboretum. Open daily during daylight hours.

The last of Clark County's **prune driers** is at 2109 Northwest 219th, Ridgefield. Built in 1899, this one still operates each fall. For tours, starting in September, call 887-3128.

For further information, contact the **Tourist Regional Information Program**, Box 128, Longview WA 98632. Telephone 577-3321.

Battle Ground

Stories spread rapidly in days gone by. This busy town is named for an Indian fight which was far from a battle. A.H. Richter built a store here in 1886 and platted the town in 1902, naming it after what he had been told was the site of an Indian battle years before. Historians now say records from Fort Vancouver indicate only that a posse came here to capture some Indians suspected of stealing livestock, apparently carrying out the mission by killing the leader of the Indian band. The plains around Battle Ground were farmed for grain sold at Fort Vancouver. This later became an orchard district.

Attractions

Battle Ground Lake State Park has day use and overnight facilities located less than two miles from town. This is a popular area resort with a sandy beach for swimming.

Two **motor tours** are suggested by the Battle Ground Chamber of Commerce. One is laid out to take a single day, the other, two days visiting scenic and historic sites on Lucia Falls Road and County Road 16. Among the sights are a Lutheran Church built in 1883, a grist mill constructed in 1876, and snags from the devastating Yacolt Burn which swept timberlands in 1902. Call the Chamber for detailed information.

Chelatchie Prairie Railroad rumbles out of a depot on Main Street from late June through early September each year. The route to Yacolt includes a 300-foot tunnel, a timber trestle over the East Fork of Lewis River, plus views of Lucia and Moulton Falls. The train turns around at Moulton Falls Park, where the timbermen who built the railroad hatched their idea in 1898. They were going to lay track over the Cascades to Yakima but loss of timber in the Yacolt Burn of 1902 snuffed the dream and made this a shortline. Reservations and special excursion rates can be made by calling 687-7428.

For information, contact **Battle Ground Chamber of Commerce**, Box 366C, Battle Ground WA 98604. Telephone 687-1510.

Clark County

Brush Prairie

Golf Course

CEDARS GOLF CLUB
15001 N. E. 181st St.
Brush Prairie, WA 98606
Tel.   WA (206)   687-4233
         OR   (503)   285-7548
Hrs: Golf course   Dawn to Dusk
         Restaurant   Mon. - Fri.   10:00 a.m - dusk
                              Sat. - Sun.   Dawn to Dusk
Reservations suggested for tee time.

    Picture yourself amidst rolling lush green countryside, interspersed with patches of tall, aromatic cedar forest and an occasional deer nibbling on the rough--you must be at the Cedars Golf Club. The Cedars is located on the outskirts of Battle Ground in the little town of Brush Prairie, only a fifteen minute drive from downtown Vancouver and a half hour from downtown Portland. Although a little off the beaten track, the Cedars is well worth the trip.
    The Cedars Golf Club, once a private country club, was recently opened to the public and has quickly become a favorite course among Northwest golfers. This 18 hole course is not only beautiful, but also challenging with lots of water and tight fairways. The Cedars also offers a driving range, full service pro shop, spacious locker rooms and practice greens. Golf lessons and rental clubs are available at reasonable rates.
    After your round of golf, be sure to adjourn to the restaurant and cocktail lounge in the sumptuous clubhouse. Relax, dine leisurely or enjoy a cocktail or two and watch big screen TV. Be sure to try their famous "Billyburger," omelets and delicious homemade soups.
    The Cedars also has meeting rooms and large banquet facilities available for your wedding reception, reunion or other special event. A perfect setting for celebrating with family and friends.
    To get to the Cedars: From downtown Vancouver, take Highway 500 east to Highway 503 (117th Avenue). From Portland take I-205 north across the Columbia River; take Exit 30 to the right; follow the road straight which will become Highway 503. Continue north on Highway 503 to Brush Prairie. Turn right on 159th Street, turn left on 152nd Avenue, go one mile and you will see the clubhouse on your left. Cedars Golf Club, a Washington "Best Choice" for relaxing amidst the splendors of the great Northwest.

Vancouver

Washington's southern gateway at the Columbia River and I-5 is closely aligned with the economy of the Portland area to the south. But the city of 43,000 has a history which predates most of that in Oregon, and with its unincorporated suburbs such as Hazel Dell, accounts for much of the county population. About sixteen square miles were within city limits in mid-1985.

This is the oldest permanent non-Indian settlement in the state. A tourist information center, at the Fourth/Plain exit from I-5, has detailed maps of all historic sites in the city and surrounding Clark County. Fort Vancouver, which opened as a Hudson Bay Company post in 1824, is next to I-5 and is now partially restored.

Today, a forty-foot channel in the Columbia River is dredged to the docks of the Port of Vancouver, continuing the ocean shipping trade which began with the fur traders.

Attractions

Six buildings and the stockade of **old Fort Vancouver** are now restored to Hudson Bay Company specifications. The National Historic Site also includes a group of Victorian homes built as officer's quarters while the fort was an active U.S. military post. On the reservation is a monument to the three Russian aviators who landed here in 1936 after pioneering the transpolar route between Russia and America. Take the East Mill Plain Boulevard exit from I-5, follow the signs south on Fort Vancouver Way, then take East Evergreen Boulevard to the visitor center. Half hour tours of the Chief Factor's house and kitchen are given daily starting at 10:00 a.m. from mid-June through the end of August. The visitor's center is open from 9:00 a.m. to 5:00 p.m.

The **U.S. Grant Museum**, 1106 East Evergreen Boulevard, is in the old post headquarters of Vancouver Barracks. The former president served here while a young man. Open Tuesday through Friday from 1:00 p.m. to 4:00 p.m. Saturday and Sunday open 1:00 p.m. to 5:00 p.m. Telephone 693-9743.

Clark County Historical Museum, 1511 Main Street, uses the community's old Carnegie Library building to house exhibits. There is a collection of goods from an 1890 country store, the piano shipped here in 1836, and several other displays. Open Tuesday through Saturday from 1:00 p.m. to 5:00 p.m. Telephone 695-4681 for information and group tour reservations.

Clark County

Columbia Arts Center, 400 West Evergreen, is an art gallery and has a performing arts schedule. Open daily. Call 693-0351 for hours and current attractions.

Covington House, 4201 Main Street, is a log cabin built in 1848 and later the first school house for the area. Open daily June through August, from 10:00 a.m. to 4:00 p.m.

The former **Providence Academy**, 400 East Evergreen Boulevard, is now a collection of shops and businesses. This was constructed by the Sisters of Providence in 1873. The chapel is restored. Open daily. Telephone 694-3271.

Also in business these days is the one-time **home of L.M. Hidden**, 100 West Thirteenth Street. Built in 1885 for a prominent businessman, this residence is now a French restaurant and an art gallery. Call 696-2847 for hours and meal reservations.

Lloyd Parson built a replica of Dodge City, Kansas in his backyard as a hobby. It is now open to the public during daylight hours as **"Old West In Miniature,"** Fifteenth and Harney Streets.

Charter **boat tours of the waterfront** are offered by some commercial operators. A call to the Chamber of Commerce will put you in touch with companies currently running tours of the port and as far beyond as you would like to go.

For further information, contact **Greater Vancouver Chamber of Commerce**, 404 East Fifteenth Street, Vancouver WA 98663. Telephone 694-2588.

Accommodations

RED LION INN AT THE QUAY
100 Columbia Street
Vancouver, WA 98660
Tel. (206) 694-8341
Visa, MasterCard, AMEX, Carte Blanche, Diner's Club and Discover cards are accepted.

Red Lion Inn at the Quay is in an old building which was unusable for sea going vessels after the nearby bridge was built. In 1960 the building was purchased and completely renovated into a delightful hostelry by Red Lion Inns. *Consumer Reports* has rated Red Lion Inns second nationwide in customer satisfaction in a comparison of all major motel chains.

The Red Lion Inn at the Quay is very conveniently located. It is three minutes from downtown Vancouver, fifteen minutes from the Portland Airport, a shuttle is available and ten minutes from downtown Portland. This is a good place to stay and explore Portland Vancouver and the surrounding areas. The beach is eighty miles away, Mount Hood skiing is fifty miles away and the scenic Columbia Gorge and Multnomah Falls are only thirty minutes away. There are 160 recently remodeled guest rooms, each with queen or king size beds. Three suites offer larger accommodations, one has kitchen facilities and two have in room jacuzzis. All river view rooms have balconies overlooking the river.

Much of Red Lion Inn at the Quay's business is from conventions and corporations, but tourism is a close second. The Inn has complete convention facilities on the premises with excellent food and beverage service for banquets of up to 1,300 people. The restaurant offers fine dining with an emphasis on fresh seafood. Whether you are travelling for business or pleasure, Red Lion Inn at the Quay will meet your needs.

SHILO INN HAZEL DELL
13206 Highway 99
Vancouver, WA 98686
Tel. (206) 573-0511
      (800) 222-2244

Shilo Inns are known for their comfortable, well appointed and moderately priced rooms. The Hazel Dell Shilo Inn is no exception. A free Continental breakfast, complimentary *USA Today* newspaper, satellite TV, in room movies, free popcorn and fruit await you at this fine motel. There is an indoor swimming pool, spa, sauna and steam room. A restaurant and lounge adjoin the inn.

There are sixty-seven rooms which are comfortable, nicely furnished and decorated. Units with kitchenettes are available, as well as guest laundry facilities. The motel offers free airport shuttle service. Clark County Fairgrounds and Equestrian Center are nearby and it's less than an hour's drive to the Mt. St. Helen's Visitor Center.

The Shilo Inns are an Oregon based chain with motels in most western states. They offer group rates and senior discounts. Shilo Inns are known for their "Affordable Excellence;" they are an excellent choice when travelling or vacationing.

Antiques

HOUSE OF VAGABONDS
606 Main Street
Vancouver, WA 98660
Tel. (206) 693-2653
Hrs: Mon. - Sat.   10:00 a.m. - 5:00 p.m.
Visa and MasterCard accepted.

Variety is a real key to an interesting antique shop. It's a pleasure to look at many different items from a span of time and imagine what the item was used for, by whom, and how it would look in your home. Antique lovers appreciate the time invested and the craftsmanship that is evident in the old fashioned.

House of Vagabonds will certainly keep your interest; there's costume jewelry, glassware, pottery, pictures and lithographs, carved frames, oriental rugs and vintage clothing. The inventory is constantly growing and changing.

If you're a record collector this place is a must...there are from fifteen to twenty thousand vintage records here. The music spans jazz, early rock, easy listening, bluegrass, country and folk. Coleen and Terry Baldwin, the owner, purchased a small used record shop to augment the already fast growing antique shop; little realizing at that time the immense popularity of old recordings.

So, with a little imagination and verve, this shop could furnish the vintage clothing, tableware and background sounds for a Great Gatsby party, or a Elvis Is Back gathering, a romantic evening with your Valentino, or...........

Bakery

GOODY'S BY GOLLY, 611 West Eleventh Street, Vancouver, Washington. Freshly-baked breads, pastries, and desserts, and gift items for any occasion.

Craft Supplies

OPAL'S CHATTERBOX
5601 St. John's Road
Vancouver, WA 98661
Tel. (206) 693-8180
Hrs: Mon. - Sat. 10:00 a.m. - 5:00 p.m.

Mildred Hooper, along with her son Jay and daughter Mary, have been operating this wonderful store for the past ten years. Opal's Chatterbox is a converted house and is full of every type of craft supplies anyone might ever need. Mildred made most of the samples throughout the store. Currently she is specializing in silk flower arrangements for weddings and has been so successful that plans are underway to create a complete wedding section which will feature anything one might need for a wedding. In addition to silk flowers there will be candles, cake pieces and even champagne fountains.

One of the specialties at Opal's Chatterbox is the plaster craft section. They have pieces ranging in size from two foot statues to delicate figurines. Mildred and Mary conduct classes to show you how to paint figures yourself; once finished they make lovely and unique gifts.

Opal's Chatterbox carries supplies for handcrafts that you might not find elsewhere. They have a good selection of beads and "eyes" for animals and dolls. No matter what craft or hobby interests you, you'll find what you need in this well stocked store, in addition helpful advice from the friendly proprietors.

Delicatessen

AL'S BROADWAY DELI, 1717 Broadway, Vancouver, Washington. A delicatessen open for lunch and dinner, and featuring open mike on Wednesday evenings. Enjoy a selection of micro-brewery beers and listen to music and comedy, no cover charge.

COFFEEVILLE, U.S.A., 1003 Main Street, and 9803 Highway Ninety-Nine, Vancouver, Washington. Both locations of Coffeeville, U.S.A. specialize in a vast assortment of coffees from around the world.

Clark County

Leaving Oregon, traveling along I-5, the first city to greet you in Washington is Vancouver. Introductions are in order.

WELCOME TO WASHINGTON			
a.m.	Totem Pole	Best breakfast	Van/Restaurant
a.m.	Covington house	Best log cabin	Van/Attraction
a.m.	Opal's Chatterbox	Best crafts	Van/Craft
a.m.	Old West In Miniature	Best setting	Van/Attraction
p.m.	L.M. Hidden	Best French food	Van/Restaurant
p.m.	House of Vagabonds	Best antiques	Van/Antiques
p.m.	Fort Vancouver	Best historic site	Van/Attraction
p.m.	Club Green	Best sports	Van/Sport
Now that your appetite's back, take yourself out to dinner.			

There's no better Introduction to Washington than Vancouver, the southern gateway to the Great White North.

Florist

KEL'S FLOWERS AND GIFTS, 7700 Northeast Hazeldell Avenue, Vancouver, Washington. A full-line florist also featuring baskets, candy, and gifts. Their chocolate molded pieces are award winning, and any figure can be custom ordered.

LUEPKE FLORIST, 1300 Washington, Vancouver, Washington. Luepke's carries a wide selection of floral arrangements, gifts, and seasonal specialities.

Food Store

VANCOUVER FOOD CENTER, Twelfth and Main, Vancouver, Washington. A full-line grocery store with a very popular coffee shop attached.

Gift Shop

COLLECTOR'S GIFT GALLERY, 700 Southeast Chaklov Drive, Number Eleven, Vancouver, Washington. A gift shop specializing in collector plates, lithographs, Hummels, Precious Moments, Tom Clark and David Winter gifts.

COUNTRY STYLE GIFT SHOPPE, 1013 Main Street, Vancouver, Washington. Explore these charming country gift selections for giving--or for your home.

Golf Course

CLUB GREEN MEADOWS
7703 NE 72nd Avenue
Vancouver, WA 98661
Tel. (206) 256-1510
Hrs: Mon. - Sun.   6:00 a.m. - 11:00 p.m.

Club Green Meadows has come a long way from its inception in the mid 1960s as a small nine hole golf course, to one of the Northwest's largest and most complete private recreational facilities. The dream for owners Leo Frank and Don Grimm is rapidly becoming a reality. Club Green Meadows offers the ultimate fitness, sports and social environment with over 180,000 square feet of indoor facilities to go with the now private eighteen hole championship golf course. There are fifteen racquetball courts, eight bowling lanes, three basketball courts, an indoor jogging track, and two swimming pools with jacuzzis. The 7,000 square foot weight room is completely equipped and has trained professionals to assist customers in planning individual fitness programs. There is a pro shop, beauty salon, tanning beds, sauna and massage facilities. Green Meadows offers training programs and classes in everything from aerobic exercise to basketball. They are the training center for the Portland Trailblazers.

On the second floor at Green Meadows is a charming deli/restaurant/lounge combination. It has beautiful oak woodwork and brass fixtures and offers a view of the golf course. There is a TV viewing room and deli seating overlooking the racquetball courts. It has been recently remodeled and redecorated offering members a charming place to enjoy good food, drink and conversation. The newly redecorated ballroom offers elegant facilities for up to 300 guests.

The Meadows Kitchen and Lounge, a restaurant near the entrance to the parking lot, is open to the general public and offers fine food in relaxing

Clark County

surroundings including patio dining overlooking the tenth tee. A visit to Club Green Meadows will be a busy and enjoyable time. The club is located just off I-205 and just north of Vancouver Mall at 78th Street and Anderson. Stop by and see one of the premier recreational facilities anywhere.

Restaurant

THE CROSSING, Eighth and Jefferson, Vancouver, Washington. All dining areas are inside vintage 1900 railroad cars. Their slogan: "On track with fine food!"

DYLAN'S RESTAURANT, 1004 Main Street, Vancouver, Washington. A full-service menu with sandwiches, chicken, and seafood. Also enjoy sundaes, cones, frozen yogurts with over forty toppings.

SPICY MAMA'S RESTAURANT, LOUNGE, AND BANQUET HOUSE, 7909 Northeast Sixth Avenue, Vancouver, Washington (At Ferryman's Inn). Over 200 spicy choices from four complete menus of homemade food.

THEO'S RESTAURANT AND LOUNGE, 109 West Fifteenth Street, Vancouver, Washington. Theo's specializes in pasta and pizza and is open for lunch and dinner.

TOTEM POLE
7720 Highway 99
Vancouver, WA 98665
Take the 78th Street exit off I-5 going north or south.
Tel. (206) 694-2541
Hrs: Mon. - Thu.   6:00 a.m. - 11:00 p.m.
       Friday   6:00 a.m. - 12:00 midnight
       Saturday   6:30 a.m. - 12:00 midnight
       Sunday   6:30 a.m. - 11:00 p.m.
VISA, MasterCard, Diner's Club cards accepted.

The Totem Pole legend of hospitality dates back more than one hundred years, for on the site of this modern dining facility weary travelers paused on their journey from Kelso to Fort Vancouver to rest, learn the news of the day, share a modest meal and be refreshed. The road over which the horse drawn wagons and buggies traveled was little more than a trail, rutted and muddy in winter, dusty in summer. In 1929, when U.S. Highway 99 was constructed in front of the old farm home, it was converted into a restaurant named the Totem Pole. Through the years the original home has gradually disappeared and today the Totem Pole can accommodate up to 250 patrons and each year serves nearly a half million travelers and residents of Vancouver.

Two breakfast, lunch and dinner specials are offered daily while the menu offers popular favorites such as Tee-Pee chicken, seafood and U.S. choice broiled or grilled steaks. There are banquet facilities for up to a hundred persons and the Canoe Room Lounge has live music from the 50s and 60s.

Despite the physical changes over the years, the same warm western hospitality which made this corner a landmark has prevailed. The legend of welcome to people of every walk of life, creed and race is as sincere today as it was a hundred years ago.

Wine

AFFAIRS OF THE HEART, 1006 Main Street, Vancouver, Washington. A specialty wine shop with many appealing gifts for the home.

THE OLD WINERY
10311 NE Highway 99
Hazel Dell, WA 98686
Tel.   (206) 573-7510
Hrs: Lunch   Mon. - Fri.   11:00 a.m. - 2:00 p.m.
          Dinner   Mon. - Fri.   4:00 p.m. - 10:00 p.m.
                             Sat. - Sun.   4:00 p.m. - 11:00 p.m.
Visa, MasterCard, Carte Blanche accepted.

When asking the whereabouts of a good restaurant in Hazel Dell, you're likely to receive the same answer from all of it's residents. They'll sit there and point a finger down the road and say, "The place you're looking for is The Old Winery. It's the best one around for miles."

The Old Winery used to be just that, an old winery. Today, after extensive reconditioning, this delightful building serves as a fine dining establishment. It's decorated in old world style with lattice work between each of the dining booths. Looking around, you'll notice Italian prints on stucco walls with an occasional patch of exposed brickwork. Plenty of plants hanging there and there lend a fresh, lively atmosphere to this unique restaurant. However, ambiance apart, a description of the food is due. The menu's main emphasis is on Italian food, but the chef, Timothy Winner (how could you go wrong with a name like that), also cooks up a mean steak.

When it's time for wine you'll be presented with an extensive selection ranging in price from inexpensive to very expensive. Choose a favorite and enjoy it on either of the two patio dining areas featuring a herb garden and a serene waterfall. The Old Winery, ever conscientious, also provides handicapped access to the entire restaurant. Ahhh, now it's easy to understand why the locals refer to The Old Winery as being the "Best Choice." Stop by and judge for yourself.

Yacolt

Railroad tracks of the Longview, Portland and Northern Railroad snaked from Vancouver to the Lewis River basin, making Yacolt a sizable community during the days of railroad logging. This is the northern terminus of the Chelatchie Prairie Railroad's excursion trains which run out of Battleground during summer months.

Attractions

About one mile north of town, where the county road and railroad grade meet on the shore of Cedar Creek is the **campsite** of George McClellan. The Civil War general, then a company officer at Fort Vancouver, camped here July 25, 1853 while on an army expedition mapping inland areas of Washington.

Attraction

POMEROY LIVING HISTORY FARM, Route One, 20902 Northeast Lucia Falls Road, Yacolt, Washington. Pomeroy Farm depicts 1920's farm life with its log house, blacksmith shop, barn, granary, separator shed, displays of antique farm equipment and more. Tours, hayrides, and seasonal activities are available.

COWLITZ COUNTY

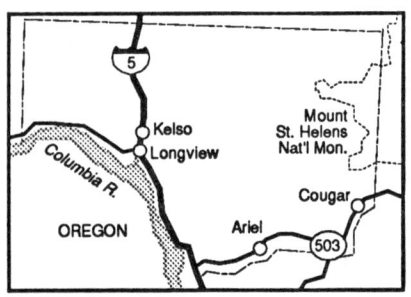

This Columbia River county shares about forty miles of its southern border with Oregon. Little Wahkiakum County is to the west and giant Lewis County stretches across the northern border, including with it headwaters of the Cowlitz River. The Cascade summit, with the peak of Mount Saint Helens, rises in the east, just over the line in Skamania County. The Willapa Hills of the Coast Range on the west are low; the Cascade foothills in the east are about 4,000 feet above sea level. There are 1,146 square miles of mostly lowlands in Cowlitz County, and perhaps 80,000 people, over half living in one urban area where the Cowlitz and Columbia meet.

Cowlitz, the county name and that of the major river draining from the north to the Columbia, was the designation given the Indian people of the Salish tribe who lived here. They used a large prairie as their place to commune with the Great Spirit. Chinook jargon roughly translates cowlitz as one who catches the "medicine spirit."

Much of today's local spirit comes from being the front door to the Mount Saint Helens National Volcanic Monument. Toutle River, which enters the Cowlitz north of Castle Rock, provides drainage from Spirit Lake on the very flanks of the mountain that blew its north side in 1980. Woodland, at the county line on I-5, has a secondary gateway up the Lewis River valley with its many lakes. Silt from the eruption is still significant in the Toutle river's flows and in sand bars which build up in channels of the Cowlitz and Columbia Rivers. From extensive scientific references to touristy-gee gaws, the mountain's life is recounted time and again.

This is a country where winter and spring bring lots of rain. About forty-five inches a year fall in Longview, and much larger totals are recorded in the foothills. The growing season is 203 days. The mild temperatures--the July high averages 77.8 and the January low 31.8--are well-suited for dairy and vegetable farming. But, it is timber, not agriculture which drives the economy. There are over 100 lumber and wood products employers in the county, plus eight manufacturing paper and another seven in the chemical business associated with both primary industries.

Cowlitz County

Well over half the total county population, 42,000 out of 80,000, live within the twin cities of Kelso and Longview which are neighbors on opposite banks of the Cowlitz. The industrial giants of Longview initially processed not only the logs from timberland up the valley, but from rafts of logs towed down the Columbia. The port offered vast acreage where ocean-going vessels could load the finished product processed in uniquely designed plants. Longview Fiber built its first paper mill in 1927 to utilize the sawdust and other waste generated by the area sawmills. Since 1941, the waterfront has held a Reynolds Metal Company aluminum plant which uses low-cost hydroelectric power to smelt bauxite brought from afar. Primary aluminum, wire and cable are turned out in the Reynolds complex.

Settlers came to the county during the days of Hudson Bay Company trading. In 1849 they created a community on what is now the industrial part of Longview. This is where Washington's 1852 convention was held that resulted in separation from the Oregon Territory. Monticello, the town established here, was named the Cowlitz county seat when the county was formed in 1854. A winter of floods in 1866-67 swept away the town and the courthouse moved to Kelso. R.A. Long, founder of Long-Bell Lumber Co., picked the flood plain in 1923 to lay out a planned community and build his mills.

Mount Saint Helens
National Volcanic Monument

Since the eruption of May, 1980, the nation's second volcanic national monument has stabilized and seismic activity indicates that a period of dormancy is returning. The preserve is mostly in Skamania County, with little fingers in Cowlitz and Lewis counties. Pumice from a big eruption of 1840 used to cover much of the country north of the peak, and probably formed Spirit Lake which was part of the Indian's lore. Spirit alludes to tales that the ghost of a bull elk is said to rise from the waters on occasion. Windy Ridge, forest road 99, leads to a dramatic overlook of the lake and the north face, altered in the recent eruption. The route is only open in the summer.

Deposition of the three or four billion cubic yards of debris and the lateral blast effect on the north side gave scientists an explanation for similar deposits seen north of Mount Shasta next to I-5 and Highway 97 in northern California. Geologists are still studying effects of the May, 1980 eruption here. Several research sites are marked for continuing work, including 250 within the monument and about 150 in the national forest which lies beyond. Tags and colored ribbon warn the curious to leave research areas to the scientists. The peak itself reopened to climbing from the south side in the spring of 1987 under a permit system. About 170 miles of foot trails are open or under development in the monument area.

The main visitor information center is east of Castle Rock on Highway 504. For planning, it takes about two and a half hours to drive from the west side to the Spirit Lake viewpoints on the east side. A summer loop route which circles the mountain will provide a full day of exploring and sight-seeing.

One of the longest lava tubes known is at **Ape Cave**, on U.S. Forest Service Roads 83 and 8303 south of the mountain. Take forest road 90 east from Cougar, turn north at the junction eight miles out and follow signs to the cave. Wear warm clothes, carry a flashlight if you are going to explore. The name comes from the cave's young discoverers, who called themselves the "cave apes."

Lava River Falls, in a canyon off forest road 83 on the south side, is a mixture of lava formations and runoff water with sounds of the waterfalls that in some places can be heard but not seen. From the Lahar Mudflow viewpoint, a one-and one-half mile hike into the canyon. Ranger tours are offered three times a week in summer months.

Meta Lake, on forest road 99 on the east side route to Windy Ridge, is a place bypassed by the eruption of 1980. The small lake survived, but the motor vehicle of a miner was trapped. Ranger walks are given here three times a day during summer months.

For further information, contact the **Mount Saint Helens National Volcanic Monument Headquarters**, telephone 247-5473, or call 864-6699 for a 24-hour recording on current information from the **Visitor's Center**.

Attractions

On the Cowlitz, which used to have regular steamboat service upstream as far as Toledo, stands **Castle Rock**, a 150-foot high crag in a flat valley. The area's first settler, William Huntington, came in 1852. The century-old town of Castle Rock, now with a population of about 2,000, is on the east bank where dikes protect the land from flooding. The town had to rebuild itself after floodwaters and mud from Mount Saint Helens' eruption devastated much of the little community. Low grade coal, the first found in Washington, was discovered here by fur traders but never mined commercially.

The **Henry Jackson house**, built in 1857 and later made into an inn, is two miles west of Castle Rock on a county road. Ask for directions in town.

Silver Lake, on Highway 504 east of Castle Rock, is said to be one of the best warm-water fishing lakes in the state. It is only about ten feet deep, storing water which runs to a tributary of the Toutle River.

The **Museum of Mt. Saint Helens**, 4004 Spirit Lake Highway near Silver Lake, is a private collection of memorabilia of the eruption. There is a part of the Cowlitz River mud flow with a motorcycle in it, a replica of Spirit Lake Lodge with proprietor Harry Truman at the bar before both vanished in the discharge of gas and volcanic ash. Open daily. Telephone 274-7011.

Ostrander, off I-5 between Castle Rock and Kelso, is a village that has generated some of Washington's best stories about gold. No one has struck it rich in Ostrander Creek, site of homesteads on its banks since 1852, but prospectors did come more than once, some drawn by the tale that a woman found two nuggets in the craw of a chicken she butchered. A mill was here in 1910 with railroad tracks extending forty miles into the woods. Everything was taken away to another location when logging ended.

Hulda Klager Lilac Gardens, South Pekin Road in Woodland, are a national historic site. It was here that Klager, in 1903, began breeding lilacs, eventually producing ten new varieties. Gardens are open daily. The house is a museum. Tours by appointment, call 225-8996.

The **Lewis River Salmon Hatchery**, 4404 Lewis River Road eight miles east of Woodland, welcomes visitors. Call 225-7413.

Kalama, a town of 1,200 persons on the Columbia River, was the home of John Kalama who came from Hawaii to work for Hudson Bay Company. The Northern Pacific Railroad made this a ferry crossing for trains in 1870. As it laid tracks north to Seattle, 1,200 laborers lived here. The town boomed, than shrank to a trans-shipping point for grain and a processing point for the salmon taken in days of commercial fisheries on the lower river.

Today there is a large marina for pleasure craft adjoining the commercial piers on a seven-mile long waterfront. The totem pole in Marine Park, carved by Chief Don Lelooska of Ariel, is said to be the tallest totem in the world carved from a single tree. In downtown, ask for the historic home brochure, which leads you by several Victorian houses.

For information, contact **Tourist Regional Information Program**, Box 128, Longview WA 98632. Telephone 577-3321.

Ariel

Ariel, a tiny community, is at the downstream end of the lake formed by Ariel Dam. Several communities could claim a link with the 1971 aircraft highjacker D.B. Cooper, but Ariel turns it into a festival with a Thanksgiving celebration and search for the elusive man and his money, not seen since he exited the rear door of a southbound jet, popping a parachute above the forest.

Gift Shop

MT. ST. HELENS VIEW PARK AND GIFT SHOP
239 Highway 503
Ariel, WA 98603
Tel. (206) 231-4333
Hrs: May - Nov. Mon. - Sat. 9:00 a.m. - 5:00 p.m.
Sunday 10:00 a.m. - 5:00 p.m.

Peter Kraakman, proprietor of the Mt. St. Helens View Park and Gift Shop came to the West Coast from Holland in 1971 as a bulb grower. He purchased the property that makes up the park in 1981 because of the fabulous view and proceeded to develop the park and shop. There is no admission charge into the park, which has the best view of Mt. St. Helens in the whole area. The park itself is lovely, with two and a half acres of beautiful dahlias, gladiolus and other flowers, some rare varieties not usually found outside of Holland.

The Gift Shop has an extensive selection. Peter and his wife Linda select their stock carefully to offer their customers a choice of beautiful and unique gift items. They have handmade cuckoo clocks from Germany, "Delft Blue" china from Holland, and handmade table linens imported from Europe. There are ceramics, crystal, pottery, pewter and the largest selection of Mt. St. Helens glass in the state.

There are hiking trails near the park, and for the less energetic, the Mt. St. Helens View Park and Gift Shop is a wonderful place to just relax and enjoy a truly remarkable view in serene and lovely surroundings.

Cougar

Cougar, located upstream almost at the boundary of the monument, is a resort community on the shores of Yale Reservoir. Helicopter rides to view the mountain take off from Cougar. Mountain lakes nearby attract fishermen and campers. Several hydroelectric turbines are powered by the water flowing through the Lewis River basin.

Chamber of Commerce

COUGAR-YALE CHAMBER OF COMMERCE
P. O. Box 117
Cougar, WA 98616
Tel. (206) 238-5253

If you know in advance that you'll be heading through this neck of the woods, it'd be a cryin' shame to just drive by on the freeway and never know what you missed. Get in touch with the Cougar-Yale Chamber of Commerce so you can plan a stop or two.

Mt. St. Helens is the big draw here, but not the only one you'll want to visit. The Lewis River Recreation Area has facilities and opportunities to accommodate almost every outdoor sport, as well as historical buildings and cultural events. Two national historic sites, the Hulda Klager Lilac Gardens and the Cedar Creek Grist Mill, are nearby, as is Kalama, the world's largest single tree totem pole.

While wandering the banks of the river perhaps you'll catch a glimpse of "Sasquatch," or "Bigfoot," an elusive man-like beast the locals say lives near Mt. St. Helens. If you're really lucky, you'll catch a trace of D.B. Cooper, an elusive man who skyjacked a jet and parachuted into this area with $200,000 in 1971. Most of the money and all of the man have never been found.

Market

COUGAR STORE
16842 Lewis River Road
Cougar, WA 98616
Tel. (206) 238-5228
Hrs: Winter   7:00 a.m. - 6:30 p.m.
      Summer   7:00 a.m. - 8:30 p.m.

What do you need right now? If you're passing through Cougar, Dorotha Elmire's got whatever you need down at the Cougar Store.

Dorotha's got food, film, gifts, beer, wine and soda. She's got gas for your R.V. She's got fishing licenses for trout, and fishing gear, too, if you need it, as well as mementos from Mt. St. Helens.

The Cougar Store is the one place for supplies you can count on to be open 362 days a year - except for Thanksgiving, Christmas, and New Year's. Dorotha invites you to come visit and enjoy the beauty of the mountain.

Pottery

COUGAR CERAMICS
16834 Lewis River Road
Cougar, WA 98616
Tel. (206) 238-5253

In case you haven't realized it yet, you're now in the shadow of one of the most phenomenal natural events of the century - the June 12, 1980 eruption of Mt. St. Helens. People in towns like Cougar can tell you stories about the ashfall that are stranger than science fiction, and they've got the ash to prove it.

Lynne Birch, however, proves it in a classy way. Lynne owns Cougar Ceramics, a shop which produces fine ceramic products using ash that fell on Cougar from the June 12, 1980 eruption of Mt. St. Helens. Lynne adds the ash into her clay and pours it in a special manner which gives a marbled effect. The white part is regular ceramic clay, while the brown is the color the ash turns when fired at nearly 2,000 F. There is no coloring added, as this is the natural color of the ash from Cougar.

You won't find ceramics like this elsewhere. Stop in and take a look for yourself. Exit from I-5 at Woodland and travel east on State Hwy 503 for thirty miles to get to Cougar.

Restaurant

THE LANDING RESTAURANT
16849 Lewis River Road
Cougar, WA 98616
Tel. (206) 238-5312
Hrs: Winter 5:00 a.m. - 8:00 p.m.
　　　Summer 3:00 a.m. - 11:00 p.m.

　　This may well be the only eatery listed in this book that opens for breakfast at 3:00 a.m. and don't confuse it with some truck stop.
　　Everything here is made from scratch -- no chemicals added -- and the food here is good! Prices are very reasonable, too, and there are senior citizen discounts.
　　Breakfasts range from the traditional to the daily specials; lunch features a variety of soup and sandwich combos; and dinners offer seafood, steaks and poultry. Halibut is the Friday special, and Tuesday is Taco Night at the Landing. The fresh shrimp dinner is sauteed, grilled, or poached. Hallelujah! Do you realize how hard it is to find shrimp that isn't deep-fried? The portions are generous, too, so you can be assured you won't walk away hungry.
　　To find the Landing, take the Woodland/Cougar exit and go right on Lewis River Road for twenty-eight miles. It's worth the trip, even if you don't keep early hours.

Kelso

　　Kelso, on the east bank of the Cowlitz, was founded by Peter Crawford, a Scotsman who came here in 1847. Hudson Bay Company shipped cattle and grain from here in pioneer days. When Crawford platted the town in 1884, he named it for his hometown of Kelso, Scotland. This was an important logging town for years, the site of a commercial smelt fishery at times, and the junction with what is now Highway 4, the traditional down-river route to the ocean beaches. The county seat, disposed from Monticello after the floods of 1866-67, was officially designated as Kelso in 1923.

Attractions

　　Cowlitz County Historical Museum, 405 Allen Street Kelso, presents information on much of southwestern Washington's heritage. A log cabin is recreated and furnished in period articles. Dolls, Indian artifacts, war memorabilia, wildlife displays and ever-changing exhibits featured.

The new building is designed for handicapped access. A tour of ten historic homes can begin here following directions in a self-guiding brochure. Call 577-3119 for more information.

Kelso Volcano Tourist Information Center is at 105 Minor Road. Displays show the progression of the l980 eruption of Mt. St. Helens. There are photographs, a large scale model and rock and pumice samples from the area. Open daily. Call 577-8058 for further information.

The **Kelso Chamber of Commerce** is located at 105 Minor Road, Box 58, Kelso WA 98626. Telephone 423-0900.

Accommodations

THUNDERBIRD MOTOR INN
510 Kelso Drive
Kelso, WA 98626
Tel. (206) 636-4400

The Thunderbird Motor Inn is your "Best Choice" for accommodations in Kelso. With a hundred and sixty-three units located in two wings, there are rooms with single queens, double queens and kings, as well as two executive suites from which to choose.

The dining facilities, overseen by Chef Scott Brown, accommodate ninety people and are open from 11:00 a.m. until 2:00 a.m., Monday through Friday. The coffee shop is open from 6:00 a.m. until 10:00 a.m. during the week and until 11:00 a.m. on Friday and Saturday. The Inn also contains seven banquet rooms, three of which can be opened up to make one large room to accommodate five hundred people. The lounge offers live music starting at 8:45 p.m. Thursdays through Saturdays. On all other evenings, music videos are displayed.

The Thunderbird Motor Inn is within walking distance to the Mount Saint Helens Visitor Center, a shopping center and fine restaurants.

Antiques

GREAT NORTHWEST TRADING COMPANY
100 South Pacific
Kelso, WA 98626
Tel. (206) 425-9610
Hrs: Mon. - Sat. 12:00 noon - 5:00 p.m.

"There's probably nothin' that we don't carry" says LaRue Heiner, owner of what looks like an old time general store and offers almost anything one can imagine.

LaRue and Toddy shop the auctions for merchandise, especially furniture, but most of the items in the store are brought in by folks who want to buy, trade or sell. Have some good ole timey fun browsing through the antiques of all sorts; china cabinets, toys, tools, old books, English bone china, cups and saucers, wrought iron beds, cook stoves, guns, trophies......well, LaRue wasn't spinnin' any yarns!

And don't go away yet! Toddy provides a unique service of printing antique looking marriage licenses fit for framing along with wedding pictures. So C'mon in and take a look-see. If they've got it, they'll get it for you and if they haven't got it, they'll show you how to get along without it!

Restaurant

HIGHLANDER RESTAURANT
1509 Allen
Kelso, WA 98626
Tel. (206) 423-1500
Hrs: Mon. - Sun. 7 a.m. - 12:00 midnight

The Highlander Restaurant, aptly named for mountainous portions of food at a molehill of a price, seems to offer something for everyone. Besides the restaurant and lounge, called the Scotland Yard, there is a sixteen lane bowling alley, which hosts the Mount St. Helens Invitational, the Mount St. Helens World gift shop and a photo lab on the premises.

Tailored for petite, regular or hearty appetites the restaurant goes against traditional rules of business by providing very large meals for little money. A hearty order of veal cutlets yields three veal cutlets and the omelettes are gigantic. "If you don't get filled up here you can't anywhere!" says owner Jim Springer. The menu offers over one hundred different items.

Located across the street from the Chamber of Commerce, the Volcano Center, and the new mall, come on in and have a bite to eat! And eat, and eat, and eat, and........

Longview

This is a major port on the vast Columbia and Snake river system that moves bulk cargo from the interior of the Pacific Northwest. Longview has a deep-draft port sixty-six miles above the Pacific Ocean that is a transshipment point for grain brought down the river by barge and by rail. The lumber, pulp and aluminum plants have their own shipping terminals at factory side.

In 1923 Robert A. Long began his planned city on the old site of Monticello. Long was a big operator in the days of "big operators." He came out from the eastern forests, then cut over to Longview, bought 60,000 acres of timberland, and set out to locate a handy millsite where the Cowlitz emptied into the Columbia. The mill and the town grew together.

Highway engineers from Oregon and Washington followed up with a graceful steel bridge over the Columbia to the town of Rainier on the Oregon shore. From the high bridge, Longview spreads itself in testimony to the planning launched by Long's employees.

Attractions

Port Longview, operated by a public Port Commission, on a 177 acre site just upstream from the highway bridge over the Columbia, bustles with shipping activity. For tours, call 425-3305. Offered between 10:00 a.m. and 1:00 p.m. daily.

McClelland Arts Center, Longview has a changing schedule of exhibits by local artists. Open Monday through Friday, 10:00 a.m. to 4:00 p.m. Telephone 577-3356.

Hotel Monticello commemorates the town, on this site, that was washed away by flood waters. The public lobby has sixteen historic paintings by Joe Knowles, an artist of the 1920s. To find this gem from another era, drive to the southern end of Washington Way when you enter Longview. Call 425-9900 for reservations. The downtown shops, which repeat some of the tradition of the town, are in a six block area on Commerce Avenue due east of the Monticello.

Lake Sacajawea, a park created in the new town, matured into a place of tranquility surrounded by a city of over 30,000 people. Commercial and residential areas touch this network of paths and picnic benches next to public schools.

Columbia Theater, a downtown architectural gem that has stained-glass in its box office windows, has a fully-restored interior with a 1,000 seat house used for road shows and local performances. The most recent restoration work was planned to replace the old roof, protecting the sculptured plaster ceiling from damage.

For information: **Longview Chamber of Commerce**, 1563 Olympia Way, Longview WA 98632. Telephone 423-8400.

Antiques

LOLA'S ANTIQUES, 5401 Ocean Beach Highway, Longview, Washington. Furniture, miscellaneous collectibles, and lots of glass--some very, very, old and from famous European glassmakers.

Art Gallery

BROADWAY GALLERY
1418 Commerce
Longview, WA 98632
Tel. (206) 577-0544
Hrs: Mon. - Sat.   10:00 a.m. to 5:30 p.m.

Five years ago three artists came up with the idea of a "co-operative" gallery. They invited thirty of the best artists from this area to a "meeting of the minds." Ideas were expressed for owning and operating a gallery, and out of the thirty artists present, seventeen strong willed and very creative individuals now run the gallery as a team.

They started out in a tiny little shop just off Commerce Avenue and their recent move to their present location was very beneficial. Now they are out where they can really be noticed. The Gallery has thirty artists represented. The members are very selective of whose work is displayed. The work of guest artists is featured several times during the year.

The Broadway Gallery is the place to see the best available by local artists. Much of the art displayed can be rented either for business or private use. The Gallery offers custom matting and framing, art supplies and art classes for both children and adults. This is a great place to shop when looking for that really special gift.

Books

VISTA COMICS, 901 Fifteenth Avenue, Longview, Washington. Collectibles, mint condition comics, baseball cards and accessories, balloons, music boxes, and other novelty gifts are here.

Delicatessen

APPLE A DAY SANDWICH SHOP
930 Fir
Longview, WA 98632
Tel. (206) 423-9600
Hrs: Mon. - Fri.   9:00 a.m. - 4:00 p.m.

Although everything served at the Apple A Day Sandwich Shop is good for you, this is not a health food store. Owner Cindy Norton named the shop "Apple a Day" because of its location in the Medical Arts Plaza. She opened the shop to provide a place for lunch for those who work in the Medical Arts Plaza, but as it's reputation for excellence has grown, many others from around the community have found their way here.

Cindy is dedicated to providing quality, quantity and fast friendly service. She uses only the best quality ingredients available. Soups and desserts are made from scratch. The delicious taco soup is a house specialty and also available are the usual deli favorites as well as vegie specials, taco salad and nachos. Cindy's desserts are continuously changing and in the spring she incorporates fresh fruit into them.

Apple a Day Sandwich Shop is an excellent choice for a delicious, nutritious, fast and friendly lunch.

Florist

FLOWERS, ETC.
330 Triangle Mall
Longview, WA 98632
Tel. (206) 425-7460
Hrs: Mon. - Fri.　9:30 a.m. - 9:00 p.m.
　　　Saturday　　9:30 a.m. - 5:00 p.m.
　　　Sunday　　 11:00 a.m. - 5:00 p.m.
and,
JANSEN FLOWERS AND GIFTS
1346 Vandercook Way
Longview, WA 98632
Tel. (206) 423-0450
Hrs: Mon. - Sat.　8:00 a.m. - 6:00 p.m.

Harry and Clara Renick have created two lovely stores with a large selection of flowers and gift items. This has been a family business since Clara's father opened the original store over thirty years ago and they have a well established reputation for quality and excellence.

Flowers, Etc. is primarily a gift shop with a large selection of porcelain collectables, dolls, plates, they are an authorized Bradford dealer, Hummel and Precious Moment figurines, Anri wood carvings and Chilmark pewter figurines. You will also find stuffed animals and a good selection of Mt. St. Helens collectables. Jansen Flowers carries a selection of gift items, too, but are known for their contemporary floral designs using unusual and exotic flowers that come from such places as Africa, Israel, Europe and South America.

Nationally known artists make guest appearances at the stores, which allows collectors the chance to meet them and have collectables signed. Recently artists Dr. Tom Clarke and Lucy Riggs have visited the store. When Harry and Clara visit the shows around the Northwest on buying trips, they purchase gifts they know you will enjoy giving. Both stores are full of beautifully displayed merchandise that make browsing a pleasure.

LONGVIEW FLORAL, 1201 Commerce Avenue, Longview, Washington. Of course, flowers. You'll also find gifts by Hagar, and in back, an attractive little wine shop with northwest and imported wines and wine-related gifts.

Cowlitz County

Is the touring vehicle getting a little bit crowded? The RV is so full of souvenirs and strewn maps that you've nicknamed it flotsam and jetsam? If so, stretch out and take advantage of Longview's break from cramped quarters.

	A REFRESHING CHANGE		
	Hotel Monticello	Best accommodations	Longv/Acc.
	After that pleasant sleep, go and see the town.		
a.m.	Apple A Day	Best sandwiches	Longv/Rest.
a.m.	Port Longview	Best tour	Longv/Tour
a.m.	Lake Sacajawea	Best park	Longv/Park
a.m.	Broadway Gallery	Best art	Longv/Art
p.m.	Boondocks	Best seafood	Longv/Rest.
p.m.	Flowers, Etc.	Best gifts	Longv/Gift
p.m.	Columbia Theatre	Best entertainment	Longv/Ent.
p.m.	Henri's	Best rack of lamb	Longv/Rest.

Now that you've had a refreshing change, gather your souvenirs, toss them in the RV and head out. It's crowded, but no one ever said touring was an easy life!

Restaurant

BOONDOCKS ON THE COWLITZ
1826 1st Avenue
Longview, WA 98532
Tel. (206) 423-7110
Hrs: Mon. - Thu.   10:30 a.m. - 10:00 p.m.
     Friday   10:30 a.m. - 11:00 p.m.
     Saturday   10:30 a.m. - 11:00 p.m.
     Sunday   10:00 a.m. - 9:00 p.m.
and,
BOONDOCKS RESTAURANT
1015 Robert Bush Drive
South Bend, WA 98586
Tel. (206) 875-5155

   The Boondocks restaurants are a family owned and operated business with Rex and Elly Gray and their children in charge. Their philosophy is that a stranger is a friend you haven't met yet. That is the way you are treated when you dine at Boondocks, like a guest in their home.

John Gray is the executive chef and eldest son, brothers Dan and Peter along with brother-in-law Tom Martin maintain food quality. John and Peter trained at the Culinary Institute of America in New York and offer a varied and interesting menu featuring many seafood selections at both restaurants. The decor of the Cowlitz restaurant is unique. The centerpiece is three huge cottonwood trees growing straight up through the middle of the restaurant. From the restaurant you can watch the boats work the river as fishermen catch fresh smelt. The South Bend Boondocks is located on the waterfront where one can watch gill netters at work in the waters in front of the restaurant.

Both of the Boondocks restaurants offer a well rounded menu with many choices in addition to the seafood they feature. There are family members to be found on both premises, overseeing the operation, which insures a friendly and rewarding dining experience in congenial and attractive surroundings.

HENRI'S
4545 Ocean Beach Highway
Longview, WA 98632
Tel. (206) 425-7970
Hrs: Mon. - Fri.   11:00 a.m. - 10:00 p.m.
       Saturday   4:30 p.m. - 10:00 p.m.

Proprietors Henri and Cathy Paul have created a warm and delightful restaurant which has been family owned and operated for the past twenty-two years. Henri, who is also the chef, has been in the food service business since 1951 and has assembled a varied and interesting menu which is served in charming surroundings.

The restaurant is large and each room is named after one of the Paul's children. There is the Vincentian which is done in Italian decor, the Elizabethan, done in British decor, and the Gregorian and Michel which are done in French decor. The main dining room is circular and in it's center is a beautiful walk in wine cellar from which the customer can choose wine.

You may choose to feast on rack of lamb or Oregon quail, which are raised just across the Columbia River, both of which Henri highly recommends, or any of the other wonderful dishes offered. Whatever your selection, the excellent cuisine and unique atmosphere will delight you.

GRAYS HARBOR COUNTY

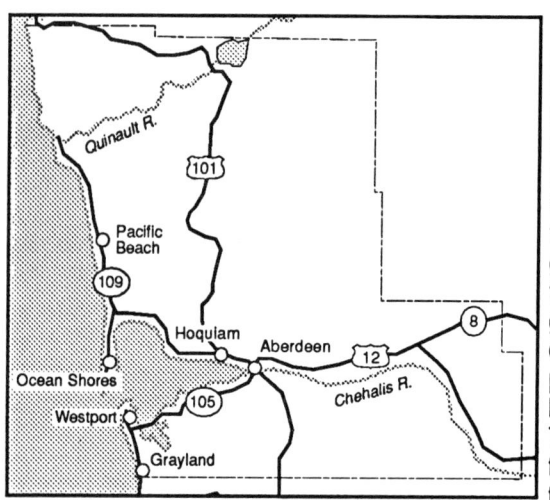

After the height of the mighty Olympic Mountains to the north, the Willapa Hills of Grays Harbor County and its neighbors to the south are geological afterthoughts. These gentle hills are some of the most productive timberland in the world. The elevation is less than 3,000 feet on the highest ridge. Flat prairies in between lend themselves to farming. The big coastal county includes the Quinault Indian Reservation on its northern beaches, the deep-draft harbor which Robert Gray discovered and at the east, the divide with Puget Sound that local people call the Black Hills.

There are 1,918 square miles in Grays Harbor County. Farming, fishing and forestry support a population of about 67,000 people. Aberdeen and Hoquiam, located at the neck of the bay first charted in 1792, are homes for almost half the county's people and most of its industry. Many other folks live in a scattering of communities along the freeway to Olympia in a valley where rivers by the dozens drain the rainfall toward Grays Harbor, a big bay. On the south spit is Westport, home to a sport and commercial fishing fleet. On the north spit is the planned vacation community of Ocean Shores.

History came early to this county with Robert Gray's three days of trading before he sailed south to the Columbia river in 1792, but there was little more than fur trading going on here until the immigrations of the 1850s. The first permanent settler in the county, William O'Leary, built among the Chehalis Indians in 1843. Montesano, the county seat since formation of the county in 1854, was settled only two years before and most of its present buildings date from the 1880s. Aberdeen, the largest town, wasn't much of anything until George R. Hume opened a fish packing company in 1878. Hoquiam, site of George Simpson's sawmill, was platted in 1885.

The beaches around Grays Harbor are popular during summer months. Many resorts, including several catering to recreational vehicle owners, dot the shoreline from border to border.

Attractions

See Clallam County for a description of **Olympic National Park**. A portion of the park, including the **Quinault Rain Forest**, lies within Grays Harbor County.

Lake Quinault, east of Highway 101 at the north county line, is one of those deep lakes formed when material pushed by glaciers created a dam after ice receded. The lake is within Quinault Indian Reservation, where tribal permits are required for fishing. Giant stands of Sitka Spruce, western hemlock and western red cedar are under study in a U.S. Forest Service research area where the average tree is 400 years old.

Pacific Beach, on Highway 109 a few miles short of the mouth of the Quinault River, has a large state park operated by a concessionaire. It includes 118 campsites, another twenty hookups for recreation vehicles. The beach is popular for surf fishing and clamming.

The **bay of Grays Harbor** itself is worth exploring. It is twelve miles wide, and reaches inland seventeen miles to the mouth of the Chehalis River. There is a two-mile channel between the spits to reach the ocean, giving a high-tide area of ninety-seven square miles of water within the bay. Boat rentals are available at several locations. A **passenger ferry** plies the bay daily from Aberdeen at South Newell Street, Hoquiam on Levee Street at Eighth, and at the Westport dock's float number six. This is a fun excursion. Call 268-0047 for schedules. Daily service is offered Memorial Day to Labor Day, and weekend trips in September.

The **domed county courthouse**, in **Montesano**, has murals showing historic events in the county's history. The **city hall**, with classical architecture, is recently restored. The name is a compromise for Mount Zion, which the wife of town founder Isaiah L. Scammon wanted. He thought Montesano more pleasant to the ear. Several Victorian homes, and a church built in 1882, can be seen while touring this little town.

Satsop Bulb Farm, west of Elma on Highway 12, is full of bright blooms each spring. Tours are available. Call 482-4223.

One of the Pacific Northwest's famed political topics of the 1980s, Washington's plan to build five nuclear power plants, can be updated by visiting **Satsop Nuclear site**, where the debt-ridden consortium's plants are in varied degree of completion. A visitor's center is on Highway 12 at Schouweiler Road. Tours are offered to some plants.

Between Elma and Oakville is the state's **Capital Forest**, a vast parkland of hiking trails, campsites and recreation areas. Over 110 miles of trails are within the forest. Open year around. Watch for the signs while driving on Highway 12.

The entire town of **Oakville**, on Highway 12 next to Chehalis Indian Reservation, is a trip back in time. Businesses continue to operate in buildings dating to the turn of the century. The showplace is a restoration of the Oakville Bank.

A **state salmon hatchery** is on the Humptulips River at the town of Humptulips on Highway 101. It is open daily until sunset. Exhibits tell the salmon's life cycle. Call 533-9372. Humptulips is Chinook jargon for hard-to-pole, as in hard to pole a canoe upstream.

For further information, contact **Grays Harbor Chamber of Commerce**, 2704 Sumner Avenue, Aberdeen WA 98520. Telephone 532-1924.

Aberdeen

Aberdeen Packing Company, already working at Ilwaco, had a packing house on the Wishkah River when Samuel Benn in 1884 turned his farm into the plat for a city and called it: Aberdeen at the suggestion of the packing house owner. Within ten years, the Tacoma, Olympia and Grays Harbor Railroad linked Puget Sound with the twin cities of Aberdeen and Hoquiam. Aberdeen now has about 19,000 residents.

Attractions

Replicas of two sailing vessels, the **Columbia** and **Lady Washington**, are under design at Aberdeen harbor. The state-financed project will eventually have both ships in port here. Matching funds from private donations are being raised to get the construction completed.

Polson Museum, on the right just before Riverside Bridge, features logging equipment. Open Wednesday through Sunday, 12:00 noon to 4:00 p.m. during summer months, and the same hours Saturday and Sunday the remaining nine months of the year. Call 533-5862.

For further information, contact **Grays Harbor Chamber of Commerce**, 2704 Sumner Avenue, Aberdeen WA 98520. Telephone 532-1924.

Accommodations

NORDIC INN
1700 S Boone Street
Aberdeen, WA 98520
Tel. (206) 533-0100

The Nordic Inn, located at the south end of Aberdeen, is a sixty-six unit motel with rooms to accommodate one person or a family. They are the only motel in town with a coffee shop and dining room right on the premises and there are banquet facilities for up to 300 people. Nordic Inn is conveniently located close to the South Shore Mall and Pioneer Park is nearby.

The Inn was built in 1969 and has recently undergone an extensive renovation, including the coffee shop and dining room. The rooms are spacious and comfortable, and nicely decorated. The coffee shop is open until 9:00 p.m. everyday and offers casual dining. The menu in the dining room offers very good fresh fish everyday, including live Maine lobster, as well as fresh local fish, such as salmon and crab, in season. There is live music every evening except Sunday in the Viking Room Lounge.

This is a good place to stay while in Aberdeen. The staff is courteous and helpful and will make your stay as pleasant as possible.

Delicatessen

SIMPSON AVENUE DELI
2600 Simpson Avenue
Aberdeen, WA 98520
Tel. (206) 538-1391
Hrs: Mon. - Thu.   6:00 a.m. - 7:00 p.m.
      Friday   6:00 a.m. - 9:00 p.m.
      Saturday   6:00 a.m. - 7:00 p.m.
      Sunday   10:00 a.m. - 5:00 p.m.

The Simpson Avenue Deli is a family affair. Gordon and Mari Miller own and run the deli and Bob, Mari's son, is the baker. He bakes fresh rolls and croissants every day. The deli offers a good selection of cheese, meat, wine, beer and daily specials to suit every taste.

One of the specialties found only at Simpson Avenue Deli is Porketta, a delicious "pasty" with meat, potatoes, and onions in a crust, very unusual and very delicious. There are always Italian specials available, such as lasagna, canneloni and ravioli. There are wonderful, fresh home made salads including potato salad, Greek salad, cole slaw and a pasta artichoke salad that is excellent. Some of the cheeses to be found are havarti, French raclette, Swiss, brie, romano and parmesan. This is fine deli with lots of interesting gourmet items in addition to the usual meat and cheese selections.

The Simpson Avenue Deli offers delicious home made deli style food, many different kinds of wine and beer to choose from in attractive and comfortable surroundings. Friendly people eager will help you find anything you need and are ready to offer suggestions. They do catering for groups and offer delivery on big orders. You'll find lots of goodies at this enjoyable deli.

Farm

BRADY'S OYSTER FARM
Star Route Box 700
Aberdeen, WA 98520
Tel. (206) 268-0077
Hrs: Tue. - Sun.   8:00 a.m. - 5:00 p.m.

In Westport, Washington at the west end of the Elk River Bridge on Highway 105, is a very unusual farm. This farm, owned and operated by Brady K. Engvall and his family raises only oysters. Oysters of all sizes, the best oysters to be found in Washington. The oysters are grown in suspended culture and they are the only retail farm that sells exclusively suspended oysters.

The unique way the oysters are grown at Brady's ensures that they are in great condition when sold. There are many sizes of oyster available, extra small, small, medium, and yearlings. The oysters are packed in ice before they leave the shop and they are so fresh that they will keep for two weeks under refrigeration. They are available in pints, quarts, and half gallons, as well as in the shell.

Brady's Oyster Farm started in 1970 and has been at this location for the past eight years. Brady and his family are committed to bringing you the freshest oysters possible. They have accumulated many different recipes over the years which they will share with you so that you can create your own delicious oyster dishes with the freshest oysters possible.

Gift Shop

THE GIFT HAUS
601 W Wishkah
Aberdeen, WA 98520
Tel. (206) 532-8261
Hrs: Mon. - Sat.   9:30 a.m. - 5:30 p.m.

Loraine Gibson and her daughters Terri Cady and Janet Boora are proprietors of The Gift Haus, one of the largest, most complete gift shops on the West Coast. They have been in business for sixteen years and have amassed a considerable knowledge of the gift market and offer a large and comprehensive selection. There are gifts here for every budget and the friendly staff are more than happy to answer questions or offer suggestions.

They offer a large selection of collectors plates and figurines including Hummel, Anri wood carvings, Precious Moments and many others. They are members of NALED, National Association of Limited Edition Dealers, and the Bradford Exchange. Browse through the children's section, dinnerware and kitchen departments. Choose from crystal, brass, china, wood and jewelry items, with major companies represented, such as Lenox, Swarovski, Waterford, Gorham, Mikasa and Black Hills gold.

They have a gift catalogue that is available in October in full color with unique gift ideas for Christmas. They offer free gift wrapping and will ship your purchase anywhere in the United States. A delightful place to browse and a must for collectors!

Restaurants

DUFFY'S
1605 Simpson Avenue
Aberdeen, WA 98520
Tel. (206) 532-3843
Hrs: Mon. - Sun.   6:00 a.m. - 11:00 p.m.
and,

1212 E. Wishkah	825 Simpson Avenue
Aberdeen, WA 98520	Hoquiam, WA 98550
Tel. (206) 538-0606	Tel. (206) 532-5419

Duffy's is a family run business that offers some of the best family dining in Aberdeen. The original Duffy's was established in 1945, and now Ralph Larson and his family have two other locations to serve you. All three locations specialize in quality, service, and price. They serve delicious, homestyle food in a casual family atmosphere at very reasonable prices.

Duffy's menu is extensive. To begin the day they have wonderful country breakfasts that are fantastic. The made from scratch Swedish pancakes are a real treat. Lunch features salads, sandwiches, everything from a hamburger to sliced turkey breast from a freshly roasted turkey. There are some delicious home style specials too, such as Irish stew, beef stroganoff and spaghetti. For dinner there is beef, chicken, pork chops and fish, including fresh salmon year round. One of the salad dressings, Mrs. Larson's creation, is a wonderful sweet and sour dressing and may be purchased to take home.

Duffy's offers an unbeatable combination of very reasonable prices for very generous portions of excellent home style food. The casual family atmosphere has made Duffy's a favorite of tourists and local residents alike. Try it, you won't be disappointed.

MISTY'S
116 W Heron Street
Aberdeen, WA 98520
Tel. (206) 533-0956
Hrs: Mon. - Sun.   11:00 a.m. - 9:00 p.m.

Misty's specializes in healthfully created cuisine with a gourmet touch. Owner Tracy Walthall searches the area to find the freshest ingredients possible for her deliciously different cuisine. The restaurant is not large, and the art deco interior adds to the intimate feeling. Tracy makes every effort to become acquainted with her customers and meet any special requests they might have.

Lunches feature a wide range of salads, such as "Chicken Oriental Salad" and sandwiches. There are daily specials for dinner, such as chicken Vermouth, or shrimp Dijon. The food has an international flavor with selections of Chinese, Italian, or French which can appear on any given day. The "just caught or just bought" special of the day is always interesting and prepared with flair. The sauteed mushrooms appetizer and the spinach salad are a delightful beginning to dinner. There is a fine wine list and this restaurant is one of only two in the area to feature beers from micro breweries.

In addition to the wonderful dining available at Misty's, there is a gift shop that carries gourmet coffees and condiments, as well as cookbooks. The emphasis is on delicious food at reasonable prices in this intimate restaurant. Tracy's innovative cooking and devotion to freshness and quality shine through in any meal you order. You will enjoy your dining experience at Misty's.

ROY'S WESTERN BUFFET
2701 Sumner Street
Aberdeen, WA 98520
Tel. (206) 533-0282
Hrs: Tue. - Sat. 11:00 a.m. - 8:00 p.m.
Sunday 12:00 noon - 7:00 p.m.

If you are traveling in Aberdeen and want a good, casual meal, this is the place. Roy's Western Buffet, as the name indicates, is a buffet, with a tremendous selection available from which you serve yourself. This is a great place to bring the kids, and they are oriented towards families and seniors. There are special children's prices, and the price of the meal includes everything, from salad to dessert to beverage.

For lunch, every day there is fried chicken, steamed vegetables, mashed potatoes, dressing, gravy, and three other entrees that are featured on a rotating basis. Dinner offers the same selection with the addition of roast baron of beef, baked ham and barbecued spare ribs. A salad bar and dessert bar are included with every meal. On Friday nights there is a special seafood buffet featuring shrimp, oysters, salmon, clam strips, pollock and more.

The food at Roy's Western Buffet is freshly prepared from scratch every day on the premises. The results are hearty and delicious and you can have as much as you want. There is lots of parking available, including many spaces for R.V.'s. This is a fine choice for casual dining in Aberdeen.

SIDNEY'S
512 W Heron
Aberdeen, WA 98520
Tel. (206) 533-6635
Hrs: Open 24 hours everyday.

Sidney's family restaurant brings you a large selection of delicious food for any time of the day. They serve only USDA choice meat and use no chemicals or preservatives. They take special pride in making all of their own sauces, gravy, potatoes, biscuits, pies, soups, salads and dressings to assure that there are no chemicals.

The menu at Sidney's is extensive. For breakfast they offer hearty country style breakfasts, as well as a good choice of a la carte items for the lighter eater. House specialties such as pork chops and eggs or Polish sausage and eggs are served with hash brown potatoes and toast. Lunches feature clam chowder, chili, soup of the day and salads along with gourmet sandwiches. The list of sandwiches is extensive with everything from croissant sandwiches to burgers. For dinner there is a large selection of pasta, meat and fish from which to choose. Dinners come with soup and potato and a salad bar is available at a slight additional charge. The homemade desserts are a delicious way to round out your meal.

Sidney's caters banquets for all occasions either at Sidney's or at the Ocean Shores Convention Center. The menu selection and prices are unbeatable and you can be sure of good fresh food at Sidney's.

Copalis Beach

Art Gallery

COVE GALLERY
P.O. Box 536
Copalis Beach, WA 98535
Tel. (206) 276-4360
Hrs: April 1st thru December 1st   11:00 a.m. - 5:00 p.m.

Art for the home or office is what you'll find at Cove Gallery. No, not the ordinary type of art that you might expect to find just about anywhere at any art gallery. But rather, at this gallery, you'll find unique, one-of-a-kind pieces crafted just for you.

Owner David Waller is also the gallery's artist, and a very talented one. David's custom, made-to-order paintings grace many fine homes throughout the Northwest. David creates the perfect masterpiece for your home as well. After viewing your furniture design and home setting, he will fit the painting to match your home by size, color and, of course, theme. All of this is done with a keen eye and sharp perceptions, which are very evident in the painting created just for you.

So, now you can understand the reasoning behind this gallery's success. Cove Gallery, producing custom art for those with a taste for excellence.

Gift Shop

TOP CAT GIFTS/SEAWAY FLEA MART
Benner Road
Copalis Beach, WA 98535
Tel. (206) 289-3423
Hrs: Wed. - Sun. 10:00 a.m. - 5:00 p.m.
and,
114 W Wishkah
Aberdeen, WA 98520
Tel. (206) 538-0123
Hrs: Tue. - Sat. 10:00 a.m. - 5:00 p.m.

Seaway Hall in Copalis Beach houses a flea market and a special gift shop called Top Cat. Both Seaway Flea Mart and Top Cat Gifts are owned and operated by Margaret and Harold McLaughlin. Seaway Hall is a quonset type building which was built in 1949 as a combination dance hall and movie theater. The flea market has three dealers and the Alley Cats Cache at the rear of the building. The Top Cat gift shop has extended into part of the flea market to have more room to display the extensive collection of gift items available.

There is another Top Cat location in downtown Aberdeen. Both stores have an excellent selection and are fun places to shop and browse. You are certain to find just the right thing for that hard to buy for person or something special just for you.

Both Top Cats offer a good selection and good prices. They carry craft supplies, as well as gift items. There are many things to be found, among them are lots of cookie cutters, feathered birds, sea shells, souvenirs, wicker, Chinese fans, jewelry, doll house furniture and miniatures, folk arts and crafts, wind chimes and a great selection of kites. They have a lot of interesting prints and many unique gift items that you won't find anywhere else.

Grayland

This unincorporated community on the county line is a major cranberry production area. Ocean Spray Cooperative markets the berries screened from the bogs each October. The flat land and tempering ocean-borne moisture protect crops for near ideal growing. To reach the bogs, which are a mass of cranberry flowers in June, take any of the small roads which lead east of Highway 101. There were native berries in the marshes when settlers arrived, and the founder of Aberdeen turned it commercial in 1912 by introducing rootstock from the east coast cranberry bogs. A similar ocean-side growing area is located near Bandon on the Oregon coast.

Attractions

Twin Harbors State Park, Highway 105 just north of Grayland, has 272 campsites and another 49 developed RV or trailer hookup points. Sand dune nature trails, surf fishing, and other attractions.

A short drive to the south, in Pacific County, takes you to **Tokeland**, a small resort community on the north shore of Willapa Bay. The Tokeland Hotel and restaurant are restored and continue to operate commercially. Highway 105 joins Highway 101 at Raymond, making possible a scenic drive down the coast and then back to Aberdeen and Hoquiam.

For further information, contact the **Westport-Grayland Chamber of Commerce**, Box 306, Westport WA 98595. Telephone 268-9422.

Gift Shops

DRIFTWOOD GIFT SHOP
1820 Highway 105
Grayland, WA 98547
Tel. (206) 267-2225
Hrs: Summer   Mon. - Sun.   10:00 a.m. - 8:00 p.m.
     Winter   Mon. - Sun.   12:00 noon - 6:00 p.m.

In business for the past twenty-five years, the Driftwood Gift Shop is the oldest gift store in Grayland. Owner Pauline Slover offers a vast selection of momentos and gifts which should satisfy nearly everyone, young and old.

An interesting motif is woven among the displays, cranberries! There are cranberry scented soaps, as well as European perfumed soaps, and cranberry glass collectibles. Also available are windsocks and wind chimes, animal ceramics, silkscreen prints created by local artists, stuffed toys for the children, kites of all shapes and sizes, and candles. Perhaps the most unusual are sea animals which have been handcarved from Mount St. Helen's ash.

If it is fun, unique and collectible, you'll find it at the Driftwood Gift Shop. Be sure to drop in and browse.

SEASON'S
P.O. Box 335
Grayland, WA 98547
Tel. (206) 267-4673
Hrs: Mon. - Sun.   10:00 a.m. - 6:00 p.m.
Visa and MasterCard are accepted.

Season's is the cottage industry and country gift shop. Emphasis is on old style mercantile and dry goods. They have a little bit of everything from German clocks and beautiful quilts from Kentucky and Tennessee, to unusual plants, baskets and dried flowers.

Manager and owner Greg Tumidanski says, "We want the people to have fun here. We're very homey. We love to give everyone a free cup of tea when they visit." Greg goes on to explain that the numerous reproductions of things from the past cause people to come into the shop to reminisce.

There's a great deal to reminisce about! Handmade country toys, a wide selection of cranberry items, wonderful wooden calendars, terrific cards for tourists, and an astonishing bear collection, as well as stuffed pigs and swans. The handmade Christmas decorations are favorites all year round. Don't miss Season's. The kettle is on and waiting for you!

Restaurant

SEA STAR RESTAURANT
P. O. Box 335
Grayland, WA 98547
Tel. (206) 267-1011
Hrs: Summer   Wed. - Mon.   8:00 a.m. - 9:00 p.m.
       Winter   Wed. - Mon.   8:00 a.m. - 8:00 p.m.
Visa and MasterCard are accepted.

The Sea Star's salad bar has been described as "a bottomless plate." Not only are the portions generous, but you can always come back for more. All the salads and dressings are homemade.

"Homemade," in fact, is the password to the Sea Star Restaurant. They have so many delectable specialties that it is difficult to know where to start. Maybe at the end, fresh strawberry pie! All their pies are made from scratch and are simply droolable.

Breakfast, lunch and dinner all feature something scrumptious. Although the breakfast menu is traditional, the fresh shrimp or crab and cheese omelette is delicious. Luncheon specials change frequently, however the Starburger deluxe remains a stable favorite, as does the "bottomless" salad bar. The dinner menu features sauteed prawns, a lovely fourteen ounce New York steak and, on Saturday and Sunday, mouthwatering prime rib. Decorated with Americana memorabilia and handmade Disney art, the Sea Star restaurant delights the eyes, as well as the palate.

Hoquiam

The township at the mouth of Hoquiam River was opened to settlers in 1856, with the option of proving up a homestead, or buying land from the government at $1.25 an acre on the "cash entry" basis. First commercial ventures were across the river at Cosmopolis where a brick yard and tannery. Hoquiam now has about 10,000 residents.

Attractions

The stately old house at 515 Cenault Avenue, Hoquiam, is a former lumber baron's home now open to public tours. Local people call it **Hoquiam's Castle**. Daily tours during summer from 11:00 a.m. to 5:00 p.m. Open the same hours Saturday and Sunday during the rest of the year. Telephone 533-2005 for off-season tours.

Some **king-sized log-stackers** handle timber at the export docks in Hoquiam where logs are sent by ship to Japan and other far east countries. There are viewpoints in the port which are out of the way of the bustling machinery.

For further information, contact **Grays Harbor Chamber of Commerce**, 2704 Sumner Avenue, Aberdeen WA 98520. Telephone 532-1924.

Bed and Breakfast

THE LYTLE HOUSE
509 Chenault
Hoquiam, WA 98550
Tel. (206) 533-2320

The Lytle House is a bed and breakfast establishment in a Victorian house that is very conveniently located near all the historic sites of Hoquiam. Hosts Elsie and Jim Reynolds make their guests feel warmly welcome from the very beginning of their stay. The first night you're a guest, but by the second night you feel a part of the family.

The house is lovely and beautifully furnished with Victorian antiques. The two bedrooms available for guests share a "guest" bathroom. The rooms have been recently redecorated, but the Victorian decor is intact and each has a Victorian bedroom suite. One of the rooms features a balcony with a beautiful view of the city and the bay. The Reynolds serve their guests a delicious full breakfast.

This lovely, big, rambling house with its oriental rugs, antique clocks and Victorian decor is a charming headquarters for a vacation exploring the Olympic Peninsula. There are many points of interest within driving distance of Lytle House.

Grays Harbor County

A tour that provides a driving and viewing tour of lighthouses, canneries, log booms and other recreational and historical activities. Interspersed are amusing side trips to gift shops, an oyster farm, early mansions and formal gardens. A little something for everyone's interests.

HOQUIAM - ABERDEEN COUNTRYSIDE TOUR

a.m.	The Lytle House	Best B&B	Hoq/B&B
a.m.	Memory Lane	Best ant.glass	Hoq/Gift
a.m.	Hoquiam's Castle	Best mansion	Gray H. Co.
a.m.	Polson Park	Best gardens	Hoq/Intro
	lunch		
p.m.	Museum of History	Best area history	Hoq/Intro
p.m.	The Gift Haus	Best collectibles	Aber/Gift
p.m.	Brady's Oyster. Farm	Best oysters	Aber/Farm
	For evening dining, your "Best Choice" in a light dinner,		
	a huge repast, or a sumptuous meal:		
p.m.	Misty's	Best intimate	Aber/Rest.
p.m.	Nordic Inn	Best casual	Aber/Acc.
p.m.	Roy's West. Buffet	Best buffet	Aber/Rest.
p.m.	Simpson Ave. Deli	Best International	Aber/Deli
p.m.	Sydney's	Best seafood	Aber/Rest.
p.m.	Duffy's	Best American	Aber/Rest.

Gift Shop

MEMORY LANE
815 1/2 Simpson
Hoquiam, WA 98550
Tel. (206) 532-5561
Hrs: Mon. - Thu. & Sat.   11:00 a.m. - 6:00 p.m.
   Friday   11:00 a.m. - 9:00 p.m.
   Sunday   11:00 a.m. - 5:00 p.m.

 Marilyn Wilson, the owner of Memory Lane, has assembled a unique collection of gift items that won't be found in other shops in this area. She also carries selected period antiques and estate jewelry on a limited basis. This is the only store in the area featuring "country French gift items."

In Memory Lane you will find everything from paintings, blankets, and wall hangings to hand cut crystal. There is a selection of cranberry glass, cloissonne items, ceramics from Italy, country dolls, ducks, pillows and beautiful pigs. Marilyn features Elton Bennett framed prints, all signed and depicting local settings and historical sites.

This is the place to look for a unique, one of a kind gift, perhaps something by one of the local artists featured here. Memory Lane has something for everyone and, most importantly, something to fit everyone's budget.

Moclips

Accommodations

OCEAN CREST INN
State Highway 109
Moclips, WA 98562
Tel. (206) 276-4465

Located one mile north of Pacific Beach, Ocean Crest Inn features exceptional dining with spectacular panoramas of the Pacific in a natural forest setting.

The luxury rooms and apartments, some featuring fireplaces, have cable T.V. and sun decks. There is an indoor heated pool, therapy pool, exercise room and a playground on the premises. The dining facilities offer a beautiful view of the water, and there is a glassed-in patio for pleasant dining and conversation.

After a day of sun and surf, drop into the Crest Room Lounge for relaxing entertainment and your favorite libation.

Ocean Shores

Once little more than a developer's dream on the sandy north spit of Grays Harbor, Ocean Shores has come of age in two decades. Now it is an incorporated city, with about 1,700 full time residents, has a convention center that attracts groups from across the state, and is host to an annual Dixieland jazz festival and other events. Most of those who live here are retired.

Attractions

The south end of Ocean Shores Boulevard is the north **jetty** of Grays Harbor. This passage is a favorite for folks who like to watch the fishing boats and ocean-going vessels which enter and leave the harbor. Waters lapping the jetty also yield good catches of fish.

Much of Ocean Shores is built around a system of canals which interconnect with **Duck Lake**. The combination provides boaters with miles of fishing. Several launching ramps are spotted along the system. Swimming, surf fishing, clam digging, kayaking, horseback riding and golfing opportunities abound.

Ocean City State Park, two miles north of Ocean Shores on Highway 115, provides camping and picnicking areas in the lee of the sand dunes, just east of the beach. The **Marine Interpretive Center** is located at this park. Twenty-seven miles on continuous beach stretch in both directions from here, with fourteen state access points north to **Pacific Beach State Park** which is a day use area with a concessionaire-operated campground.

For information, contact **Ocean Shores Chamber of Commerce**, Box 382, Ocean Shores WA 98569. Telephone 289-2451.

Accommodations

THE CANTERBURY INN
Ocean Shores Boulevard
Ocean Shores, WA 98569
Tel. (206) 289-3317
Visa, MasterCard, AMEX, Diner's Club and Carte Blanche accepted

The Canterbury Inn is a luxury condominium beach resort with each unit individually owned and furnished. All units have fully equipped kitchens and fireplaces. All ocean side units above the first floor have an unobstructed view of the Pacific Ocean.

The quality and service at the Canterbury Inn make it very special. The managers are very responsive to the needs of their guests and large number of repeat guests attests to their hospitality. The staff at the Inn is also ready to handle conventions and a better spot to combine work and play would be hard to find. Access to the beach is located directly in front of the Inn and many rooms have charming balconies from which to enjoy the view of the beach and ocean.

This is a great place to stay on the Washington coast. The beachside location and the many amenities, including swimming pool and spa make it a very relaxing spot for a vacation.

THE DISCOVERY INN
1031 Discovery Avenue SE
Ocean Shores, WA 98569
Tel. (206) 289-3371
    (800) 882-8821

This charming inn is the nature lover's delight. It is off the main track, a perfect place to watch birds. It is located on the Grand Canal, with a private dock where you can rent boats and motors. Duck Lake is accessible from the canal, and the bass and trout fishing there are good.

The Discovery Inn is a condominium motel with a variety of outstanding accommodations. They offer an outdoor pool and spa, family units with fireplaces and kitchen facilities, views of Grays Harbor Bay, boat and moped rentals nearby, and shuttle bus service to Olympia.

The Discovery Inn is one of Ocean Shore's best kept secrets. It's a wonderful place to stay, offering peace and quiet, and many interesting things to do.

OCEAN SHORES INN
Ocean Shores Boulevard
Ocean Shores, WA 98569
Tel. (206) 289-2407
Hrs: Sun. - Fri.   7:00 a.m. - 10:00 p.m.
     Saturday   7:00 a.m. - 12:00 midnight
     Lounge   12:00 noon - 2:00 a.m.

This is an incredibly large restaurant offering many services, including a coffee shop, dining room, and banquet facilities and a two gift shops. The quality and service here have always been excellent, and the new chef, Randy Nyland, has revamped the menu and offers some really exciting dining.

Breakfast is served all day, and there are lunch specials in both the coffee shop and dining room, as well as the regular menu which is extensive. The food is always excellent, and prepared from only the freshest ingredients. The restaurant's owners also own a grocery store so they have access to the best produce of anybody in town. The view of the ocean is wonderful, and storm watching from here while dining is really an experience. The prices are moderate which makes this a very good choice for dining in Ocean Shores.

One of the most unique features of the Ocean Shores Inn is the Golden Gull Gift Shop, which is open every day. They have a wonderful selection of gift items to suit every taste and every budget. There is fine crystal, pewter, jewelry, porcelain dolls, Austrian crystal, music boxes and ladies apparel. Children and adults alike will be delighted by the selection of plush animals. In the Golden Gull you will find collector's items of every kind, but you'll also find things you can use every day in your own home.

POINT BROWN RESORT CONDOMINIUMS
Chance ala Mer and Ocean Shores Boulevard
Ocean Shores, WA 98569
Tel. (206) 289-4421
(800) Pt-Brown in WA

This lovely resort condominium development is a wonderful place for the vacation of your dreams. The resort won the International Design Award given by Resorts Condominium International. This is one of the best beach locations in Washington, and is the perfect place for a special event, whether a honeymoon, anniversary, or family reunion. All units are available on a limited basis and it is wise to call well in advance for reservations.

Every unit here is spacious, beautifully appointed and fully furnished. Units are owned on a time share basis and are the ultimate in luxury living, with fireplaces, built in stereo, television, VCR, marble floored bathrooms with jacuzzis, and unsurpassed ocean views. The kitchen are fully equipped, with microwaves, dishwashers, self-cleaning ovens and more.

This is a perfect spot for whale watching, salmon fishing, storm watching or just beach walking and relaxing. You'll never forget your vacation at the Point Brown Resort, and you'll want to come back again and again.

Apparel

JUICY FRUITS
Chance Ala Mer
Ocean Shores, WA 98569
Tel. (206) 289-2959
Hrs: Mon. - Sat. 10:00 a.m. - 5:00 p.m.
Sunday 11:00 a.m. - 3:00 p.m.
Closed Tuesdays in the winter.

Juicy Fruits--A Tasty Bite of Fashion is the creation of owner Susan Hoyt. Susan seeks out the unusual for her shop. There are unique things here from small vendors and craftsmen, things you won't find in large department stores. She travels extensively to find the quality items she carries in her shop.

The emphasis at Juicy Fruits is on pastels and colors. There are many accessories here, such as scarves, beads and jewelry. The jewelry featured here comes from all over the world. There are designer necklaces and bracelets of leather and mixed media pieces. There is a French or New York flair to everything offered in this delightful shop.

From the moment you enter Juicy Fruit, the soft jazz sets the tempo for an elegant time of browsing through the many, varied and uniquely wonderful things to be found here.

Art Gallery

GALLERY MARJULI´
865 Point Brown Avenue
Ocean Shores, WA 98569
Tel. (206) 289-2858
Hrs: Mon. - Sun. 10:30 a.m. - 5:00 p.m.
Closed Christmas and Thanksgiving

The Gallery Marjuli´ carries a wide range of art works in different media, as well as a good selection of gift items. It is unique in the Ocean Shores area. The approach here is upscale, but there are items of interest for every budget. Many Northwest artists and artisans are featured.

Marjuli offers beautiful serigraphs by a number of artists, including David Trask, John Morgan, Roger Berghoff and Walton Butts. There are original paintings by a number of artists. Also to be found are glass pastels, prints, Mt. St. Helens glass and jewelry, enamel ware and cloisonne. Art supplies are available on a limited basis and there is a selection of cards, books and stationery.

The Gallery Marjuli´ has a wide selection of many different art forms. Many local artists are featured, and many of the paintings are sea and landscapes. This is a family run business and they go out of their way to serve you and answer any questions you may have.

Bed and Breakfast

OCEAN FRONT INN
N Ocean Shores Boulevard
Ocean Shores, WA 98569
Tel. (206) 289-3036

Are you looking for a place to stay while visiting or traveling through Ocean Shores? Well if you are, the Ocean Front Inn is a bed and breakfast that's ready, willing and able to please you.

Here, a Continental breakfast consisting of croissants, fruit juice, wonderful breads and gourmet coffees will be formally presented to you every morning as you sit in the beautiful dining room overlooking the ocean. After breakfast, stroll out to the courtyard and sunning area and enjoy the enclosed hot tub. When you've dried off, relax in the elegantly appointed living room accentuated with an open hearth fireplace. There's also a full service salon on the premises for your convenience. Dutch is spoken at this bed and breakfast, and you'll find an amazing air of international flair to this wonderful little inn.

Owner Charmaine Tipsen is sure you and your party will consider the Ocean Front for a truly remarkable getaway on one of the nicest spots of Ocean Shore's beaches. Stop by and savor a warm and sunny experience with a most hospitable host.

Books

MARJA'S BOOKS
168 Ocean Shores Boulevard
Ocean Shores, WA 98569
Tel. (206) 289-2075
Hrs: Tue. - Sun. 10:00 a.m. - 5:00 p.m.

Marja's Books is a very well stocked book store, presided over by genial owner Jim Everman. Jim is an former elementary school principal whose enjoyment of books brought him to his present situation. This probably accounts for the wonderful children's section of books in his shop. He has the experience to know what pleases children, and what pleases their parents.

Marja's offers a wonderful, cozy, warm setting in which to peruse the latest literary offerings, everything from best sellers to travel guides. Jim also sells a variety of gourmet coffees which you can enjoy as you browse. There is also selection of cards, gifts, and book accessories.

This is a very welcoming, well stocked shop, and your shopping or browsing experience will be pleasant and fruitful.

Delicatessen

DICK'S FOOD CENTER, Chaunce ala Mar and Point Brown Boulevard, Ocean Shores, Washington. This super super market and full-service deli also has a fish market, pharmacy, magazine and book department, video rental area, and more, and caters to tourists' special needs.

Gift Shop

LIL' IODINE'S, on Point Brown <u>and on</u> Cardinal Street, Ocean Shores, WA. Original floral arrangements, custom silk floral designs, brass items with nautical themes, stuffed toys, and assorted gifts.

TIDE CREATIONS GIFT SHOP
<u>Wa-a-ay</u> down Point Brown Avenue SW
Ocean Shores, WA 98569
Tel. (206) 289-2550
Hrs:　Mar. - Oct.　Mon. - Sun.　　　　10:00 a.m. - 5:00 p.m.
　　　Nov. - Feb.　Mon., Wed., Fri.　　11:00 a.m. - 4:00 p.m.
　　　　　　　　　Sat. - Sun.　　　　　10:00 a.m. - 5:00 p.m.
Closed Tuesday and Thursday in the winter only.

Tide Creations Gift Shop owners Erma and "Doc" Bedilion welcome you to "The Happiest and Craziest Shop In Town." This is the most fun you'll ever have shopping! Be sure to talk to the magic mirror and push the start button!

Famous for their unusual shop and different gifts, from crazy gag items to the rare and beautiful, they feature wonderful gourmet Fudge, freshly made on the premises with ten to twenty-six delicious varieties always available. Also a fantastic selection of sweatshirts and t-shirts from sizes toddler through adult extra large are offered. Seashells, puzzles, toys and stuffed animals, seagulls, coffee mugs and greeting cards are just a few of the thousands of things available in their store.

Another claim to fame is the twenty-four feet of miniature town and village on display - along with waterfalls and curtains of driftwood. A trip to Ocean Shores isn't complete without a visit. As Erma and Doc put it, "Browsers Welcome - Buyers Adored!" You will adore shopping at Tide Creations Gift Shop! Remember - go waaay down Point Brown Avenue (almost to the Marina.) They are located on the Grand Canal, so you can even arrive by boat, as well as car and bus.

Restaurant

DUGAN'S PIZZA
Ocean Shores Boulevard
Ocean Shores, WA 98569
Tel: (206) 289-2330
Hrs: Mon. - Thur..   4:00 p.m. - 11:00 p.m.
       Friday   4:00 p.m. - 1:00 a.m.
       Saturday   11:00 a.m. - 1:00 a.m.
       Sunday   11:00 a.m. - 11:00 p.m.
Visa and MasterCard are accepted.

"One bite and we gotcha." That's the slogan of Dugan's Pizza in Ocean Shores. How true it is. A bite into one of their delicious homemade pizzas is all it takes to set the hook.

Owner Dugan Wilgus is very proud of the fact that Dugan's Pizza holds no rival. Many pizza places have tried to emulate Dugan's, but it all comes to naught; perfection can't be matched. What's the reason for their outstanding success? It's the right kind of atmosphere mixed with the right kind of food. There, amidst lovely cedar booths, you'll find a game room containing over twenty games, a birthday party room and a large dining area, wherein the best pizza around is served. Everything is made from scratch and only the finest ingredients are used in the creation of such things as the world's largest spin pizza. Measuring twenty-six inches in diameter, this pizza is hand spun just like they did it in the old days.

Apart from pizza, Dugan's also serves lasagna, cannelloni, manicotti, sub sandwiches and crisp, homemade salads. With the sponsoring a yearly Saint Patrick's Run, Dugan's Pizza is as much a boon to the community as it is to the traveler in search of good food. Stop by, take a bite and get hooked.

HARBOR LANDING RESTAURANT
Point Brown Avenue
Ocean Shores, WA 98569
Tel. (206) 289-3171
Hrs: Sun. - Thu.   5:00 p.m. - 11:00 p.m.
       Fri. - Sat.   4:00 p.m. - 1:00 a.m.
Visa, MasterCard, AMEX accepted.

When traveling through Ocean Shores, one can't miss out on the finest dining experience in that fair town. The Harbor Landing Restaurant, Ocean Shore's newest and most gorgeous gourmet dining house, offers you an experience that can best be classed as an adventure in dining.

Harbor Landing is one of Ocean Shore's finest dining establishments. From the moment you walk in you'll bask in the air of casual elegance that pervades there. It's a very relaxing restaurant and produces the type of atmosphere that is conducive to gourmet dining. What dining it is! A unique blend of American and continental cuisine featuring seafood, milk-fed veal, European pasta, thick steaks and much more, all await your eager palate.

For those who are in the mood for a little more than good food in an unparalleled ambiance, Harbor Landing also features live entertainment on Friday and Saturday nights. This entertainment comes in the form of beautiful melodies drifting from a piano to your table. If you've got a special event on the horizon, Harbor Landing has the banquet facilities available for almost any occasion. Ahhh, paradise on earth in the form of a gourmet dining house. When in the area, don't miss experiencing this "Best Choice."

THE MISFIT RESTAURANT
Ocean Shores Golf Course
Ocean Shores, WA 98529
Tel. (206) 289-3376
Hrs: Mon. - Thu.　7:00 a.m. - 10:00 p.m.
　　　Fri. - Sun.　　7:00 a.m. - 11:00 p.m.

Ray Sundquist, the owner of the Misfit Restaurant has created a terrific dining place. It has the best location in Ocean Shores with the best view of the beach.

The wonderful view is matched by the wonderful cuisine. The emphasis is on seafood, but beef is plentiful, too. Steaks range in size from six ounces to twenty-four ounces, something for every size appetite. The seafood is always fresh. Especially delicious are the oysters Rockefeller and the Petrale sole. The pies here are a house specialty and the perfect finish to your gourmet dinner.

The Misfit Restaurant offers gourmet dining, a wonderful view, and those little extras like fresh flowers on the table that make a dining experience so special.

Travel

OCEAN SHORES RESERVATION AND CONVENTION BUREAU
Ocean Shores Boulevard
Ocean Shores, WA 98569
Tel. (206) 289-2430
 (800) 562-8612
Hrs: Mon. - Sat. 9:00 a.m. - 11:00 p.m.
Credit cards accepted depend upon facilities being reserved.

Everyone likes it when their affairs run smoothly, but sometimes they don't. Reservations can get cancelled and mixed-up, leaving you out in left field with nowhere to turn. When planning a trip to Ocean Shores, don't let this happen to you. Call ahead and let Ocean Shores Reservation Bureau handle all of your accommodation needs.

With the help of Ocean Shores Reservation Bureau you can rest assured that all your reservations will be in perfect order and that everything will run smoothly. You can call months ahead of time to reserve rooms in the finest resorts and hotels in the city. For a more secluded getaway, let the Reservation Bureau set aside a privately owned home or condominium. These enchanting accommodations are available for nightly, as well as weekly rental. There's nothing better than the feeling you get when you know everything is planned out, set and sure.

Whether it's business or pleasure that brings you to Ocean Shores, the Reservation Bureau will make your trip a much more pleasant one. If its a family gathering, reunion, wedding and reception...call Ocean Shores as they're able to reserve the hall, the banquet, the band, photography and the bar. Call them, set up your itinerary and relax with the knowledge that you're being taken care of.

Pacific Beach

Pacific Beach, on Highway 109 a few miles short of the mouth of the Quinault River, has a large state park operated by a concessionaire. It includes 118 campsites, another twenty hookups for recreation vehicles. The beach is popular for surf fishing and clamming.

Grays Harbor County

Accommodations

THE SANDPIPER BEACH RESORT
P. O. Box A
Pacific Beach, WA 98571
Tel. (206) 276-4580

The Sandpiper Beach Resort is a wonderful place for a "get away from it all" vacation. It is located right on the beach, with miles of beach combing available. Every unit has an ocean view, and there are all sizes available to accommodate from one to twelve people. Hosts Betty and Dick Winders do everything possible to make your stay enjoyable. They will probably greet you accompanied by their dog, Barney, a local celebrity who has been on several television programs. All Dachshunds are Barney's guests at no charge.

This is a place to relax. For one thing, there is no television, just spectacular uninterrupted views of the ocean and the accompanying sound of the surf. All units feature handsome fireplaces, beachside decks, well equipped kitchens and a casual decor. The ambiance is that of a European resort, with a Northwest feeling. Slow down and savor life, fly a kite on the beach, hike or pitch horseshoes. Browse through the library located in Sandpiper's gift shop where you will find exciting gifts from throw pottery to high fashion sweat shirts and a fantastic selection of kites, but above all, enjoy yourself.

The Sandpiper Beach Resort is a special place for a family vacation, and intimate getaway, or a family reunion. Whatever the reason that brings you here, you'll have a great time and want to return again and again.

Point Roberts

Bed and Breakfast

OLD HOUSE BED & BREAKFAST INN
674 Kender
Point Roberts, WA 98281
Tel. (206) 945-5210

You can only get to this part of the United States by car by traveling through Canada. And what a drive! On the north is Canada, south and west, the Strait of Georgia and to the east, Boundary Bay. Point Roberts offers the finest viewing location of the Straits, the Canadian Gulf Islands and San Juan Island and the Olympic Mountains.

A special amenity of Point Roberts is the Old House Bed and Breakfast. This estate home, circa 1928, has housed three families thus far. Innkeepers Jack and Glenda Fraser bought the home in 1984. In 1983, the Old House had suffered a fire that gutted the structure, so Jack and Glenda completely modernized the water and electrical systems before restoring the home to its original glory. Charming and comfortable guest rooms are done in the style of the period. Glenda, a gourmet cook is famous for her breakfasts, including a yummy assortment of home-baked pumpkin, blueberry and blackberry muffins.

If you come to Old House by boat or plane, Jack and Glenda will be happy to pick you up at the local marina or airport. You'll only be ten minutes from the Victoria ferry terminal, twenty five minutes from Vancouver, B.C., five minutes from two golf courses, and twenty minutes from an international airport. Pastimes to please most guests include fishing, crabbing, bicycling, or just gazing at the Straits from a private beach or the second floor of Old House. You may arrive at Old House as guests of the Frasers, but be assured you will leave as friends.

Restaurant

ROOF HOUSE, 398 Marine Drive, Point Roberts, Washington. A combination restaurant/gallery filled with fine paintings; there's also a small gift area. Pastries are a specialties of the restaurant.

Westport

This vacation and fishing community on the south spit of Grays Harbor has been the Coast Guard's base of operation for years protecting small craft that cross over the sometimes stormy bar. The marina is home to a large fleet of charter fishing boats and nearly as many commercial fishing vessels which work offshore endeavoring to fill their holds with salmon and tuna.

Wind has carved giant mountains out of sand on the beach side and you find several homes built in the lee of the stabilized dunes. About 2,000 people live in Westport's city limits, and more make their homes in Bay City and other villages on the south shore of Grays Harbor.

Attractions

The **lighthouse**, built in 1898, is located on the seaward end of Ocean Avenue. Call 268-0121 if you would like to tour it.

Westport Aquarium, 321 Harbor Street in the boat basin area, has a collection of seals as well as many of the fish and other creatures of the sea. Telephone 268-0471.

The **South Jetty** begins at the north end of the harbor development. This is a location for fishing and boat watching. A viewing tower is nearby. For many years the mouth of Grays Harbor was just an opening washed in the sand, but Army Engineers built the jetties in hopes of cutting down on dredging costs required to reduce sand build up on the entrance bar.

An 1800 foot walk and bridge enable fishermen to fish from the breakwater area as well as the jetties. There's **ferry service** daily, June thru August, to Aberdeen and Hoquiam.

There is a **local museum** at 2201 Westhaven Drive which features maritime history. This is the old Coast Guard Station. Open Wednesday through Sunday, 12:00 noon to 4:00 p.m. from June through Labor Day. Open same hours on weekends in April and May.

Westport city park, 306 West Washington Street, has overnight camping facilities. **Westhaven State Park,** at the north end of Montesano Street, provides access which continues south on the beach to the Point Chehalis lighthouse. See Grayland listing for **Twin Harbors Park,** three miles south of Westport.

For further information, contact the **Westport-Grayland Chamber of Commerce,** Box 306, Westport WA 98595. Telephone 268-9422.

Accommodations

THE ISLANDER
Westhaven and Revetment Drive
P. O. Box 488
Westport, WA 98595
Tel.   (206)   268-9166
         (800)   562-0147

Overlooking the ocean and fishing harbor, The Islander features a restaurant, motel, R.V. park and charter service.
From the standard accommodation to the luxurious two- bedroom suite overlooking the marina, The Islander offers all the comforts necessary to make your holiday a memorable one. The coffee shop is open daily, there is deluxe

dining and dancing in the meeting room and a gift shop and beauty salon on the premises. There is convenient parking and the fishing marina and swimming pool are at your door.

A complete fishing package is available, including all fishing equipment and live bait, and all vessels are equipped with Coast Guard approved safety devices. Tuna fishing, which begins in July and lasts through October, are of twenty-four hours duration with three meals and individual beds, with all gear and live bait furnished. All you need to bring are your fishing clothes, your camera and your enthusiasm!

Art Gallery

COHASSETT STUDIO GALLERY
2603 S Forrest
Westport, WA 98595
Hrs: Winter   Thu. - Mon.   10:00 a.m. - 5:00 p.m.
       Summer   Wed. - Mon.   10:00 a.m. - 5:00 p.m.
Visa and MasterCard are accepted.

Located on Highway 105, a quarter mile north of Twin Harbor State Park, Cohassett Studio Gallery sits above a stable off the road. This small gallery contains the works of painters from New York City, as well as local artists from Grays Harbor.

Owner and proprietor Frances Morgan Lew is also a painter, specializing in water colors, and has won numerous awards for her work. The studio also features beautiful ceramics, pottery and clay sculptures.

On display in the gallery are contemporary paintings, abstracts, sumi-e, oils, Japanese and screen paintings. Here is an excuse to get off the beaten track and spend a bucolic afternoon....enjoying the scenery without....and within!

Bed and Breakfast

GLENACRES INN BED AND BREAKFAST
P.O. Box 1246
Westport, WA 98595
Tel. (206) 268-9391

Beautifully secluded among tall, stately evergreens, Glenacres Inn stands back from the highway on eight wooded acres. Like a pioneer's dream, it has character bursting from its seams.

The history of Glenacres Inn began in 1861 when a document in the abstract of title was signed by Abraham Lincoln's secretary to transfer title from the government. Shortly after, the Benjamin Armstrong family came into possession of the land and began building. It must have seemed like a dream home to pioneer logger and half-blood Indian Benjamin Franklin Armstrong and his resourceful wife, Minnie, who in her horse and buggy, drove guests to the house for bed-and-breakfast style lodging. In the house's heyday in the early 1900's, crystal chandeliers glowed from its windows. These days, the lights are shining as brightly as ever. Luckily for fun seekers, history has repeated itself. With its story book past and a cast of hundreds, Glenacres once again offers bed and breakfast to Westport's visitors.

Today, Glenacres Inn offers guests a range of accommodations from formal to casual, for individuals, couples, families and small conferences. Those who stay in the house itself will find five bedrooms tastefully furnished with lace curtains, quilted comforters, brass beds and private baths.   House guests can linger over a Continental breakfast in the dining room, enjoying the bay windows, antiques, (some for sale), photographs and memorabilia. Others may prefer the more informally furnished rooms, which open onto a massive deck with a hot tub and gazebo. Families and larger parties can choose among cottages of various sizes, the most spacious of which sleeps twelve, with kitchens, fish and clam cleaning facilities and extra privacy. Also, a recreational area has been added providing volleyball, badminton and horseshoes.

Bakery

THE BAKERY COTTAGE RESTAURANT
389 W Ocean Avenue
Westport, WA 98595
Tel. (206) 268-0318
Hrs: Mon. - Sat.   8:00 a.m. - 3:00 p.m.
                                      6:00 p.m. - 10:00 p.m.
Visa, MasterCard accepted.

One of the Bakery Cottages favorite recipes includes delightful ingredients like ocean breezes, a pinch of silvery sand, the sound of the surf mixed with pleasant company and a loaf of freshly baked bread. This cozy little place, set in soft pastels, crystal, and touched with antique paintings has a warm spirit well matched to the fresh wholesome cooking.

Everything is made from scratch and prepared the old fashioned way. The menu has a message which says, "If there is some food you want and it isn't on the menu - Ask! We may be able to accommodate!" Gourmet dinners on Thursday, Friday and Saturday evenings are prepared from scratch. The attitude and service here is as refreshingly old fashioned as the food preparation! The Bakery features fantastic cookies and pies, French breads, sourdough rolls, and enormous made fresh daily cinnamon rolls.

Everything from the light pancakes to the soups, sandwiches, salads and crepes are well prepared and beautifully presented. Combine all that, bake at a pleasant temperature and yield fond memories, a rested spirit and a happy tummy!

Restaurant

ARTHURS
2681 Westhaven Drive
P.O. Box 1159
Westport, WA 98595
Tel. (206) 268-9292
Hrs: Tue.- Sun.　　Lunch　　11:30 a.m. - 2:00 p.m.
　　　　　　　　　　Dinner　　5:00 p.m. - 10:00 p.m.
Open Mondays in the summer. Reservations are recommended.

Arthur Laurence went to school and trained in Southern California. He moved to Washington for the weather, but the always the same Southern California weather got boring after a while. Arthur is the owner and chef of a fine restaurant in Westport. The specialty is fresh seafood and prime rib. The ambience is elegant, with simple white tablecloths and great service.

Some of the favorite lunches at Arthur's are the Arthurburger, fish and chips, fresh oysters and the crab sandwich. The spinach salad is delicious and the soups are always excellent. At dinner there are different soups every night and a selection of salads, such as antipasto and fettucini. There are fresh seafood specials everyday and a favorite dish is cioppino. Truffles fettucini is a superb dish, which Arthur is happy to prepare if you call ahead. The delectable desserts are prepared from scratch and feature such delights as Mud Pie, peanut butter ice cream, fudge ice cream and mocha cheesecake.

The cuisine at Arthur's is excellent and the service couldn't be better. Arthur personally trains his servers to insure that your dining experience will be pleasant. Don't miss Arthur's when you're in Westport.

CLAM-ITY JANE'S
260 E Dock Street
Westport, WA 98595
Tel. (206) 268-0545
Hrs: Winter   Mon. - Sun.   7:00 a.m. - 9:00 p.m.
     Summer   Mon. - Sun.   4:00 a.m. - 10:00 p.m.

Tired of pretentious, over priced "eateries" with poor food? Looking for a clean, family style, back to basics restaurant? Clam-ity Jane's has the quality, atmosphere and personal attention you are craving! Speaking of craving...whatever your palate desires you can be sure to find.

Breakfast starts early, 4:00 a.m. in summer for those early rising fisherman, and is available all day. Some of your day starting choices are eggs with sausage or chicken fried steak or spicy hot Italian links or ground round steak or,...well you get the idea. Omelets offer an equally large selection and there are pancakes, French toast, biscuits and gravy, oatmeal and maybe best of all ... Clam-ity fritter critters. A plethora of sandwiches, salads, and luncheon meals provide a pleasant mid day break. Dinner runs the gamut from steak to salmon, oysters, halibut, scallops, prawns, clam strips, veal, salads and more. Everything is made fresh from scratch, even the salad dressings and hash browns.

The prices at Clam-ity Jane's are modest and the portions more than generous. Be sure to visit this "Best Choice" restaurant where you will find that value is an honored tradition.

COLONIAL CAFE
P.O. Box 845
Westport, WA 98595
Tel. (206) 268-9726

The Colonial Cafe is located across from Float 7 in Westport and is the place to go for breakfast before your fishing trip. Sandy and Dick Simmons describe their cafe as, "Where the fishermen meet and eat." Breakfast is served all day and features hearty portions of deliciously prepared home style food. A favorite is biscuits and gravy and the pancakes are the largest in town. There are several interesting omelettes, featuring such ingredients as hot sausage, mushrooms, chives, cheese and more. For the really hearty eater,there is rib eye steak and eggs. Sandy and Dick offer the lowest price cup of coffee in town. Breakfast is served all day.

Lunch at the Colonial Cafe offers a selection of sandwiches and burgers. Try the bacon burger, or the primo burger with bacon, ham, Swiss and American cheese with sauteed fresh mushrooms. Dinners feature local fresh seafood and bottom fish. Enjoy such selections as halibut, ling cod, prawns, oysters and scampi. All dinners come with soup or salad and a choice of potatoes and bread. For dessert, be sure to try one of the delectable homemade pies.

The Colonial Cafe offers delicious, well-prepared food in hearty portions at reasonable prices. Children are always welcome here and it's a good place for family dining. After dinner take time to enjoy the comfortable atmosphere and watch the cribbage game that's always in progress. For great food, especially fresh seafood and fish, eat where the fishermen do, the Colonial Cafe.

DEE'S CAFE
203 S Montesano Street
Westport, WA 98595
Tel. (206) 268-9737
Hrs: Winter   Mon. - Sun.   7:00 a.m. - 8:00 p.m.
      Summer   Mon. - Sun.   4:00 a.m. - 11:00 p.m.
Visa and MasterCard are accepted.

What's the secret to success? In the case of Dee's Cafe, it's the fantastic secret recipes and fresh seafood used in the cooking. The restaurant specializes in fresh fish and has been labeled as one of the ten best eateries in Washington.

With seating for approximately forty people the place fills up fast and stays busy...all day. There is a "no-frills" decor, as the emphasis here is on the quality of the food, however, the service is excellent.

There is a full breakfast, lunch and dinner menu. The Razor clams with eggs, when in season, are excellent. The fish is extremely fresh, and the sea bass, ling cod, halibut and petrale sole is very well prepared. Why is the food here so good? Straightforward, fresh, and very well prepared. That's the secret!

Tours

NEPTUNE'S CHARTERS AND GIFTS
2601 Westhaven Drive
Westport, WA 98595
Tel. (206) 268-0124
Reservations are advised.

Bill Hoffman has been in the charter business since 1954 and really knows how to please his customers. He and his wife, Sue, run Neptune's

Charters and Gifts. They offer fishing trips for salmon, tuna and bottom fish. Charters leave at 6:00 a.m. and return about 3:30 p.m. Neptune's Charters is the only charter company in this area that is open all year. In addition to fishing trips, there are also whale watching excursions. Bill knows the best times to be sure of seeing whales, which is in March, April and May. Their whale-watching cruises are great fun.

The gift shop specializes in nautical brass, but also has a good selection of varied gift items. They carry a good selection of Mt. St. Helen's glassware, crystal, handblown glass and wood carvings. There's something for everyone and the prices are very reasonable. The atmosphere is cozy and friendly, enhanced by a fireplace. Take time to relax by the fire while you sip a cup of coffee and watch whale tapes.

All of Neptune's Charters' boats are comfortable and safe and the skippers are picked for their experience and friendliness. Overnight charter trips are especially fun and are very popular. You can be certain of a pleasant and rewarding fishing trip or pleasure cruise when you use Neptune's Charters.

ISLAND COUNTY

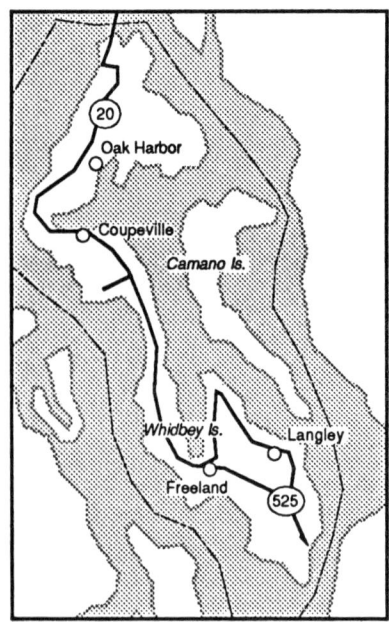

Isolated from the mainland by the waters of Puget Sound, but a short ferryboat ride from the populated Everett area, Island County is a 212 square mile collection of shoreline, farms, parks and homes on Whidbey and Camano islands. One of the nation's major naval air stations is in the northern portion of skinny Whidbey, the guardian of the Strait of Juan de Fuca.

Oregon's Territorial Legislature designated this county in 1853. The boundaries stood through Washington's territorial days and statehood. Missionaries were here as early as 1840. The Skagit Indians, adept at growing potatoes as well as fishing, lived here long before that and ranged inland up the Skagit River which empties into the sound between the two islands. George Vancouver brought his ship to an anchorage in Port Susan, the waters between the mainland and Camano Island, in June 1792.

Camano, the smaller of the two main islands, is named for Jacinto Caamano, a Spaniard who charted the coast of Vancouver Island the same year Vancouver explored the sound. The longer Whidbey Island honors Joseph Whidbey, sailing master on Vancouver's vessel. Today 44,000 people live on the two islands, over 12,000 of them in Oak Harbor, another 8,000 close by this major town.

The islands are a popular weekend spot for visitors from Seattle. Inns, motels and bed and breakfast establishments are everywhere. Resorts are on many small harbors. Fine dining is offered at quaint cafes and rustic restaurants.

Whidbey Island can be reached from the north on Highway 20 by a bridge spanning waters of Deception Pass. Keystone, at mid-island on the west shore, has ferry service to the Olympic Peninsula. At Clinton on the south tip, it is a fifteen minute ferry ride to Mukilteo on the mainland. Camano Island is connected to the mainland by a causeway that carries Highway 532. Several county roads loop the island's shoreline. Like the San Juan Islands to the north, Whidbey enjoys temperate weather with a long summer dry spell and heavy rains during winter months. Most of the early residents came here to farm.

Attractions

Clinton and **Bayview** are two unincorporated villages which greet most visitors arriving on Whidbey from the Mukilteo ferry. Bayview has several lakes around it which attracts freshwater fishermen. Clinton is the ferry landing and for years was a community of summer homes; the owners attracted by beaches close by the dock.

South Whidbey State Park, on Smugglers Cove Road south of Greenbank, is one of the most popular spots from which to make photographs of the Olympic Mountains. Eighty-seven acres of old growth forest are on a bluff which slopes 300 feet to the beach. There are campsites, and a sandy beach for clam diggers. Other points north and south yield goeduck and butter clams.

Encompassing 17,00 acres in central Whidbey is **Ebey's Landing National Historical Reserve.** It protects a variety of natural and historic sites including military fortifications, farms and pioneer buildings. SR 20 and county roads provide the link to Eoupeville, Smith Prairie, Crockett Lake and Uplands, Ebey's Landing, Grassers Hill and Lagoon, Monroe Landing, Fort Casey and Fort Ebey State Parks.

Deception Pass State Park, at the north tip of Whidbey Island, has extensive facilities and is a launching point for divers and fishermen. There is freshwater swimming in **Cranberry Lake**. Over 20 rustic park buildings were constructed by the depression-era Civilian Conservation Corps. There are 246 campsites within the park. Strong currents sweep the channel which is only 40 yards wide at one point. The name comes because many explorers were deceived, and did not believe it a passage at all between Skagit Bay and Rosario Strait.

Deception Pass Bridge was an engineering feat of the 1930s. Completed in 1935 with federal funding, is is 1,350 feet long and 182 feet above the water at its highest point. The tidal flow beneath it is logged at five to eight knots, the channel four fathoms at its shallowest sounding.

Fort Casey State Park, on the west shore at Admiralty Head, is a U.S. Coast Artillery post that once commanded the entrance of the Strait of Juan de Fuca. Concrete bunkers were built between 1898 and 1907. The Admiralty lighthouse, which ceased operation in 1954, is relocated from its original placement in 1861. On the point's south side is **Keystone Underwater Park,** set aside for scuba divers. Strong currents sweep the abandoned jetty, making diving dangerous except during the slack water between tidal shifts.

Camano Island State Park, near the village of Camano, has eighty-seven campsites, and provides access for year around salt water fishing. The park displays vegetation of a Mediterranean climate with fifteen inches of rain a year, caused by moisture being taken from storms passing over the Olympic Mountains to the west. Nature trails tell the story.

For further information, write the **Whidbey Island Visitor's Council,** Box 809, Coupeville WA 98239.

Coupeville

Thomas Coupe founded the town in 1853 after Indians discouraged earlier settlers attracted to the prairies above Penn Cove. Several sea captains chose the little community for retirement and built Victorian homes which are undergoing restoration in modern times. The prairie which Isaac N. Ebey claimed in 1852 is now part of a 17,000 acre National Historic Preserve. Fort Ebey State Park, off Libbey Road, is the site of a defense point established during World War II to block water entrance into Puget Sound.

Attractions

A **walking tour map** is available at the **Island County Historical Society Museum** on Alexander Street at Coveland Street. The museum contains exhibits that pertain the the early history of Whidbey Island. A collection of dolls, Alaskan Indian baskets and the furnishings from the 1891 county courthouse.

Old stores on Front Street and many of the restored residences are described in the walking tour brochure. The historic district contains forty-eight buildings which are part of the National Historic Reserve. There is an exhibit of Indian canoes and a restored blockhouse across from the museum.

The **city pier**, which dates back to times when large ships sometimes called at the cove, is now restored as a tourist attraction and greets the people who tour the sound by boat. There is a store right on the pier.

Sunnyside Cemetery is southwest of Coupeville, on Sherman Road south of its intersection with Highway 20. This is where many early settlers are buried. Two blockhouses were built here and down the road in 1855 by the Ebey family. When they arrived on the scene, the Sachet tribe of Skagit Indians lived behind stockades with thirty-foot high plank walls as protection against slave-hunting tribes from the north who landed unannounced on the island.

West of town is Madrona Drive, a four mile **scenic drive** that winds along the shores of Penn Cove. For information, contact the **Coupeville Chamber of Commerce** at 678-5434 or the **Coupeville Harbor Store**, Box 869, Coupeville WA 98239. Telephone 678-3625.

Accommodations

CAPTAIN WHIDBEY INN
2072 W Captain Whidbey Inn Road
Coupeville, WA 98239
Tel. (206) 678-4097

Simply described as "an inn by the sea," this is one of the most famous and venerable of Washington's hospitality institutions. Built in 1907 by Judge Lester Still, this huge, two story structure of chinked madrona logs was used for years as a retreat for well heeled guests arriving here by steamer from Seattle.

Today, the inn retains its original charm. A comfortable sitting room with a huge beachstone fireplace occupies the ground floor. Upstairs, along with a well stocked library, are thirteen sleeping rooms, all with log exposed walls. Feather filled pillows and down filled comforters add to the rustic mood. Guests can choose from these old upstairs rooms, the modern "lagoon" rooms, the cottages or the duplex. The Lagoon rooms have their own porches and a sweep of well kept lawn sloping down to a lagoon off Penn Cove. A nostalgic gazebo graces the lawn. It's simply romantic, nothing in the city could compete with this serene, idyllic setting.

The dining room, with its beautiful land and water views, has been deservedly famous for eighty years. It features Northwest regional cuisine, including fresh salmon, crab, oysters, mussels and other seafood specialties. Outside the kitchen window the chefs grow their own herbs for seasonings.

To find the Captain Whidbey from Oak Harbor, go south on Hwy 20 for ten miles and turn left at the sign onto Madrona Road. If coming from Coupeville, simply go three miles north of town.

THE COUPEVILLE INN
200 NW Coveland Street
Coupeville, WA 98239
Tel. (206) 678-6668

Coupeville is one of the historic jewels of Whidbey Island, once known as the "town of sea captains" because so many of the original settlers were sailors. The inn sits on an imposing rise just outside the main business area and enjoys a magnificent view of Coupeville and Penn Cove, and the Saratoga Passage.

A conference room on the upper level becomes the gathering spot for the complimentary breakfast of freshly ground coffee and fresh fruit-filled muffins, a specialty of the house. The fruit comes from nearby orchards, and ranges from pears to apples and blueberries, depending on the season. Coupeville Inn is within walking distance of Coupeville's antique shops, art galleries, bakeries and waterfront restaurants. Guests with mid-July reservations can see the famous Whidbey Island Yacht Race from their rooms or from one of the many vantage points within a few blocks of the inn.

Northwest residents and tourists alike have discovered this place in its first two years of operation, so advance reservations are essential, especially during the busy summer months.

Island County

Freeland

Freeland began life as a cooperative colony whose residents ran a sawmill. The colony disbanded in 1904, the little town continues as a resort.

Bed and Breakfast

PILLARS BY THE SEA
1367 E Bayview Avenue
Freeland, WA 98249
Tel. (206) 221-7738
Visa and MasterCard are accepted.

Founded near the turn of the century in a small settlement known as Freeland, the graciously renovated original building now housing Pillars By The Sea combining the picturesque charm of eight decades plus all modern conveniences. Overlooking a serene inlet, Pillars By The Sea derives its name from the elegant white pillars across the long, front porch.

Gracious living is suggested in every room of this lovely charming inn. Geraniums bloom in window boxes whose windows are framed with lace and a piano awaits in the parlor. The rooms are luxury plus! The East Room, with private bath, is decorated with antique furniture and old fashioned print wallpaper. Best of all is the view, serene forested green hills that gently slope down to the harbor. The West Room, with its antique mahogany bed and cozy down comforter, sports a special writing area with a Victorian desk.

Luxury doesn't stop with the surroundings. Every morning a gourmet breakfast is served on china plates with sterling silverware. The menu may include sour cream eggs a la crepe, or special corn-apple hot cakes with ham and eggs. Fresh fruit in season and freshly ground coffee always provide a lovely accompaniment. Elegance and comfort are hallmarks at Pillars By The Sea.

Langley

Langley, on Saratoga Passage on the eastern shore of Whidbey Island, is a small town which prides itself in being an arts colony. The Island Arts Council keeps its headquarters here in a community of 700 people. The name comes from J.W. Langley who invested in a wharf that became the place where steamers on the sound called for cordwood to fire their boilers.

Island County

Bed and Breakfast

LOG CASTLE BED AND BREAKFAST
3273 E Saratoga Road
Langley, WA 98260
Tel. (206) 321-5483

Bed and breakfast inns have been a tradition in British countries and Europe for well over a century. Now Whidbey Island also welcomes visitors with this type of accommodations. One of the most enjoyable and uniquely Northwest experiences to be found there is the Log Castle Bed and Breakfast. It is located a few miles outside of Langley, looking across to Camano Island and the mainland.

The term "castle" is truly appropriate for this delightful bed and breakfast lodge. The 5,000 square foot structure has an octagonal shaped tower that makes it look like an authentic castle. The arched, handcrafted, thick planked door opens into a forty foot living room with a spectacular view of the inland waters. Two of the guest rooms are located in the tower and each has its own bath and a catwalk for sun bathing and water watching. Hostess Norma Metcalf offers a wonderful country breakfast, accompanied by the sweet recorded dulcimer music of a Bainbridge Island group called Magical Strings.

After enjoying your bountiful breakfast, you can stroll down the path to the beach which offers miles of beach combing for shells, clams, mussels and driftwood. The Los Castle Bed and Breakfast is a delightful place to stay and to savor the historical flavor of the area.

LONE LAKE COTTAGE AND BREAKFAST
5206 S Bayview Road
Langley, WA 98260
Tel. (206) 321-5326

Lone Lake Cottage and Breakfast is located on 150 feet of lakeside setting and is delightful. This is an unpretentious place, and the warm hospitality of the owners Ward and Delores Meeks make it a wonderful place to stay. The architecture and decor are Oriental, unusual for Whidbey, and delightful for the guest.

The Terrace Cottage is decorated in rose, with Oriental vases, fans, and brilliant inlaid mosaic wall pieces. It has a bedroom, living room with fireplace, kitchen, and its own covered deck with a barbeque grill. The Garden Cottage is away from the house and has two bedrooms, sitting room with fireplace, color cable television and VCR with a well stocked library of films.

Island County

The grounds and gardens are delightful for strolling and exploring. Adjacent to the Terrace Cottage is a huge aviary, stocked with cardinals, budgerigars, canaries and other exotic birds.

There is a very special treat in store for guests at Lone Lake Cottage. Ward has created a forty foot stern-wheeler pleasure launch from which you can explore the lake. It has plush seating in a glassed in cabin and even a glass window in the bottom for viewing under the lake. Truly this is a unique and unusual extra to add to your memorable stay at Lone Lake Cottage.

When you're looking for scenery, it's time for:

	PITCHING TENT, LANGLEY STYLE		
	Deception Pass	Best camping	Lang/Camp
	For those who don't like backpack provisions:		
a.m.	Mike's Place	Best meals	Lang/Restaurant
	Now for some leisurely hiking and:		
a.m.	South Whidbey Park	Best clam digging	Lang/Park
p.m.	Historical Reserve	Best history	Lang/Park

Langley can be reached either by Highway 20 or ferry. The campgrounds, some of the best in the Northwest, offer a variety of activities, such as clam digging, photography, hiking and swimming. Pounding tent stakes was never so much fun.

Restaurant

MIKE'S PLACE
215 1st Street
Langley, WA 98260
Tel. (206) 321-6575
Hrs: Summer   Mon. - Sun.   8:00 a.m. - 10:00 p.m.
         Winter   Sun. - Thu.   8:00 a.m. - 9:00 p.m.
                          Fri. - Sat.   8:00 a.m. - 10:00 p.m.
Visa and MasterCard are accepted.

Mike Rosenberg, proprietor of Mike's Place, recently remodeled the kitchen of his popular restaurant located on the main street of Langley. Fortunately, he didn't change the warm and comfortable street side dining room that is so well suited to the old fashioned charm of Langley. From that remodeled kitchen and into the dining room, warmed by a woodstove, come a tempting variety of meals and treats.

Baker lladeene Leierer creates a dozen different, delicious items every day. These are not run of the mill bakery items. For example, there's Mexican Mocha Cake, Viennese Torte, and fresh pear pie to name only a few of the unusual specialties she creates. Breakfasts include lots of waffles, omelettes and crepes, as well as the standards. The lunch menu offers a variety of sandwiches, burgers, specials and there's a salad bar. Dinner fare runs from fresh seafood, pasta and steaks to sauerkraut and bratwurst.

All the meals offered at Mike's Place are satisfying and reasonably priced. Mike and his staff create an enjoyable dining experience pleasant and relaxed surroundings and this is a restaurant prized by local residents and visitors alike.

Oak Harbor

Oak Harbor, settled in 1849, and the community of Crescent Harbor to the east, settled in 1851, grew into farming towns supporting emigrants from Holland. Barrington Avenue gives a flavor of the old business district which existed here until the post-war period created a booming community. The headquarters of the island's Naval Air Station, which actually has two airfields and a seaplane base, is part of Oak Harbor which numbers close to 20,000 residents in its urban area. Oak Harbor's name comes from the groves of oak trees on the prairie behind it, testimony to a climate far drier than most in western Washington.

Attractions

Holland Gardens, 500 Avenue West, has a Dutch windmill and several plantings that honor the area's first white farmers. The gardens are open all year.

Ault Field, northwest of town on Ault Field Road, is headquarters for a naval electronic warfare wing and the Pacific Fleet's reserve aviation training. For group tours, call 257-2286 and ask for the public affairs office.

The L.P. Byrne house, Midway at Thirtieth Avenue, was built in 1894 and is typical of much of the original construction. There is an "old town" portion of the business district dating back to a time of creameries and farm supply stores.

Crescent Harbor, east of the navy station, has several historic homes. The first settler here, Richard Lansdale, paddled a canoe up from Olympia, checking out the sound as he worked his way north.

For information, contact **North Whidbey Chamber of Commerce**, Box 883, Oak Harbor WA 98277. Telephone 675-3535.

Accommodations

AULD HOLLAND INN
5861 Highway 20
Oak Harbor, WA 98277
Tel. (206) 675-2288

One of the landmarks in Oak Harbor is the round stucco windmill tower with its forty-eight foot diameter wind vanes. It's a real windmill built by Joe Franssen, a structural engineer, who along with his wife Elisa are the innkeepers of the Auld Holland Inn. The windmill is the inn's office. The whole building is done in old Dutch architecture and features stucco and exposed wood beams.

The Dutch theme design continues in the guest rooms which are decorated with antiques and provincial print wallpaper. Honeymoon suites with fireplaces and family kitchen units with refrigerators are available. Extra amenities include a heated pool, hot tub, tennis and basketball courts, laundry facilities, and the elegant but relaxed Kasteel Franssen restaurant right next door.

Joe designed and built the Kasteel Franssen Restaurant, too. The old Dutch country theme is also carried out here, with stucco and wood, a real working water wheel, and authentic old framed prints. Master Chef Jean Paul Combette, specializes in French and American cuisine, and has fifty-five years experience in France, Italy, England and the United States. The Auld Holland Inn and Kasteel Franssen Restaurant are the perfect places to stay and to dine to savor an old world experience.

Restaurant

CHAR'S COVE
2068 200th Avenue SW
Oak Harbor, WA 98277
Tel. (206) 679-2515

Hrs:	Lunch	Mon. - Fri.	11:00 a.m. - 2:00 p.m.
	Dinner	Sun. - Thu.	5:00 p.m. - 9:30 p.m.
		Fri. - Sat.	5:00 p.m. - 10:00 p.m.
	Brunch	Sunday	10:00 a.m. - 2:00 p.m.

Note: 200th Avenue S.W. is also locally known as Flintstone Freeway and may be shown that way on some directories and street maps.

Char's Cove is not only one of the best restaurants in Oak Harbor, but it also seems to be the live entertainment center for the town. Live music and dancing is featured Tuesday through Saturday nights from 9:00 p.m. - 1:30 a.m. and on Sunday evenings top West Coast comedy artists play to full houses.

Char's Cove is the only waterfront restaurant in the town, and the view from the second level is spectacular. The menu offers a variety of choices including steak, prime rib, seafood and pasta. There are two fresh seafood and two pasta specialities featured nightly. The wine list is impressive with something to please every palate and features Northwest as well as imported wines.

JEFFERSON COUNTY

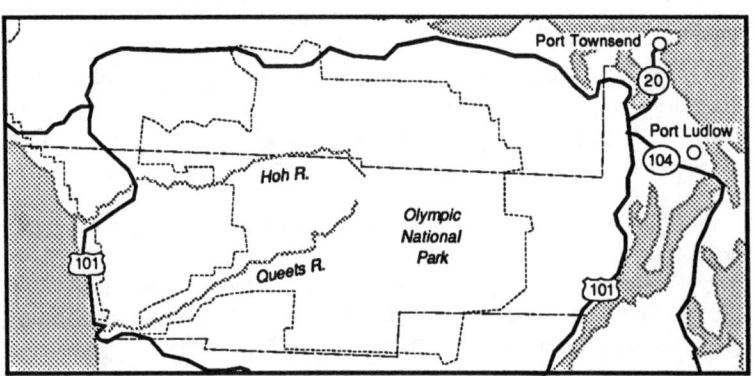

Reaching from the Pacific Ocean beaches across the middle of the Olympic Peninsula to Hood Canal and Puget Sound, this 1,805 square mile county is a land of trees and small ports. At last count, about 16,000 people live here, almost all of them on the county's eastern shores either in Port Townsend, or in the unincorporated communities around Oak Bay, just a few miles south.

The Olympics dominate the geography and climate of Jefferson County. Mount Olympus, at 7,965 feet above sea level the highest of the mountain range, is within the county. But, there are only a few roads and a network of foot trails to reach the national park and national forest lands (see Clallam County listing for details on all routes into Olympic National Park).

Port Townsend, a community started in 1851, became the county seat in 1852 when the Oregon Territorial Legislature was creating counties. Jefferson County continued through statehood, but promoter's dreams of a big seaport disappeared with emergence of Tacoma and Seattle. Military engineers picked several locations in the county for coast artillery batteries, and manned forts Worden and Flagler through World War II even as aircraft extended defensive strategy off-shore and made the guns obsolete. Today both are unique state parks operated as cultural and convention centers.

ATTRACTIONS

Fort Flagler State Park, on **Marrowstone Island**, was a coast artillery battery site created in 1900 and manned through most of World War II. Guns

Jefferson County

from here, Fort Worden and Fort Casey on Whidbey Island were to lay a "triangle of fire" which would deny an invading navy access to Admiralty Inlet and Puget Sound. Now home of a music camp sponsored by Seattle Youth Symphony, the park has camping, boat launching and a youth hostel. Call 385-1259.

On the Discovery Bay side of Quimper Peninsula is **Cape George**, a land mark first charted in 1846. This is one of the recommended viewpoints for pictures of the Olympic Mountains to the west, and for watching ships passing to the north through the Strait of Juan de Fuca.

Quilcene, on Highway 101 in the south county, is a fishing and oyster processing community settled about 1860. This is an important information place for travelers heading into national forest or national park lands. **Quilcene Ranger Station** has maps. A national salmon hatchery, producing about eight million fish a year, is on the Quilcene River. It welcomes visitors.

For further information, contact the **Chamber of Commerce**, 2437 Sims Way, Port Townsend WA 98368. Telephone 385-2722.

Port Ludlow

This was once the scene of one of the area's major sawmills. There was a large Indian village here when George Vancouver called to trade in May, 1792. After the sawmill began, a shipyard operated here in the 1880s. Today it is an unincorporated community with a large resort complex including golf course, marina and other facilities.

For further information, contact the **Chamber of Commerce**, 2437 Sims Way, Port Townsend WA 98368. Telephone 385-2722.

Resort

THE RESORT AT PORT LUDLOW
781 Walker Way
Port Ludlow, WA 98365
Tel.   (206) 437-2222
         (800) 732-1239 WA

You'll be happy as a clam when you comb the beach at low tide for fresh shell fish just a few steps away from your comfortable condo at the Resort at Port Ludlow.

It's been called the ultimate meeting and vacation spot on the Washington coast. Just twenty-eight miles from Seattle and a short ferry ride, the 210 deluxe accommodations and 50 fireplace suites sit on the edge of Port Ludlow Bay on Admiralty Inlet, just north of the Hood Canal. The resort offers such a wide variety of features you'll never be bored. There's the indoor and outdoor swimming pools, the seven tennis courts, and the sauna, beach club and a golf course that's been ranked among the top one percent in the nation by the American Society of Golf Course Architects. Available are bike rentals, paddle boats and recreation activities for the kids. At low tide clams and oysters emerge on the beach for shucking. For an incomparable evening, sail out on a champagne cruise and return for dinner at the resort's Harbor Master Restaurant.

When it's all over, you have something to talk about. No one will accuse you of clamming up.

Port Townsend

Residents of this small community beside the entrance to Puget Sound bill their place as a Victorian seaport. The description fits the homes and buildings which date from a time when 7,000 people lived here and many thought this would be a major shipping point for goods in the Alaska and Pacific trade. The most recent census gives a population of 8,500. Antiques and art galleries, restaurants and clubs with live entertainment cater to the thousands of visitors drawn here.

Attractions

Jefferson County Historical Museum contains a library of maritime history, Indian artifacts, a record of turn-of-the century trade in Port Townsend and a Victorian-style parlor and bedroom. The museum is in the **City Hall** at the foot of Water Street. Open Monday through Saturday, 11:00 a.m. to 4:00 p.m. Sundays, 1:00 p.m. to 4:00 p.m.

Sailors use the 100-foot high tower of the **Jefferson County Courthouse**, on Jefferson Street at Cass Street, as a bearing while running Admiralty Inlet. Built in 1892, it is one of the two oldest courthouses in Washington still in use. The architecture employed is a mixture of Romanesque and Gothic as well as an element of "fairytale castle."

The county honors Thomas Jefferson, and was named by the Oregon Territorial Legislature. In 1914, after Washington had long-since taken jurisdiction of its territory as a state, Oregon created another Jefferson County in central Oregon.

A walking tour of Port Townsend, one of the oldest cities in this state, will provide you with numerous examples of Victorian architecture, complete with turrets, towers and carpenter-Gothic trim. A tape recording telling of area history, keyed to a tour map, can be rented or purchased at the museum. Maps detailing more than sixty historical sites in the town are available at the Visitor Center, 2437 Sims Way. Telephone 385-2722.

Rothschild House, on Franklin Street near Taylor Street, built in 1868, is now kept up by the state park commission. From April 1 through October 1, it is open daily between 11:00 a.m. and 4:00 p.m. The rest of the year, it is open Saturday and Sunday, 11:00 a.m. to 4:00 p.m.

Fort Worden, at the tip of Quimper Peninsula, was a coast artillery post. It is now a 338 acre state park. **Point Wilson light house**, placed where the channel turns from the Strait of Juan de Fuca to Admiralty Inlet, was rebuilt in 1914.

The old military officer's quarters are used for conventions and cultural activities which draw artists from across the country. The commanding officer's house is a **museum** open April through October from 10:00 a.m. to 5:00 p.m. There is a campground. Telephone 1-800-562-0990.

Old Fort Townsend State Park is three miles south of town and east of Highway 20 on Old Fort Townsend Road. Created after an Indian disturbance in 1855-56, the post operated briefly, then was activated for a twenty year period beginning in 1874. Seven miles of trails wind among sites of old buildings and to a public beach.

Washington State Ferries offer daily service from Port Townsend to Keystone on Whidbey Island. Telephone is 542-7052.

For further information, contact the **Chamber of Commerce**, 2437 Sims Way, Port Townsend WA 98368. Telephone 385-2722.

Events

Port Townsend's semiannual **Victorian Homes Tour** is held the first weekend in May and the third weekend in September. An admission fee is charged.

The annual **Rhododendron Festival** is held in mid-May, just after the Victorian Homes Tour.

Accommodations

MANRESA CASTLE
7th and Sheridan Street
P. O. Box 564
Port Townsend, WA 98368
Tel. (206) 385-5750

Manresa Castle perches on a hill overlooking Port Townsend. If you have ever wanted to stay in a castle, here is your chance, and you don't even have to go to Europe. The castle was built in 1882 by a wealthy Prussian merchant who wanted to impress his bride by building a turreted castle reminiscent of those along the Rhine. He lived there only until 1905 and it was sometime later that the castle was purchased and renovated by group of Jesuits. They named it Manresa after a town in Spain where St. Ignatius of Loyola underwent great austerities. In 1973 the building was purchased by Ronald Smith and his wife Carol, who completely refurbished it into a charming hotel.

A variety of rooms are available, with or without private baths. The rooms are comfortable and charmingly furnished, reminiscent of days long ago. The turret suites are particularly popular. Many of the rooms have color televisions and phones and three have whirlpool baths. The hotel grounds are delightful with a charming English garden and the view overlooking the town, the mountains and bay is unbeatable. There is a dining room which serves, among other things, excellent fresh seafood.

For a delightfully different place to stay with a touch of old world elegance, Manresa Castle is perfect. The charming surroundings and friendly and accommodating staff will make your stay here a vacation to remember.

PALACE HOTEL, 1004 Water Street, Port Townsend, Washington. A downtown turn-of-the century hotel furnished in Victorian antiques. Enjoy mid-week winter rates. MasterCard and American Express accepted.

Jefferson County

STARRETT HOUSE INN
744 Clay Street
Port Townsend, WA 98368
Tel. (206) 385-3205
Visa and MasterCard are accepted.

Port Townsend is a town of charming Victorian houses, and the Starrett House inn is one of the most beautiful. It is a classic Victorian home built in 1889 by George Starrett for his bride. From the moment you enter the house, you know you are somewhere really special. The truly spectacular entry way, circular stairway in the tower and George Chapman's painted allegorical figures of the four seasons on the ceiling set this house apart from all others of the era. The Inn offers nine non-smoking guest rooms, each of which is furnished in antiques of the Victorian period and has a view of either Puget Sound or Port Townsend.

Starrett House offers something very special for guests, mystery weekends. On special weekends throughout the year you can become a character in a complex mystery, or become another person for the first twenty-four hours of your visit. A crime will be committed and no one may leave the inn until the mystery is solved. Solstice Performance Arts, a Tacoma based production company, has built an elaborate cast of characters and intriguing mystery for your enjoyment. The group festivities begin with a reception in the parlor, followed by a delightfully catered dinner and drawing room diversions. When the crime is discovered, the search is on until Saturday afternoon when the mystery is resolved and justice is served.

If you're a mystery fan, you'll love the ambiance during the mystery weekends - you'll feel as though you stepped into an Agatha Christie book. If mysteries aren't your cup of tea, however, you'll enjoy a stay at Starrett House Inn on any other weekend. The surroundings are truly magnificent and the friendly and courteous staff will make your visit delightful. When in Port Townsend, don't miss this opportunity to experience a taste of an earlier, gracious era.

Antiques

PORT TOWNSEND ANTIQUE MALL
802 Washington Street
Port Townsend, WA 98368
Tel.   (206) 385-2590
Hrs: Mon. - Sat.   10:00 a.m. - 5:30 p.m.
          Sunday   11:00 a.m. - 5:00 p.m.
Closed on Christmas Day and Thanksgiving Day.
Visa, MasterCard, AMEX and checks are accepted.

Kitty and Bill Sperry had been interested in antiques and quality furniture for years when Starrett House Antiques came up for sale in 1980. They bought the shop and moved from Gig Harbor to start their new life in Port Townsend. After several successful years they wanted to expand into a larger location and try something different and exciting. Thus was born Port Townsend Antique Mall.

The Sperry's specialize in English furniture and they have assembled under one roof, twenty antique dealers who specialize in many different things. There are dealers who carry antique clocks, fine jewelry and cut glass. There are musical and surveying instruments, tools, nautical accessories, duck decoys and fishing lures. The mall includes a gemologist, an antique appraiser and an area which provides coffee, pastries and light lunches.

The Port Townsend Antique Mall is a must for the antique connoisseur and the novice antique shopper. You will find something to please everyone with the wide selection this mall offers. Make this a stop during your stay in Port Townsend and enjoy yourself browsing among all the unique collectibles and antiques you will find.

Apparel

CHINA BLUE, 912   Water Street, Port Townsend, Washington. Natural fiber women's clothing in junior sizes. Visa, MasterCard accepted.

Art Gallery

THE FRANKLIN HOUSE GALLERY
636 Water Street
Port Townsend, WA 98368
Tel. (206) 385-0478
Hrs: Mon. - Sun. 10:30 a.m. - 5:00 p.m.
Closed on Christmas, Thanksgiving and New Year's Day.
Visa, MasterCard and personal checks are accepted.

Franklin House was one of Port Townsend's first galleries. The shop is located on the north end of the main street and is a wonderful, eclectic shop that highlights artists from Port Townsend and the State of Washington. There is a unique collection of toys, gifts and art work.

There is something for everyone at The Franklin House Gallery. You will find tapestries, etchings, jewelry, dolls, antiques, woven rugs, photographs, wood block prints, numerous items from Nepal, handpainted eggs and masks and a large selection of toys and greeting cards. The art gallery in the back of the store has one wall dedicated to displaying Centrum, the State Art Commission's works. Centrum also puts on concerts in the backyard garden area during the summer months.

The Franklin House Gallery is a unique place to shop. Be sure to note the handcarved oyster fisherman in the store when you visit. The artist, Stanley Rill lives in Port Townsend. You will be delighted by the varied and imaginative selection of art work and gifts that you find here, don't miss it when you're in Port Townsend.

Bed and Breakfast

THE HASTINGS HOUSE INN, 313 Walker Street, Port Townsend, Washington. Non-smokers welcome at this lovely B&B furnished in fine antiques. House tours daily; checks, MasterCard and Visa accepted.

HERITAGE HOUSE, 305 Pierce Street, Port Townsend, Washington. This 1870 Victorian provides a view of the bay and Mount Olympus. Six lovely rooms.

Jefferson County

INN DEERING AND THE APARTMENT
523 Fillmore
Port Townsend, WA 98368
Tel. (206) 385-6239
Visa and MasterCard are accepted.

Joan and David Deering moved to Port Townsend in 1984 after falling in love with the town's quaint, seaport charm. They purchased a house that was built in 1877 in the historical uptown section of Port Townsend and have completely renovated it into a lovely family home and Inn.

Inn Deering has three bedrooms in the main house that are beautifully furnished and decorated with antiques. The sunroom has a lovely view of Quimper Sound and is furnished with one hundred year old wicker furniture. The largest bedroom provides a view of the Sound from its private deck. Next door to the main house is a nicely decorated apartment which is a self-contained guest house designed to accommodate two to four people. It has a completely equipped kitchen and a nice view of the sound from the parlor.

The Inn has bikes for rent and is within walking distance of downtown. Children are welcome and the Inn provides a dog kennel for pets. Joan and David will make your stay in this tranquil spot a relaxing and enjoyable time.

JAMES HOUSE, 1238 Washington Street, Port Townsend, Washington. This grand Victorian mansion built in 1891 offers bay and mountain view from rooms furnished in period antiques. A garden cottage with private bath also available.

LIZZIE'S VICTORIAN INN
731 Pierce
Port Townsend, WA 98368
Tel. (206) 385-4168
Visa and Master Card are accepted.
Reservations are recommended.
Children over ten are welcome.

Lizzie's Bed and Breakfast is a special place. The house was built in the 1880s by a well to do woman named Lizzie, whose photograph still hangs in the living room. Hosts Patti and Bill Wickline have created a quiet, relaxing environment where it is a pleasure to stay. The house is filled with Victorian antiques, leather sofas, books, great fireplaces and a grand piano in the parlor. You are encouraged to look, touch and enjoy yourself.

There are seven guest rooms, each unique in its own way. Charlie's Room is furnished with an antique double bed and private shower. Daisy's

Room provides a king size bed and goose down pillows; Daisy signed her name on the wall in 1894. Jessie's Room has a half bath and queen size bed. Sarah's room has two double beds, a sitting area with bay windows overlooking the bay and mountains. Georgia's Room has a giant armoire, a high double bed and shower. Hope's room shares a hallway bath, has a double bed and a view of the backyard. Finally, there is Lizzie's room which has the only bedroom fireplace. Lizzie's Room is also known as the honeymoon suite and has an old fashioned tub and Lizzie's own brand of bubble bath and lotion in the bathroom.

No matter which room you choose, you'll enjoy your stay in this charmingly renovated Victorian home. Your hosts are warm, welcoming and make you feel at home. Lizzie's bubble bath is available for all baths with tubs. This is a very popular place, so don't miss it in your excursions in the Port Townsend area.

Delicatessen

WATER STREET DELI-RESTAURANT, 926 Water Street, Port Townsend, WA. Sandwiches, soups and salads for lunch; dinner gourmet seafoods and steaks.

Florist

HOLLY'S FINE FLOWERS
220 Taylor Street
Port Townsend , WA 98368
Tel. (206) 385-5428
Hrs: Mon. - Fri.   9:30 a.m. - 5:30 p.m.
          Saturday   10:00 a.m. - 5:00 p.m.
Visa and MasterCard are accepted.

Holly Mayshark moved to Port Townsend in 1981 to escape the hectic life of the city in this tranquil town. She opened her flower shop and was a success from the beginning. Holly moved to her present location in 1985 and can boast that her shop is the oldest and best flower in Port Townsend.

What sets Holly's shop apart from others is the quality of her floral designs, they are beautiful works of art. You can find something to please any taste, from sophisticated high style designs to charming European garden style arrangements. Holly and her assistants specialize in fanciful, old fashioned dried flower wreaths. Their cut floral bouquets are also extremely popular.

The shop is open, airy and the flowers are nicely displayed. They offer a full line of floral services including delivery to outlying areas and are associated with four floral wire services. Stop in at Holly's Fine Flowers to see for yourself what sets this shop above others, and enjoy browsing in this delightful, fragrant store.

Gift Shop

THE GREEN EYE SHADE
720 Water Street
Port Townsend, WA 98368
Tel. (206) 385-3838
Hrs: Mon. - Sat.   10:00 a.m. - 5:30 p.m.
          Sunday   11:00 a.m. - 5:00 p.m.
Closed major holidays.
Visa, MasterCard, AMEX and Discover cards are accepted.

When Port Townsend residents are shopping for a special gift, they go to The Green Eye Shade gift shop. Owners Thorne and Dorine Edwards opened their shop in 1970 and are the only remaining original store owners still on the main street. Since they are both potters, they began by carrying their own pottery along with 18th century English antique furniture , cards, jewelry and women's wear from India. The shop has evolved over the years and now carries a large selection of unique gifts at reasonable prices. Teddy's House is a charming playroom for children while mothers shop.

When the Edwards go on buying trips to Seattle, Los Angeles, or New York, they purchase quality items they know their customers will like. They have unique jewelry in sterling, brass and ceramics and lovely Sasaki Crystal. There is a selection of attractive and functional linens and flatware. The kitchen shop is well stocked and there is a delightful gourmet section.

The staff at The Green Eye Shade is knowledgeable and eager to serve their customers. They will special order items not in stock, offer complimentary gift wrapping and have a bridal registry. They will pack your order, if you wish, and ship it anywhere. The Green Eye Shade is the place to find just the gift you need, no matter what the occasion.

MARY KAISER DESIGN CO., LTD., 807 Washington Street, Port Townsend, California. An unusual selection of accessories, gifts, linens and furniture. Visa and MasterCard accepted.

Ice Cream

ELEVATED ICE CREAM
627 Water Street
Port Townsend, WA 98368
Tel. (206) 385-1156
Hrs: Winter Mon. - Sun. 11:00 a.m. - 10:00 p.m.
     Summer Mon. - Sun. 9:30 a.m. - 10:00 p.m.

Julie and David McCulloch established the Elevated Ice Cream shop in 1977. The name derives from the fact that its first home was in a Victorian elevator cage. They bring you some of the best, high quality, fresh and delicious ice cream you'll ever eat. There is a selection of specialty desserts, full fountain service and an espresso bar.

Choosing what to indulge in at Elevated Ice Cream can be quite a decision. In addition to the homemade ice cream made with the freshest ingredients possible, including Sequim strawberries, Marrowstone Island raspberries, Northwest filberts and Guittard chocolate direct from the factory, there are fresh Italian fruit ices and chocolate covered espresso beans. There are ice cream pies, such as S'mores pie, Oreo cookie pie, mint mountain pie, Swiss orange pie and mud pie to name a few. Then, of course, there are the hand dipped chocolate truffles made on the premises with flavors such as Amoretto, Grand Marnier and many more.

"The nicest thing about the ice cream business," says Julie, "is that we're generally dealing with happy people. If they're not happy when they come in, they're usually smiling when they leave." Make yourself happy and enjoy one of the delicious treats offered by Elevated Ice Cream.

Market

ALDRICH'S
940 Lawrence
Port Townsend, WA 98368
Tel. (206) 385-0500
Hrs: Mon. - Sun. 8:00 a.m. - 10:00 p.m.
Closed on Christmas Day.

John Clise, owner of Aldrich's Neighborhood Food Store, is a remarkable man and has created an equally remarkable store. Before moving to Port Townsend in 1983, John was executive director of the Pike Place Market in Seattle. He was born and raised in Seattle, and loved the challenge of his job. Also, he realized a desire to become part of a small community and to operate a business on a small scale. Aldrich's was ready and waiting for him. The Aldrich family had owned and operated the store on the same spot in Port Townsend for ninety years, but were ready to sell and their store was just what John Clise had in mind.

Aldrich's was the opposite of everything John knew about modern high tech merchandising. The store was designed to be a friendly, comfortable place to do business, not to manipulate the customer into buying. John has retained this comfortable ambiance, while developing what he calls his "schizophrenic" concept of a grocery store. On one hand Aldrich's remains the friendly little neighborhood grocery it always was; on the other hand, John offers high-quality specialty items unavailable elsewhere in the area.

John has brought together in this store a small community of merchants under one roof, sort of a mini Pike Place Market. Shopping at Aldrich's is fun and rewarding. Take the time to browse through this interesting store when in Port Townsend, you'll love the gourmet selection and the neighborhood atmosphere.

Restaurant

THE FOUNTAIN CAFE, 920 Washington Street, Port Townsend, Washington. Open 10 a.m. - 10 p.m. Monday - Saturday, the Fountain features lots of daily specials, fresh local seafood, great desserts. Also beer, wine, and expresso.

HALF SHELL
630 Water Street
Port Townsend, WA 98368
Tel. (206) 385-6677
Hrs: Wed. - Sun. Dinner 6:00 p.m. - 10:00 p.m.
Visa and MasterCard are accepted.

Joan and Robert Allen opened the Half Shell in 1984 and divide their time between the restaurant and their bed and breakfast, The Lincoln Inn. The Half Shell is charming, with narrow brick walls decorated from items purchased during their travels around the world. There are rugs from Baghdad and copper from Iran, a cosmopolitan touch to the decor that is also reflected in the menu selections.

The house specialities are fettucini Alfredo and calamari Provencal. Candlelight, fresh flowers and linen tablecloths add to the ambiance in the evening. Begin with an appetizer, such as calamari kamikaze. Entree selections are varied, there is a good selection of seafood and meat dishes. The dessert cart rolls around after dinner with a yummy selection of cheesecake, English truffles and strawberry mousse and many others from which to pick.

The Allen's bed and breakfast offers three rooms with private baths in a Victorian house and is the perfect place to stay while in Port Townsend. The Allens will make your stay in Port Townsend enjoyable with their comfortable accommodations at The Lincoln Inn and the fine dining at the Half Shell.

LA FONDA MEXICAN RESTAURANT
2330 Washington Street
Port Townsend, WA 98368
Tel. (206) 385-4627

Hrs:	Winter	Mon. - Fri.	11:30 a.m. - 9:00 p.m.
		Sat. - Sun.	4:00 p.m. - 9:00 p.m.
	Summer	Mon. - Fri.	11:30 a.m. - 9:30 p.m.
		Sat. - Sun.	4:00 p.m. - 9:30 p.m.

Closed Christmas, New Year's, Easter and Thanksgiving.
Visa and MasterCard are accepted.

Gary and Sue Wall opened La Fonda in 1981 and it has been a hit with the local people ever since. The Walls and Chef Daniel Knudson have developed the recipes used. You can always expect consistently good food and service. The restaurant is not large and has a quiet, relaxed atmosphere, enhanced with white stucco, overhead fan and nice Mexican art work. In the winter months there's a cozy fire to take away the chill.

The menu emphasizes fresh seafood with a Mexican touch, such as red snapper in chili red wine sauce, salmon in cinnamon clove sauce and seasonal specials such as Dungeness crab and shrimp chimichangas. All sauces were developed in La Fonda's kitchen and are uniquely delicious. There are numerous a la carte selections and combination dinners. A full service cocktail bar exists where they make margaritas with freshly squeezed lime juice and their own Sangria to complement your meal.

La Fonda is located near the Boat Haven, one block toward the water off the main highway. Don't hesitate to ask for directions, you'll be glad you did when you relax in the congenial south of the border atmosphere and enjoy some uncommonly good Mexican food.

Jefferson County

LIDO'S RESTAURANT AND INN
925 Water Street
Port Townsend, WA 98368
Tel. (206) 385-7111

Hrs:	Winter	Sun. - Thu.	11:00 a.m. - 9:00 p.m.
		Fri. - Sat.	11:00 a.m. - 10:00 p.m.
	Summer	Sun. - Thu.	11:00 a.m. - 10:00 p.m.
		Fri. - Sat.	11:00 a.m. - 11:00 p.m.

Visa, MasterCard, AMEX and Diner's Club are accepted.

"Our goal is to provide the best food and service possible. The chefs are continually updating their skills with cooking classes and the servers go through extensive training," said owner Rudy Valiani while explaining just what makes Lido's one of the best restaurants in Port Townsend. The restaurant is on the Bay and has view seating. It's a comfortable place with high ceilings and brick walls. It is the excellence of the cuisine and the selection which ranges from seafood to chicken to meat that really sets it apart from other restaurants.

For lunch there is a good selection of seafood depending on what is fresh that day. There are homemade soups, salads and such entrees as stuffed salmon, quiche and the pasta or crepe of the day. Pink scallops come directly from Port Townsend Bay and clams, oysters and mussels are from the peninsula. The wine list is extensive and all servers have been through numerous wine tasting sessions to advise you on the best selection to enhance your meal. After a sinfully rich dessert and some delicious espresso, venture downstairs for live jazz every weekend.

Above the restaurant is Lido Inn. These charming, light, airy rooms are furnished with antiques. The suite has a bedroom, loft and private bath with the added attraction of a view of the water. It is a delightful place to stay on the water in Port Townsend and the Lido Restaurant is an equally delightful place to dine. Try one or both to make your stay in Port Townsend more memorable.

WATER STREET DELI-RESTAURANT, 926 Water Street, Port Townsend, Washington. At lunch, design your own sandwiches, enjoy good soups and salads. Gourmet dinners include steaks, seafoods, and more.

Jefferson County

THE SYBARITES   LOOSE IN PORT TOWNSEND

Where would a Sybarite stay?		
Inn Deering	Best seaview comforts	PortT/B & B
Lizzie's Victorian Inn	Best family charm	PortT/B & B
Manresa Castle	Best old-world elegance	PortT/Acc

What would a Sybarite do with their day?		
Aldrich's	Best edibles	PortT/Market
The Wine Cellar	Best award-winning wines	PortT/Wine
Visitors Center	Best walking tour guidebook	PortT/Attrac.
Port T. Antique Mall	Best antique collectibles	PortT/Ant
The Green Eye Shade	Best handling gifts	PortT/Gift
Port T. Bay Company	Best sporting goods	PortT/Sport
Lido's Restaurant & Inn	Best oysters and jazz	PortT/Rest.

Syb·a·rite (Lat. Sybarita, native of Sybaris<Gk. Subarités<Subaris, Sybaris, Italy) One fond of pleasure and luxury.

Sporting Goods

PORT TOWNSEND BAY COMPANY, INC.
1042 Water Street
Port Townsend, WA 98368
Tel. (206) 385-5279
Hrs: Mon. - Sat.   9:00 a.m. - 6:00 p.m.
        Sunday   11:00 a.m. - 5:00 p.m.
Closed on Thanksgiving, Christmas, New Year's and Easter.
Visa, MasterCard and personal checks are accepted.

When Port Townsend Bay Company first began doing business years ago, it was a small-town department store. When Vance Jacobsen purchased it several years ago, he envisioned a different future for the store. He has built it into one of the best sporting goods and outdoor supply stores on the Peninsula. Each member of the staff has an area of expertise, but is also trained and familiar with other areas to better serve the customer. There is always someone to answer any questions you have about your particular area of interest. An information area in the store has handouts and video tapes on many different sports.

Fishermen will find just what they need at Port Townsend Bay Company, whether it's equipment or information. They have an extensive line of salmon, fly fishing gear and keep current on the best fishing place in the area. Hikers and backpackers will find the latest trail information and topographical maps, as well as a complete line of hiking equipment. In the winter, there is cross country skiing equipment for sale and rent. The store carries one of the largest selections of Patagonia clothing in the Pacific Northwest. If you are an experienced runner, or are just getting started, Port Townsend Bay Company has just what you need. Experts are available who will use different techniques to analyze your shoe needs for a perfect fit.

No matter what sport or outdoor activity interests you, you'll find just what you need at Port Townsend Bay Company. They have as complete a selection of equipment as you'll find anywhere, and the expert sales people are friendly and waiting to help you. Before you head out to enjoy the outdoor activities and beauty of the Pacific Northwest, plan a stop at Port Townsend Bay Company.

Tavern

RUSSELL'S BACK ALLEY
P. O. Box 1347
West end of Tyler Street
Port Townsend, WA 98368
Tel. (206) 385-6536
Hrs: Mon. - Sun. 12:00 noon - closing
Visa and MasterCard are accepted.

The building that houses Russell's Back Alley was a turn of the century Chinese laundry at one time, and had been vacant for forty years before being completely renovated by proprietor Russell Williams, a musician. He used white stucco and wood along with the existing brick and turned the old building into a two story split level night spot.

Russell's Back Alley has a show stage and features popular rock and roll bands on the weekends, and Jazz on Sundays. Occasionally major acts such as Taj Mahal, Maria Muldaur and Jazz greats Bud Shanks and Barney McClure appear at this night stop. In the summer months there is a courtyard which features live music on Sundays. Plans are underway for an enclosed deck for the winter months.

The menu at Russell's Back Alley features chili and Cajun items, such as gumbo. Of course, beer and wine are available. Russell's Back Alley is unique in

Port Townsend, plan to spend some time there enjoying the great entertainment offered.

Wine

THE WINE SELLER
940 Water Street
Victorian Square
Port Townsend, WA 98368
Tel. (206) 385-7673
Hrs: Mon.-Sat.   10:30 a.m.-6:00 p.m.
       Sunday   11:00 a.m.-5:00 p.m.
Extended hours in the summer.
Most major credit cards are accepted.

It doesn't take a bank roll to buy a fine wine, but it does take knowledge. That's where Wine Seller owner Joe Euro comes in. Joe or one of his trained and knowledgeable staff can point you in the direction of a five dollar wine that many expensive labels would have trouble measuring up to in quality and taste. Because Joe stays on top of the news of the wine world, reading every review he can get his hands on, he knows the gems that crop up from time to time and stocks many of them.

In this 1,000 square foot shop you'll find many top rated and award winning wines. Case discounts are offered. Now, if you are extravagant, and appreciate one of the world's great wines, you can take home one of six or seven vintages of Mouton Rothschild, Lafite Rothschild, Chateau Margaux, Dom Perignon, etc. The real emphasis is on fine Washington and West Coast wines and there are plenty in stock!

Besides wine, the shop offers an espresso bar, deli items, and a selection of beers, coffees, teas. So when you make an informed selection, you'll be able to rest your case on its quality.

KING COUNTY

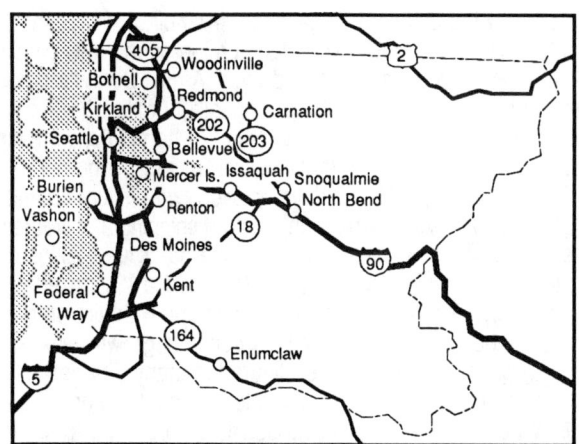

The contrasts are many in this big, 2,128 sq. mile county. On the hilly land between Puget Sound and Lake Washington is Seattle, a city of 500,000 people. More than twice that many people live in an urban corridor stretching south to Tacoma and north to Everett. From the Alpine Lakes Wilderness of Mount Baker National Forest, it is less than thirty-five miles airline miles west to the busy urban area. In between are farms, sawmill towns, coal mines, and access to a water wonderland. Rural Vashon Island, with about 7,400 residents, stands off East Passage just a ferry-boat commute from a busy West Seattle. Towering office buildings, glittering with modern glass and burnished metal exteriors, loom above squat brick structures constructed when this was the best place to ship out for the Alaska gold fields.

The county's west boundary is in the sound at sea level. It's eastern limits follow the crest of the Cascade Mountains where elevations approach 8,000 feet and tend to be 3,500 in the passes and 6,000 feet above sea level at the ridge tops and mountain crests. Large quantities of rain fall on the foothills of the Cascades, creating productive forest land managed by the U.S. Forest Service and several private timber companies plus hundreds of small woodland owners. Greenwater River, at the county's south boundary with Pierce County, is one of hundreds of streams draining this forest. The northern boundary with Snohomish County is a surveyor's line running east and west that begins in the sound just off Point Wells.

Industrial development has long-since lifted the western county from its heritage of timber and farming. Soft coal and iron ore combined to make steel rolling mills viable in Seattle. Ship and aircraft building are major industries, and factories at Renton which began turning out cars for logging railroads have diversified their output. Coal was mined from a seam discovered on the eastern shore of Lake Washington, now called the Newcastle coal fields, as early as 1863. Black Diamond, a much more reliable coal field in the Green River valley of the south county, was linked to Renton by railroad in 1885.

Modern history of King County begins with the landing of a party of twenty-four emigrants in November 1851 at a place on the sound now called Alki Point. Alki in Chinook jargon was "bye and bye." Arthur Denny's party joked that their town by the water would be "New York alki," or New York, bye and bye." It was a far cry from New York four years later when Indians raided the settlement despite the presence of the naval vessel Decatur in the harbor. Those days turned to a time of building. Seattle enjoyed two distinct booms. One was the 1897 gold strike in Alaska which emphasized shipping and created more docks for the export of lumber and coal. As in the other large cities of the Pacific Coast, the economic boom of World War I had a lasting effect, creating industrial capability. The area's modern boom came with aircraft and ship manufacturing demanded by World War II. Economic growth was not without labor strife. King County working men figured in many tiffs between managers of lumber companies and locals of the International Workers of the World union, called "Wobblies" by the people. Seattle emerged as a strong union city; producing national leaders in the labor movement. Tradition of organized labor continues in the county's industrial working places, and elsewhere, even among its performing artists who are many these days.

King County also took the lead in developing the state's educational system. The Organic Act creating Washington as a territory specified a university which actually opened in 1861 on land donated by Arthur Denny. That ten acre site in Seattle was too small. As the new century opened, the University of Washington campus moved to its present location on Lake Washington where logging engineering and aeronautical engineering are among the fields of study, reflecting the industrial roots of the growing community.

ATTRACTIONS

Blake Island State Park, located west of Seattle in Kitsap County, can be reached by boat only and the ferry shuttles from the Seattle waterfront. There is bottom fishing, eight miles of foot trails and tent campsites for boaters.

Tillicum Village, a commercial concession on the island, packages a salmon dinner with tours from Pier 56 at the foot of Seattle's Seneca Street. Indian dances, a traditional cedar longhouse are part of the experience. Call 329-5700 for rates and reservations.

King County

Snoqualmie Pass, on I-90, has **major winter ski areas** and is the summer entry to the **Pacific Crest Trail** and the vast National Forests which include the Cascade Mountains and their foothills to the west. During ski season, regular bus service connects the pass with Seattle. Call 236-1000 for road and snow reports.

Puget Sound Railroad Museum, 109 King Street, Snoqualmie, is part of a steam train ride which leaves from a depot built in 1890. If you take the excursion ride offered weekends from April through October, the train will loop close to Snoqualmie Falls. Call 746-4025 for museum hours and train departure times. The line runs to North Bend and back.

Snoqualmie Valley Historical Museum, 320 North Bend Boulevard, North Bend, has one of the area's best collections of Indian artifacts from tribes living west of the Cascades. Also on display are a 1910 kitchen recreation and a diorama of early logging techniques. From March 1 through October 1, open Saturday and Sunday from 1:00 p.m. to 5:00 p.m. Open the rest of the year by appointment, call 888-3200 or 888-0062.

Mount Si, a lone peak northeast of North Bend, is a popular **hiking spot**. The 4,190 foot summit is a day's hike off Mount Si Road. For a map and complete directions, check with the North Bend Ranger station. Several other hiking trails are east of here in the Cascades including one from Alpental Ski area that leads up to jagged and scenic granite peaks.

East of Seattle is **Snoqualmie Falls**, a 268-foot sheet of water which creates its own little falls of wind-blown moisture condensed on the rock walls of its canyon. There is a viewing platform at the top, a restaurant and view point near the base of the falls.

Sixty-two miles from Seattle and two miles beyond the little community of Snoqualmie, on Highway 202, Puget Power built the state's **first hydroelectric plant** in 1898. They run the park and own the falls.

Tokul Lake State Fish Hatchery, north of the falls, was the first trout hatchery in Washington state. Visitors are welcome. This reach of the Snoqualmie has been a favorite of trout fishermen for decades.

Fall City, on Highway 203 northwest of the falls, is still a logging town and celebrates the fact each June. Many buildings in town show the architecture popular, at that time, for commercial construction in the 1880s. Each summer an open-air theater presents drama which runs from

Shakespeare to religious passion plays, with an optional steak barbecue before the show. **Raging River**, south of Fall City, is popular with fishermen and campers.

Coal Creek Park, east of I-405 next to Newport, preserves the first low-grade coal mine in King County. A seam of lignite was opened here and strip mined over a long period of time. The county park includes part of the reclaimed area.

Flaming Geyser Recreation Area, on Highway 169 at Green River, is a 1500-acre forested area. It adjoins **Nolte Recreation Area** on Deep Lake with self-guided nature trails. Flaming Geyser once flamed as natural gas mixed with saltwater belched occasionally from the ground. Those in the know would run over and ignite the gases. A smaller geyser was also uncovered when geologists explored for the McKay coal seam by drilling far beneath the surface.

For further information, contact the **Seattle/King County Convention and Visitors Bureau**, 1815 Seventh Avenue, Seattle WA 98101. Telephone 447-7276.

Auburn

Auburn has roots as a trade center for hop farms along the Green River. The original plat of 1886 honored Lt. William Slaughter who had died in the Indian wars of 1855. Residents found themselves the butt of jokes and went to the legislature in 1893 for a special law renaming the town for a New York state hop-growing center, Auburn. Modern Auburn has its own "way," the state's West Valley Freeway on Highway 167 that whisks motorists north to Seattle without ever getting on the old parallel federal way.

Attractions

The **Auburn Railroad Depot**, on C Street, is an historic building at what is a major division point created when the Northern Pacific Railroad reached here in 1883. Architects also study the 1923 city hall located at 25 West Main Street as an example of government structures of that era.

The regional headquarters for the **Federal Aviation Center**, from which its aircraft controllers direct instrument flights in the Pacific Northwest, is in

Auburn. If you are interested in touring the Seattle Center, as it is called, telephone 833-6800 for an appointment and directions.

For further information, contact the **Auburn Chamber of Commerce**, 24 B Street Northeast, Auburn WA 98002, telephone 833-0700.

Bellevue

Like a puddle of water fed by a brisk northwest rain, Bellevue spread over the timbered hills on the east shore of Lake Washington and north of I-90. City limits now reach east to Lake Sammamish. Bellevue numbers over 74,000 residents, many living on large lot homes and in subdivisions which sprouted as rural developments in the 1950s and 1960s.

Bellevue's post office was designated in 1887, the original town platted around it in 1904. This is now Washington's fourth-largest city, with major hotels catering to conventions, shopping centers, its own symphony orchestra, and art museum. Bellevue is a center for distributing, light manufacturing and high-technology industries.

Attractions

The original townsite, platted by Isaac Bechtel, is now a **chic shopping area** with over ninety shops on streets decorated with flowers. High fashion clothing and antiques are among the merchandise which draws shoppers here.

Bellevue Art Museum, 301 Bellevue Square, features changing exhibits. Local and regional artists' works are regularly displayed along with some international fine art. This is on the third story of a collection of shops which are the Bellevue Square shopping center. Open Tuesday through Friday 12:00 noon to 8:00 p.m. Saturday 11:00 a.m. to 5:30 p.m., and Sunday 11:00 a.m. to 5:00 p.m. Telephone 454-3322.

Bellevue remembers the area's roots as a farm community in **Kelsey Creek Community Park.** There are barns, farm animals and pony rides along with a forest full of hiking trails. Take 132nd Place east from I-405. It becomes Southeast Seventh Place. Turn left on 130th and follow signs to park entrance.

One of Washington's first premium winemakers is **Columbia Winery**, 1445 120th Avenue Northeast. The vineyard and winery are together, and visitors are welcome. Open daily, 10:30 a.m. to 4:30 p.m.. Telephone 453-1977.

There's a candy shop and tours at **Vernell's Fine Candies**, 11959 Northup Way. Tours take about forty-five minutes among the machines and hand-dipping operations. Open Monday through Friday from 8:00 a.m. to 3:00 p.m. for tours. The candy shop stays open until 4:00 p.m. Call 455-8400.

Beaux Arts Park, on the shore of Lake Washington just north of I-90, is a model of an English garden village created in 1908 by Sidney Lawrence, an artist known for his landscape paintings of Alaska. Bellevue surrounds the town now. It was to be an artists' colony, but by the 1930s it had become an exclusive residential area.

Bellevue's harbor, now devoted to pleasure craft, was for decades the home port of American-Pacific Whaling Company which operated steam whalers in Alaskan waters from June through October then brought the vessels here for maintenance and storage. Houghton, to the north on the shore, was a shipyard town where whaling vessels and others underwent repairs.

For further information, contact the **King County East Convention and Visitors Bureau**, 515 116th Avenue Northeast, Bellevue WA 98004. Telephone 455-1926.

Accommodations

BELLEVUE HILTON
100 112th Avenue NE
Bellevue, WA 98004
Tel. (206) 455-3330

It would be easy to simply say the the Bellevue Hilton lives up to the already established reputation of the other Hiltons, but that wouldn't be doing it justice. Even by the most exacting standards, this hotel is a pleasure. The Bellevue Hilton, conveniently located off of I-405 in the heart of Bellevue, offers a seven story hotel complex with tastefully decorated rooms designed for both comfort and security. In addition to the usual amenities, the hotel also features twenty-four hour room service, complimentary Movie Channel and direct dial phones.

Here, after a fun-filled day, you can enjoy a relaxing dip in their pool or jacuzzi. They've also got a private health club with raquetball, tennis, and basketball courts, as well as a full-sized gym. Once you've worked up a hearty appetite, assuage your hunger by choosing a dining place from among three speciality restaurants and lounges, such as Sam's Restaurant, offering an elegant menu amidst the oak and velvet of turn-of-the-century Seattle; or The Cork N' Cleaver, specializing in fine wines and steaks; and finally, the El Torrito, a spicy Mexican restaurant.

For special events, there are banquet, convention and group services available for accommodating as many as 400 people. And if you're a parent, there is no charge for children, regardless of age, when they occupy the same room as yourself. For an encounter with casual elegance in a style all it's own, the Bellevue Hilton is a "Best Choice."

BELLEVUE HOLIDAY INN
11211 Main Street
Bellevue, WA 98004
Tel. (206) 455-5240

For the past sixteen years, Sam Saleh and Dietmar Jaeger have made the Bellevue Holiday Inn one of the best operated and designed inns in the Northwest. Their staff is dedicated to quality and service. Lush gardens and tall evergreens surround these environs and invite the traveler to a serene respite from the fast pace of nearby Seattle.

Each of the 182 well-appointed rooms is designed with comfort in mind, air conditioning, color television, room service and many other amenities are provided.

The inn's restaurant is Jonah's which has been newly remodeled, is open and airy in a park like setting. Featured is Northwest cuisine, with the best fresh seafood, chicken, beef, pasta, garden fresh salads and even Sunday Brunch. The Jonah Lounge features a big screen TV, cable, movies and special sports events. Live entertainment is presented every Friday and Saturday.

With airport transportation available, free parking and banquet facilities for parties of up to 500, the Bellevue Holiday Inn provides a wide range of quality services at excellent values.

BELLEVUE RED LION INN
300 112th Avenue, S.E.
Bellevue, WA 98004
Tel. (206) 455-1300

Only ten miles from downtown Seattle, the Red Lion Inn of Bellevue rises dramatically alongside Interstate 405. Nestled between busy Lake Washington and serene Lake Sammamish, the Red Lion is an integral part of the rapidly-expanding Eastside.

From the moment you enter the spectacular lobby with its soaring glass canopy, you know you've entered a world of first-class accommodations. The glittering smoked-glass elevators silently whisk you toward one of the 355 luxurious guest rooms. Each spacious room features air conditioning, direct-dial telephone, double vanities, color television, and king and queen-sized beds.

Guests at the Red Lion have their choice of convenient services; there is ample free parking, room service, valet and laundry service, a hair salon, a travel agency, and car-rental desk. The magnificent pool area, surrounded by a landscaped deck and complete with its own waterfall, gives guests an opportunity to relax, swim, and sunbathe.

Excellent dining is a Red Lion tradition. Guests can select from two different restaurants and two lounges, each with its own unique atmosphere. Misty's Dining Room, on the Mezzanine, is well-known in the area for its outstanding cuisine and elegant setting. The Coffee Garden, amidst the sky-lit main lobby, surrounds guests with foliage while they enjoy a tasty snack or a complete meal. Misty's Lounge, a prime spot in Bellevue's nightlife, features dancing on two sunken dance floors. Or, need a little serenity? slip into the plush, Quiet Bar and sip on your favorite refresher.

The Red Lion, one of the première hotels in the Northwest. A "Best Choice" for offering you the selection of ambiance to match your mood.

THE RESIDENCE INN SEATTLE EAST
14455 NE 29th Place
Bellevue, WA 98007
Tel. (206) 882-1222
      (800) 331-3131

The Residence Inn is an all suites hotel with one and two bedroom units, each with a fully equipped kitchen with everything necessary to cook for and serve to a family of four. Each unit is like a condominium, with a separate entrance, fireplace, and even a popcorn popper for those quiet evenings reading or watching television. Guest laundry facilities are provided and there are laundry and valet services six days a week and daily housekeeping. The helpful staff at The Residence Inn will even do your grocery shopping for you at no charge and there is free parking.

The Gatehouse is the center for additional services. Here you'll find the reservation desk, complimentary coffee at all times, complimentary dessert in the evening and buffet continental breakfast in the morning. The Gatehouse lobby has a television, fireplace, chairs, tables and an assortment of games, cards, and books. It has a number of social functions in which you may wish to participate. The Residence Inn provides three jacuzzis, a swimming pool, volleyball and basketball courts. You can order a meal sent to your room from Houlihan's, a wonderful restaurant located adjacent to the Inn.

The Residence Inn is a perfect "home away from home." Whether you are visiting Seattle for an extended period or just a few days, you'll find this an ideal spot to stay. The rates are comparable to corporate rates at major hotels and decrease with the length of your stay. You'll receive outstanding value for your money at The Residence Inn and receive personalized service from the staff.

Antiques

DAYS GONE BYE ANTIQUE MALL
2209 N.E. Bel-Red Road
Bellevue, WA 98052
Tel. 206 641-7452
Hrs: Mon.-Sat.   10:00 a.m. - 6:00 p.m.
          Sunday   12:00 noon - 5:00 p.m.
Visa, MasterCard, and Discovery Card accepted.
Personal checks, Canadian currency accepted.
Financing available on approved credit.

Every antique shop offers a slice of time, but with 12,000 square feet, Days Gone Bye Antique Mall comes a lot closer to putting you in touch with the old world.

The Mall's specialty is quality furniture. You can enjoy free coffee as you browse leisurely among the historic treasures in air conditioned comfort. The displays are well displayed and the wide aisles provide for handicapped access, which is unusual in an antique shop. If you find something you like among the 25,000 items, staff members will be happy to take a Polaroid picture of the item for you to compare with the rest of your furnishings at home. Shipping will also be arranged. An interior decorator is available to help with design coordination for your home.

If you have a hunger for the past and its memories, stop in and satiate that craving...at Days Gone Bye Antiques.

(See special invitation in the Appendix.)

Apparel

MARGEO'S
10042 Main Street
Bellevue, WA 98004
Tel. (206) 451-9100
Hrs: Mon. - Fri. 10:00 a.m. - 6:00 p.m.
Saturday 10:00 a.m. - 5:00 p.m.
Visa, MasterCard and AMEX are accepted.

Located on Bellevue's quaintly-restored Main Street, Margeo's offers the finest in women's apparel for the discriminating shopper. Fashion-conscious without being faddish, Margeo's goes the extra step in ambiance and service to make the customer feel special. From the antiques which decorate the shop, to the individually-chosen fashions, no amount of effort has been spared to make the shop unique, and to give it a warm and friendly feeling.

The Zoffel family have, for the past four and one-half years, made twice-annual trips to New York, Dallas, and Europe to assure their patrons more in selections and style. Margeo's features labels such as Alfred Sung, Le Painty, accessories by Alexis Kirk, and elegant handknit sweaters created by local designers.

As is usually the case with traditional fashions, it's not so much the textures and patterns which one uses, but how they are put together which makes the difference. The staff at Margeo's are experts in the area of wardrobe consulting and color coordination. For more in service, selection, and style, Margeo's is worth the visit.

PAPILLON
608 Bellevue Way NE
Bellevue, WA 98004
Tel. (206) 454-7324
Hrs: Mon. - Sat. 10:00 a.m. - 6:00 p.m.
Visa, MasterCard and AMEX are accepted.

For the past ten years, from her location adjacent to Bellevue Square, June Baschen has offered the finest in women's apparel and wardrobe services. By offering a wide range of better goods, June and her manager, Tassie Pember have carved out a popular niche in the local clothing-conscious community.

Papillon suits the woman with classic tastes, yet one who prefers a fresh, modern look. Careful selection of patterns and textures enables the shop to provide unique fashions to its patrons. Canadian and American designers rub shoulders with European designers and give the shop an international flavor.

In addition to a complete line of accessories such as belts, jewelry, handbags, and hosiery, the shop also stocks such favorites as Le Painty pants and Berek sweaters.

In a successful attempt to provide that extra measure of service, Papillon provides personal wardrobing by appointment, color analysis, gift wrapping, and alterations.

Art Gallery

KENNETH BEHM GALLERIES
109 Bellevue Square
Bellevue, WA 98004
Tel. (206) 464-0222

With three galleries, one in Seattle's Rainier Square and two in Bellevue, Kenneth Behm has one of the largest collections of fine art, prints, and reproductions in the Northwest. The galleries provide a comfortable setting for browsing.

The Northwest artist collection at the Behm Galleries is extensive; with such artists as Michael Cobb, Robert Addison and Max Hayslette well represented. The selection of contemporary artists includes Chagall, Miro, Picasso, and the largest collection of Salvador Dali's works in the Pacific Northwest. Other contemporary artists displayed are Alvar, Aldo, Luongo, Patrick Nagel, Harold Altman, Leroy Neiman, Uzilevsky, Erte, Gorman, Kipniss and local artists Lee Bogle and Robert Allen.

Kenneth Behm Galleries offers innovative purchase plans which include a five year exchange privilege and extended financing terms. A visit to the Behm Galleries will be visually rewarding for those seeking the best selection possible of contemporary and Northwest artists.

Bed and Breakfast

PETERSEN'S BED AND BREAKFAST
10228 SE 8th
Bellevue, WA 98008
Tel. (206) 454-9334

While on a European vacation, Carl and Eunice Petersen enjoyed the traditional European bed and breakfast inns they encountered. They wanted to share this type of accommodation with others and started their own bed and breakfast at their home in Bellevue. They are conveniently located near downtown Bellevue in a charming setting.

Their house is surrounded by greenbelts, giving it a country feeling in the city. Their hospitality and old world charm make their guests feel very welcome. They have a beautiful backyard with a lovely garden where guests enjoy quiet strolls. They always serve their guests a delicious homemade breakfast which includes fresh fruits and vegetables in season.

The Petersen's do their best to make their guests feel at home. They offer such extras as airport pickup service to add to the convenience. Once you try the bed and breakfast concept, you'll want to return again and again to this charming kind of accommodation.

Candy

ELMER FUDGE
Eastside Public Market
15600 N. E. 8th Street
Bellevue, WA 98008
Tel. (206) 643-5312
Hrs: Mon. - Fri. 10:00 a.m. - 9:00 p.m.
 Saturday 10:00 a.m. - 6:00 p.m.
 Sunday 12:00 noon - 5:00 p.m.
Closed Christmas, New Year's, and July 4th
and,
401 Broadway East
Seattle, WA 98102
Tel. (206) 328-1216

For twenty-seven years, Phil Kropelnicki day-dreamed about owning a candy store. When he announced to his friends that he had found some great fudge recipes, had purchased a fudge machine and was going into business, one dubbed him "Elmer Fudge" and the name stuck. Phil created some of the finest fudge you will ever taste.

When Gary Rands of Grand Design created a logo and signs for Elmer Fudge, he hardly expected to buy the store a year later. He had watched the store grow with great interest and as Elmer Fudge began to expand, he and his wife Marilyn, bought the Eastside Public Market Elmer Fudge. Phil and his wife, Pattie, opened another Elmer Fudge on Broadway in Seattle.

Both stores carry some twelve to fifteen different flavors of fudge, including such treats as Vanilla Praline, Chocolate Amaretto Nut, Chocolate Peanut Butter, Rocky Road and many more. When local strawberries are ripe, you must try the Strawberry Devonshire and Strawberry Nut. Free samples are offered to help you decide which of the delicious concoctions you want to buy. The fudge is made fresh daily using the best natural ingredients, real butter, without any fillers or preservatives. You will want to try a fudge dipped Oreo cookie and in season, a fresh fudge dipped strawberry.

It's fun to go to Elmer Fudge, because in addition to trying samples, you often can watch the fudge being made. Both stores also carry an assortment of other candies including Jelly Bellies, Gummy candies and a delightful sugar free line of confections that match the sugar candies in taste. For a fun and delicious time be sure to visit Elmer Fudge in either Bellevue or Seattle.

Farm

THE GARDEN PATCH
Crossroads Public Market
15600 NE 8th
Bellevue, WA 98008
Tel.   (206)   641-6223
Hrs: Mon. - Fri.   9:00 a.m. - 9:00 p.m.
          Saturday   12:00 noon - 6:00 p.m.
          Sunday   12:00 noon - 5:00 p.m.
Closed Christmas and New Years
No credit cards accepted, personal checks okay.

There is a lot to learn about the fruit and vegetable delicacies of the world, and The Garden Patch is the place to start your education. There are 14,000 edible plants in the world, and we eat only 2,400! Mel Grondahl and his wife, Gail assisted by their children Trent, Melody, and Todd and employee Melissa Basinger, will expand your knowledge of specialty fruits and vegetables. Mel has been in the produce industry for many years and uses his expertise to obtain only the finest and freshest produce for his market.

The Garden Patch likes to feature gourmet fruits and vegetables not found in grocery stores. Among the produce on their shelves are Tamerillos, Jacima, Spanish black winter radishes, all squashes in season, beet and turnip greens, Belgian endive, and many, many more. To maintain freshness, Mel and his crew refrigerate all fruits and vegetables each night and recreate the attractive displays again each morning. Their efforts keep their produce at its highest quality and insure customer satisfaction. Recipe sheets are available for many of the specialty fruits and vegetables and Mel and Gail are happy to explain how to prepare and serve the produce.

Do your produce shopping at The Garden Patch for outstanding value and selection in very friendly surroundings. This is a fun place to shop and to

King County

begin, or continue, your education on gourmet fruits and vegetables from all over the world.

Adventurous? Enjoy a challenge?? Want to decorate, spruce up, and just in general reinvigorate your home's decorating style??? Import your ideas and your furnishings from Washington.

BELLEVUE'S DOYENNE OF DESIGN			
a.m	Austrian Design	Best furniture	Bell/Furn.
a.m.	Country Kitchen	Best gourmet	Bell/Kitc.
a.m.	Scandell's Ice Cr.	Best ice desserts	Bell/Ice
a.m.	Distinctive Designs	Best silk florals	Bell/Gift
p.m.	Bellevue Hilton	Best luncheon	Bell/Acc.
p.m.	Days Gone Bye	Best antiques	Bell/Ant.
p.m.	Cuttysark	Best nautical	Bell/Naut.
p.m.	Pioneer Maps	Best maps	Bell/Map
p.m.	Wang's Garden	Best "imperial"	Bell/Rest.

Note: Pioneer Maps was included, it's part of the challenge; how to get the loot home by the shortest possible route!

Florist

CROSSROADS FLORIST
Crossroads Mall
156th and NE 8th
Bellevue, WA 98008
Tel. (206) 747-5654
Hrs: Mon. - Fri. 9:00 a.m. - 5:30 p.m.
Saturday 9:00 a.m. - 4:00 p.m.
Major credit cards are accepted.

Crossroads Florist is truly a full service florist. Established in 1970 by Jon Bergstrom and his mother, Crossroad Florists is a family business with Jon's wife, Chris and brother, Sten joining the superb team of "floral artists." Manager Lan Opheim, an honorary member of the family, has been with them for 12 years and is Jon's old high school friend. As John says, "Our family are everyday people who chose flowers as an avocation to be good at."

Truly beautiful flower arrangements require the highest quality, freshest flowers. Jon insures that the shop has nothing but the best by buying the flowers fresh daily, individually selecting only the freshest available. The floral artists who create the masterpieces keep contemporary by either attending or teaching floral design classes. Everything they produce is unconditionally guaranteed. You will also find a selection of vases to complement the flowers as well as mylar balloons to carry your special message with the arrangement. Additionally, Crossroads Florist has a fine selection of green and blooming plants.

Crossroads Florist will deliver anywhere in the greater Seattle area or through FTD. Let them serve you the next time you need flowers. Whether you need a large arrangement or something small and simple, they will work their magic and create the perfect arrangement just for you.

Furniture

AUSTRIAN DESIGN
Crossroads Mall
15600 N E 8th
Bellevue, WA 98008
Tel. (206) 643-0710
Hrs: Mon. - Fri. 10:00 a.m. - 9:00 p.m.
     Saturday 10:00 a.m. - 6:00 p.m.
     Sunday 12:00 noon. - 5:00 p.m.
Closed Christmas, Thanksgiving, and New Years.
Visa and MasterCard are accepted.

Austrian Design President Richard Ellert grew up in the furniture business in Austria where, after many years of education and training he became a Master Builder. He came to the United States seventeen years ago and was a furniture salesman for many years. He started Austrian Design two years ago in an effort to bring this unique and totally new style of quality furniture to the Northwest.

The furniture in Austrian Design is designed and built by two manufacturers in Austria. The quality of the construction is excellent, all drawers and cabinets are finished inside and out and the chairs have hardwood supports for the seats to provide strength not found in standard furniture. A variety of woods are used, including pine, oak, and spruce. Featured items in Austrian Design are the varied and stylish breakfast and dining nooks. They are very uniquely designed and the craftsmanship is of the highest quality.

Browsing through Austrian Design, you will find yourself impressed with the quality and selection of furniture offered. To appreciate the full

King County

range of cabinets, tables, dining nooks, chairs and wall and corner units available, take time to browse personally, or ask for their catalog. All items are available and can be shipped anywhere in the country. Don't hesitate to ask Richard for details, he loves to help his customers make quality furniture purchases that will please them for years.

Gift Shops

DISTINCTIVE DESIGNS
Crossroads Mall, G-16
15600 NE 8th Street
Bellevue, WA 98008
Tel. (206) 643-7079
Hrs: Mon. - Fri. 10:00 a.m. - 9:00 p.m.
Saturday 10:00 a.m. - 6:00 p.m.
Sunday 12:00 noon - 5:00 p.m.
Major credit cards are accepted.

You'll appreciate the warmth and comfort of the Distinctive Designs shop with its natural wood floors and service with a smile from owner Marcia Schuelke. Marcia is a specialist in silk floral design, creating unique and lasting arrangements that will complement the decor of your home or business.

Plan to spend some time browsing as Marcia has on display an outstanding collection of specialty gifts including some limited prints. Her philosophy is to provide decorative items at reasonable prices to enable people to accent their homes with beautiful accessories. Marcia has displayed her wares by color to make selection easier.

Make Distinctive Designs a stop during your travels and enjoy the "forever fresh" silk flowers at this "Best Choice" shop in Bellevue.

ELLE SACS/KILIMANJARO TREASURES
Crossroads Mall
156000 N. E. 8th Street, G-4
Bellevue, WA 98008
Tel.   Elle Sacs (206) 747-9221
       Kilamanjaro Treasures (206) 584-2864
Hrs: Mon. - Fri.   10:00 a.m. - 9:00 p.m.
      Saturday   10:00 a.m. - 6:00 p.m.
      Sunday   10:00 a.m. - 5:00 p.m.
Closed Christmas and New Years
Visa and MasterCard accepted.

Leo Clark, owner of Elle Sacs and John and Alice Kimani, owners of Kilimanjaro Treasures, decided to share retail space when they realized that their businesses complimented one another when they had shared adjacent space at another location. It was an excellent business decision for Leo, John, and Alice, and the shoppers are the real winners.

Elle Sacs is _the_ place to go for eel skin shoes, purses, wallets, jewelry and other accessories. Leo is happy to tell you about the unique features of the skin of the Conger eel, found only in the waters off Korea and Japan. The Conger eel is excellent for leather products since it is plentiful (not an endangered species) and the meat is a delicacy for the local population. Leo imports only the highest quality eel skins, which are 150% stronger than leather of equal thickness. He imports directly from the factories in Korea and his prices are the best in town.

Kilimanjaro Treasures has a diverse selection of African designs, arts, and crafts. John is always looking for new art objects and crafts and makes frequent trips to Kenya. He has provided an enlarged market for the Kenya artisan and reasonably priced authentic African crafts for his customers. Some of the more impressive items are ceremonial shields and spears from the Masai tribe of Kenya and carvings of elephants, zebras, tigers, lions, etc. from the Akamba tribe. There is lovely custom made jewelry, batiks, and clothing with wildlife designs. A visit to Elle Sacs/Kilimanjaro Treasures is a unique and interesting shopping experience.

Golf Course

STUDIO FORE
Professional Indoor Golf Instruction, Gifts and
Practice Facility
#56 Brierwood Center
12003 NE 12th Street
Bellevue, WA 98055
Tel. (206) 454-6766

Studio Fore is the place to go if your golf game needs help. Their motto is, "It's difficult to correct something you cannot see." They use a combination of teaching and technology to improve your swing. The teacher is Lesley Holbert, LPGA professional golfer and instructor. Lesley spent seven successful years on the LPGA tour before beginning her teaching career in 1972. She coached the University of Miami Women's Golf Team to two national championships before returning to her hometown of Bellevue in 1982.

With the aid of two video cameras and a computer swing analyzer, Studio Fore is able to record and analyze your swing from two angles at the same time. Lesley explains both the positive and negative aspects of the swing and sends you home with a computer analysis of your swing and a color tape to study. If there's an easy way to improve or learn golf, this is where to start.

If you like to practice on your own, a practice tee is available. You can practice indoors in a perfect climate. It is equipped with a color video camera, microphone and a swing analyzer which offers you the opportunity to record and view your practice sessions. Lesley has written helpful instructions of what to look for in your swing and on the computer. It's fun and easy and will improve your game.

King County

When visiting...it's best to just get out there and experience everything the locale has to offer. So, get up and get going!

\	\	BELLEVUE'S GET GOING TOUR	\
a.m.	Red Lion Inn	Best breakfast	Bell/Acc.
a.m.	Kenneth Behm Gall.	Best selection/art	Bell/Art
a.m.	Elle Sacs	Best eel skin shoes	Bell/Gift
a.m.	Kilimanjaro Trea.	Best African art	Bell/Gift
\	\	lunch	\
p.m.	Papillon	Best classic clothes	Bell/Apparel
p.m.	Margeo's	Best contemp. fashion	Bell/Apparel
p.m.	Studio Fore	Best swing	Bell/Golf
p.m.	Crossroads Florist	Best blooms	Bell/Florist
p.m.	La Cantina Wine	Best N.W. wines	Bell/Wine
\	\	An ethnic dinner at:	\
p.m.	Angelo's Ristorante	Best Italian	Bell/Rest.
p.m.	Torero's Family	Best Mexican	Bell/Rest.
\	\	A good nights rest at:	\
p.m.	Peterson's B & B	Best hospitality	Bell/B & B
p.m.	Residence Inn	Best equipped	Bell/Acc.

Ice Cream Parlor

SCANDELL'S ICE CREAM
800 156th Avenue NE
Bellevue, WA 98008
Tel. (206) 746-8518
Hrs: Mon. - Fri.   10:00 a.m. - 9:00 p.m.
        Saturday   10:00 a.m. - 6:00 p.m.
        Sunday   11:00 a.m. - 5:00 p.m.
Closed July 4th, Thanksgiving, Christmas and New Year's.
No credit cards accepted, personal checks okay.

Scandell's Ice Cream offers delicious ice cream and yogurt treats. Owner Stewart Luce has been catering to people with a sweet tooth since 1981 when he purchased the business. Scandell's is named after the scandalous cone that was born of necessity in 1902 at the Philadelphia World's Fair when an ice cream vendor ran out of cones and used waffles from a vendor in the next booth.

Scandell's serves Vivian's Pride ice cream which is locally produced by Theno's Dairy in Redmond and rated twentieth overall in a recent national taste test. They feature sixteen flavors, among them French vanilla, chocolate chip mint, caramel, coconut cashew, and mocha almond fudge. The waffle cones have also been shaped as bowls to hold classic banana splits and sundaes. You can personalize your dessert by adding selections from the "mix-ins", including nuts, candies, malted milk balls, Oreo cookies, and yogurt covered raisins. The frozen yogurt served comes from Honey Hill Farms and Colombo. Among the nine flavors available are White Chocolate, Macadamia, Murphy's Irish Cream, and Chocolate Grand Marnier.

Scandell's offers a delicious way to top off your shopping trip at the Eastside Public Market at Crossroads. Whether you want one of the specials, like the Whopper Shake with crushed malted milk balls or a Scandell's Cooler containing two scoops of vanilla ice cream and either orange or strawberry fruit whip, or just an ice cream or frozen yogurt cone, you'll by delighted by the selection and taste at Scandell's.

Kitchen Supplies

THE COUNTRY KITCHEN STORE
Eastside Public Market
15600 N. E. 8th Street
Bellevue, WA 98008
Tel. (206) 643-5312
Hrs: Mon. - Fri.   10:00 a.m. - 9:00 p.m.
       Saturday   10:00 a.m. - 6:00 p.m.
       Sunday   10:00 a.m. - 5:00 p.m.
Visa, MasterCard, and Discovery accepted.

The Country Kitchen Store is more than just a store, it is an experience in creative kitchenry. Owners Patty and Phil Kropelnicki have gathered just about anything and everything that is needed for a smooth running kitchen, and then some. Patty has an extensive background on the consumer side of the kitchen and she tries everything before deciding if it has the quality and uniqueness required by The Country Kitchen Store. She searches high and low for truly unusual and useful items.

The Country Kitchen Store has one of the largest collections of refrigerator magnets you'll ever see (including some that are living plants). There are all types of regular and espresso coffee makers, gourmet coffees, and beautiful and humorous coffee mugs. You can even pick up some tasty gourmet food items such as jams, jellies, mustard and vinegars to accent your favorite recipes. Patty keeps a selection of products from Northwest artisans and craftsmen, and from international markets, including some very interesting wall hangings from Haiti.

Whether you are looking for recipe books, kitchen tools or decorations, jars and labels for your own homemade jams, or practically anything else for your kitchen, The Country Kitchen Store is the place to go. It's almost impossible to see everything they have to offer on one visit, you'll want to return again and again to this wonderful store.

Maps

PIONEER MAPS
14125 NE 20th
Bellevue, WA 98007
Tel. (206) 746-3200
Hrs: Mon. - Fri. 9:30 a.m. - 6:00 p.m.
Saturday 10:30 a.m. - 4:00 p.m.
Major credit cards are accepted.

Whether you need a map of the city of Agra, India or Bellevue, Washington, you'll find what you need at Pioneer Maps in Bellevue or Metsker Maps in Seattle. Owner Howard Burd stocks any kind of map you might possibly want, from small maps you can carry in your pocket to nine foot by twelve foot murals. As Howard proudly states,"We have a fun store to visit to look at where you've been and where you're going!" Walker Willingham, manager of Pioneer Maps, knows maps as well as anyone in the Northwest and is more than able to help you find what you seek.

Pioneer Maps carries photo maps from space, contour maps, raised relief maps, cartoon maps, and marketing maps. There is a large selection of atlases, as well as an excellent selection of globes. They also have an extensive selection of United States and foreign travel books. Howard features books including "off the beaten track" books for the person who wants something different than the usual travel experiences. They also have a good selection of nautical charts.

No matter where you want to go, Pioneer Maps will have a map and information for you. The staff is knowledgeable and eager to be of help. Whether you want a map of where you're going or where you've been, Pioneer Maps is the place to go.

Nautical Equipment

CUTTY SARK OF BELLEVUE
10235 Main Street
Bellevue, WA 98004
Tel. (206) 453-1265
Hrs: Mon. - Fri.   9:30 a.m. - 5:30 p.m.
 Saturday   9:00 a.m. - 5:00 p.m.

Even the most ardent landlubber will feel nautical stirrings when they open the door to this fantastic shop. Somewhere, within the beautifully arranged interior of this store is everything and anything having to do with ships and the sea. You wouldn't be a bit surprised to stumble into Davy Jones; he probably does his shopping here.

While pursuing a career as a consulting Marine Engineer, with offices in the United States and the Philippines, owner Dennis Wood-Gaines found himself in possession of a great deal of nautical memorabilia. His wife suggested opening a shop; he took her up on it and a new career was born.For the past ten years, Dennis and Audrey, with loving help from employees Meredith Gaskill, Pat Fox and Ann Davis, have operated The Cutty Sark.

Looking for a ships' flag, porthole, telescope, lantern?...perhaps you'd like to call the kids in, to do their homework; use a foot-operated fog horn. If they don't have it here, Dennis has a man scouring the south seas, full-time, looking for more brass and hardware to fill the already bursting shop.

Want to turn your taco stand into a seafood restaurant? Dennis has a booming mail order business and does consulting with restaurants in search of the right nautical motif. Getting to the Cutty Sark is the easy part. Getting back out is somewhat harder. It is truly a fascinating shop.

Party

BIRTHDAYS!
Overlake Square
15171 NE 24th Street
Bellevue, WA 98052
Tel.   (206) 747-6757
Hrs: Mon. - Fri.   9:30 a.m. - 9:00 p.m.
          Saturday   9:30 a.m. - 6:00 p.m.
          Sunday   11:00 a.m. - 5:00 p.m.
Visa, MasterCard and AMEX are accepted.
and,

Northgate Village   Parkway Plaza
11016 8th NE   17312 Southcenter Parkway
Seattle, WA 98125   Tukwila, WA 98188
Tel. (206) 365-4774   Tel. (206) 575-3135

"Birthdays are a celebration of life!" - the foundation of BIRTHDAYS! your "one stop birthday shop" in Bellevue. Started in 1983 by Charlotte Killien, Marvetta Healy and Rob Harden to focus on the positive marks in life, <u>fun</u> is an accurate description of shopping at BIRTHDAYS!

Gifts such as exquisite chocolate candies, fine champagne, balloons and party favors are just some of the items you'll find. Displayed are a full selection of tasteful cards including varieties from one to sixty-five, birthday buttons from one to one hundred and special packages to celebrate those benchmark days of 30th, 40th and so on. Browsing through the store you will find gourmet gifts, stationery, stuffed animals, coffee mugs and party baskets with themes such as, "Over the Hill." BIRTHDAYS! also caters events, books clowns and entertainers, custom orders loot bags, even rents a pop-out birthday cake for the hit of any party!

The staff is full of imaginative, creative ideas to help you coordinate that special day in the life of a loved one. This is a definite "Best Choice" for shopping in Bellevue.

(See special invitation in the Appendix.)

Restaurants

ANGELO'S RISTORANTE
1830 130th Avenue, N.E.
Bellevue, WA 98005
Tel. (206) 883-2777
Hrs: Mon.-Sat.   11:00 a.m.-11:00 p.m.
          Lunch   11:00 a.m.- 2:30 p.m.
          Dinner   5:00 p.m.- 10:00 p.m.
      Closed major holidays
and
601 Southwest 153rd
Burien, WA 98166
Tel. (206) 244-3555

If you haven't experienced the warmth and friendliness of a close Italian family, a visit to Angelo's Ristorante is a must! And if you have, you already know how you will be treated at Angelo's. Be prepared to enjoy some delectable Italian cuisine.

Angelo's began as a deli in Burien 31 years ago and evolved to the fine Italian restaurant it is today. According to Angelo, the restaurant's success is due to his philosophy, "buy the best you can buy, treat people decently, and you'll succeed." Angelo's in Bellevue opened 11 years ago and sons Ron and Rich are managers and chefs of the restaurant. All of the employees, though, are part of the extended Ricci family.

Some of the features on the menu are: Seafood Cannelloni (egg crêpes filled with shrimp, crab, and mushrooms covered with a cream sauce and mozzarella), Linguini with Fresh Clams, Italian Sausage and Peppers, Veal Parmigiana, and on Friday and Saturday only, Chicken Cacciatore. All meals are served with soup or salad and pasta. Angelo's features 15 different imported Italian pastas.

Choose from a selection of 170 domestic or Italian wines. After dinner, select an espresso coffee, port, sherry, or another fine liqueur and/or desserts such as spumoni, gelati, sorbet, or Ameratto di Lucca.

Angelo's also has banquet facilities for 40 and a full-service lounge open from 11:00 a.m.-11:00 p.m. Whether having a private dinner for two or a large party, Angelo's provides wonderful food and service at reasonable prices. VISA, Mastercard, and Diner's Club accepted.

(See special invitation in Appendix.)

DAS KRAUT HAUS
Eastside Public Market at Crossroads
15600 N.E. 8th Street, Suite 27
Bellevue, WA 98008
Tel. (206) 641-3392
Hrs: Mon.-Sat. 9:00 a.m.-8:00 p.m.
   Sun. 11:00 a.m.-6:00 p.m.
   Hours extended during the Holiday season
   Closed major holidays
Manufacturing plant:
West 11 First Avenue
Odessa, WA 99159
Tel. (509) 982-2701

Using old family recipes, Jerry and Ellen provide a variety of foods for your eating enjoyment either at the Eastside Public Market or at home. They also ship anywhere in the U. S. Das Kraut Haus has a variety of special taste delights including their Smoked Sausage and Summer Sausage, both of which have no water added and are made from choice cuts of beef. For lunch at the Public Market there are several sandwiches to select, including smoked sausage, liverwurst, summer sausage, and smoked turkey. Try the Kraut Ranza, a traditional pocket bread containing a filling of cooked cabbage, ground beef and onion, and then sealed and baked. Finish your meal with one of the five delicious Kuchen, a traditional dessert of fruit pastry topped with custard.

Jerry and Ellen also invite you to attend the Deutsches Feste in Odessa in the third week of September. As many as 15,000 merrymakers per day enjoy three days of drinking, dining, dancing, and entertainment. It is an event to experience and enjoy. For details contact the Odessa Chamber of Commerce, Odessa, WA 99159.

So, experience and enjoy some fine German delicacies from Das Kraut Has during your visit to Western Washington, and take home or send home your favorites. Once you have sampled the food at Das Kraut Haus, you'll be back for more!

DOMANI
604 Bellevue Way NE
Bellevue, WA 98006
Tel. (206) 454-4405
Hrs: Lunch   Mon. - Fri.   11:30 a.m. - 2:30 p.m.
     Dinner   Mon. - Fri.   5:30 p.m. - 10:00 p.m.
              Sat. - Sun.   5:30 p.m. - 10:00 p.m.
Visa, MasterCard and AMEX are accepted.

The first inkling that you may be onto something really special comes when you notice there are numbers of patrons standing outside of Domani each day waiting for the restaurant to open for lunch. This pre-lunch gathering might lead one to the conclusion that its either the world's choicest soup kitchen, or a restaurant of unusual distinction. Domani's falls into the latter category.

The owner Steve Cohn and chef Michael Cowart have made Domani one of the Eastside's most popular restaurants for the past twelve years. Although the decor creates just the right touch, it is the food that is the main attraction. The menu changes monthly; the quality and presentation do not.

Domani specializes in pasta, veal dishes, and fresh Northwest seafood; such dishes as prawns in a demi-glaze and sherry lobster sauce, fresh northwest seafood pasta, tuna with a honey-mustard glaze, and veal in a port wine sauce keep the patrons coming back again and again. The wine list features California wines, premium and vintage wines. There is an excellent selection of beer and ales from small Northwest breweries. Make your reservation early - this establishment isn't exactly a secret!!!

EBRU
Eastside Public Market/Crossroads
15600 N. E. 8th Street
Bellevue, WA 98008
Tel. (206) 641-4352
Hrs: Mon. - Fri.   9:00 a.m. - 8:00 p.m.
     Saturday   10:00 a.m. - 6:00 p.m.
     Sunday   11:00 a.m. - 6:00 p.m.
No credit cards or personal checks are accepted.

The word "ebru" means a traditional high quality Turkish art dating back to the mid-1500s. Bulent Aki and Sharrie Nailon chose that name for their restaurant, because they provide food and service that are traditional and of high quality. Bulent has an in depth knowledge of the preparation of traditional Turkish and Mediterranean food, and Sharrie has extensive business and restaurant experience. Together they have created Ebru.

Mediterranean salads are a specialty of Ebru. Try the Tabouli (parsley, mint, bulgar, and lemon), the Mediterranean Rainbow (a three pasta delight), or the House Special, containing fresh vegetables and Turkish pasta. There are also sandwiches for lunch, dinner, or to take home. The hot Gyros Sandwich is a specialty, with beef, tomatoes, onion, and a special cucumber sauce in hot homemade pita bread. Spanakopita, spinach and Feta cheese wrapped in phyllo pastry, is another favorite. There are several great Turkish espressos to enjoy with your meal.

If you are planning a party, call Ebru and have them prepare a party tray for you. Your guests will love trying the new and interesting foods, and so will you, when you visit Ebru. It's a wonderful family meeting place, at the Eastside Public Market in Overlake.

LIL JON
3080 148th Southeast
Bellevue, WA 98007
Tel. (206) 746-4653
Hrs: Mon. - Fri.   5:00 a.m. - 10:00 p.m.
                   11:00 a.m. - 2:00 a.m.
     Sat. - Sun.   6:00 a.m. - 4:00 p.m.
                   11:00 a.m. - 7:00 p.m.

Little John, one of legendary companions of Robin Hood, was a big man with a little name. The same goes for a family restaurant in Bellevue. It's called Lil Jon, and like the man, it has a few surprises for anyone who comes into contact with it.

This restaurant, owned by Judy and Al Sjolander, who have been in business for over twenty years with forty-two persons under their employ, isn't small. Nor is it so large that they have forgotten what service is all about. In fact, because the service is so good you'll find people here from all walks of life. Professors, police, church groups, truck drivers and many more, all frequent Lil Jon. But apart from atmosphere and patronage, the food there is excellent. They serve breakfast, lunch and dinner, with breakfast being served at any time of day. The desserts, such as their famous cinnamon rolls, are as delicious as the main courses. For libations, they've got a large variety of beers, wines and liquors.

If you're in a hurry, but don't want fast food, you can order anything you like from the menu for take-out, as do many of the people from the local businesses. Just like Little John, Lil Jon is quite a package. Unfortunately, Robin Hood's companion isn't around to take the merry band to enjoy his namesake. On the other hand, you are, and your merry little band is sure to thank you for it.

NEPTUNE'S
Crossroads Mall
15600 N. E. 8th
Bellevue, WA 98008
Tel. (206) 746-3655
Hrs: Mon. - Sat.   9:00 a.m. - 8:00 p.m.
      Sunday   ll:00 a.m. - 6:00 p.m.

A visit to the Eastside Public Market in the Crossroads Mall isn't complete without a stop at Neptune's. Savor the flavor of the best smoked salmon available -- owner Ron Kucheran and his staff will help you expand your knowledge of the variety of uses for smoked salmon. While establishing Neptune's, Ron had visited more than fifty different smokehouses from Seattle to Alaska to taste-test the quality of their products. The result was a selection of five premier products. Ron features low salt salmon for most dishes, and you will also find unique treatments of salmon such as teriyaki smoked salmon.

A major concern of the staff at Neptune's is to educate the consumer on the variety of different dishes that can be created with smoked salmon. With few exceptions, Neptune's will provide you with a recipe of your favorite dish sampled and thereby you can recreate it for your family or guests.

Although the menu is always changing as new and interesting items are added, there are six to eight bagel sandwiches with different smoked salmon spreads and a form of salmon baklava containing smoked salmon and marinated artichokes prepared with filo and served as snacks, appetizers, or meals. There are also smoked salmon paté, mousse, quiches, cream spreads and even pickled smoked salmon.

Ron will ship either cold-pack or non-refrigerated smoked salmon to your home. Orders are received and shipped direct within 48 hours of receipt. Neptune's backs their product with a money-back guarantee of satisfaction. Call or write for a brochure describing the smoked salmon products available from Neptune's. Visa or Mastercard accepted.

(See special invitation in Appendix.)

THE PUMPHOUSE
11802 NE 8th
Bellevue, WA 98005
Tel. (206) 455-4110
Hrs: Mon. - Sat. 10:00 a.m. - 12:00 midnight

The Pumphouse in Bellevue is a lively dining and drinking establishment. Much like the setting on the TV show "Cheers," you know as soon as you step in, you're going to have a good time.

One of the busiest times at this friendly restaurant/tavern is lunch. People from all walks of life enjoy a hearty meal in an atmosphere of laughs and warm feelings. The menu includes delicious hot and cold sandwiches and special Pumphouse hamburgers with a secret sauce, lean beef and all the traditional toppings. There's also several speciality salads, fish and chips, chicken filets, clam strips and chips and the biggest chili dog in town. Be sure to enjoy the nightly steak special at a very reasonable price. If you've come to enjoy the night life, you're sure to enjoy the selection of beers, over 29 varieties, wine and music.

Owners Bob and Danielle Griffith have really outdone themselves with this remarkable establishment that's such a popular favorite in Bellevue. It's well worth a visit for lunch, dinner or evening entertainment and socializing.

(See special invitation in the Appendix.)

THE SARATOGA TRUNK
2239 148th Avenue NE
Bellevue, WA 98008
Tel. (206) 641-6666
Hrs: Restaurant Mon. - Sun. 5:00 p.m. - 10:00 p.m.
     Lounge Mon. - Sat. 4:00 p.m. - 2:00 a.m.
Closed Christmas and New Years
Major credit cards accepted.

Until you've experienced The Saratoga Trunk and its famous 'Salad Car,' you've missed something special! That's right, a Salad Car. The salad bar at this unique restaurant is in a 1953 red MG convertible. There is a variety of dining experiences available here. You can dine in regal splendor with lots of red velvet, or enjoy a cozy dinner for two in the Pepsi can. Children particularly enjoy the Pepsi can, the TeePee, they get a button verifying that they've eaten in an authentic teepee, and the Snoopy Booth. For groups of ten to fourteen there is the Cave, with a huge, beautiful table surrounded by walls and ceiling of stone. Smaller groups may prefer the Shake cottage. To make your evening even more enjoyable, you may be served by a Ninja warrior, a Royal Canadian Mounted Police, Supergirl, Peter Pan or one of a number of other delightfully costumed people.

Not just the atmosphere is special here, the food is memorable too. The menu has such culinary delights as steak Saratoga, Hazelnut chicken, lobster tail, scallops Dijon and much more, all at reasonable prices. For dessert try the scrumptious Saratoga Surprise, Mud Pie Saratoga, or any of several special desserts of the day. For a perfect end to a unique dining experience visit the lounge for one of the Saratoga Trunk specialty drinks and enjoy the live entertainment. There is dance floor and featured events every night, such as lip synch contests and ladies' night.

The Saratoga Trunk is truly a one of a kind dining experience. It's fun for the whole family, and is an experience you'll remember for a long time. It's definitely not to be missed, you'll want to include The Saratoga Trunk on your itinerary.

THE THAI KITCHEN, 114115 Northeast Twentieth Street, Bellevue, Washington. Five different tastes at this authentic Thai restaurant--hot, spicy, sour, sweet, and salty. Choose how hot you like it--from one star (mild) to five star (extra hot).

TORERO'S FAMILY MEXICAN RESTAURANT
3720 128th Avenue SE
Bellevue, WA 98006
Tel. (206) 643-5585
Hrs: Mon. - Thu. 11:00 a.m. - 10:00 p.m.
Fri. - Sat. 11:00 a.m. - 11:00 p.m.
Sunday 3:00 p.m. - 9:00 p.m.
Closed major holidays.
Visa, MasterCard, AMEX and Diner's Club are accepted.

Camilo and Kim Mora opened their Torero's Family Mexican Restaurant at Loehmann's Plaza in Factoria in July, 1984. Chef Enrique Sanchez and most of the staff have been with them since they opened and are all dedicated to providing for their customers the best possible Mexican food and service in congenial surroundings.

The portions at Torero's are very generous so bring a big appetite when you come for lunch or dinner. Favorites among the lunch crowd are the chimichanga and the half order of super nachos. Super nachos, with beef or chicken, beans, cheese, chopped tomato, onions, guacamole, and sour cream are an outstanding appetizer for afternoon gatherings. The full dinner menu offers twenty-five different combinations for large and small eaters. There are specialties too, such as tacos al carbon, tacos rancheros and camerones con arroz - luscious shrimp simmered in a spicy sauce and served with Mexican-style rice. The most popular dinner selection is carnitas de res - sliced, fried top sirloin with green pepper, onions, and spices.

Torero's Family Mexican Restaurant offers delicious, well prepared Mexican food at reasonable prices. The people are warm and friendly and will make your dining experience as pleasant as possible. You'll enjoy your visit to Torero's and will want to return often.

TWELVE BASKETS RESTAURANT AND CATERING
201 106th Ave. N.E.
Bellevue, WA 98004
Tel. (206) 455-3684
Hrs: Lunch   Mon. - Sat.   11:00 a.m. - 5:00 p.m.
     Dinner Mon. - Sat.   5:00 p.m. - 8:30 p.m.

Since 1976, John and Jamie Bagge have sought to provide Eastside residents with something a little different. They have succeeded admirably. If you want quality food, in a relaxed atmosphere...it's Twelve Baskets you've been seeking.

From the full-length fireplace to the antique quilts hanging on the walls, the charming country decor makes patrons feel as they have found a home away from home. Twelve Baskets provides quality, wholesome food without actually categorizing itself as a health-food restaurant. Everything is made from scratch; with a special eye for quality control. While Twelve Baskets offers a number of vegetarian specialities, they also serve beef, pasta, fish and chicken. Regardless of your menu choice, you'll get a great meal, prepared with attention to detail, using only the freshest ingredients and served in a non-smoking, non-alcoholic environment.

A special attempt is made to make children and families feel welcome. It's the kind of place one can take the family and feel good about it. If you've had enough of headwaiters or fastfood, give Twelve Baskets a try!

WANG'S GARDEN RESTAURANT
16444 140th NE
Bellevue, WA 98005
Tel. (206) 641-6011
Hrs: Restaurant

Mon. - Thu.	11:30 a.m. - 9:30 p.m.
Fri. - Sat.	11:30 a.m. - 10:30 p.m.
Sunday	4:00 p.m. - 9:30 p.m.

Lounge

Mon. - Sat.	12:00 noon - 12:00 midnight
Sunday	4:00 p.m. - 11:00 p.m.

Closed major holidays
Visa, MasterCard, AMEX, and Diner's Club are accepted.

    C.C. Wang, proprietor and chef of Wang's Garden Restaurant is one of the world's best Chinese Master Chefs. He has a long history of preparing traditional Chinese food for local, national, and international dignitaries at top restaurants across the United States. When China's highest ranking dignitaries, including ambassadors, governors, and the Vice Premier visit Seattle area they go to Wang's Garden Restaurant for imperial Chinese cuisine. Dishes at Wang's are prepared according to the five tenets of imperial cuisine: color, smell, taste, sound, and shape. In imperial cuisine everything has to look good, as well as taste good, and C. C. Wang is a true artist when it comes to creating beautifully carved flowers, animals, and dragons from foods and vegetables.

    Imperial cuisine uses many fresh vegetables and fruits and the more expensive items such as duck, oysters, prawns, and shark fin. At Wang's you can experience such delicacies as Imperial Shark Fin Soup, and you don't have to plan ahead twenty-four hours to enjoy Peking Duck as you do in so many Chinese restaurants. This traditional Peking Royal presentation, as well as Imperial Peking Roast Duck can be enjoyed shortly after placing your order. For dessert try a house specialty, Imperial Flaming Bananas, or one of the other delicious offerings.

    Dining at Wang's, you experience the ultimate in fine Chinese cuisine. C. C. Wang's artistry allows you to learn about truly traditional imperial Chinese cooking. You have not experience the finest in Chinese dining until you have visited Wang's Chinese Garden.

Did you ever, as a kid, go to a party that originated at one friend's house for salad, another's house for the pizza, and someone else's for the dessert? It's called a progressive dinner party. For a fun tour, try the progressive approach while tasting your way thru Bellevue's "Best Choices" for your dining pleasures.

BELLEVUE DINING AROUND TOWN		
Ebru	Best Turkish coffee	Bell/Rest.
Red Lion Inn	Best croissant & jam	Bell/Acc.
Das Kraut Haus	Best sausage snack	Bell/Rest.
Columbia Winery	Best wine tastings	Bell/Wine
Beaux Arts Park	Best walk-about	Bell/Intro
Neptune's	Best shrimp cocktail	Bell/Rest.
The Saratoga Trunk	Best salads	Bell/Rest.
Kelsey Creek Park	Best hike	Bell/Intro
Domani	Best dinner	Bell/Rest.
Twelve Baskets	Best dessert	Bell/Rest.
Elmer Fudge	Best candies	Bell/Candy
Garden Patch	Best fruit	Bell/Farm

WHEW! The only item missing from the tour was a "Best Choice" for tailoring. Too much of this "good life" could lead to a major overhaul of your closet's contents!

Wine

COLOMBIA WINERY
1445 120th Avenue, N.E.
Bellevue, WA 98005
Tel. (206)453-1977

In an effort to sell more wine, many wineries claim to be the oldest, the biggest, or the best. Thus, it is refreshing when one finds a winery which may well be all of those things---but makes very little noise about it. Colombia Winery doesn't have to boast; it just keeps making and selling world-class wines with the quiet confidence of a virtuoso.

In 1962, a group of Seattle businessmen pooled their resources and wine expertise to plant a small vineyard in the Yakima Valley. In 1967, convinced of Washington's potential to make fine wines, the men began Associated Vinters. The winery was renamed Columbia Winery in 1984.

Colombia has consistently created fine wines. Winemaker David Lake joined Colombia in 1979. Lake, who holds the world's most distinguished wine title, that of "Master of Wine," personifies Colombia. He is soft spoken, yet intense; confident yet speaks with humility. Rarely will you hear him praise his own wines. Rather, he'll say, "Let's taste some wines," preferring to let the wines speak for themselves.

Call for the time for tours and tastings. Enjoy both the tours and the tastes of a vintage stop on your trip to Bellevue. You may want to ask for what Lake feels is his finest wine...it's the Millennium Cabernet. Lake so named this special 1979 wine as he feels it will continue to improve into the next millennium.

LA CANTINA WINE MERCHANT
10218 N.E. Eighth Street
Bellevue, WA 98004
Tel. (206) 455-4363
Hrs: Mon. - Sat. 10:00 a.m. - 6:00 p.m.
Visa, MasterCard, AMEX and Discover cards are accepted.

La Cantina Wine Merchant of Bellevue is one of those shops which takes the guesswork out of buying wine. Specializing in French wines, La Cantina provides you the opportunity to taste and purchase rare wines, each of which has been pre-tasted and selected for its quality rather than its reputation. By making yearly trips to France, the owner is able to purchase wine from generally unavailable small vineyards and provide you with an unusual array of fine wines. The selection of wines from California and the Northwest is made with equal care.

Located across the street from Bellevue Square, La Cantina is convenient and manages to avoid the pomp and circumstance often associated with buying fine wines. The relaxed atmosphere allows a casual buyer to feel free to ask questions and seek recommendations from the knowledgeable staff.

While browsing through the Red Bordeaux, the Burgundies, and some fine Champagnes, don't forget to check out the selection of wine books, wine glasses, and domestic and imported beers. Ask owner Tom Cottrell, or a friendly staff person, what you should serve at your special occasion. ... you won't be disappointed.

Bothell

It may be hard to imagine as the modern traveler drives into the crossroads community of Bothell where Highway 522 from around the north shore of Lake Washington intersects with I-405's neat north-south freeway, but when the town started the only way to travel from it was by steam launch. A boat threaded the twisting Sammamish River to Lake Washington carrying shingles milled on the Bothell family farm. From David C. Bothell's mill of 1886, the community has grown to about 8,000 residents.

Attractions

Bothell Historical Society Museum, 9919 Northeast 180th Street, has exhibits on development of communities on the north end of Lake Washington. Open Sundays 1:00 p.m. to 4:00 p.m. Also open by appointment, call 486-1889 or 448-8408.

Bothell Landing, site of the original steam launch moorage, is now a city park. From here the Sammamish River Trail follows the stream to Marymoor Park in Redmond.

Flowers by the building-full greet visitors at **Molbak's Greenhouse**, 13625 Northeast 175th Street. Indoor plants are propagated here, and are offered for sale. Many of the twenty-eight green houses are open to visitors. Open daily, 9:30 a.m. to 6:00 p.m. Call 483-5000.

For information, contact the **Bothell Chamber of Commerce**, 18925 Bothell Way Northeast, Bothell WA 98011, telephone 486-1245.

Antiques

THE RED BARN ANTIQUES
23929 Bothell Highway, S.E.
Bothell, WA 98021
Tel. (206) 486-7309
Hrs: Wed. - Sat. 11:00 a.m. - 5:00 p.m.
Or by appointment.

Owner Barbara McArdle says that the motto of the Red Barn is: "We have everything. We may not be able to find it....but we have it!" This is an apt description of this unusual antique shop. It is jammed to the rafters with an incredible array of trash and treasures.

The Red Barn was constructed in 1901 as part of the Henderson Boys' Ranch called Sunny Heights Boys Ranch. In 1978, it was recycled into The Red Barn Antique Shop. At least once a month, someone who lived at the Sunny Heights comes in to reminisce and talk over the good old days at the ranch, when there were horses instead of collectors items in the barn. Mrs. Henderson, 94, lives in Oswego, Oregon and drives alone to the Red Barn about every six months.

Barbara, who has taken her good friend Carol Nelson as a partner, laughs when she recalls that opening the shop was more an act of survival than of commerce. She and her husband, Pat, had been collecting antiques for years. Finally, they either had to open a shop, or move out of the house.

In the past nine years, the collection of goods in the shop has grown to include American antiques, china, glassware, European items, pine furniture, pictures, books, jewelry, and about anything else your heart desires.

A wonderful service called "Antique Finders," at The Red Barn, will help locate and then ship anywhere in the world. Barbara and Carol love to buy and will hold estate sales and even garage sales. Happy hunting!!!

Rafting

DOWNSTREAM RIVER RUNNERS
12112 N.E. 195TH
Bothell, WA 98011
Tel.   (206) 483-0335
          Toll free 1-800-732-RAFT
Hrs: Weekdays 9:00 a.m.-6:00 p.m.

Looking for something a bit different? Whether it's the tranquil beauty of a quiet river float or the excitement of whitewater rafting that you crave, Downstream River Runners has just what you're looking for. Fourteen years of outfitting river tours has made Downstream the foremost outfitter of its type in the state. Float through dense forests ringed by towering snow-capped peaks or along sagebrush canyons under clear blue skies. Whether you're eight or 80, Downstream River Runners has a trip which is just right for you.

For each well-planned trip, owners Casey and Karen Garland provide: experienced professional guides, each with years of river experience; wetsuits with boots; a wonderful buffet lunch, and a van and bus shuttle. By providing the best equipment and service available, Downstream has earned both a solid reputation and a perfect safety record.

While Downstream's programs operate year-round, the primary season is April through July. Downstream offers one-, two-, three-, and five-day trips on the foremost rafting rivers of Washington and Oregon. Eastern Washington trips include the Wenatchee, Methow, Tieton and Klickitat Rivers, while western Washington offers the Lower Skykomish, Middle Skagit (an unforgettable float through one of the largest concentrations of bald eagle habitats in the United States), Upper Skagit, Suiattle, and Green River Gorge. Oregon river trips include the Grande Ronde and the Owyhee.

Make your reservations early. Trips are generally booked six weeks to four months in advance. Grab a paddle and enjoy the grace of motion that only nature can provide.

Restaurant

CLIFFORDS RESTAURANT
6251 NE Bothell Way
Bothell, WA 98155
Tel. (206) 485-7585
Hrs: Lunch   Mon. - Fri.   11:30 a.m. - 2:00 p.m.
             Dinner   Mon. - Sun.   5:00 p.m. - 10:00 p.m.

With its panoramic view of Lake Washington and the downtown skyline, Cliffords Restaurant has long been a favorite of north shore residents. Watch the sea planes take off and land while you dine on fresh seafood from the Pacific northwest, pasta dishes and good American cuisine.

Owner-Chef Paul Kolden believes in the finest and freshest ingredients and prepares them in such a way as to allow the natural flavors to assert themselves. Entrees are nicely cooked yet unpretentious. The wine list provides an excellent selection of well priced northwest and California wines.

Cliffords is easily accessible and has valet parking. It is a nice casual neighborhood restaurant, and a good choice for any occasion.

King County

Shopping Mall

COUNTRY VILLAGE
23710-23806 Bothell Way SE
Bothell, WA 98021
Tel. (206) 483-2250
Hrs: Tue. - Sat.   11:00 a.m. - 5:00 p.m.
      Sunday   12:00 noon - 4:00 p.m.

If you are looking for something special which doesn't seem to be in your local chainstores or shopping malls, or if you have grown tired of mall shopping, Country Village may be just the alternative you've been seeking. With thirty shops in one convenient, garden like location, Country Village harkens back to an era of unhurried shopping and personal attention. A wide array of shops, services, and special events guaranteed to please the entire family await you. While the kids play at the playground or get an ice cream cone, you can stroll leisurely among the gardens and choose from the following shops:

Belle Province - A place to find enchanting gifts and home accessories from around the world.

Busy B Collectiques - Lots of collectible glassware, fine china, jewelry, silk flowers arrangements and more.

Buttons and Bows - The children's cottage with affordable clothing, accessories and gifts for your special "little one," sizes one through fourteen.

Chloe's Antiques, Etc. - Dealers in fine collectibles, antiques, glassware, pottery, china, furniture and primitives. A unique cross section of merchandise.

Classics Northwest - Dresses, interchangeable separates and accessories to build a successful wardrobe.

Country At Heart - Carries antique furniture with folk art accents for your home, as well as custom lamp shades.

Country Cafe - "Down home cooking," specializing in homemade bread, burger buns and pies.

Country Cradle - A unique collection of baby and children's gifts and room accessories.

Country Gourmet - Choose from a wide selection of gourmet foods and coffee, kitchenware and country decorating items.

Country Pickins - Colorful plants, gifts, cards, baskets and fun decorating ideas.

Distinctively Yours - Personalized gift baskets with items for all occasions and holidays. Gourmet foods, birthdays, bath, home fragrances and more.

King County

Farmer's Daughter - Antiques and collectibles of all kinds. Country crafts, bears, folk art, etc., in a welcoming atmosphere.

Farmhouse Antiques - Enjoy a cup of Market Spice Tea while browsing through quilts, old lace, handcrafted folk art, primitives and collectibles.

Favorite Things - Fun things to own, everything from toys to clothing for children and adults.

Flowers For You And Me - Fresh cut flowers and floral displays for all occasions.

For All Occasions - A charming assortment of cards, paper and gifts.

Golden Fleece Yarn Shop - A friendly little yarn shop bulging with a huge variety of yarns and threads. Classes in knitting, crochet, weaving, spinning and tatting.

Golden Goose - Beads, gifts and the latest in fashion jewelry. Create your own necklace or have one custom made.

Grandma's Nook - Take a step back to the "good old days". Ask about the appraisal service.

Gramma's Sweet and Snack Shoppe - Sandwiches, soup, muffins, pie, cake, ice cream, candy and much more.

Heartland Interiors - A fresh new look in country interiors. Specializing in creating custom gifts with a very personal touch.

Heather House - A unique country gift shop specializing in hand crafted gifts from England and America.

Keepsake Cottage Fabrics - Featuring calicos, quilting supplies, DMC floss, cross stitch books, stencil and smocking supplies. Classes offered.

Milk Shed - A cozy new handcraft shop for country collectibles, oak crates, framed labels and pictures, miniatures, stenciled items and gift ideas. Custom orders welcomed.

Northcreek Mercantile - A browser's paradise of antiques, primitives, glassware and collectibles.

Paradise - A unique art gallery.

Scotland Yard - Specializing in European furniture at "thrifty" prices. Tools and marine items, too.

Second Best - Quality women's clothing and accessories on consignment.

Shaker's Cottage - Dedicated to bringing you the best in American country. Specializing in stoneware, redware, tin lighting, pine furniture and folk art.

Taylor Topper - Specialists in men's, women's and children's hair replacement. The finest in hairstyling too.

The Weed Patch - A great shop to find that touch of country charm in gifts, baskets, dried flowers, ribbons and craft ideas.

King County

    <u>Town Hall and Auction House</u> - A space available for entertainment, special events, auctions, etc.
    <u>Ye Olde London Bus Gift Shop</u> - Toy metal cars, S. Gibson and porcelain dolls, Steiff and collectible teddy bears, wood nutcrackers, music boxes, ornaments and other neat stuff to browse.
    A variety of special events are held throughout the year. Below is a general listing of the events and dates. For more information call (206) 483-2250 or (206) 483-0253.
    First week of May - Country Touch Craft Show
    First week of June - Anniversary Celebration
    Middle of October - Harvest Festival
    First Week of November - Holiday Open House.

Burien

    Seattle Tacoma Airport, Sea-Tac to most, is in the center of this unincorporated community south of Seattle proper. Both areas are now highway crossroads.
    Burien claims about twenty-six square miles of hills and within the Highline School District, which now defines the area, there are perhaps 107,000 residents. The area was a summer playground for the rich of Seattle, who had homes on Lake Burien. The name is an incorrect spelling honoring Gottlieb Burian who built a cabin on the lake shore in 1884.

Attractions

    The **Olde Burien district**, on Southwest 152nd Street between Ambaum Boulevard and Tenth Southwest, has taken on a turn-of-the-century look much as it did when the streetcar ran from here to Seattle. About thirty specialty shops are part of this district.

    Sea-Tac is an international hub of air travel, handling more than twelve million passengers a year. The first landing strip was built here in 1942 to relieve congestion at Boeing Field closer to Seattle. The passenger terminal was not built until 1949. Now the Port of Seattle estimates that 20,000 jobs are linked to airport activity. Call 433-4644 for the airport's community relations department.

    Each Saturday, the area's farmers set up an **outdoor market** in the Metro Park and Ride lot at Southwest 148th and Fourth Avenue. The market operates from late June through September each year.

Seahurst Park, at the foot of 152nd Street, has a sandy beach on the shore of the sound's East Passage. This beach was one of the attractions which created the original summer home development here.

Restaurant

ANGELO'S RISTORANTE, 601 Southwest 153rd, Burien, Washington. With over thirty years experience, Mark and Phil Ricci create fine Italian dishes in a warm and friendly atmosphere at Angelo's. See the Bellevue section of this book for a more complete description.

SATSUMA JAPANESE RESTAURANT
14301 Ambaum Boulevard S.W.
Burien, WA 98166
Tel. (206) 242-1747
Hrs: lunch: Mon., Wed., Fri.   11:30 a.m. - 2:00 p.m.
             dinner: Mon. - Sun.   5:00 p.m. - 10:00 p.m.
Closed on all major holidays.
MasterCard, Visa, AMEX and Diners' Cards accepted

This is an authentic, well-established Japanese restaurant in an unassuming, out-of-the-way location, in Burien. Owner/chef Takeyuki Suetsugu has been delighting connoisseurs of Eastern cuisine for twenty-five years.

The luncheon menu ranges from sashimi to chicken teriyaki to deep fried tofu. The dinner ambience is more subdued and the friendly, quiet atmosphere provides a pleasant gathering place for the visitor, as well as, the local area regular.

Takeuki is a perfectionist. This is reflected in his bill-of-fare. Start your dinner with one of Tak's original creations, like: Mt. St. Helen's Surprise, a seafood and vegetables medley in a steaming volcano made out of egg whites. The Ika Satsumayaki is pan-fried squid, laced with satsuma sauce. Dinners include sunomono (cucumbers marinated in rice-vinegar dressing), or tempura and soup, rice and green tea. The most popular entree is the Satsuma Ozen Special, nine courses, selected and prepared daily by the chef.

Two years ago, Takeyuki made the decision to share his expertise with the public when he started his cooking school. His students are a varied bunch that include hotel chefs, housewives, and college professors. It's a nine week course and he offers his students step-by-step instructions.

If nine weeks is too long to wait for your dinner--let Takeyuki do the cooking.

Carnation

Scandinavians, engaged in farming and dairying, settled this area in 1865. Carnation took its name from the neighboring dairy farm which is famous for its superior dairy herds.

Attractions

Carnation, the big animal feed and dairy product company, has its **research farms** in the town of Carnation, east of Bellevue. There is a showplace English garden and a self-guiding tour. Open Monday through Saturday, 10:00 a.m. to 3:00 p.m. Call 788-1511. Leave Highway 202 at Ames Lake Road, keep bearing right and it becomes Carnation Road. If you approach on Highway 203 from the town of Carnation, turn left on Carnation Farm Road and follow it to the 1,200 acre site.

Farm

CARNATION FARMS
28901 Carnation Farms Road NE
Carnation, WA 98014
Tel. (206) 788-1511
Hrs: Mon. - Sat. 10:00 a.m. - 3:00 p.m.

Farming is one of man's oldest and most important activities. Years ago, man learned how to utilize animals and plants to provide himself with food, clothing and shelter. Today, this kind of activity still goes on in many areas, such as Carnation Farms in Carnation, Washington. Carnation Farms offers an opportunity to tour one of the largest farms of its kind.

Its an educational experience that the whole family can enjoy. During your tour you'll be able to view the development of new breeds of farm animals and new milk products that have been marketed all over the world. You'll also enjoy hearing about the history of this type of farming as told to you by your experienced and educated guide. Carnation Farms is an actual working dairy that, after one visit, will heighten your appreciation for those products that too many people take for granted every day.

The entire farm is set in a beautiful country atmosphere with clean air and the sounds of animals all around. Stop by for a tour of this innovative farm, see progress in action and learn all about the farming process that has evolved throughout mankind's existence. Carnation Farms, a farm that's educating the populace, while at the same time producing better foods.

REMLINGER FARMS
P.O. Box 177
32610 NE 32nd
Carnation WA 98014
Tel. (206) 451-8740
(206) 333-4135
Hrs: Apr.15 - Dec. 21 Mon. - Sun. 8:00 a.m. - 8:00 p.m.
Closed January, February and March.

A visit to Remlinger Farms is a unique experience. It is much more than just a farm. You can choose to pick your own fruit, buy from the market located at the farm, lunch, or shop in the craft shop full of creations by local artisans. Remlinger Farms is the largest and oldest "u-pick" farm in the area. It is a family operation, now managed by Gary and Bonnie Remlinger. Floyd Remlinger founded the farm in 1940. In addition to the land in King County, Remlinger Farms also owns land in Yakima which produces peaches, apricots, apples and acreage near Qunicy where they grow sweet corn.

There is something different to pick or buy each season. In the spring look for asparagus and rhubarb, while summer brings juicy berries. The farm sells strawberries which are the farm specialty. Cucumbers, carrots, beets, squash, beans, potatoes, and onions are also available. For those who like their produce already picked, the market at the farm has everything they produce in each location for sale. In the fall you will find acres of pumpkins and at Christmas time there are trees to cut.

In addition to the wonderful fresh produce available at Remlinger Farms, there is a craft shop which carries unique items handcrafted by local artisans. It's a great place to browse for a special gift. The Farm deli offers great, fresh homemade food to eat there or take home. The fresh fruit and berry pies are outstanding and they are fresh frozen so you can take them home and bake them. This family run farm is a great source of delicious, wholesome fresh produce, fruit and a fun outing for the whole family.

(See special invitation in the Appendix.)

King County

Golf Course

CARNATION GOLF COURSE
1810 W Snoqualmie River Road NE
Carnation, WA 98014
Tel. (206) 454-7543
Hrs: Dawn to Dusk
Closed Christmas Day

Even non-golfers will enjoy a day at the eighteen hole Carnation Golf Course, tucked away from it all in the lovely Snoqualmie Valley. Mountain scenery delights the eye, and wildlife abounds. The course is completely surrounded by the Snoqualmie River.

Owner/pro Dan Tachell describes the course as excellent challenge for the average handicapper. It is a flat course of medium length and the course offers a full service pro shop, quality instruction, plenty of golf carts, and friendly service. Carnation Golf course welcomes tournaments, and men and women's clubs encourage new members. A special discount exists for an active "Swinging Seniors" group. The snack bar features sandwiches, beer and wine all year round; in the summertime, the Tachell family fires up the barbeque and prepares some of the tastiest outdoor eating to be found.

The Carnation Golf Course is located eight and one half miles from Redmond on Red-Fall City 202. Take a left on Tolt Hill and go two miles. Just before the bridge, turn right.

Des Moines

There is a long, crescent-shaped beach framing this city of 7,400 located on I-5 just a few miles south of Sea-Tac Airport. This was a promoter's town envisioned by the Des Moines Improvement Company, which in 1889 sold lots for summer homes. One of the company's principles was from the Iowa city of the same name. Modern Des Moines is a commuter's town, with a reputation for its restaurants.

Attractions

More than 800 boats make the **Des Moines Marina** their home port. The facility serves owners from Tacoma north to Seattle, providing docks and dry storage. A public fishing pier attracts many visitors. Call 824-5700 for city marina information.

Normandy Beach and **Des Moines Beach** are just north of town off Marine View Drive. To the south is **Saltwater State Park**, with fifty-two campsites, lots of foot trails into **Kent Smith Canyon** east of the beach, and clamming on the swimming beach

Southwest King County Art Museum is on the fifth floor of the Highline College Library building, east of Highway 99 on South 240th Street. Call 878-3710 for hours and current exhibits.

For information, contact the **Des Moines Chamber of Commerce**, 21630 Eleventh South, Des Moines WA 98198. Call 878-7000.

Restaurant

D'ANDREA
22308 7th Avenue S
Des Moines, WA 98188
Tel.   (206) 824-7083
Hrs: Mon.- Fri.   11:30 a.m. -   2:00 p.m.
                        5:00 p.m. - 10:00 p.m.
         Saturday   5:00 p.m. - 10:00 p.m.
         Sunday   4:00 p.m. - 10:00 p.m.
Visa, MasterCard, AMEX and Diner's Card are accepted.

When they say this is pasta just the way Mother made it, or the bread just like Mom's, you can believe it. That's because owner and Chef Andy D'Andrea Jr. works with his mother in the kitchen.

That's one reason why D'Andrea has built the reputation it has earned as a fine Italian restaurant. Originally from Pittsburg where he learned his trade from his family, Andy opened the restaurant in Des Moines in 1980. It became an instant success, primarily because it was one of the few places at the time to offer superb homemade pastas. But if you are looking for something a little lighter on the carbos, there's also a fresh catch of the day, which ranges from prawns to salmon. The menu features a total of ninety tempting items, from veal pepperoni with roasted peppers and pimentos, to fettucini with sausage and mushrooms.

So if you're looking for authentic Italian restaurant, try the place with an authentic Italian mother.

Enumclaw

Enumclaw, on Highway 164 east of Auburn, is the gateway to ski areas on the east shoulder of Mount Rainier, and to coal fields in the White River basin. The railroad came through in 1884, and farmers created strong cooperatives which made the community a major trade center.

The name Enumclaw, "place of the evil spirits," is derived from the name the local Indians allegedly gave to a nearby mountain after they were frightened by a severe thunderstorm while camping.

Attractions

The first building here was **Enumclaw Hotel**, erected at 1704 Railroad Avenue. Now exhibits in **Enumclaw Public Library**, 1309 Myrtle Avenue, recount that past. Open Monday through Saturday 10:00 a.m. to 5:00 p.m.

Farman Pickleworks processes nearly 5,000 tons of cucumbers a year here and offers tours of the plant.

Mud Mountain Dam off SR410 on Mud Mountain Dam Road is an earth and rock flood-control dam. Of interest is the cableway tower and samples of rock cores drilled with a 36 inch calyx drill. A park here includes overlooks, a children's wading pool, hiking trails and a playground. Open daily from 9:00 a.m. to 8:00 p.m. Call 825-3211 for further information.

Black Diamond, on Highway 169 north of Enumclaw, shows off its coal mining history in a **museum** at the restored railroad depot. Open Thursday from 9:00 a.m. to 3:00 p.m., and Saturday and Sunday from 12:00 noon to 3:00 p.m.

Accommodations

KING'S MOTEL
1334 Rossevelt Way E
Enumclaw, WA 98022
Tel. (206) 825-1626
Mastercard and Visa are accepted.

A royal welcome is what awaits you at the King's Motel, a complete home away from home for the traveler. Whether you decide to stay here for a day, a weekend or a month, you'll be pleased with the consistent quality, comfortable rooms, amiable service and every amenity needed to make your stay a memorable one.

The welcome includes rooms featuring air conditioning, balconies, whatever size bed you may need, color TV and a few other personal touches by the owners, Bob and Sarah Boli. For your seasonal use, they offer a heated swimming pool. Besides being a great place to lodge and relax, the King's Motel also provides you with a good pivot point for exploring the Cascade Range. It is the nearest deluxe accommodations to Mount Rainier, Chinook Pass and Crystal Mountain recreation area on Highway 410. Golfing, hiking, fishing, skiing and much more can be enjoyed in this magnificent location.

This motel has accommodated groups as varied as loggers, a Danish bowling team, dog groomers and triathalon athletes. These groups all received the royal welcome and the red carpet treatment. The King's Motel bids the same to you. Come on out and experience a first class motel in a first class setting.

Art Gallery

COUNTRY GALLERY FINE ARTS
22531 SE 436th Street
Enumclaw, WA 98022
Tel. (206) 825-7451
Hrs: Tue. - Sat. 11:00 a.m. - 5:00 p.m.

Ida Morin saw a definite need in Enumclaw for an art gallery to carry original art works. She fulfilled that need with her Country Gallery Fine Arts. The gallery features Northwest artists, displayed in a relaxed Western setting. There is plenty of space here to step back and take a good look at the works displayed. You will find only high quality art at this fine gallery.

The artists featured at the Country Gallery are Ida Morin, who specializes in wildlife, Fred Oldfield, whose specialty is western art, Ron Smith, another western artist, and Jan Westland, wildlife. There are a number of open houses throughout the year which features one particular artist each time. You will find works in a number of media, including oils, watercolors, acrylics, bronzes, wood carvings and pottery. Ida's studio is located at the gallery, she is very helpful, informative and loves to discuss art with her customers. She also has a custom framing shop on the premises.

Country Gallery Fine Arts is a worthwhile stop when in the Enumclaw area. You'll enjoy browsing in the relaxed, attractive surroundings. Northwest and Western art lovers will find a wealth of fine works.

Gift Shop

VILLAGE SHOPPE
1444 Cole Street
Enumclaw, WA 98022
Tel. (206) 825-6481
Hrs: Mon. - Fri.   10:00 a.m. - 5:30 p.m.
          Saturday   10:00 a.m. - 5:00 p.m.
Visa and MasterCard are accepted.

Oh no, you've driven all the way to Enumclaw and have forgotten the present! Quick it's time to get another one, but where do you go? Now, now, let's not get frantic. There's always a way out. Wait a minute, that's it, all you need to do is make a trip to the Village Shoppe where you're sure to find the perfect gift for just about anyone.

Upon stepping through the door at Village Shoppe, your troubles are ended and your dreams fulfilled. Here, you can browse among the many wares while partaking of a delicious cup of gourmet coffee. Candies, chocolates, jelly beans, baskets, kitchen gadgets, mugs of all kinds, crystal sets, tea pots, pewter items, music boxes, prints and much, much more are all displayed in this unique gift shop. If you like the coffee you're drinking, you may wish to investigate their remaining flavors, such as golden pecan, carviolli and many other rich blends.

Owner Vera Anderson and her husband Alan, are proud of their shop that started out four years ago as a small kitchen store. Come on in, browse around and share in their enthusiasm. You see, there's always a solution to any dilemma.

Restaurant

VELVET GOOSE
1218 Griffin Avenue
Enumclaw, WA 98022
Tel. (206) 825-7581
Hrs: Tue. - Fri.   11:00 a.m. - 8:00 p.m.
          Sat. - Sun.   9:00 a.m. - 8:00 p.m.
Closed Christmas and New Year's Day

Sandy Terou, with the help and support of her husband and daughters, started this successful business, which combines an antique store and restaurant, five years ago. She was originally in the catering business and this seemed a logical progression when she wanted to start a business of her own.

The food at the Velvet Goose is delicious. Some of the food Sandy serves is made from Danish family recipes, such as the Ebelskiver and the oven pancakes which is served for lunch, as well as breakfast. There are a good selection of sandwiches for lunch, including many which are served on freshly baked croissants, there are salads and soups from which to choose. Dinner offers such selections as pan fried oysters, shrimp stuffed sole, chicken Cordon Bleu and more. The desserts are freshly made on the premises and are great.

The Velvet Goose is attractively furnished with antiques, all of which are for sale. When you are out for a nice Sunday drive, plan a side trip to Enumclaw to enjoy some truly outstanding food in attractive and congenial surroundings.

Fall City

Farm

THE HERBFARM
32804 Issaquah-Fall City Road
Fall City, WA 98024
Tel. (206) 784-2222
Hrs: March - October Mon. - Sun.
Call for winter hours.

Fourteen years ago Lola Zimmerman grew herbs as a hobby and to share them with her neighbors she filled a wheelbarrow and set it out under the walnut tree. From this modest beginning The Herbfarm has evolved. There are over 400 different kinds of live herb plants and 120 species of succulents from around the world. Any number of interesting activities and classes are available at The Herbfarm. It's a great place to visit and enjoy a unique experience.

The Herbfarm offers ongoing programs of educational classes and instruction from experts in cooking, crafts and gardening. The luncheon programs feature a six course meal of regional cuisine with cooking instruction included. There are many special events here that the whole family will enjoy. On the 4th of July weekend there is a llama festival, a harvest fest on Labor Day, and weekends in the fall there is a cider pressing from fresh apples picked in the local area. The Herb Shop has a variety of interesting items. In addition to herbs there are food, books, and unique gift items.

Write for The Herbfarm's interesting brochure which lists many of the things they have for sale, as well as a schedule of the events held throughout the year. A trip to The Herbfarm will be a unique and enjoyable experience for the whole family.

Golf Course

SNOQUALMIE FALLS GOLF COURSE
35109 SE Fish Hatchery Road
Fall City, WA 98024
Tel. (206) 222-5244
 (206) 392-1276
Hrs: Mon. - Fri. 6:00 a.m. - 9:00 p.m.
 Sat. - Sun. 5:00 a.m. - 9:00 p.m.

Snoqualmie Falls Golf Course is located along the Snoqualmie River and is very scenic. It is easy to play and well maintained. With an PNGA rating of 64.8 for men and 67.8 for women, the course is easy to walk, with a nice layout spread between fir trees. The front nine is 2820 yards with the back nine bringing the total to 5427 yards. This is one of the driest winter courses in the Seattle Area.

John Groshell, co-owner and pro, along with W. M. Porter, co-owner and manager, and Chris Dowd, co-owner and superintendent, keep Snoqualmie Falls Golf Course an attractive, nice course to play. There is a fully stocked pro shop that carries a full line of equipment and clothes. Golf carts are available, and the pro shop rents clubs. Golf instruction is available by appointment, and a driving range complete with mats or grass will help you get warmed and ready to play. This facility is open to the public and anyone will feel comfortable in the casual atmosphere. A restaurant serves meals, beer, and wine.

Snoqualmie Falls Golf Course equals good golfing. Plan to stop here when you are in the area, and look to score one of your better rounds.

Federal Way

This community in the south county has grown in recent years, a short commute from jobs in either the Seattle or Tacoma areas. Federal Way is one of those phenomena of the linear community. Its name comes from what local people called Highway 99, the Pacific Highway, when it was constructed with federal funds. It was a "federal way." Then came a high school which adopted the name, and finally, after I-5 became the new federal way, between the two came Sea-Tac Mall, a modern shopping center.

Attractions

Federal Way has two theme parks. One is **Wild Waves**, full of water sides, man-made river rapids, and the like. The other is **Enchanted Village** with sixteen rides, a doll museum and a petting zoo. Use exit 142 B from I-5. Call 838-8828 for Wild Waves information, 838-1700 for Enchanted Village.

Dash Point State Park overlooks the sound at the south end of **Vashon Island**. About 400 acres are now in the park, which is reached from Highway 509, Dash Point Road. On the Sound tides often carve steep drop-offs from the beach, but here is an exception, a sandy expanse even at low tide. The slope of one percent reaches 2,200 feet out from the high tide mark, giving shallow and warm water favored for swimming. There are 136 campsites, twenty-eight with hookups for recreational vehicles.

For further information, contact the **Federal Way Chamber of Commerce**, 32015 First Avenue South, Federal Way WA 98003, telephone 838-2605.

Gift Shop

THE WINNER'S CIRCLE
2020 S 320th Building O
Federal Way, WA 98003
Tel. (206) 941-0597
Hrs: Mon. - Thu.   9:30 a.m. - 6:00 p.m.
　　　Friday   9:30 a.m. - 9:00 p.m.
　　　Saturday   9:30 a.m. - 6:00 p.m.
　　　Sunday   11:00 a.m. - 5:00 p.m.
All major credit cards are accepted.

Rhinoceroses, alligators, elephants, sharks, ostriches, snakes and kangaroos all contribute to one of The Winner's Circle's specialties: very elegant Western boots and accessories.
Also featured is a large selection of high quality Western cut jeans, slacks, suits, skirts, and sport coats. Western hats are available in qualities to match your budget - from economy models to the finest obtainable.
It's authentic Americana at its best. If it is a standard, brass belt buckle, or one that has been handtooled in gold or silver, you'll find it at The Winner's Circle.

Golf

GOLFUN
31531 1st Avenue S
Federal Way, WA 98003
Tel. (206) 941-8933
Hrs: Mon. - Sun. 9:00 a.m. - Dusk

Do you want to golf but can't afford the stiff fees charged by private clubs? Or can't stand the long delays on the public links? Are you a beginner, who might be a little intimidated by the big traps and silly, little balls? Maybe you feel left out because everybody says you're too young or too old? Well, you've found the answer, Golfun.

Golfun is a brand new, patented golfing game that uses oversized, air filled balls on a compact and playable course contained on six and one half acres. People of all ages, shapes and sizes can play Golfun, all you need is a desire to have a good time.

Plan a tournament, a corporate picnic, or have a birthday party in the clubhouse and then take off to the links for an afternoon of fun and play. Golfun - "It's not full-size, it's fun size."

(See special invitation in the Appendix.)

Issaquah

Seattle residents brag about being in the country after a half-hour drive. Often, they are thinking of Issaquah, a community of 5,500 on I-90 about half-way to Snoqualmie Pass. City limits include a large area of rural homes and farms around this trade center which started in 1862. A million dollar coal mining venture flopped here during World War I, but coal seams are productive in other locations. Formed of peat laid down about fifty million years ago when this valley was the swamp behind a coast line, many of the deposits were later buried by masses of rock and soil carried down with glaciers.

Attractions

Lake Sammamish State Park, and a commercial **Waterworks Park**, are located near Issaquah. Both are summer attractions in a climate several degrees warmer than the sometimes foggy days in Seattle. Call 435-5555 for Waterworks information. Sammamish is no small lake; nine miles long, its east shore has summer homes, its west is now part of sprawling Bellevue.

At the same freeway exit is the Issaquah airport, a popular target for hundreds of **sport parachutists** in the area. The best watching for skydivers is during spring and summer weekends.

Gilman Village, on Gilman Road at exit 17 from I-90, has a group of shops and restaurants which cater to visitors from Seattle and beyond. Historic buildings from several locations were moved here and restored into this unique shopping center. Phone 392-7024.

Boehm's Homemade Swiss Candies, 255 Northeast Gilman Boulevard, Issaquah, offers tours of its plant. Julius Boehm, who came from Switzerland, started the operation but it now makes peanut brittle along with European chocolates. Call 392-6652.

For further information, contact the **Issaquah Chamber of Commerce**, 145 1/2 NW Gilman Boulevard, Issaquah WA 98027. Telephone 392-7024.

Antiques

HAUS OF ANTIQUES and TEAROOM, 157 1/2 Front Street, North, Issaquah, WA. Furniture, glass, collectibles; tearoom attached.

MICHELE LeROUX ANTIQUES & FINE OLD BOOKS
710 Fifth Avenue Northwest
Issaquah, WA 98027
Tel.   (206)   392-9536
Hrs: Tue. - Sat.   11:00 a.m. - 5:00 p.m.
         Sunday   1:00 p.m. - 5:00 p.m.

The charming white house framed by ivy, surrounded by a white picket fence, accented in the summertime with flowers bursting with color; the old riding harrow in the front yard, the milk cans on the porch, the welcome wreath and mat; immediately take you back to a place familiar in your childhood, Grandmother's, or Aunt Hattie's, or......Your trip of nostalgia continues when you step through the front door, heralded by the merry jingle of sleigh bells, you're greeted warmly by Michele LeRoux, the charming mistress of this time lapse.

Your fantasy continues as you wander through the rooms, burgeoning with treasures of bygone days. The rooms are arranged to give the impression that the owners have just stepped out, and will be back in a moment. In the bedroom, clothes and linens hang in the closet, a pair of shoes are left carelessly tumbled beside the bed.

The rooms look lived in and the lovely antiques and collectibles relative to each room are arranged in creative and useful ways. Even in the bathroom, antique shaving mugs, straps, linens; all give the impression of a frozen moment in time. The kitchen is filled with cookware, cookbooks, implements, and pottery. Old ice tongs hang near the sink, pinching a modern roll of paper towels within their iron fingers. It's a wonderful place to get ideas on how to use and display your antiques.

You'll find a wonderful collection of old books to peruse. There's Chippendale, Staffordshire, and other "name" antiques. Wonderful rugs, furniture with the original upholstery, old magazines, lamps, toys, jewelry, primitives and Victorian pieces. The price range is wide, and fair. You could spend days here wandering...and find pleasurable every hour of the time spent.

Apparel

SOMETHING KNITTED, Gilman Village, Issaquah, WA. Handmade clothing and jewelry.

Art

ISSAQUAH GALLERY
49 Front Street North
Issaquah, WA 98027
Tel.   (206) 392-4247
Hrs: Mon. - Fri.   10:00 a.m. - 6:00 p.m.
           Saturday   10:00 a.m. - 5:00 p.m.
Closed Sundays and major holidays.

Gallery owners/artists Judith and Albert McNea moved to Issaquah from Michigan in 1978 to fulfill a lifelong dream, opening an art gallery in a small town.

Since Issaquah Gallery opened, it has attracted a select following of clients who know that the work they will find featured represents the very best in quality and talent of over fifty Northwest artists. Hundreds of pieces of work are collected there ranging from oils, watercolors, prints, pottery and sculpture, photography, stained glass, bronzes, jewelry, weavings and textile art. In addition to showing the McNea's own work, Judith teaches watercolor classes at the gallery throughout the year. A different artist is featured monthly at Issaquah Gallery, with two or three major shows happening annually. Custom framing is available and on-going client education is an important service of the gallery.

"Art is very personal" says Judith. She and Albert are always ready to provide a friendly consultation to assist with making your selection at Issaquah Gallery one you'll treasure for a lifetime.

Bakeries

DESSERTS, ETC., 1640 Northwest Gilman Boulevard, Meadows Shopping Center, Issaquah, Washington. Breads, cakes, pies, cookies, cheesecake. Wedding cakes a speciality.

PETITE BOULANGERIE, 1175 Northwest Gilman Boulevard, Issaquah, WA. French breads, croissants, bagels, soups and sandwiches.

Bed and Breakfast

WILDFLOWER INN
25237 SE Issaquah-Fall City Road
Issaquah, WA 98027
Tel. (206) 392-1196

Everything about the Wildflower Inn says welcome. It is a warm, lovely bed and breakfast lodge built in 1983 by its gracious hostess, Laureita Caldwell. You'll feel at home the moment you enter. On chilly days a cozy fire in the open hearth stove in the kitchen-dining area welcomes you. The beautiful golden brown log walls are an appropriate backdrop for the lovely antique quilts, most of which were quilted by Laureita's grandmother. The braided rugs, early American furniture and the piano just waiting for frequent sing-alongs enhance the welcoming atmosphere.

Upstairs are four guest rooms, each decorated beautifully in the colors and motif of its wildflower namesake. The rooms Daisy and Rose share a bath and Fern and Strawberry each have their own private facilities. The rooms are large and comfortable and feature window seats overlooking the forest. Coffee and tea are always available and breakfasts are bountiful and delicious. There are paths cleared for walks through the forest and to a small meadow not far from the house.

Reservations are required and pets and children under twelve cannot be accommodated. This authentic log lodge in a quiet forest setting will delight you and is located only five minutes from Issaquah, fifteen minutes from Bellevue, and twenty-five minutes from Seattle. It's a wonderful spot for skiers too, only thirty minutes from the closest ski area.

Books

GILMAN VILLAGE BOOKS
Gilman Village
Issaquah, WA 98027
Tel. (206) 392-3766
Hrs: Mon. - Sat.   10:00 a.m. - 6:00 p.m.
         Sun.   12:00 a.m. - 5 p.m.
Visa and MasterCard accepted.

    Children, the future leaders of our society, should be educated well. One of the best foundations for a good education is learning to read at an early age. But that's not where it stops. Children should also enjoy reading, because by doing so they will learn even more. Teaching children the value of books is one of the reasons Gilman Village Books exists. However, that's not the only reason. It's also a great place for gifts and general reading for adults.
    Owned by Gerry and Paul Hargraves, Gilman Village Books has been in business since 1979 and is a first-class establishment with a lot of extras. As far as the children are concerned, they'll love it. Many special events take place, such as personalized readings for children, costume readings, and autograph parties. For the adults, Gilman Village Books features a wide selection of books in various topics. Science fiction, self-help, cookbooks, fiction, exercise books and many general publications are all included in their inventory.
    The shop also carries book-related gifts such as calenders, magnifying glasses, chess sets, greeting cards, book markers, books on tape, videos and much more. Gilman Village Books, with friendly service and a wide variety of reading material, is a perfect place to learn and have fun at the same time. For children or adults, it's a "Best Choice" in Issaquah.

For those of you who love to eat, here's a tour that'll fill your stomach, as well as your day.

	ISSAQUAH, A TOUR DE FOOD		
	Wildflower Inn	Best lodging	Issa/B & B
a.m.	Anglomania	Best gifts	Issa/Gift
a.m.	The Feed Store	Best specials	Issa/Restaurant
a.m.	The Goldworks	Best jewelry	Issa/Jewelry
a.m.	Boarding House	Best brunch	Issa/Restaurant
p.m.	Leroux Antiques	Best collectibles	Issa/Antiques
p.m.	Mandarin Garden	Best lunch	Issa/Restaurant
p.m.	Omar	Best woodcarver	Issa/Wood
p.m.	Harry O's	Best supper	Issa/Restaurant
	Now to work off those calories:		
p.m.	Front Street Workout	Best gym	Issa/Sport
	Hungry again ?		
p.m.	Golden Pheasant	Best late supper	Issa/Restaurant

Candy

BOEHMS CHOCOLATES, Edelweiss Chalet, 255 Northeast Gilman Boulevard, Issaquah, WA. Delicious candies, art gallery and an Alpine chapel.

Delicatessen

J. M. BIBBS, 1175 Northwest Gilman Boulevard, Issaquah, WA. Find tasty cheeses, breads, wines, and more at this delicatessen.

Entertainment

THE VILLAGE THEATER, 120 Front Street North, Issaquah, WA. Live theater performances every weekend at 8:00 p.m.

Gift Shop

ANGLOMANIA
Gilman Village
Issaquah, WA 98027
Tel.   (206)   392-2842
Hrs: Mon. - Sat.   10:00 a.m. - 6:00 p.m.
            Sunday   12:00 noon - 5:00 p.m.

Brightly-colored windsocks, with the Commonwealth's insignias, bob at the front door and herald your entrance into this bit of Britain. When owner Susan Jarrett welcomes you in her lovely British accent, you may develop a sudden urge for a cuppa tea. If so, you're in the right place. Susan's shop has a wonderful selection of genuine English teapots, teas and biscuits. Although Susan has lived in the United States for more than twenty-one years, she still returns to Britain at least twice a year to bring back things for her shop.

Anglomania is crammed from floor to ceiling with collectors' items: fine china like Royal Doulton, Beleek, Royal Albert, Wedgwood, and Royal Worcester. There are Wade porcelains, Bossons hand-painted plaster faces, royal family memorabilia, Pimpernel matching coasters, placemats, trays, trivets, tiny hand-painted tins, thimbles, cups and saucers, flags and maps.

For the children, there are Beatrix Potter items, Paddington Bear, Bunnykins, Pen Delphin rabbits, little tin soldiers, and beautiful books.

You can outfit yourself in a wool sweater from England or Ireland, wrap a lovely, soft woolen scarf about your neck and top it off with an authentic cap or hat. Set off across the moors grasping your walking stick in leather gloved hands and enjoy the view. Have an English Christmas with plum pudding and Christmas crackers, trim the tree with ornaments, put the wrapped perfume, soap, talcum powder and linens under the tree and relax.

THE GRASS ROOTS, Gilman Village, Issaquah, WA. Plants, baskets, gifts and dried flowers.

THE KITCHEN CUPBOARD, Gilman Village, Issaquah, Washington. Kitchen decorations, and everything for the gourmet cook.

TRIVIA AND MORE, Gilman Village, Issaquah, WA. Glassware, china, linens, kitchen items and MORE.

Gym

THE FRONT STREET WORKOUT AND NAUTILUS
485 Front Street N
Issaquah, WA 98027
Tel. (206) 392-FITT
Hrs: Winter Mon. - Thu. 6:00 a.m. - 9:00 p.m.
             Friday   6:00 a.m. - 8:00 p.m.
             Saturday   8:00 a.m. - 4:00 p.m.
             Sunday   9:00 a.m. - 2:00 p.m.
     Summer Saturday   8:00 a.m. - 1:00 p.m.
             Sunday   9:00 a.m. - 1:00 p.m.

With a wide range of Nautilus and free weight equipment downstairs, plus a large, mirrored exercise room upstairs, the Front Street Workout is the most complete health and fitness facility in Issaquah. For owners Brad and Jan Horrigan, the well being of their clients is their main concern. They can design an individual program for anyone to progress safely at his or her own rate to optimum physical fitness.

There are various aerobic programs available for all different levels, everyday. Instructors are highly qualified and certified by the International Dance and Exercise Association. There are showers, a sauna, free weights, exercise bikes and a rowing machine. A physician and dietician act as consultants to offer a holistic approach to fitness. A small shop offers the latest in exercise wear.

Several different types of memberships are available. Brad feels that the Nautilus and aerobic programs together offer the best way to develop strength, coordination and endurance. Combine them with a nutritious diet and you're on your way to a new, healthier you.

(See special invitation in the Appendix.)

Ice Cream

THE SWEET ADDITION, Gilman Village, Issaquah, Washington. This ice-cream parlour features Italian ice cream, chocolates, candies, and serves lunch.

Jewelry

DIAMOND LIL'S, Gilman Village, Issaquah, Washington. Antique and estate-sale jewelry and gifts.

THE GOLDWORKS
Gilman Village
Issaquah, WA 98027
Tel. (206) 392-6622
Hrs: Mon. - Wed. 10:00 a.m. - 6:00 p.m.
    Thursday   10:00 a.m. - 6:00 p.m.
    Fri. - Sat. 10:00 a.m. - 6:00 p.m.
    Sunday   12:00 noon - 5:00 p.m.

This unique jewelry store offers much more than beautiful works of gold. There are lovely pieces of sterling silver and other precious metals, plus collector's items of hand blown glass, handmade porcelain and hand crafted metal. The jewelry displayed here is all gallery quality and fashioned by hand. Many of the pieces are fashioned by Northwest artisans.

Diane Frizzell established The Goldworks when she realized the need for a retail outlet for Northwest jewelry artists. There is a designer available in the shop who will work out an individual design just for you. They will mount unset stones, or redesign heirloom jewelry. The Goldworks offers two special "Remount Events" each year, one in the spring and one in the fall. They also do repair work and more than seventy-five jewelers contribute their expertise to the store.

This is certainly the place to find unusual and precious gifts. The hand blown glass pieces and handmade porcelain are exquisite. The Goldworks is a real treat for lovers of jewelry and art.

Restaurant

THE BOARDING HOUSE
Gilman Village
Issaquah, WA 98027
Tel. (206) 392-1100
Hrs: Mon. - Sun. 10:00 a.m. - 5:00 p.m.

The first thing you notice when you enter The Boarding House is the wonderful aroma. The next impression is the decor, with its antique tables and straight back chairs, walls adorned with pictures from days gone by, and an old style, ceramic jar with a push spigot from which the water is drawn. The kitchen of this charming restaurant is open to view so you can watch cook Yutta Nelson peeling and cutting vegies to pop into her soup cauldron or slicing freshly baked bread. Owners Dianne Cole, Gerrie Armbruster, Lee Berry and Lu Tochterman have become successful by offering a simple and delicious menu.

There is a choice of two hearty, tummy warming soups each week, such as split pea, clam chowder or vegetable. You can order a Boarding House salad, which is a tasty melange of greens, marinated beans, mushrooms, ham or turkey, cheese and croutons topped with your favorite of the homemade dressings. Sandwiches are thick and fresh. They include ham and Swiss on rye, turkey on wheat or tuna on egg bread. For blissful desserts try warm apple crisp, carrot cake with cream cheese topping, cheesecake with strawberry sauce, brownies or special pies.

The popularity of this "Best Choice" restaurant shows in the return of customers year after year, and in the praise of the delicious goodies.

THE FEED STORE
Gilman Village
Issaquah, WA 98027
Tel. (207) 392-1297
Hrs: Mon. - Sun. 9:00 a.m. - 4:00 p.m.

An authentic, 1920 Issaquah Feed Store was moved several years ago to Gilman Village and is now home of The Feed Store restaurant. Owners Dianne Cole, Lee Berry and Linda Welsh insist on high quality, fresh ingredients for the tasty concoctions they serve.

Freshly made soup makes a great beginning, followed by a chicken salad sandwich, herbed cream cheese with roast beef or maybe a terrific seafood salad. Three different entrees are featured each day, such as spinach cheddar pie with cheese sauce, chicken cheese crepes, quiche, roast beef or turkey breast with homemade cranberry chutney. To complement your meal, The Feed Store carries domestic and imported beers, espresso, juice and a superb wine list available by the glass or bottle. Champagne can be ordered by the split or the bottle.

The warm pub-like atmosphere and friendly service provide a relaxing experience at this "Best Choice" restaurant, The Feed Store.

GOLDEN PHEASANT
1580 NW Gilman Boulevard
The Meadows Shopping Center
Issaquah, WA 98027
Tel. (206) 392-8372
Hrs: Mon. - Fri. 11:30 a.m. - 2:00 a.m.
Saturday 4:00 p.m. - 2:00 a.m.
Sunday 4:00 p.m. - 10:00 p.m.

The Cantonese and Mandarin cuisine offered at the Golden Pheasant is always delicious. Co-owner Danny Chinn is also the head chef and he has been cooking professionally in the Seattle area for more than forty years. He trains all of the chefs and insists on the best quality and freshness for all his creations.

The Chef's choice is the "Golden Special", a family style dinner with barbecued pork, egg roll, chow mein, Mongolian beef, sweet and sour chicken, sauteed scallops Chinese style and special fried rice. There is a tank of live lobsters and crabs from which you make your selection for lobster or crab with ginger sauce, an outstanding entree. There are daily luncheon specials and an American menu is available, too. Food service is available in the full service bar which has a large screen television and a dance floor.

A kitchen tour of the Golden Pheasant is available. It's fascinating to see the giant woks, the refrigerated storage, the huge oven full of hanging strips of barbecued pork, the activity and the cleanliness. The tour is almost as much fun as eating the delicious food at the Golden Pheasant.

HARRY O'S
719 NW Gilman Boulevard
Gilman Square
Issaquah, WA 98028
Tel. (206) 392-8614
Hrs: Lunch Mon. - Fri. 11:30 a.m. - 2:00 p.m.
Dinner Sun. - Thu. 5:00 p.m. - 9:00 p.m.
Fri. - Sat. 5:00 p.m. - 10:00 p.m.
Brunch Sunday 10:00 a.m. - 2:00 p.m.

Tucked away in a shopping center, Harry O's offers fine dining in a lovely atmosphere. The decor is done in pink, gray and mauve for a quiet, relaxed effect. The best American and Continental cuisine is featured and in the summer diners can enjoy the sidewalk cafe. Susan Davin is the manager and along with Chef Sara Barclay, they offer their patrons a memorable dining experience.

Susan's staff is well trained and provide unobtrusive good service. One of her waiters, Lloyd Lluellyn, is so efficient and so popular, that people make reservations just to get one of his tables. There are two dinner specials nightly, some of the favorites from the regular menu are veal Philip - veal medallions sauteed with Cointreau, veal Oscar and beef medallions Diane. The menu is extensive.

There is a comfortable bar, made cozy by an open fireplace. The wine list is extensive with many Northwest wine choices, as well as French vintages. Harry O's pleasant atmosphere, excellent service and unbeatable cuisine offer a delightful dining experience.

MANDARIN GARDEN
40 E Sunset Way
Issaquah, WA 98027
Tel. (206) 392-9476
Hrs: Tue. - Wed. 11:30 a.m. - 9:30 p.m.
     Thu. - Fri. 11:30 a.m. - 10:00 p.m.
     Saturday   4:00 p.m. - 10:00 p.m.
     Sunday   4:00 p.m. - 9:30 p.m.
Closed Monday

This little restaurant is known as one of the finest Chinese restaurants in the Puget Sound area. There is usually a line waiting for tables on weekends, so come early with a good appetite, and prepare to enjoy some excellent Northern Chinese cuisine, featuring Mandarin, Szechuan and Hunan selections.

Owner Andy Wang sets the highest standards for his food. He feels the reason the Mandarin Garden has been voted "best" by several area newspapers is his insistence on freshness. Every dish is cooked to order, using the finest fresh vegetables, meats and seafoods available. The chef's recommendation for a succulent chicken dish is Kung Pao Chicken, chicken breasts stir fried with walnuts, peppers and onions. The most popular beef dish is Mongolian Beef, spicy and delicious. Seafood dishes are a specialty of the house and the Peking Duck is outstanding, but must be ordered at least one day ahead so Andy can prepare it properly.

The authenticity of this restaurant is underscored by the wait staff. They are all Chinese and the bill at the end of the meal is written in Chinese characters. The Mandarin Garden offers an unbeatable experience in fine Chinese dining.

Signs

OMAR THE WOODCARVER
240 NW Gilman Boulevard
Issaquah, WA 98027
Tel. (206) 392-7512
Hrs: Mon. - Sat. 9:00 a.m. - 4:30 p.m.

Just off I-90, Front Street Exit, fifty feet from the railroad tracks where trains still chug through downtown Issaquah, sits a genuine 1920's Great Northern Railroad caboose. Sitting permanently on a set of tracks going nowhere, this little red caboose is the shop of Omar the Woodcarver, also known as Jerry Whitmire. Jerry wears the traditional striped bib overalls and trainman's cap as he welcomes you to his unique sign making shop.

Jerry has been in the sign making business for more than twenty-five years, and has a selection of beautiful signs of every size and type. There are hand carved signs, sand blasted signs and wooden signs with vinyl computer cut lettering. Jerry said, "If someone can draw it or find a picture of it, I can do it." The largest sign he's done is eight inches thick, seven feet tall and twenty-two feet long. There's no sign too big for Jerry to make.

Jerry loves his work which gives him a chance to release his creativity through wood. He takes great pride in his signs which are in great demand. The signs are made mostly from redwood or cedar and will last for years. There is a second Omar's location at Pier 55 in Seattle and a visit to either is an interesting shopping experience.

Kent

Apparel

THE WINNER'S CIRCLE, 27117 Soos Creek Drive, S.E., Kent, Washington. The store carries a western apparel and boots, as well as a full line of tack and feed.

Kirkland

Lake Washington's east shore community of Kirkland was once a small village connected to Seattle by ferry service. An English industrialist, Peter Kirk, wanted to capitalize on iron ore discovered up the Snoqualmie River and the coal fields to the south on the lake to make this the site of a large steel factory. The town was platted in 1886. When the ore proved of such low grade that mining was uneconomical Kirkland became a trade center for farms in the area. Kirk, by the way, moved to a farm of his own on San Juan Island, ignoring the community which bears his name. Now with the Evergreen Point floating bridge bringing autos almost to Kirkland's doorstep, both farms and trade center have merged into another residential suburb of Seattle.

Attractions

The business district has grown into a collection of shops, including some mall-style antique offerings, that bring shoppers from the metropolitan area and beyond.

Off **Houghton Park** is the submerged wreckage of the steamer **Bremerton,** which went down in 1909.

The **John Kellett House**, 526 Tenth Avenue West, was built about 1890 and is one of several homes which date from platting of the town. Houghton, a nearby community, was started in 1875.

Peter Kirk's office building, Seventh Avenue Northeast and Market Street, is a bit of nineteenth century commercial architecture in the midst of development that is seventy years younger. There were four buildings when Kirk readied his foundry, three remain. All were built in 1891.

For information, contact **Kirkland Chamber of Commerce**, 301 Kirkland Avenue, Kirkland WA 98033. Telephone 822-7066.

Accommodations

SILVER CLOUD INNS, 12202 Northeast 124th Street, Kirkland, Washington. Moderate prices, immaculate rooms, queen-sized beds, free local calls, jacuzzi, swimming pool, free guest laundry, valet service, complimentary coffee bar, and more.

Antiques

ALEXANDER MCCALLUM TOPPIN AND SONS ANTIQUES
217 Lake Street South
Kirkland, WA 98033
Tel. (206) 827-6593

What makes Alexander McCallum Toppin and Sons Antiques different from the run-of-the-mill antique shop is not only the diversity of the merchandise, but the care with which each piece is selected. Regardless of price, each piece has been tastefully chosen and contributes to the overall effect of the store.

Thirty-five years of collecting and travelling the world are manifested in the shop. The love the owners have put into this business shows in every antique. An Audubon print hangs over an exquisite piece of Georgian silver artfully displayed on an ornately carved 1880s sideboard. Fine Ming porcelain reflects the opulent colors of Kashan carpets that are on display next to the delicately-carved pieces of nineteenth-century Chinese ivory. A Chien Lung funeral piece rests among the prints, porcelain, paintings, crystal, silver, ivories and collectibles of another age.

Located in picturesque downtown Kirkland this is the type of shop one can spend a happy afternoon browsing. It provokes memories of times when life embodied different values and a calmer pace, and greater importance was placed on aesthetics and home environs. Today, for those same aesthetics in craftsmanship it is necessary to look to the past, and antiques, like those carried by Alexander McCallum Toppin and Sons.

ANTIQUE CONNECTION
147 Park Lane
Kirkland, WA 98033
Tel. (206) 828-0778
Hrs: Mon. - Sat. 10:00 a.m - 5:30 p.m.
　　　Thursday 10:00 a.m. - 8:00 p.m.
　　　Sunday 12:00 noon - 5:00 p.m.

While working in interior design, Debora Trepus discovered that what interested her more than design work were the antiques gracing the homes. Not surprising, as Debora's family has been in the antique business for seventeen years. So eventually Debora and her husband, Marvin gave into her primary interests and opened The Antique Connection.

A store in which the merchandise is so varied you are almost certain to find something that you have been looking for for just ages, and couldn't find. If perchance its not there, they will gladly help you find it.

The shop carries a collection of primitives, prints, English silver, rare books, jewelry, quilts, and other memorabilia. Furniture, vintage clothes, dolls and glassware are also among the treasures at The Antique Connection.

For the manually-inclined, there is an interesting assortment of antique hardware, furniture refinishing supplies, and knowing professionals to share your challenges. The Antique Connection also provides local delivery, nationwide shipping, glass repair, and other amenities that keep their customers satisfied and loyal.

Apparel

THE SILVER WILLOW
123 Lake Street, South
Kirkland, WA 98033
Tel. (206) 827-2597

The first impression the visitor to the Silver Willow perceives is the international flavor; Korean character masks gaze at you from one wall; an Edwardian Jester head laughs at you from another. The shop features numerous handwoven items, tapestries, and wall hangings, a selection of local and internationally-handcrafted goods, all made from natural fibers. The shop feels more like a gallery than a clothing store; some of the items look as if one should frame them as fabric art instead of wear them.

Owner Becky Willow provides her customers with clothes having a sense of personal character. The items come from Ireland, Iceland, Japan, Uruguay, Peru, Nepal, Tibet, and a host of equally-exotic locations. Each item in the store has been chosen with comfortable quality in mind, and with a style to be found only at the Silver Willow.

Art

THE LAKESHORE GALLERY
15 Lake Street
Kirkland, WA 98033
Tel.(206) 827-0606
Hrs: Mon. - Wed.   10:00 a.m. - 6:00 p.m.
      Thu. - Fri.   10:00 a.m. - 9:00 p.m.
      Saturday   10:00 a.m. - 5:30 p.m.
      Sunday   12:00 noon - 5:00 p.m.

The Lakeshore Gallery fits well into the chic, small town atmosphere of Kirkland. The shop manages to capture both the friendly, relaxed surroundings and the general air of sophistication in the area.

The focus is on Northwest artists, whether original fine art, handcrafted jewelry or handwoven textiles, each piece is well chosen. Woven art, blown glass, lamps and sculpture, all created by local artisans, add to the overall effect of the shop.

Featuring one person and group shows, owner Georgie Kilrain also arranges individually commissioned pieces. Georgie also sells custom wind socks, planters, hats, crockery, pottery, woodware, paintings and stained glass.

Bed and Breakfast

THE SHUMWAY MANSION
1410 100th Ave. N.E.
Kirkland, WA 98033
Tel. (206) 823-2303

Sitting regally on a wooded hillside overlooking Juanita Bay, the Shumway Mansion depicts the elegance of a bygone era. A sense of permanence here belies the mansion's actual history, for the building was moved intact to its present location in 1985. By conquering what seemed at times to be insurmountable problems in moving such a historic structure, Dick and Salli Harris have provided their guests with a rare and unusual opportunity to step into the past.

The 10,000 square-foot structure was originally built in downtown Kirkland in the early 1900s. It was considered to be one of the finest mansions on Lake Washington's east side. When Dick and Salli saw the mansion for the first time, they were charmed by this reminder of the past.

The mansion has seven bed and breakfast rooms, all with private baths. Five rooms face the lake, two have private balconies, and all possess an old-world charm. In addition to the bed and breakfast rooms, and the sumptuous gourmet breakfasts served by daughter Julie Blackmore, the mansion is also available for weddings, receptions, business meetings, and seminars. Recently, the Washington Trust for Historic Preservation awarded The Shumway Mansion its highest award as Best Restoration for Commercial Use.

Treat yourself to a unique experience. Visit the Shumway Mansion. You'll be glad you did.

Gift Shop

AIRY GREETINGS
14330 124th Avenue NE
Kirkland, WA 98034
Tel.   (206)   771-4661
         (206)   821-3442
Hrs: Mon. - Fri.   7:30 a.m. - 8:00 p.m.
         Saturday   9:00 a.m. - 6:00 p.m.
Closed Sunday, except for deliveries.
Visa, MasterCard and AMEX are accepted.

Founded five years ago by mother and daughter Joan Thomas and Kathy Koch, Airy Greetings has met and conquered every challenge presented them in the area of creative ballooning. Whether you need a multitude of balloons for a special celebration, a comic mylar balloon or a 10 1/2 foot polypropylene balloon to draw attention to your business or special event, you'll find what you need at this uplifting store.

A visit to the Airy Greetings store is fun and exciting. There are over 300 mylar balloons on display, along with gifts and novelties for all occasions. Every day you can see clowns coming and going with balloon bouquets for various occasions, except, of course, on Easter when only Easter Bunnies are seen delivering balloons. The staff at Airy Greetings has extensive experience with large or small parties and will arrange for balloon deliveries around the country through a network much like FTD floral deliveries.

Joan and Kathy love their work and love a challenge. The photograph album in the store will show you their creative and innovative ways with balloons. Whether you want just a simple balloon to say "Thank You" or "I Love You" or a balloon sculpture to enhance that special event, Airy Greetings won't let you down.

Restaurants

THE FAMOUS KIRKLAND FISH COMPANY
452 Central Way
Kirkland, WA 98033
Tel. (206) 827-8700

One of life's simple pleasures is finding a nice informal restaurant which has a very definite idea of what its goals are and succeeds in accomplishing them. The Famous Kirkland Fish Company fits this description to a tee.

Sitting squarely on Kirkland's busy Central way, The Famous Kirkland Fish Company provides one of the best price-to-value menus in the greater Seattle area. They offer the best quality seafood at moderate prices.

Inside the glassed-in kitchen area, you can see the meals artfully cooked to perfection before your eyes. Only the freshest seafood from the Northwest and the Gulf and Atlantic coasts are used. The combination of well-prepared food and a relaxed, congenial atmosphere make The Famous Kirkland Fish Company a favorite with local residents.

The interior decor is assertively nautical with boats, buoys, nets, and mounted fish hanging from the walls and ceiling. There is an abundance of well-placed natural lighting which lends intimacy without feeling cluttered. As strange as it may seem, the combination f decor and lighting create the feeling of eating right down on the waterfront.

The front bar, which seats about 25, features an interesting array of beer and ales from some of Washington's most successful micro-breweries. The restaurant's wine list offers a well-chosen selection of Northwest wines. Do yourself a favor and find out for yourself why Kirkland's Fish Company became famous.

IZUMI
12539 116th NE
Totem Lake West Shopping Center
Kirkland, Wa 98034
Tel. (206) 821-1959
Hrs: Mon. - Fri.   Lunch   11:30 a.m. - 2:00 p.m.
                   Dinner   5:30 p.m. - 10:00 p.m.
     Sat. - Sun.   4:30 p.m. - 9:30 p.m.
Closed Christmas, New Years and first Monday of each month
Visa and MasterCard accepted.

If you are looking for one of the best sushi chefs on the West Coast, you'll find him at Izumi. Mr. Matsushima presides over the newly expanded Sushi

Bar, where he enlightens the intellect and delights the palate with his creations. At Izumi you will not only taste Japanese food, but also savor the Japanese atmosphere, enhanced by the traditional dress worn by the staff.

The menu at Izumi offers a variety of dinners, combination dinners, and a la carte meals. Especially popular is the Makunouchi, an assortment of Japanese style dishes, served with Japanese soup, salad, rice and tea. Enjoy the Tokoju-sushi, a special assortment of sushi or try tempura or teriyaki. To complement your meal, there is a selection of Japanese and American beer, Japanese plum wine, domestic wines and soft drinks.

Izumi opened in the spring of 1985 and has since doubled its original size. It's fine Japanese cuisine and authentic atmosphere have made it a favorite dining spot in the Seattle area.

PELICAN'S WHARF
15 Lake Street
Kirkland, WA 98033
Tel. (206) 822-FISH

Hrs:	Lunch	Mon. - Fri.	11:00 a.m. - 2:30 p.m.
		Saturday	10:00 a.m. - 3:00 p.m.
	Dinner	Mon. - Thu.	5:00 p.m. - 10:30 p.m.
		Fri. - Sat.	5:00 p.m. - 11:30 p.m.
		Sunday	4:00 p.m. - 10:00 p.m.

The Pelican's Wharf Restaurant, with its antique stained glass dome over the bar fits right into the charming waterfront atmosphere of Kirkland.

Kirkland has avoided the urban sprawl so prevalent on the Eastside, and instead created an atmosphere of chic civility reminiscent of Fisherman's Wharf in San Francisco, and Sausalito in Marin County, California.

Pelican's Wharf manages to be sophisticated without being ponderous, with just the right combination of great food and spectacular scenery. As the name implies, the speciality of the house is a well-chosen array of fresh fish and seafood. From the calamari to the fresh mussels, each entree is splendidly-prepared. Most dishes are grilled over a mesquite broiler in full view, making the experience a treat for both the eye and the palate.

The Pelican's Wharf, a soaring experience, a full catch, and a comfortable place to land in which to enjoy it all.

Tours

BUFFY BUS
222 Park Place Center
Kirkland, WA 98033
Tel. (206) 827-632

Whoever it was that said that, "there is no substitute for a good idea" must have been thinking of the Buffy Bus. The Buffy Bus has as its motto, "Take Off A Day." If taking a day off for a guided shopping tour sounds good to you, the Buffy Bus certainly has your choice. Fourteen different tours around Puget Sound cover a wide range of taste and interests.

With box lunches provided, and a stewardess to help with your every need, a Buffy Bus tour is just the ticket for serious bargain hunters. Tours include: The Fashion Fling, a fantastic one-day tour of Seattle's best sample shops and factory outlets. All well-known brands, high-quality merchandise at UNBELIEVABLE PRICES. Mai Fest, a bit of Bavaria by bus. Celebrate the arrival of spring in the little alpine town of Leavenworth. Arrive in time for the spring festival and plenty of shopping. This tour is available either as a one-day spree or as an overnight getaway. For the serious bargain-hunter, there is Wholesale Heaven, inside the Seattle Trade Center with over 100 different wholesale reps and over 400 different lines of merchandise--all at or below wholesale prices. For collectors, there is the Junky Jaunt, which takes you to liquidators, warehouses, second-hand shops and even an antique shop or two. Big bargains on everything from food, clothing, and fabrics--to tools, furniture, and camping gear. These are but a few of the tours available; other tours include the Tacoma Treasure Hunt, The Port Townsend Prowl, the Tulip Trek, The Coastal Express, Portland for Penny-Pinchers, and Vintage Vancouver.

"Take Off a Day".....just remember to make your reservations well in advance, as seating is limited, and these trips are popular.

Wine

THE GRAPE CHOICE
436 Central Way
Kirkland, WA 98033
Tel.   (206) 827-7551
Hrs: Mon. - Fri.   10:00 a.m. - 7:00 p.m.
            Saturday   10:00 a.m. - 6:00 p.m.

A trip through The Grape Choice is a trip through the major wine growing regions of the world. This is exactly the type of friendly, unpretentious wine shop that everyone hopes to find. Larry Springer and Penny Sweet have assembled the finest vintages from France, Spain, Australia, Italy, California and the Pacific Northwest in an amiable atmosphere conducive to the appreciation of fine wines.

The spacious cellar-like interior houses an excellent collection of fine Northwest and California Boutique Wines. Of special note are the wines from Walla Walla, Washington. Not only are the wines excellent, but you find the largest selection at The Grape Choice, complete with the intriguing story behind the production of each one. Domestic and imported cheeses and beers are also available.

The Grape Choice has weekly tasting sessions and a newsletter that is sent to customers. The owners are friendly and helpful and will aid you in selecting just the right wine for that special occasion.

Leavenworth

Ski

STEVEN'S PASS
P.O. Box 98
Leavenworth, WA 98826
Tel.   (206) 973-2441
Hrs: Winter Mon. - Sun. 9:00 a.m. - 10:00 p.m.

Here's something new. Two new lifts, "Double Diamond" and "Southern Cross," open the Mill Valley area with 360 acres of terrain not previously accessible, with both intermediate and advanced runs. The area's steepest, longest run, also named "Double Diamond," is new this year. This season marks the area's 50th year of operation — 1937-1987. It began with a single rope tow!

A Total of 10 lifts accommodate 12,000 skiers per hour so that the management can live up to its motto, "Cater to the Skier." The skiers they are talking about include every member of the family and every ability level. A ski school is available if you'd like to get even more out of those new runs. Accommodations are available twenty to thirty minutes away.

If skiing make you feel good, at Steven Pass you'll feel like a million dollars.

Maple Valley

Bed and Breakfast

MAPLE VALLEY BED AND BREAKFAST
20020 SE 228th
Maple Valley, WA 98038
Tel. (206) 432-1409
Children are welcome.

Jayne and Clarke Hurlbut moved to Maple Valley to raise their family in 1971. With the help of their three children and Jayne's expertise in decorating and entertaining, they opened a charming bed and breakfast inn.

Located on a knoll overlooking a pond frequented by blue heron and ducks, this beautiful country home is the perfect place to relax. A picnic table and a near by children's wading pond offer guests a place to ruminate in the great outdoors. The interior of the home has an abundance of cedar panelling throughout with a woodburning stove and stone fireplace that lend a cheery warm in cold weather. There are two beautifully appointed, spacious guest rooms, one with twin beds and one with an unusual big log bed. Breakfast is splendid with "hootenanny" pancakes with strawberries, whipped cream and slivered almonds, fresh eggs and freshly ground coffee.

The Hurlbuts will gladly suggest recreational activities in the area such as innertubing down Green River, a visit to Crystal Mountain and more. Discounts are offered on longer stays, so be sure to visit this "Best Choice" - Maple Valley Bed and Breakfast Inn.

Mercer Island

Squat and substantial, the timbered mass which is Mercer Island rises from the southern arm of Lake Washington. The island is named for Thomas Mercer, captain of a wagon train which arrived in 1853. Mercer named Lake Washington and in later years was a Seattle judge. His brother Asa was first president of the University of Washington and had a summer home on the island. Six miles long, about one mile wide on the plain above bluffs which drop to the shore, the island has fifteen miles of shoreline. It contains a collection of houses marked by the time before and the decades after World War II. Before the war, homes were on the shore or with a view of the lake, served by a road looping around the rim. The floating bridge which carries I-90 eastward reached here in June 1940, but the interior housing development did not come until the 1950s. There are now 21,500 residents who have incorporated as a city their collection of homes and subdivisions built in times before comprehensive planning. Mercer Island has no downtown but most of its commercial offices and stores congregated between Island Crest Way and 76th Avenue to the south of I-90. Without a street map, it is difficult to find an address, because many interior streets stop and then begin again on the other side of large tracts of forest or parklands.

Attractions

Luther Burbank Park, on North Mercer Way near the Island Crest Way exit, is a product of planning in the midst of ad hoc community. A unique children's play area has objects to climb on, over and under. The waterfront provides recreation for adults.

Just south of the Seattle side of the bridge, on Sixtieth Avenue, are a group of homes with lake views which show the work of several of the Northwest's top architectural firms. Take the West Mercer Way exit to the south, turn east on 27th street to reach Sixtieth. It is **one of the earliest residential areas** on the island. Mercer Way loops the entire island.

For information, contact the **Mercer Island Chamber of Commerce**, Box 111, Mercer Island WA 98040.

Antiques

END OF THE RAINBOW
7831 SE 27th
Mercer Island, WA 98040
Tel. (206) 232-0676
Hrs: Tue. - Sat. 11:00 a.m. - 5:30 p.m.

Island Market Square on Mercer Island is the location of End of the Rainbow which specializes in antique pieces with a country flavor. Owner

Nadine Parker has been an antique dealer for many years and handpicks her pieces on frequent buying trips.

There are many antiques of 19th century pine along with walnut, cherry and other period woods. Copper and brass items, quilts, wicker, duck decoys and oriental porcelain are displayed with unique accessories. There is a wide selection of early prints and unique items such as rocking horses, stoves and hall trees to be found here.

End of the Rainbow is full of unique, carefully selected antiques that will delight the shopper. Nadine's warm and comfortable hospitality and extensive knowledge of the antique business make this shop a very pleasant experience.

Apparel

RILEY'S
7811 SE 27th
Mercer Island, WA 98040
Tel. (206) 232-0833

Riley's offers a great selection of both functional and impulsive items for everyone from infants to adults. Owner Gloria Riley supervises a sales staff well versed in the possible selections.

The infant section is especially attractive with a large inventory of knitwear, dolls, bedding, clothing and furniture. There are clothing departments for the rest of the family too, no matter what their ages. Riley's is one of only a few stores offering authentic Amish furniture. The housewares department has a large selection, including silver, crystal, Hadley hand painted pottery and Royal Copenhagen porcelain figurines. There is a section of superb glassware and gift cards for all occasions.

Riley's offers a nearly department store size selection, but the warmth and hospitality of a smaller, individually owned establishment. The selection of unique and unusual gifts can't be beat and there is truly something for everyone at this quality store.

Bed and Breakfast

MERCER ISLAND HIDEAWAY
8820 SE 63rd Street
Mercer Island, WA 98040
Tel. (206) 232-1092
No smoking is allowed indoors.

Hosts Bill and Mary Williams love to entertain and the result is one of the best bed and breakfast establishments to be found anywhere. Located on scenic Mercer Island adjoining Pioneer Park, Mercer Island Hideaway offers an idyllic setting for a bed and breakfast stay. Situated fifteen minutes from the attractions of Seattle and Bellevue, they have the best of both worlds. The lush green wilderness trails of forty acre Pioneer Park, only steps away, provide a tranquil setting for an early morning walk in the forest.

Mercer Island Hideaway offers two guest rooms with private bath, each beautifully furnished and appointed. The rooms have either king, queen or twin beds. One is a suite with private entrance adjoining a ground floor patio. Bill provides the full breakfasts which are varied, delicious and served in a dining room appointed with a round Danish table. The spacious cathedral ceilinged living room contains two grand pianos, harpsichord and reed organ. It is a music lover's paradise! Mary is a professional musician and loves to share the instruments.

Mercer Island Hideaway provides the perfect setting for small celebrations. No pets, smoking or RV parking. There is a two night minimum stay and children are welcome. Bill and Mary enjoy entertaining in their home and their guest reap the benefits. They provide quiet luxury in a beautiful setting, big beds, delicious meals and great company.

Delicatessen

C'EST CHEESE
7525 SE 24th Street
Mercer Island, WA 98040
Tel. (206) 232-9810
Hrs: Mon. - Fri.   7:00 a.m. - 8:00 p.m.
     Saturday   8:00 a.m. - 8:00 p.m.
     Sunday   9:30 a.m. - 5:30 p.m.

The words "say cheese" are what photographers generally use to bring a smile to their their clients. A visit to C'est Cheese, a wonderful delicatessen on Mercer Island, will bring a smile to anyone fortunate enough to walk in the door.

For the past nine years, Mary Lou, Gary, and Kim Smith, with the help of their staff, have provided the residents of Mercer Island and the Eastside with fare fit for a king. C'est Cheese carries an incredible array of deli meats and cheeses. There are also prepared entrées designed to please even the most discriminating palates. Try our Sunday Brunch for a special treat.

In addition to both take-out and on-the-premise dining, C'est Cheese also boasts mercer Island's most complete selection of French, California, and Northwest wines. An excellent custom catering service, wine tastings, fresh baked goods, wedding cakes, custom picnic baskets and imported and domestic beers are also offered.

Come to C'est Cheese and smile-- you'll have a wonderful culinary experience.

Gift Shop

FINDERS
7607 SE 27th
Mercer Island, WA 98040
Tel. (206) 236-1110
Hrs: Mon. - Sat. 10:00 a.m. - 6:00 p.m.

Judy Abrahamson was an employee of Finders a year and a half ago when the current owner decided to sell the shop. A little voice inside Judy said, "If you don't buy this store, you'll wish you had." So, following her intuition, Judy bought the store. She's glad she did and you will be too when you shop at Finders.

Judy has some of the best country home furnishings and gifts in her shop. You'll find handcrafted pine furniture, clocks, hatboxes, Shaker reproductions, handwoven rag rugs, baskets, hand dipped candles and some particularly interesting willow furniture crafted in Oregon. Nearly everything in the shop is handcrafted, many by local artisans. The handmade afghans and handwoven towels are beautifully done and will enhance any home. There is a good selection of limited edition lithographs, all in keeping with country decor.

If you are looking for something even vaguely connected to the "country look", you are almost sure to find it in this well stocked shop. Virtually nothing here is a run of the mill gift shop item; well chosen stock and a good job of merchandising make Finders a good place for the discriminating shopper.

Ski Resort

ALPENTAL*SKI ACRES*SNOQUALMIE
3010 77th Avenue SE #201
Mercer Island, WA 98040
Tel. (206) 232-8182
        (206) 434-6112 Alpental
        (206) 434-6671 Ski Acres
        (206) 434-6161 Snoqualmie

    Located just forty-seven miles from Seattle, is the ultimate ski area for Western Washington.   Known as "The Big Three", Alpental*Ski Acres*Snoqualmie, it offers complete skiing for everyone from beginner to expert. This is the largest ski area in the state, with half a million visitors a year. It also has the largest night skiing area in the world. People have been enjoying skiing here for the past fifty years, ever since present owner, David Moffett's father, started the resort area in 1937. Many special events are planned for their fiftieth anniversary celebration.
    Big Three customers get a lot for their money. Lift tickets are reasonably priced, and are interchangeable among the three areas. There are many runs, some brand new, some upgraded old runs. New lighting has opened up even more of the area for night skiing. There are twenty chairlifts (including a brand new four-seater beginner chair at Snoqualmie) and an uphill capacity that rivals that of Vail. Remodeled food and rental services, improved restrooms, and permanently graded lift line mazes are all recently completed projects that make skiing at The Big Three even more enjoyable. The Ski Acres Cross Country Ski Center has twenty kilometers of machine groomed trails, fifteen kilometers lighted, offers lessons, rentals, and provides a day lodge for those who enjoy cross country rather than downhill skiing. Alpental offers miles of untracked back country skiing for the intrepid.
    No matter what your skiing preference, cross country, well groomed trails, night skiing, or back country skiing, you'll find just what you need at The Big Three - Alpental*Ski Acres*Snoqualmie.

North Bend

    This is where the Snoqualmie River takes a bend to the north. Scattered settlers came to the open prairie here and built a blockhouse in 1856 as a shelter point during possible Indian raids. The town itself was laid out in 1889. Samuel Hancock, who came on the wide river plain in 1850 wrote a description which still fits today "...snow-capped mountains around, while the air echoed with the music of birds, and on the beautiful prairie could be seen the deer quietly feeding.

Attractions

Snoqualmie Valley Historical Museum, 320 North Bend Boulevard, North Bend, has one of the area's best collections of Indian artifacts from tribes living west of the Cascades. Also on display are a 1910 kitchen recreation and a diorama of early logging techniques. From March 1 through October 1, open Saturday and Sunday from 1:00 p.m. to 5:00 p.m. Open the rest of the year by appointment, call 888-3200 or 888-0062.

For years, the town has boasted one of the few **covered bridges** built for railroad use. Ask for directions at the museum or from local stores.

Mount Si, a lone peak northeast of North Bend, is a popular hiking spot. The 4,190 foot summit is a day's hike off Mount Si Road. For a map and complete directions, check with the North Bend Ranger station. Several other hiking trails are east of here in the Cascades including one from Alpental Ski area that leads up to jagged and scenic granite peaks.

Bakery

GEORGE'S BAKERY
115 Main Street
North Bend, WA 98045
Tel. (206) 888-0632 Bakery
      (206) 888-3222 Marketplace
Hrs: Bakery   Tue. - Sun.   8:00 a.m. - 6:00 p.m.
      Marketplace Mon. - Sun.   9:30 a.m. - 6:00 p.m.

George's Bakery is much more than a bakery, it's also a unique gift shop, full service delicatessen and art gallery. It's a wonderfully diverse establishment that is a "Best Choice" in North Bend.
In the deli section you'll find such delectables as homemade breads, Cornish pasties, ham and cheese croissants. Some of the other sandwiches include turkey and cheddar on crushed wheat, German sausage, sauerkraut on rye and Italian meatballs on French bread. The Marketplace, home of speciality foods, features many exquisite offerings including Starbuck's coffee and tea, Washington and Snoqualmie Valley wines, imported beer, Greek speciality foods, imported candies, Northwest postcards, souvenirs and a terrific catering service for special events.

The special and unique gift selections feature imported German steins, plush animals, English decorative tins, champagne and wine glassware. For your aesthetic senses, you'll enjoy Snoqualmie Valley photographs, handcrafted pottery, needlework, collectables and paintings by Snoqualmie Valley and Northwest artists. Wow, diversity at it's finest! What started out as a small bakery in the first half of the century, has emerged into a first class attraction. Stop by, taste good food, buy fine wine and admire this work of art.

Restaurant

**KEITH'S HOMESTEAD STEAKHOUSE
AND SPORTS BAR**
101 West North Bend Way
North Bend, WA 98045
Tel. (206) 888-0431
Hrs:Mon. - Sun. 7:00 a.m. - 10:00 p.m.
Bar open until 2:00 a.m.
Closed Christmas Day.

Headquarters to those who like to gather for food and libations before or after golf, skiing, hiking, biking, or getting fit in a health spa, Keith's Homestead has the kind of ambiance that makes one want to stay and regain the calories which may have just been burned off by vigorous exercise.

Specialties of the house at dinner time are prime rib, steak, and lobster. You can grill your own steak outdoors on the huge barbeque grill, or have dinner served as you sit toasting your toes and contemplating your sore muscles before the roaring fireplace. Breakfasts are varied and generous and will get you fueled for an all-day workout, or tide you over until you can enjoy some of the delicious homemade soups and sandwiches served on the lunch menu. A full service bar with creative bartenders serving great mixed drinks, as well as domestic and imported beer provides a great gathering spot before or after eating.

Parking to the rear of the building is convenient. Last, but not least, you'll find Keith's Homestead Steakhouse and Sports Bar so easy on the pocketbook, you won't mind making this great restaurant a frequent stop when you want to eat in North Bend.

SEATTLE EAST AUTO AND TRUCK PLAZA
Exit 34 I-90
P. O. Box 363
North Bend, WA 98045
Tel. (206) 888-1119
Hrs: Always open.

    Ken Rogers started serving the travelling public on I-90 in 1941 and now his oldest son, Hadley, heads the operation. It has expanded tremendously since Ken opened his restaurant. The complex now features full services for travellers and truckers, a restaurant, gift shop, and traveller's store. This is a very large facility, and the area for trucks is separate from the one for cars. It's close enough for the kids to enjoy watching the trucks, though. There is a mechanic on duty twenty-four hours a day.
    The restaurant is large and serves good, hearty, homemade food. Breads, pastries, soups, and chili are made fresh daily. Breakfast, lunch, and dinner are all offered at any time of the day. The gift shop is located in the restaurant and has hundreds of interesting things from which to choose. The travellers store has anything you would possibly need on the road, from flashlights and flares to sunglasses. There is even a non-denominational chapel in this large complex which is open from 7:00 a.m. - 10:00 p.m.
    This is a family run operation whose main focus is on helping travellers. The Seattle East Auto and Truck Plaza can't be seen from the interstate, so make sure you watch for exit number thirty-four when you are travelling.

Redmond

    Luke Redmond settled here in 1861, became the postmaster and had the post office and town named after him. For years this was a sawmill town that provided a place for farmers to shop. The town incorporated in 1912 when it had about 350 residents.
    One of its most notable moments in history was in 1935 when a black bear came to town, and remained treed for three days while game wardens and townspeople watched and the nation's press reported. The bear finally ambled back to the woods and the reporters left town. Those days are long-gone with the suburban housing boom of the 1960s which leaves Redmond with 28,200 residents, and presumably no bears.

Attractions

Marymoor Park, on the north shore of Lake Sammamish, is the largest park in the county system. There is a **museum** in the mansion house of this former estate, 6046 West Lake Sammamish Parkway, Northeast. Telephone 885-3684 for current hours. A partially-excavated **Indian village** site nearby is part of the exhibits.

The **Marymoor Velodrome**, in the park, is a competitive speed track for bicycle racers with banked turns tilting at twenty-five degrees. Weekend races for local and national speed events are staged from May through the fall. For the amateur, there are bike rentals here, and a host of park trails on which to ride. Telephone 329-2453 for event information.

Sammamish River Trail, which follows the stream from the lake down to Bothell, begins in the park. Farms and forests touch the corridor, along with some of Redmond's newer homes.

For information, contact the **Redmond Chamber of Commerce**, Box 791, 16210 NE 80th, Redmond WA 98073. Telephone 885-4014.

Accommodations

REDMOND MOTOR INN, 1760 Redmond Way, Redmond Washington. A quality motel with 140 units, rooms for smokers and non-smokers, wuites, handicap rooms, guest laundry , valet service and meeting rooms. The motel is located between two golf courses and minutes to shopping malls.

SILVER CLOUD INNS
15304 NE 21st Street
Redmond, WA 98052
Tel. (206) 746-8200
      (800) 231-1311 WA
      (800) 551-7207 Western USA
and,
12202 NE 124 Street   13050 48th Avenue S
Kirkland, WA 98034   S. Seattle, WA 98168
Tel. (206) 821-8300   Tel. (206) 241-2200

19332 36th Avenue W
Lynnwood, WA 98036
Tel. (206) 775-7600

The Silver Cloud Inns offer immaculate rooms, a warm and friendly atmosphere and professional treatment at moderate rates. Each Silver Cloud Inn has free guest laundry facilities, as well as a valet service available. The lobbies have comfortable furniture and complimentary coffee bar, Continental breakfast is offered except at the Silver Cloud Inn in S. Seattle. There is a jacuzzi to help you relax after a hard day. The rooms have queen and king size beds for your comfort. No smoking rooms are available.

All Silver Cloud Inns are located close to freeways and regional shopping areas. Free local calls are provided, a feature much appreciated by business travelers and tourists alike. Meeting rooms are available and accommodate up to forty people. All inns are located within easy walking distance of restaurants.

The management of the Silver Cloud Inns are eager to serve you and to be of help. The guests are their first consideration and are made comfortable from the beginning to the end of their stay.

Bed and Breakfast

CEDARYM - A COLONIAL BED AND BREAKFAST
1011 240th Avenue NE
Redmond, WA 98053
Tel. (206) 868-4159
No children and no smoking allowed inside.

Your hosts at Cedarym Bed and Breakfast, Mary Ellen and Walt Brown, have painstakingly created a home styled after 17th Century colonial living. Built in 1981, no detail has been overlooked in this beautiful reproduction.

Even before you enter the house, you will notice the detailing such as the panes of bull's eye glass over the front door and the hand forged lift latches used in place of modern day door knobs. Once inside, everywhere you look you will see functional and attractive features that complete the mood. The Keeping Room is the "living" area with a large brick fireplace where Mary Ellen often cooks over the open flame. All the floors in the house are either pine planks or red brick and even the staircase leading to the second floor has been built with a steep pitch in keeping with the design of the colonial days. Two rooms are available to guests, the Tulip Room and the Anchor Room, each with decor fitting their names. The stenciling on the walls and the furnishings, complete with brass beds, further the ambiance of the house. Breakfast time brings a feast served in front of the fireplace in the dining room with hand dipped candles in brass holders lending a pleasant aura.

In the garden there are beautiful flowers, herbs and dozens of roses; paths leading through the woods and a gazebo covered spa for relaxing. These lovely gardens have become increasingly popular for weddings and receptions.

For a restful, relaxing step back in time, be sure to visit the Browns at this "Best Choice" bed and breakfast - Cedarym.

Delicatessen

FILL YER BELLY DELI
8461 164th Avenue NE
Redmond, WA 98052
Tel. (206) 883-1080
Hrs: Mon. - Fri.   7:00 a.m. - 3:00 p.m.
    Saturday   10:00 a.m. - 4:00 p.m.
Closed Sunday and holidays
No credit cards accepted, personal checks okay.

The Fill Yer Belly Deli was established in 1984 by Joanne Bagge and Diane and Mike Tice, the same Mike Tice who plays tight end for the Seattle Seahawks. As a matter of fact, the deli caters lunches for the Seahawks, and don't those guys look like they'd know where to find the best food in town? Mike, Diane, and Joanne, who is Diane's sister, are all from New York and they have brought to Redmond all the positive features of a real New York style deli and added some of their own, such as a comfortable place to sit and enjoy your meal.

Everything in the deli is fresh, homemade, and cooked by Diane and Joanne. In addition to the normal deli sandwiches, salads, and soups, they prepare a couple of featured sandwiches, including the Fill Yer Belly Deli super sub - ham, bologna, salami, pepperoni, provolone and American cheese, pepper, oil, and vinegar, and Mike Tice's New York Sandwich - hot pastrami and Swiss cheese with horseradish and mustard on rye. There is also a good selection for breakfast. Catering is a specialty here and everything is fresh and homemade.

When in Redmond, don't miss the Fill Yer Belly Deli and let Diane, Mike and Joanne feed you some of the best deli food this side of New York.

Florist

FLOWER STOP
16150 NE 85th #127
Redmond, WA 98052
Tel.   (206)   881-1096
Hrs: Mon. - Fri.   8:00 a.m. - 6:00 p.m.
          Saturday   9:00 a.m. - 5:00 p.m.
Closed Sunday and holidays
Most major credit cards are accepted.

Kathy Nussbaumer has been arranging flowers since she was twelve years old, working in her mother's shop in Alaska. She opened Flower Stop in 1983 and with her husband John offers customers a wonderful selection of flowers, plants, and gift items. She continually searches for the unusual and unique gifts and vases with which to complement the floral masterpieces she and her staff create.

Flower Stop has many selections to delight you, especially interesting are the English gardens and European gardens, in which there are many plants, each in its own pot, which allows you to care for them individually and change the arrangement at will. In the gift section there is a variety of Northwest foods, as well as unique gift items. Kathy will prepare a Northwest gourmet food basket which will include premium wine, Grandma Pfeiffer's Cake in a Jar, Buckeye Beans and Herbs Soup or any number of other unique Northwest offerings.

Flower Stop is much more than just flowers, which it offers in abundance, beautifully arranged by Kathy and her staff. There are gifts and accessories for every taste and every budget. A visit here is a visually delightful experience and highly recommended.

Furniture, Children's

A CHILD'S PLACE, 15163 N.E. 24th Street, Redmond, Washington. A large selection of children's furniture, plus bedding, wallpaper, and other accessories to create a special room for your youngsters.

Gift Shop

BOWS N' CALICOS, Village Square Shopping Center, 16150 Northeast Eighty-Fifty, #Seven, Redmond, Washington. Local craftspeople have created the array of gifts you find here. Pleasant setting, friendly service.

Glass

GLASS DESIGN GROUP
16540 Redmond Way
Redmond, WA 98052
Tel. (206) 885-5955
Hrs: Mon. - Sat. 10:00 a.m. - 6:00 p.m.
Visa, MasterCard and AMEX are accepted.

What began as a hobby twelve years ago for owner Chuck Paulson became a business five years later. For the past seven years Chuck has been creating beautiful stained glass pieces at the site that was formerly Lesko Stained Glass. With fellow artisans Rob Paulson and Maureen Gummeson, the Glass Design Group has been designing and assembling custom windows for commercial and residential buildings. Many new homes and businesses in the Redmond area contain custom stained glass windows designed to accent the decor of the home or office.

The Glass Design Group employs all modern techniques including the use of beveled glass and glass etching to create pieces that vary from business card holders and decorative boxes to cabinet doors, lamp shades, and large windows. Sets of etched wine glasses are also available. In addition to creating custom glass art, Chuck and his colleagues have the largest repair studio in the area.

For those who wish to participate in the creation of their own stained glass pieces, the Glass Design Group has a full complement of necessary materials including more than 400 types and colors of glass. Classes are available so these masters can pass along their techniques to the new hobbyist.

Restaurant

THE BRITISH PANTRY, LTD.
8125 161st Avenue, N.E.
Redmond, WA 98052
Tel. (206) 883-7511
Hrs: Mon.-Sat.   10:00 a.m.-5:30 p.m.
   Tea Room closes at 4:30 p.m.
   Closed Sundays, major holidays,
   and Boxing Day
Additional location:
119 West Dayton
Edmonds, WA 98020
Tel. (206) 771-3967

Where do you suppose Prince Charles and Lady Diane got their sausage rolls, afternoon pastries, and British apple pie when in route from Japan to London? Right here in Redmond, from The British Pantry. And The British Pantry also catered the Children's Orthopedic Hospital Tea for Queen Elizabeth on her visit to Seattle. These two experiences not only highlight the culinary career of owner Mavis Redman, but also attest to the quality and authenticity of the fare offered. Mavis represents the third-generation baker, with son Neville, who is the fourth-generation baker at the Edmond's store. Many of the recipes come directly from hand-written documents of Mavis's great grandfather. The Edmond's store also enjoys the expertise of daughter Alvia Redman.

The store was opened in Redmond to fill a need for transplanted Britons wanting "a little bit of home." Both British Pantry locations carry British biscuits, sauces, pickles, jams and jellies, cheeses, candies and chocolates, and beers. A large variety of distinctive gifts have also been imported from Britain.

The refrigerated display cases are filled with items to tantalize the palate. Afternoon pastries are, of course, a specialty of the house and you'll find a nice variety from which to choose. In season, do not miss Christmas pudding and British Christmas cake. There is also a supply of British style sausage ("bangers") made from whole pork butts.

The Tea Room (only available in the Redmond British Pantry) serves a variety of sandwiches including the British-style tongue sandwich as well as 10 varieties of savory pies (pasties) and sausage rolls. While it is recommended that you eat in the relaxing environment of the Tea Room, the treats are also available for carry out.

Don't miss the opportunity to experience the authenticity and flavor of The British Pantry, Ltd., your one-stop British shopping experience. Keep your eyes open for a third British Pantry Ltd. opening on the Eastside in 1987.

(See special invitation in Appendix.)

BUD'S THE PLACE IN REDMOND
16101 Redmond Way
Redmond, WA 98052
Tel.   (206)   881-9917
Hrs: Mon. - Fri.   6:00 a.m. - 3:00 p.m.
           Saturday   7:00 a.m. - 2:00 p.m.
No credit cards are accepted, personal checks okay.

This is a fast food restaurant where people prefer to spend time. It is owned and operated by Walt and Marilyn Grosjean with help from their daughter Jody. Bud's provides the kind of service and atmosphere enjoyed by all. One of its most interesting features is the "middle table." This table seats eighteen to twenty interested and "conversationally active" people. Many regulars meet here daily and discussions on how to solve the world's problems abound.

Walt and Marilyn serve the best hamburgers in Redmond. Here everything is fresh and made to order. Breakfasts vary from pancakes and omelettes to corned beef hash and eggs. The homemade cinnamon rolls and muffins round out your breakfast selection perfectly. The lunch menu is extensive with lots of hamburger specials and sandwiches and the prices are reasonable.

Visit Bud's the Place in Redmond for fine food in a friendly and warm atmosphere. If you're in a hurry, the service is fast, but if you're not, gather 'round the "middle table" for some lively conversation while you enjoy some of the best food in town.

KIKUYA
8105 161st Avenue NE
Redmond, WA 98052
Tel. (206) 881-8771
Hrs: Lunch   Tue. - Fri.   11:00 a.m. - 2:00 p.m.
      Dinner   Tue. - Fri.   5:00 p.m. - 10:00 p.m.
                 Sat. - Sun.   4:30 p.m. - 9:30 p.m.
Closed Monday and major holidays.
Visa and MasterCard are accepted.

Horaki Ito and his wife Miyoko established Kikyua in 1981. Horaki has been cooking all his life and prepares some of the best Japanese food you'll ever eat. He was trained in Japan and first came to the United States when he was chef for the Japanese Ambassador to the United Nations. Although he returned to Japan, he liked the U.S. and eventually returned to cook in San Francisco and Portland before opening his fine restaurant in Redmond.

The lunch and dinner menus are extensive and the selection of sushi is good, with larger portions than are usually found in sushi restaurants. For the adventurous sushi novice, there is a sushi plate for variety. In addition to sushi there are seafood, beef and chicken selections, including many combinations. The Japanese and local beers, sake, and wines go well with the meals, and the prices are very reasonable.

Kikuya is a family restaurant and children are welcome. The goal here is to provide the best Japanese food possible in pleasant surroundings so you go home happy and satisfied, and they succeed admirably.

REVEL CAFE
2424 148th Avenue N.E.
Redmond, WA 98052
Tel. (206) 747-0452
Hrs: Mon.-Thur.   7:00 a.m. - 10:00 p.m.
      Friday   7:00 a.m. - Midnight
      Saturday   11:00 a.m. - Midnight
      Sunday   1:00 p.m. - 10:00 p.m.
Credit cards not accepted.

Are you looking for the finest frozen yogurt and espresso shop in the Overlake area? Do you enjoy sinfully delicious desserts? Do you want a lunch menu that offers healthy, nutritious food? All can be found at George Prudhon's Revel Cafe!

Originally opened a few years ago as "Desserts Are Us," the Revel Cafe has developed a unique expanded menu for you to savor. Enjoy fresh soups, salads, and bagel or whole-grained sandwiches. The sugarless desserts are truly wonderful. Select from cheesecakes, tortes, pies, carrot cake or chocolate decadence. You can order whole desserts two days in advance and receive a discount.

Honey Hill Farms' frozen yogurt is a special feature at Revel Cafe. There is a wide selection of flavors from which to choose, you can also select your own toppings of nuts, candies, coconut, granola, crushed cookies, and fresh fruits. Frozen yogurt tastes like premium ice cream, with a fraction of the calories or cholesterol.

Special coffees made with Starbuck's include espresso, cappucino, mocha, cafe almonde, and cafe latte. For the incomparable taste treat try steamed milk flavored with cherry, almondine, or raspberry. Bottled water, non-alcoholic beer, seltzer, and soft drinks are available.

When looking for that special place for lunch and/or dessert, with the finest coffee available, join the regulars at the Revel Cafe for a taste treat you'll never forget. The Revel Cafe is a light, bright, comfortable setting in which to enjoy the special items George has placed on his menu.

(See special invitation in Appendix.)

RUTH E'S
706 228th Avenue, N. E.
Redmond, WA 98053
Tel. (206) 868-4484
Hrs: Mon. - Fri.   8:00 a.m. - 8:00 p.m.
     Saturday   9:00 a.m. - 6:00 p.m.
     Sunday   9:00 a.m. - 5:00 p.m.

Would you believe that some of the finest chocolates and desserts in the Seattle area are prepared and/or served by a dental hygienist and a dentist! Ruth E's, owned and operated by Ruth Dingfield (hygienist) and her father, Oscar Schmuland (dentist), is a restaurant and confectionery shop that is a must on your list of things to experience in Western Washington. Be prepared for some unique and unusual foods, candies, bakery items, and services.

The chocolates are truly delectable custom creations that are hand-dipped, extremely rich, and contain no preservatives. They are prepared fresh by local chocolate designer Joanne Armstrong.

Oscar has developed quite a reputation for his excellence in baking. The popularity of his cookies prompted the packaging of a mix, "Oscar's Outstanding Cookie Mix", so you can bake them yourself at home. Oscar also has a special fruitcake that is worth trying.

The restaurant features only home-style cooking and includes a Continental breakfast, homemade soups and sandwiches, and fresh brewed Starbucks coffees. Ruth E's has also created the VCR (Very Complete and Reasonable) Dinner, a hot and delicious meal to enjoy at home. Each day there is a special entree including seafood fettucini, steamed halibut, etc. and, on Fridays the Frisbee Burger (1/2 pound of beef on a six-inch bun). Try the quarter-pounder, believe it or not, chocolate hamburger with fries! Everything on the restaurant menu is available for take out.

Ruth E's offers a unique service--"Breakfast in Bed", which is particularly popular on Mother's Day and Valentine's Day. Also, one Saturday night a month Ruth E's presents "Dinner at Eight"--candlelight, linen tablecloths, fine wines, crystal and china service, and gourmet cuisine for ten couples. Call for dates, menu, and entertainment. Reservations are required.

Last, but certainly not least, Ruth E's does custom catering for groups from two people to six hundred. If you're entertaining, bring in your serving pieces and desserts or hors d'oeuvres will be arranged on them for you.

Ruth and Oscar (and spouses) are truly creative individuals and enjoy bringing special services to their customers while providing outstanding foods and confections.

SABRINA'S BISTRO, 16150 Northeast Eighty-Fifth Street, Redmond, Washington. For a little bit of Europe, visit Sabrina's Bistro, featuring breakfast, lunch and dinner. There's delectable desserts, deli items to take out, and affordable catering.

Wine

FRENCH CREEK CELLARS
15372 NE 96th Place
Redmond, WA 98052
Tel. (206) 883-0757
Hrs: Thu. - Sat. 12:00 noon - 5:00 p.m.
Or by appointment.

In 1973, three families of wine enthusiasts began making varietal wines for fun. Their history and experience with wines, several grew up in wine regions of Europe, produced several excellent varieties. In 1983 some of their wines were made available with the French Creek Cellars label. French Creek Cellars is a small premium winery and its partners are intimately involved in the production of high quality varietal wine. They produce three red and five white varieties.

The fine wines of French Creek Cellars are available to sample in the tasting room. Informal tours are conducted during tasting room hours, and one of the principals of the winery is always available to answer your questions. Their 1985 Muscat Canelli is a particularly fine wine, a very fragrant and flowery dry cocktail wine that won a gold medal at the 1986 Northwest Enological Society competition. Also be sure to sample the reserve bottling 1985 chardonnay which is fermented in small French oak barrels for a unique flavor. In 1985 a new wine, Lemberger, was released. This is made from a noble, but extremely rare grape variety grown in a few isolated places in Europe, and now in Washington State.

When on a wine tasting trip, getting there is part of the fun. To reach French Creek Cellars, take exit 18 from I-405. Go east on highway 908, turn left onto Willows Road, then right on N.E. 95th St. Follow 95th through Willows Business Center, turn left on 153rd, N.E. and follow the sign to the winery in Building C, Suites 11 and 12. Now you're ready to taste, and enjoy the enthusiasm of the owners as they convey to you their satisfaction and enjoyment in creating fine wines.

Renton

Renton rises at the south end of Lake Washington, the industrial community born of King County's coal fields. It was in 1853, out at the end of what is now Williams Street that Dr. R. H. Bigelow discovered coal. William Renton, after whom the town is named, organized the mining company which was in operation by 1873. Foundries, kilns producing industrial clay pipe, and a host of other industrial operations followed. Pacific Foundry Company began building cars for logging railroads, and evolved into military vehicles and truck bodies as well as FMC rail car production.

Attractions

Lake Wilderness, ten miles southeast of Renton on Highway 169, is now a King County park utilizing a development created by private capital in 1950. The **Lake Wilderness Lodge**, which won several architectural awards is now a conference center for the University of Washington. The park was completed in 1973.

Downtown Renton has a **reminder of the past** on Wells Street between Second and Third streets, where the volunteer firemen presented a horse watering trough to the city in 1910. A bust of Chief Seattle was erected above drinking fountains for people who came with the horses.

King County

Renton Historical Museum, 235 Mills Avenue South, has an old fire engine, displays on early coal mining, and artifacts from logging conducted in Maple Valley and elsewhere. Open only on Tuesday and Sunday, from 2:00 p.m. to 4:30 p.m.

Happy Trails Horseback Riding Ranch, 10719 142nd Place Southeast provides a modern place for riders. There are lessons for beginners, day or overnight excursions for more experienced riders. Telephone 226-7848.

Longacres Race Track, on the outskirts of Renton just south of I-405, has an April through October season of thoroughbred horse racing. There are tours of the stables and practice areas by calling 226-3131. Race days are Wednesday through Sunday with post time at 4:30 p.m. on week days and 1:00 p.m. Saturday and Sunday.

For information, contact the **Renton Chamber of Commerce,** 300 Rainier Avenue North, Renton WA 98055. Telephone 226-4560.

Antiques

ST. CHARLES PLACE ANTIQUES & RESTORATION
230 Wells Avenue South
Renton, WA 98055
Tel. (206) 226-8427
Hrs: Mon. - Sat.   9:30 a.m. - 6:00 p.m.
          Sunday by appointment.

If you like to spend hours browsing through an incredible number and variety of antiques; then this is a place you must visit. You'll feel like a kid in a candy store. There are three floors with 12,000 square feet, packed with antiques.
Owner, Charles Divelbiss said he has the widest variety of quality antiques in King County. He travels to Europe three times a year to find and bring back the finest 18th and 19th century French, English and Austrian pieces.
All you have to do is bring in a drawing or a picture of the desired piece and he'll find it for you, at a reasonable price. "Service is our Hallmark," he said. Charles opened St. Charles Place in 1971 and knows antiques. He's always willing and able to answer your questions and help in your search.
The store offers full-service restoration and appraisals. The staff can do everything from furniture stripping and refinishing, repairing porcelain and

glass, rewiring, brass polishing, clock repairing, reupholstering, duplication of antique hardware, and leather retooling.

It's a great place to find a gift for the person who has everything. There is even a "Bargain Basement" for that find of a lifetime.

Anything purchased can be returned, in good condition, for credit on a more appropriate piece if your taste changes, or if you move to another place and the piece doesn't fit the decor. Charles will also exchange, trade, or buy antiques. Some pieces are taken on consignment. Shipping arrangements can be made for your purchase.

Delicatessen

RENTON CENTER SEAFOODS
458 Hardie Avenue, SW Renton Center
Renton, WA 98055
Tel. (206) 228-0971
Hrs: Sat. - Sun. 10:00 a.m. - 6:00 p.m.
and
MARKET PLACE DELI
Tel. (206) 226-4780

Owners Don and Marlene Kean have been gratifying the local tastebuds for the last ten years. Marlene manages the deli and Don supervises the only fish market in Renton.

The seafood center carries fresh fish caught in local waters and those brought in from the Alaskan waterways. The house special is a mouth-watering bite of custom smoked salmon. For the gourmet in your life...he will ship this smoked salmon anywhere in the United States.

The wine cellar carries a large stock of all varieties. Marlene said, "If there's a bottle you've looked for an can't find, you're most likely to find it here."

The Market Place Deli has incredible homemade soups: cream of broccoli, seafood chowder, cheddar cheese and chicken noodle. There are scrumptious salads, old fashioned cookies, rolls and pies. Walking in the door to the Deli you wonder why Marlene doesn't tack on an extra charge just for the good aromas.

Restaurant

ANDY'S TUKWILA STATION, 2408 West Valley Road, Renton, WA. Steak, seafood, sandwiches served in an authentic 1930s railroad car.

DIAMOND LIL'S
321 Rainier Avenue, South
Renton, WA 98057
Tel. (206) 226-2763
Hrs: Mon. - Sun. 9:00 a.m. - 2:00 a.m.

Diamond Lil's caters to the finer dining atmosphere. Specializing in seafood: the jumbo prawns are stir-sauteed with green peppers, onions, mushrooms, and tomatoes...plus a liberal dollop of white wine, or, try the scallops, shrimp or seafood medley.

For dessert try the Texas Hold'em, or low ball draw and high stud poker. Yes...besides food they serve the biggest, little card room in this state. For your pin-money there are limited games with five and ten dollar stakes. Unbeatable -- dinner and entertainment.

LER MONDS OF RENTON
111 Airport Way
Renton, WA 98055
Tel. (206) 255-2221
Hrs: Mon. - Thur. 5:00 a.m. - 9:00 p.m.
     Friday   5:00 a.m. - 10:00 p.m.
     Saturday   5:30 a.m. - 10:00 p.m.
     Sunday   6:00 a.m. - 10:00 p.m.

The 4th of July, bubble gum, a teddy bear with one eye = Ler Mond's of Renton. Tradition, value and warm memories. When you leave Ler Mond's, you do so with the desire to come back often.

If you're looking for brass rails, fancy lights and waitresses with painted smiles; you'll have to go elsewhere. Ler Mond's is old-fashioned American cooking--the way grandma used to do it. Portions large enough to satisfy your appetite without your wallet feeling starved.

The sign out front reads, "We're good food--fast food is up the street." Owner Dick Ler Mond, and his wife Faye, are at the restaurant daily and have been serving great meals for the last eleven years. Dick turned a hobby into a avocation when he opened this restaurant.

The house special is Yankee pot roast; slow cooked, basted with beer, special seasonings, side-dressed with potatoes and vegetables. (Dick says to assure you the potatoes come from the ground, not a freezer!) Add a slice of fresh baked bread, some fresh ground coffee and a piece of strawberry shortcake with ice cream and topped with real whipped cream...m-m-mmmm Heaven.

There's a house special everyday: chicken and dumplings, Swiss steak or sauteed halibut to name a few. Ler Monds is old fashioned and proud of it.

RIFFLESTEINS
317 Main Street
Renton, WA 98055
Tel. (206) 226-6663
Hrs: Mon. - Sun. 10:00 a.m. - 2:00 a.m.

At Rifflesteins it's all play. Newly renovated by the owners, Fred Steiner, Keith Quale and Herb Frei, into a 1890's saloon theme with red plush, brass rails, ferns and an array of old-time photos of Renton.

There's a newly built card room catering to the younger players; games are kept to a low limit. This is where you can sit down with twenty dollars and play for hours. Rifflestein's also offers poker lessons to teach the art of play.

There are two pool tables and four pull-tabs and all the liquor and great food you can handle.

Seattle

Set between the waters of Puget Sound on the west and Lake Washington on the east, Seattle is a city which grew late, and then flowered quickly as the Pacific Northwest's industrial giant, dominant urban center, and cultural gem. Temperatures are mild. Snow is so rare than when it occurs traffic on the many hills of the city slides almost to a halt until ice melts away. Rain is so frequent that most visitor guides carry special indoor attractions to take care of those who don't follow the local lead and put up an umbrella or pull on a slicker for an outing. Like most of the northwest coast, Seattle in fact has long periods of sunshine, a boon to its residents who take to the water in small craft by the thousands.

The first settlers did not land here until 1851. For years it was one of many small logging and mill towns on a timber-fringed Puget Sound. Alaskan gold rush commerce before the turn of the century brought the area's first boom, which was hardly over before industrial demands of World War I moved this place beyond the time when people thought of lumber and logs skidded down a road to waterfront mills. It was aviation and the Boeing Company which brought Seattle to full flower. From those interested in aircraft design gathered in a barn on the Duwamish River by William E. Boeing in 1915 sprang the state's largest employer with factories in several locations. Boat shops, military space contracts, and now development of a new turbo-prop 150-passenger aircraft which will replace medium range jets are part of Boeing's evolution.

Seattle is cosmopolitan. Live music and drama can be found every night of the week. Big band music plays in historic dance halls, strains of the classics come from remodeled churches and the modern Seattle Center stages, while jazz and rock vibrate in busy nightclubs. The nation's third largest Asian population creates a colorful International District which includes a Japanese supermarket. Three major-league professional sports teams, the football Seahawks, basketball Supersonics, and baseball Mariners, make their home in the indoor Kingdome which rises above the city's King Street railroad station at the edge of old town.

Seeing Seattle is a matter of picking from its neighborhoods, which now reach beyond the original seven hills to include communities once part of the suburbs. Seattle is now hemmed in on all sides by other municipalities. Unless it grows upward, the county seat of King County is mature at half-a-million residents and will probably never become more populous. Here is a brief look at those neighborhoods.

Alki and West Seattle

Alki, the peninsula of West Seattle which is formed by the Duwamish River's channel, is where it began. "Come as soon as you can, we have found a valley that will support a thousand families," Arthur A. Denny declared in an 1851 letter to his brother's party waiting in Portland.

The movers-and-shakers would leave Alki within the year for a better sawmill and harbor location. They left behind one of many Seattle suburbs slow to mature. West Seattle incorporated in 1902 and annexed to Seattle in 1907. An electric railroad connected the communities and until a fire in 1931, brought passengers to a large amusement park on Duwamish Head. West Seattle Freeway carries cars over the river now to reach the original settlement.

Attractions

The **Denny family monument** is on Alki Avenue at 63rd Street. A lighthouse was built on the western tip of the point in 1916. The city's **Alki Beach Park** sweeps northeast from the point around Duwamish Head where there is a public boat-launching ramp.

Alki Point Lighthouse, 3201 Alki Avenue Southwest, has open house every Saturday, Sunday and holiday from 1:00 p.m. to 4:00 p.m. The duty lighthouse keeper for the Coast Guard will describe the equipment and working schedules.

Bernard House, a private residence at 2717 61st Street, is a landmark built in 1903 of logs taken from Alki Beach. This was once part of an estate which extended more than a block south away from the water. The former stables at 6301 Southwest Stevens Street have been remodeled into a residence.

Lincoln Park, on Fauntleroy Way south of the point, is an old city recreation area set aside to preserve a natural area. When the Denny's arrived much of the peninsula had been burned by a forest fire which made land clearing easier for people bent on farming. Timber remained in the Lincoln Park area.

Boeing Field, on East Marginal Way, became a prime aircraft manufacturing site. The **Museum of Flight**, 9404 East Marginal Way South, is a 142,816 square foot building on the location of the first powered flight in the region in 1910. Early biplanes and a replica of the Mercury space capsule share display space. Next to the museum is a restoration of the "red barn" in which Boeing's first assembly line operated. Telephone 767-7373 for museum hours.

Downtown Seattle

Pioneer Square, Second Avenue at King and Jackson Streets, is focal point of the original municipal plat. It was here that the entrepreneurs of Alki came to start Henry Yesler's sawmill in 1853. Within thirty-five years about 12,000 people lived in the community which reached little more than ten blocks in each direction off of Yesler Way.

The businesses moved north after the Alaska gold rush boom which ran about eight year starting in 1897. Now the historic district is a tourist attraction with its old buildings, the commercial center towering above it with skyscrapers and the redevelopment area to the south anchored by Kingdome and King Street Station.

Attractions

This is a city of art galleries, both downtown and in many other locations. Seattle/King County visitor information services publish a seasonal listing of "events" which lists current displays at all of the popular **galleries and museums**, plus many concerts, sports and special events. Call 447-4240 or visit an information center for your copy.

Volunteer Park, 15th Avenue at Prospect Street, includes **Seattle Art Museum** and the city's **plant conservatory** with five greenhouses filled with collections from palm trees to seasonal flowers. Open daily in the summer from 10:00 a.m. to 7:00 p.m. and until 4:00 p.m. for the rest of the year.

Pioneer Square is a triangle where the original Denny plat came together with the Maynard development. On the square in 1909 was built a cast-iron and glass shelter for people waiting the catch the trolley. Restored in 1970, **the pergola** is at the center of an area of buildings which are an easy walking tour of what was built after a fire. Construction around the square dates from 1890, although two structures at 208 First Avenue and 91 South Main, were completed in 1889.

Seattle's first house was at Second and Cherry Street, where the **Hoge Building** was built in 1911 as the commercial district moved north. Terra cotta and brick give relief to the exterior design. The original log cabin is a footnote in history books.

Antique street cars first put into service in 1927, have been rescued from their second duty station in Melbourne, Australia and returned to the Seattle tracks. They rattle along the waterfront next to Elliott Bay. The car barn is across from Pier 70, and the trolleys run south from there daily between 6:00 a.m. and 6:00 p.m.

King Street Station, a 1906 terminal for the Great Northern Railroad, stands on Third Avenue. The **Union Station** of the Northern Pacific, Milwaukee Road and Union Pacific was a 1911 project. To the south at the time were tideflats, and trains approached on trestles. Today Amtrak rolls into King Street Station, and on days of sports events fans walk to the **Kingdome** constructed by the county in 1976 as part of a redevelopment project.

On the waterfront south of Kingdome is the **U.S. Coast Guard Museum**, 1519 Alaskan Way South. Exhibits from the Alaska and Pacific Northwest duty stations of the Coast Guard are on display every weekday afternoon except

Thursday, from 1:00 p.m. to 5:00 p.m. Beyond the museum on Pier 36 are berths for two icebreakers and several other cutters. Visitors are welcome each Saturday and Sunday afternoon aboard which ever vessels are in port.

Pier 57 downtown is home port for **Grayline Sightseeing**, with daily water cruises at 12:00 noon and 3:00 p.m. that include the waterfront, Lake Washington ship canal and Elliott Bay. At the foot of University Street. Telephone 441-1887.

At **Pier 54**, home of the famed Ivar's Restaurant, the sternwheeler Emerald Princess sails from May through October making one hour water tours of Elliott Bay each day. Near the Aquarium and Waterfront Park. Telephone 783-8873.

The **Seattle Aquarium**, between Pike and Union streets on the bay, replicates the underwater life of the sound. Seals and otters cavort, there's a tidepool where visitors can handle some of the creatures. Open daily. Summer hours 10:00 a.m. to 7:00 p.m., winters from 10:00 a.m. to 5:00 p.m. Telephone 625-4357.

Museum of Sea and Ships is on Pier 59, located between Pike and Union streets. Open daily. Summer hours are 9:00 a.m. to 7:00 p.m., in the winter 10:00 a.m. to 5:00 p.m. Telephone 628-0860.

Merchants gather fish, vegetables, flowers and works of local artists at the venerable **Pike Place Market**, on First Avenue at Pike Street. Restaurants and street musicians make this a festive place. Started in 1907 on a small scale, this public market is now a series of buildings climbing up a hillside above the waterfront. Open Monday through Saturday from 9:00 a.m. to 6:00 p.m. There are guided tours from May through October which leave at 10:00 a.m., 11:00 a.m., and 1:00 p.m. from the market information booth. Telephone 587-0351 for market information.

Downtown is linked by **monorail** to Seattle Center on Fifth Avenue, site of the 1962 World's Fair and the landmark **Spaceneedle** with its celebrated restaurant. This is home of **Pacific Science Center** with several buildings of exhibits, the city's **Opera House, Bagley Wright Theater**, and **Seattle Museum of Modern Art**. Those who know say up to six hours is needed to "do" the center. Call 625-4234 for general information, 443-2001 for the Science Center.

First Hill, the neighborhood rising above downtown, was once the home of the rich who lived above Yesler Way's steep grade. Now I-5 separates the area from downtown, leaving a group of houses from the early 1900s and modern hospitals, mixed with large churches. **Seattle Buddhist Church**, 1427 South Main Street, was built in 1914.

Lake Union and the Canal

Seattle has not lacked for engineers with vision. One of the earliest major projects was Denny Regrade near Seattle Center in which a hill too steep for development was washed flat into Elliott Bay by the hydraulic techniques of gold miners. In 1916 the Lake Washington Ship Canal was completed. Locks and fish ladders built at Ballard on what was known as Salmon Bay were key to the project. Water levels on Lake Washington were dropped eight feet to match the canal and lock system. Lake Union became a port for ocean-going vessels. Towns on Lake Washington had residents talking of industry tied to water-born freight. Suburbs such as Ballard, which had 18,000 residents and a Scandinavian flavor, came into Seattle in this era. The city's population more than doubled in the first decade of the new century.

Attractions

Hiram M. Chittenden Locks, on Northwest 54th Street, are busy almost constantly moving the parade of working vessels and pleasure boats between fresh and salt water.

It is at the **fish ladder** that sea lions gather to eat salmon and steelhead migrating inland. Herschel the sea lion, who defied game wardens for two seasons, earned national press for the locks in the late 1980s. A visitor's center and ornamental garden are next to the locks. Open daily, 7:00 a.m. to 9:00 p.m. From the city, drive over Ballard Bridge, turn left on Market Street then south on 54th. Call 783-7059.

Ray's Boathouse, on Seaview Avenue off Market Street, is headquarters for charter fishing and tour boats. Regular water tours leave at 6:00 a.m. daily in the summer, 7:00 a.m. in the winter. Call 783-8873 for information and reservations.

The **Nordic Heritage Museum**, 3014 Northwest 67th Street, tells the stories of Scandinavian settlers who came to the Ballard district along the canal and to other parts of the Pacific Northwest. Open Tuesday through

Thursday from 11:00 a.m. to 3:00 p.m.; Saturday and Sunday from 1:00 p.m. through 5:00 p.m. Telephone 789-5707.

Over 34,000 full and part time students flock to classes on the **University of Washington** campus, located between Northeast 45th Street and the canal to the south. Buildings reflect work since 1895 when the University was moved here from a hill overlooking downtown. Most construction dates after the 1909 Alaska-Yukon-Pacific Exposition which used much of the present campus. Denny Hall, the oldest building, was joined by two dormitories in 1896, all grouped around the old Seattle-Snohomish Road.

The **Campus Visitor Information Center**, 4014 University Way Northeast, is open Monday through Friday from 8:00 a.m. to 5:00 p.m. with maps of the campus, its art galleries and museums.

The oldest museum of Washington history and natural resources, the **Thomas Burke Memorial**, is on the campus of the university. Started in 1885, its collections are extensive. Open Tuesday through Friday from 11:00 a.m. to 5:30 p.m. and Saturday and Sunday from 9:00 a.m. to 4:30 p.m.

Trees and their management are a big part of the University of Washington forestry program. At the **Washington Park Arboretum**, Lake Washington Boulevard at East Madison, over 5,000 varieties of trees, shrubs and plants are on display for botanical research. A Japanese garden is included. Open daily 8:00 a.m. to sunset. Tours are available by calling 625-2635.

Woodland Park and **Green Lake**, north of the University District on Phinney Avenue at the West 50th street exit of I-5, include a world-class zoo. Exotic animals live in replications of native habitat. Open daily at 8:30 a.m. The closing hour is 6:00 p.m. from April through September; 5:00 p.m. in October and March; and 4:00 p.m. from November through February. Telephone 789-7919. Green Lake is a water recreation site surrounded by city. Speedy hydroplanes use the lake for weekend races in the summer.

For further information, **Visitor Information Centers** are located on the lower concourse at SeaTac Airport, and at 666 Steward in downtown Seattle. Write or call **Seattle/King County Convention and Visitors Bureau**, 1815 Seventh Avenue, Seattle WA 98101. Telephone (206) 447-7276.

Accommodations

APPLE INN
20651 Military Road S
Seattle, WA 98198
Tel. (206) 824-9902
All major credit cards are accepted.

Whether you're driving or flying into Seattle, you'll find the Apple Inn very convenient. Only five minutes from Sea-Tac airport and right on the freeway, the Apple Inn provides free airport pickup and delivery. But apart from the convenience, this inn has a lot more going for it.

Since its opening in 1983, the Apple Inn has been serving the Sea-Tac area traveler in a fashion that can't be matched elsewhere. Their slogan, "comfort and service at a very low price," is something that attracts many people to this delightful inn. All the rooms, recently remodeled, are designed with comfort in mind and each has a telephone and television. If you're looking for a place to host a special occasion, look no further, because the Apple Inn has space available for parties, banquets and business meeting.

This hotel, being mid way between Seattle and Tacoma, is the perfect place to relax away from it all, yet be in touch with everything both cities have to offer. Now doesn't this sound like the ideal spot to lodge? The Apple Inn, offering convenience and solace, is an accommodation that has been pleasing travelers for years. Let it please you too.

BEST WESTERN EXECUTIVE INN
200 Taylor Avenue N
Seattle, WA 98109
Tel. (206) 488-9444

Comfort and convenience are highlighted in this luxurious hotel. Just one block from Seattle's Space Needle, a warmly colored, cheerful foyer greets guests as they enter this conveniently located hotel. Rooms are spacious and comfortable with mini-suites featuring couches, wet bars, refrigerators, and whirlpool baths.

Additional amenities available for the guests' convenience include covered parking and complimentary limo service provided to downtown Seattle. A gift shop and both men's and women's hair service is available.

Live entertainment is featured in the Acorn Lounge and the Oak Tree dining room offers excellent cuisine. Centrally located, the Executive Inn is a city within a city, ready to serve.

King County

THE BEECH TREE MANOR
1405 Queen Anne Avenue North
Seattle, WA 98109
Tel. (206)281-7037
Open Year Round

A massive copper beech tree greets guests of Virginia Lucero's bed and breakfast inn, reminiscent of an English country home. Choose from four comfortable and tastefully-furnished bedrooms with two baths. Blue pastels create a constant spring-like atmosphere, and art collectors will appreciate Virginia's original artwork adorning the halls. Beech Tree Manor, conveniently located near Seattle Center, offers guests a remarkably peaceful atmosphere. The handsome parlor features a comfy fireplace and several relaxing easy chairs.

Virginia is a "hands-on" hostess. She personally oversees everything for her guests' comfort from freshly-ironed linens to generous breakfasts of just-baked cinnamon rolls or scones. A special touch here is the complimentary sherry served in the evenings amid the glow of a hearty fire burning in the hearth. You can catch a Metro to downtown Seattle right in front of the manor. A variety of restaurants and shopping areas are within walking distance.

For relaxed, comfortable lodging and personable hospitality, visit the Beech Tree Manor.

CAMLIN HOTEL
1619 9th Avenue
Seattle, WA 98101
Tel. (206) 682-0100

This well known Seattle hotel has recently been renovated from the ground up and is now known as "The New Camlin Hotel." It is located near downtown Seattle and is convenient to business and shopping.

Rooms feature warm tones and charming furnishings. Baths are tiled in European fashion and closets are roomy. Suites are available and are actually complete apartments, with private dining rooms. A heated pool with a spacious deck is available for guests in the summer. The Cloud Room and Lounge offers delicious cuisine that can be savored while enjoying a sweeping view of Seattle.

This charmingly renovated landmark has kept its character and is a delightful place to stay during your visit to Seattle.

King County

FOUR SEASONS OLYMPIC
411 University Street
Seattle, WA 98101
Tel. (206) 621-1700
All major credit cards are accepted.

Four Seasons Olympic Hotel was restored with one purpose in mind; to create a grand hotel that adapts itself to your lifestyle. That means you don't have to worry about acclimating yourself to a new environment, because it's already done for you. There, anticipating your needs, your normal routine is never compromised. This grand idea provides a strong foundation for a grand hotel.

At Four Seasons Olympic Hotel you can begin your day with a refreshing 6:00 a.m. dip in the spacious swimming pool. Go ahead, get a good swim, a full workout and sauna, then partake of a leisurely breakfast. At day's end, when you've completed the business at hand, relax with a massage, ease into the whirlpool or recline on the private sun deck. You can also experience the personal concern shown by everyone of the hotel's 450 staff members. For example, take the chef de cuisine, he understands your tastes and your inhibitions about indulging. With this in mind, he creates a unique cuisine featuring the area's famous fresh fish specialties. The end result, gourmet food without gourmet calories.

Most other fine hotels would consider a full health spa and special menu not necessary luxuries, to Four Seasons Olympic Hotel, it's only a small part of the grand idea. The idea based on a simple philosophy of adapting to you and your needs. Not the other way around. For business or pleasure, make your reservations today, and see how easy it is to enjoy gracious accommodations.

THE HILTON SEA-TAC
17620 Pacific Highway S
Seattle, WA 98188
Tel. (206) 244-4800

For the weary traveler "Best Choices" presents The Hilton at Sea-Tac. In the tradition of Hiltons this is a quality establishment designed to cater to the needs of the discriminating traveler.

The hotel complex is centered around a beautifully lush courtyard in the center of which is a heated swimming pool and jacuzzi. The attractively furnished rooms, the largest of any at the Sea-Tac airport, all have private patios many of which open into the courtyard. Once checked in, there is no need to travel anywhere else for services. On the premises is the award winning restaurant, Buckwell's. Evening dining in the quiet surroundings allows a fine selection of seafood such as fresh salmon and scampi. There are also several veal and steak entrees. For lunch, The Hilton offers the only soup and salad bar in the Sea-Tac area. Sunday is buffet style with a wonderful selection of entrees and desserts.

Business or vacation traveler, you will find The Hilton a first class stop on your itinerary. Maybe it's time now for you to stop into their lounge and relax.

HYATT SEATTLE
17001 Pacific Highway South
Seattle, WA 98188
Tel. (206) 244-6000
(800) 228-9000

There is always something going on at the Hyatt Seattle. A hotel of distinction, guests can revel in the comfort of their comfortable rooms or engage in one of the many activities or services offered to customers.

Besides 305 spacious guest rooms and suites plus a variety of meeting and banquet facilities, the Hyatt offers an Olympic size heated pool, sauna, massage services, women's boutique and salon and a gift shop. For those who seek the exclusive in accommodations, there is the Regency Club, a privately secured area of the hotel that offers guests the additional amenities of a private lounge, cocktail hour, guest robes in each room and a complimentary Continental breakfast. Choose from two fine restaurants in house, the Market Place and Hugo's Restaurant. Hugo's is the formal dining area with a menu of first class full course meals. The Market Place is a bit more casual and is arranged around a lovely garden setting. At least once each month the Hyatt hosts a planned event open to guests and the public as well. For example, recently chefs from around the states gathered for a feast of America best cooking. Once a year the Hyatt boasts "The World's Largest Office Party".

Convenient to air travelers and freeways , it makes sense to stop at the Hyatt in Seattle.

MAYFLOWER PARK HOTEL
405 Olive Way
Seattle, WA 98101
Tel. (206) 623-8700

The Mayflower Park Hotel, a Seattle landmark, will soon celebrate its sixtieth year as a warm and gracious hotel. The hotel's size, under 200 rooms, brings to mind the quality European hotels where personal and individual service is the order of the day. From the moment guests are greeted in the inviting lobby that's decorated in soft green pastels, until they are bid farewell at the end of their stay, the efficient staff does everything in its power to make their visit pleasant and memorable.

The hotel has been thoroughly remodeled and offers air conditioned rooms with sound insulated windows. There are meetings rooms available for seminars, weddings and banquets. Lunch and cocktails are available in the delightful Oliver's Lounge which overlooks both Fourth and Olive Streets. The main restaurant is Clippers which offers excellent Northwest cuisine and is open for breakfast, lunch and dinner. The restaurant renovation took first place honors in the 1983 Designer's Circle Awards and is a beautiful place to dine.

The Mayflower Park Hotel is conveniently located in the heart of Seattle, only a five minute walk from Pike Place Market and one block to catch the monorail to the Space Needle and Seattle Center. With it's old world charm and courtesy, it is a very special and enjoyable place to stay.

MEANY TOWER HOTEL
4507 Brooklyn Ave., N.E.
Seattle WA 98105
Tel. (206) 634-2000

The Meany Tower Hotel is a multi sided architectural masterpiece with central core construction that rises 15 stories. When it opened in 1931, its claim was "Every room has a corner view." This feature is even more appreciated today. A total renovation in which it was completely remodeled has made it virtually a new hotel.

The hotel offers 155 guest rooms and 8 banquet rooms. General Manager Jim Veenhuizen is a cordial host and takes pride in showing off the outstanding interior design with its warm peach pastels complemented by tasteful art. The lower level has a spacious lounge and dining room done in soft greens with contrasting peach and brass. American cuisine is served from 6:00 a.m. to 10:00 p.m. daily. Guest rooms are spacious, decorated in warm pastels with expensive furnishings, including 25 inch television sets enclosed in cabinets. Double thermal windows eliminate exterior noise and a quiet heat pump system insures year round comfort.

Located in the heart of the University District, the Meany Tower Hotel is within walking distance of the University of Washington campus and shopping. It has received the AAA four diamond award, a tribute to the quality of services and accommodations offered here.

King County

NENDELS SEA/TAC
16838 Pacific Highway South
Seattle, WA 98188
Tel. (206) 248-0901

There is a very homey atmosphere at this Nendels and you will feel welcome from the moment you enter the large attractive foyer. You will be greeted by one of the friendly, helpful staff members and know you are in good hands. Many of the guests have been coming here for years because they know they can expect consistently good service and comfortable accommodations.

All of Nendel's 151 rooms offer comfortable queen beds and free first run, in-room movies. There are non-smoking rooms available, balcony rooms and rooms for the handicapped. Two meeting rooms are available, the largest holds a maximum of forty people. A complimentary continental breakfast is offered every morning.

Nendels provides transportation to nearby restaurants and lounges on a twenty-four hour basis, as well as twenty-four hour shuttle service to Sea-Tac Airport. You won't be disappointed in your stay at Nendels, they live up to their motto, "The best value and warmest welcome."

PACIFIC PLAZA HOTEL
4th Avenue at Spring Street
Seattle, WA 98104
Tel. (206) 623-3900
  (800) 732-1235 CA
  (800) 426-1165 USA

A jewel of an inexpensive hotel, Pacific Plaza is located in midtown Seattle. This intimate and lovely European style inn conveys a warm ambiance with an abundance of wood, warm, cinnamon colored rugs, accents of brass and marble and porcelain trimming.

The rooms are attractively appointed and spacious. Two restaurants, the Red Robin and City Picnics serve delicious meals at moderate prices. Continental breakfast is served in a restful common room.

This wonderful hotel is conveniently located within walking distance of shopping and the waterfront. Be sure to stay in this "Best Choice" accommodation while in Seattle.

King County

THE RED LION INN
18740 Pacific Highway S
Seattle, WA 98188
Tel. (206) 246-8600
All major credit cards are accepted.

Are you going to be flying into Sea-Tac airport anytime in the near future? If you are, you're probably going to be looking for accommodations in the local area. Well, there's no more need to search for that facility that can handle your specific needs, because The Red Lion Inn, offering full airport service and recognized as the leader in western hospitality, is the destination that can satisfy all of your needs.

This hotel has been a part of the Sea-Tac area since the airport's beginning days. So you can rest assured that they have plenty of experience dealing with travelers and their desires. They welcome with wide arms the individual, as well as the large group, knowing both will be satisfied with their stay. How can they be so confident? Well, just one look at the hotel and that question will be answered. A gracious and contemporary ambiance is blended with a spacious lobby and handsomely appointed rooms and suites to create the perfect atmosphere for any occasion. For special services, all one has to do is ask.

For dining, you can take in a terrific airport view while eating in the hotel's restaurant, which also features a comfortable, quiet lounge. They say that experience molds perfection. In the case of The Red Lion Inn, this saying has proven to be correct. The next time you fly into Sea-Tac airport, be sure to have reservations at The Red Lion Inn. You're anticipation will only be a glimmer of what awaits you.

RESIDENCE INN - SEATTLE SOUTH
16301 West Valley Highway
P. O. Box 88904
Seattle, WA 98188
Tel. (206) 226-5500
and,
14455 29th Place Northeast
Bellevue, WA 98007
Tel. (206) 882-1222

A home away from home...certainly describes this beautiful, new, all-suites hotel. The friendliness and helpfulness of the staff, combined with the comfortable, spacious rooms makes your stay here a "Best Choice" experience.

There are charming one and two bedroom suites, complete with a full kitchen; featuring a refrigerator that has an ice maker, a coffee server, fireplace, television, capacious living room, a comfortable bed and a well-lit bathroom.

Manager Denise Swarat trains her staff to deliver personal service-- the hallmark of the Residence Inn. You can even drop off your grocery list at the desk in the morning and someone will do your shopping for you!!! at no extra charge!!!

A complimentary Continental breakfast is served in the main lobby, where there is a large double-faced fireplace and plenty of tables and chairs; making it conducive to congenial conversation. At night, join the others for complimentary evening snacks. Sit by the fireplace and read the paper, books or magazines that are provided. The coffee pot is always on. Every effort is made to make you feel right at home.

Once a month there is a "Get to know your neighbor party." Invitations are placed in all the rooms and everyone is invited. At holiday times there are special theme parties, and on Monday nights, during the football season, fanatics can meet over snacks and watch the games in the lobby.

There are three conference-meeting rooms, a swimming pool, three jacuzzis, a sports court for volleyball, basketball and pickle ball, a coin-operated laundry, laundry and dry cleaning services and complimentary shuttle service to and from the airport. The Residence Inn is five minutes from SeaTac Airport, fifteen minutes to downtown Seattle, across the street from Longacres Racetrack and just a few minutes from Southcenter for shopping.

SEATTLE MARRIOTT HOTEL
3201 S 176th Street
Seattle, WA 98188
Tel. (206) 241-2000

The Seattle Marriott is an airport hotel, but its formidable award-winning atrium gives it a resort quality. A huge multi-angled swimming pool fills the center of this indoor, a half acre atrium and is surrounded by a variety of lush Northwest flora, Indian art and flowing water. It is a lovely and inviting setting which welcomes the visitor.

Each of the hotel's 462 guest rooms is smartly furnished and provides quality guest amenities. The Yukon Landing is the hotel's restaurant and it manages the transition from a coffee shop by day to a fine dining room by evening gracefully and competently. The hotel's chef has been with the Marriott corporation for over fifteen years and brings a wealth of experience to the cuisine offered nightly. Each night there are several choices of fish fresh from the Pike Fish Market. There is also light dining daily in the lovely atrium setting with a lavish all you can eat buffet.

The Seattle Marriott offers impressive accommodations and quality, caring service. The Corporation's motto is "Marriott People Know How," and they certainly do.

SORRENTO HOTEL
900 Madison Street
Seattle, WA 98104
Tel. (206) 622-6400

The Sorrento Hotel was opened for the Yukon Pacific Exposition in 1909 and has aged most admirably. It was completely remodeled in 1981 and is an excellent example of renaissance architecture. It features a large courtyard leading into a richly hued lobby with a huge fireplace. Honduras mahogany surrounds the lobby which doubles as a cozy lounge.

There are 76 rooms with two penthouse suites. There were originally 150 rooms, so the restoration created very spacious and comfortable suites which are decorated in soft tones. The elegant Hunt Club Restaurant was renovated in shades of wild rose combined with the original dark mahogany paneling. Tempting menu items include warm quail salad, smoked duck with mango, sauteed halibut with crayfish and prime aged sirloin, among others.

The Sorrento conveys an old world charm with its Italian character. It is located four blocks east of the downtown Seattle business district, and is a lovely place to stay, or just to have "high tea" in the lounge to escape the ordinary.

STOUFFER MADISON HOTEL
515 Madison Street
Seattle, WA 98104
Tel. (206)583-0300

The Stouffer Madison Hotel is located at Sixth and Madison in heart of Seattle's financial district. Catering to the business traveler, the hotel's facilities include The Madison Club, two "concierge floors" offering an added dimension of service.

Guest begin their day at the Stouffer Madison with a cup of coffee and morning newspaper delivered with their wakeup call. Fine dining is at hand at Prego, the hotel's prestigious rooftop restaurant. For more casual fare, visit Maxwell's a cozy American style cafe located on the second floor. Exercise facilities including health club and spa are capped off by a twenty-seventh floor swimming pool that offers a panoramic view of the Seattle harbor and

Olympic Mountains. The hotel has several meeting and conference rooms and a ballroom that will accommodate up to 600 people.

Easy freeway access, friendly service, underground parking and complimentary in-town transportation all add to the convenience and comfort of the Stouffer Madison.

VANCE HOTEL
620 Stewart Street
Seattle, WA 98101
Tel. (206) 426-0670
     (800) 426-0670

Located in the heart of downtown Seattle, The Vance Hotel is operated in the heritage of old European hotels.

There, hospitality is everything. From room service to free covered parking, they cater to the frequent traveler. Recently, they added a rather unusual option to their rooms, breakfast or dinner at the Gas Lamp Restaurant. For just a few dollars more, you can reserve a room with a full country style breakfast. Or, for a few dollars more than bed and breakfast, they will give a room and a full course dinner.

Plus, their Sixth and Stewart places them in the midst of Seattle's best banks, retail stores, recreation and restaurants. Prices, double or single occupancy, start at $49 (at the time of this publication.)

WEST COAST SEA TAC HOTEL
Formerly Vance Airport Inn
18220 Pacific Highway South
Seattle, WA 98188
Tel. (206) 246-5535
     (800) 426-0670

The newly renovated West Coast Sea-Tac Hotel is directly across from Seattle-Tacoma International Airport. Courtesy limousine service twenty-four hours to and from the airport is provided. The hotel also offers free covered parking to its guests.

The sleeping rooms are spacious with queen or king size beds and panoramic bay windows. The Executive fifth floor rooms all have king beds, mini bars, robes, shoeshine machines and hair dryers for the person who likes to travel in luxury. There is an outdoor heated swimming pool, as well as a year round jacuzzi and sauna.

Gregory's Bar and Grill serves a wide variety of meat and seafood entrees. The food is expertly prepared and professionally served in a congenial and warm atmosphere. Live entertainment is featured Tuesday through Saturday nights in Gregory's Lounge. There are meeting and banquet facilities available for groups up to 200.

The West Coast Sea Tac Hotel's convenient location combined with its first class facilities, reasonable rates, and courteous staff make it the right choice for travelers on business or pleasure.

Antiques

ANTIQUE BROKERS INTERNATIONAL
2613 California Southwest
Seattle, WA 98116
Tel.   (206) 938 -5322
Hrs: Tue. - Sat.   12:00 noon - 7:00 p.m.
Visa and MasterCard are accepted.

Steve Lapham, owner of Antique Brokers International, is a consignment specialist, and welcomes good condition quality furniture and collectibles. Steve knows how to help you price your merchandise, and displays it in a way which is eye-pleasing.

In addition to taking consignment merchandise, Steve combs the nation and the world for fine antiques and collectibles to sell outright. There is something for everyone at Antique Brokers International, including mission oak, Victorian pieces, glassware, roll-top desks, armoires, chests, sterling, silver, and small collectibles. Steve is a licensed state appraiser and will gladly examine and appraise your collection of antiques for resale or insurance purposes.

Antique Brokers is located in the Admiral Junction ten minutes from downtown Seattle in a two story building chock-full of antiques. You'll feel you have made a "Best Choice" of antique stores when you shop at Antique Brokers International.

ANTIQUE FINDERS
22444 Pacific Highway South
Seattle, WA 98198
Tel. (206) 878-7338
Hrs: Tue. - Sat.
Visa and MasterCard are accepted.
and,
AREAWAY ANTIQUES
400 Occidental South
Seattle, WA 98104
Tel. (206) 382-9440

Owner Mike Wall started Antique Finders on Pacific Highway South in 1975. As an art history major at the University of Washington specializing in furniture, Oriental, East Indian and Egyptian art. Mike's studies made him aware of how much there is to know about antiques. Graduation wasn't the end of Mike's education. Since opening his business, he has avidly devoted himself to furthering his knowledge in ways which will benefit the customer fortunate enough to find Antique Finders.

Mike is a certified antique appraiser, but doesn't hesitate to call in other experts in special fields if he needs them. Some advice from Mike: "Buy what you like. You have to be your own expert most of the time."

The Antique Finders shops are filled with unique pieces. Low cost and bargain treasures can be found next to quality works of art, so there is something for everyone's taste and pocketbook. Mike considers fine art anything which is original, handmade, and tastefully designed. Glassware and silver settings, rare prints, ivory, bronze and fine furniture are featured.

Both stores are filled with treasures, however, the time you take to stop and talk with Mike could well be the most rewarding part of your visit to Antique Finders.

THE ANTIQUES GALLERY
123 S Jackson Street
Seattle, WA 98104
Tel. (206) 340-0444
Hrs: Mon. - Sat.   10:00 a.m. - 5:30 p.m.
     Sunday   12:00 noon - 5:00 p.m.

The Antiques Gallery came about in July, 1985 when a group of professional antique dealers with a common interest in fine antiques wanted an environment of quality and beauty in which to display and sell their merchandise. There is a comprehensive range of wonderful items from the last

King County

three centuries. Whether your interest lies in the primitive, country or formal, in items of utility or those of sheer beauty, you will find a selection to delight you in this gallery setting.

The amazing selection includes, antique furniture, American, English and Oriental from the 1600's through the 1800s; fine English, Japanese, and Chinese porcelain; glassware - both English and American-cut, blown, and pressed; cloisonne; graphic art, including oils, watercolors, and prints; bronzes; pottery of many kinds; primitives; jewelry and folk art; Arts and Crafts Period furniture, pottery, metal ware and lighting and fine quilts. These are only some of the wonderful pieces you will find displayed here.

This is the perfect setting to display the fine pieces found in The Antique Gallery. There is truly something for everyone, from the novice to the antique connoisseur at this distinctive gallery.

AREAWAY ANTIQUES, LTD.
400 Occidental Avenue S
Seattle, WA 98108
Tel.   (206)   382-9440
Hrs: Mon. - Sat.   10:00 a.m. - 5:30 p.m.
          Sunday   11:00 a.m. - 5:00 p.m.

Areaway Antiques, Ltd. has eighteen spaces leased to local antique dealers. There one can find a large and varied selection of antiques. There is Oriental porcelain, furniture, fire arms, suits of armor and swords. In addition to antiques, there are ancient artifacts, jewelry, fine art and much more. Each dealer has their own specialty, and browsing through the many treasures is delightful.

Areaway Antiques, Ltd. offers such a selection in so many different shops, that browsing there is a fascinating pastime. This is definitely a must for the antique connoisseur, as well as anyone seeking a special or unusual gift.

BOB ALSIN ANTIQUES
1114 Post Avenue
Seattle, WA 98101
Tel. (206)   6224-9799

The red brick walls of this pleasant shop provide the perfect background for Bob Alsin's large collection of 18th and 19th century English and French country antiques. The shop is located near Seattle's waterfront, between Seneca and Spring Streets.

Bob Alsin Antiques features fruitwood, pine and oak furniture along with such items as paintings, prints and mirrors. There is a varied assortment of accessories, such as brass, copper and pewter pieces, as well as porcelains, Oriental rugs and clocks.

Bob has been a professional antique dealer for many years and his interior design ability serves him well when advising clients on their selections. He makes three trips annually to Europe to insure and interesting and changing inventory for his customers.

CAPITOL HILL ANTIQUES AND CLOCKS
203 14th Avenue E
Seattle, WA 98112
Tel. (206) 323-5120
Hrs: Mon. - Sat. 12:00 noon - 6:00 p.m.

Capitol Hill Antiques and Clocks has found a wonderful new home at the top of Capitol Hill on the corner of Fourteenth Avenue E and E John Street. As you pull into the large parking area and gaze at this stately old home built in 1895, you notice that even the front porch is lined with the overflow of fine old furniture (weather permitting of course.)

After perusing the porch display you saunter through the large front door into the foyer. Your ears immediately tune to the gentle ticking of dozens of old clocks, your feet step quietly over handmade Oriental carpets, your eyes glide from stately pier mirrors to dainty crystal stemware, all illuminated by the hundreds of old lights and chandeliers waiting for their next home.

Introduce your children to the fun of a player piano or let them pump an old reed organ, there is nearly always one in stock. By now your heart will be won over by this shop with its diverse inventory and very reasonable prices. You can find anything from a $2 depression glass cup to a $3,000 wall clock.

Specialties: clocks, clock repair, full time repair/refinish shop, light fixtures and parts, extensive selection of brass replacement hardware.

CARRIAGE HOUSE GALLERIES
5611 University Way NE
Seattle, WA 98105
Tel. (206) 523-4960

Robert "Buzz" Shaw is the congenial owner of this unusual antique shop which has been serving clients for more than thirty years. The entire antique spectrum is well represented at Carriage House Galleries, with two floors full of rare pieces.

Of particular note, is the solid oak dining table with high backed chairs and two large matching credenzas, which put one in mind of the days of King Arthur. You will find chandeliers, pewter, flatware and a large selection of bone china, to mention only a minute portion of Buzz's stock. His position as a qualified estate appraiser provides him with a prime source of inventory.

This delightful shop is located in the University District, near Ravenna Park and has ample parking.

CONNOISSEUR ANTIQUES
713 Broadway E
Seattle, WA 98102
Tel. (206) 322-1222

Owner John Yaconetti's shop has an aura of rural England and sets the stage for his merchandise. Located in the handsome Loveless Building on Capitol Hill, its lead framed windows, parquet floor and cosy fireplace provide a beautiful and elegant background for the treasures it encloses.

Mr. Yaconetti chooses his eighteenth and early nineteenth century English and continental pieces three times a year when he travels to Europe. Always searching for quality silver, Sheffield plates, paintings, porcelain, and furniture, he has succeeded in filling his shop with one of the largest selections of antiques and accessories to be found.

Mr. Yaconetti holds exhibitions twice annually. He also provides custom buying for special clients, as well as painting restoration and reguilding. Connoisseur Antiques is for the connoisseur and collector alike.

DAVID WEATHERFORD
133 14th Avenue E
Seattle, WA 98102
Tel. (206) 329-6533

David Weatherford's 1895 "home turned studio" is located on Capitol Hill in the midst of Seattle's historical district. David's specialization in antiques is focused primarily on the periods of Jacobean, William and Mary, and Georgian, including fine French and Italian period pieces. He also has a superb collection of Oriental screens, Korean Tansu pieces, as well as collectible porcelain, mirrors, and an excellent stock of reproduction chairs.

David, a noted interior designer, is a member of the American Society of Interior Designers, and caters to a well established clientele in many of Seattle's finest homes. His staff includes two professional interior designers for consultation.

Everything you need to know or need to own can be satisfied with the assistance of David Weatherford. His frequent buying trips to Europe and the Orient, combined with years of proven expertise, are well evidenced by the inventory in his splendid studio on Capitol Hill.

GAINES HALLIDAY ANTIQUES
1121 First Avenue
Seattle, WA 98101
Tel. (206) 464-0807
Hrs: Mon. - Sat. 10:00 a.m. - 5:30 p.m.

Antique connoisseurs will find this shop a rewarding stop on their map. Gaines Halliday Antiques is a gallery of distinction that features antiques primarily from the 18th and 19th centuries.

Visitors are received into an elegant showroom that is immaculately kept. Period pieces from Europe, America and Asia are displayed throughout the premises which is floored in rich marble. As a collector, or just an interested browser, you'll find the representative pieces to be a lovely assortment of fine quality original woods such as mahogany, rose wood, fruit wood and satin wood. Amongst the large variety of tables, chairs, dining and bedroom furniture, there are also various art objects and paintings.

Accommodating and comfortable, this well lit, clean and organized shop makes for a very pleasant stop on your journey.

HAGEMAN ANTIQUES
119 South Jackson Street
Seattle, WA 98104
Tel. (206) 467-1535
Hrs: Mon. - Sat. 10:00 a.m. - 5:00 p.m.

Peter Hageman's antiques store, located in Seattle's Pioneer Square area, is a store with a European flair. Peter, who is originally from The Netherlands, has assembled an interesting collection of different styles and period European antiques. He has been collecting antiques since he was a child and his years of expertise are obvious when you view the wonderful collection assembled. This shop has the largest collection of antique paintings in the Northwest.

Peter imports regularly from Europe, where he believes there is still a wealth of excellent pieces to be obtained. Different from the American antique trade where Peter feels there are 200,000 people looking full time for the furniture of 200 families. In contrast, European furniture is still in excellent supply and well represented in this shop. The furniture available is carefully chosen and reasonably priced, in keeping with Peter's belief that antiques should circulate, rather than sit for years in shops.

Hageman Antiques also does business on a wholesale basis, importing containers of antiques directly from Europe. With Peter's contacts in Europe, he has been able to assemble an interesting and varied collection of European antiques which the antique shopper will find worth viewing.

KAGEDO
55 Spring Street
Seattle, WA 98104
Tel. (206) 467-9077
Hrs: Mon. - Sat. 10:30 a.m. - 5:00 p.m.
Or by appointment.

Close to the waterfront you will find Kagedo, Japanese Antiques and Folk Art. Their collection of investment quality Japanese art is personally selected by the owners who spend many months each year traveling extensively in the Japanese countryside.

Their collection includes fine tansu chests, paintings, sculpture, ceramics, architectural pieces, and a wide variety of decorative art.

Architecture art is an area of particular interest to Kagedo, and they recently place a rare Meiji Era Shinto Shrine at the Art Gallery of Greater Victoria in British Columbia. This full scale village shrine is one of the few examples of period Japanese architecture outside of Japan.

LES THERIAULTS
106 N 36th Street
Seattle, WA 98103
Tel. (206) 547-3489

Les Theriaults is located in Seattle's Fremont District in what was formerly a church. This is a unique antique shop owned by three very knowledgeable and hospitable people, Philip, Jeanette, and Lawrence Theriault. They have a large selection of china, silver, screens, paintings and objets d'arts.

Philip lived in Japan for thirty years and is knowledgeable in the subject of Asian art. The china collection includes an exceptional twenty-two karat gold demitasse service for twelve. There are both original and reproduced paintings available. Their furniture pieces are of exceptional quality and there is a truly outstanding European walnut armoire which will delight antique furniture lovers.

The Theriaults have arranged chairs to provide a seated view of some of their items. This allows the shopper to gain a different perspective than while walking around the shop and to further enjoy the warm and tidy atmosphere while making a selection. Les Theriaults is a shopping experience that antique connoisseurs will thoroughly enjoy.

MARVEL ON MADISON
69 Madison
Seattle, WA 98104
Tel. (206) 624-4225
Hrs: Mon. - Sat. 11:30 a.m. - 5:30 p.m.

Maneki Neko, the beckoning cat, is the symbol of welcome at Marvel and Phil Stewart's Asian antique shop in Cornerstone's Waterfront Place. The Stewart's have collected a varied assortment of Asian fine art and folk art, ranging from lacquerware to carved jade beads.

Marvel and Phil started collecting in 1955 and have a unique network of sources in Japan, China, and Thailand. Their interest and knowledge encompasses not only antiques, but contemporary art as well. Their inventory includes Imari porcelain, stoneware, textiles, jewelry, rugs, scrolls, hibachi dolls, candlesticks, lamps and obi. Items are primarily from the Edo Period (1615-1868) and the Meiji Period (1868-1912).

Marvel will give you tips on innovative ways to display your antiques. Their prices are moderate and the Stewart's extensive knowledge and gracious hospitality make shopping at Marvel on Madison a pleasure for the novice antique shopper, as well as the connoisseur.

N. B. NICHOLS AND COMPANY
1924 Post Alley
Seattle, WA 98101
Tel. (206) 448-8906
Hrs: Tue. - Sat. 10:00 a.m. - 5:30 p.m.

Located in Post Alley in the famous and historic Pike Place Market, N.B. Nichols and Son is an antique shop of unusual charm that offers quality items hand selected by owner Nancy Nichols on her many buying trips throughout Europe.

This includes antique furnishings for every room in the home, artifacts and handmade objects representing cultures from around the world. Discover fine pieces of quality furniture that are both fully restored or waiting for you to finish yourself at extraordinary prices. Find also handwoven rugs from Greece, pottery from Italy, bell wheels from France, masks from Vienna, or perhaps a tiny Egyptian bronze ibis. All items found in the shop are handcrafted with a sense of artistic skill.

Because owner Nancy Nichols has an experienced eye, the shop has gained a reputation among collectors and decorators throughout Seattle. The interior of the rustic and high ceiling shop offers a sense of history and the romance of a bygone era. One can just browse among the unusually wide selection or make an exciting and one of a kind finds on two large floors of inventory.

For those who want the excitement of finishing a piece of fine English furniture, Nancy is pleased to offer skilled guidance and suggestions. You'll find this a surprisingly affordable antique store with quality items, because the owner personally visits European markets, auctions and out of the way places in an effort to locate antiques objects that will last many lifetimes more.

PELAYO ANTIQUES
3236 N. E. 45th Street
Seattle, WA 98105
Tel. (206) 525-1444
Hrs: Mon. - Sun. 11:00 a.m. - 6:00 p.m.
and,
8421 Greenwood Avenue N
Seattle, WA 98103
Tel. (206) 789-1333

Pelayo Antiques has two locations, one a veritable warehouse in the Greenwood District, the other a smaller shop in the university area. Proprietor Pedro Pelayo specializes in English and Danish pine antique country furniture.

The Greenwood store stocks a variety of furniture pieces, bookcases, desks, credenzas, dressers, tables and even a sleigh. Many of the pieces were originally painted, but now they have been restored to their natural finish and waxed. European China is featured, as well as brass and copper accessories. Most of the collection dates from the 19th and 20th centuries.

Pelayo Antiques offers one of the largest collections of European furniture to be found. A visit is well worth while for the antique hunter looking for quality furniture at moderate prices.

THE SINGER GALLERIES
1621-B Queen Ann Avenue N
Seattle, WA 98109
Tel. (206)285-0394
Hrs: Tue. - Sat. 10:00 a.m. - 5:00 p.m.

Situated on the highest hill in Seattle, The Singer Galleries presents an interesting and tasteful collection of antiques, from jewelry to furniture. The shop is comfortable, spacious and visitors appreciate the unhurried ambiance in this neighborhood setting.

Proprietor Scott Singer is a qualified estate appraiser with a consummate knowledge of both European and Oriental antiques. He has assembled a wonderful Asian collection which attracts out of town visitors looking for the best, at affordable prices, as well as local residents. Porcelain and silver, brilliant cut glass, exquisite jewelry and fine furniture are beautifully displayed for close inspection.

Antique enthusiasts will appreciate The Singer Galleries' outstanding collection and browsing in such congenial and attractive surroundings.

THE TIMELESS TRAVELER
5424 Ballard Ave. N.W.
Seattle, WA 98117
Tel. (206) 789-2452
Hrs: Tues. - Sat. 10:30 a.m. - 6:00 p.m.
        Monday by appointment only.

Stepping into The Timeless Traveler is like stepping into the past. Located on Ballard's quaint Ballard Avenue, the shop exudes an eclectic feeling. Russell Peterson and his partner Ken Newberg, who runs the Salt Lake City store, County Antiques, have between them more than 50 years of experience in the business.

Well-chosen pottery, paintings, china, jewelry, toys, antique handmade linens, original and restored furniture and a bevy of items too numerous to catalogue, make the shop a delight. The shop specializes in delights such as an Art Nouveau lamp circa 1915, an Art Deco shade from 1920, or a beautiful opalescent swirl fixture from 1895. Each fixture is restored to its original condition, using only original parts.

So, if your life could use a little lighting up, stop by The Timeless Traveler and let Russell Peterson shed a bit of light on the subject.

WEST SEATTLE COINS
ANTIQUES AND COLLECTIBLES
4500 California Avenue, S.W.
Seattle, WA 98116
Tel. (206) 932-3328
Visa and MasterCard card are accepted.

This shop carries a tremendous selection of coins, including pennies from 1796 through 1807, 1800 to 1808 half pennies and even an 1875 twenty cent piece. There is also a wide selection of silver dollars and commemorative coins. Owner Beverly Dinger first carried only coins, but has now branched into jewelry and fine art pieces.

You will find a nice selection of beautiful rings, necklaces and bracelets of silver. There are exquisite handpainted pins and brooches from the 1840s to the 1920s. There are pictures, posters, quality crystal and china, collector's plates and cups, unique decorative lamps and a large variety of sterling silver items.

Several antique shops exist in West Seattle, but West Seattle Coins, Antiques and Collectibles is by far the "Best Choice"for finding truly unique and lovely pieces.

Art, Artists and Galleries

ADVENTURE UNLIMITED
1906 Pike Place - Stewart House
Seattle, WA 98101
Tel. (206) 448-9520

This is a unique shop featuring ethnic artifacts from remote areas of Africa, Papua New Guinea, Burma, India and Peru. The masks, statues, jewelry, clothing and musical instruments presented will appeal both to the art investor and the curious.

The most singular aspect is that owner Ginny Thome, a seasoned traveler, has developed a travel service specializing in adventure destinations in combination with the resale of the arts of those regions. A safari to East Africa, Nepal trek, hiking the Milford Track in New Zealand or investigating Papua New Guinea are just a few of the many possibilities.

A visit to Adventure Unlimited is an exciting experience for the prospective traveler or the appreciative collector because it conjures up the essence of cultures we know so little about.

CAROLYN HARTNESS FINE ART
83 South Washington
Seattle, WA 98104
Tel. (206) 441-9360

Surreal connoisseurs will delight in the visionary paintings displayed at Carolyn Hartness' cozy Pioneer Square gallery. Ilene Meyer is exclusively represented, as well as, Rob Schoeten. There are interesting ceramic lite masks by Gayle Lutschg.

Many of the artists portray a humorous vein in their work. The gallery is a real find for those seeking the unusual.

CAROLYN STALEY - FINE PRINTS
313 1st Avenue S
Seattle, WA 98104
Tel. (206) 621-1888
Hrs: Tue. - Sat. 11:00 a.m - 5:00 p.m.

Carolyn Staley - Fine Prints is a gallery specializing in fine original prints. The gallery's inventory includes antique maps and decorative prints such as botanicals and natural history subjects. Sixteenth through twentieth century master prints by artists including Durer, Beham, Callot, Hogarth, Goya, Daumier, Whistler, Renoir, Bonnard, Maillol, Chagall and others are featured. American prints of the 1930s and 40s are another area of focus - both well known artists nationally and regionally, especially depression era works by Northwest artists Jacob Elshin, Fay Chong, Harold Keeler, William Cumming, Helmi Juvonen, George Tsutakawa and more. A major specialty of the gallery is Japanese woodblock prints, from Utamaro to Yoshitoshi - in traditional ukiyo-e (images of the floating world) and modern Japanese prints, especially from the period before and following World War II up through the 1960s. Northwest historical subjects are also exhibited in the gallery, including rare views of Seattle, Tacoma, Spokane, Portland and other regional centers.

The gallery endeavors to provide a wide range of fine prints, and focuses on works by artist who are no longer living, although Northwest book arts, prints by some established contemporary Northwest artists, and illustrated antiquarian books are also available.

Diverse and interesting exhibits are rotated every four to six weeks and the variety of shows has involved all of the above subjects. The following are exhibited annually: master prints, traditional and modern Japanese woodblocks and American prints of the 1930s and 40s. Past exhibits have included: Piranesi, James Gillray caricature, Hiroshige, Osaka Actor Prints, Kuniyoshi and Yoshitoshi, Fay Chong Block Prints, Rediscovered Northwest Artists, Northwest Town and City Views, Pierre Josheph Redoute's Les Liliacees, Karl Bodmer's Travels to the Interior of North America, La Belle Epoque: Art Noveau Posters and Prints, European Master Prints and Antique Maps.

The gallery works with individuals, interior designers, art consultants, corporate collections and museums. The price range is as broad as the inventory - from $5 to $15,000 and they invite both browsers and connoisseurs.

CRACKERJACK CONTEMPORARY CRAFTS
1815 N Forty-fifth #212
Wallingford Center
Seattle, WA 98103
Tel. (206) 647-4983
Hrs: Open daily

Crackerjack Contemporary Crafts is an elegant shop in historic Wallingford Center, a remodeled elementary school built in the early 1900's. The shop specializes in the quality crafts of over 100 artists working in jewelry, ceramics, fiber, wood and hand blown glass.

Owner Kathleen Koch seeks the unique at craft fairs and national craft shows, working directly with artists when choosing items for her store. You will find silver and natural stone earrings, enticing necklaces made of antique and hand blown glass beads, a wide selection of ceramics, silk and mohair scarves, hand painted sweatshirts and many other intriguing items.

The selection of crafts is well displayed in an atmosphere which invites browsing.

THE CRANE GALLERY
1203-B 2nd Avenue
Seattle, WA 98101
Tel. (206) 522-7185

Attention collectors of high quality Oriental art! The Crane Gallery, owned by Cheney Cowles, is one of the few galleries in the northwest that concentrates on Oriental antiques.

In the display window is a seventeenth century Chinese cabinet, as well as a moderate offering of other fine Asian pieces, giving you an idea of what lies within. One of Mr. Cowles' specialties is antique Japanese netsuke. Also displayed are Japanese, Chinese and Korean ceramics, paintings, elegant screens, delicate porcelain items, and fine Chinese snuff bottles.

The Crane Gallery is located in the heart of Seattle's financial district and Mr. Cowles' discriminating and elegant collection offers pleasant respite from the grating pressures of daily commerce. For Asiaphiles, The Crane Gallery should not be missed.

DAVIDSON GALLERIES
1915 1st Avenue
Seattle, WA 98101
Tel. (206) 441-6699
and,
313 Occidental Avenue S
Seattle, WA 98101
Tel. (206) 624-7684

Books! Manuscripts! Antique Art! These are the passwords to Dan Davidson's First Avenue Gallery. The gallery is divided into three sections. The first contains European and American manuscripts, antique original prints, and original manuscript fragments and maps from both the East and West. The middle section is devoted to Donnally books, offering both new and used specializations in art, architecture, photography and literature. The last section is a gallery with changing shows primarily of Japanese wookblock prints and exhibits of Goya.

Dan's Occidental gallery is located in the heart of Pioneer Square. Thirteen years ago, the gallery started with original prints and other works on paper and now stocks the largest print inventory in the Northwest. It also was the first gallery in the United States to exhibit and sell mainland Chinese paintings.

While now featuring contemporary work by both national and international artists, the gallery also represents such notables as Carl Summers, Art Hanson, and Scott Smith, to name a few. Davidson also publishes posters and catalogs to compliment his changing exhibitions.

DUNVILLE GALLERY
9025 35th Avenue SW
Seattle, WA 98126
Tel. (206) 935-7557
Hrs: Mon. - Fri.   10:00 a.m. - 6:00 p.m.
     Saturday   10:00 a.m. - 4:00 p.m.
AMEX, Mastercard and Visa are accepted.

If you're traveling in the Northwest and viewing the sights, you're probably interested in art. Nature's masterpiece, in many people's opinion, is this beautiful area of America. That's why it should come as no surprise that one of the most beautiful and respected galleries in the Northwest, Dunville Gallery, is located in Seattle.

Dunville Gallery, established since 1975, specializes in fine art and custom picture framing. Owner, Mel Neville, features some of the Northwest's finest artists, such as Sue Ellen Ross, Yvonne Davis and many others; as well as world class artists like Robert Bateman, Ron Parker and Nita Engle to mention only a few. Also featured, are numerous handcrafted original gift items by very talented Northwest artisans.

For custom picture framing, this gallery's professionalism is impeccable, winning national framing honors for their creative designs. In fact, the Seattle Art Museum has asked on two separate occasions for Mr. Neville to give lectures pertaining to the delicate art of framing.

Overall, Dunville Gallery is a warm and inviting place in which to view and purchase some of the finest pieces of art in this area of the Northwest.

(See special invitation in the Appendix.)

FINE IMPRESSIONS GALLERY
7714 Greenwood Avenue N
Seattle, WA 98103
Tel.   (206) 784-5270
Hrs: Tue. - Fri.   11:00 a.m - 7:00 p.m.
           Saturday   11:00 a.m. - 5:00 p.m.

At Fine Impressions Gallery they help you find that special handmade print or fine art poster which expresses your individuality and provides a stimulating focus for your home or office.

Their personally selected inventory represents work by European, Asian and Northwest artists of the 19th and 20th centuries who have mastered the complex techniques of printmaking. Most of the imported museum posters, antique prints and original works are not available elsewhere.

To protect and display your artwork they offer a large selection of fine handcrafted frames, hand painted watercolor French mats and years of experience in planning classic frames to complement artwork. Their high standards of framing will protest and preserve your art.

Artwork and framing from Fine Impressions Gallery will give you years of enjoyment at prices you can afford.

FLURY AND COMPANY
322 First Avenue South
Seattle, WA 98104
Tel. (206) 587-0260
Hrs: Tue. - Sat. 11:00 a.m. - 6:00 p.m.
Or by appointment.

Lois Flury has assembled the largest collection of master photographer Edward Curtis' work to be found. These vintage photos of North American Indians are well displayed in this Pioneer Square gallery. In addition to the originals, prints of Edward Curtis' work are available.

Flury and Company also exhibits a full spectrum of American painters from 1860 to contemporary art. The gallery has also arranged sales of paintings by such masters as Monet, Van Gogh, Frederick Remington and C.M. Russell.

Flury and Company complements its art displays with Native American blankets, rugs, wood carvings, baskets and pottery. With so much to see and buy, you will understand why Flury and Company is a "Best Choice" in Western Washington.

FOLK ART GALLERY/LA TIENDA
4138 University Way NE
Seattle, WA 98105
Tel. (206) 632-1796

The two floors and six rooms of the Folk Art Gallery/La Tienda are a vital, special place to visit. Four months of the year the owner, Leslie Grace and her staff travel in search of pieces. A balance these past ten years has been reached between contemporary pottery, clothing and jewelry from the United States and ethnographic pieces such as: musical instruments and textiles from other parts of the world.

The orientation of this gallery/shop is towards the functional - the usable and wearable. Care and time is taken in search of these pieces and in displaying them. Presently the Folk Art Gallery works with over five hundred sources.

This unique place with its knowledgeable staff and fascinating selection is well worth repeated visits. Folk Art Gallery/La Tienda is located one block from the University of Washington campus - two blocks from the Burke Museum on the campus.

FRAME IT ON BROADWAY
1822 Broadway
Seattle, WA 98122
Tel. (206) 322-4455

This poster, print and framing workshop is in a charming Victorian house on Broadway and offers both custom and "do it yourself" framing. Owner Linda Meier has occupied this house for over eleven years and has expanded her extensive poster collection to the second floor. These posters feature European artists and some fine limited editions. Linda frequently offers exhibitions of Japanese and local artists.

The actual framery offers a wide selection of wood, metal and lacquer frames, as well as elegant matting materials ranging from silk and other elegant fabrics to more traditional mats. A friendly and knowledgeable staff will help you select appropriate mats and mouldings. Those "do it yourself" patrons also will be assisted with the assembling of their artwork, and tools and tables will be furnished without cost.

FRANCINE SEDERS GALLERY
6701 Greenwood Avenue N
Seattle, WA 98103
Tel. (206) 782-0355

Since 1970, the Francine Seders Gallery has displayed the works of local artists like Guy Anderson, Jacob Lawrence, Mark Tobey, Karl Benjamin, Fay and Robert Jones, Norman Lundon, and Michael Spafford, to name a few. Exhibitions change every month and Francine continues to promote young, practicing, local artists.

The gallery is enclosed in an elegant former home with tiered hardwood floors in the main showroom. Located close to Woodland Park, the ambiance is one of quiet contemplation, perfect for viewing.

This is a golden opportunity to find an up and coming artist among the gallery's collection of paintings, sculptures, ceramics, and limited edition prints by those artists represented. Don't miss it!

King County

HONEY CHURCH ARTIQUES
1008 James Street
Seattle, WA 98104
Tel. (206) 622-1225
Hrs: Mon. - Sat. 10:00 a.m. - 6:00 p.m.

Fanciers of Asian art, artifacts and furniture will enjoy Honeychurch Artiques. John Fairman's superb collection is reflective of his years of living in the Orient and the influence of his parents who own a shop in Hong Kong.

Honeychurch's extensive variety ranges from artifacts dating from the Third Millennium B.C. to early Twentieth century. Considerable effort is spent in researching the history of each piece and significant facts and background are well documented. Many pieces from John's exhibits have been featured in leading Asian art publications.

It is worth a visit to experience John's infectious enthusiasm for Asian culture and his fine displays of art.

KIDDER GALLERY OF AMERICAN INDIAN ART
87 S Washington
Seattle, WA 98104
Tel. (206) 340-1048
Hrs: Mon. - Sat. 11:00 a.m. - 6:00 p.m.

Spirits of the totems, spirits of the earth, water and sky welcome you to Kidder Gallery. Located in historical Pioneer Square, they are dedicated to showing the folk art of our native people.

Along the coast: the ever workable cedar. The people of this region did not have to wander or wonder where their next meal was coming from, for everything of bounty came from the limitless ocean. In the midst of such graciousness came some of the finest and most decorative art in wood, copper, slate, basketry and clothing the world has ever seen.

Tribes of the southwest: Apache, Navajo, Pueblo. Mountain traveling, mesa dwelling, far seeing people of the high desert. It is believed the Navajo and Apache were once one tribe, a tribe that split and went separate yet similar ways. Sandpaintings for healing are done by both and explain their nomadic ways - coming with the dust and going with the wind. From these people came the most versatile and best weavers, pot makers and silver workers in the country.

Of the plains, of the great open spaces the tipi dwelling, buffalo hunting warriors of time immemorial. All part of a great Siouan family. It is from this name they got the tribal name Sioux. Beadwork, headbands and chockers, buffalo hide paintings, bright displays of earth mother love Wankentaka blessings.

The American says, "To eat you must have a prayer, to pray you must have dreams," and so the dreams are kept alive.

KIMZEY MILLER GALLERY
1225 2nd Avenue
Seattle, WA 98101
Tel. (206) 682-2339
Hrs: Mon. - Sat.   8:30 a.m. - 6:00 p.m.
         Sunday   12:00 noon - 6:00 p.m.

During a visit to the city of Seattle, many people would find a visit to a local art gallery a fine distraction to fill a few hours of the day. Fine art is satisfying to the soul, a meal of gratification to the aficionado, an adventure to the uninitiated.

Patrick Kimzey and Terry Miller have created a gallery that specializes in a collection of contemporary fine art. Represented are works in most major mediums, oil, watercolor, graphics and a unusual selection of glass. After a viewing of the Impressionist, Abstract, Art Deco, and Jazz Art pieces in the gallery, visitors are sure to come away with an appreciation for the quality of art work displayed. Pegge Hopper, Russell Chatham, John Powell, Pierre-Marie Brisson, and Bernard Gantner are among the artists represented.

For a diversion into the world fine art, Patrick and Terry welcome you to their "Best Choice" - Kimzey Miller Gallery.

THE LEGACY
1003 1st Avenue
Seattle, WA, 98104
Tel. (206) 624-6350
Hrs: Mon. - Sat. 10:00 a.m. - 6:00 p.m.
Visa, MasterCard and AMEX are accepted.

This land was once populated by a people close to the earth. Legends passed down through the generations spoke of the creators of the of local land. These people, the Native Americans of the Northwest, are survived by their progeny, with whom they have left their legacy. In the spirit of these people, The Legacy is an art gallery of Northwest Coast Indian and Alaskan Eskimo artifacts.

Come journey into another culture with a visit to The Legacy. A ten foot totem pole greets you as you enter the gallery. Numerous masks hang on the walls. A fascinating collection of stone carvings, blankets, and baskets done only in the way Indians can, impart a sense of their mystical heritage. More recent art work is also on display including a selection of serigraph prints.

Whether a collector or an interested spectator, you will find a wonderful trove of treasures here. Complimenting the gallery is a fine library of Indian history with ivory pieces and native knives. In this land that is so over populated, take some time to appreciate the legacy of those that have gone before us.

LEGENDS
1421 1st Avenue
Seattle, WA 98101
Tel. (206) 622-6630
Hrs: Mon. - Sat. 10:00 a.m. - 6:00 p.m.
Sunday 12:00 noon - 4:00 p.m.
Winter hours may vary.

Located near Seattle's Pike Place Market, Legends is a two level art gallery that features works primarily by Northwest artists. There are more than 150 artists represented. Their work encompasses a variety of media, including wood, ivory, glass, pottery, metal and fibers.

The handcarved original wood artwork at Legends is in a class by itself. Wood enthusiasts will appreciate the skill involved in constructing the large wooden clocks with their hyper extended working gears. Also on display are very unique pottery tables and chairs, which are finished in soft pastels.

Legends offers the shopper a host of unusual and unique art objects to choose from. Whether you prefer wood, three dimensional stained glass, jewelry, or any of a number of other interesting art forms, you'll find something to catch your fancy at Legends.

LISA HARRIS GALLERY
1922 Pike Place
Seattle, WA 98101
Tel. (206) 443-3315
Hrs: Mon. - Sat. 11:00 a.m. - 5:30 p.m.
Sunday 12:00 noon - 5:00 p.m.

Lisa Harris's comfortable gallery is located upstairs in the north end of the Pike Place Market, with a panoramic view of Elliott Bay and the Olympic Mountains. The magnificent view is matched by the magnificent selection of art to be found. Northwest, national and internationally known artists are featured.

The gallery specializes in contemporary works on paper in a variety of styles, from realistic to abstract and serves both the serious collector and those seeking art for the home or office. There are paintings, lithographs, serigraphs, etchings, wood block and monoprints from which to choose. A substantial collection of mezzotints by internationally known artists Hwang and Yokoi can be found together with superb photographs by Northwest photographer Deborah DeWit. Other artists include Victoria Adams, Heidi Blackwell, Brian Chapman, Russell Chatham, Allen Cox, Joan Gold, Nelleke Langhout-Nix, Richard Morhous, Royal Nebeker, James Rizzi, Susan Schneider, Bruce Weinberg and Ron Westman.

The Lisa Harris Gallery has a wide selection from which the discriminating buyer may choose. Through its affiliation with Christie's Contemporary Art of London and New York, the gallery also presents original prints by modern masters. This is the place to go for contemporary art.

LYNN MC ALLISTER GALLERY
601 2nd Avenue
Seattle, WA 98104
Tel. (206) 467-0277

This gallery is located in the beautiful old Butler Block Hotel in Pioneer Square. It features mostly contemporary art by Northwest artists. The works displayed range in style from abstract to representational in a variety of media.

Lynn McAllister, who holds a Ph.D. in art history, carries an impressive portfolio and exclusively represents Max Benjamin, Joe Fedderson, Shirley Gittelsohn, Sally Haley, Manuel Iziquierdo, George Johanson, Mel Katz, Michihirao Kosuge, Daniel Russell, Stephen Yates, Wattana Wattarapun, Hans Schiebold, Kirby Kallas-Lewis and Michele Russe. Original graphics by national print makers include Pat Stier, Andy Warhol and W. Dekooning.

Monthly shows are held and Dr. McAllister's expertise covers appraisals, private and corporate consulting and estate valuations. Those with an interest in fine art by emerging and established artists will find a wide range of styles subjects, sizes and prices at the Lynn McAllister Gallery.

MARKET GRAPHICS
1935 1st Avenue
Seattle, WA 98101
Tel. (206) 682-7732

Market Graphics, located just above Pike Place Market, has the most extensive poster collection in the Northwest, covering such subjects as photography, music, humor, Seattle and the Pacific Northwest. Reproductions of noted artists such as Gauguin and Brian Davis are available, framed in clear acrylic or metal. There are glossy prints by Ansel Adams, Patric Nagel, George Seracot and Richard Avedon.

Prints and posters are organized to conveniently locate a certain artist or type of print. Partners Ann Tucker and Sharon Hamilton frequently change the displays and they also provide a custom framing service.

With over 3,000 poster and prints in stock, browsers and art collectors will find an abundance of affordable art in the international collection at Market Graphics.

NANCY TEAGUE GALLERY
1512 5th Avenue
Seattle, WA 98101
Tel. (206) 447-9166

The Nancy Teague Gallery is located on fashionable Fifth Avenue and is one of the largest galleries in Seattle, with two floors and 4500 square feet, Nancy Teague has been serving patrons for eleven years, offering well displayed art by internationally recognized artists.

Among the artists represented in the gallery are Altman, Delacroix, Earle, Gartner, Gorman, Miro, Moti, Tanayo and Tobey. Fine art is displayed on the ground floor and the lower level features limited edition prints, posters and custom framing.

The Nancy Teague Gallery is well known for its extensive collection of fine art, glass sculpture and art posters. It is open every day and shipping service is available. The knowledgeable gallery staff, eager to assist both the novice and the experienced collector, and the wonderful selection of fine art work make shopping at the Nancy Teague Gallery a pleasant and rewarding experience.

NATIVE DESIGN GALLERY
108 S Jackson in Pioneer Square
Seattle, WA 98104
Tel. (206) 624-9985
Hrs: Tue. - Sat.   11:00 a.m. - 5:00 p.m
       Summer Tue. - Sat.   10:30 a.m. - 6:00 p.m.

The owners of Native Design Gallery, David and Pat Logan, have lived and worked in many of the countries from which their gallery's art originates. They met in Africa in 1975 and the gallery grew out of their desire to provide

Seattle and the Pacific Northwest with an opportunity to understand, through art, something of the lifestyles and cultures of other parts of the world.

Celebrating ten years at this address, the gallery hosts changing exhibits of traditional art from Asia, Africa or the Americas, west room gallery. Featured and for sale are collector textiles, ritual masks and carvings, baskets, puppets, beadwork and other handmade items reflecting an art form indigenous to other cultures. Seattleites and visitors from across the continent make it a point to visit, and re-visit, this unique gallery as a year round source for important world wide ethnic and primitive art. As African art specialists, the owners can provide appraisal services or custom made mountings for your important masks and carvings, by appointment only.

Native Design Gallery is conveniently located on the Kingdome side of Pioneer Square and within Seattle's free downtown bus zone. In addition to regular gallery hours, they are open every first Thursday and on most Sundays from 1:00 p.m to 5:00 p.m. By calling or writing in advance of your expected visit, the owners will be glad to accommodate appointment customers.

NORTHWEST ART AND FRAME
4733 California Avenue SW
Seattle, WA 98116
Tel. (206) 937-5507

Located in the heart of West Seattle's main shopping area is Northwest Art and Frame, which is well known for it's excellent selection of prints, custom frames, art and regular cards and gifts.

The owner, Dan Reiner and his staff believe that a frame can make or break a fine piece of art. Because of this, Dan creates frames that enhance the beauty and the drama of the art while taking into account the decor of the room in which it will be displayed.

This marriage of fine selection and professional service combine to make the Northwest Art and Frame shop a "Best Choice" you will be glad you visited.

PRINTLAND
111 First Avenue S
Seattle, WA 98104
Tel. (206) 622-3887
Hrs: Mon. - Sat.   10:30 a.m. - 6:00 p.m.
       Sunday   11:00 a.m. - 4:30 p.m.

Located in Pioneer Square is a shop named Printland that carries a wide selection contemporary prints by established and classical artists, as well as, a variety of modern posters.

Owner Marv Mc Connell along with framer Tim Ross are available to help you with any questions you may have and help you pick mattings and frames to highlight the beauty of the art. Tim was selected Framer of the Month by *Decor* magazine in December, 1986 and May, 1987. You will understand why when you see the creativity and assortment of materials that are special to Printland. One of their specialties is Art Deco mats which lend themselves beautifully to a variety of art and decor.

Printland will ship to any location, so you can pick your favorite piece of art, matting and frame and it will be waiting for you when you return home.

SNOW GOOSE
4220 Northeast 125th Street
Seattle, WA 98125
Tel. (206) 362-3401

Proprietor Jane Schuldberg is justly proud of the authenticity of the Eskimo and Northwest Coast Indian art and artifacts displayed in her cozy Snow Goose Gallery.

The quality of Snow Goose's collection is unparalleled. Both rare and contemporary trinket baskets share space with a variety of Alaskan native ivory carvings of soapstone objects. The Canadian collection of prints and posters is unexcelled, and there is a well-presented library chronicling Northwest Coast Indian history.

Jane travels twice annually to Canada and Alaska researching and locating the skilled handicrafts of native artists. She is an expert on the work of Inult, Eskimo, Aleut, and various Northwest Coast and other Indian artists. Several special shows are held annually which showcase particular artists.

STONE PRESS GALLERY
91 Yesler Way
Seattle, WA 98104
Tel. (206) 624-6752

The Stone Press Gallery is located in Pioneer Square and displays a number of current American print makers, hand printed intaglio, lithography, wood block and monoprints.

Master printer Kent Lovelace utilizes his stone lithography to hand print original lithographs of his own superb artwork as well as other artists. Printmaking is a fascinating medium and Kent is certainly one of the most skilled artists in this field.

Exhibitions are held regularly, highlighting Northwest artists. A visit to the Stone Press Gallery is both interesting and educational. Browsing among the wonderful work displayed here is a very rewarding experience.

STONINGTON GALLERY
2030 1st Avenue
Seattle, WA 98121
Tel. (206) 443-1108
Hrs: Mon. - Sat. 10:00 a.m. - 5:30 p.m.

In a spacious and welcoming ambiance, the Stonington Gallery displays the finest work of those who have contributed to the heritage of Alaska and the Northwest. Located only one block north of the Pike Place Market, the Stonington has a collection of paintings, limited edition prints, sculpture, carvings, fiber arts and jewelry.

Nancy Taylor's watercolors are featured, as well as the complete collection of her prints, which chronicle the Northwest landscape and capture the special quality of its environment. Over thirty-five other artists represent all the cultures of Alaska and the Northwest: the Eskimo, Aleut, Northwest Coast Indian and the non native adventurers that settled the region.

Special shows highlighting original works, often based on a theme, are hosted several times annually. The gallery also provides full framing and shipping services. The Stonington Gallery presents its varied and interesting collection of artworks in pleasant, well arranged surroundings and is well worth a visit.

T & N ASIA GALLERY
1220 First Avenue
Seattle, WA 98101
Tel. (206) 622-0516
Hrs: Mon. - Sat. 10:30 a.m. - 5:00 p.m.

T & N Asia Gallery has a unique combination of antiques and Asian folkart. Proprietor Tony Ventura travels annually throughout Asia locating unusual and interesting textiles, furniture and artifacts for his shop.

Here the antique connoisseur will find an 18th century bronzed urn from Java sharing space with Korean and other Asian cabinets. A 19th century Borneo warrior's festival jacket and 20th century Butanese women's sashes are only part of the extensive textile collection. A magnificent 18th century Korean temple painting hangs across from Timor funeral masks. There is also a large collection of ethnic jewelry.

T & N Asia Gallery is a delightful shopping experience. Tony displays his varied collection to advantage and those seeking the unusual in Asian artifacts will be delighted.

WILD WINGS GALLERY
1312 5th Avenue
Seattle, WA 98101
Tel. (206) 622-1384

Wild Wings Gallery has an impressive collection of wildlife artwork. Nature lovers will be delighted with the paintings, limited edition prints, sculptures and carvings displayed in this gallery.

There is a wonderful selection of carved wooden ducks, geese, and swans. A variety of high-quality gift items depicts wildlife in native habitat. There are lamps, clocks and tables along with paintings and prints of all sizes.

This spacious gallery, located in downtown Seattle, is the perfect spot to find just the right piece of wildlife artwork.

King County

A day filled with sweets, fun and excitement isn't just for kids.

	CAREFREE AND CAPRICIOUS		
a.m.	Salty's On Alki	Best breakfast	Sea/Restaurant
	Since you're going to be gone for a while, better pack lunch now		
a.m.	City Picnics	Best picnic lunch	Sea/Restaurant
	Hi ho, hi ho, it's off to the San Juan Islands we go.		
a.m.	Kenmore Air Harbor	Best transportation	Sea/Tour
	Picnic's over. Back to Seattle for more fun.		
p.m.	West Seattle Coins	Best collectibles	Sea/Antiques
p.m.	Greetings	Best gifts	Sea/Gift
p.m.	Big People Toys	Best toys	Sea/Toy
p.m.	Wedgewood Broiler	Best steaks	Sea/Restaurant

Now that's quite a day! To accomplish all of the above, you don't have to be young, just carefree and capricious.

Bakeries

AU GAVROCHE
1530 Post Alley
Seattle, WA 98101
Tel. (206) 624-2222
Hrs: Mon. - Sat. 7:00 a.m. - 6:00 p.m.

Cathy Conner has a winner in her fine bakery, Au Gavroche. Her background is impressive, she studied at Cordon Bleu in Paris for the full four quarters and received the Grande Diploma. She then went on to attend the "ecole de patisserie de France a Paris," French Pastry School, and passed the Practical French CAP de Cuisine. It was while working at a large catering concern in Paris that she earned the nickname "Gavroche" which is used to describe a mischievous urchin type of character.

When Cathy returned to Seattle, she opened Au Gavroche in 1981, doing all the pastry work herself. She was instantly successful and now has a staff of seventeen, including three pastry people and four bakers. Most of the pastries are French in nature and all are made with only the finest and freshest ingredients. The list of selections is mouth-watering, featuring such delights as chocolate mousse cake, gateau citron, chocolate italien fan torte and many,

many others. She offers breakfast, lunch, wine, and espresso, as well as pastries in her Pike Place Market location.

A visit to Au Gavroche confronts one with an irresistible array of delectable pastries. Be sure to stop by when shopping at Pike Place Market and enjoy something delicious.

CHEZ DOMINIQUE EUROPEAN PASTRIES AND CAFE
77 Spring Street
Seattle, WA 98104
Tel. (206) 623-2219
Hrs: Mon. - Fri.   6:45 a.m. - 6:00 p.m.
     Saturday   8:00 a.m. - 6:00 p.m.

Chez Dominique is for those with a discriminating sweet tooth. Authentic European pastries are featured here from exquisite five tiered wedding cakes, made to order, to delectable puff pastries.

Owner Dominique Le Marrec is from Nantes, France, where he was a master French pastry chef since the age of fourteen. He imports jams, jellies and chocolate from Europe to create his masterpieces. They include such delicacies as croissants, Danish, scones and muffins. True buttercream fillings are prepared with a light meringue and unsalted butter. Highly recommended are the fruit plan and the layered chocolate Mozart torte.

In keeping with the European tradition, breakfast and luncheon sandwiches are served outside, using croissants and freshly baked bread. Chez Dominique's truly is a civilized treat for a jaded palate.

THE CRUMPET SHOP
1503 First Avenue
Seattle, WA 98101
Tel. (206) 682-1598
Hrs: Mon. - Sat. 7:30 a.m. - 5:00 p.m.
Closed major holidays.

Baking truly good crumpets is an art which Gary Lasater mastered during his training in Victoria, B.C. Making crumpets is a very delicate process, the room temperature and the batter temperature, in addition to the temperature of the griddle are critical to producing perfect crumpets. Gary now produces perfect, delicious crumpets at The Crumpet Shop in Seattle. The recipe he uses is the same one that has been used for more than sixty years in Victoria.

The Crumpet Shop offers just about anything you might want to spread on your crumpet. They have wonderful Northwest jams and jellies such as wild huckleberry and blackberry. For those who want something different, or don't have a sweet tooth, they offer such exotics as smoked salmon and English cheese. The Good Coffee Company coffee is featured here as an accompaniment to the crumpets and they offer three different sizes of espresso, eight, ten, and twelve ounce. Other beverages such as hot chocolate, milk, tea, and more are also served. Kids love to come here for crumpets and hot chocolate and to enjoy the Alice and Wonderland mural painted on the west wall.

People come from all over the world and all walks of life to enjoy Gary's crumpets. He doesn't allow smoking in his shop, but there are tables outside for the smokers who stop by. Visit The Crumpet Shop and try Gary's delicious crumpets yourself, you'll want to take home lots for yourself and your friends.

PIKE PLACE BAKERY
Pike Place Market
1501 Pike Place
Seattle, WA 98104
Tel. (206) 682-2829
Hrs: Summer Mon. - Sun. 7:00 a.m. - 6:00 p.m.
     Winter   Mon.- Sat.   7:00 a.m. - 6:00 p.m.
Closed on major holidays.
and,
CAKE MASTER BAKERY
Renton Center
Renton, WA 98055
Tel. (206) 682-2846

Got a hankering for a huge, tasty, home baked Texas size pastry freshly baked with the freshest ingredients? A stop at The Pike Place Bakery or Cake Master Bakery will delight your palate, and your pocket book!

Third generation bakers Genaro and Nedy Perez and family bake from scratch, using only the choicest ingredients. The Perez's day starts in the wee dark hours, before the roosters crow or the cows are milked. By the time you arrive, you'll have a delicious freshly baked selection of donuts, cookies and cakes to start your day. In addition to standard American pastries, the bakeries feature German, French, Swedish and Italian delectables. Ask for what you want and your special order will be ready when you call.

Conveniently located in a corner stall in the Pike Place Market and in the Renton Center, this family owned bakery is a great way to please all the Texas sized appetites in your group at any time of the day you decide to take a break.

(See special invitation in the Appendix.)

THREE GIRLS BAKERY
1514 Pike Place Stall #1
Seattle, WA 98101
Tel. (206) 622-1045
Hrs: Mon. - Sat. 7:00 a.m. - 6:00 p.m.
Closed Sundays and major holidays.

Brother and sister team Jack Levy and Zelda Dixon literally grew up in the Pike Place Market. They used to work in their father's produce shop when they were kids and always wanted to own their own shop in the Market. They are now the proprietors of the second oldest business in Pike Place Market. The Three Girls Bakery was founded in 1912 and has gone through several owners. The bakery is full of glass framed bins which hold loaves of bread and has a sandwich bar that does a booming business.

You will find lots of different kinds of breads in this fine bakery. Sourdough is their most popular bread, with rye a close second. They sell fresh pastries every day, and also feature bagels and rolls. The sandwiches served here are huge and made with a delicious nine grain bread. They custom make sandwiches to order so you get just what you want. There is a wide variety of kosher products, too. This is a very popular spot with locals and tourists alike.

For a delicious lunch in a uniquely Pike Place Market setting, or for some of the best and freshest bread in town, visit Three Girls Bakery.

Banquets

THE STIMSON GREEN MANSION
1204 Minor Avenue
Seattle, WA 98101
Tel. (206) 624-0474

The Stimson Green Mansion is a fine example of turn of the century construction. Tudoresque in appearance, the half-timbered house stands as one of the few remaining residences to use this style of architecture. It has 10,000 square feet of floor space and is situated on a 19,350 foot lot. It is richly panelled with imported hardwoods and beautifully preserved. This magnificent residence is a State and National Historic site and is available for special events.

The house is furnished with rich tapestries, antiques and the rooms are decorated with finely carved ornamentation which creates an elegant atmosphere for those wishing a special ambiance for their special celebrations. The Mansion is very popular for weddings, receptions, anniversaries, birthdays and other special occasions. The entire main floor is open to guests and will accommodate 200 people. When larger groups wish additional space, the downstairs is also available. The Mansion Catering Department offers a complete menu prepared and served on the premises.

The Mansion offers truly memorable surroundings for your special celebration and to prolong the experience, an overnight guest suite is available, complete with chauffeured limousine to airport or home the next day. Reservations are required for functions to be held at the Mansion and calling well in advance for specific dates is recommended.

Bed and Breakfast

CHAMBERED NAUTILUS
5005 22nd Avenue NE
Seattle, WA 98105
Tel. (206) 522-2536

Kate McDill and Deborah Sweet are the hosts at this classic University District Inn. The Chambered Nautilus, a perfect example of Georgian Colonial architecture, reflects the English heritage of its first owners. Perched on a hill with fine views of the Cascade Mountains, the inn is within walking distance of the University of Washington campus and only ten minutes from downtown Seattle.

There are six guest rooms available and all are large, airy and furnished with a mixture of English and American antiques. Japanese yukatas are supplied to guests using the three full baths. Kate is a professional baker and creates bountiful breakfasts in her large, commercial style kitchen. Her specialty is orange souffle, served with fresh muffins and scones. The dining room has a cozy fireplace, but if you wish, breakfast can be served in your room.

This fine inn frequently hosts scholars and an international clientele while they are visiting the University. Full catering service is available, for events held either at the inn or elsewhere. You'll feel very pampered during your stay at the Chambered Nautilus.

CHELSEA STATION BED AND BREAKFAST INN
4915 Linden Avenue N
Seattle, WA 98103
Tel. (206) 547-6077

Chelsea Station is located next to Woodland Park in a tranquil and woodsy setting, yet is only five minutes from downtown Seattle. Within walking distance is Green Lake where you can take a leisurely stroll along one of the waterfront trails.

This elegant 1920 Federal Colonial brick home was converted by owners Dick and Marylou Jones into a splendidly comfortable five bedroom bed and breakfast. Chelsea Station features two spacious suites with serene pastel furnishings. The cozy parlor off the dining room invites guests to relax with a cup of tea and cookies. The library is brimming with information about nearby restaurants, entertainment and sightseeing.

Luxury is uppermost. Sumptuous breakfasts include ginger pancakes with lemon sauce, and you'll love soaking in the relaxing hot tub. If you yearn for the scent of pine trees, first class hospitality and service, plus a fabulously convenient location, visit Chelsea Station where you'll be welcomed warmly by Dick, Marylou and their amiable Yorkshire terrier, "Chelsea."

GASLIGHT INN
1727 15th Avenue
Seattle, WA 98122
Tel. (206) 325-3654

Imagine yourself as a turn of the century aristocrat traveling first class. After a long steamer voyage, your secretary has made arrangements for you to stay at an exclusive guest residence of one of your business associates. Picture yourself at the Gaslight Inn.

Remodeled from a 19th century boarding house, this elegant bed and breakfast is a cut above in style and service. Of the nine available rooms, half have private baths. The master suite has the added luxury of a private sitting room with fireplace. All rooms are equipped with the 20th century conveniences of television, refrigerators, alarm radios and guest robes. Conduct your traveling party onto the main where the choice of living room, parlor or library awaits your presence. There are no servants; however, owners Trevor Logan and Steve Bennett provide a Continental breakfast in the dining room. In the warm months enjoy the afternoon beside a heated pool or be served a wine cooler deckside. The entire place is done in rich antique furnishings with original wood fixtures refinished to reveal their beauty.

In the evening relax in the parlor by the warm glow of authentic gaslights. Imagining can be very satisfying, but experiencing the reality of this wonderful inn is better. Make your reservations soon, the Gaslight Inn is usually and understandably well occupied.

GENIE'S BED AND BREAKFAST
3498 West Blaine
Seattle, WA 98199
Tel. (206) 282-2583

Quiet and cozy, Genie's Bed and Breakfast provides a tranquil retreat on the west side of Seattle's Magnolia district. Not being one of the larger inns is an advantage of Genie's, which is carefully run by proprietor Eugenia Nault.

From its vantage point, Genie's opens to a sweeping view of the Puget Sound as passing freighters cruise the distant shipping lanes. Since there are only two bedrooms, guests will never have the feeling that they are crowded out by others and each room has its own private entrance. As a departure from the traditional Continental breakfast of these types of establishments, visitors at Genie's are treated to a full breakfast the likes of eggs Benedict, fresh fruit and pastry.

Outside is a peaceful Japanese garden for relaxing, or during inclement weather, indoors is equally delightful in the sitting room by the warmth of a fireplace. Not more than ten minutes from downtown Seattle, Genie's gives the best of both worlds when looking for accommodations.

HANSON HOUSE BED AND BREAKFAST
1526 Palm Avenue SW
Seattle, WA 98116
Tel. (206) 937-4157

Of all of the bed and breakfast houses in Seattle, Hanson House has the finest view and friendliest service available. The Hanson House sits a top a bluff looking across Elliott Bay to the skyline of Seattle and the Cascades. As spectacular as the view is, it is matched by the warm hospitality of Jody Weaver and her lovely home. She has recently added an art gallery. In the galleria, there are changing exhibits of contemporary arts and photographs. The works, representing a wide spectrum of current impressions by American and Pacific Northwest artists, will be for sale.

While you have breakfast, you can gaze at the view in the quiet relaxing atmosphere as you prepare for a day of adventurous shopping, going to theaters and sightseeing just ten minutes drive over the new West Seattle bridge. You are just minutes away from golf, tennis, swimming and boating. See what Seattle's all about.

Pacific Bed and Breakfast Reservation Service has recommended the Hanson House as one of the 100 best bed and breakfasts in Frommer's North American Guide Book. Be sure to call for reservations as this guest house is very popular and books up far in advance.

Jody Weaver, your resident concierge and innkeeper, will help you with your Grey Line Tours, restaurant reservations and "where to go and what to do" while you are in Seattle. She is currently authoring a new cookbook-guidebook entitled "Favorite Recipes of the Washington State Bed and Breakfast Innkeepers", which is a guide through the nooks and crannies of the great state of Washington. (Cat and dog in residence.)

THE COLLEGE INN
4000 University Way N.E.
Seattle, WA 98105
Tel. (206) 633-4441
Open Year Round

James and Judith Oliver are the owners of Seattle's original European-style bed and breakfast inn. Located next door to the University of Washington, The College Inn is minutes away from Lake Washington, Lake Union and down town Seattle.

You'll be struck by the warmth of the inn from the time you set foot on the burgundy carpets complementing the red brick foyer. The College Inn is on the National Register of Historic Places as a restored historic Tudor hotel. Window seats, antique writing tables and pastel comforters provide a glowing ambience. The Inn currently boasts 27 rooms, each with a personal sink, and newly-tiled bathrooms conveniently located on every floor. James and Judith's future plans include adding conference rooms.

There's a deli in the building open until 2:00 a.m., a cafe which conveniently operates 24 hours a day, and even a pub on the lower level for socializing. The College Inn offers some nice extra touches. Coffee and tea are available at any time and a pleasant Continental breakfast is included with your room. There's a living room for guests to read the morning paper or take time to write the letter to the folks back home. Rates here are quite reasonable and children are always welcome.

King County

THE LOGAN LOFT
7045 Beach Drive SW
Seattle, WA 98136
Tel. (206) 938-3129

Pat and David Logan are the hosts of this delightful single room bed and breakfast which is located at the north end of West Seattle's Lincoln Park. Their English tudor home is on the waterfront with beach access and a sweeping view of Puget Sound and the Olympic Mountains.

David is an architect who designed the very warm hemlock lined upstairs studio-loft. This cozy addition has it's own private entrance. It features a balcony, sitting room, a double bed in the sleeping loft and it's own bathroom. A continental breakfast is served with fresh croissant, juice and coffee or tea. A small refrigerator, toaster-oven, and coffeemaker are also provided in the room.

This is a perfect spot for relaxation and quiet just twelve minutes from downtown Seattle and within walking distance of the Vashon Island Ferry. This is a popular bed and breakfast spot so it is advisable to call well in advance for reservations.

THE SHAFER MANSION
907 14th Avenue East
Seattle, WA 98102
Tel. (206) 329-4628
Personal checks are accepted.

The Shafer Mansion was completed in 1914 at a cost of over $100,000. The 14,000 square foot home was sold to Julius Shafer in 1927 and was his private residence until 1957. In 1979 Lee Vennes and Erv Olssen purchased the house and restored it to its former glory. There is lovely solid oak panelling, the original chandeliers, sconces and leaded glass windows. The mansion has three stories, a billiard room, library, solarium, in addition to the guest rooms.

There are five non smoking guest rooms available. The executive suite features an antique mahogany sleigh bed, private bar and sitting area, private shower and a bright southern exposure overlooking the courtyard. The Walnut room and Maple room both have western exposures and views of the Olympic Mountains and Space Needle. Breakfast each day consists of fresh fruits, homemade muffins, coffee, tea, or orange juice served in either the dining room or solarium. During the summer months you may enjoy a stroll in the lovely garden filled with roses and geraniums.

The house and garden are available for parties, dinners and receptions of up to 150 people. Limousine service is available to and from the airport, train and bus depots. Downtown Seattle and the University District are just minutes away and there is excellent bus service. For a relaxing change from hotel life, try The Shafer Mansion. Your gracious hosts will provide you with a truly enjoyable visit.

Books

METSKER MAPS, 702 First Avenue, Seattle, Washington. A complete inventory of maps and travel books to help you see the Northwest and the world. See detailed description for Pioneer Maps in the Bellevue section of this book.

Bowling

SKYWAY PARK BOWL
11819 Renton Avenue South
Seattle, WA 98178
Tel. (206) 772-1220
Hrs: Bowling: Mon. - Sun.   open 24 hours
Cocktails: Mon. - Sun.   10:00 a.m. - 2:00 p.m.
Card room: Mon. - Sun.   9:00 a.m. - 2:00 a.m.

When Fred Flintstone says, "Let's go bowling Barney!" he has in mind the kind of bowling the Skyway Park Bowl offers; home of the professional bowlers tour being held this June. A bright colored, ultra-modern bowling center, one of the finest in the Seattle area. It features forty lanes with the Brunswick A-2 Automatic scoring system; that's computerized scoring!

The Skyway Park Bowl is more than a bowling phenomenon, this very special center has videos, pool tables, the Washington State Lotto machine and a full-service restaurant that specializes in home-cooked food. Parents will be happy to know that the bowl has a nursery for children so they too can enjoy the action.

The philosophy, as expressed by partner, Dave Pardey is that, "If you've happy, so are we." To stay on top, the center is always looking to improve. The newly remodeled cocktail lounge with a card room offers the popular Texas Hold'em, with a $10 limit. The restaurant features home-baked pies, a salad bar that will challenge your stacking abilities and the tastiest hamburgers and steaks to be found. There are also banquet rooms with twenty-four hour service. Dave says, "We try harder. Anyone traveling through can stop and bowl--cause we'll be open. This is a modern, up-dated bowling center, not one of those typical dingy, dark, older bowls."

Imagine bowling, with cocktail service on the lane and after the game cutting into a juicy top quality steak, then sitting in on a hot game of poker. What a life! Barney would love it!

Cannery

PORT CHATHAM PACKING COMPANY
632 N. W. 46th Street
Seattle, WA 98107
Tel. (206) 783-8200
Hrs: Mon. - Fri. 8:00 a.m. - 5:30 p.m.
        Saturday   9:00 a.m. - 5:00 p.m.

For more than fifty years the Port Chatham Packing Company has been providing its customers with to be some of the world's finest smoked seafood. Founded in Alaska in the village of Portlock, on Alaska's Port Chatham Bay, Port Chatham makes the type of products you are proud to send to your friends. The company specializes in both cold-smoking and hot-smoking Northwest seafood. Cold smoking is a process in which the fish is cured in a special formula and then smoked slowly and carefully at no more than 70 degrees. Hot smoking is a process in which the fish is cooked and smoked simultaneously at about 180 degrees. Either way, the end result is equally delicious.

Port Chatham offers such a wide range of smoked products for the consumer that you can decide to buy through mail order or at the retail outlet. The list includes several types of hot and cold smoked salmon, a wonderful hand-packed smoked albacore tuna, smoked rainbow trout, smoked sturgeon, and some particularly delicious Pacific Northwest oysters.

The number of products is far too long to list, so come to the cannery and enjoy the incredible array.

Candy

ELMER FUDGE, Two locations in Seattle: Columbia Center, and 425 Broadway, East. For the finest fudge around, visit Elmer Fudge! (See Bellevue Eastside Public Market for complete article.)

OLD WORLD FUDGE
1530 Post Alley
Seattle, WA 98101
Tel. (206) 682-6579
Hrs: Mon. - Sat. 9:00 a.m. - 6:00 p.m.
Extended hours in December and summer.
and,
297 Gilman Boulevard
Issaquah, WA 98027
Tel. (206) 391-2779

Fudge is probably the only well known candy that had its origins in North America. It first appeared in the Northeast United States in the late 1700s. At Old World Fudge they make their fudge using the same kind of equipment and the same methods as candy makers of that era. Old World Fudge is owned by Hazelgrove Chocolate, Inc. and is operated by Lance Haslund, his sister Rondi, and his wife Laurie.

All ingredients used at Old World Fudge are of the highest quality and freshness, including real butter, cream, sugar, cocoa, and the best of flavorings. The flavorings have been formulated specifically for Old World Fudge and are not available to any other candy manufacturers. They use an old family recipe and each batch is strictly controlled. Several different flavors are available, including milk chocolate with or without walnuts, dark chocolate, also with or without nuts and chocolate amoretto, among others. The product is sold to fine food and specialty shops in the area, as well as at both store locations.

Old World Fudge is famous locally for its caramel apples, too. During strawberry season a special treat is very large fresh strawberries dipped in your choice of chocolate. Gift certificates are available if you can't make up your mind or want the recipient to have the fun of sampling and deciding himself which delicious fudge to buy. Stop in at Old World Fudge for a mouth-watering treat.

(See special invitation in the Appendix.)

Coffee

CULPEPPERS
2217 NW Market Street
Seattle, WA 98107
Tel. (206) 784-5400
Hrs: Mon. - Sat. 10:00 a.m. - 6:00 p.m.
Visa, MasterCard and AMEX are accepted.

Coffee gourmands take note! Culpeppers has it all! Over forty different kinds of coffee from as many countries are available here. Also, for those who wish to avoid the caffeine, Culpeppers stocks over twenty kinds of decaffeinated coffee. And, as always, the staff cheerfully will custom grind your favorite morning miracle especially for you.

Along with all manner of coffee and tea related items, such as coffeepots, mugs, espresso machines and accessories, Culpeppers also features a beautiful espresso bar and serves espresso imported directly from Trieste.

That's not all. Culpeppers also caters to your sweet tooth with a full array of chocolates and candies from top-of-the-line gift boxes of chocolates, to less esoteric favorite collections like gummy bears and worms. The Pacific Northwest also is highlighted by a specialty selection of regional wines, jams and gourmet pickled asparagus. Culpeppers is a treat waiting just for you. The carefully selected stock is wide ranging and certainly worth your visit.

STARBUCKS COFFEE
2010 Airport Way S
Seattle, Washington 98234
Tel. (206) 447-1575
Coffee by Mail
Tel.   (206) 447-1580 WA
       (206) 445-3428 USA
and,
Pike Place Market   University Village
516 Broadway East   4555 University Way Northeast
Fourth and Spring   10213 NE 8th, Bellevue
           Bear Creek Village, Redmond

Starbucks in the Pike Place Market is synonymous with excellence in coffee in the Northwest. Starbuck's coffee buyer travels the world, from East Africa to Central America in search of the best beans....and brings them to you at seven Starbucks locations in the Seattle area.

Starbuck's commitment to quality and taste is a fifteen-year tradition. Each batch of coffee beans is custom roasted. Daily. Careful quality control and taste tests are made several times a day; the end product is dark, full-bodied, and worth a drive to the Seattle area to enjoy!

Knowing that freshness is a critical factor in good coffee flavor, Starbucks delivers all coffee sold to stores within 48 hours after roasting, and all roasts are date-coded. Any coffee that gets to be a week old, without selling, is donated to charity! Fastidious attention to freshness and excellence has created a demand for Starbucks coffee which allowed expansion to six locations outside the Pikes Place Market.

Yearning for some of this fresh brew and don't know when you'll get to Seattle? It's easy to order by mail by calling the number listed above during the hours of 9 a.m. to 5 p.m. Monday through Friday. (Pacific Time)

You'll also want to request Starbucks brochure which provides some great coffee brewing tips, a dictionary of coffee types, and the story of good coffee in the Pacific Northwest.

Collectables

GOLDEN AGE COLLECTABLES, LTD.
1501 Pike Place Market
Seattle, WA 98101 #401 Lower Level
Tel. (206) 622-9799
Hrs: Mon. - Sat. 10:00 a.m. - 5:30 p.m.
Open Sundays during the summer.
and,
Collectors Bookstore, Ltd.
1501 Pike Place Market #432 Lower Level
Seattle, WA 98101
Tel. (206) 622-5182

Take a journey down memory lane at Golden Age Collectables. Nostalgia buffs never had it any better. The collection of 1940 to 80s movie memorabilia, classic comic books, posters and baseball cards will stagger the sensory receptors of even the most jaded minds.

Since opening in 1970, owners Rod and Colleen Dyke have amassed the largest collection of vintage collectables available on the West Coast. Start with over 1,000,000 comic books from a 1938 edition of Superman #1 to the most recent Spiderman. This is truly a collection without parallel. For the movie fan there is a sizeable trove of such gems as theater posters from "Gone with the Wind" and "The Wizard of Oz". Original movie scripts are available, as are some 5,000 photos of stars like Marilyn Monroe, James Dean and Humphrey

Bogart, plus many autographed photographs!. Not to be left out are the Sci-Fi fans, who can search through a unreal selection of books and at their associate store Collectors Bookstore, Ltd., 300 feet up the hall!. Original radio programs of yesteryear are on cassette tape for sale. Take of these home for an exciting diversion from the VCR next evening. Throw in the gigantic collection of rare and recent baseball cards and there is probably more to look over then the mind can handle in one day.

Ready for a trip down memory lane?

Delicatessen

THE CRUMPET SHOP
1503 1st Avenue
Seattle, WA 98101
Tel. (206) 682-1598
Hrs: Mon. - Sat.   7:30 a.m. - 5:00 p.m.
         Sunday   8:30 a.m. - 5:00 p.m.
Closed major holidays. No smoking allowed indoors.

The Crumpet Shop is a Seattle jewel that the rest of the country is beginning to discover. The Crumpet Shop is one of only two locations in North America where freshly baked crumpets are available, and people from all parts of the country are dropping in. Imagine the famous English crumpet spread with delicious Northwest jams and jellies such as, wild huckleberry, or covered with chocolate, English cheese, or sumptuous smoked salmon. The mouth waters at the idea.

Owner Gary Lasater trained in Victoria, BC, and uses the same famous Victoria English crumpet recipe which has been popular for over sixty years in Canada. Lasater explains that the creation of a perfect crumpet requires the merging of many critical factors. He says that not only must the temperature of the griddle be rigidly controlled, but also the temperatures of the batter and the room in which they're being prepared. The results are delicious.

Also featured in the charming and delightfully decorated Crumpet Shop is freshly ground coffee from The Good Coffee Company. Plus, Lasater offers three different sizes of espresso.

King County

LOUIE'S
1926 Pike Place
Seattle, WA 98101
Tel. (206) 621-1035

The delectable aroma of rich cheeses and smoked seafood greet you as you enter this large and comfortable deli, located in the heart of the Pike Place Market.

Louie's offers such treats as smoked salmon, rainbow trout, sausages, and a variety of delicious jams and jellies. There is a considerable inventory of Northwest wines as well as import reds and whites.

In addition to the large deli selection available, Louie's also has several aisles of regular household needs.

Furnishings

CURRENT
1001 Western Avenue
Seattle, WA 98104
Tel. (206) 622-2433

Current is the essence of contemporary Italian furniture. State of the art suspension lighting shares the spacious showroom with examples of the best of Italian craftsmanship. The selection of furniture spans chairs, tables, wall sections, couches and floor lamps mostly in muted black, white, gray and tones of tan. All the best names are featured, Imports Driade, Palliello, Zanotta, and Fontana Arte in leather, fabric, steel, wood and granite.

Owner Ron Gawith has arranged the selections elegantly and, with the judicious use of avant-garde lighting, has achieved excellent distance perspectives within the pieces.

For a truly contemporary experience in light and exciting Italian furnishings, visit Current, located in the south corner of the Cornerstone Redevelopment Project on Western Avenue.

THE GOLDEN HORN
323 First Avenue South
Seattle, WA 98104
Tel. (206) 464-0578
Hrs: Mon. - Sat. 10:00 a.m. - 6:30 p.m.
 Sunday 12:00 noon - 5:00 p.m.

Centuries ago the caravans of the east brought the wares of the Orient to Europe. Gentry of feudal period came to highly value these imports, especially the beautifully woven rugs. Today the commerce continues as people still value the fine craftsmanship of these Oriental rugs. The Golden Horn in Seattle is today's version of the ancient trade routes.

Run by a third generation rug dealer, The Golden Horn stocks over 3,500 rugs from India, China, Turkey, Pakistan, Afghanistan and Tibet. Proprietor Ali Bozatli personally oversees the selection and importing of these handmade works of art. Displayed in their huge showroom are wool and silk rugs of every size. The capable and knowledgeable staff is ready to assist you with your home decorating needs.

No need to travel to China to find that rug you've been envisioning in that blank spot on your floor, just journey to The Golden Horn.

KEEG'S
310 Broadway East
Seattle, WA 98102
Tel. (206) 325-1771
Hrs: Mon. - Fri. 10:00 a.m - 8:00 p.m.
 Saturday 10:00 a.m. - 6:00 p.m.
 Sunday 11:00 a.m. - 5:00 p.m.

Keeg's offers Seattle's finest selection of contemporary home furnishings and gifts. You'll find the best in Danish light woods, sleek Italian lamps, classic wicker chairs, and hand woven rugs from India, Hungary and Sweden.

Keeg's carries a wide variety of traditional and contemporary dinnerware, flatware and glassware from around the world. In Keeg's cookware room you'll find essentials for the beginning cook and elegant tools of the trade for the gourmet. Peruse Keeg's collection of greeting cards, fabulous jewelry and whimsical toys that delight children and adults alike!

If you're looking for something out of the ordinary, you'll certainly find it at Keeg's.

PERIOD. FURNISHINGS
2200 1st Avenue
Seattle, WA 98121
Tel. (206) 443-1909
Sales and Rentals
Hrs: Tue. - Fri.   11:00 a.m. - 6:00 p.m.
     Saturday   11:00 a.m. - 5:00 p.m.
     Or by appointment.

Period. is an exciting top end mid-century modern home furnishings gallery which will take you back to the 1950s. A very enthusiastic owner, Geraldine Zelinsky, showcases an impressive twenty year collection of furniture, home furnishings, and collectibles dating from the mid 1900s.

Having accumulated some 5,000 square feet of showroom and warehoused merchandise, Geraldine is continually buying, selling and trading merchandise which keeps the gallery interesting and creative. Production and/or window display rentals and mail order are all available at Period.

Additionally, Period. serves as a resource and network center for mid-century designs. Open house is held on the first Thursday of each month from 6:00 p.m. until 9:00 p.m. This boutique is a unique experience in nostalgia and should not be missed.

Garden Center

SEATTLE GARDEN CENTER
1600 Pike Place Market
Seattle, WA 98101
Tel. (206) 624-0431
Hrs: Mon. - Sat. 9:00 a.m. - 5:30 p.m.
     Sunday   10:00 a.m. - 4:00 p.m.

A trip to Seattle's beautiful Pike Place Market would not be complete without a stop at the Seattle Garden Center. This shop, in business for over forty years, appeals to a wide variety of shoppers from virtually all over the world. What is it that attracts these people, you ask? Well, it's a combination of the staff's excellent service and the shop's quality supplies.

The Seattle Garden Center is well known for its vegetable, herb and flower seed selection, which is one of the largest in the Pacific Northwest. The Garden Center imports seeds from many countries, such as England, Germany, Canada, France and Italy. If you're looking for bulbs for spring and summer bloom, the Center is an excellent source for that as well. When working in the garden, discovering you need special tools, you can be secure in the knowledge that Garden Center carries just about any tool you might need.

Whether its herbs, annuals, perennials or houseplants, you're sure to find them at the Garden Center, where quality is a high priority. If it's a special gift item for yourself or a friend, be sure to check the Center's wide selection of Bonsai, flowering plants, containers, baskets and "Gifts for Gardener's. Whatever the reason or occasion, Seattle Garden Center can fill your agricultural needs.

Gift Shops

THE BEST OF ALL WORLDS
523 Union Street
Seattle, WA 98101
Tel. (206) 623-2525
Hrs: Mon. - Sat. 10:00 a.m. - 5:30 p.m.
Extended hours during the Christmas season.

As the name suggests, the best from all around the world can be found in this delightful shop, conveniently located on the corner of Sixth and Union. The shop is charming, with wood-beamed ceilings. Proprietor Eriann Davis has spared no effort in providing unusual and elegant selections from which to choose.

The Best of All Worlds has a variety of European imports. French, Italian and Portuguese faience dinnerware is complemented by a large selection of table linens. There is excellent flatware, such as Scof from France. An imposing brass and copper weathervane with a sailboat mounted on top is sure to catch your eye. There are handsome furniture pieces, too.

Whether you are seeking unique and unusual jewelry from France, sterling silver ornaments from Portugal, or something truly different and unique from some exotic spot, you'll find an unbeatable selection at The Best of All Worlds.

BEST REGARDS
2211 N. W. Market Street
Seattle, WA 98107
Tel.   (206) 783-4562

Hrs:	
Mon., Tues., Weds., Fri.	10:00 a.m. - 5:30 p.m.
Thurs.	10:00 a.m. - 8:00 p.m.
Saturday	10:00 a.m. - 5:30 p.m.
Sunday	12:00 p.m. - 5:00 p.m.

    For that special occasion, Best Regards is the place to shop. If you're looking for just the right card or gift wrap to compliment the occasion, you're almost guaranteed to find precisely what you're looking for among the seemingly endless collection of cards, wraps and party favors.

    If a gift shop is defined by the variety and quality of its merchandise, then Best Regards is very well defined indeed. There is an excellent selection of fragrant soaps, handcrafted lamps, clocks, frames, painted party trays and a vast selection of ceramic masks.

    It is, however, the dollar-to-value relationship which makes this shop special. Whether you want a champagne bucket or special English Christmas crackers, you will find what you are looking for. All of the items are tastefully displayed and reasonably priced. Stop in, and receive friendly service at Best Regards.

THE BLUE PARROT
1815 N 45th Street
Seattle, WA 98103
Tel. (206) 547-8871

    When The Blue Parrot's proprietor, Susan Godfey, lived in the Caribbean, she involved herself in co-op projects and developed an appreciation for native handcrafts. The Blue Parrot reflects her interest and expertise with shelves full of traditional and contemporary folk art from the Caribbean and Latin America.

    There are handpainted balsa birds from Ecuador, worry dolls from Guatemala, alpaca sweaters handwoven in Peru, assorted Mexican piñatas, and baskets of multicolored seed beads. Displays are changed with the seasons and Susan is delighted to help with useful gift suggestions.

    The Blue Parrot offers a colorful array of goods to please every taste. The prices are very reasonable and this is an interesting place to shop for something out of the ordinary.

King County

DEUX AMIS
85 Yester Way
Seattle, WA 98104
Tel. (206) 624-3545

Located near the picturesque waterfront, this cozy shop offers a wide range of gift items. There is a generous selection of gifts to choose from which are imported from England and France, as well as soaps and sweets. Deux Amis also carries a large variety of antique collectibles, featuring delightful stuffed bears and other children's toys.

The eclectic inventory also includes glittering crystal from Russia, Turkey, Romania and Poland, gleaming brass items from India and China, and charming pottery from England.

Those searching for quality table linens will be pleased by Deux Amis' wide variety. Blankets, towels and numerous plants also are available to round out your gift list. This charming shop will be a great asset to your gift and decorating needs.

If you find yourself lacking in culture, after this tour you'll be able to converse with the best of them.

	THE WORLD IN SEATTLE		
a.m.	Chez Dominique	Best French breakfast	Sea/Rest.
a.m.	Uwajimaya	Best Asian goods	Sea/Gift
a.m.	Best of All Worlds	Best imports	Sea/Gift
a.m.	Kagedo	Best Japanese art	Sea/Art
a.m.	Norwegian Sausage	Best sausage	Sea/Food
p.m.	Mama's Mexican Kitc.	Best Mexican lunch	Sea/Rest.
p.m.	Golden Horn	Best Persian rugs	Sea/Furn.
p.m.	Scandinavian Gift	Best heritage selection	Sea/Gift
p.m.	Norway Knits	Best Norse goods	Sea/Yarn
p.m.	Blue Parrot	Best Caribbean goods	Sea/Gift
p.m.	Saleh Al Lago	Best Italian cuisine	Sea/Rest.

Who wants to go around the world in eighty days when they can do it in eight hours?

EGBERT'S
2231 1st Avenue
Seattle, WA 98121
Tel. (206) 624-3377

In the middle of Seattle's historic Belltown on Upper First Avenue is Jim Egbert's modern and contemporary housewares shop. Items include sparkling beads, jewelry, rich table linens and handwoven rugs from Finland. Egbert's inventory primarily is drawn from Northern Europe, although there is a smaller selection of Asian items.

A collection of furniture is offered in light hardwood, birch, beechwood, and white oak. Presented exclusively are Juhava stearine candles from Finland and Pott stainless steel tableware from Germany.

Jim also carries Jukka toys and games made from light hardwood from Finland. These high-quality items are a delight for children and have won numerous awards. A true potpourri of gifts, accessories, furniture and unique housewares is available from this top exclusive shop.

EXCLUSIVELY NORTHWEST
415 Stewart Street
Seattle, WA 98101
Tel. (206) 622-9144
Hrs: Mon. - Thu.   10:00 a.m. - 5:30 p.m.
      Friday   10:00 a.m. - 7:00 p.m.
      Saturday   10:00 a.m. - 5:00 p.m.

Exclusively Northwest is a delightful gift shop that is really more like an art gallery, situated in The Times Square Building just across from the Mayflower Hotel and The Bon. Owner Miki Brostrom has arranged her handcrafted items from all over the Northwest in a relaxing and well-lighted showroom.

There is an excellent selection of colorful porcelain and stoneware pottery displayed on oak shelves. Gourmet food such as smoked salmon, blackberry preserves and hazelnut honeybutter share space with sterling silver jewelry, sculpture and books. Woolen throws and wraps, fascinating Northwest Coast Indian masks and original wall art are creatively exhibited.

As the name explains, Exclusively Northwest is the "Best Choice" for special mementos of your travels.

FIREWORKS CERAMIC GALLERY
210 First Avenue S
Seattle, WA 98104
Tel. (206) 682-8707

Seattle is well known for its seemingly everlasting cloud cover. With the exception of a short period in the summer, this city sees very little sun. Because of this, it's nice to know where you can go to get out from under the clouds and have a little fun. Warm laughter, exquisite works of art and personal attention all await you at Fireworks Ceramics Gallery in Pioneer Square.

Step into this gift shop/gallery and step into another world, one of humor and unique wares. The assortment of artwork includes such items as The Insane Asylum Salt and Pepper Shakers. What in the world could that be, you ask? Well, come by and find out while looking at the many other pieces displayed here. Microchip earrings, stuffed purple pigeons, Raku vases, etched porcelain by Dan Hoskisson and contemporary dishware are only a few of the objects this gallery has to feature.

The proprietor, Michele Manasse is justly satisfied with her varied collection that consists of something to please or surprise anyone. She's done a good job providing a little bit of sunlight to the Emerald City of Seattle. Stop by for a visit that is sure to arouse a few giggles.

THE GIFT GALLERY
4530 California Avenue SW
Seattle, WA 98116
Tel. (206) 932-9275
Hrs: Mon. - Sat. 9:30 a.m. - 5:45 p.m.

When you are shopping in West Seattle, be sure to visit The Gift Gallery. The shop is managed by Rebecca Buxbaum and assistant manger Margaret Winter. This team has knowledge to share in everything from crystal to miniatures.

Some of the interesting treasures to be found are a fantastic selection of Waterford and Gorham crystal or glass made from Mt. St. Helens ash. There is a special collection of carousel horses by Willits, handsomely displayed, and collectible figurines by Precious Moments, Robert Olzewski, De Drazia and Hummel. Additionally, there is adorable children's tableware by Brambly Hedge and Beatrix Potter and Bunnykins, all by Royal Doulton. Also carried are crystal by Riedel, and Swedish crystal from Kista Boda and many other gift items by Goebel, Royal Doulton, Reflections, Toby Jugs, floral baskets, Capodimonte florals, and Irish bone china from Belleek.

The staff of the Gift Gallery are always enthusiastic and willing to answer any questions you may have, so be sure to drop by to find that special gift at this "Best Choice" shop in Seattle.

GREETINGS
106 1st Avenue South
Seattle, WA 98104
Tel. (206) 624-7713
Hrs: Mon. - Sat.   10:00 a.m. - 6:00 p.m.
         Sunday   12:00 noon - 5:00 p.m.

If you like <u>fun</u> shopping, the kind of place that features pink flamingos, inflatable dinos and the latest creations for gifts and cards, Greetings is a must. Owner Dan Jeske has put together an eye-catching shop with something for everyone.

If gifts for those back home are high on your list, the selection of artistic, unusual custom t-shirts is a great beginning place. Cards, stationery, jewelry, watches and decorative items with a unique twist are displayed.

The Greetings approach is to find those gifts that make the ordinary into the extraordinary. Whether it's neon art or cards, shopping at this "Best Choice" will be an experience in merriment.

J. F. HENRY
4540 California Avenue SW
Seattle, WA 98116
Tel. (206) 935-5150
Hrs: Mon. - Thu.   9:00 a.m - 6:00 p.m.
         Friday   9:00 a.m. - 9:00 p.m.
         Saturday   9:00 a.m. - 6:00 p.m.

Patty and Tom Henry have created a gift and tableware store that must be seen to be appreciated. The Henrys have taken their many years of retail experience and opened a store that allows them to use their creativity.

Among the items at this store are china, silverware, linens, exquisite crystal and ceramics plus fabrics for the table in a variety of stunning colors. The Henrys are delighted to help you when selecting something new for your home or gifts for weddings and anniversaries. The Henrys also carry a wonderful collection of cute animals and cuddlies for the young ones on your list.

Whatever your gift needs, or needs for the home, Patty and Tom invite you to come in and browse through J.F. Henry.

MADE IN WASHINGTON
1530 Post Alley
Seattle, WA 98101
Tel. (206) 467-0788
Hrs: Mon - Sat.   9:00 a.m. - 6:00 p.m.
     Sunday   11:00 a.m. - 5:00 p.m.

Just as the name indicates, Made in Washington carries only things produced in the state of Washington. There is a large selection of food items, crafts, books, cards, posters and gift items.

Jack and Gillian Mathews have assembled a wide selection of Washington-produced goods for their shop. There are berry jams, smoked salmon and other seafood and Washington wines and cheeses available in the food section. You can make up your own gift pack of unique Washington items and they will take care of shipping for you, anywhere in the U.S. Choose from the extensive selection of craft items, local pottery, prints, Christmas ornaments and Mt. St. Helens glass.

This is the place to shop for things that are uniquely Washington. Whether you are seeking a gift or a remembrance of your vacation, you'll find it at Made in Washington.

MR. PEEPERS GIFT SHOP
6200 San Point Way NE
Seattle, WA 98115
Tel. (206) 522-8202
     (206) 524-6464
Hrs: Mon. - Sat.   10:00 a.m. - 6:00 p.m.
     Thursday   10:00 a.m. - 8:00 p.m.
     Sunday   12:00 noon - 5:00 p.m. Winter only

Mr. Peepers has the finest and most complete selection of miniature furniture, accessories, kits and dollhouses in the Pacific Northwest. It is located past Children's Hospital and Medical Center three blocks south of the San Point Naval Air Station, northeast of the University District. It is certainly worth the trip just to view the magnificently detailed dollhouse by nationally recognized miniaturists.

The store has a fine selection of handcrafted items from artisans of the area, as well as from others throughout the country. Owners Allan Davis and Barbara Raftery celebrate each major holiday by decorating the store and featuring items characterizing the season.

There is a wide variety of toys, stuffed animals, nutcrackers, smokers, ornaments, paper goods and exceptional gifts from which to choose. All items are hand selected and the discerning and "young at heart" shopper will be delighted in what Mr. Peepers has to offer.

NONPAREIL
705 Broadway East
Seattle, WA 98102
Tel. (206) 328-2810

Nonpareil is a warm and interesting shop offering an unparalleled selection of contemporary Asian gifts, accessories and furniture. Co-owners are Deborah Fairman and Suzanne McNamara. Deborah grew up in the Orient and her parents own a shop in Hong Kong. This experience provides a unique background to customers.

The array of items includes pottery, porcelain dolls, jewelry, paintings, pillows and vintage Japanese furniture and more. Deborah and Suzanne publish a newsletter in which they share travel tips and information on Asia, and will gladly assist in your home decorating needs.

PANACHE
1015 Western Avenue
Seattle, WA 98104
Tel. (206) 223-1151

The modern motif and spacious, mauve-colored interior of this recently-opened gift shop is a real asset to Seattle's waterfront. Proprietor Patricia Tall is a cordial host and ensures customer satisfaction. Panache's gift selections include linens for bed, bath and table, flatware, and dinnerware ranging from Limoges china to handmade ceramic items. All glassware is handblown, and Patricia personally selects all merchandise.

Panache is the exclusive representative of the Swid Powell collection of china, glassware and silver designed by American architects. Gift shoppers seeking tasteful, superlative offerings will enjoy visiting Panache.

PERGOLA WEST GIFT SHOP
600 Western Avenue
Seattle, WA 98104
Tel. (206) 622-0816
Hrs: Mon. - Sun. 10:00 a.m. - 6:00 p.m.
Visa, MasterCard and AMEX are accepted.

Stroll on in to the Pergola West Gift Shop and you are immediately aware you are surrounded by Northwest artists' creations. Tastefully displayed in an uncluttered, open-space shop.

Planned to take home "a little something" from your trip? This is the place to be. You will find a fabulous assortment of Mt. St. Helens glass that has been interpreted into jewelry and ornaments. Native American art and designs, totems from four inches to seven feet! Eskimo-carved pieces in soapstone and stone, scrimshaw ivory, handcrafted sterling silver jewelry, an assortment of stuffed animals for the young, and Emerald City truffles or Aplets & Cotlets to munch on the way, or to ship home.

A complete selection of Northwest kitchen art, capable of functionality or as wall-hangings awaits your choice. You'll also find locally produced tote bags, T-shirts, carved wooden ducks, and an impressive collection of pottery.

This shop is a "Best Choice" for people looking for gifts which typify the best the Northwest has to offer--Pergola West.

THE SCANDINAVIAN GIFT SHOP
2016 NW Market Street
Seattle, WA 98107
Tel. (206) 784-9370
Hrs: Mon.-Sat. 10:00 a.m.-5:30 p.m.
    Call for holiday hours.

Ballard, located in the northwest section of Seattle, is justly proud of its Scandinavian heritage. Among the multitude of shops on Ballard's thoughtfully restored Market Street, The Scandinavian Gift Shop offers the visitor a rare opportunity to sample the best of Scandinavia without ever having to leave Seattle.

In addition to an excellent selection of imported goods such as crystal, pewter, solje pins and earrings, and handmade sweaters suitable even for the fabled Seattle weather, The Scandinavian Gift Shop also offers such related items as Scandinavian books and records, and even t-shirts with a Scandinavian theme such as, "You can always tell a Swede, but you can't tell him much."

The warm, friendly atmosphere created by the Hatley family make the shop a delight. The Hatleys cordially invite you to visit their store which is "just like a visit to the old country."

TRADITIONAL PICNICS
2948C Eastlake Avenue, East
Seattle, WA 98102
Tel. (206) 328-4474
Hrs: Mon. - Fri.   10:00 a.m. - 5:00 p.m.
           Saturday   12:00 noon - 5:00 p.m.

If you are running out of ideas for special occasions and holiday gifts, you are going to love what Traditional Picnics has to offer. For the past three years, the owners of Traditional Picnics have been providing a wonderful alternative to run of the mill gifts –fabulous gift baskets and unique picnics for special occasions.

Traditional Picnics provides a wide array of deliciously filled picnic baskets available for pickup or delivery on a twenty-four hour notice. Try "The All Occasion" basket for two which includes fresh pesto and walnut salad, imported cheeses, fresh baked bread, fresh fruit, a homemade dessert and your choice of imported or non-alcoholic wine. For something a little more elaborate, there is "The Northwest Splurge" which features smoked trout, French potatoes, blackberry marinated carrots, fresh baked bread, imported cheeses, fresh fruits, homemade dessert and wine. Once you have finished the contents, you get to keep the basket.

Traditional Picnics offers a "Working Lunch" and "Working Dinner" both of which can be delivered to your place of business. Baskets can be picked up, delivered or shipped within twenty-four hours of ordering. Custom baskets are available and they sell a wide range of gourmet items. For a delightfully different and unusually delicious gift, visit Traditional Picnics.

THE WAYSIDE
4507 SW Wildwood
Seattle, WA 98136
Tel. (206) 932-4147
Hrs: Tue. - Sat. 10:00 a.m - 6:00 p.m.

For Ellen Anderson, bringing beauty to the world is a way of life. She dedicates her time and efforts to acquiring things of beauty and delight for her customers. Located on a quiet street near Fauntleroy ferry dock where the Vashon Ferry connects to West Seattle, Ellen invites you to explore her exquisite shop and revive your spirit.

The best dried florals that nature can provide are featured with the finest silks, offered by the stem or in custom designs. Special, unique gifts are hand selected for quality and charm. Baskets range from pure elegance to rustic elegance to wild and woodsy. Ellen selects cards and gift wraps aimed at touching the spirit by expressing the beauty in each of us. Seasonal decorations are designed with an emphasis on the "simple yet elegant."

If you are looking for a different shopping experience, one that will nurture, as well as excite, The Wayside is your "Best Choice" in Seattle.

YE OLDE CURIOSITY SHOP, 601 Alaskan Way, Seattle, Washington. National Geographic says this shop is "Seattle's most fantastic store...a landmark of the whole Northwest."

Glassware

GLASSHOUSE ART GLASS
Pioneer Square
311 Occidental Avenue S.
Seattle, WA 98104
Tel. (206) 682-9939
Hrs: Mon. - Sun. 10:00 a.m. - 5:00 p.m.

The fine art of glass blowing and glass art have found a home in the Pacific Northwest. One of the finest examples of what this means can be found in Pioneer Square.

The GlassHouse, started in 1971, has evolved to become not only one of the most exciting galleries in the Northwest, but one of the most interesting places to visit. Why??? Because not only can you see the beautiful results of fine craftsmanship and artistry in glass, but you can actually watch as the glass blowers create their art.

At the rear portion of the GlassHouse gallery and studio, enclosed behind large glass partitions, is the actual furnace and work area where the artists perform their magic with glass. Watch the speed and grace of an expert blower as they manipulate a heavy, glowing ball of the hot glass, and then turn that molten lump into a work of art of rare beauty and grace. It's pure fascination!

One of the joys of glass is that it offers function, as well as beauty. A specialty of The Glasshouse is their display of lamps and lighting pieces. The fluted Art Nouveau lighting fixture with delicate shade, combined with the drama of light, creates an overall effect that would enhance anyone's decor. One outstanding aspect is the palette of colors available to the glass artists.

With color they can "paint" patterns of reality or the abstract into a eyecatching piece of art.

NINETY-SIX-3-PIECE DUCKS
214 1st Avenue S Lower Arcade
Pioneer Square
Seattle, WA 98104
Tel. (206) 624-4041
Hrs: Mon. - Sat.   11:00 a.m. - 5:00 p.m.
         Sunday   12:00 noon - 5:00 p.m.

Ninety-Six-3-Piece Ducks is as unusual, fascinating and unique as its name. Located in the lower arcade of the Grand Central Building, the shop features the art of glass. The three dimensional quality of the works attain a transcendental beauty that will grace your home.

Owners Debra and Brian Dameron are glass artists who specialize in Tiffany style creations, using modern colors and designs. Other techniques used in their art include etching on glass and the use of kilns to melt and bend glass. Since the work is done in the shop, you will enjoy the added pleasure of watching art in the making. You will also find the works of other outstanding artists, featuring neon sculptures and blown glass using the ash from the May 18, 1980 eruption of Mt. St. Helens.

When you find that exquisite item you simply can't resist, and are dreading the task of getting it home in one piece, don't despair, they will ship it there...anywhere in the world.

Golf Course

TYEE GOLF COURSE
2401 South 192nd
Seattle, WA 98105
Tel. (206) 878-3540

For the traveller to Seattle who enjoys a game of golf, Tyee Golf Course is perfect. It is an eighteen hole course located just minutes from Sea-Tac Airport. It has a slope rating of 113, which puts it exactly in the middle of the course ratings. There are longs, shorts, uphills, downhills and dog legs to challenge the golfer.

The course definitely represents Northwest golf, with several ponds, a creek and even a lake on the course. It is a lovely course, with a nice variety of Northwest plants, including pine and willow trees. There are very active men and women clubs which have a number of competitions during the year with various activities during the summer. Tyee is a member of the Washington Golf Association and P.G.A.

The clubhouse is open daily for breakfast and lunch where you can enjoy your meal outside on the patio during the summer months. The pro shop carries a full line of clubs, clothing and shoes. For an enjoyable day of golfing, take the time to play Tyee Golf Course when you're in Seattle.

Hats

WE HATS
105 First Avenue S
Seattle, WA 98104
Tel. (206) 623-3409
Hrs: Mon. - Thu.   10:00 a.m. - 6:30 p.m.
      Fri. - Sat.   10:00 a.m. - 12:00 midnight
      Sunday   12:00 noon - 6:00 p.m.

Hats are fun and WE Hats has the best selection of them that you'll ever see. Owner Leone Ewoldt has been in the hat business for more than thirteen years. She learned to make hats from renowned milliner John Eaton and her creations reflect her delight in her work.

There are all kinds of hats at WE Hats. Many are interesting and unusual creations made right there on the premises, but there is also a selection of "serious" hats in traditional styles for both men and women. These are hats that add a touch of class and style to your outfit that no other accessory can. WE Hats can block your hat to restore size and quality, refurbish your hat or make you a new one either using your design or designing one for you. One of the local favorites is the Duckbill hat, which local fisherman have pronounced perfect for the wet Northwest climate.

WE Hats is a Pioneer Square landmark. On a warm spring or summer weekend night, you might find as many people at WE Hats as the local night spots. It's that kind of place, a place to have fun and find the hat of your dreams.

Herbs and Spices

MARKET SPICE
85A Pike Place
Seattle WA 98101
Tel. (206) 622-6340
Hrs: Mon. - Sat.   9:00 a.m. - 6:00 p.m.
      Sunday   11:00 a.m. - 4:00 p.m.

Market Spice, a Seattle landmark since 1911, is famous world wide for its Market Spice tea. The wonderful, spicy aroma of this shop beckons you as you shop at Pike Place Market. When you enter the store, you will be amazed at the stock of tea, spices, and herbs available. There is always a pot of the famous Market Spice Tea brewing and customers are urged to sample. The staff is friendly, helpful and very knowledgeable about their product.

Market Spice carries in bulk more than 500 different herbs and spices. Here you will find anything you might ever want for even the most exotic recipe. This is the place to get, whole or ground foenugreek, juniper berries, kelp powder, Chilean mushrooms, psyllium seeds and other exotic items. Of course, there is a complete selection of more common herbs and spices, too. Literature is available explaining about many of the products and tips on how to use them. Gift packs are available, too - the perfect answer for someone who thought they had everything. In addition to the selection of herbs, spices, and seasonings, you will find a complete selection of coffees and teas.

Market Spice ships their products all over the world. They will help you make interesting selections that will meet your needs and choose unusual gifts of fine seasonings, coffees and teas that will please even the most discriminating. Don't miss a visit to Market Spice when you're in Seattle.

Ice Cream

CRAIG'S ICE CREAM, 614 First Avenue, Seattle, Washington. Enjoy the wide assortment of delicious flavors and creative cold and sweet concoctions at Craig's.

King County

THE SHY GIANT
1500 Pike Place Market #16
Seattle, WA 98101
Tel. (206) 622-1988
Hrs: Summer   Mon. - Sun.   9:00 a.m. - 6:00 p.m.
         Winter   Mon. - Sun.   9:00 a.m. - 5:00 p.m.
Closed Sundays in the winter.

    Paul Billington, owner, considers himself a contemporary version of the shy giant, and thus, has named his friendly one man shop.
    The Shy Giant is one of the first frozen yogurt shops to open in the Pike Place Market and the Northwest, having opened in 1977. Enjoy the Shy Giant's all natural yogurt with any number of delicious fresh fruit toppings, or have one of the other frozen dessert specialties. Dankens and Dryers gourmet ice creams are featured, along with Island Springs frozen tofu. A special treat are the dessert fraze's, the frozen fruit whips, and the hand-rolled Norwegian waffle cones.
    In the Market, The Shy Giant is behind Three Girls Bakery and kitty corner from Crystal Meats. Don't be shy. Go on and try. You'll like this guy, and his frozen desserts.

(See special invitation in the Appendix.)

Jewelry

SOLSTICE ON THE WATERFRONT
Pier 55
Seattle, WA 98101
Tel. (206) 624-9057
Hrs: Summer: Mon. - Sat.   10:00 a.m. - 6:00 p.m.
                      Sunday   11:00 a.m. - 6:00 p.m.
         Winter: Mon. - Sat.   11:00 a.m. - 6:00 p.m.
                      Sunday   12:00 noon - 5:00 p.m.
Visa, Mastercard, and AMEX cards.

    Amidst the exciting bustle of Seattle's waterfront, there is a quiet little jewel awaiting your discovery. It's a shop called Solstice; inside the mood is relaxed and friendly, a place where you can choose among the offerings of handwrought gold and silver, as well as every color under the sun in gemstones, porcelain, cloisonné and niobium jewelry. The style is an artful blend of contemporary and classic, each piece chosen for its beauty and timeless appeal.

King County

Featured are fine inlay, sterling (casual and dressy), vintage glass beads, natural crystal, art nouveau and marcasite designs, and original work by local artists. Earrings are a specialty and the imaginative collection has won rave reviews for years. In addition, there is a wonderful array of luminous Mt. St. Helen's art glass and stunning emerald obsidianite jewelry as a special remembrance of your trip.

Moderate prices and personal attention at Solstice make gift shopping a rare treat you won't want to miss!

A tour for the those who don't like ordinary tours.

	FAIR WIND AND FOLLOWING SEAS		
a.m.	Three Girls Bakery	Best mini-breakfast	Sea/Restaurant
	Now to acquire the food for the day's highlight.		
a.m.	Magnano Food	Best pack-up foods	Sea/Food
	You've got to have the perfect hat.		
a.m.	We Hats	Best hats	Sea/Apparel
	Now for the wine.		
a.m.	Station Hills Winery	Best wine	Sea/Wine
	Here comes your boat.		
a.m.	Sailboats Unlimited	Best sailing	Sea/Boat
	It's time to soothe those sore muscles.		
p.m.	Tubs Seattle	Best sauna	Sea/Spa
p.m.	Franco's Harbor	Best seafood	Sea/Restaurant

You're no ordinary person, and this is no ordinary tour!

Kitchen Supplies

A COOK'S TOUR
Pier 56 Alaskan Way
Seattle, WA 98101
Tel. (206) 623-7277
Hrs: Mon. - Sun. 10:00 a.m - 9:00 p.m.
Visa and Mastercard are accepted.

You buy gifts for people when you wish to show your appreciation of them, but have you ever bought a gift for your kitchen? Why not? Your kitchen does so much for you every day. It endures awful heat in the summer, puts up with nasty spills during the preparation of meals and looks nice for you when you have guests. Yes, your kitchen deserves a token of your appreciation. And for this, a visit to A Cook's Tour is in order.

A Cook's Tour is a delightful shop specializing in anything that a kitchen might need. It's a kitchen person's paradise. You'll have fun as you browse through the many imported and domestic items featured in this bonanza. Cutlery, potware, miscellaneous supplies, flatware, dinnerware and much more, all await your eager eye. You can buy something either for yourself or for a friend. Whatever the motive, you're sure to find exactly what your looking for and have fun in the process.

The next time you're in the Seattle area and are looking for something that will be useful in your's or a friends kitchen, stop by A Cook's Tour. It's a charming place to visit when the kitchen needs a gift.

KITCHEN 'N THINGS
2322 NW Market Street
Seattle, WA, 98107
Tel. (206) 784-8717
Hrs: Mon. - Sat.   10:00 a.m. - 5:30 p.m.
      Thursday   10:00 a.m. - 8:00 p.m.
      Sunday   12:00 noon - 5:00 p.m.
Visa and MasterCard are accepted.

For every chef with a domestic flair and for every homemaker with an eye for the finest, your "Best Choice" is Kitchen 'N Things. Here is a gift shop par excellence that carries a complete line of goods pertaining to the art of cuisine.

As with many shops in Ballard, the emphasis is on the Scandinavian. The European flair is consistent throughout the store. One of the first things the visitor may notice is a display of well-placed crystal that catches the sunlight, reflecting it around the walls of this airy shop. Kosta Boda crystal from Sweden and iittala from Finland highlight the display. Strolling through the aisles, you will encounter an engaging arrangement of table accessories, kitchen appliances and gadgets. Among the table service items are pottery by Bing and Grøndahl, Porsgrund china, and Portmerion English ceramics and pewter plates. There are also quality kitchen names such as Cuisinart and Calphalon cookware.

Kitchen 'N Things makes a special effort to put on the ritz for Christmas with a complete selection of handcrafted Scandinavian items.

SEATTLE KNIFE SUPPLY
1920 Pike Place Market
Seattle, WA 98101
Tel. (206) 441-8988
Hrs: Mon. - Sat. 9:30 a.m. - 6:00 p.m.
Extended hours in December and summer.
Closed major holidays.

Andre Espinosa has been in business in this location since 1979, offering a wide variety of quality knives and accessories. The staff is very professional, knowledgeable and will help you with your cutlery needs. Many chefs and cooks in the Seattle area come here for their knives because they know that they will find the quality and selection they need.

Seattle Knife Supply carries all kinds of knives from many different manufacturers, they have Forschner, Henckels, Trident, Chicago Cutlery, and more. You will find pocket knives, sushi knives, Swiss army knives, and a large selection of kitchen knives of all sizes. In addition to knives, there are a large selection of manicure implements, scissors, cutting boards, knife storage blocks, kitchen gadgets, bottle openers, zesters, tenderizers, pizza cutters, knife sharpeners, and more. A knife sharpening service is offered to clients. You will find a selection of custom, handmade knives with lovely carved handles.

For the best selection of knives and cutlery in Seattle, visit Seattle Knife Supply. You will be astounded by the assortment and variety from which to choose.

SUR LA TABLE
84 Pine Street
Seattle, WA 98101
Tel. (206) 448-2244
Hrs: Mon. - Sun. 9:00 a.m. - 6:00 p.m.

If you're looking to find something for the kitchen, Sur La Table, a favorite for professional chefs in Seattle, is the place to go. They offer the most extensive pastry department in the Northwest, with over 300 pastry tips and a large variety of molds and other baking equipment.

Sur La Table, in business for fifteen years, is owned and operated by Shirley Collins. Under Shirley's deft supervision, Sur La Table offers a grand selection of cooking products and services for the novice, as well as the professional cook. There's a large selection of European cookware, cookbooks, cookie cutters, blenders, kitchen knives, British teapots, speciality items and so much more that a visit is necessary to view all the wares offered. Sur La

Table also sponsors special events throughout fall including book signings and cooking demonstrations.

The entire staff at Sur La Table is well versed in every aspect of kitchen expertise. If you have a question when you walk in, you won't when you leave. If this isn't enough, when it comes to cooking instruction, they feature a most extensive video tape library that deals with many areas of the kitchen. Sur La Table, providing more than just tabletop needs, is the place to visit when you find yourself or your kitchen lacking in what it takes to cook that great meal.

(See special invitation in the Appendix.)

Kites

GRAND CENTRAL MERCANTILE CO., INC.
316 1st Avenue S
Seattle, WA 98104
Tel. (206) 6623-8894
Hrs: Mon. - Sat.   10:00 a.m. - 6:00 p.m.
      Sunday   11:00 a.m. - 5:00 p.m.
Visa and MasterCard are accepted.

It's always hard to beat Mom's cooking and even harder to beat Grandma's cooking, so who should know better about the kitchen than Grandmother herself. Bettye Greig's knowledge of cookware is both seasoned and up-to-date, as a visit to her business, Grand Central Mercantile, will attest.

A source of kitchen supplies and dinnerware for the novice and gourmet alike, Grand Central Mercantile is well-stocked and staffed by people who care about people. In the appliance department, you will find quality brand names of countertop cooking accessories, as well as qualified instruction. The dinnerware selection is attractive and functional. Bettye will be more than happy to help the new homemaker. The Grand Central Mercantile maintains an active bridal registry with shipping available nationwide via UPS.

Have you got a question for the kitchen? Who should know better than Bettye?

GREAT WINDS KITE SHOP
402 Occidental Avenue
Seattle, WA 98104
Tel. (206) 624-6886
Hrs: Mon. - Sat.   10:00 a.m. - 5:30 p.m.
      Sunday   12:00 noon - 5:30 p.m.
Visa, MasterCard and Travelers checks are accepted.

Maybe you've seen them on the beaches of the Northwest coast, those high flyers in a myriad of bright colors. Perhaps you've stopped along the highway to stare at the fantastic aerobatics they preform. These are the kites and windsocks that have been experiencing a resurgence of popularity in the past decade. Right on the forefront of this renaissance are Ken Conrad and Suzanne Sadow who opened their Great Winds Kite Shop back in 1972.

This is truly a pastime with universal appeal. Every kid has at some time been fascinated with those colorful kites they've seen in the air. Every big kid could probably pull out that fascination from the dusty confines of past memories. Great Winds Kite Shop is the a toy shop for the young and old, the serious and the frivolous flyer. This is a full service store; if you need raw materials to design and build your own, they have it and will help you with any questions or problems that arise. Not that ambitious? Then buy one of many kits that are easy to assemble. Still too much? Then they have many kites all ready to go. For the Charlie Brown flyers out there Great Winds carries the "Frustrationless Flyer." Windsocks can be made to order if the large selection doesn't suit you. There are many other air toys like boomerangs, wind-up planes and gliders.

Fancy stunt kites to docile winds socks, Great Winds Kite Shop is selling fun for all. Conveniently located in the Pioneer Square District just a block from the Kingdome, the staff knows all the great location to let your line out without get caught in the trees. Now, go fly a kite.

Knitting Supplies

NORWAY KNITS
2320 N. W. Market Street
Seattle, WA 98107
Tel. (206) 782-5775
Hrs: Mon.-Sat. 10:00 a.m.-5:30 p.m.

By the time you've motored your way down Ballard's beautifully restored Market Street, you will probably feel sufficiently Scandinavian for a visit to one of Ballard's many Scandinavian accented shops. Norway knits is a good place to start.

The inside of the shop is a veritable rainbow of colored yarns and Norwegian handmade goods. Definitely a paradise for the knitting and stitching enthusiast, Norway Knits features a complete collection of fine quality knitting supplies, patterns, and imported and domestic yarns in a variety of weights and textures.

Should you happen to need a wee bit of help in turning these raw materials into beautiful finished goods, owner Solveig Howland will be more than happy to help. Norway Knits offers customers both free instruction and the kind of personal service so often missing these days. Should you, on the other hand, rather have your sweater already made, Norway Knits features a wonderful collection of handknit Norwegian sweaters guaranteed to keep the chill from your bones.

Other interesting items include Scandinavian needlepoint wall hangings, and a variety of very interesting handmade and painted wooden items, which are produced locally by Norwegian craftsmen. If quality goods and personal service are what you have in mind, give Norway Knits a try.

Markets

CRYSTAL MEATS
94 Pike Street
Seattle, WA 98101
Tel. (206) 622-5499
Hrs: Mon. - Sat. 9:00 a.m. - 6:00 p.m.
Closed Sunday and major holidays.

Michael Greenblat and his wife Delores own and operate this fine meat market which was founded by Michael's father Harry S. Greenblat in 1947. Mike's sister Mary also helps out in this family run business. They have a well trained, knowledgeable staff to assist customers in the selection of meats and poultry. Meats are cut fresh daily and they offer a full line of meat and poultry. Mike is constantly striving to find the highest quality sources for his meats, such as cattle ranches and chicken farms.

Everything carried is of the highest quality and is as fresh as possible. The short ribs, thick cut bacon, pork, beef and sausage are outstanding. They make their own corned beef and link sausages. Ground beef is made daily, and fresh lunch meats are sliced daily. For diet conscious customers, Crystal Meats offers lean beef, lamb, pork, and chicken. They carry a full line of meat products, this is the place to find beef tongue or oxtails for those special recipes.

Crystal Meats has served generations of the same families since it opened. People know that they can expect the best. If you are looking for fresh Washington meats and poultry, Crystal Meats is the place to find just what you want.

MAGNANO FOOD
Pike Place Market
Seattle, WA 98101
Tel. (206) 223-9582
Hrs: Mon. - Fri.   9:30 a.m. - 5:30 p.m.
      Saturday   9:00 a.m. - 5:00 p.m.

Magnano Foods, located on the Mezzanine level of the Pike Place Market, is packed full of natural, delicious food where you are met by a wonderful aroma the minute you enter. Ann Magnano, the owner, is an outdoor oriented person who has developed a unique store with all kinds of fresh, natural foods that will appeal to health conscious people.

Magnano Foods has every kind of dried fruits and trail mixes, plus a large variety of the freshest nuts making the store the perfect stop for backpackers and kayakers who want to stock up on nutritious foods for their trips. The store isn't just for healthful snacks, as it is fulled with a large variety of natural, gourmet foods including bulk olive oils, pastas, beans, ten different kinds of rice, every grain and flour for all your baking needs, low salt, chemical free sauces, soups; everything for the health conscious chef. Magnano Foods also has a large selection of Northwest wines and over ninety-five varieties of beer available, also organic coffees, teas and juices.

When you are shopping at the Pike Place Market, be sure to make Magnano Foods a stop on your itinerary. You will marvel at all the wonderful, healthful, delicious foods.

PIKE PLACE MARKET CREAMERY
1514 Pike Place Stall #3
Seattle, WA 98101
Tel. (206) 622-5029
Hrs: Mon. - Sat. 9:00 a.m. - 6:00 p.m.
Closed Sundays and major holidays.

The Pike Place Market Creamery is a little country milk barn right in the middle of town. Nancy Nipples Douty, who owns the Creamery, treats her customers to an amazing array of dairy products you won't find in many stores.

Of course there's milk, ice cream, goats milk, butter, yogurt, cottage cheese, eggs, ice cream sandwich bars, honey, and a selection of health food and soy products...but where else can you find fresh quail eggs? Or heavy cream with all the butter fat left in or milk in glass bottles? Nancy and her crew, who she refers to as "the Milk Maids", have loyal customers who have been coming since the Creamery opened in 1978 and some customers come from not-so-nearby Bellingham and Bellevue. The Creamery buys products fresh daily from a number of local independent dairies and egg growers. The Creamery's wholesale business delivers to numerous bakeries and restaurants in the Seattle area.

If you are in Seattle on Halloween, you won't want to miss the Creamery's now-famous annual Mooing and Clucking Contest, which usually receives lots of media attention. As you can tell, Nancy's and her crew enjoy a good time; her name, and how she got into the business are stories worth hearing.

SCANDINAVIAN SPECIALTY PRODUCTS, INC.
8539 15th Avenue NW
Seattle, WA 98117
Tel. (206) 784-7020
Hrs: Mon. - Sat. 9:00 a.m. - 6:00 p.m.
Call for holiday hours.

Just up the hill from Ballard, Seattle's Scandinavian enclave, the little neighborhood of Crown Hill has what may be the true flavor of Scandinavia. Here is the shop known as Scandinavian Specialties or The Norwegian Sausage Company, which offers a wonderful selection of Scandinavian food.

Owners Herb and Ruby Anderson serve the type of authentic fare which is seldom available outside of the old country. Among the delicacies available are, Fleskepose, which is pork sandwich spread, Kalvsylta Lungemos, which is meat in gelatin form, Rullipolse - lamb roll, Sylte - pork roll and Kalveroll - veal roll all of which are luncheon meats and should be eaten cold. Scandinavian Specialty also makes Knakkwurst, Wieners and dinner sausage with only four percent fat, no preservatives and if you can't wait till you get home, they will heat them for you.

The visitor is encouraged to taste his way through the shop while browsing. In addition to the various kinds of sausage, there are homemade fish cakes and various imported cheeses, breads and crackers. Do your tastebuds a favor, try this wonderful shop.

UWAJIMAYA
6th South and South King
Seattle, WA 98104
Tel. (206) 624-6248
Hrs: Mon. - Sat.   9:00 a.m. - 7:00 p.m.
      Sunday   10:00 a.m. - 6:00 p.m.
Closed Christmas, New Year's and Thanksgiving.
Visa, MasterCard, AMEX accepted for non food items.

Uwajimaya is the largest Asian retail store in the Pacific Northwest. It began in 1928 when Fujimatsu Moriguchi began selling his homemade fishcakes to Japanese loggers, farmers, railroad workers and fishermen in the Tacoma area. The Seattle store opened in 1945 and has grown over the years, moving to its present location, with 35,000 square feet, in 1970. There are also stores in Southcenter and Bellevue. It is still a family business, with Tomio Moriguchi serving as President and his three brothers, sister and mother responsible for various aspects of the business. Mrs. Fujimatsu Moriguchi can still be found supervising the sushi bar at the Seattle store.

Uwajimaya is a one stop supermarket and gift shop which brings the East to the West. Here you will find unique seafood, octopus, abalone, squid, eel and geoduck, as well as the more common shellfish. Fresh produce includes taro root, Chinese cabbage, bamboo shoots, snow peas and much more. Here is everything you need to prepare oriental specialties, including meat, groceries and more than thirty different cooking classes.

The gift shop offers treasures from throughout the Orient. There is precious China, practical pottery, clothing, exotic jewelry and much more. For those unable to pay a visit in person, a mail-order catalog may be obtained by calling or writing. Shopping at Uwajimaya is a special experience, and a good way to learn more about the Orient.

Museum

NORDIC HERITAGE MUSEUM
3014 NW 67th Street
Seattle, WA 98117
Tel. (206) 789-5707
Hrs: Tue. - Sat.   10:00 a.m. - 4:00 p.m.
      Sunday   12:00 noon - 4:00 p.m.
Admission is charged.

The Nordic Heritage Museum is located in a renovated 44,000-square-foot building in Ballard, the Scandinavian enclave in Seattle. It was founded to collect and preserve objects that relate to the work and lifestyles of the Pacific Northwest settlers who came from the five Nordic countries of Denmark, Finland, Iceland, Norway and Sweden.

The museum has a full time exhibit which chronicles the long and arduous journey from Scandinavia to the Northwest. It also offers a superb schedule of traveling and on-loan exhibits from the Nordic countries themselves. The collections date from the 18th century to the present and include costumes, textiles, wooden utensils, maritime and logging equipment, paintings and photographs. The museum's programs include lectures, concerts, film series and Nordic language classes.

No visit to Ballard would be complete without a visit to the Nordic Heritage Museum. Take a little time to step back into history and savor a taste of Scandinavian culture. The museum is a private non-profit organization which is well worth your support.

Nautical

CAPTAIN'S NAUTICAL SUPPLIES
Salmon Bay Fishing Terminal
Seattle, WA 98119
Tel.(206)   283-7242
Hrs: Mon. - Fri.   8:00 a.m. - 5:30 p.m.
            Saturday   9:00 a.m. - 5:00 p.m.
Visa and Mastercard are accepted.
and,
1324 2nd Ave.
Seattle, WA 98101
Tel. (206) 622-3305

In 1897, Max Kuner opened the doors in Seattle.   Since then, Captain's Nautical Supplies has provided a wide selection of nautical supplies and fine service to commercial and pleasure boaters alike.

The current owner, Leonard Shrock, has been a familiar face on Seattle's waterfront scene since 1947. A trip through the shop is almost guaranteed to give even the most landlocked visitor an urge to "put to sea". The shop carries a world-class selection of charts, maps, books and navigational information, one of the largest selections in the Northwest.

Arranged within the shop are binoculars, spotting scopes, marine clocks, and barometers by Chelsea and Boston. You will also find code flags, magnetic compasses, course plotting instruments, sextants, chronometers and traffrail logs. A wide and well-chosen array of nautical gifts is also available.

In addition, Captain's offers professional service on all types of nautical gear as well as expert compass adjustment by some of the most highly-skilled staff in the Northwest. Not only are the staff knowledgeable and helpful, they also make a visit to Captain's enjoyable and productive. If you can't get to Seattle, call or write and your phone or mail order will be promptly filled.

Party Supplies and Costumes

CHAMPION DISPLAY AND COSTUME
1928 Pike Place
Seattle, WA 98101
Tel. (206) 441-1925
Hrs: Mon. - Sat. 9:00 a.m. - 6:00 p.m.
Open Sundays during October 12:00 p.m. - 5:00 p.m.

Robert Champion founded his business in 1920. Originally he painted vaudeville act signs and eventually evolved into window display signs, continuing on to produce ever more elaborate window displays. He supplied theatrical people with such things as feathers, sequins and rhinestones. Over the years the store, which is now owned by Beau Champion, Robert's son, has evolved into a costume and party shop.

At Champions you can find a costume for any occasion for people of all ages. There is a full line of adult costumes, rubber masks, and children's costumes. They offer costume rentals, as well as sales. In addition to the multitude of costumes from which to choose, there is a full line of party supplies. Everything you might ever need for the perfect party can be found. Weddings are a big part of the party business and they do custom party designs, napkins, matchboxes, balloons or anything else you want.

When planning the perfect party, a stop at Champions is a must. You'll find everything you need with one stop and have the best party yet.

Pizza

GUIDO'S PIZZERIA
7902 East Greenlake Drive N
Seattle, WA 98103
Tel. (206) 522-5553
Hrs: Tue. - Sat.   9:00 a.m. - 10:00 p.m.
     Sunday   9:00 a.m. - 9:00 p.m.

Directly across the street from Greenlake Park, Guido's caters to the hungry public with a selection of homemade, hand-built New York style pizza along with a few things you might not expect from a standard pizza parlor.

All the ingredients of a Guido's pizzeria are concocted right there. Four different tomato products are used just to make the sauce. One of their specialties, Sicilian thick crust pizza, is baked twice to insure a moist delicious quality. Pick your own favorite combination from their long list of toppings. At Guido's they don't just bake pizza. You can pick out a piece of coffee cake from the case of baked goods and settle down over a cup of espresso. Greenery lovers will appreciate Guido's special spinach salad. Any pizza will taste better with a glass of fresh made real fruit lemon or limeade. There are also fresh fruit juices in season. Try one of these with seltzer water for a real lift on a hot day.

Guido's is not a standard pizza parlor. Pizzas, calzones, salads, cold drinks or coffee - everything is created with a full measure of care at Guido's.

Restaurant

ACRES OF CLAMS, Pier 54, Seattle, Washington. A Seattle tradition since 1938 on the historic waterfront with a great view of Puget Sound. Limitless seafood in a nautical decor. Casual dress, families welcome.

CITY PICNICS
999 Third
Seattle, WA 98104
Tel. (206) 467-8995

City Picnics is a versatile restaurant that started out as a catering service for the business community in downtown Seattle. The restaurant has evolved into a great place to have breakfast or lunch in-house or to go.

For breakfast there is a wide selection of choices from fresh baked pastries to waffles, oatmeal or delicious omelets. There are a variety of juices and coffee to top off your meal and start your day off right.

If you are ready for lunch you can eat at one of the locations of City Picnics, pick up a lunch to take with you or have your meal delivered via yellow cab sandwich service. The lunch menu offers gourmet sandwiches of only the freshest ingredients, featuring Northwest produce and meats. There are beers and Northwest wines to complement your lunch. In addition to breakfast and lunch, there are light dinners available for a quick meal before the theater or a concert.

If the weather is nice, be sure to order a picnic and enjoy the beauty of the Seattle area.

Seattle, also known as The Emerald City, acts like a powerful magnet for artists and art enthusiasts alike. Here's a tour designed specifically for those of you who have been pulled hither to view the magnificence of the Northwest.

	SEATTLE'S ART UNVEILED		
a.m.	Au Gayroche	Best breakfast	Sea/Rest.
a.m.	Carolyn Hartness	Best visionary art	Sea/Art
a.m.	Stonnington	Best Alaskan culture	Sea/Art
a.m.	Stone Press Gallery	Best lithographs	Sea/Art
a.m.	Crumpet Shop	Best crumpets	Sea/Bakery
a.m.	La Tienda	Best folk art	Sea/Art
a.m.	Francine Seders	Best novice artists	Sea/Art
a.m.	Flury And Company	Best photographs	Sea/Art
p.m.	Fine Impressions	Best framing	Sea/Art
p.m.	Copacabana	Best lunch	Sea/Rest.
p.m.	Davidson Gallery	Best literature	Sea/Art
p.m.	Glass House	Best glass art	Sea/Art
p.m.	Native Design Gallery	Best African art	Sea/Art
p.m.	Nancy Teague	Best display	Sea/Art
p.m.	Lisa Harris Gallery	Best contemporary art	Sea/Art
p.m.	Northwest Art	Best atmosphere	Sea/Art
p.m.	Yung Ya	Best supper	Sea/Rest.

COPACABANA
1520-1/2 Pike Place
Seattle, WA 98101
Tel. (206) 622-6359
Hrs: Winter Mon. - Thur. 11:30 a.m. - 4:00 p.m.
          Fri. - Sat. 11:30 a.m. - 9:00 p.m.
     Summer Mon. - Sun. 11:30 a.m. - 10:00 p.m.

This interesting little restaurant is owned and operated by a family who has been in and out of the restaurant business for years. It was originally established in 1964 by Ramon and Hortenzia Pelaez who are from Bolivia where Ramon was a gourmet cook. The restaurant closed after they died, but was reopened in 1975 by their children, Mike, Maretha, and Fernando. They moved from their old location to their present spot in 1978 and they still retain the open kitchen arrangement which was a tradition of the original restaurant.

The recipes used at Copacabana are the ones used by the family when they lived in Bolivia. They serve delicious, authentic Bolivian food. The paella with saffron rice, chicken, pork, chorizo, shrimp, and clams is a real treat. The menu selection has changed little from the original restaurant, the food is delicious. Try such selections as Picante de Pollo - breast of chicken simmered in a zesty sauce of onions, tomatoes and green peas or Fritanga - boneless pork cubes simmered in a mild, rich Andean sauce, served with white hominy. There are several salads and desserts available, among which Tres Leches, a Nicaraguan cake, stands out.

Copacabana has pleasant outdoor tables at which one may dine in the summer. This is a real favorite among the local population. For fine South American dining in pleasant and congenial surroundings be sure to try Copacabana.

EL PUERCO LLORON
1501 Western Avenue
Seattle, WA 98101
Tel. (206) 624-0541
Hrs: Mon. - Sat. 11:30 a.m. - 9:00 p.m.
     Sunday 12:00 noon - 7:00 p.m.

El Puero Lloron has been in business since 1982 and is a real favorite of Seattle's Mexican food aficionados. From the moment you enter the establishment you will feel like you are in Mexico. It is attractively decorated with folding metal tables and chairs with Mexican beer advertisements splashed on them and colorful piñatas hanging from the ceiling. Mexican posters decorate the walls, as do posters of pigs; El Puerco Lloron means The Weeping Pig. Lively Mexican music adds to the ambiance.

The food at El Puero Lloron is delicious, made fresh daily from old family recipes handed down through generations. As you enter, you move to the open kitchen and ordering counter to select your meal from the items listed on the chalkboard. There are many great Mexican food choices including taquitos - beef, chicken, or pork, tacos, tostada's tamales, picadillo, carnitas, and carne asada, all served with rice and beans. The corn tortillas, made fresh every morning, are among the best you'll ever taste. At the end of the counter there are salsa, peppers, and mixed vegetables to add to your plate. This is also where you order your beverage, they have a large selection of Mexican and domestic beers and soft drinks.

Once you have your food and beverage, you're all set to sit back and enjoy the lively atmosphere and some delicious Mexican food. This is a great place for families and it's easy on the pocketbook. Watch for new El Puero Lloron locations in the Northwest in the near future.

EMMETT WATSON'S OYSTER BAR
1916 Pike Place #16
Seattle, WA 98101
Tel. (206) 448-7721
Hrs: Mon. - Sat. 11:45 a.m. - 6:00 p.m.
Closed Sunday and major holidays.

This fine restaurant in Seattle's Pike Place Market was established in 1978 by current owner San Bryant and Emmett Watson. Emmett had experience with an oyster bar in New Orleans and they were a success from the start. They moved to their present location in May, 1985. The oyster bar has received a lot of praise and national publicity for its wonderful food. It is a fun place to eat in a casual, relaxed atmosphere. Outside dining is available in the summer.

The emphasis is on seafood. The menu, printed on a brown paper lunch sack, offers a variety of seafood selections, such as oysters, shrimp, steamed mussels, fish and chips, and much more. The oysters come from Canterbuy Farms in Quilcene on the Columbia. One real favorite that was introduced to Seattle by Emmett and Sam is toasted seafood ravioli, a unique and delicious dish. There is a good selection of beer and wine to complement your meal.

This is a great place to eat, very popular locally and with tourists. It is very reasonably priced and you can be sure of delicious, fresh seafood.

King County

ENOTECA
Times Square Building
414 Olive Way
Seattle, WA 98101
Tel. (206) 624-9108
Hrs: Monday   7:00 a.m. - 6:00 p.m.
     Tue. - Sat.   7:00 a.m - 9:00 p.m.
Visa, MasterCard and AMEX are accepted.

This combination restaurant and wine shop provides a charming and refreshing change from the usual. Emphasis is on fresh, seasonal dishes and Northwest wines. Enoteca long has been known for serving innovative food and wine combinations. The menu includes tomato-pesto tart with Oregon blue cheese, curried corn fritters with Wax Orchards cranberry chutney, grilled Isernio sausages and peppers, Enoteca duck salad, Penn Cove mussels, and many other regional specialties.

Enoteca's wine shop contains over 500 labels reflecting the Northwest's best vineyards, and also contains an extensive wine book library. Wine tastings are held every Tuesday and over thirty wines are available at the wine bar.

Wine appreciation classes are offered and a meeting room capable of accommodating twenty people is available for special meetings. For a new and zesty experience, don't miss Enoteca.

THE FISHERMAN'S RESTAURANT
1301 Alaskan Way, Pier 57
Seattle, WA 98101
Tel. (206)623-3500
Hrs: Lunch   Mon. - Sun.   11:00 a.m. - 4:00 p.m.
     Dinner Mon. - Sun.   11:00 a.m. - Closing.
Reservations are accepted September through May only.
Visa, MasterCard and AMEX are accepted.

Established in 1979, the expert staff of The Fisherman's Restaurant are ready to cater to your smallest needs. A unique approach to the art of serving food has been developed in this restaurant.

The Fisherman's Restaurant specializes in a four course, family style feast. Your meal begins with a bucket of clams served by an appointed "host" in your party, followed by a tureen of soup and a crisp, tossed salad. The entrees of filet of salmon and three choices of crab, Dungeness, Snow and King, are served on wooden platters that are a foot and a half long. There are seven different entrees, luscious salads including, Chef, tuna, salmon and seafood, and daily specials for both lunch and dinner and even a la carte options from which to choose. A full selection of Northwest wines will complement any meal.

With a 180° view of Puget Sound and a staff that takes pride in offering a genuine "Northwest Experience," this is your "Best Choice" for enjoying the warm, friendly hospitality and delicious food that the Northwest offers.

FRANCO'S HIDDEN HARBOR
1500 Westlake North
Seattle, WA 98109
Tel. (206) 282-0501
Hrs: Mon. - Sat. 11:00 a.m. - 1:00 a.m.
     Sunday   12:00 noon - 8:00 p.m.
Visa, AMEX, Diners Club, Carte Blanche,
Discover cards are accepted.

Located on the shores of Seattle's beautiful Lake Union, Franco's Hidden Harbor is aptly named, as it is both somewhat hidden and it is indeed in a harbor. Long a favorite with Seattle's boating set, this delightfully unique restaurant has been quietly providing its customers with the finest in both waterfront dining and fresh Northwest seafood for the past forty years.

Yes, as a diner one really receives a double pleasure of truly fine fare with a location usually reserved for members of an exclusive yacht club. Rather than having an overlooking view of the harbor, Franco's is literally part of the harbor. The house specialty is Dungeness Crab served in at least ten equally appetizing ways. Other fresh seafood, as well as "turf" selections of prime cut steaks, receive the same excellent treatment though the combined efforts of hosts Robert Stilnovich and Robin Day

Out on the water, the finest of Seattle's pleasure fleet glides by peacefully easily seen from the patio dining or indoor seating. Be sure to make this "Best Choice" one of your ports of call.

GRECIAN CORNER
901 Madison Street
Seattle, WA 98104
Tel. (206) 623-6333
Hrs: Mon. - Thur. 6:00 a.m. - 11:00 p.m.
Fri. - Sun. 6:00 a.m. - 2:00 a.m.

Kali sperah filos! For those who haven't had the opportunity to learn Greek, this means "good evening." And a good evening is what it will be at Grecian Corner in Seattle.

Grecian Corner is an authentic Greek restaurant in the best tradition of that idyllic Mediterranean paradise. The restaurant's walls are adorned with original oil murals depicting lovely Grecian scenes which make you feel as if you were really there. After you have become acclimated to this delightful ambiance, it's time to order. There are many traditional Greek dishes to choose from including Bouzouki, Tragoudi, Siritaki and Moussaka. As it would take many pages to fully describe each one of these tantalizing entrees you'll just have to go in and find out what they are by tasting.

If the food isn't enough, Grecian Corner also features nightly entertainment in the form of exotic belly dancing! Ahhh, the hot-blooded Greek spirit unveils itself at this restaurant. Was spirit mentioned? Well, an evening in Greece can't be spent without partaking of their well-known liqueur, Ouzo. Be careful though, it packs quite a punch. Come on out to Grecian Corner where your always welcome. Yasoo filos.

IVAR'S CAPTAIN TABLE
333 Elliott Avenue West
Seattle, WA 98104
Tel. 206) 284-7040
Hrs: Mon. - Thu. 11:00 a.m.- 10:00 p.m.
Saturday 4:00 p.m.- 11:00 p.m.
Sunday 4:00 p.m. - 10:00 p.m.

Having carried on a love affair with Seattle and the waterfront for years, Ivar's is one of Seattle's finest seafood restaurants. You'll experience the best seafood the Northwest has to offer in a scenic waterfront atmosphere with a spectacular view of the Olympic Mountains.

The service is impeccable, the staff friendly are quick to anticipate your every need, and the decor is pleasing. You'll find Ivar's at the foot of Queen Anne Hill near the waterfront.

Easy off-street parking makes it convenient to eat lunch or dinner at Ivar's without the hassle of searching for where to put your car. Start your own love affair with Ivar's Captains Table. It could last a lifetime.

IVAR'S SALMON HOUSE
401 Northeast Northlake Way
Seattle, WA 98104
Tel. (206) 632-0767
Hrs: Mon. - Fri.   11:30 a.m. - 2:00 p.m.
                    5:00 p.m. -10:00 p.m
     Saturday   4:00 p.m. - 11:00 p.m.
     Sunday   10:00 a.m. - 2:00 pm.

Designed and decorated in the style of an authentic Indian longhouse, Ivar's Salmon House features Seattle's finest alder smoked salmon, barbequed ribs, and prime rib.

While you dine, you can enjoy watching the activities of Lake Union, in the University District, from the inside or outside tables. There is also an outdoor fish bar where you can get take-out orders. A staff whose primary goal is to make your dining experience unforgettable is a bonus to the exceptional cuisine and atmosphere.

Ivar's Salmon House is a "Best Choice" for seafood in Seattle.

LOWELL'S RESTAURANT AND BAR
1519 Pike Place
Seattle, WA 98101
Tel. (206) 622-2036
Hrs: Mon. - Fri.   7:00 a.m. - 5:00 p.m.
     Saturday   7:00 a.m. - 5:30 p.m.
     Happy Hour   5:00 p.m. - 7:00 p.m.
Visa, MasterCard and AMEX are accepted.

You won't have any difficulty finding a table with a view at Lowell's. All three floors of the restaurant overlook the Seattle waterfront and offer different perspectives of the bay from each floor.

Lowell's excellent food and reasonable prices have earned this restaurant a reputation among the folks who live and work at the market and on the waterfront. Leave your camera in the car, don your fishing cap, and mingle with the crowd, and experience the feeling of fitting right in to a favorite spot in Seattle. For breakfast, try one of Lowell's specials, trout and eggs, corned beef hash and eggs, or steak and eggs. Be sure to ask for a bran muffin, so tasty that the special Lowell's muffin recipe has been featured in *Gourmet*

Magazine. Lowell's lunch menu is filled with fresh fruits, seafood, breads, and dairy products of the Pike Place Market; you can't go wrong with any of the delicious sandwiches, salads, or hot entrees of the day at this restaurant. Starbuck's famous coffee is served, along with a line of fine northwest brewery beers. Appetizers are served from 3:00 p.m. to 8:00 p.m., daily.

This spacious restaurant welcomes groups, and the 150-person seating capacity frequently allows for impromptu planning of meetings. This is your "Best Choice" for great food and company.

MAMA'S MEXICAN KITCHEN
2234 2nd Avenue
Seattle, WA 98121
Tel. (206) 728-MAMA
Hrs: Mon. - Thu.   10:30 a.m. - 10:00 p.m.
     Fri. - Sat.   10:30 a.m. - 11:00 p.m.
     Sunday   12:00 noon - 9:00 p.m.

Mama's Kitchen is the creation of transplanted Southern Californians Mike and Marie McAlpin, a brother and sister team. The restaurant is named Mama's after their grandmother. They use her recipes for the Southern California style Mexican food. The restaurant offers outside dining during the summer and is large enough to accommodate groups. The decor and atmosphere are very inviting,d this is a good place to bring the family.

The menu selections at Mama's are extensive, from appetizers to desserts. Whether you prefer tamales, burritos, enchiladas, chili rellenos, tostadas, or tacos, you'll find something to please you. There are a la carte items available, as well as full meals served with beans and rice. A nice selection of combination plates will be appreciated by people who can't make up their minds and want to try more than one. There are a number of specials such as chile verde and steak picado available. Children's portions are served to those under ten.

When you are looking for good Mexican dining in the Seattle area, be sure to visit Mama's Mexican Kitchen for some of the best food in town.

PARKER'S RESTAURANT, 17001 Aurora Avenue North, Seattle, Washington. A casual restaurant open for lunch and dinner and featuring top forties and rock music for your dancing pleasure on one of Seattle's largest dance floors.

PIKE PLACE FISH
86 Pike Place
Seattle, WA 98101
Tel. (206) 682-7181
Hrs: Mon. - Sat. 9:00 a.m. - 6:00 p.m.
Extended hours in summer.
and,
Eastside Public Market
156th & N. E. 8th
Bellevue, WA 98008
Tel. (206) 644-7402

 Pike Place Fish is owned by John Yokoyama who used to help his father in his produce shop next to the fish market at Pike Place. John was always interested in the fish market and bought the business in 1965. He is assisted in this venture by his brother Dick and assistants Dereck DeJong, who manages the Pike Place location, and Rick Cavanaugh. Quality and service are the watchwords of this fine fish market. They bring you only the freshest, finest quality fish and seafood available.
 The selection offered at Pike Place Fish is tremendous. Fish from all over the world may be obtained. In addition to Pacific Northwest salmon, for example, there are also salmon from Chile, New Zealand, Norway, and Canada. You will find mahi mahi, yellowtail, opakapaka, many different kinds of crab, and over 100 varieties of prawns and shrimp. They have things that you have probably never heard of, let alone eaten. Fortunately, the staff knows all about every kind of fish they sell. They will tell you where it came from, how to keep it fresh, and how to prepare it to your liking.
 Pike Place Fish is tourist oriented and will pack fish in ice in leakproof containers guaranteed to keep it fresh for forty-eight hours. Shopping there is a real education in fish and seafood of the world. For some delightfully different taste treats, or for tried and true familiar fish, shop at Pike Place Fish. They have the best selection of fish you'll ever find anywhere.

SALEH AL LAGO
6804 E Greenlake Way N
Seattle, WA 98115
Tel. (206) 524-4044
Hrs: Lunch Mon. - Fri. 11:30 a.m. - 2:00 p.m
 Dinner Mon. - Thu. 5:30 p.m. - 10:00 p.m.
 Fri. - Sat. 5:30 p.m. - 11:00 p.m.
Visa, MasterCard, AMEX and Diner's Club are accepted.

To be pampered and have palate pleasing foods, one of the "Best Choices" in Seattle is Saleh al Lago. At Saleh's (pronounced Sollie's) your desire is their command. Want a different sauce on the pasta? No problem? Want to see how it's prepared? Please come watch. Saleh says that when he grows old, he wants to think back on having made people happy with what he does. What he does is cook wonderful Italian meals.

His menu is reflective of Central Italian cuisine, so your won't find heavy tomato sauces, what you will find is antipasta, pasta, salads and entrees of beef, veal and seafood. Ingredients are of the highest quality or "I don't touch them." says Saleh. Many of the ingredients, in fact, come from Italy; others are fresh from Seattle area suppliers. All the pasta is made fresh at Saleh's and sauces are only prepared once they have been ordered.

One of the interesting features of Saleh's is the open kitchen. Surrounded by a divider of curved glass, the cooks can watch the customers enjoying their meals, while the diners observe the action in the kitchen. A full bar and an extensive wine and champagne list, some by the glass, are available to complement your meal.

It is Saleh's intention to cook "...as if you hired me to come into your home to prepare your meal." Attention is paid to every detail, so come with a big appetite and enjoy Italian cooking at its finest.

SALTY'S ON ALKI
1936 Harbor Avenue SW
Seattle, WA 98116
Tel. (206) 937-1600
Hrs: Open Daily
Reservations and major credit cards are accepted.

Anchored on the waterfront overlooking Elliot Bay, Salty's has been voted "The Best New Restaurant" by *Seattle Magazine*. The historic location (built in 1893) is situated to provide guests with a place they may relax and enjoy the exclusive panoramic view of the entire Seattle skyline, from the Space Needle to the Kingdome.

Savor the spectacular view while enjoying the Northwest's freshest seafoods and finest meats, expertly prepared for your dining pleasure. Banquet facilities are located at sea level, featuring the unique view, with the ability to accommodate groups from 10 to 400. At Salty's, Seattles largest waterfront patio is available for your day of fun in the sun, be it lunch, dinner, brunch or just relaxing with your favorite beverage.

An exciting Sunday brunch buffet offers you a bountiful selection of omelettes, pastas and Belgian waffles all cooked to order. There are also pastries, fresh salads, desserts, plus an array of the Northwest's favorite seafood entrees.

THE SKIPPER'S GALLEY
2223 California Avenue S.W.
Seattle, WA 98116
Tel. (206) 937-7445
Hrs: Wed. - Sat. 5:00 p.m. - 10:00 p.m.

The Skipper's Galley is a pleasant small house near the main intersection of the Admiral Junction section of West Seattle. The nautical decor of the restaurant provides a comfortable, unpretentious atmosphere. Walt Fisher, chef and host, is a charming man with an easy going style. For the past twenty-two years he has been at this spot, preparing fine food and building his reputation as chef extraordinaire.

After you are welcomed, seated and have made your selection, the feast begins and feast it is. Twelve courses are presented, featuring fish prepared to perfection. The largest prawns and scallops available are used. This is seafood so delicious and cooked with such expertise, that it's like tasting seafood again for the very first time. Walt 's cooking experience goes back almost fifty years and he offers some of the best food you will ever eat.

Those who truly love great food find their way to The Skipper's Galley, including an astounding list of celebrities, ranging from John Wayne to Steven Spielberg. The relaxed atmosphere, the huge portions, the no-rush attitude and the best seafood in town make this a truly memorable dining experience.

VINCE'S ITALIAN RESTAURANT & PIZZERIA
8824 Renton Avenue S
Seattle, WA 98118
Tel. (206) 722-2116
Hrs: Mon. - Thu.   11:00 a.m. - 2:00 a.m.
     Fri.- Sat.   11:00 a.m. - 2:00 a.m.
     Sunday   4:00 p.m. - 12:00 midnight
Closed Thanksgiving, Christmas and New Year's Day.
and,

2815 NE Sunset Boulevard	605 Queen Anne N
Renton, WA 98056	Seattle, WA 98109
Tel. (206) 226-8180	Tel. (206) 283-9353
32411 Pacific Highway S	6218 6th Avenue
Federal Way, WA 98003	Tacoma, WA 98406
Tel. (206) 839-1496	Tel. (206) 564-7994

15223 4th Avenue SW
Seattle, WA 98166
Tel. (206) 246-1497

    Vince Mottola serves the finest and most authentic Italian cuisine possible in his family-owned and operated restaurant. Attention to detail and quality are of utmost importance and the results are outstanding.

    Vince's menu offers many southern Italian dishes not commonly found in Italian restaurants in the United States. The pasta alla carbonara is a favorite with a rich cream sauce, bacon, Parmesan cheese, egg and a lot of pepper. Also delicious are pasta alla matriciana, pasta all' arrabbiata and pasta alla puttanesca with hot spicy tomato sauce, calamata olives, capers and a touch of anchovy. What has made Vince's famous from the beginning is their wonderful hand tossed pizzas. A real treat is the authentic Neapolitan pizza that features tomatoes with olive oil, fresh garlic and spices.

    Everything at Vince's is carefully prepared from scratch with the freshest ingredients possible. The homemade pasta and pizza are created from original recipes brought from Naples. There is a wide selection of imported Italian wine to complement your meal. This is truly an Italian dining experience not to be missed.

WEBSTERS REAL FOOD
5261 California Avenue SW
Seattle, WA 98136
Tel. (206) 932-3120

The goal of Websters Real Food is to serve the kind of hearty, wholesome, great tasting food that you had as a child. They serve high quality, delicious food made with strictly fresh ingredients.

Websters offers the kind of wonderful fluffy waffles and tender pancakes that are hard to find these days, but they also offer fresh seafood and salads and other menu selections that allow the diet conscious to enjoy a great meal without pangs of conscience afterwards. They do all their own baking everyday, from scratch, and the results are stupendous.

The unfailingly high quality and reasonable prices for generous portions make Websters a great choice for delicious "real American food."

WEDGWOOD BROILER
8230 35th Avenue NE
Seattle, WA 98115
Tel. (206) 523-1115
Hrs: Mon. - Thu. & Sun.   11:30 a.m. - 12:00 midnight
       Fri. - Sat.   11:30 a.m. - 1:00 a.m.
Visa, MasterCard and Diner's Club are accepted.

The Wedgwood Broiler is reminiscent of the friendly neighborhood broiler of the past, where families went to have a quiet, comfortable steak dinner in congenial surroundings. Owners Jim Anderson and Glen Jensen have recreated that friendly atmosphere with the highest quality food and service. They offer fine family dining with something for everyone.

Lunch and dinner is served seven days a week. Lunch selections are plentiful, from sandwiches, salads and steaks to the daily specials which include a choice of soup or salad. For dinner, sizzling broiled steaks of Colorado corn-fed beef, ordered "by the ounce." There are daily Chef's Selections too. They are particularly proud of their homemade soups and a special recipe for bleu cheese dressing. Children and seniors have a wide choice.

The Wedgwood Broiler provides fine dining in a relaxed and casual atmosphere. The service is excellent and your meal will be a very memorable experience.

YUNG YA
4841 California Avenue SW
Seattle, WA 98116
Tel. (206) 935-9200
AMEX, Mastercard, and Visa are accepted.

Terrific Chinese cuisine, a warm, friendly atmosphere and beautiful decor in a Chinese motif, are what you'll find at Yung Ya. It's a Chinese restaurant that has been pleasing Seattle residents, as well as those traveling through, for over six years.

You know you've found a good Chinese restaurant when you enter and discover that many of its patrons are of Oriental heritage. Yung Ya is rated very high by the local Chinese population, as well as Chinese food fanatics. Here, amidst an authentic Chinese ambiance, you can enjoy such dishes as Szechwan prawns, Szechwan ginger beef, chicken entrees, steaks and much, much more. They've also got some terrific cocktails that will take the edge off of any day and allow you to relax before dinner.

This is the kind of place where you can bring a few friends, the entire family or just yourself, to enjoy a delicious, filling meal in an unmatched setting. A "Best Choice" for Chinese food in a town that loves Chinese food, Yung Ya is waiting for your approval.

Sailing

SAILBOATS UNLIMITED WEST, INC.
2046 Westlake N
Seattle, WA 98109
Tel. (206) 283-4664
Hrs: Monday 9:30 a.m. - 5:30 p.m.
    Wed. - Sun. 9:30 a.m. - 5:30 p.m.

The Puget Sound area offers unlimited opportunities to enjoy sailing. Sailboats Unlimited, with the largest fleet of sailboat rentals and charters in the Northwest, has just what anyone needs to get out on the water. Owners Helen and Dick Ulm have been helping people to fulfill their nautical dreams for the past twenty-five years.

From its offices on Lake Union, Sailboats Unlimited offers day rentals of sailboats of all sizes, sailing lessons and a full service marina. They also sell the complete line of Catalina, O'Day, Endeavor, Capri and Cal sailboats. From its base in Anacortes, Sailboats Unlimited offers charter boats ranging in size from twenty-five to thirty-nine feet, sleeping between five and nine people and completely equipped. They'll even supply a skipper if you don't sail yourself.

Whether you want to learn to sail, buy a small boat, buy a large boat, cruise the San Juan Islands or just spend a few hours on Lake Union, Sailboats Unlimited is the place for you.

Spa

TUBS
50th & Roosevelt Way N.E.
Seattle, WA 98105
Tel. (206) 527-8827
Hrs: Mon. - Sun. 7:00 a.m. - 2:00 a.m.
and
11023 N.E. 8th
Bellevue, WA 98004
Tel. (206) 462-TUBS
Hrs: Mon. - Sun. 12:00 noon - 2:00 a.m.

What better escape from the Seattle weather than Tubs Seattle. Since opening in 1982, Tubs has become both a local landmark and an industry standard for commercial spa operation and design.

The friendly staff and beautiful Art Deco design compare favorably with the very best European and Japanese luxury baths. Each individually-designed tub room includes a sparkling acrylic spa with hydro-therapy jets, swedish dry-heat sauna, spa-side cold spray, shower, shampoos, towels and linens, stereo sound system, fresh-squeezed juices and mineral waters, and a private intercom system.

The wholesome atmosphere makes Tubs suitable for the whole family (children are always free). In addition, business and social groups can be accommodated.

Tubs Seattle also has a modern up-to-date tanning facility. While Tubs are on a first come-first serve basis, reservations are recommended for tanning.

(See special invitation in Appendix.)

Sporting Goods

ATHLETIC SUPPLY COMPANY
901 Harrison Street
Seattle, WA 98109
Tel. (206) 623-8972
     (800) 732-9259
Hrs: Mon. - Sat. 9:00 a.m. - 5:30 p.m.
Major credit cards accepted

The Athletic Supply Company was established in 1932 and is one of the oldest sporting goods stores in Seattle and the Pacific Northwest. The University of Washington Huskies and Seattle Seahawks buy their gear there, as have three generations of young athletes in the Seattle area. There is now a second Athletic Supply Company store in Redmond which supplies the same quality equipment and service.

Owners Steve Engstrom and Mike Lambert have assembled a staff which can assist you whatever your sporting goods needs, whether it's a simple pair of goggles for swimming or a complete home fitness center. Let John Anderson design your own personal fitness room, or have Scott Warren show you the latest in hi tech squash and tennis rackets.

Whether your athletic supply needs are large or small, you want quality equipment that will do the job. Athletic Supply is the place to go, they serve the needs of the community by supplying the best equipment possible and highly qualified staff.

Stationery

PAPER MOON CARD SHOP
1906 Pike Place #3
Seattle, WA 98101
Tel. (206) 443-0675
Hrs: Mon. - Sat. 9:30 a.m. - 5:30 p.m.

The Paper Moon card shop, located in Stewart House at the famous Pike Place Market, carries a huge selection of cards, stationery, posters, souvenirs, as well as fun party supplies and gift items.

Owner Betty Johnson shops the trade shows in New York and Los Angeles to find the latest in unusual lines of cards and gifts. She has assembled a large collection of greeting cards from which to choose, including the most complete inventory of the "Far Side" by Northwest native Gary Larson, whose comic strip is nationally syndicated. There are also an excellent selection of prints by several local artists that capture the flavor of the market, as well as a whimsical series of posters, greeting cards and post cards of the many statues to be found in and around Seattle.

All of this can be found in less than 500 square feet. So, for that unusual card, fun gift, interesting print, great souvenir or just an enjoyable browsing experience, be sure to visit the Paper Moon!

Tours

KENMORE AIR HARBOR
6321 N.E. 175th
Kenmore, WA 98155
Tel. (206) 486-1257
Hrs: Sun. - Sat. 8:00 a.m. - Dusk

The Pacific Northwest being a land of rivers, lakes and ocean, opportunity for travel by air are opened up through the pontoon airplane. Kenmore Air Harbor, located on the north shore of Lake Washington, provides recreational and business air taxi service with the largest floatplane installation in the U.S.

With a fleet of more than 120 seaplanes, Kenmore Air Harbor stands ready to fill your flying order whether it be a sight seeing tour of the regional beauty or a commercial venture. Services offered include aircraft and float sales, airframe and engine maintenance, avionics and flight instruction along with their flight services. A popular destination for the vacationer is the salmon fishing camps throughout British Colombia. When was the last time you went to the San Juan Islands? This time why not see it from the air and arrive there in a fraction of the time? A spectacular vantage and more leisure time, sure sounds appealing.

Next time you take out the map and start drawing lines on it, think of Kenmore Air Harbor, a unique and pleasurable way to travel.

Toy Store

BIG PEOPLE TOYS
110 Alaskan Way S
Seattle, WA 98104
Tel. (206) 583-0160

A toy is a toy is a toy, not so. Toys are made in a wide variety of ways for a wide variety of interests. These interests range from simple to intricate and entertain both the young and the old. At Big People toys, although the name implies otherwise, not only will you find toys for the big people, but you'll also find some for the little ones as well.

The Owner of Big People Toys, Victor Voris, has done something that many dream of, but few achieve. He is surrounded by, plays with and makes a living off of toys! Toys of all kinds. Antique toys, modern toys, decorator toys and items, coin operated toys, juke boxes, arcade games and much more are all a part of his everyday life. Remember those toys you played with as a child? Well, it's almost a certain bet that you will find either the same thing or something similar in Victor's store. You can enjoy it once again or stir fond memories of your growing years by giving it to your child.

Another special feature of this shop is its rustic atmosphere. It makes you feel as if you were walking backward in years. Visit Big People Toys for yourself or a child. You'll find out that a toy is not just a toy, its a plaything containing memories.

TEDDY'S ON ROOSEVELT
6420 Roosevelt Way
Seattle, WA 98115
Tel. (206) 524-7004
Hrs: Mon. - Sat. 10:00 a.m. - 5:30 p.m.
        Sunday   12:00 noon - 4:00 p.m.

When you enter Teddy's on Roosevelt, you are confronted by bears, dozens of them gazing benevolently at you from the walls of the shop. Owner Carol Pang wanted to open a teddy bear theme store and when she found a convenient location on Roosevelt Way in Seattle, the name Teddy's on Roosevelt just seemed to naturally follow.

In addition to teddy bears of every size, style and description, the shop has a well chosen collection of cards, gifts and party supplies. The younger set will adore shopping among all the lovely fuzzy creatures, and adults will be pleased by the nice selection of gifts available.

Whether you are looking for the perfect bear, or the perfect gift, Teddy's on Roosevelt will have what you want.

Wine

LA CANTINA - THE WINE MERCHANT
2601 University Village Mall
Seattle, WA 98105
Tel. (206) 525-4340

La Cantina has been in business for more than eighteen years. Between owner Michael Dodson and assistant manager Oliver Beck, they have thirty years of experience in the wine trade. Their expertise helps customers choose wine for quality and value, not just its reputation.

Every year Michael journeys to France to select and purchase the best available wines. La Cantina offers a vast selection of Burgundy, Bordeaux and Champagne. In addition to the French wines, La Cantina also carries an excellent selection of California, Italian and Spanish wine. There are also wine tastings and wine classes.

If you are looking for a quality wine and knowledgeable, friendly service, La Cantina is exactly the shop for which you have been searching.

LE SOMMELIER
3131 East Madison
Seattle, WA 98112
Tel. (206) 322-7754
Hrs: Mon. - Thur.   8:00 a.m - 9:00 p.m.
       Fri. - Sat.   8:00 a.m. - 10:00 p.m.
Visa, Mastercard and American Express are accepted.

Le Sommelier has just recently moved to a spiffy new complex that's located just across from the Arboretum. It's well lighted, airy and has plenty of room to display the numerous choices. The host, Marc Laderriere provide an excellent selection of imported, domestic and Northwest wines.

A unique addition is a wine bar; where tasters may purchase just a glass to comparison shop prior to purchasing a bottle of wine. A Wine-keeper, with nitrogen added, preserves these tasting wines. Various cheeses and other suitable condiments complement the tasting in this casual and relaxing atmosphere. Wine tasting bars originated in Paris and have proven a popular success in both San Francisco and New York.

Marc, formerly from Paris, knows his wines and stocks a wide range. Choose a superb Chateau Margaux or a local vintner's quality wine. *A votre sante* !!!

STATON HILLS WINERY
1910 Post Alley
Seattle, WA 98101
Tel. (206) 443-8084
Hrs: Mon. - Sat. 11:00 a.m. - 6:00 p.m.
Extended hours in December and summer.

For more than eighty years, Washington farmers have carried their products to the market stalls in Seattle's historic Pike Place Market. Since the late 1960s a new Washington taste has come from the rich farmland of the Yakima Valley, Northwest wines. Washington has gained a world class reputation for its varietal wines. Dave and Susanne Staton, along with the internationally known and respected wine artist, Sebastian Titus, opened Staton Hills Seattle Winery and Tasting Room in 1986.

Staton Hills is housed in the J.P. Jones Building and retains the charm and spirit of the market while incorporating the modern technology necessary for a fully equipped, working winery. The facility features a tasting bar, gift gallery, gourmet food shop, and barrel room. They have a unique wine making exhibit that uses an electronic display to show the various stages and procedures involved in the wine making process. A variety of award winning wines are offered for tasting at the winery, including Chardonnay, Chenin Blanc, Gewurztraminer, Johannisberg Riesling, White Riesling, Sauvignon Blanc, Semillon, Cabernet Sauvignon, Merlot, and Baco Noir Blanc.

Several original wine art works by Sebastian Titus, who has designed more than 175 wine labels for wineries from California to Europe, are on display at the winery. You'll enjoy a visit to Staton Hills Winery and the opportunity to sample their fine wines.

Snoqualmie

Sixty miles from Seattle off I-90 on Highway 202, Snoqualmie blossomed with the coming of the railroad in 1887. The name mean moon to the Snoqualmie Indian people, whose legend had the source of life originating with the moon.

Attractions

Puget Sound Railroad Museum, 109 King Street is part of a steam train ride which leaves from a depot built in 1890. If you take the excursion ride offered weekends from April through October, the train will loop close to Snoqualmie Falls. Call 746-4025 for museum hours and train departure times. The line runs to North Bend and back.

Snoqualmie Falls is a 268-foot sheet of water which creates its own little falls of wind-blown moisture condensed on the rock walls of its canyon. There is a viewing platform at the top, a restaurant and view point near the base of the falls. Puget Power built the state's first hydroelectric plant here in 1898. They run the park and own the falls.

Accommodations

THE SALISH LODGE
P. O. Box 1109
Snoqualmie, WA 98065
Tel.   (206)   888-4230
          (800)   826-6124
Hrs: Mon. - Sat.   8:00 a.m. - 10:00 p.m.
            Sunday   8:00 a.m. - 9:00 p.m.
Visa, MasterCard, AMEX and Discover cards are accepted.

When traveling through beautiful Snoqualmie Washington you'll want to lodge at a place that is as beautiful as the surroundings. The Salish Lodge, located next to the magnificent 268 feet Snoqualmie Falls, is managed by Salishan Lodge. It allows you the elegance you have worked so hard for and deserve on your vacation or business trip.

This ninety-one room luxurious country inn, to be opened the summer of 1988, is the perfect place from which to plan and ready yourself for all of Snoqualmies attractions. The list of features includes such things as a marvelous main restaurant which provides gourmet dining in a country style; the Country Cafe with summer barbecues and many other delightful offerings, skiing thirty minutes away, fishing, hiking, picnic tables and even a sun dial, bicycles and other outdoor equipment for rent, and space for parties, business meetings and banquets. Most rooms have decks or patios which face the river and have woodburning fireplaces and refrigerators.

Probably one of the best features of The Salish is its location. Just a half hour from Seattle and only ten minutes from four golf courses, this lodge gives you the tranquil feeling of remoteness. Yet, at the same time, on a whim, you're able to be in touch with the outside world. The Salish is truly a paradise well worth any visit. On your next vacation or business meeting, remember this "Best Choice."

Farm

NORMAN BROOK FARM MILK BARN
39155 SE Snoqualmie-North Bend Road
Snoqualmie, WA 98065
Tel. (206) 888-1209
Hrs: Mon. - Sun. 6:00 a.m. - 12:00 noon
Closed Christmas Day

Bill Venn and his family have operated this dairy farm for two generations and had retail outlets off and on during during this time. This is a working farm and dairy which supplies milk to retail stores. They are one of the few places that still bottles their milk in glass bottles. They produce good, high quality dairy products on a limited scale. They don't try to compete with the big dairies like Darigold or Carnation, they just try to bring you the better dairy products than you can buy anywhere else.

The Milk Barn has more than just dairy products, though. There is a grocery store, a bakery selling fresh baked goods, a delicatessen that offers salads, sandwiches, and pizza and an area of tables at which to enjoy your food. They serve fountain drinks and ice cream cone too. Bill is very proud of the quality of the products the store sells and you will appreciate the clean, family oriented surroundings. Be sure to try their chocolate milk, it is outstanding.

Take time to stop at Norman Brooks Farm Milk Barn. You'll find Bill Venn very knowledgeable about the history of the area and a good source of information about happenings in the Snoqualmie Valley. You'll really enjoy their outstanding food and dairy products, too.

Golf

MT. SI GOLF COURSE
9010 Meadowbrook-North Bend Road Southeast
Snoqualmie, WA 98065
Tel. (206) 888-1541
Hrs: Summer   Dawn to Dusk
     Winter   7:30 a.m. to Dusk

What was once the largest hops farm in the world, is now a beautiful eighteen hole golf course set in the Snoqualmie Valley with Mt. Si rising in the background. The Mt. Si Golf Course first opened in 1927 as a nine hole course and expanded to eighteen holes in the late thirties. The course is challenging, but not so difficult that the average hacker can't have a terrific time.

This course, offering gently rolling, easy-to-walk hills, consists of a variety of challenging holes and shots. For example, hole number three is a five par shot in 520 fun filled yards. For a real challenge, wait until you experience hole number seventeen. It's 515 yards, a par of five and filled with all kinds of surprises. But whatever hole you're shooting, everyone of them offers a beautiful view and an abundance of wildlife. You need to go to the Pro Shop before golfing, you say? That's no problem, because Mt. Si Golf Course has a well-stocked shop and offers rentals, golf carts, equipment repair, lessons and much more.

When it's time to sit down and discuss the day's golfing over a meal, you'll enjoy the Club House. There you can partake of excellent food ranging from hamburgers and hot dogs to steak and other fine dishes. So, when you're in the area and feel like participating in a good game of golf, visit Mt. Si Golf Course. You'll challenge your skills, shop for quality gear and dine in style.

(See special invitation in the Appendix.)

Wine

SNOQUALMIE WINERY
1000 Winery Road
Snoqualmie, WA 98065
Tel. (206) 888-4000
Hrs: Mon. - Sun. 10:00 a.m. - 4:30 p.m.
Closed Christmas and New Year's Day.

On the north slope of Rattle Snake Ridge in Snoqualmie, overlooking the Snoqualmie Valley and Mt Si, is one of the finest wineries in Washington. The Snoqualmie Winery, founded in 1983 by Joel Klein produces fine varietal wines and is a major force in the Washington Wine business. The setting is reminiscent of Bavaria, but has rustic, rugged Northwest scenery. If you are lucky, you will see some of the abundant wildlife, ranging from deer and elk to birds of prey on your visit.

Snoqualmie Winery offers seven different varieties of wine. Their Semillon is unsurpassed and their Cabernet has won double gold medals at the San Francisco wine fair. They market their product in two dozen states and export to Japan and England. The wine is made in Eastern Washington, aged in oak casks at the Snoqualmie Winery and then returned to Eastern Washington for bottling. Tours of the winery are held daily and samples of the wines are available for tasting. The winery is equipped to handle weddings, receptions, or parties for private.

Plan a trip to Snoqualmie Winery when you are in this area. You will enjoy the lovely setting and the informative tour of the winery. There are facilities for picnicking on the grounds so take time after touring and tasting to relax and enjoy the views of the Cascade Mountains and Snoqualmie Valley.

Tukwila

Tukwila, on the east side of the airport nearer the Duwamish River, was originally called Garden City. Residents in 1905 adapted the name Tukwila from an Indian word said to mean land of the hazelnuts. This area was farmed intensively for years to supply produce for the city. With the development of the airport and construction of I-405, which branches here from I-5, Tukwila became what it is today, a collection of shopping malls and popular stores.

Accommodations

NENDELS INN
15901 West Valley Road
Tukwila, WA 98188
Tel. (206) 226-1812

Nendels of Tukwila is nestled in a quiet, pastoral setting. Soothing mauve colors and a modern decor create a very luxurious atmosphere. Surrounding the area of Nendels on the south is the majestic Green River. On the north is a rustic farm built in the early 1900's.

The excellent service makes Nendels a "Best Choice." In 1934, Margaret Nendel started with a restaurant near Beaverton, Oregon. As a result of sticking with her tradition of service with care, the company now has thirty-one convenient locations throughout the Northwest and has received numerous five-star awards.

Already, Nendels of Tukwila has received a four-star rating by the AAA since it opened its doors on June 20, 1986. The hotel features a fitness room, sauna, outdoor pool and jacuzzi, an outdoor wading pool for the kids, and a 24-hour courtesy car service to nearby Sea-Tac Airport and the Southcenter area for local shopping.

In each of the 147 rooms you will find plush carpeting, warm beds, AM/FM radio, remote control TV, and stylish decor. There are four elegant suites each featuring a private jacuzzi and an outside deck overlooking the river.

Spend a night at Nendels and experience excellent personalized service, a beautiful interior, and gorgeous surroundings. Dine in Victor's Restaurant and Lounge which features exhibition cooking.

SILVER CLOUD INNS, 13050 Forty-eighth Avenue South, Tukwila, Washington. Moderate prices, immaculate rooms, queen-sized beds, free local calls, a jacuzzi, swimming pool, free guest laundry, valet service, and much more.

Vashon Island

Located near the south end of the Puget Sound, and between Seattle and Tacoma; Vashon Island is a treasure true unto itself. Discovered by Captain George Vancouver on May 28, 1792, Vashon Island was named in honor of Vancouver's friend, Captain James Vashon. Before his arrival, Snomamish Indians, a tribe of hunters and gatherers, periodically occupied the island and feasted upon its wild cherries, blackberries and other fruits, as well as fish and game.

As white settlers came in, they supported themselves on timber, farming, fishing, shipbuilding and brickmaking. Today, most of those early industries have dwindled and now this most self-sufficient island is home to small manufacturing firms, retail businesses, specialty food producers, cottage industries, and a variety of artists and craftspeople. Collectively, they are the mainstay of the island economy. Probably no other place in North America has such a collection of enterprises which has attained the coast to coast critical acclaim as the people and products of Vashon Island.

Formed by glacial deposits, Vashon Island is approximately twelve miles long and five miles wide and dotted with small communities. The island's population fluctuates around 8,000, with approximately twenty per cent of the residents working off the island.

Vashon is a fifteen minute ferry ride from Fauntleroy Dock in Seattle and the Southworth dock on the Kitsap Peninsula to Heights Dock on Vashon's north end. Or, if you are traveling from Tacoma, you can take a ferry from Point Defiance and dock fifteen minutes later at Tahlequah on Vashon's southern tip.

Once on Vashon you will find forests, highlands and stretches of protected beaches. Inland roads will take you through a rural countryside of small farms, orchards, vineyards and cottage industries, many of which have products for you to sample. To complete your Vashon experience, you can hike, ride a bike, water ski, ride a horse or sail a boat, and enjoy small town comforts just minutes away from the big city.

Vashon Islanders are independent, self-sufficient people who value their rural island lifestyle and willingly make concessions to maintain it,

King County

concessions such as ferry travel, risk-taking, patience, and putting in the hard work and long hours necessary to be small but competitive. In return they are rewarded with independence and the joys of supporting themselves with dreams they have brought to life. The industrious nature of the island's people have combined with its good soils and mild, year-round maritime climate to provide not only a bounty of delightful, quality, products for visitors, but to be a sensual inspiration as well.

Island communities and merchants host a variety of events during the year, but the island's summer highlight is the Strawberry Festival and parade in mid-July. This is a time when local artists, craftsmen and merchants throughout the island collectively display their wares and restauranteurs offer especially good things to eat. But any time is a good time to experience Vashon Island. So hurry to Vashon and see what community-minded, creative, people can do, then take your time while you're there.

Attractions

Ober Park, just north of downtown Vashon, is the center for all community functions and is the site for the summer arts and crafts fair and the fall harvest fair.

Dockton, at a point where Maury Island hooks into Quartermaster Harbor, was site of a dry dock built in 1892 to handle seagoing vessels. The dock was 325-feet long and handled both steamers and sailing ships. For a time there was a large plant which dried and cured codfish which were then shipped east from Tacoma by railroad.

Dockton Park is about two miles north of Burton on the Island Highway. It has a swimming, boat ramp, a large dock and picnic areas. Hiking trails are nearby.

Another popular park is **Jensen Point Park**, just west of Burton. Lying in a protected harbor, this park has a boat launching, picnic areas and hiking trails.

Point Robinson Park, on the Maury Island Peninsula, has picnic facilities and an old U.S. Coast Guard light house on the beach below.

A trip up to **Inspiration Point**, either by car or bike, is a treat. This scenic vista is on the main highway half way between Burton and the Tahlequah ferry dock.

The Tramp Harbor Fishing Pier is a newly renovated public fishing pier on the east side of the island south of Heyer Point.

Washington State Ferry system docks are at both north and south ends of the island. For schedule information, call 800-542-0810.

Vashon, four miles south of the ferry dock when coming from Seattle, has been the island's population center for years. This was once the primary source of cut flowers for the Seattle market and greenhouses produced off-season vegetables such as cucumbers and tomatoes at premium prices. Businesses are clustered around the highway where Bank Road becomes Southwest 176th Street.

Ellisport, due east of Vashon on the county road, gives a flavor of the way summer homes were before the turn of the century. Three clergymen, including the Ellis family, took up homesteads here in 1879.

The road to **Maury Island** crosses a sand spit at Portage, the small village on the main island. Maury is about five miles long, forming Quartermaster Harbor as it parallels the larger island with long beaches and sheltered waters. Point Robinson has a lighthouse built in 1915, which replaced a structure that began operation in 1887.

For information, contact Vashon Business Association, Box 1035, Vashon WA 98070. Telephone 463-3804.

Accommodations

THE SWALLOWS NEST, Route 3, Box 221, Vashon, WA. Individual cottages located on twenty view acres.

Antiques

OWEN'S ANTIQUES
Main Highway, Mid-Island Route 5, Box 240
Vashon Island, WA 98070
Tel.   (206)   463-5193
         (206)   567-4827
Hrs: Wed. - Sat. 11:00 a.m. - 5:00 p.m.
Expanded summer hours.
Visa, AMEX and MasterCard are accepted.

A surprise is in store for you at Owen's Antiques. Inside the Victorian house on Vashon Island's main highway are eleven rooms full of antiques beautifully displayed. Antique American furniture, Oriental rugs on the floors, fine old paintings and prints on the walls, with china, glass, and silver adding sparkle and gleam.

Three rooms make up the "Country" section. There you'll find old quilts, antique country furniture, kitchen primitives, duck decoys and antique baskets. There's an "ethnic" section with a fine selection of Northwest Indian baskets, Navajo rugs, Southwest pottery and other native arts. Baubles, bangles and beads fill two cases with both costume and fine jewelry. The knowledgeable staff will show you antique and estate pieces, and point out some marvelous reproductions of Victorian rings. The shop offers a wide variety of china and pottery: French Haviland, Irish Belleek, American Art Pottery, Satsuma, Majolica and Roy Doulton to name just a few.

Owen's Antiques is like a fine department store of antiques and decorative arts, the merchandise is logically arranged, well identified and tidy. It is located about six miles from either the West Seattle or Tacoma ferry landing, on the main highway at the old time "Center" of the island. In fact, the building was Vashon's first general store when it was built in 1884. Visit and see why this shop was featured in *Sunset Magazine* and on King TV's "Evening" program.

Apparel

BUGSY'S
P.O. Box 463
Vashon, WA 98070
Tel.   (206)   463-3464
Hrs: Mon. - Fri.   10:00 a.m. - 6:00 p.m.
         Saturday   10:00 a.m. - 5:00 p.m.
         Sunday   11:00 a.m. - 3:00 p.m.
Visa, MasterCard and Discover cards are accepted.

Elise Hass opened her first shop on Vashon Island nine years ago. It was a successful home furnishings store, but five years ago Elise decided to change her focus to women's clothing. She and her sister Barbara Hawkins recognized the need for a quality women's apparel store on Vashon so they opened Bugsy's (Elise's nickname). The sisters both love clothes and had a good idea of what lines they should carry to meet the needs of women in their thirties and forties. By paying much attention to their customer's taste, they have evolved into a popular island boutique.

Elise and Barbara's buying trips take them to San Francisco, Los Angeles and even Hong Kong. They focus on clothing made with quality construction from quality fabrics. Many of their customers are career women, but since styles have become less structured over the years, Bugsy's also carries casual clothes and soft, feminine styles. At least forty percent of Bugsy's inventory is accessories, which allows the customer to put together a complete outfit, or wardrobe.

Bugsy's is a bright and colorful boutique with every display focussing on a variety of interesting color combinations. Elise and Barbara are knowledgeable and eager to help you select the perfect clothes and accessories for your lifestyle. Be sure to stop at Bugsy's when you are exploring Vashon.

Bed and Breakfast

ISLAND INN BED AND BREAKFAST, Rt. One, Box 950, Vashon, Washington. Experience island living at this lovely Victorian farmhouse with views of Mount Olympus, the Sound, and farmhouse gardens.

THE SWAN INN, Route Five, Box 454, Vashon, Washington. You'll think you're in a Fourteenth Century English country inn when you stop over at this island bed and breakfast.

King County

Bakery

BOB'S BAKERY, Main Highway, Center of Vashon, Vashon, Washington. A delicious assortment of baked goods here!

Gift Shop

THE COUNTRY STORE AND FARM
Route 2 Box 304
Vashon Island, WA 98070
Tel. (206) 463-3655 or Seattle 622-3072
Hrs: Mon. - Sat.   9:00 a.m. - 6:00 p.m.
       Sunday   12:00 noon - 5:00 p.m.
Visa, MasterCard and AMEX are accepted.

A unique turn of the century building, The Country Store and Farm sits off the road on ten acres of productive farmland. Customers are welcome to stroll the fields, stop by the plant tables or to enjoy a picnic under the trees!

Discover perennial and annual herbs, flowers and edible greens, plants for garden and landscape, trees and shrubs. The old-fashioned store carries an incredible array of merchandise from natural fiber clothing to rubber boots, pet and garden supplies and a selection of Northwest and Vashon products. There are fruit spreads, jams and jellies, confections, herb vinegars and glazes, nuts, salmon and gift packs.

The Country Store and Farm also operates a personal mail order service through their retail catalog and they'll be happy to ship anywhere. Located on the main highway, mid-island, The Country Store and Farm is just a hoot 'n a holler from either the Seattle, Southworth or Tacoma ferry.

THE LITTLE HOUSE
P.O. Box 865
Vashon Island, WA 98070
Tel. (206) 463-9033
Hrs: Mon. - Sat.   10:00 a.m. - 6:00 p.m.
       Sunday   11:00 a.m. - 4:00 p.m.
Visa and MasterCard are accepted.

You'll have to journey one block off the main street of Vashon proper to find The Little House, but it is well worth it. The Little House is owned by Dan and Bettie Snyder, who have put time and care into making this a special shop. As Bettie said, "There is never a time I'm not excited about coming to work!"

The old house is filled with the unique and unusual. The Snyders carry stock not found just anywhere.

You will find contemporary sports clothing, great for casual wear while traveling and clothing for the kids in the children's room of the house. In addition to clothing, everything from toys to books will entertain the kids while you browse the rest of the house. One entire room is filled with kitchen ware, while another, the party room, carries everything from personalized napkins to fun, whimsical gifts, many under one dollar in price. Children can spend a lot of time in this room also, putting little inexpensive packages together as gifts. Bettie is constantly asking local children what they want to see carried in the store and because of this the inventory is up-to-date. You can purchase candies by the ounce and she even has penny jawbreakers. For the older kids, there are unique jewelry items, earrings and necklaces in porcelain and sterling silver. The aroma of select coffee from Kenya, Guatemala and Antigua fill the house; available by the whole bean or ground while you wait.

Keep browsing and you'll discover adorable stuffed animals, candles, bathroom soaps and fragrances, fine, highfire functional pottery and even a selection of Washington wines.

At Easter Dan plays Easter Bunny and at Halloween, Bettie dresses as the Wicked Witch. Notice the backyard tree; it's used for Vashon's Christmas lights when Santa arrives by sled the first Friday in December.

The Little House has wonderful gifts and is staffed by energetic, caring people. Don't miss it on your tour of Vashon Island!

MINGLEMENT, Island Highway at 204th Street, Southwest, Vashon, Washington. Healthfoods, vitamins, and gifts. Open daily. Visa, MasterCard accepted.

Restaurant

CASA DEL SOL
Route 1, Box 692
Vashon, WA 98070
Tel. (206) 567-5249

Hrs:	Winter	Lunch	Tue. - Sat.	11:30 a.m. - 2:30 p.m.
		Dinner	Tue. - Sat.	5:00 p.m. - 9:00 p.m.
			Sunday	4:00 p.m. - 8:00 p.m.
	Summer	Lunch	Tue. - Sat.	11:30 a.m. - 2:30 p.m.
		Dinner	Tue. - Sat.	5:00 p.m. - 9:00 p.m.
			Sunday	1:30 p.m. - 8:00 p.m.

Closed New Year's Day, July 4th, Thanksgiving and Christmas Eve
Visa, MasterCard, Discover cards and personal checks are accepted.

Vashon Island is easily accessible by ferry and Casa del Sol is located right at the island's north end ferry dock. The restaurant is small and bright on the waterfront with a magnificent view of Puget Sound and Seattle. Michelle Altier and Gloria Maimer own and operate Casa del Sol and produce some of the best Mexican food to be found in the Seattle Puget Sound area. Both women are from Mexico and Michelle's parents owned a restaurant in Mexico City. She grew up loving to cook Mexican food and produces wonderful dishes for the restaurant.

Casa del Sol has an extensive menu featuring delightful dinners such as Pollo en Mole (chicken in a sweet, spicy sauce), chili Colorado (chunks of beef in chili sauce) and Camaron al Mojo de Ajo (shrimp sauteed in a delectable garlic sauce). There are numerous burrito and enchilada dishes and all dinners are served with rice and beans. Daily specials which change regularly are offered. If you have a favorite dish that isn't listed, Michelle will prepare it for you. There is a good selection of Mexican beers to accompany your meal, but wine is limited to house wines.

Children are more than welcome here and it has become a favorite spot for many of the kids from Vashon. There are plans for a deck to provide al fresco dining. A trip on the ferry and a meal at Casa del Sol are a delightful way to spend a relaxing afternoon or evening. The restaurant is especially accessible to foot passengers arriving on the island without cars since it is reached by only a short walk up the ferry dock.

SOUND FOOD
Route 2, Box 298
Vashon, WA 98070
Tel. (206) 463-3565

Hrs:	Summer	Mon.-Thu.	7:00 a.m - 9:00 p.m.
		Friday	7:00 a.m. -10:00 p.m.
		Saturday	8:30 a.m. -10:00 p.m.
		Sunday	8:30 a.m. - 9:00 p.m.
	Winter	Mon.-Thu.	7:00 a.m. - 8:00 p.m.
		Friday	7:00 a.m. - 9:00 p.m.
		Saturday	8:30 a.m. - 9:00 p.m.
		Sunday	8:30 a.m. - 8:00 p.m.

Closed Tuesdays, Christmas and Thanksgiving.
Visa and MasterCard are accepted.

A bright and airy restaurant with a casual atmosphere, situated in a country setting, Sound Food serves Pacific Northwest style breakfast, lunch and dinner fare that is fresh and wholesome.

Weekend brunch features such popular dishes as blintzes, potato pancakes and a variety of seafood specials like trout, snapper or scallops with Hollandaise. The luncheon menu includes roast beef sandwiches, pasta dishes and daily specials. Dinner begins at 5:15 p.m. and offers delicious homemade soups, entrees such as stir-fry chicken or pan-fried oysters, and always, a fresh fish special. There is an extensive wine list, and a bakery where the cinnamon rolls are renowned.

There are freshly cut flowers on the tables and patio dining during the summer months. A popular spot with both locals and off-islanders alike, dining at Sound Food is a sound idea!

Woodinville

To the west of Bothell is Woodinville, another farming community named after its first resident, Ira Woodin, who settled in 1872. Just off Highway 202 which links the urbanized communities on the shores of Lake Washington, Woodinville remains a rural community. Its citizens have not felt the need to incorporate into city-style government.

Attractions

Chateau Saint Michelle, one of Washington's best known wineries, is on Stimson Lane in Woodinville. The vineyards and underground cellar are open

King County

daily, and a tasting room greets visitors from 10:00 a.m. to 4:30 p.m. The turn off is two miles south of Woodinville on Highway 202. Call 488-1133.

For further information contact the Woodinville Chamber of Commerce, 17601 140th Northeast, Woodinville WA 98702, telephone 481-8300.

Antiques

PUTNAM ANTIQUE MALL
14450 Woodinville-Redmond Road
Woodinville, WA 98072
Tel. (206) 485-5555
Hrs: Mon. - Sat. 10:00 a.m. - 6:00 p.m.
Sunday 11:00 a.m. - 6:00 p.m.
Closed major holidays.

Putnam Antique Mall is a 12,000 square foot building that offers the best and largest selection of antiques in the Northwest. There are 148 displays and booths in an elegantly appointed setting. The building was designed specifically to house the antique mall. It features a lovely, warm interior decorated in mauve with lovely custom made display cases. The selection available is astounding, everything from a pillbox to a Picasso is available. There is an art gallery and a jewelry gallery in addition to the shops that feature antiques and collectibles.

Pam Putnam is the owner of this delightful antique mall, and they have assembled a staff that is knowledgeable and ready to help you find just what you are seeking. You will find dealers offering antique books, Victorian furniture, country furniture, office furniture, toys, juke boxes, quilts, military antiques, and much more. There are antiques from around the world. Pam also offers dealers rental space with a beautiful atmosphere to display their merchandise.

This is a fun place to spend an afternoon browsing. Include Putnam's Antique Mall on your itinerary when you are in the Woodinville area, you won't be disappointed.

Attraction

GOLD CREEK FISH FARM, 15844 148th Avenue, Northeast, Woodinville, Washington. Just a few miles south of Hollywood, owner Newt Olson has created a rustic and relaxing fish farm; just visit, or catch your own succulent trout dinner.

Florist

CHATEAU FLORAL
14461 Woodinville/Redmond Road
Woodinville, WA 98072
Tel. (206) 486-0640
Hrs: Mon. - Fri. 9:00 a.m. - 6:00 p.m.
      Saturday 10:00 a.m. - 5:00 p.m.
Closed Sundays, Christmas and New Year's Day.
Extended hours during the holiday season.
Visa and MasterCard are accepted.

    At Chateau Floral, owners Connie Adams and Patty Sego have pooled their extensive expertise and talents to provide a European market type of florist to serve you. Connie has been a wholesale flower buyer for several years. Patty has considerable experience as a design coordinator and uses her training at Master Designer in Holland. Both are very knowledgeable about flowers and bring you cut flowers that are the freshest possible. They will also share with you techniques for getting the longest possible life from the arrangements or flowers you purchase.
    While at Chateau Floral you'll find buckets and buckets of fresh cut flowers from which you select what pleases you. You may take them home to arrange yourself, or have them arranged in European tradition. Most of the flowers are imported, which provides a diverse selection from which to choose. Of course, Chateau Floral also has a delightful collection of arrangements in their cooler and the staff welcomes the opportunity to create custom arrangements. They will deliver in the local area.
    When touring the Hollywood Vineyard area south of Woodinville, plan a stop at Chateau Floral. In addition to the beautiful flowers, you'll find delectable fruit baskets which include some nice Northwest wines. You'll find Chateau Floral a lovely and enjoyable place to shop.

Garden Center

MOLBAK'S
13625 NE 175th
Woodinville, WA 98072
Tel. (206) 483-5000
Hrs: Sat. - Thu.   9:30 a.m. - 6:00 p.m.
       Friday   9:30 a.m. - 9:00 p.m.
Open until 8:00 p.m. during the month of May.
Closed Thanksgiving, Christmas, and New Year's Day.

Molbak's is an extraordinary nursery and garden center. It is an ten acre complex with twenty-eight greenhouses, a large garden store building, an outdoor nursery, and a flower and gift shop. They grow most of their own plants and you can see plants in various stages of development, from seedlings to the finished plant that is ready to take home. There is a large staff, all very knowledgeable about flowers and plants and able to answer any questions you might have.

Molbak's is a great place to find flowers and plants all year round, but there are three special times of year to visit. May is the most colorful month with lots of blooming plants and flowers. October is floral fairyland time with a fairy tale theme, employees in costumes, puppet shows and other things of interest for children. From Thanksgiving through Christmas is the poinsettia festival. At this time there are hundreds and hundreds of beautiful poinsettias. Customers come from all over the state to shop. Molbak's is internationally known as a garden center, and the selection of everything from annuals to potted houseplants is tremendous.

Molbak's is a family oriented business and there is something here to please everyone. Be sure to stop by for a visit your whole family will enjoy.

Gift Shop

THE FRAZZLED DUCK
14473 Woodinville-Redmond Road
Woodinville, WA 98072
Tel. (206) 485-2294
Hrs: Mon.-Fri.   10:00 a.m.-7:00 p.m.
      Sat.   10:00 a.m.-6:00 p.m.
      Sun.   Noon-5:00 p.m.
      Closed major holidays

    Betty and Jim Marth have created a specialty antique and gift shop that is a real pleasure to visit and shop. Upon entering The Frazzled Duck, you will note the aroma of fresh brewed coffee. Enjoy a complimentary cup while you browse through the shop. With fine coffee in hand, you become aware that you are in an old country general store displaying many fine antiques.
    The Frazzled Duck also displays many beautifully carved and painted decoys and duck heads as well as numbered prints of wildlife paintings. There are even shell boxes decorated with handcarved decoys. The expertly crafted jewel boxes of rare woods are worth the visit themselves and make outstanding gifts. The Frazzled Duck also offers specialty candies, linens, baskets, towels, men's soaps, and handmade quilts. Betty and her staff will be happy to help you create that custom gift for your favorite person(s) from any or all of the above items.
    When in the Hollywood area, "step into the past" and visit The Frazzled Duck, a fun country store, and a place you will enjoy and return to often.

(See special invitation in Appendix.)

Jewelers

KASHMIR CUSTOM JEWELERS
Hollywood Schoolhouse
14810 NE 145th
Woodinville, WA 98072
Tel. (206) 487-1010
Hrs: Tue. - Sat. 10:00 a.m. - 6:00 p.m.
Or call for appointment.
All major credit cards are accepted.

    Enter the main portal to the Hollywood Schoolhouse and find Kashmir Custom Jewelers. Kashmir....the rarest and bluest sapphires known to man.

Owners Mike and Vicki Spelman, raised near the Yogo Sapphire Mine in Montana have a special fascination for sapphires, a fascination that has led to the acquisition and marketing of the highest quality, unusual and exotic stones. The Spelmans have a combined gemological background of over fifty years and their son, Trevor, follows in their footsteps as a creator of fine custom jewelry.

Stop by this comfortable shop for a free ring polishing, cleaning, inspection and appraisal. The Spelmans have the expertise to beautifully rebuild and restore your fine pieces and stay within your budget - and you can participate in the process!

Come in and linger over the large variety of natural gemstones - select one, choose a setting and Viola! Create your own heirloom! Kashmir Custom Jewelers for one of a kind jewelry that will be enjoyed for generations.

Pottery

WOODINVILLE POTTERY
14810 NE 145th Street
Woodinville, WA 98072
Tel. (206) 481-1435
Hrs: Tue. - Sat.   10:00 a.m. - 5:00 p.m.
        Sunday   12:00 noon - 5:00 p.m.
Closed Monday.
MasterCard and Visa are accepted.

Woodinville Pottery is owned and operated by master potters Jensen and Karen Wilkins. They have personally selected only the best artisans from craft shows across the country for their store, thus creating one of the most distinctive gift shops on the West Coast.

Jensen and Karen offer handmade objects from thirty potters and over forty crafts people at very reasonable prices. Amongst the many unique items offered are the eastside's largest selection of handmade pottery sinks, many of them hand painted to match wallpapers. They also offer an old-fashioned candy store, within the store, offering very special candies for you to enjoy - ask for a free sample!

They are located in Woodinville's most famous historical landmark, the Hollywood Schoolhouse. The building is a classic three story brick schoolhouse with beautifully landscaped grounds, antique windmills and a stream wandering through. They are within walking distance of two wineries and the Northwest's largest antique mall. Mr. Stimson of the Stimson Lumber Co. built the school in 1912 and donated it to the county so that his children would have a school nearby, as their home was the Stimson Mansion located on land now known as the Chateau Ste. Michelle Winery.

Restaurant

CHIN'S PALACE
13317 NE 175th Street
Woodinville, WA 98072
Tel. (206) 486-6252
Hrs: Mon. - Fri.   11:30 a.m. - 10:00 p.m.
     Sat. - Sun.   3:00 p.m. - 10:00 p.m.

Kon and Ophelia Chin, owners of Chin's Palace, have created a pleasant, family oriented restaurant which specializes in Mandarin, Szechuan, and Cantonese cuisine. Kon was in the restaurant business with his family in Illinois for years before moving to the Northwest. He learned his trade from his parents and uses family recipes for the dishes he serves. The restaurant is attractively decorated, fish tanks greet you as you enter. The walls have flowered wall paper and are decorated with oriental paintings. Fresh flowers adorn the tables set with pink and white linens. The entire effect creates a charming and relaxed atmosphere.

Family's are welcomed, kids love it, and there are special children's portions available. Several family style dinners offering a number of dishes are available. Dinner A, for example, has barbecued pork, almond fried chicken, pork Chow Mein, pork fried rice, sweet and sour pork, tea, and fortune cookies. There are also individual combinations which feature three or four different dishes. A number of chef's specials are delicious and unusual, such as the Happy Family which features shrimp, scallops, chicken, and barbecued pork stir fried with vegetables in a harmonious blend. With a couple of days advance notice, a special cake or treat will be provided for anniversaries or birthdays.

You'll enjoy the delicious selections available at Chin's and the reasonable prices. They can accommodate large groups, and the entire restaurant can be reserved for special meetings or parties. Dining at Chin's Palace is fun and delicious for the whole family.

CREEKSIDE RESTAURANT
13120 NE 177 Place Suite A-201
Woodinville, WA 98072
Tel. (206) 485-0721

Hrs:	Mon. - Thu.	11:00 a.m. - 10:00 p.m.
	Fri. - Sat.	11:00 a.m. - 11:00 p.m.
Lounge	Mon. - Thu.	open until 12:00 midnight
	Fri. - Sat.	open until 2:00 a.m.

This delightful addition to the Woodinville dining scene has been in business since 1985 and is delighting the local population for both lunch and dinner. Helle Bey Larsen was in the restaurant business in Denmark before opening at her present location. She designed the kitchen and the charming interior of the restaurant, which has a very warm atmosphere with peach and light blue accented with light wood trim. There is a deck for outside dining during the spring and summer. The menu was designed by Chef Rod Brown who has studied with gold medal winning chefs.

Lunches feature such items as sandwiches, omelettes, oysters, sole, salads, hamburgers and a delightfully different Danish specialty called Frikadeller - fresh ground pork pan fried with sweet and sour cabbage and mashed potatoes. The dinner menu has a good selections of appetizers with which to begin, including smoked salmon, escargot, cheeses, and more. Soup and salad are available and entrees feature chicken, steak, and fresh seafood. Wonderful freshly made pastries are a perfect finish to a delicious meal. There is a good selection of wine available and the bar serves many different wines, beer and also snack foods.

The Creekside Restaurant is very popular locally and people come from all around the area for dinner. Helle and Rod are very friendly and like to visit with their dinner guests. You'll enjoy the warm and comfortable atmosphere and the delicious food.

LE COURTYARD
17705 140th Avenue Northeast
Woodinville, WA 98072
Tel.   (206) 483-1088
Hrs: Lunch   Mon. - Fri.   11:30 a.m. - 3:00 p.m.
       Dinner   Mon. - Sat.   6:00 p.m. - 9:30 p.m.
Reservations are recommended.
Visa, MasterCard and AMEX are accepted.

Located in a house in Woodinville, Le Courtyard is a restaurant with changing personalities. This charming country house is decorated in pastels of mauve and plum, with lovely art adorning the walls, comfortable high back chairs and ceiling fans lending the finishing touches.

At lunch the atmosphere is relaxed and comfortable, providing a pleasant noontime break from the rigors of the work day. At night the restaurant is transformed to provide an ambiance of elegance and sophistication.   White linen tablecloths and burgandy napkins accented with fresh flowers and candle light are the graceful touches that start an unforgetable meal at Le Courtyard.

The focus of the menu is upon Northwest and Continental cuisine. Luncheon choices include veal, seafood and fresh seasonal fish. Be sure to sample such delicacies as Penn Cove mussels or Canadian smoked salmon. For dinner you will want to choose from a wide variety of appetizers and continue with fresh salmon or specialties such as, fresh pheasant or quail. A wine list with numerous Washington wines featured is available, as well as full bar services to complement your meal.   Be sure to enjoy this "Best Choice" restaurant for excellent meals and unequaled atmosphere.

TEXAS SMOKEHOUSE BAR BQ
14467 Woodinville-Redmond Road
Woodinville, WA 98072
Tel. (206) 486-1957
Hrs: Mon.-Thur.   11:00 a.m.-8:00 p.m.
       Fri.-Sat.   11:00 a.m.-8:30 p.m.
       May 1-Aug. 31   open till 9:30 p.m.

Be prepared and hungry for a special treat when you visit the Texas Smokehouse Bar BQ! Located in the Hollywood Vineyards shopping mall in close proximity to St. Michelle and Haviland wineries as well as the Sammamish bike trail, the Putnam Antique Mall and the schoolhouse, the Texas Smokehouse Bar BQ is a convenient stop for refueling in a comfortable, family-style setting. Not only is this the only eating establishment between Redmond and

Woodinville, it is also one of the very few barbeque restaurants in greater Seattle.

The Texas Smokehouse Bar BQ is a family owned and operated restaurant that is oriented toward family enjoyment. Owners Scott and Suzi Powell, and parents Doris and Maurice Powell (all native Texans and recent transplants to the Northwest) will make your visit comfortable and memorable. They also do their best to obtain the finest ingredients for the restaurant.

The specialty of the house is the smoked beef brisket served sliced or chopped. You'll also find plenty of homemade potato salad, coleslaw and barbeque beans. Another specialty--a potato that weighs in at one pound or more that is baked and dressed with sour cream, chives, cheese and topped with chopped Bar BQ beef! You better be hungry to attack this one!

Personal checks accepted, no credit cards.

Sporting Goods

GOLDEN EGG SKI AND SPORT FACTORY OUTLET
12609 NE Woodinville Drive
Woodinville, WA 98072
Tel.   (206) 488-8444
Hrs: Winter   Mon. - Fri.   10:00 a.m. - 9:00 p.m.
                Saturday   10:00 a.m. - 5:00 p.m.
                Sunday   10:00 a.m. - 5:00 p.m.
       Summer   Mon. - Fri.   10:30 a.m. - 5:00 p.m.
                Saturday   10:00 a.m. - 5:00 p.m.
Closed major holidays.
MasterCard, Visa and AMEX are accepted.

For first quality active sportswear and accessories at discounted prices visit the Golden Egg Ski and Sport shop. Owners Dora and John Coughlin give you the benefit of their long experience in the sportswear field. Hailing from New England, they are experts in cold weather dress.

John has over twenty-five years of experience in the manufacturing and marketing of ski and outer wear. In addition to retail experience, Dora has been a clothing buyer, is extremely knowledgeable about fabrics and colors and has a personal knowledge of both cross country and downhill skiing. She will provide the expertise necessary to select and fit you for the sporting activities you enjoy and knows what you need to keep warm and dry.

In addition to ski wear, Goretex of different weights, the newest fashion accessories, underwear (wool, silk and poly pro), all kinds of socks and children's clothing, the Golden Egg stocks backpacks, tents, hiking boots, foul weather gear and accessories. For summer activities you'll find triathalon apparel, sun care products, a nice selection of swim wear and proper bicycling attire. Satisfy all your sportswear needs in the small shop with the big inventories.....and even bigger savings! You will find Golden Egg Ski and Sport Factory Outlet on the road to the famous Woodinville wine country. Free maps are available.

NEW WEST PROSPECTING AND MINING SUPPLIES, INC.
12637 Woodinville Drive
Woodinville, WA 98072
Tel. (206) 487-MINE
Hrs: Tue. - Fri.   10:00 a.m. - 6:00 p.m.
          Saturday   9:00 a.m. - 5:00 p.m.
Closed Sunday and Monday

Get your donkey, pans and provisions. We're going for gold!!! And it's a lot easier these days than before. How does one find this gold? And if you find it, how do you sell it? The place to start is New West Prospecting and Mining Supplies. Tex and Elly Loftin, who have been prospecting for years, established their business to promote recreational gold prospecting. At their new location they have the room to carry out the many aspects of their business.

Education is a major part of their program. Classes, field trips and workshops are directed toward teaching how and where to find gold, how to recover it, and how to sell it. There are classes on geology, claim staking and map reading. You'll learn about the equipment needed for different methods of recovering gold - from panning to using sluice boxes. A phone call will provide you with the dates of the classes and field trips of interest to you. New West carries a full line of supplies including pans, sluice boxes, dredges and gold recovery systems, as well as a complete selection of "how to" books and maps.

Elly emphasizes that prospecting should not be taken seriously. "If you want to strike it rich, buy a lottery ticket, your odds are better. If you want to have a lot of fun, and make gas money, then prospecting is what you should do." Prospecting is a great family activity and kids usually do real well. Their sharp eyes and their attention span is sometimes better than adults when rocks, water and gravel are involved.   Call or stop by New West Prospecting and Mining Supplies and get involved with an exciting way to experience the great outdoors. New West can help you have fun looking for gold whether you have only a few days or want to get more serious about your prospecting.

TACK SHACK INC.
13400 NE 175th Street
P. O. Box 116
Woodinville, WA 98072
Tel. (206) 481-8875
Hrs: Mon. - Sat. 9:30 a.m. - 6:00 p.m.
Extended hours during Christmas Season. Closed major holidays.
Visa, MasterCard, BankCard and checks are accepted.

Whoa there Pardner! For the finest western wear for man and beast the Tack Shack is your one stop shopping experience for everything western. Belly up to the antique 1880's hat bar and have owner Winnie Russe fit and style your western hat. This classy lady will style all western hats purchased at the Tack Shack free for as long as the hat can take it!

Daughter Nancy Drake, master of the tack department is responsible for fitting tack to horses she doesn't see, as well as selling medicines and leg care items. The tack department is large and contains everything needed to properly equip your mount, including custom designed tack and sterling silver accessories. The Tack Shack carries a large selection of western cut clothing for men, women and children including jeans, western shirts, business suits, stylish western wear for women and all varieties of accessories such as belt buckles, ties and boots.

Professional rodeo hands buy their gear at the Tack Shack - where else can you get a ninety foot lariat? Conveniently located in downtown Woodinville and easily accessible from I-405 and I-5 from the Highway 522 exit, mosey on in to the Tack Shack and make yourself at home! Yaa-Hooo!

Wine

CHATEAU STE. MICHELLE
14111 NE 145th
Woodinville, WA 98072
Tel. (206) 488-1133
Hrs: Mon. - Sun. 10:00 a.m. - 4:30 p.m.
Extended hours in summer. Closed major holidays.

Chateau Ste. Michelle is a pioneer in Washington winemaking and vineyard research. They began producing sweet dessert wines from Washington fruits, berries, and grapes in the 1930s. In the early 1950s they began planting acres of classic varietal grapes native to Europe. After many years of testing and developing, the first Ste. Michelle wine was produced in 1968. From the very beginning they have been able to hold their own against the premier wines of California. This facility in Woodinville has been in operation since 1976 and it, along with the other locations, makes Chateau Ste. Michelle the largest wine producer in Washington.

Plan to spend an afternoon when you visit Chateau Ste. Michelle. You will want to take the tour and spend some time tasting the wines they have available for sale. You will also want to browse in the gift shop, which has many interesting gift items. In addition to wines, they offer gifts and special gourmet food. They also have picnic items and the grounds surrounding the winery are perfect for picnicking. The winery is set in eighty-seven acres of parklike grounds and there are areas where you can relax and enjoy some of their wonderful wine with your picnic.

There are many activities that take place at the winery. There is an outdoor theater where Shakespeare plays are presented during the summer. A series of concerts, ranging from Blue Grass to classical are also held during the summer. Be sure to plan a stop at Chateau Ste. Michelle when you are in the area; it is a lovely place and you will enjoy the interesting selection of wines available.

HAVILAND WINERY
#1 Manor Lane
14030 NE 145th
Woodinville, WA 98072
Tel. (206) 488-0808
Hrs: Mon. - Sun. 10:00 a.m. - 5:00 p.m.

Haviland Winery is the owner of the oldest producing vineyard in the Northwest, a Cabernet Sauvignon vineyard located in the Yakima River Valley Basin. The winery at Woodinville is one of the few wineries in Washington where a visitor can see the full process of hand crafting wines. The knowledgeable tour guides will conduct you on a visit and explain the wine making process from start to finish. In the tasting room you can sample the finished products. The new Manor House is a state of the art 30,000 square foot winery equipped to produce 125,000 gallons of wine per year. The 1987 crush is anticipated to be 90,000 gallons.

Manor House also features a large visitor's center with a tasting room, retail store, and banquet facilities which will serve 120 for weddings, receptions, or private functions. Haviland has won national and international awards for their Merlot and Chardonnay, which is fermented in brand new oak barrels for each batch. You can purchase Haviland Winery wines and other wine related products in the store. It also has anything you might need for a picnic in the park like grounds which surround the winery.

King County

Haviland Winery is an interesting place to visit. You will find the lovely new buildings and grounds a very attractive place to spend a few hours. The tour guides and retailers are knowledgeable, helpful and will help you gain new insight into the wine making process. You'll leave the winery feeling richer for the experience.

KITSAP COUNTY

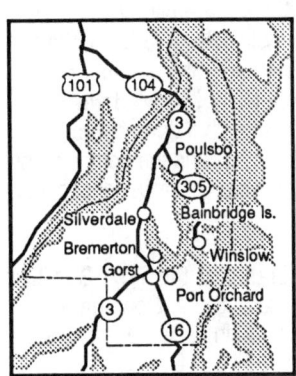

Named in honor of a local Indian chief who fought to evict white settlers during the wars of 1855-56, Kitsap County includes 393 square miles of peninsula and island lands amid waters of Puget Sound. The county also does homage to modern warriors of the U.S. Navy, providing a place for repair of their ships, berths for their nuclear submarines, and home port for vessels moth-balled in readiness for war in places not yet imagined.

Kitsap was created by the Territorial Legislature of 1857. The county seat moved in the early days, finally coming to Port Orchard in 1893. Bremerton, site of a naval yard since 1891, houses over one-fifth of the county's 150,000 residents. Timber, fishing and farming sustain those families not linked to the navy or businesses supporting it. Bainbridge Island, a thirty-minute ferry ride from Seattle, has much of the mixed rural and commuter quality found on Vashon Island in King County's part of the Sound. Hood Canal, on the peninsula's west side, has a distinct rural flavor to its shores, broken by the super-secret Trident submarine base at Bangor, and the massive floating concrete highway bridge which links Port Gamble with the road to Port Angeles far to the west across the sometimes choppy water.

Like the hills marching to Hood Canal from the Olympic Mountains, the lower Kitsap Peninsula has prime sites for growing timber. Most of the trees were cut for the first time between 1850 and the turn of the century and have now grown back. Its miles of beaches, most of them cobbled with rounded gravel and washed by brisk tidal flows, yield oysters and clams at low tide. Its channels are home to many varieties of saltwater fish. Several small resorts and camps greet vacationers who come to enjoy these attractions. Summer homes cluster around the small inlets and bays of the coastlines.

Attractions

Suquamish Museum is part of the **Port Madison Indian Reservation** near Winslow. Indian history comes alive in exhibits and on the grounds of the scenic reservation next to Agate Passage. From Winslow ferry dock, eight miles north on Highway 305 to Sandy Hook Road, then left to the museum. Open daily 10:00 a.m. to 5:00 p.m. in the summer. Hours for the rest of the year are Tuesday through Friday 11:00 a.m. to 4:00 p.m. and Saturday and Sunday from 10:00 a.m. to 5:00 p.m. Telephone 478-4819.

North of Hood Canal Bridge (Highway 104) is the quaint town of **Port Gamble**, and across its small bay the **Port Gamble Indian Reservation**. Pope and Talbot, one of the west's famous ocean shipping and lumber firms, had its start here in 1853. The lumbermen sailed out from Maine, prowled the Sound and sent the crew ashore to build their mill on the small but deep harbor. New England architecture is everywhere in the public buildings and the homes of the company town. The company once owned 160,000 acres of timberland to feed the mill's hungry headsaws.

The northwest's lumber industry is celebrated at the **Port Gamble Historical Museum**, on the lower level of the General Store. Open daily from 10:00 a.m. to 12:00 noon and 1:00 p.m. to 4:00 p.m. during summer months, by appointment at other times of the year. Telephone 297-3341.

The second and third levels of the Port Gamble General Store house a private collection of sea shells which is part of the **Of Sea and Shore Museum**. Open Monday through Saturday from 9:00 a.m. to 6:00 p.m. and on Sundays between 10:00 a.m. and 6:00 p.m. Telephone 297-2426.

Highway 104 begins at the small community of Kingston, where there is ferry service to Edmonds on the Seattle side of the Sound. This is the most direct route from the mainland to the Olympic Peninsula by using the ferry and the mile-long floating bridge over Hood Canal.

Indians had a word meaning "long nose" for the sandy spit reaching eastward into the main channel at the north of Kitsap peninsula. The mapping crew of the 1841 Wilkes expedition dubbed it **Point No Point**, a name which sticks and applies to a twenty-five acre park and a lighthouse. Historians disagree on the reason for the name, but note a similar designation on the Hudson River where as mariners get closer to the promontory it seems less significant. A treaty with Clallam and Skokomish Indians was signed here in 1855, placing Point No Point in history books as well as mariner's charts. The lighthouse carries a reminder of damage from a 1930 lightening strike.

For further information, contact the **Bremerton/Kitsap County Visitor and Convention Bureau**, Box 836, Bremerton WA 98310. Telephone 479-3588.

Bainbridge Island

This island is named after William Bainbridge, captain of the U.S.S. Constitution in the Revolutionary War. Indians lived here with little trouble from settlers until a sawmill was built in 1853. When the timber was cut over the mill ports gave way to vacation camps for Seattle's well-to-do families.

Attractions

In **Winslow**, the harbor was once the site of a large ship yard which turned out U.S. Navy minesweepers before World War II. This was also home port for several off-shore commercial fishing vessels.

Port Blakely, due south of Winslow is a quiet inlet named after a naval hero of the war of 1812. William Renton opened a sawmill here in 1863 and expanded it several times. Fire swept the plant in 1888, and in 1907. The mill closed in 1914, with little trace of it remaining. Once 1,200 men worked here producing 400,000 board feet of lumber a day.

Fort Ward State Park, on the shore west of Bean's Point, is a day use area popular with SCUBA divers. Built in 1910 as a coast artillery battery, the 330-acre reservation was held by the navy for years and its gun mounts remain. Above the post are a group of summer homes at South Beach.

Port Madison, on the far north of the island, curves around a small harbor. A lumber mill established in 1853 was followed by a machine shop, foundry and other industrial operations. This was Kitsap County seat in 1861, the result of an election.

Fay Bainbridge State Park has overnight camping facilities. **Port Madison Indian Reservation** is located on the main peninsula across the waters of Agate Pass. A treaty designated the reservation in 1855 but it did not begin operation until 1864.

Strawberry Hill Museum, on High School Road in Strawberry Hill Park, houses a collection of island history. Open Saturdays from 11:00 a.m. to 3:00 p.m. and by appointment. Telephone 842-3433.

For further information, contact **Bainbridge Island Chamber of Commerce**, Harold's Square 153 Madrone Lane North, Bainbridge Island WA 98110. Telephone 842-3700.

Accommodations

THE BOMBAY HOUSE
8490 Beck Road NE
Bainbridge Island, WA 98110
Tel. (206) 842-3926

High on a hill overlooking Rich Passage in the southwest part of Bainbridge Island, sits The Bombay House, a lovely turn of the century bed and breakfast establishment. The setting is wonderfully reminiscent of the past, with a widow's walk, a gazebo, and masses of flowers. Nearby you can enjoy hiking, biking, beachcombing, shopping, and fine dining. Your hosts, Bunny Cameron and Roger Kanchuk will go out of their way to make your stay as delightful and relaxing as possible.

The house is beautifully restored and offers charming guest rooms furnished in country antiques. The King's room offers a tin soaking tub and king-size bed while the Captains room has a beautiful view of the passage below. The breakfast presented each morning includes fresh fruits and juices, cereals, and freshly baked croissants and pastries. Your hosts are very flexible and with advance notice will prepare special diet foods, make dinner reservations, or even pick you up at the ferry terminal.

Prices at The Bombay House are surprisingly reasonable and it offers the weary traveler, or even locals who just want to step back in time for a moment, a giant dose of relaxation.

SKIFF POINT GUEST HOUSE, 11040 Mountain View Road, Northeast, Bainbridge Island, Washington. A spacious, furnished guest house perched on Skiff Point overlooking Puget Sound. Day-conferences, small groups welcome. Checks accepted, no credit cards.

Seclusion, a time to get away and relax, to gather your thoughts and to enjoy the solitude of nature. This isn't a hustle and bustle tour. It's a slow and leisurely visit to beautiful Bainbridge Island.

SLOW DOWN AND SMELL THE ROSES

	First, you'll need lodging. Here are two wonderful B & B inns:		
	The Bombay House	Best lodging	Bain/B & B
	Skiff Point	Best lodging	Bain/B & B
	Now for your relaxing tour.		
a.m.	Fort Ward Park	Best scuba	Bain/Attraction
a.m.	Port Madison	Best atmosphere	Bain/Attraction
a.m.	Strawberry Hill	Best museum	Bain/Attraction
p.m.	Fay Bainbridge Park	Best camping	Bain/Camp
p.m.	Pleasant Beach Grill	Best seafood	Bain/Restaurant

Take several days to see it all. Once you're relaxing, you'll find time working for you instead of against you.

Restaurant

PLEASANT BEACH GRILL AND OYSTER HOUSE
4738 Lynnwood Center Road
Bainbridge Island, WA 98110
Tel. (206) 842-4347
Hrs: Mon.-Sun.   5:00 p.m. - Closing
     Sunday Brunch   10:00 a.m. - 2:00 p.m.

The Pleasant Beach Grill and Oyster House is located in Lynwood Center, approximately four miles outside of Winslow, in what was once a private mansion built in the late 1920's for one of the island's most prominent families. Co-owner Jeffrey Erickson and his family have created an elegant restaurant in a very romantic setting. From the cozy fireplace in the study and lounge to the white linen tablecloths and fresh cut flowers, the ambiance leaves nothing to be desired.

The Ericksons firmly believe in the Northwest seafood approach. "Only the best and freshest possible," says Jeffrey. The menu features a full page of oyster specialty dishes ranging from curried oysters to oysters pepperpan. The grill page has a variety of steaks, lamb chops, chicken and veal. There are nightly specials listed on the blackboard. The fresh salmon with fresh basil and raspberry butter is an outstanding selection. There is an extensive wine list featuring many award winning local labels.

If you don't happen to be staying on Bainbridge Island, The Pleasant Beach Grill and Oyster House is well worth the short ferry ride over from the mainland for dinner. This charming restaurant offers a truly unique Northwest dining experience.

(See special invitation in the Appendix.)

Bremerton

When William Bremer came to this harbor in 1888, historians say the hillsides were a mass of stumps from decades of logging. The town was platted in 1891, and Bremer is credited with selling the navy on locating a dry dock at what is now Puget Sound Naval Shipyard. The modern city surrounding the yard has an estimated 36,000 residents. About 700 acres with a multi-million dollar investment in facilities now comprise the yard. Much of the Pacific Fleet comes here for overhaul and repairs, with about 3,000 crew members in port at any given time. This became the home port for U.S.S. Nimitz, a large aircraft carrier, in 1987. About 5,000 people including ship's company and dependents, moved to Bremerton and its environs as a result of the Nimitz move. About 12,000 civilians work in the several naval facilities which are part of the yard.

Attractions

Illahee State Park, three miles north of town on Highway 306, has almost 1,800 feet of frontage on an inlet. Much of the original development was carried out in the late 1930s by federal Civilian Conservation Corps crews. Two naval guns, memorials to sailors who died in World War I, came from the U.S.S. West Virginia. Camping, boat launching and moorage are part of this seventy-five acre park. Open April 1 through October 15 from 6:30 a.m. to 10:00 p.m. and the rest of the year from 8:00 a.m. to 5:00 p.m.

Puget Sound Naval Shipyard Museum, 120 Washington Avenue, located near the ferry terminal, contains ship models and other artifacts from the navy's near-century here. Open daily from 9:00 a.m. to 5:00 p.m. Telephone 479-7447. The area visitor information center is next door.

U.S.S. Missouri, the decommissioned battleship, is the most famous of mothballed vessels in the shipyard. The Japanese treaty ending World War II was signed on her decks. NOTE: At the time this book was published the U.S.S. Missouri had just been recommissioned and sent to the Mediterranean to take part in the "peacekeeping" of maintaining the waterways for oil shipments.

For information, contact the **Bremerton Area Chamber of Commerce**, 837 Fourth Street, Bremerton WA 98310. Telephone 479-3579.

Accommodations

BAYVIEW INN, 5640 Kitsap Way, Bremerton, Washington. You will appreciate this landmark hotel for its comfortable accommodations, fine restaurant, and great view of the bay.

BEST WESTERN WESTGATE INN
4303 Kitsap Way
Bremerton, WA 98312
Tel. (206) 377-4402
      (800) 826-7162

Bremerton is mid way between Seattle and Olympic National Park which makes it an ideal location from which to explore the entire area. The Best Western Westgate Inn in Bremerton is a good place to make your headquarters when vacationing in this region.

Each of the 102 units at the Inn is an over size suite with a living room, kitchen and sleeping area. The Inn was recently redecorated in warm, natural colors and furnished with oak to provide a pleasant ambiance. Large suites are available with color cable television, laundry facilities and complimentary charge accounts. There is a playground for children and a heated swimming pool. Westgate Inn is conveniently located within walking distance of several nice restaurants and shops.

Best Western Westgate Inn's primary emphasis is tour and travel trade visiting the park, which makes them knowledgeable and helpful when you are planning your itinerary. There is pickup service from the Bremerton airport and it's only fifty minutes from the Seattle Tacoma Airport and ten minutes from the Bremerton ferry terminal. For a comfortable, convenient place to stay on your visit to the Seattle Olympic Peninsula area, try the Best Western Westgate.

Kitsap County

RAFFLES OYSTERS BAY INN, 4412 Kitsap Way, Bremerton, Washington. 4412 Kitsap Way, Bremerton, Washington. There's an excellent view of the bay from the inn and a quality restaurant serving steak and seafood. AMEX, Diner's Club, MasterCard accepted.

WESTGATE SUITES
4303 Kitsap Way
Bremerton, WA 98312
Tel. (206) 377-4402
      (800) 826-7162

Bremerton is midway between Seattle and Olympic National Park which makes it an ideal location from which to explore the entire area. Westgate Suites in Bremerton is a nice place to choose as your vacation hide-away visiting this region.

Westgate Suites have 100 rooms along with a luxurious Jacuzzi Suite. There are various types of accommodations to fit your needs, as well as regular rooms, non-smoking, kitchenettes, and complete one or two bedroom suites are available. Many amenities are also offered, cable TV, on-site laundry facilities, a playground for the children and a heated swimming pool. Westgate Suites is conveniently located to several nice restaurants and shops, all within walking distance.

Westgate Suites' primary emphasis is tour and travel trade visiting the Olympic National Park. Transportation from Bremerton Airport is provided upon request. There is transportation from Sea-Tac International Airport provided by Bremerton-Kitsap Airporter which leaves from the airport approximately every hour. Westgate Suites is approximately fifty minutes from Sea-Tac International Airport and five minutes from the Seattle-Bremerton Ferry Terminal. For a comfortable, convenient place to stay on your visit to the Seattle/Olympic Peninsula area, try the Westgate Suites.

Farm

SILVER BAY HERB FARM
9151 Tracyton Boulevard
Bremerton, WA 98310
Tel. (206) 692-1340
Hrs: Tue. - Sat. 11:00 a.m. - 5:00 p.m.
Visa, MasterCard and personal checks are accepted.

The land where the Silver Bay Herb Farm is located has a rich history. Stone artifacts found there indicate that at one time it was a gathering place for Indians. It was settled at the turn of the century by a German family who were dairy farmers. In later years, this area had been the site of an oyster farm and a strawberry farm. Mary Preus, owner and operator, began raising vegetables, herbs and flowers in the late 1970s with the intention of making it a family farm once again. Her interest in herbs grew and by 1981 she put out the sign making it an official herb farm.

Silver Bay is located beside Dyes Inlet, just north of Bremerton. The farm offers a peaceful setting in which to wander through the lovely gardens and a place to picnic on the beach. The gift shop is full of dried floral bouquets, lavender fans, wreaths, bags of dried herbs, herbal honeys, vinegars and numerous books on herbs. When Mary designs bouquets for weddings, a card which discusses each herb's symbolic meaning is enclosed.

Mary has a stall in Pike Place Market, where she sells her wonderful herbal products and has two special annual events at the farm, a Mother's Day sale and a Christmas sale. Area craft people bring their plants and handiworks for the sale days and there is a wonderful selection. For a pleasant country experience, plan a trip to Silver Bay Herb Farm, you'll enjoy the pastoral setting and Mary's selection of items for sale.

Restaurant

BOAT SHED, 101 Shore Drive, Bremerton, Washington. One mile from the ferry, there's a great view from the Boat Shed. Excellent seafood, sandwiches, and salads for lunch and dinner.

Gorst

Located at the head of Sinclair Inlet, Gorst is one of the major crossroads of Kitsap County. Samuel Gorst, the original settler here, could probably not have imagined the traffic that travels the roads nowadays.

Highway 16 from Tacoma to Bremerton jogs through, Highway 3 which takes travelers to Belfair and the south Hood Canal, begins in Gorst. A major county road to the lake-filled western county alongside Hood Canal winds away from Gorst, too.

Golf Course

GOLD MOUNTAIN GOLF COURSE, Old Belfair Highway, Gorst, Washington. A good public course with eighteen holes, pro shop, instruction, driving range, lounge, and restaurant. Visa and MasterCard accepted.

Port Orchard

The south county, with Port Orchard as its anchor, is a popular place for bicycle tours over a gently-rolling countryside.

Another of William Renton's sawmills was established here, in 1854, on an inlet first named by explorer George Vancouver for H. M. Orchard, clerk of the ship Discovery. Sidney Stephens platted the town in 1886 and dubbed it Sidney.

The legislature, at the request of residents, christened it Port Orchard in 1903 and also affirmed the fact that the county seat had moved here. Port Orchard Naval Station post office actually received the mail for the much larger Bremerton yards that sprouted on the inlet's north shores. East of the business district, a residential area on terraced streets mounts the hill. At its top is the courthouse. About 4,900 people live inside city limits.

Attractions

Passenger ferries from the marina, and from tiny Annapolis to the east, ply Sinclair inlet to Bremerton on a regular schedule. The Southworth ferry on the peninsula's east shore provides a connection to West Seattle by way of Vashon Island.

Sidney Art Gallery, and the **Log Cabin Museum** next to it in the 200 block of Sidney Avenue, give a look at the town's culture. The gallery is in the Masonic Lodge Building constructed about 1908. Open Tuesday through Saturday from 11:00 a.m. to 4:00 p.m. and Sunday from 1:00 p.m. to 5:00 p.m. In the gallery is the county register of historic sites, with maps to assist the curious. The cabin museum was put up in 1913, and is open Sundays from 1:00 p.m. to 4:00 p.m., Monday from 10:00 a.m. to 12:00 noon. Call 871-1104 for an appointment to view the museum on other days.

Restil, on the hill above Annapolis, has a campus-like Washington Veteran's Home set among weeping willow trees, madronas and sweeping lawns. About 500 veterans are housed here following a tradition of state care which began after World War I.

Blake Island Marine Park (see King County listing) is just off the coast, accessible by boat and site of old Indian villages and the modern Tillicum village operated by a concessionaire. People touring the sound by boat call at Blake where a campground is maintained by the state park department.

For information, contact the **South Kitsap Chamber of Commerce**, 727 Bay Street, Port Orchard WA 98366. Telephone 876-3505.

Antiques

OLDE CENTRAL ANTIQUE MALL, 801 Bay Street, Port Orchard, Washington. Right downtown, you'll enjoy browsing in the sixty distinctive shops in this mall which caters to lovers of antiques, collectibles, and memorabilia. Visa and MasterCard o.k.

Art Gallery

SIDNEY ART GALLERY, 202 Sidney, Port Orchard, Washington. Northwest artists display oils, photography, watercolors, pottery and more. Visa and MasterCard accepted.

Bed and Breakfast

OGLE'S BED AND BREAKFAST, 1307 Dogwood Hill, Southwest, Port Orchard, Washington. Look out at Sinclair Inlet and Mount Olympus from the quiet hillside on which this comfortable bed and breakfast inn resides.

Golf Course

CLOVER GOLF COURSE AND COUNTRY CLUB, 5180 Country Club Way, Southeast, Port Orchard, Washington. Excellent eighteen-hole public course.

Restaurant

TWETEN'S LIGHTHOUSE
429 Bay Street
Port Orchard, WA 98366
Tel. (206) 876-8464
Hrs: Sun. - Thu.   11:00 a.m. - 10:00 p.m.
         Fri. - Sat.   11:00 a.m. - 11:00 p.m.
Visa, MasterCard, AMEX and Discover cards are accepted.

For boaters arriving at Port Orchard, the fine service of Tweten's Lighthouse begins at the Marina. Restaurant staff often pick up boaters and take them straight to the dining room overlooking Sinclair Inlet and the Bremerton's shipyards.

The restaurant is handsomely decorated, open and airy. The menu features dishes acquired from restaurants across the country, as well as some of their own. Lunch at the Lighthouse can be anything from fresh Northwest seafood to a fancy croissant sandwich. The dinner menu is extensive. Try starting with an oyster shooter or baked stuffed mushrooms. Your entree can be anything from prawns and scallops, or sole Normandy, rack of lamb or veal Marsala. The smoked salmon fettucini is a delight.

When someone suggests the Lighthouse, tell them it's a bright idea. They'll be beaming.

Poulsbo

Say it PAWLZ-boh and you'll be close to the Norwegian pronunciation of the name given this little fishing village on the twisting shoreline of Liberty Bay. The name came from a fjord community in the old country, meaning "Paul's place."

Fishermen began anchoring here in 1882, creating a home port for trawlers which regularly worked the Alaskan waters in season. Pacific Coast Codfish built a plant to process the catch through open-air drying and salting. Several farms are in the area, where the stumps left by early loggers gave the settlers a head-start on clearing for cultivation and pasture. Poulsbo's Norwegian heritage is celebrated with festivals three times a year.

Attractions

Marine Science Center, 17771 Fjord Drive, maintains most of the underwater creatures of Puget Sound in its display tanks. Some critters may be handled as part of the tours. Call 779-5549 for current hours.

For information, contact the **Greater Poulsbo Chamber of Commerce**, Box 1063, Poulsbo WA 98370. Telephone 779-4848.

Events

Mid-May and Paulsbo celebrates its Norwegian heritage with the **Vikingfest**. In mid-June the **Skandia Midsommarfest** and in late November the **Yule Log Festival**.

Accommodations

POULSBO'S EVERGREEN MOTEL, 18680 Highway 305, Poulsbo, Washington. Sixty spacious private rooms near heart of Poulsbo. Color television, queensize beds, some kitchen, non-smoking and view units. Visa, MasterCard,AMEX, and Diner's Club accepted.

Art Gallery

PERIPHERY
18937 Front Street
Poulsbo, WA 98370
Tel. (206) 779-3024
Hrs: Mon. - Sat.   10:00 a.m. - 5:30 p.m.
 Sunday   11:00 a.m. - 4:00 p.m.
Visa, MasterCard, AMEX and Discover cards are accepted.

Steve and Karen James acquired Periphery, which means "outer perimeter," in 1985. They have expanded the store so that they offer both a gallery and custom framing. Steve has a strong background in custom framing and says he can frame anything. Some of his past framing projects include an antique nail, a broken dish, and a small boy's art project consisting of a stick with a ladybug attached. The frame shop offers free estimates.

The gallery is full of original and limited edition art work. Northwest artists are featured. There is also handmade jewelry, bronze and paper sculptures, pen and ink drawings, pottery, and lovely Mesolini glassware.

Whether you are looking for the perfect piece of art work for yourself or someone special or have what you thought was an "impossible" framing job, you'll find Steve and Karen at Periphery will meet your needs.

Gift Shops

CARGO HOLD
P.O. Box 712
Old Front Street Building
Poulsbo, WA 98370
Tel. (206) 697-1424
Hrs: Tue. - Sat. 10:30 a.m. - 5:30 p.m.
     Sunday   12:00 noon - 4:00 p.m.
Visa, MasterCard, AMEX and personal checks are accepted.

Poulsbo, a charming Scandinavian village, is a very popular vacation spot, particularly among boaters. There is a marina where you can dock your boat while you spend the day exploring the town. Nicky Olson, owner of Cargo Hold, recognized the need for a shop catering to those in need of nautical gifts and wares. Her shop is filled with a delightful selection that will please both boat owners and land lubbers.

Nicky has a nice selection of wood and teak accessories, maritime brass and everything from clocks to barometers. She and her husband have owned a power boat for years, so she knows what works for a boat and what doesn't and is able to select unique and useful items on her buying trips for the store. One area of the shop is dedicated to the galley. There is a complete line of lovely and functional non breakable acrylics that would be appropriate for the most elaborate yacht in the harbor. One of the most popular gift items in the store is a Mt. St. Helen's ash oil lamp which is made by a Seattle artist.

The Cargo Hold is a fun place to shop whether or not you are a boat owner. The selection of items available is varied and interesting and the friendly, helpful staff will assist you in finding just the gift you need.

HOLLY HAUS
18937 Front Street
Poulsbo, WA 98370
Tel. (206) 779-5581
Hrs: Mon. - Sat.   10:00 a.m. - 5:30 p.m.
          Sunday   12:00 noon - 5:00 p.m.
Visa and MasterCard are accepted.
and,
HEARTS AND HOMESPUN
18850 A Front Street, NE
Poulsbo, WA 98370
Tel. (206) 697-6699

    Holly Haus began as a small Christmas shop, but its popularity grew rapidly and so did its inventory. Owners Ann Mossman and Kathy Holodnak have more than 400 artists, primarily from Washington and many from Poulsbo, who supply the shop with art work and crafts of all kinds. There is a wonderful selection of pottery, handmade silver jewelry, water colors and limited edition artwork, woven baskets, dried floral arrangements, wreaths, crocheted picture frames, handmade toys and clothes for children and much more.
    On the second Saturday and Sunday of November, there is an open house at Holly Haus which features Christmas items. The store is filled with hundreds of Christmas ornaments and five decorated Christmas trees. Each tree has a different theme, and vary from year to year. The Christmas displays are enchanting and will delight everyone.
    Holly Haus's Country Corner was so popular that Kathy and Ann opened a new shop called Hearts and Homespun in 1987. The shop is located just down the street from Holly Haus and has a wonderful selection of country arts and crafts. There is antique and willow twig furniture, European lace curtains, country pottery, rugs, brooms and woven art. Both shops are extremely popular locally and are very successful with their mixture of artist's works and high quality retail items. The staff is friendly and helpful and the inventory constantly changing. A visit to Holly Haus and Hearts and Homespun is a delightful experience and a must when in Poulsbo.

Restaurant

    FRONT STREET CAFE, 18820 Front Street, Poulsbo, Washington. You'll find homemade soups, baked goodies, espresso, and authentic Cajun cooking here.

SCANDIA GARDENS, 18830 Front Street, Poulsbo, Washington. Serves Scandinavian fare including a full smorgasbord buffet, lunch, and dinner. Visa, MasterCard accepted.

Textiles

MARIE'S WILD AND WOOLY
17791 Fjord Drive NE
Poulsbo, WA 98370
Tel. (206) 779-3222
Hrs: Tue. - Sat. 10:00 a.m. - 5:00 p.m.
Visa and MasterCard are accepted.

When she graduated from high school four years ago, Marie Miller decided to take a chance and open the shop of her dreams. She had been knitting since she was a child and wanted to turn her hobby into her livelihood. She has succeeded admirably. Since opening Wild and Wooly she has moved and expanded three times and the shop is now located in Liberty Bay Marina at the very end of the pier. This is as cheerful, comfortable, and colorful a yarn shop as you could hope to find.

Marie's Wild and Wooly has every color yarn you could imagine, and then some. Marie takes pride in selecting only quality yarns which come from all over the world. Almost all the yarns are natural fibers, wools, silks, cottons, cashmeres and mohairs. If there is something special you want that Marie doesn't carry, she'll order it for you. You'll also find a large selection of knitting catalogs and magazines and all the accessories you'll need to become an accomplished knitter.

If this all sounds wonderful, but you don't know how to knit, don't despair. One of the services Marie offers is private knitting lessons. Of course, she is happy to answer any questions that come up or help you solve any problems that arise in the course of your knitting. She really knows her business, and with her help you'll find knitting easy and fun.

Silverdale

This was once a bustling port town, with produce from farms coming to the wharves set on the head of Dyes Inlet. The trade disappeared and commercial attention focused on Bremerton at the head of the inlet, leaving several buildings as monuments to times past.

Attractions

Kitsap Historical Museum, 3343 Northwest Byron Street, is in an old bank on the waterfront where busy farmers used to ship eggs by the hundreds to Seattle. Open Monday through Friday from 10:00 a.m. to 6:00 p.m. and Saturday, Sunday from 1:00 p.m. to 4:00 p.m. Call 692-1949.

Restaurant

SANDPIPER RESTAURANT, 3113 Northwest Buckland Hill Road, Silverdale, Washington. Specialties are steaks, prime rib and seafood. Visa, MasterCard, and AMEX accepted.

Winslow

Washington State Ferries shuttle between Winslow and Seattle over twenty times a day, making this island of timber and farms a rural extension of the city.

From Winslow on Eagle Harbor where the ferry docks, Highway 305 heads north to the bridge at Agate Pass which connects motorists with the rest of Kitsap County and the Olympic Peninsula. Winslow, with about 2,400 residents, is the only incorporated municipality among the island's twelve communities. The total population is about 12,300. Many residents commute to jobs in Seattle.

Bakery

BAINLERIDGE BAKERS, Winslow Green, Winslow, Washington. Fine European pastries, breads, and baked goods. Closed Sundays.

Delicatessen

THREE SISTERS DELI
100 Winslow Way North
Winslow Green
Winslow, WA 98110
Tel. (206) 842-8280
Hrs: Mon. - Fri. 9:00 a.m. - 7:00 p.m.
      Saturday 9:00 a.m. - 5:30 p.m.
Visa and MasterCard are accepted.

Three Sisters Deli opened in 1984 and has been delighting Bainbridge Island residents and visitors ever since. Mrs. Zawideh and her daughter, owners of the deli, were in the food service in Michigan for thirty-five years. The knowledge and experience gained in those years in Michigan have been put to excellent use in this fine delicatessen.

The menu is varied and new selections are constantly being added. The most popular items include the six-cheese lasagna, oriental chicken salad with toasted almonds and sesame oil dressing and tabouli (green salad composed of bulgar, parsley, fresh mint and lemons). A deliciously different treat is mulligatawny soup which combines curried chicken broth with apples, rice and carrots. The deli's coleslaw is made from a thirty-year-old family recipe, which you'll think it's the best you've ever tasted. Baklava is just one of the many homemade desserts and is "Grandma's" recipe from the old country. There is a limited breakfast selection, but it does include a ham and Swiss croissant and smoked salmon on a bagel.

The Three Sisters Deli is a good stop when you visit Bainbridge Island. You will not be disappointed in the variety and quality of the delicious food served here.

Gift

THE BERRY PATCH
Winslow Mall
Winslow, WA 98110
Tel. (206) 842-3593
Hrs: Mon. - Sat. 10:00 a.m. - 5:00 p.m.

The Berry Patch is primarily a kitchen and bath shop, but owner Jane Pomeroy carries a wide selection of other gift items to appeal to her sophisticated clientele. Jane has items from Mexico, the Orient and the United States. She stocks one of a kind gifts. You'll find such diverse items as a tortilla fryer basket for making homemade tortillas and handcrafted, floral-painted teddy bears.

In addition to operating the gift shop, Jane has other enterprises. With twenty-four hours advance notice, she will prepare a delicious picnic lunch for you. She also runs a catering service called "Berry Best" which is known for its fabulous desserts and specialty items. Jane and her artists friend, Dick Baker, have started a line of t-shirts and sweatshirts called "Sweatshirts by Dick and Jane."

FOX PAW
160 Winslow Way West
Winslow Green
Winslow, WA 98110
Tel. (206) 842-7788
Hrs: Mon. - Sun. 10:00 a.m. - 6:00 p.m.

Linda Allen opened Fox Paw in Lynwood Center in 1978. She was successful from the start and expanded to her present location in Winslow in 1984. The shop has a wonderfully eclectic collection of unique gift items, exquisite white linens, baskets, Orientalia, jewelry, accessories and metaphysical books. Everything reflects Linda's sophistication and good taste. The secret of her success with Fox Paw is that she buys only those items she would be willing to take home.

Linda has devoted one area of the shop to interior design. She works with clients in selecting fabrics, wall coverings, window treatments and furniture. There is an attractive selection of merchandise to enhance the decor of any house.

The book section carries publications that Linda feels will "enhance reality and make our planet a safer and more pleasant place to live." She also carries an extensive collection of stones, crystals, and one of a king jewelry items.

The discriminating selection that Linda chooses for Fox Paw attracts people from off the island and even out-of-state. Be sure to take time to stop in and browse when you are exploring Winslow. For a special treat, ask to see the mink teddy bear, and meet the shop kitty "Olivia."

Kitsap County

Restaurant

THE SALTWATER CAFE
403 Madison South
Winslow, WA 98110
Tel. (206) 842-8339
Hrs: Mon. - Sun. 11:30 a.m. - 9:30 p.m.
Visa and MasterCard are accepted.

The Saltwater Cafe has a loyal following of local residents and travelers who journey here to enjoy not only the flavorful food but also the casual, fun atmosphere. The cafe is located next to the Winslow Wharf Marina and offers it's diners a sweeping view of Eagle Harbor and is the only waterfront restaurant on Bainbridge Island.

One glance at the bill of fare and you know there is something there for even the most discriminating palate. The lunch menu ranges from Cajun file gumbo to bay shrimp salad dijon. Other choices include Alaskan cod fish and chips or a bowl of creamy New England chowder.

Dinner offers a more extensive selection from fresh seafood to several chicken dishes and daily specials. For a real treat, try the Cajun barbeque shrimp and jumbo Gulf Stream prawns. All dinners are served with a fresh green salad and bread. The wine list features wines from Bainbridge Island Vineyards and there is an impressive variety of imported beers.

There is no better way to spend an afternoon than lounging on the deck of the Saltwater Cafe feasting on delicious clams or mussels. Enjoy!

SAN CARLOS RESTAURANT
279 Madison Avenue N
Winslow, WA 98110
Tel. 206) 842-1999
Hrs: Lunch   Tue. - Fri.   11:30 a.m. - 2:00 p.m.
     Dinner   Mon. - Sun.   5:00 p.m. - 9:00 p.m.
Visa, MasterCard, Discover and checks are accepted.

This is Mexican food at its best. San Carlos' food is authentic, yet with an approach almost French in style of preparation. It is always unique and delicious. All foods are prepared from scratch on the premises.

Each week the lunch menu offers a special from fresh tamales to smoked salmon enchiladas. Every evening there's a seafood special such as, poached sea bass in cream salsa sauce or Panamanian scallops in Spanish champagne sauce. Once a month they make fresh tamales. Believe it or not, they have a list of customers they phone to tell what night they're serving them! The menu also contains the usual bill of fare like burritos, tacos and enchiladas. The wine list is limited, but there is a wide selection of imported Mexican beers and the fresh fruit margaritas are excellent.

The restaurant is tastefully decorated in a Mexican folk art style of original oils, photographs and prints by Georgia O'Keefe. In the summer months, you'll enjoy dining on the garden patio surrounded by colorful and fragrant flowers. You'll be hooked on San Carlos after your first visit.

STREAMLINER DINER
397 Winslow Way
Winslow, WA 98110
Tel. (206) 842-8595
Hrs: Mon. - Fri.   7:00 a.m. - 3:00 p.m.
                     5:30 p.m. - 9:00 p.m.
      Saturday   8:00 a.m. - 3:00 p.m.
      Sunday   8:00 a.m. - 2:00 p.m.
Closed major holidays.
Visa and MasterCard are accepted.

When the Streamliner Diner was put up for sale in 1984, the idea of buying it seemed far out of reach to employees Judith, Irene, Alexandra and Elizabeth. After it had been on the market for a while, they began to seriously consider ways to purchase it. Fortunately for the culinary life of Bainbridge Island, they succeeded. January 1, 1987 marked their second anniversary as proprietors of this fine restaurant.

The Streamliner Diner serves breakfast, lunch and dinner. Breakfasts are hearty and creative with twelve different omelettes. All omelets are served with fresh fruit and a homemade muffin. There is a daily egg special, homemade granola and buttermilk waffles served with real maple syrup. All baking is done on the premises and the pastries are delicious. Lunch offers fresh soup with a daily special, such as acorn squash with wild rice and sausage stuffing, spanakopita, stroganoff, pasta carbonara, blue cheese hamburgers, lentil burgers, Mediterranean plates, or shrimp curry over rice. The dinner menu changes nightly. Each has a different style so you will enjoy a diverse selection of such things as salmon-filled pastry, champagne chicken, or greens and ham.

The philosophy shared by all four owners of the Streamliner Diner is to serve only the freshest ingredients combined in great recipes. They offer ample portions which are reasonably priced. This is home-style cooking at its best and you'll have money left over for the ferry ride home.

Yarns

M. L. MALLARD LTD.
169 Winslow Way
Winslow, WA 98110
Tel. (206) 842-7792
Hrs: Mon. -Fri. 10:00 a.m. - 6:00 p.m.
 Saturday 9:30 a.m. - 5:30 p.m.
Visa, MasterCard, AMEX cards are accepted.
Additional location:
1012 Western Avenue
Seattle, WA 98104
Tel. (206) 621-0632

Some of the world's finest yarns, needlework and custom designs give M. L. Mallard the distinction of being a premier yarn shop. Owners Kerry and Stuart Ferguson left the sun of southern California several years ago seeking a place similar to the Lake District of Stuart's native England and they found it in Winslow.

When a yarn shop came up for sale they purchased it with a goal of developing the shop into a stimulating place where people would have access to all the latest trends in knitted fashions. Believing that good design should be affordable, they seek an honest value in their purchasing and take buying trips to Los Angeles, Chicago and New York to locate new and exotic fibers and fashions.

The shop is attractive and the colorful arrangements and displays are warm and inviting. The staff is trained to meet each customer's needs and they offer classes and workshops for the beginner and the pro. Be sure to visit their new branch shop in Seattle.

LEWIS COUNTY

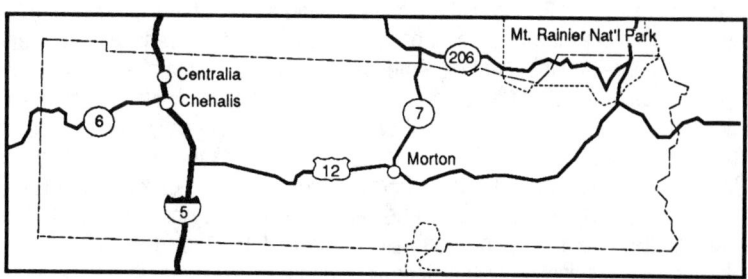

Neatly drawn boundaries, map-makers lines every one except that following the Nisqually River and that along the crest of the Cascade Mountains, enclose a 2,409 square mile county. This was the second county created by Oregon's territorial legislature on lands north of the Columbia River. Lewis honors Meriwether Lewis of the 1804-1806 expedition which brought Americans overland to the Pacific Coast. The Chehalis River which flows north, then west to Grays Harbor, drains the valley which attracted most settlers. The Cowlitz, a major tributary of the Columbia River, reaches its smaller valleys far to the east into the Cascade Mountains.

Technically this is the oldest county to carry the same name in what is now Washington State. When it was created August 21, 1845 it extended from the Columbia River north to fifty-four degrees forty minutes north latitude which is now in British Columbia, and from the crest of the Cascades to the Pacific Ocean. Later legislatures, most notably the 1852 Territorial assembly of Oregon, trimmed this first county down to its present dimensions.

Geographically, Lewis marks the mid-point of a trip between Portland and Seattle. Centralia is eighty-four miles from both metropolises, but that had nothing to do with selection of the name (see Centralia listing, below). Lewis County is also the mid-point between two imposing Cascade Mountain peaks. Mount Saint Helens (see Clark County for details) sent vast clouds of waste from its 1980 eruption northward into Lewis county forests. Mount Rainier National Park (see Pierce County for details) can be reached by following roads which trace the Cowlitz River to its headwaters.

The western county is in an area called the Willapa Hills which was once on the floor of the Pacific Ocean and is now a combination of timber and farm lands. South of Chehalis where massive deposits dropped by glaciers cover the older landforms, there was a natural gas field which played out and is now used to store gas moved to Washington by pipeline. From about Salkum on the

Cowlitz River eastward the geology reflects volcanic activity from several eras. The resulting hills and mountains are fertile timberlands, with heavy amounts of precipitation each year.

One of the state's bitterest disputes came in Lewis County on Armistice Day, 1919. The national press called it the "Centralia Massacre." A local war hero at the head of a parade of uniformed veterans was shot and killed with three members of the American Legion, as the marchers halted near the headquarters of the Industrial Workers of the World. Another Legionnaire died later. Nine Wobblies, as the IWW union people were called, were arrested and their offices sacked. One of the accused was taken from jail that night, killed and his mutilated body hung from a bridge over the Skookumchuck River. Seven Wobblies were convicted and sent to prison. No one was arrested for the killing of the man taken from jail. From that 1919 incident IWW activity declined in Washington, with historians saying public fear played a hand in the organization's demise.

Attractions

The **small church in Claquato**, a town two miles west of Chehalis on Highway 6, is restored through an American Legion project. Just twenty by thirty feet, the structure was built by hand in 1858, boards cut by whipsaw, timbers morticed by hand. It is the area's oldest church that remains standing. Closed except for special occasions. For information contact the Historical Society, 748-0831.

Jackson Prairie, off Highway 12 on Jackson Highway, is one of the first settlements north of the Columbia River. The John R. Jackson House built in 1845 is part of **Lewis and Clark State Park**. Lewis County's first courthouse is here. Jackson Prairie School, 4128 Jackson Highway, is now an antique shop.

Toledo, a small town east of I-5 in the south county is near the site of Cowlitz Landing. The first trail to Puget Sound crossed here and later Hudson Bay Company farms used the landing to ship produce to Fort Vancouver. Floods washed away the wharf. Toledo was the head of navigation in days of shallow-draft steamboats.

East of Longmire on Highway 706 is **Alexander's Inn**, one of the oldest buildings in the Mount Rainier area. A homestead in 1892 grew into the 1912 inn for travelers bound for the mountain, and its guest book includes at least two U.S. presidents. The hostelry was restored in 1984. Telephone 569-2300.

They call it the **Tin Bridge**. The covered bridge is on Muller Road, out of Pe Ell, is a combination of wood and iron truss construction built in 1934 when covered bridges were going out of style. The town's water supply pipe crosses the river on the bridge. From Highway 6, turn south on Third Street, then right on Muller Road.

Onalaska, east on Highway 508 from I-5, is a ghost of itself. The 225-foot high smokestack of Carlisle Lumber Company remains as a monument to the mill which operated from 1913 to 1942.

Packwood, sixty five miles east of I-5 on Highway 12, has a hotel which has operated since 1911. Among its antique guest rooms is one in which President T.R. Roosevelt is said to have slept. Telephone 494-5431. Several other newer inns and vacation cabin rentals are grouped in this community deep in the National Forest.

For further information, contact the **Twin Cities Chamber of Commerce**, 1611 National Avenue, Chehalis WA 98532. Telephone 748-8885.

Centralia

Coal mining sets this town of 11,500 residents apart from other communities in the mid-section of Western Washington. The Centralia Steam Plant, 913 Big Hanaford Road, employs about 250 people who convert the deposits to electrical power. Other manufacturing firms turn out products as varied as leather gloves and liners to contain oil spills.

George Washington, a slave born in Virginia in 1817, and the adopted son of a couple from Missouri, who freed him, emigrated to Oregon. With his adopted parents he took up land claims on the Chehalis River at the mouth of the Skookumchuck river. Washington was logging and farming the property when the railroad came through and bought the right-of-way.

Washington filed a plat for Centerville, later changed to Centralia, on both sides of the tracks. Center, he said, meant center of the valley, and Centralia was a fine name to end confusion with Centerville in Klickitat County.

Washington helped many get started in business and assisted people caught in the depression of the 1890s. The town shut down for a day of mourning when Washington died in 1905.

Attractions

The residential areas of town contain several Victorian and early 1900s homes set back from pleasant, tree lined streets. An old school, complete with woodsheds and outhouse, is located about two miles east of the center of town on Summa Street. Ask for directions to Salzar Valley School, and you will see some of the residential areas, too.

The former Elks Lodge, 201 South Pearl Street, opened in 1986 as **Centralia Square**, a collection of shops that may be the antique supermarket of Washington. The developers had sixty-five dealers when they opened the doors, plus restaurants and other shops. Telephone 736-6406.

The **Centralia Massacre** site is 807 Tower Avenue, which was a hotel in 1919 where some IWW organizers had set up headquarters after being run out of town earlier in the year. The bridge which figured in public display of the body of the IWW man taken from jail is on Mellen Street.

Perhaps the most visited building in town is **Borst Blockhouse** in the park on Belmont Street off Harrison Avenue. Built in 1855 when settlers feared Indian attack, it was mostly used to store the grain harvested by Joseph Borst, a well-heeled farmer.

The **Joseph Borst Home** is a Greek Revival style mansion built in 1857. To see this creation, drive west on Borst Avenue, left on Allen, then left on Bryden for half a mile and turn left again on a gravel road. The house will be on the right.

For further information, contact the **Twin Cities Chamber of Commerce**, 1611 National Avenue, Chehalis WA 98532. Telephone 748-8885.

Accommodations

FERRYMAN'S INN
1003 Eckerson Road
Centralia, WA 98531
Tel. (206) 330-2094

The Ferryman's Inn is the newest motel in the Centralia area and offers special treats to make you feel right at home in any of its fifty-nine units. With your room, you receive a Continental breakfast of coffee, donuts, and freshly squeezed orange juice.

Innkeepers Ken and Gladys Hinkle have twenty years of providing hospitality to weary travelers and are happy to assist you with special needs. There are six kitchen units, thirty-one queen units, and three handicapped units at The Ferryman's Inn. Non-smokers will find choices of rooms also. All rooms have telephones and cable TV and there's a spa/jacuzzi to help you unwind.

Located close to the freeway, The Ferryman's Inn is convenient to north and southbound traffic on Interstate Five.

Antiques

CENTRALIA SQUARE, 201 South Pearl Street, Centralia, Washington. The Northwest's antique trading center, exactly equi-distance between Portland and Seattle, just off I-5. Fifty Northwest dealers carry everything from estate jewelry to massive pieces of highly-carved furniture.

Apparel

BOUTIQUE EUROPA
604 W Cherry
Centralia, WA 98531
Tel. (206) 736-3167
Hrs: Tue. - Fri. 10:00 a.m. - 5:00 p.m.
Or by appointment.

Flossie and Riley Kaufman have traveled the world. Their daughter Kay has lived in Italy for the past ten years with her husband Victor Falda. Because of the Kaufman's buying contacts in Europe they are able to offer fine clothing at very affordable prices.

Their offerings include Italian hand painted art, Italian brass, silk clothing - ties, scarfs, suits, Italian leather and Italian silver. They have silk pillow cases, silk rugs. Individual selections of clothing for both men and women including Sahara Club shirts.

You will also find here many beautiful arts from China and the Philippines - ornate furniture, silk pictures and wall hangings, as well as figurines and vases.

To find this fascinating boutique take the Mellen Street exit from I-5 for approximately one mile and look for the small house on the left at Cherry and Alder.

Lewis County

Restaurant

THE COLLECTOR'S CHOICE II RESTAURANT
202 West Locust
Centralia Square
Centralia, WA 98531
Tel. (206) 736-1183
Hrs: Mon. - Sun. 11:00 a.m. - 9:00 p.m.
Closed Christmas, Thanksgiving, Easter and July 4th.
Visa and MasterCard are accepted.

"Casual elegance" is a good description of the ambiance offered by The Collector's Choice II Restaurant which is located in Centralia Square, a magnificent edifice built as an Elks Lodge in 1920. Owners John and Donna Hager renovated their portion of the building to take advantage of the high ceilings and created a comfortable feeling of openness. This is a place where you'll feel at home whether dressed casually in sportswear, or dressed in your "Sunday best." The restaurant opens into one of the finest antique malls in Western Washington and is a convenient stop for lunch, coffee and pastry or dinner.

Lunch entrees at Collector's Choice II are varied, with everything from homemade lasagna to fish and chips. The Monte Cristo sandwich and spinach salad, with their own sweet and sour dressing, are popular items from the extensive selection of sandwiches and salads. For a light lunch try the homemade soup and the salad bar. For dinner there are appetizers, soups and salads to begin your meal. The selection of steaks is excellent, and there are seafood choices, chicken and pasta from which to choose. Dinner sandwiches are available for the lighter eater or those who want to be sure to have room for one of the scrumptious treats from the dessert menu. The homemade pies are a real favorite.

Whether you are shopping for antiques at the mall, passing through Centralia on vacation, or live in the area, you can't do better than The Collector's Choice II Restaurant for a pleasant dining experience in congenial surroundings.

Chehalis

Travelers called this Saunder's Bottom in the old days, a muddy place on the square mile claimed by Shuyler Saunders in 1852.

Now about 6,100 people live in the southernmost of what local boosters call the "twin cities" of Centralia and Chehalis. The name comes from the Indian people who had a village far down stream at Grays Harbor, but was given to the post office here in 1870.

Northern Pacific Railroad tracks, bound from Kalama to Tacoma, came in 1874 and businesspeople of Claquato moved a couple of miles east to what has become a bustling little town serving loggers and farmers. This became the county seat in 1883.

Attractions

The old Burlington Northern Railroad depot, 599 Northwest Front Street, is now the **Lewis County Historical Museum.** Built in 1912, the brick building was slated for demolition in 1973 when the county stepped in at the urging of citizens. Exhibits show farm, forestry and home life in earlier years. Open Tuesday through Saturday from 9:00 a.m. to 5:00 p.m. Telephone 748-0831.

The **O. B. McFadden log house,** 1639 Chehalis Avenue, was constructed by Saunders in 1859 when he split the south half of his donation land claim and sold to McFadden. McFadden, a lawyer, went on to become the state's chief justice and later a congressional delegate. A private home, this is said to be the oldest residence continuously in use in Washington.

Western testing of new varieties for the **American Rose Society** is carried out very publicly in a garden on Washington Street between the City Hall and the Library. This official garden is observed for plant performance, and is visited by rose fanciers curious about the new hybrids under development.

Highway 6 heads east from here to Raymond and Willapa Bay. Sixteen miles down the road is **Rainbow Falls State Park,** one of those creations of the Civilian Conservation Corps in the 1930s on a 120-acre parcel of old growth Douglas Fir timber. There is a swinging bridge over Chehalis River, miles of trails and the falls themselves. Open all year.

For further information, contact the **Twin Cities Chamber of Commerce,** 1611 National Avenue, Chehalis WA 98532. Telephone 748-8885.

Bed and Breakfast

THE DAHL HOUSE BED AND BREAKFAST
214 Bunker Creek Road
Chehalis, WA 98532
Tel. (206) 748-9489

Located midway between Seattle and Portland, amidst pastoral farm land and evergreen forests, is The Dahl House Bed and Breakfast Inn. The farm is just four and a half miles west of I-5. Your hosts Rebecca and Don have completely restored this three story American four square home, creating an ambiance of cozy elegance, while paying close attention to safety and comfort.

Each of the lovely rooms has a private bath and queen size bed. Don and Rebecca pride themselves in serving you a memorable breakfast. Don't be surprised to find pork chops, quiche or huge country omelets on your breakfast table, along with homemade breads, blueberry muffins or coffee cake. They raise their own honey, eggs and fresh fruit in season. You won't go away hungry and probably won't need lunch. A light supper served in your room is available for a small fee, if you feel like staying in for the evening.

If you are traveling with family or a small group, you might feel even more comfortable in the guest cottage. The cottage sleeps four adults and assorted children comfortably. There is a washer and dryer, stove and refrigerator for your use. It is also equipped with all the kitchen utensils you will need, including coffee pot and toaster.

Rebecca and Don are looking forward to meeting you. At this "Best Choice" bed and breakfast in, you are certain to have a relaxing, memorable stay.

Apparel

THE FEMALE CONNECTION
60 NW Boistford Plaza
Chehalis, WA 98532
Tel. (206) 748-1514
Hrs: Mon. - Sat. 10:00 a.m. - 5:30 p.m.
Visa, MasterCard, AMEX, and Discover cards are accepted.

What's the connection? Well, The Female Connection is a division of Schwartz Men's Wear. More important, owner Selma Schwartz has been in business for fifty-nine years, and in 1986 was awarded the title of Lewis County Businesswoman of the Year.

Selma stocks top quality clothing at discount prices. Most everything in the store is one-third off the price you'll find in major clothing stores.

Selma shops the major markets, San Francisco, Los Angeles and New York. Her store is quite sizeable and her inventory very large, consisting of clothing for women from teens to grandmothers, sizes three to twenty. "We cater to a forward thinking missy without being trendy," says Selma.

Selma's employees can help you coordinate an entire ensemble from scratch or match something you already have. Tailoring can usually be done while you have lunch. Selma will also do personalized buying for you, and can ship anywhere.

Selma also runs interesting happenings throughout the year -- seminars on skin coloring and career dressing, wine and cheese parties, and Men Only nights. If you've been feeling detached lately, this is a great place to get connected.

(See special invitation in the Appendix.)

Books

BOOK N' BRUSH, 518 North Market Boulevard, Chehalis, Washington. In books, everything from children's books to art books and bestsellers. In art, a full line of art supplies, plus classes for would-be artists. Also cards, calendars, and maps.

Country Art

CALICO CRAFTS
448 N Market Boulevard
Chehalis, WA 98532
Tel. (206) 748-6096
Hrs: Mon. - Fri.   10:00 a.m. - 5:30 p.m.
          Saturday   10:00 a.m. - 5:00 p.m.
Visa and MasterCard accepted

Calico Crafts is full of hand crafted items from local, regional, and national artists. A place where talented artists can display their wares and where customers can find a large selection of quality products.

"Only the highest quality crafts are displayed in this store," says owner Denise Nacht, "because that's what my customers have come to expect." About sixty craftspersons are represented. Most, but not all, work on rural themes. Included are tole paintings, soft sculpture, silk and dried flowers, wood carvings, clocks, ceramics, pottery, brass, folk art, primitives and, of course, Mt. St. Helens glass. For the "do it yourselfers," there are a large selection of supplies including tole wood, paint, brushes, ribbon, wreaths, flowers, wood cut-outs and kits.

Many items are available for under ten dollars. Special orders are available, as is shipping, and gift wrapping is free. If you're looking for an inexpensive, hand crafted, original gift, look no further than Calico Crafts.

	CHEHALIS TOUR		
a.m.	The Dahl House	Best farm breakfast	Che/B & B
a.m.	Calico Crafts	Best handmade items	Chel/Gift
a.m.	The Female Connect.	Best women's apparel	Chel/App
a.m.	Glass Rainbows	Best country crafts	Chel/Glass
a.m.	Heartstrings	Best fudge-to-go	Chel/Candy
p.m.	Mary McCrank's	Best lunch	Chel/Rest.
p.m.	Newaukum Val.Golf	Best relaxing afternoon	Chel/Golf
p.m.	Collector's Choice	Best International supper	Centr/Rest.

A relaxing in 'n outdoors day. If golf is not your recreation of choice...try a tour of some of the "attractions" enumerated in the Chehalis introduction. Dinner is a leisurely drive to Centralia to the Collector's Choice II. Bon appetit!

Gift Shop

HEARTSTRINGS
2100 N National
Yard Birds Shopping Center
Chehalis, WA 98532
Tel. (206) 748-3940
Visa and MasterCard are accepted.

Heartstrings is a Hallmark Shop with a twist. The twist is owner Cindy Sharp, who believes that if you treat everyone just like a good friend they will return - and they do.

Cindy stocks a wide variety of cards, candies, and gifts. She makes homemade cream-and-butter fudge right here in the store, along with famous Chehalis mints. Along with balloons, mugs, stuffed animals, toys, puzzles, candles, figurines, stationary and gift wrap, Cindy has ninety-six solid feet of nothing but cards.

Cindy's easy to find, located inside the Yard Birds Shopping Center. Let her strum your heartstrings.

Glass

GLASS RAINBOWS
509 NW Pacific Avenue
Chehalis, WA 98532
Tel. (206) 748-1156
Hrs: Tue. - Thu.   10:00 a.m. - 3:00 p.m.
          Fri. - Sat.   10:00 a.m. - 5:00 p.m.
Visa, MasterCard, and Discover cards are accepted.

If you could follow a rainbow to its end, you'd either find a leprechaun or Darleen Stanton. Darleen perfected her craft, stained glass, for ten years before going into business. Five years ago she decided to take a chance and open her own shop. Almost everything here is a display of Darleen's considerable talent.

A pastoral country theme, including geese, ducks, pigs, and such runs through much of her work. There are also original lamps and wall hangings. She teaches classes in working with stained glass, and offers supplies to that end.

Darleen does custom work, too, of course, including entire windows for homes or businesses.

Don't wait for a rainbow, you can find Darleen in Chehalis, and she's a lot more reliable than most leprechauns!

Golf Course

NEWAUKUM VALLEY GOLF COURSE
3024 Jackson Highway
Chehalis, WA 98532
Tel. (206) 748-0461
Hrs: Summer   Open 6:30 a.m. to dusk
          Winter   Open 8:00 a.m. to dusk

Been cooped up in your car for too long? Get out in Chehalis and play a few holes!

John Date and his family sold their timber company in 1975 and purchased an old dairy farm with the idea of developing a golf course. Construction began and in 1977 the first nine holes were opened. The back nine were opened in 1980, shortly after Mt. St. Helens blew her top. Recently condominiums have been built on the premises for those who can't bear to be out of sight of their beloved game.

The Dates have put in a full irrigation system which creates excellent green turf throughout the summer months, yet drains so well that the course is one of the rare western Washington courses dry enough for enjoyable winter use.

To get to Newaukum Valley Golf Course, take I-5 exit 72 five miles south of Chehalis, go north on Rush Road to Bishop Road, and right on Bishop to Jackson Highway. Turn right on Jackson and go 300 yards to the course entrance.

Restaurant

MARY McCRANK'S
2923 Jackson Highway
Chehalis, WA 98532
Tel. (206) 748-3662
Hrs: Tue. - Sat.   11:30 a.m. - 2:30 p.m.
                            5:30 p.m. - 8:00 p.m.
       Sunday   12:00 noon - 8:00 p.m.

This is a real find. Mary McCrank started this restaurant fifty years ago in a beautiful old home just four and a half miles east of Chehalis on Jackson Highway. Beautiful gardens surround the house, and beautiful aromas surround the food.

The special thing about Mary's is that, as one waitress put it to a patron, "we still cook here." What she means is that everything - that's literal, now - everything is made fresh from scratch. Nothing is frozen. Notice they don't open until 11:30. No breakfast is served. Instead, all morning is spent preparing soups and pies for that day. This is an old fashioned country kitchen, just like when it started. The time is well spent, too, because the food is absolutely delicious!

Mary passed away a few years ago, but her faithful friends and employees have kept her spirit alive. The entire restaurant is non-smoking.

Mary's is one of the very best restaurants of its kind - a real "Best Choice." Don't miss the wonderful food and atmosphere.

Morton

This community of about 1,300 residents at the base of Cutler Mountain has its roots in logging and the railroad which came through the Tilton

River Valley. In the 1930s this was a major reload point where logs cut from surrounding private and government forests were put aboard special rail cars, the trains bound for milling points in the giant establishments on Puget Sound.

A fellow named Uncle Jimmy Fletcher is said to have come here in 1871 but the records indicate it was twenty years later before anyone called the place a town. Morton gained fame in 1980 as one of those communities north of Mount Saint Helens which witnessed the build up and eruption of the volcano. Residents repeat stories of the Sunday morning the sky turned dark, lightening shot through the cloud and volcanic ash fell as temperatures rose.

Attractions

Morton's crossroads location twenty-five miles north of Mount Saint Helens makes it the starting point for several **motor tours** of the Cascades and the upper Cowlitz River Valley. One loop, east on Highway 12 through Packwood, can take in Mount Rainier National Park. Another, south from Randle on Highway 25, will go around Mount Saint Helens.

There's a **steam train excursion** from Elbe to Mineral, two communities located north off Highway 7. Mount Rainier Scenic Railroad takes ninety minutes for its round-trip runs. The Mineral depot includes an exhibit of early logging equipment. Telephone 569-2588 for schedules.

An imposing log building built in 1906 survives as **Mineral Lodge**, on Mineral Hill Road east of Highway 7. This structure has had a varied history including private hunting lodge and sanitarium. The post office building, about eight feet square, is said to be the smallest in the United States. It is just beyond the lodge.

Riffe Lake, formed behind Mossyrock Dam and its powerhouse, is a popular fishing and boating area. The Cowlitz upstream offers trout fishing and several forest camp areas.

Old Settler's Museum, the east county branch of Lewis County Museum is next to the park. Morton Railroad Depot is nearby. Tours of both can be arranged by asking at City Hall.

For information contact the **Morton Chamber of Commerce**, Box 10, Morton WA 98356. Telephone 496-5123.

Lewis County

Accommodations

THE SEASONS MOTEL, Box 567, Morton, Washington. Newly-built, The Seasons Motel offers nineteen beautifully-decorated rooms and friendly service. Reservations recommended in summer and fall.

Resort

RESORT OF THE MOUNTAINS
1130 Morton Road
Morton, WA 98356
Tel. (206) 496-5885
Reservations required.

In a beautiful, pastoral setting with rustic buildings and condos is Resort of the Mountains. Clean air and breathtaking scenery provide a relaxing retreat from life in the city. From health education to recreation, this resort is the perfect place to go for a night or a month. From artesian water to gourmet health food meals everything provided will leave you feeling invigorated.

The Settler's Inn has modern accommodations that are comfortable and colorful or, for a more rustic experience, plan to stay in the Teepee Shelter. Activities from lazing in the library to fishing in Inspiration Pond or joining a volleyball game to hiking or skiing the trails will fill your days. The resort has a natural food store, an antique and gift shop and also offers classes in weight balancing and exercise programs. A licensed massage therapist is on staff to ease your tired muscles after a day of fun.

For relaxation and education on stress reduction, proper exercise and diet programs and a welcome break from fast paced living, reserve some time to take advantage of Resort of the Mountains.

Restaurant

ROADHOUSE INN
HI-WAY ROOM
U.S. Highway 12 and Crumb Lane
Morton, WA 98356
Tel. (206)   496-5029
Hrs: Mon. - Sun.   8:00 a.m. - 11:00 p.m
         Lounge until 2:00 a.m.

    The Roadhouse Inn is owned and operated by Peggy Brown who has been offering delicious food and good service to her customers for the past eleven years at this location. The restaurant is very attractive, decorated in 1950's style and is a favorite of local residents and travellers alike.
    The menu is extensive for all three meals. Breakfasts offer a wonderful selection of great pancakes, French toast and some unusual daily specials. For lunch the soups and salad are great, with the best salad bar in the area, featuring a large array of pasta. For dinner there is an excellent selection of seafood, exquisitely prepared, as well as prime rib and daily specials. After dinner on weekends there is live music in the lounge which has a tremendous sound system. Country and contemporary music are featured.
    The Roadhouse Inn started as a dinner house, but because of its popularity and the demand for quality breakfasts and lunches, Peggy expanded the restaurant to accommodate her customers. Thanks to her, this is a wonderful place for any meal of the day.

MASON COUNTY

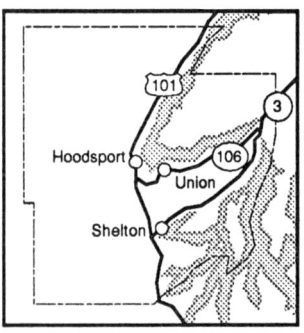

Mountainous and timbered, with the wild areas of Olympic National Park and vast tracts of national forest land, Mason County includes 961 square miles on the Olympic Peninsula plus the Hood Canal and miles of scenic waterfront on the southern-most arms of Puget Sound. About 32,000 people live here, their lives for the most part tied to the timber industry.

Mapped on its shores by the Wilkes expedition of 1841, Mason County came into being in 1854. Its productive forests yielded timber for the nineteenth century lumber boom, and now its futures are tied to second-growth yields from the Olympic National Forest. Many of the experimental long-term federal timber sale contracts are with Simpson Timber Company, which has headquarters in Shelton. The rain-drenched east slopes of the Olympics are among the most productive Douglas Fir forest lands in the west.

Fishing remains an important source of income for Mason County residents. One of Washington's first environmental conflicts was fought here in the 1930s when waste discharged from Shelton's new pulp mill sent sulphites into the oyster flats of Oakland Bay. After a lawsuit closed the plant, the company bought the oyster beds and launched experiments in culturing the shellfish, which abound on most gaveled areas of the canal and sound.

Attractions

Olympic National Park (see Clallam County listing).

Hood Canal's underwater wonders attract scuba divers, fishermen and low-tide beach walkers to **Potlatch State Park**, twelve miles north of Shelton on Highway 101. There's a beach for swimming, buoys for mooring boats if you are doing Puget Sound by water. Thirty five campsites, about half fully-developed for recreational vehicle hookup.

Potlatch, a small community near the park, was commercial headquarters for the Skokomish Indians for years, at a place where they traditionally exchanged gifts. Their large potlatch house was here.

Amid ferns and big trees at Union is the **Dalby Waterwheel**, a mill built in 1922. This tiny town was once a boom city in the 1890s when rumor came that Union Pacific Railroad would terminate here and move its trains to Seattle by barge. The depression caused by the bank panic of 1893 scuttled the project shortly after work began. The town started in 1858 as a trading post. Today it is a summer resort center.

Belfair State Park, at the head of Hood Canal on Highway 300, is a major location for campers touring the Kitsap Peninsula and Hood Canal area. There are over 180 campsites, many developed for recreation vehicles. As in most canal recreation areas, the waters yield oysters and clams at low tide. Check with the park for seasons before harvesting. Belfair's stores supply a large number of summer residents with vacation cabins on the canal or inlets to the south.

Shelton, the county seat and most populous community, has about 7,700 residents. Named for David Shelton who settled here in 1853, the town was not platted until 1884. After the early sawmill days, ITT Rayonier built a pulp plant here based on utilizing wood waste from the area's mills. A laboratory at Rayonier has for decades carried out research on other use of wood byproducts. Check with individual mills for tours.

Railroad logging, a tradition which ended in most of the west with the advent of diesel trucks and mobile yarding equipment, continues out of Shelton. A network of private railroad track goes west over the forks of the Satsop River and north into National Forest land. Vance Creek Railroad bridge near Shelton was an engineering wonder when built in 1929. Its tracks are 347 feet above the timbered canyon bottom.

For further information, contact the **Shelton-Mason County Chamber of Commerce**, Box 666 Shelton WA 98584. Telephone 426-2021. If you are in Shelton, look for the Visitor Information office in a caboose on Railroad Avenue between Second and Third Streets.

Hoodsport

Hoodsport, once a bustling logging town, now is a supply point and stop for vacationers. Among the views, about half a mile west of Lilliwaup, three miles north, is Lilliwaup Falls. The stream pours out of a swampy forest plateau, then drops 150 feet to a pool almost at sea level.

Attractions

Lake Chusman State Park surrounds a reservoir which provides one of the entrance points to Olympic National Park. The state recreation area has extensive camp grounds and resort facilities. The lake is ten miles long, with mountains towering above it on all sides. Located seven miles West of Hoodsport on a county road.

Skokomish Indian Reservation, in the elbow of Hood Canal's Great Bend, is split by Highway 101. The 1855 Treaty of Point No Point (see Kitsap County) established this reservation; now home for about 550 members of the Skokomish and Squaxin tribes.

Wine

HOODSPORT WINERY, Highway 101 (one mile south of Hoodsport), Washington. Quality wines from fine Washington grapes, fruits and berries. The tasting room is open daily 10 a.m. - 6 p.m.

Union

This tiny town was once a boom city in the 1890s when rumor came that Union Pacific Railroad would terminate here and move its trains to Seattle by barge. The depression caused by the bank panic of 1893 scuttled the project shortly after work began. The town started in 1858 as a trading post. Today it is a summer resort center.

Attractions

Amid ferns and big trees at Union is the **Dalby Waterwheel,** a mill built in 1922. This is a much photographed and painted view seen in regional art shows.

Accommodations & Restaurant

ALDERBROOK INN, Highway 101, Union, Washington. This inn, resort, and conference center offers an eighteen-hole golf course, year round swimming pool, jacuzzi and sauna, and boating and water sports. Visa, American Express and MasterCard accepted.

PACIFIC COUNTY

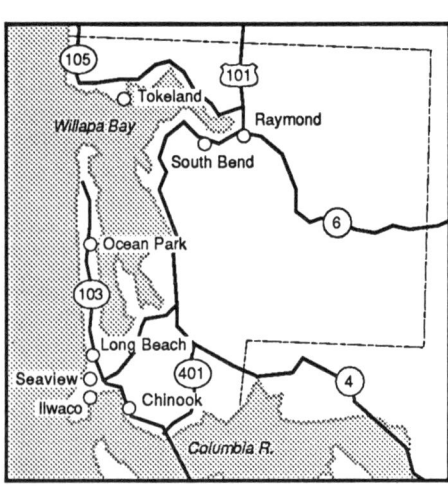

Two hours from Portland, three hours from Seattle, with a sand spit twenty-eight miles long and the Columbia River's opening to the Ocean for attractions, Pacific County can more than double its resident population of 17,700 on any weekend from late spring through the fall. This southwestern corner of Washington has the Willapa Hills in its interior, the lumber-town of Raymond on its north. Willapa Bay and the Long Beach Peninsula are the rest of this 908 square mile county. They get all of the attention.

Washington, a new state in terms of recognition, has much history in Pacific County, where the mouth of the Columbia was discovered in August, 1775 by Bruno de Hezeta. Robert Gray named it after his fur-trader's ship, Columbia Rediviva, in 1792. Willapa Bay was observed in 1788 by John Meares, who thought the bar so shallow that he dared not cross and it was not until an 1852 ground party of the U.S. Coast Survey that the county's major feature came to be part of maps. That was a year after the Oregon Territorial legislature had created Pacific County. Oysterville, which was the county seat until 1893, had settlers as early as 1841.

Geologists say the ocean rose 300-feet after the last ice age, submerging large sections of coastline. The sandy Long Beach Peninsula is said to be formed of material washed down the Columbia River, then drifted north by the ocean current during run off from glacial melt and the 8,000 years of wave-action since. Winds blow from the southwest in winter, the northwest in summer, and heavy rains soak the area each winter. Runoff inside the bay, from Naselle River at the bay's south and Willapa River near its mouth, bring more material which builds small islands and shoals behind the spit. Clams thrive here, Oysters have been a commercial crop since days of the California gold rush, and both streams have steelhead and salmon runs which draw fishermen.

Pacific County

ATTRACTIONS

Willapa National Wildlife Refuge is on Long Island and surrounding tidelands. The 11,500 acre reserve includes a red cedar forest which is about 4,000 years old. Giants of their species, they are about five to seven feet at the butt growing in a forest floor of salal, huckleberry and other brush.

Boats can be obtained at **Nahcotta Moorage Basin** on the peninsula, or at the refuge headquarters on Highway 101 twelve miles north of Ilwaco. When the tide goes out, this shallow bay is a mass of mud for hours, so travelers are advised to plan their trips. There are elk and deer on the island, and five overnight campsites. Telephone 484-3482.

The northward drift of coastal currents lodges all manner of flotsam on **Leadbetter Point** at the far northern end of Long Beach Peninsula. Eight miles of sandy roadway face travelers after the last asphalt paving. This state natural area has no overnight facilities, but is popular with beachcombers. Many make for the point after each heavy storm of the winter.

South Bend, on Highway 101 at the Willapa River, and **Raymond**, just upstream, are the largest communities in this sparsely-populated county. South Bend has about 1,700 residents, and is home of the 1911 **Pacific County Courthouse**. A glass dome draws attention while inside. The entire building, set in a landscaped park, presents a dramatic appearance. Two oyster companies have plants here. Raymond, with 3,000 residents, once had about two-dozen lumber mills but is now down to one. The Weyerhauser mill sports new technology in lumber production and welcomes visitors. Inquire at the plant office.

For further information, contact the **Peninsula Visitor Bureau**, Box 562, Long Beach WA 98631. Telephone 577-3321.

Chinook

A small unincorporated community almost at the mouth of the Columbia, Chinook takes its name from the Indian tribe which lived on the river and created a jargon which whites and Indians of several linguistic backgrounds used for communication in the Oregon country.

There are several homes here which were built before the turn of the century. This is a processing point for crab caught by the fleet which fishes these waters each winter and spring. Pacific County's first court held session here in 1853. A salmon cannery began operating at the Chinook docks in 1870. Several resorts are located on this peninsula downstream from Highway 101's Columbia River crossing.

Attractions

Astoria-Megler Bridge, which takes Highway 101 over the Columbia almost at its mouth, is a recent addition to this sometimes stormy passage where ferryboats for decades carried travelers between the shores. A visitor's information center is on the Washington side of this bridge. Open daily 9:00 a.m. to 7:00 p.m. from June through September. Call 777-8388 for seasonal information.

Sea Resources Hatchery produces salmon. The facility is open daily from 9:00 a.m. to 5:00 p.m.

Saint Mary's Catholic Church, on Highway 101 west of the bridge, was built in the cannery town of McGowan in 1904. This is a landmark for river navigation. During summer months, mass is said in the old church.

Fort Columbia, one of the more recent coast artillery defense sites, is now a state park and a youth hostel. The post was built in 1895. There is a museum on the post, and from Scarborough Hill to the rear is a sweeping view of the Columbia River mouth. Open in the summer daily from 8:00 a.m. to dusk. Open Wednesday through Sunday 9:00 a.m. to 5:00 p.m. the balance of the year. Call 642-3078 or 777-8221 for park information.

Restaurant

SANCTUARY RESTAURANT
Hwy 101 and Hazel Street
Chinook, WA 98614
Tel. (206) 777-8380

Upon emerging from the Sanctuary Restaurant customers exclaim their satisfaction. The Sanctuary Restaurant is set in an old country church which dates from the turn of the century. Owners Geno and Joanne Leech originally bought the church to make a home but found the lure of a restaurant irresistible.

The veteran chef, Fernard Lopez, born in Madrid, has cooked in the finest restaurants in France, Montreal, Washington D.C. and throughout the

West Coast. His veal dishes are highly recommended, as are the daily fresh seafood specials. The oysters casino is a popular appetizer, and the Svenska Köttbuller - Swedish meatballs, are a specialty recipe of Joanne's. Joanne is also responsible for the desserts, try the Krumkake, a Swedish dessert filled with whipped cream and topped with Lingon berries. Geno has also created a fine wine list, with a very good selection of wines from Oregon, California, Washington and imported wines.

The Sanctuary Restaurant has very fine dining, with excellent food and an unpretentious atmosphere. You don't need to dress up to take advantage of this great restaurant, absolutely a "Best Choice."

Concrete-Birdsview

Attraction

The **Puget Power Plant Visitors Center** at 102 East Main Street is open Monday thru Friday, closed on major holidays, phone 853-8341. Offering a view of replicas of the Upper and Lower Baker Dams, a display of fish indigenous to the area and an outdoor fish trap that is used in the center's stocking program.

Accommodations

CASCADE MOUNTAIN INN
3840 Pioneer Lane
Concrete-Birdsview, WA 98237
Tel. (206) 826-4333
Visa and MasterCard are accepted.

Deer graze in the meadows, songbirds beckon from the forests, and bald eagles circle overhead, occasionally stopping to perch in a nearby tree. A short walk brings you to the edge of a river, its water from the nearby mountains rushing over and around polished rocks as it makes its way to the sea. Salmon and steelhead try to avoid your lure as they fight the currents to reach their spawning beds.

After a day of hiking the picturesque mountain trails you spend your evening quietly conversing in luxurious comfort by the stone fireplace or outside by a fire pit under the stars. You sleep in crushing quiet, broken only by the coyote's howl or the occasional hoot of an owl. You awaken, refreshed, to a hearty breakfast prepared and served by sensational hosts and then - do it all over again!

A fantasy? No, rather a realistic description of a day at Cascade Mountain Inn! Owners Gerhard and Ingrid Meyer discovered the Upper Skagit Valley in the early 1970s, visited every year hiking the many trails, and finally purchased property with a view of Sauk Mountain. Their dream has culminated with the construction of their inn, designed to take advantage of all the area has to offer. Six guest rooms await you, each with a private bath. The rooms are named and furnished in the theme of a country in which the Meyers have lived, Philippines, United States, Peru, Scotland, and native Germany. The sixth room, the Studio, has a separate entrance with pictures, tiles, and wall hangings telling the story of Bremen, Gerhard and Ingrid's home town.

Cascade Mountain Inn is a lovely thirty minute drive from I-5 exit 230. Travel east on Hwy 20 about twenty-four miles and turn right on Wild Road, one mile past Baker Lane Road. Pioneer Lane is a few hundred feet further and you'll see the Inn. The city is close enough to visit but too far away to interfere. Gerhard and Ingrid love conversation and interesting people. They've hiked every trail and will help you select those that meet your interests and abilities. Visit them at Cascade Mountain Inn and you too will fall in love with the Upper Skagit Valley.

Restaurant

DEL CONTE'S TIMBERLINE RESTAURANT, 4286 Highway 20, Concrete, WA. Outstanding meals in an atmosphere best described as casual and INTERESTING.

Ilwaco

Much of the commercial and spot fishing fleet which works the Columbia River makes this small town in the shelter of Cape Disappointment its home port. The permanent population was 604 in the most recent federal census, but records at the harbormaster show about 1,000 boats carry Ilwaco on their stern and most berth here for part of the year. Charter boats and commercial trollers are most numerous during salmon season. Settled in 1851 by Henry Feister, the town's name comes from an Indian known as Elwahko Jim.

Ilwaco is protected by tall headlands to the west, just northeast of Cape Disappointment, it had been regarded as one of the most treacherous river bars in the world prior to the jetties that were erected to control the sandbar. The mouth of the Columbia River was known as the "Graveyard of the Pacific" because of those treacherous waters.

Attractions

Ilwaco Heritage Museum, in the Ilwaco Convention Center at 115 Southeast Lake Street, tells stories of logging, fishing and farming. Exhibits recall the days when a railroad carried excursion trains here from Portland and Seattle. The railway baggage depot, under restoration in recent years, is next to the museum. Open Monday through Saturday 9:00 a.m. to 4:00 p.m. and Sundays 12:00 noon to 4:00 p.m. during the summer. For the balance of the year open the same hours Monday through Saturday. Telephone 642-3446.

Descendants of the Fred Colbert family still occupy the house at the corner of Quaker and Lake Streets. Built in the 1880s by an emigrant from Sweden, it has been expanded several times.

Fort Canby State Park, on the ocean side of Cape Disappointment, has an extensive exhibit of the expedition of Lewis and Clark in the **Lewis and Clark Interpretive Center**. There are replicas of the boats they fashioned to travel down the Columbia and back up stream, plus many of the tools and weapons carried by the party. Open June through September daily from 9:00 a.m. until 6:00 p.m. The rest of the year, open Wednesday through Sunday from 9:00 a.m. to 5:00 p.m. There is a 190-site campground, access to the Columbia River north jetty and to miles of hiking trails. Call 642-3078 for reservations and park information.

Willapa National Wildlife Refuge has its headquarters just 8 1/2 miles north of junctions US 101 and US 101 alternate. The refuge contains 10,900 acres of marshland, upland forests, pastures and tidal estuary. Virgin stands of red cedars and tidal marshes that support deer, elk, coyotes, bear, beaver and smaller mammals and birds (more than 180 species of migratory birds) call this home. For further information call 484-3482.

The **U.S. Coast Guard's** only heavy-weather Motor Lifeboat School conducts training for its helmsmen at Fort Canby. Coxswains and crew are sent out into rough surf to become confident while manning self-righting boats on the Columbia River bar. Call 642-2382 for station information and access to the Cape Disappointment light house.

Two venerable lighthouses are located south of Ilwaco. **Cape Disappointment light** was built in 1856, and is the oldest lighthouse in the Pacific Northwest. Meares named the cape after his 1788 probe of the coast when he charted the location but failed to spot the entrance channel to the Columbia River.

Standing 190 feet above sea level is the **North Head light**, put into service in 1898. Among its notable log entries was a 1932 accident when a duck smashed into the window and with a shower of glass-shards broke the lens which magnifies the lamp's light seen far out at sea.

Accommodations

HEIDI'S INN
Highway 101, Downtown
Box 776
Ilwaco, WA 98624
Tel. (206) 642-2387
Visa and MasterCard are accepted.

European charm complete with gingerbread trim and flower boxes describes Swiss born Heidi Valentine's respite for weary travelers. In accordance with her European philosophy "you must try to do better than the next guy!", this restored lodging has had an immaculate overhaul, with Heidi's own decorative artwork displayed in each of the rooms.

Consisting of twenty-seven units, eight have two double beds and eight larger rooms contain a queen bed with room for a single. The two largest units are equipped with a queen bed and two singles. All of the rooms have refrigerators and coffee is available in each. There is also a large banquet room available for families or groups to gather.

Stop in and enjoy Heidi's European hospitality. She is sure to make your stay pleasant and happy!

Delicatessen

SEA-FUN GALLERY, Ilwako Boardwalk, Ilwako, Washington. A New York-style deli also featuring fish and chips and claiming to have the best frozen yogurt on the peninsula.

Having a blah day? Here's a tour that'll lighten up even the most monotonous stretch of road.

THE LIGHTHOUSES OF ILWACO			
	Heidi's Inn	Best lodging	Ilwa/Acc.
a.m.	Heritage Museum	Best museum	Ilwa/Museum
a.m.	Fort Canby Park	Best hiking	Ilwa/Park
a.m.	Willapa Refuge	Best wildlife	Ilwa/Park
Stomach grumbling? Go ahead and eat, but hurry back.			
p.m.	Disappointment Cape	Best historical site	Ilwa/Attraction
p.m.	North Head Light	Best lighthouse	Ilwa/Attraction

Florist

HERMIE'S ORIGINALS and **ARTISTIC BOUQUETS AND MORE**, Both at the Intersection of Highway 101 and 103, Ilwaco, Washington. Hermie's carries silk flowers, supplies for needlepoint, basket and rug weaving, tole painting and macrame´ and more. Artistic Bouquets is a full-service florist with an extensive array of green plants, silk flowers and gifts. MasterCard and Visa accepted.

Restaurant

DOUPES GAZEBO ROOM, First and Spruce, Ilwako, Washington. Sandwiches, famous clam chowder, ice cream, and gifts. Baskets a speciality.

Long Beach

This is the commercial center for the summer homes and resorts scattered along the peninsula. Long Beach is a popular oyster farming and vacation center; about 1,200 people make their home here year around. The wide beaches, which reach for miles, are popular for horseback riding and for driving on sand left firm by water from the receding tides. Razor clams are taken in large numbers from many places along these beaches but the surf is generally unsafe for swimming because of rapid flows and tidal fluctuations.

Attractions

Washington State's **cranberry research station** is about one mile north of Long Beach. Greenhouses are used to speed propagation. Tours are offered and a slide show fills in the plant's life-cycle for a full year. Open Monday through Friday from 9:30 a.m. to 4:00 p.m. Call 642-2031 for the research station. Harvest time on the peninsula and on the main land (see Grayland under Grays Harbor listing) is in October. There are over 460 acres in production on Long Beach Peninsula.

Cranguyma Farms at Ocean Park covers 130 acres of cranberry bogs. This is said to be the largest Cranberry farm west of the Mississippi River.

The old resort of Ocean Park, created by families from the Methodist Church in 1889, has a couple of curious buildings. **The Wreckage** is a cabin built from material salvaged off the beach. **Taylor Hotel**, built in 1887, has some of the older flavor of the town. There is an art museum here. Telephone 665-5477 for information on the Ocean Park area.

Nahcotta, on the bay side of the peninsula, almost due east of Ocean Park, has a state shellfish laboratory which concentrates on oyster culture. Open Monday through Friday from 9:00 a.m. to 12:00 noon and 1:00 p.m. to 4:00 p.m. **Northwest Oyster Farms**, one of many commercial operations in Willapa Bay, has its plant here.

For more information contact **Long Beach Merchants Association**, Box 896, Long Beach WA 98631. Telephone 642-2400.

Accommodations

THE BREAKERS
P.O. Box 428
Long Beach, WA 98631
Tel. (206) 642-4414

Located on Highway 103 and 95th, The Breakers is a seventy-two one and two bedroom unit accommodation which faces the ocean. Ideal for retreats, small conferences or family reunions, the spacious rooms, luxurious surroundings, and conference room with a seventy-five person capacity are all available at group rates.

The outdoor barbeque area has space for horseshoe games, basketball and volleyball. The ten acre, ocean front property is host to many different kinds of animals, including beautiful Chinese pheasants. Indoors, there is a new pool, a spa and a sauna.

All units are equipped with telephones, cable television, a patio, full kitchen and a woodburning fireplace. Second and third story rooms offer ocean view and convenient ground level rooms are also available. The Breakers....a resort motel that feels like the luxury of a very nice home.

CHAUTAUQUA LODGE
P.O. Box 757
West of Pacific Highway on 14th St.
Long Beach, WA 98631
Tel. (206) 642-4401

The Chautauqua Lodge offers spacious, attractively decorated rooms in a resort-like setting on the Beach. Enjoy the sunset over the beautiful Pacific from your charming ocean view room. Beachcomb along miles of sandy beach, try surf fishing, clamming or salmon fishing nearby.

Accommodations range from ocean view suites, complete with fireplace to more modest non view units. There are 60 units with kitchenettes and 120 of the 180 units available have ocean views. The units are privately owned and General Manager Lou Hermens maintains them in excellent condition. There is also an indoor pool, two hot tubs and a sauna, as well as a recreation room. The restaurant offers a good selection of steak and seafood, as well as sandwiches and salads and is open for breakfast, lunch and dinner.

This is a wonderfully relaxing place to enjoy a vacation or just a weekend. In addition to the recreational opportunities offered by the beach and ocean, there is golf available nearby. The reasonable rates make this a "Best Choice" for your stay at the beach.

EDGEWATER INN MOTEL
409 SW 10th Street
P.O. Box 793
Long Beach, WA 98631
Tel. (206) 242-2311

You'll find it easy to choose the Edgewater Inn Motel when you stay in Long Beach, as it is the only motel right on the beach!

The Edgewater gives you expansive views of crashing waves, breathtaking sunsets, and the unforgettable Washington coast from any room you choose. All rooms at the inn have cable television, queen sized beds, and are spacious and inviting. Twelve of the thirty-six rooms offer two beds, and some handicapped units are available.

Kick off your shoes, open your drapes, settle back with a cup of coffee, and watch the waves crash. Congratulate yourself that you have found one of the quality bargain lodgings of your trip.

Bakery

COTTAGE BAKERY AND DELI, Highway 103 and Second Street South, Long Beach, Washington. A full-service bakery and delicatessen.

Camera Supplies and Services

THE PICTURE ATTIC, 711 Pacific Highway North, Long Beach, Washington. One-hour developing, picture framing, photo note cards and framed photographs of local scenery.

Restaurant

MILTON YORK RESTAURANT
1st and Pacific
P.O. Box 416
Long Beach, WA 98631
Tel. (206) 642-2352

Hrs:	Winter	Sun. - Thu.	7:30 a.m. - 8:00 p.m.
		Fri. - Sat	7:30 a.m. - 9:00 p.m.
	Summer	Mon. - Sun.	7:00 a.m. -10:00 p.m.

From a tent with a simple sign pounded into the ground that said "CANDY', Milton York has evolved into an historic retail establishment and restaurant. Specialists in mouth watering confections such as crunchy peanut brittle, truffles and velvets, caramels made with pure whipping cream, succulent mints and the incomparable Milton York special: three layers of light and dark chocolate fused together, the center layer filled with fresh, chopped almonds, Milton York has been producing superlative candy since 1882.

Customers are made to feel most welcome. They can deliberate over sixteen flavors of ice-cream, or be seated for a full breakfast, lunch or dinner. Highly recommended is the Fritata, a baked vegetable omelette covered with cheese and made from scratch. Soups and chowders, unusual sandwiches, steaks and seafood are offered along with daily specials.

Milton York, where dulcification is their business. "We cater to your sweet tooth!"

Ocean Park

This old resort was created by families of Methodist clergymen. The first cabins appeared in 1889. There was already a resort hotel operating when the clergy took up their home sites and began summer trips to the peninsula with its sandy beaches.

Attractions

Cranguyma Farms at Ocean Park covers 130 acres of cranberry bogs. This is said to be the largest Cranberry farm west of the Mississippi River.

The Wreckage is a cabin built from material salvaged off the beach. **Taylor Hotel**, built in 1887, has the flavor of the older town. There is an art museum here.

Nahcotta, on the bay side of the peninsula, almost due east of Ocean Park, has a **state shellfish laboratory** which concentrates on oyster culture. Open Monday through Friday from 9:00 a.m. to 12:00 noon and 1:00 p.m. to 4:00 p.m.

Northwest Oyster Farms, one of many commercial operations in Willapa Bay, has its plant here.

For more information contact **Ocean Park Chamber of Commerce** at Ole's Nook, telephone 665-5477.

Restaurants

B. J. SQUIDLEY'S, Highway 103 and 259th Street, Ocean Park, Washington. Open 6 a.m. to 9 p.m. daily except Thanksgiving and Christmas for breakfast, lunch, dinner, this restaurant features a burger the owner call "B.J.'S Treasure--a meal and then some!"
BAY AVENUE FISH HOUSE AND OYSTER BAR, Bay Avenue and Pacific Highway, Ocean Park, Washington. Delicious fish and shellfish specialities!

Oysterville

This little Victorian resort community almost closed down in the 1970s when it shrunk to about ninety residents. There has been some resurgence since then. Oysterville was placed on the national register of historic places in 1976. Historic structures line Fourth Street on a town plat in which Front Street has already disappeared at high tide.

Indians guided Issac Clark to the native oyster beds. With his partner Robert Espy, Clark founded the town in 1854. The narrow gauge railroad being constructed up the peninsula was to reach the town. It did not. In 1869 the transcontinental railroad reached San Francisco, delivering east coast oysters to the specialty market in which Oysterville's native shellfish competed. West coast oysters lost in sales, and declined in number. Storms in 1888 damaged the wharves and apparently triggered the final decline although an oyster cannery was constructed here as recently as 1940. Morgan Oyster Co. built its plant, the first, in 1865.

The native oysters were overfished. Seed oysters were brought from Japan to replace them, and for years did not reproduce naturally in numbers to keep the industry going. Many of the homes existing today were constructed in the 1870s. Local lore is not complete without telling how court records were taken from here in the dead of night after what historians now say was a fixed election. What ever the facts, South Bend became county seat in 1893.

Attractions

The **Baptist Church** was a gift to the community from Espy, the town founder, in 1892. Regular services ended in 1940. A foundation working to restore Oysterville buildings owns the property, where restoration continues. In the vestibule of the church, visitors will find maps and historic description of the remaining buildings of Oysterville for use in walking or driving tours of town.

The oldest building left is what folks call the **Little Red Cottage**. It was built in 1863. This is where court records were first kept when Oysterville became the county seat. It is now the summer home of Willard Espy an author and member of the community's founding family.

Oysterville became a post office in 1858. Though the town has few residents the post mark is still in use at a building constructed many years later. This is supposed to be the oldest post mark remaining in continuous use in the state.

For more information contact **Ocean Park Chamber of Commerce** at Ole's Nook, telephone 665-5477.

Seaview

Just north of the bustle of Ilwaco's port is an unincorporated town which dates from the era when people came to the beach for the summer, not the weekend. Seaview, settled by vacationers who sailed down the Columbia River by steamboat, still has some homes built in its heyday of the 1880s.

Attractions

Shelburne Hotel is furnished in the style of the original town. Built in 1896 as a combination home and inn, this hostelry has operated continuously. It expanded in grand style in 1941 when the owners bought a boarding house and moved it across the street, joining the structures together. There are fifteen guest rooms in the present layout.

The **Peter Schulderman House**, on C Street, was built by a Portland family in 1888 as a summer residence. A third generation of the family now lives here full time. The Victorian structure can be seen from the street but is not open to visitors.

Highway 103 presents a choice here, left to the mouth of the Columbia, right to Long Beach Peninsula. There is a **Visitor Information Center** at the junction of Highway 103 with 101 that has current information on the area.

For more information contact **Long Beach Merchants Association**, Box 896, Long Beach WA 98631. Telephone 642-2400.

Accommodations

THE SHELBURNE INN HOTEL
THE SHOALWATER RESTAURANT
Pacific Hwy 103 and N. 45th Street
Seaview, WA 98644
(206)   642-2442

The Shelburne Inn is one of the unique Northwest country inns. Each room is decorated in beautiful European antiques of all kinds. Some of the furnishings in the rooms are for sale, the innkeepers, David Campiche and his wife Laurie Anderson are antique dealers as well. The Inn has seventeen rooms which rent for very reasonable rates.

The warm and homey atmosphere is apparent the minute you enter the lobby which looks like a living room, with a big fireplace, plush davenports and magazines. A church altar is the registration desk. A gift shops sells art work from the East Indies, Tibet and Nepal along with Oriental carpets, hand woven baskets and other collectables. The Inn's restaurant continues the antique decor with silk-fringed floor lamps and ceiling lamps with red glass shades and prisms. Chefs Eric Jenkins and Cheri Walker and owners Tony and Ann Kischner offer delicious Northwest cuisine magnificently prepared.

The Shelburne Inn is on the National Historic Registry and is a lovely retreat for the city dweller who wants to get away and relax. The gracious atmosphere and hospitality will make your stay there memorable.

SOU'WESTER LODGE
Beach Access Road 38th Place
P. O. Box 102
Seaview, WA 98644
Tel. (206) 642-2542
Visa and MasterCard are accepted.

Facing silently across the dunes towards the ocean, the historic Sou'wester Lodge has been a refuge for the urban dweller since 1892 when US Senator Henry Winslow Corbett built it as his coastal estate "Westborough House." Situated on three tranquil acres, it still offers the casual restfulness of yesteryear.

Travelers seeking its serenity will find the Sou'wester offers a kaleidoscope of lodging options. The ground floor of the Victorian lodge hosts the bed and (MYOD)* breakfast. There, in effect, each guest becomes a one-third owner of the ground floor of the lodge. Each guest has a private room and shares the bathroom, the big open-beam ceilinged living room, and an airy country kitchen where they are free to prepare their own food.

Persons seeking more solitude may prefer the fully equipped beach cottages, 1940s vintage. With two rooms, plus kitchen, bathroom and garage they sleep one to five people. All linens and kitchen equipment is included. The owners refer to the furnishings as "Early Salvation Army" decor.

Fondly nostalgic of decades of youth hosteling in different countries, the owners of the Sou'wester are developing is TCH (Trailer Classics Hodgepodge) component. These will appeal to students and outdoor types traveling on a limited budget.

In addition, a separate campground offers quiet campers grassy sites for RVs and tents. Electricity, sewer, water, hot showers, toilets, a fish and clam cleaning shed, laundromat and a barbeque patio are among the amenities offered.

For those planning a stay of at least a month, the Sou'wester offers its "Stay Awhile" plan. These are fully equipped apartments on the second and third floors of the historic lodge, with uninterrupted views across the quiet dunes to the sea.

Accommodations are casual and unpretentious. Books and magazines tumble out in profusion everywhere. Small wonder that numbers of creative folk have been attracted to what travel writers have described as a "notorious intellectual haunt." Out of such clientele have grown two unique Sou'wester activities. The first is the "Fireside Evening Series" of casual chamber music and chamber theater performances. The second is the "Sou'wester Teacup T'ink Tank (the not quite a thing tank) Series." These center on differing topics affording opportunity for lectures, discussions, dialogues and diatribes.

The Sou'wester is not everybody's cup of tea, but for those seeking the unique blend of casual hospitality if offers, it is the perfect brew, a fact attested to by the remarkably high number of guests who are returnees or coming on the basis of a recommendation.

*Make Your Own Damn

Tokeland

This one-time resort and the Shoalwater Indian Reservation just west of it are in the lee of Cape Shoalwater which guards the north entrance to Willapa Bay. An Indian chief named Toke lived on the point during the 1850s. The resort developed in the 1880s took the name. Several recreation facilities and boat launching are located here.

Attractions

Tokeland Hotel was constructed over a thirty year period beginning in 1880. The **William Kindred House** became an inn before the turn of the century and still serves guests today.

The 335-acre **Shoalwater Indian Reservation** was established in 1866. There used to be a museum here with tribal artifacts on display. Modern tribal managers have turned the building into a bingo parlor, operated under the museum facade. A smallpox epidemic in 1853 killed most of the Chinook people on Willapa Bay. Descendents of the few survivors live on this small reservation.

Restaurant

DUTCH'S TOKE POINT RESTAURANT
3284 Front Street
Tokeland, WA 98590
Tel. (206) 267-7741
Hrs: Mon. - Fri.   10:00 a.m. - 8:00 p.m.
            Sat. - Sun.   8:00 a.m. - 8:00 p.m.
Closed Wednesday.

Large windows overlook Willapa Bay at this charming restaurant - Dutch's Toke Point Restaurant. Owners Dick, Darlene and Diane Kadyk serve the best home cooked food you've every tasted with special care assuring that only the freshest ingredients are used.

Only after you have placed your order is the food prepared. Fresh seafood dominates the menu with choices such as the Dutch's Captain's Plate featuring a variety of oysters, scallops, cod and jumbo prawns prepared as you request. Dick is known for his oyster dish creations, one example is the Hangtown Fry - a mixture of oysters, vegetables and eggs scrambled to perfection. Seafood pasta salad and burgers round out the menu. Milkshakes made from hard ice cream complement any selection. Try some of Darlene's fresh baked pies.

This family restaurant is casual and does not allow smoking. Stop by this "Best Choice" - Dutch's Toke Point Restaurant to enjoy the fine view and scrumptious food.

THE STUDIO OUTPOST, On top of the Marina by the Old Tokeland Hotel, Tokeland, Washington. Gourmet soups, a limited ala carte menu, and great beers and wines are featured. This is also an art gallery displaying sculptures, photographs, and mixed media pieces. Most of the art has feminist and neo-avant garde overtones.

Seafood Market

NELSON CRAB INC.
3088 Kindred Avenue
Tokeland, WA 98590
Tel. (206) 267-2911
Hrs: Mon. - Sun. 9:00 a.m. - 5:00 p.m.

At the end of the Marina and docks in Tokeland is Nelson Crab Inc. which produces and sells wonderful delights called Sea Treats. Sea Treats are the "extra fancy" pack from the choicest of all catches processed the West's largest exclusive packers of rare sea foods. They are caught by the company's own fleet and smoked or fancy packed within a few hours using world-famous Tokeland recipes. This is a family operation dedicated to producing and selling the best quality seafood possible. They have an extensive selection of canned seafood items, more than any other business in the area.

Sea Treats are available by mail or may be purchased at Nelson Crab. The variety of products changes seasonally, for example the crab season is December 15 to September 15. They offer fresh and canned Dungeness crab during this period. You will find fresh salmon, shad roe, shrimp, and other local seafood delights. The selection of canned seafood is extensive and the company specializes in gift packs made up of a variety of canned delicacies. Gift Pack No. 1, for example, contains Dungeness Crab, smoked oysters, albacore tuna, smoked sturgeon, smoked salmon, blueback salmon, smoked shad, Pacific shrimp, and minced clams.

Visit the charming porch at Nelson Crab Inc. and enjoy a fresh crab or shrimp cocktail as you browse through the large selection of canned seafood. The gift packs they offer are a wonderfully different and delicious idea for any occasion. Gift packs are available by mail, write for a brochure or pick one up when you visit this unique seafood shop.

PIERCE COUNTY

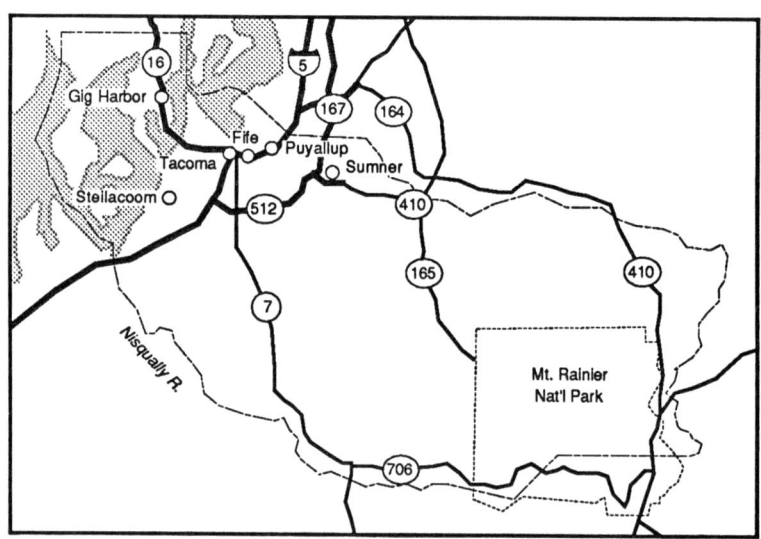

From sea level on Puget Sound, Pierce County's topography wrinkles upward to the 14,410-foot summit of Mount Rainier. Between the fast-moving tidal currents of the Sound and the rushing streams of the Cascade Mountains live about 490,000 people. Farming, lumbering, and manufacturing around Tacoma drive a local economy supplemented by one of the largest U.S. Military garrisons on the West Coast. Fort Lewis, home of a division and thousands of support troops, is next to McCord Air Force base where giant cargo planes stand ready to deploy army units to points around the world.

Washington's first incorporated city, Steilacoom, is on the sound a few miles south of modern Tacoma. Hudson Bay Company chartered the Puget Sound Agriculture Company to farm the plains above the sound. In 1849 there was a clash with international echoes when Thomas Chambers filed a land claim on lands the British company grazed. Chambers asserted rights under American law in defiance of a treaty made three years earlier between Britain and the United States. Chambers brought in other colonists and prevailed in the courts after years of unrest. The government paid damages to the trading company. Indians had dozens of villages along the food-rich sound and the rivers with their salmon runs. The county's history includes tales of several skirmishes with the natives before and after treaties established a system of reservations in the mid-1850s. Isaac Stevens, the territorial governor, made his first treaty at Medicine Creek near the delta of Nisqually River which is the boundary of Pierce and Thurston counties.

Timber, demanded by the booming California gold-rush economy, started Pierce County's first industrial boom. Tacoma emerged as one of the economical locations where large mills could process logs cut elsewhere. Timber was towed in rafts to efficient plants which replaced the early wharf-and-sawmill days on the Sound. Weyerhauser Timber Co., which got its start through purchase of over 900,000 acres of Northern Pacific Railroad grant lands, picked Tacoma for its corporate and research headquarters. The facilities shifted in the 1970s to Federal Way in neighboring King County.

Ruston, a tiny town totally surrounded by Tacoma, tells a story of other industrial development through its ASARCO copper smelter. Now idled in an environmental dispute over air pollution, the plant once thrived on low-cost electricity generated by hydroelectric projects and ore mined elsewhere that could be moved cheaply by ship to the Port of Tacoma. Other industrial plants including one aluminum reduction mill, take advantage of the area's location, bulk transportation and nearby hydro and coal energy sources.

Agriculture continues to be an important part of the county's economy in areas where good soil escaped being covered by the rocks and cobble dropped off from the last ice age's glaciers. The Puyallup valley turns out produce as varied as cut flowers and lettuce, while more marginal soils support a livestock and small wood lot economy. The climate features long growing seasons, with rainfall concentrated in winter months and occasional precipitation in early summer which reduces the demand for irrigation on some crops and pastures. Occasional winter snows in the low lands are usually water-laden and melt quickly. Massive snow packs are common in the Cascades. Flooding can cause dramatic damages at times.

Pierce County has developed its own form of government after years of sometimes stormy local politics that come with rapid urban growth, often in areas without any city services. The county charter approved in a 1980 election does away with Washington's traditional three-person county commission, and has an elected county executive who carries out legislation developed in a council chosen by district voters. Booth Gardner, a Weyerhauser executive who won the top job in Pierce County, became Washington's governor in 1985.

Mount Rainier National Park

This 337-square mile park surrounds an imposing volcano peak which dominates Western Washington's skyline. Forested valleys with hiking trails, ice caves in glaciers creeping down the mountain's flank, downhill and cross country ski areas all lay below the crest which challenges thousands of mountain climbers each year. The park is open year around, but heavy snowfall closes some areas and avalanche danger restricts some climbing routes in the winter and spring.

There are four highway entrances to the park. Beginning at the northwest corner, the Carbon River canyon leads Highway 165 to a fork going to Ipsut Creek camp or Mowich Lake. Both roads are closed in winter. From the northeast, Highway 410 follows the White River in to the popular Sunrise area high on the mountain's east flanks. The road continues south, inside park boundaries, to meet Highway 706 at Stevens Canyon where motorists can either exit the park to Packwood, or drive west to Paradise and the Nisqually entrance which is at the park's southwest corner. A park highway, closed in winter, leads from Nisqually entrance north to Klapatche Pass where there are spectacular views of the mountain's west face and Puyallup Glacier is a short, but steep, hike away.

Visitors who want to climb the mountain can get instruction and a guide through the mountaineering service which makes the trip a two-day experience. Climbers camp at 10,000-foot-high Camp Muir, then reach the summit and return the second day. The National Park Service requires registration of all independent climbing parties going above the 10,000 foot elevation. There is downhill skiing at Paradise Lodge during the winter, and several cross country ski trails are marked elsewhere on the mountain. Crystal Mountain ski area, one of the best in the state, is east of Highway 410 just outside the east park boundary.

The first exploration of the mountain was an 1833 trip by a Hudson Bay factor, William Tolmie, who set out to collect botanical samples. Work since then has identified close to 700 varieties of flowering plants within park boundaries. Hazard Stevens and P.B. Van Trump are said to be the first climbing party to reach the summit, on August 17, 1870. Congress created the national park in 1899.

Expect changeable weather on Mount Rainier, regardless of the time of year. Paradise Lodge has some equipment rentals connected with its guide service. Hikers heading for the glaciers need boots, sun glasses, and should carry a jacket or parka even in summer. Rock avalanches and mudflows can be a danger much greater than the possibility of eruption. Rangers at information centers will discuss best hiking and viewing places to avoid hazards. While several reports of "eruptions" have come over the years, the best information shows that volcanic ash on the eastern side of the mountain was deposited between 1824 and 1850, probably the last "real" eruption. Wisps of clouds swirling around the peak and dust from rockfalls often appear to visitors to be steam or ash. Those who make the peak know this remains a dormant volcano, seeing steam caves free of snow as testimony of the geothermal energy beneath the rock.

Both Paradise and Sunrise have **summer hikes** which are easy. They cross meadows where spring-like flowers bloom into August. Paradise's **Alta Vista** and **Edith Creek Basin** walks offer the bright orange berries of mountain ash in September to complement the flower display from June through August. From Sunrise, the flower walks are either the **Sourdough** or the **Burroghs** mountain trails.

Back country hiking is coordinated by the Park Service. Information on permits and camping points is available by contacting the superintendent in advance or inquiring at any park entrance or visitor center. **Wonderland Trail**, as it was christened years ago, circles the peak from Longmire and is a 100-mile, seven day trip for experienced hikers who don't take side trips.

Sunrise Point on the east side of the mountain, provides one of the most spectacular views anywhere in the park. Cascade volcanos, from Mount Adams in the south to Mount Baker on the north, can been seen on clear days. Two small mountain lakes, **Sunrise** and **Clover**, are about a half-mile away. **Emmons Glacier**, named for geologist Samuel Emmons who made the second summit climb in 1870, can be seen on the mountain itself. This is the largest ice field remaining in the United States.

Mount Rainier Guest Services operates the lodging concessions in the park including the **National Park Inn**, open year around and the old Paradise Inn which is open from late May through mid-October. For reservation information write the company at 55106 Kernahan Road East, Ashford WA 98304, or call 569-2275.

On the way to the park, at Elbe, is **Mount Rainier Scenic Railroad**, which runs excursion trains over a fourteen mile track to Mineral Lake. There's an exhibit of old logging equipment at the turn-around point. The season runs from the end of May through the second week of September with trains departing each Saturday and Sunday at 11:00 a.m., 1:15 p.m., and 3:30 p.m. Telephone 569-2588.

For further information, contact Superintendent, **Mount Rainier National Park**, Longmire WA 98397; **Rainier National Park Guide Service**, Paradise WA 98398; and for facilities outside the park entrances the **Mount Rainier Business Association**, Box 63, Elbe WA 98330. Telephone 569-2285.

Pierce County

ATTRACTIONS

Riding the ferry is one of Pierce County's adventures. Daily service from Steilacoom dock by a county-owned shuttle boat connects with Anderson Island. From Point Defiance docks, Washington State Ferries maintain service with Vashon Island (see Vashon, listed with King County). The Anderson Island boats operate from 6:00 a.m. to 6:00 p.m., the Vashon schedule is 6:20 a.m. through 10:35 p.m. Be sure to check return ferry times! There are no overnight accommodations on Anderson. Vashon's inns are often full and those who miss the boat might be without a bed.

Anderson Island Historical Society runs the **John Johnson Farm** as a demonstration of agriculture in the early 1900s. The **pilot house of the Tahoma**, the Anderson ferry until 1954, is on exhibit next to the farm. From Memorial Day through Labor Day, there are tours of Johnson's farm house each weekend between 12:00 noon and 4:00 p.m. The island also has its own park department which operates a swimming and picnic facility each summer.

Tacoma Narrows, with a mile-long suspension bridge, daily sees millions of gallons of water flow to and from the southern portion of Puget Sound. Charted in 1792 by a party off George Vancouver's ship, the narrows was spanned by a highway bridge opened in July 1940. Its decks collapsed months later in a wind storm. With a federal grant the bridge was rebuilt, hung from towers rising 507-feet above the water. The replacement bridge reopened ten years after the disaster. Highway 16 crosses the narrows to reach Gig Harbor and the Kitsap Peninsula.

Northwest Trek, on Highway 161 north of Eatonville, is a 500-acre wildlife park featuring animals of the Pacific Northwest. Moose and bison graze the meadows, owls are in the trees. Visitors ride busses with big windows to view the larger animals, or stroll through a five-mile long trail system for more leisurely viewing. Open from February 1 through October 7, daily from 10:00 a.m. to 7:30 p.m. During November through January, open weekends and holidays from 10:00 a.m. to 5:30 p.m. Telephone 832-6116.

Pierce County voted a bond issue in 1917, purchased 62,000 acres and gave it to the U.S. Army as inducement to locate a major training camp now called **Fort Lewis**.

Fort Lewis Military Museum, 4320 Main Street on the post, details some history of units stationed here. The post is named after explorer

Meriwether Lewis, whose achievements rate a special place in the museum. Take exit 119 off I-5 and follow museum signs. Open Tuesday through Sunday from 12:00 noon to 4:00 p.m. Telephone 967-7206.

Spanaway, a small community on Highway 7 south of Tacoma, is home to a popular motor racing track which stages events from March through September each Wednesday and Saturday night and Sunday afternoons. Telephone 537-7551 or 832-3126.

Wolf Haven America, 3111 Offut Lake Road, Tenino, is a wolf sanctuary which welcomes human visitors. Over thirty animals, representing several subspecies, live on the sixty-acre farm. A private foundation which lobbies for animal rights, sponsors the haven and conducts public education on wolves. From June through September, open daily 10:00 a.m. to 5:00 p.m. Special "howl-in" program at 7:00 p.m. Fridays features tour, campfire and of course howling wolves. From October through May, open Friday, Saturday and Sunday, 10:00 a.m. to 4:00 p.m. Telephone 264-2775.

For further information, contact the **Tacoma/Pierce County Visitor and Convention Bureau**, 735 Saint Helens Street, Tacoma WA 98401. Telephone 832-3291.

Crystal Mountain

Resort

THE CRYSTAL MOUNTAIN RESORT
P. O. Box 1
Crystal Mountain, WA 98022
Tel. (206) 663-2265
Hrs: Winter lift Mon. - Thu. 9:00 a.m. - 4:30 p.m.
                              Friday   9:00 a.m. - 10:00 p.m.
                              Sat. - Sun. 8:30 a.m. - 10:00 p.m.
           Summer lift Mon. - Thu. 9:00 a.m. - 4:00 p.m.
                              Fri. - Sat. 10:00 a.m. - 5:00 p.m.
Call for availability of accommodations and other facilities.

Whether it's winter snow pack or a summer pack trip, Crystal Mountain offers the best of Washington as a resort. Located at the northeast boundary of Mount Baker National Park, seventy-six miles from Seattle, Crystal

Mountain is Washington's only destination ski resort. Many consider it the best overall ski area in the state.

In the summer, the chairlifts remain open to accommodate hikers. Many of the summer visitors find the hotel and condominiums the perfect base for wilderness backpacking, day hiking and fishing. There is horse back riding, including wilderness excursions for sightseeing, fishing and hunting for elk, deer and bear. Skiers enjoy nine chairlifts offering vertical drops of 3,000 feet, making it possible to ski connecting trails for more than three miles. Lodging is just a short walk from the lifts at the hotel and condominium units. Child care is available by reservation. When all that skiing has made you hungry, take your choice of several dining and lunch facilities. The Crystal Inn Saloon features live entertainment, dancing and some of the Northwest's best bands. Refreshments are also available at the Snorting Elk Cellter, The Pub and Rafters.

This is one place that packs a lot of fun into a weekend or a week, any season and for any reason.

Fife

The Puyallup River north bank upstream from the port becomes a large industrial area. Fife, a community of manufacturing plants, is named for industrialist William Fife, the Tacoma millionaire who created it. Both I-5 and Highway 99 pass through Fife. The commercial area is along Highway 99, where Taylor Way curves northward into the Port of Tacoma industrial area.

Restaurant

THE TURNING POINT
3025 Pacific Highway E
Fife, WA 98424
Tel. (206) 922-9555
Hrs: Mon. - Sun. 6:00 a.m. - 12:00 midnight
Restaurant closes at 10:30 p.m.
Visa, MasterCard, AMEX, and Discovery cards are accepted.

The Turning Point is a stylish, yet friendly and relaxed family restaurant. A favorite of local business people, residents, and tourists, The Turning Point promises a wide array of menu selections, generous servings, and welcoming smiles during breakfast, lunch and dinner.

Breakfast features egg and meat dishes, waffles, and numerous omelettes with fresh shrimp and cheddar cheese. Also available is that hearty southern staple, biscuits and country gravy. Lunch and dinner menus are varied with daily specials. They may include anything from grilled calamari steak or sauteed fillet of sole Florentine, to roasted chicken with dressing and cranberries.

Conveniently located just off I-5, The Turning Point is a distinctive choice for dining when in Tacoma.

Gig Harbor

This little town of 2,500 is just a short trip across the Tacoma Narrows Bridge from the bustling urban area. Its harbor has moorage and anchorage for transit boats. A collection of waterfront restaurants and shops appeal to visitors arriving by land and water. Outdoor theater plays here during the summer.

The captain's gig from the 1841 Wilkes expedition sought shelter in a squall, discovering the small inlet noted as "gig harbor" on the expedition chart. The name stuck. These sheltered waters became home to a commercial fishing fleet. A shipyard, which began producing fishing vessels and then switched to small ferry boats, worked at water's edge for years. The forest marches down to the small town beside the harbor, creating a picturesque setting.

Attractions

Old Saint Nicholas Church is now a **museum** for the Peninsula Historical Society.

For further information, contact the **Gig Harbor Area Chamber of Commerce**, Box 1245, Gig Harbor WA 98335. Telephone 851-6865.

Apparel

MCBECKLANDS WOMEN'S BOUTIQUE, 30005 Harborview Drive, Gig Harbor, Washington. On the waterfront, featuring casual clothing for women.

Art Galleries

AMERICAN HEARTH BED AND BREAKFAST AND GALLERY
7506 Soundview Drive
Gig Harbor, WA 98335
Tel. (206) 851-3965
Hrs: Gallery Mon. - Sun. 10:00 a.m. - 8:00 p.m.

 Diane Wolf, hostess and owner of American Hearth and Gallery, refurbished a twenty-eight room colonial mansion in the heart of Gig Harbor and turned it into a wonderful gallery of textile arts with two charming guest suites. The Rose Room on the third floor has an airy hideaway bedroom with luxurious private bath, queen size bed and a dining and sitting area. The Executive Suite is an apartment with its own entrance, living room, bedroom, pullman kitchen and fireplace. This suite is decorated with antiques, quilts and paintings. Each morning a breakfast consisting of crepes, eggs, fruit, juice, coffee or tea and peach wine is served in your room. The mansion has a swimming pool and a spectacular view of the water.
 The Gallery portion of the mansion is called the American Gallery of Quilt and Textile Art and includes modern, traditional and antique works. You will find high quality original clothing designs, fabric that can be hung for decorative purposes, water colors, soft sculptures, glass creations and oil paintings. The quilts are a highlight of the collection. The quilts Diane carries are highly prized and people come from as far away as the East Coast to purchase them. She has a file of more than 2,000 women who work on quilts and her stock comes from all over the country.
 For an interesting and unique shopping experience, don't miss the American Hearth Gallery or pass up the chance to stay in the charming bed and breakfast accommodations offered by this delightfully restored mansion in the heart of Gig Harbor. It will be an experience to remember.

ARTIST PALETTE GALLERY
8811 North Harborview Drive
Gig Harbor, WA 98335
Tel. (206) 851-9390
Hrs: Tue. - Sat.   10:00 a.m. - 5:00 p.m.
   Sunday   12:00 noon - 5:00 p.m.
Extended hours during the summer.
Visa, MasterCard and AMEX are accepted.

 The Artist Palette gallery is located on the east side of Gig Harbor, on the waterfront with an incredible view of Mt. Rainier as a backdrop. This gallery specializes in contemporary and Northwest marine art. Owners Lee Renney and Frences Swinhart are constantly seeking the best available for their gallery. They travel to major trade shows in Dallas, Los Angeles, Hawaii and New York in search of art work they know their customers want and are very successful in their efforts. This gallery carries a fine selection and is one of the most respected and successful galleries in Gig Harbor.

Approximately half the inventory of the gallery is original art. They host six shows yearly featuring local artists such as Judy Odell and Les Barnett. Also carried are works of renowned artists Byron Birdsall, Brent Heighton and wildlife artist naturalist Robert Bateman whose talent and dedication to preserving the wilderness and its creatures has been recognized around the world. The other half of the gallery's stock is limited edition prints.

The clientele of the Artist Palette are people from all over the United States as well as local residents. Be sure to visit this distinctive gallery so you too can enjoy the fine selection of beautiful art offered .

Bed and Breakfast

OLD GLENCOVE HOTEL, 9418 Glencove Road, Gig Harbor, Washington. Built in 1898 as a hotel, this B&B overlooks a small cove and pond.

KRESTINE KETCH
3311 Harbor View Drive
Gig Harbor, WA 98335
Tel. (206) 858-9395
(206) 858-9451
Reservations are recommended.

"Shiver me timbers!" and be piped aboard the Baltic Trading Ketch Krestine, me hardys, for nautical lodging in a unique ship setting!

Gather 'round the woodstove in the grand salon in this one hundred foot coastal sailing Trader built in 1903, and spend your get away close to the sea. The dining facilities aboard the Krestine Ketch can accommodate up to twelve for breakfast and dinner, and meals are moderately priced. Sleeping accommodations are split between one double stateroom and two smaller double cabins.

There are facilities for complete small weddings, performed by the Captain. Located on the waterfront of downtown Gig Harbor, where the Cap'n says "specialty shops are a mere monkey fist heave from the ship's poop deck!", a stay aboard the Krestine Ketch will make a "tar" out of any landlubber!

Gift Shop

THE BEACH BASKET GIFT SHOP AND CASUAL SHOP
4102 Harborview Drive
Gig Harbor, WA 98335
Tel. (206) 858-3008
Hrs: Mon. - Sat.   9:30 a.m. - 5:30 p.m.
       Sunday   11:00 a.m. - 5:30 p.m.
Visa and MasterCard are accepted.

As the name indicates, this shop offers a lot, both gifts and casual women's apparel. The setting for the shop is very unusual, it's located in an old log sawmill which is a famous Gig Harbor landmark. This shop is known for its warm country style atmosphere. When you step in, you feel as though you were in a country store of the past.

An old-fashioned candy counter at this shop will attract children and adults alike. There are aisles of unique and interesting gifts. You'll find a wide selection of baskets, wicker furniture and cards. There is a large selection of Northwest gifts, including concrete and ceramic seagulls, nautical accessories, Gig Harbor t shirts, sweatshirts and coffee mugs. The casual shop carries a wide variety of quality clothing in misses and junior sizes and styles.

The Beach Basket Gift Shop and Casual Shop offers a warm and congenial shopping experience in interesting surroundings and one of the largest selections of fine gifts and clothing you'll find in Gig Harbor. Be sure to make it a stop on your itinerary.

THE COTTAGE, 3024 Harbor View Drive, Gig Harbor, Washington. A gallery of homecrafted gifts for the home. Visa and MasterCard accepted.

COUNTRY TOUCH, 3110 Harborview Drive, Gig Harbor, Washington. Fine gifts, interior and home accessories. MasterCard and Visa accepted.

Restaurant

NEVILLE'S SHORELINE
8827 N Harborview Drive
Gig Harbor, WA 98335
Tel. (206) 851-9822
　　(206) 627-1784

Hrs:	Dinner	Mon. - Sat.	5:00 p.m. - 10:00 p.m.
		Sunday	4:00 p.m. - 9:00 p.m.
	Lunch	Mon. - Sat.	1:00 a.m. - 3:00 p.m.
	Brunch	Sunday:	9:00 a.m. - 3:00 p.m.

Floor to ceiling windows reveal the views of the serene harbor and Mount Rainier from a restaurant tastefully decorated for an elegant but unpretentious experience.

The lunch menu always provides four specials like stuffed baby coho, catfish Louisiana and quite often fresh salmon and halibut. A favorite among the homemade soups is Portuguese bean. The dinner menu begins with your choice of sixteen appetizers, everything from clam fritters to mushrooms St. Michelle. Check out the dinner specials like New Zealand bass, king crab legs and steak. They also have a number of Cajun treats. Sunday brunch includes unlimited Champagne, crepes and various meats and salads.

A trip to Gig Harbor and a fine meal at Neville's can make that trip just perfect.

TIDES TAVERN, 2925 Harbor View Drive, Gig Harbor, Washington. Tie up your boat at the Tides Tavern and enjoy home cooking, pizza, soups, burgers and more. Live music sometimes. Checks ok.

W.B. SCOTTS, 3108 Harbor View Drive, Gig Harbor, Washington. Fine dining, steak and seafood specials. Visa, MasterCard, Diner's Club, AMEX accepted.

Lakewood

Three lakes, American, Steilacoom and Gravelly, form the attraction which drew residents to this large unincorporated area south of Tacoma and west of the Fort Lewis-McCord Air Force Base military reservations. Stately mansions, many almost hidden beneath the Douglas Fir trees, front on the shores of all three lakes.

About 55,000 people now live in Lakewood, which has its own large shopping center, and several multi-family and modern subdivision housing developments to complement the original estate homes constructed decades before. Fort Lewis and McChord, on the other side of I-5 from Lakewood, have another 32,000 residents among troops and their dependents living on base.

Attractions

Lakewood Players use a theater in the Villa Plaza Shopping Center for their performances. The summer offering is usually a melodrama. For information on current shows, call 588-0042 or 582-4220. Most performances play Friday through Sunday evenings with curtain time at 8:00 p.m.

For further information, contact the **Lakewood Area Chamber of Commerce**, Box 99084, Tacoma WA 98499. Telephone 582-9400.

Puyallup

This city of nearly 19,000 residents in the farm land east of Tacoma was originally called Franklin. Pioneer Ezra Meeker, who first farmed on McNeil Island, moved here and became a businessman and promoter of community development. Confusion over other Franklins in Washington including a coal company and a county by that name, caused Meeker and other residents to use the Indian name for the river in their valley as the name for the town. Roughly translated Puyallup means "generous people."

Meeker platted the town in 1887. The city incorporated in 1890. It is now the home of the long-running Western Washington Fair and each spring celebrates its commercial bulb crop with a daffodil festival.

Attractions

Ezra Meeker did well for himself in the Puyallup Valley, leaving a two-story mansion, the **Meeker Mansion**, as a monument to success. Built in 1890 by the same architectural firm which designed many of Tacoma's public buildings, the seventeen-room house is now open to the public. On East Pioneer Avenue near Pioneer Park.

The **fairgrounds** on the edge of Puyallup were constructed in 1900. Expansion has continued, making this one of the top ten fairgrounds in the United States in terms of exhibits and attendance. The fair itself is in

September, but the exhibit halls and grandstands host several other events through out the year.

Frontier Museum, 2301 23rd Avenue Southeast, has western artifacts on display, Wednesday through Sunday between 9:00 a.m. and 5:00 p.m.

Ryan House Museum, 1228 Main Street, is opened each weekend from April through October during afternoon hours. Constructed in 1875, the house is fully restored and features a local arts and crafts festival in early August.

For further information, contact the **Puyallup Valley Chamber of Commerce**, 2823 East Main Street, Puyallup WA 98371. Telephone 845-6755.

Accommodations

NORTHWEST MOTOR INN
1409 S Meridian Street
Puyallup, WA 98371
Tel. (206) 841-2600
Visa, MasterCard, AMEX, Diner's Club and Discover cards are accepted.

The Northwest Motor Inn is conveniently located just twelve minutes from the Tacoma Dome and right across the street from the Puyallup fairgrounds. The management and staff are devoted to making your stay pleasant and comfortable, and the service can't be beat.
The motel offers fifty-one pleasant units, each with a queen size bed and there are three kitchen units available. There is complimentary coffee, cable television with HBO, guest laundry facilities and an outdoor hot tub. A twenty-four hour restaurant is located across the street from the motel.
You can be sure that your stay at the Northwest Motor Inn will be enjoyable and worry free.

Antiques

HAGEMAN ANTIQUES
119 South Jackson Street
Seattle, WA 98104
Tel. (206) 467-1535
Hrs: Mon. - Sat. 10:00 a.m. - 5:00 p.m.

Peter Hageman's antique store, located in Seattle's Pioneer Square area, is a store with a European flair. Peter, who is originally from the Netherlands, has assembled an interesting collection of different style and period European antiques. He has been collecting antiques since a child and his years of expertise are obvious when you view the wonderful collection assembled. This shop has the largest collection of antique paintings in the Northwest.

Peter imports regularly from Europe where he believes there is still a wealth of excellent pieces to be obtained. Different from the American antique trade where Mr. Hageman feels there are 200,000 people looking full time for the furniture of 200 families. In contrast, European furniture is still in excellent supply and well represented in this shop. The furniture available was carefully chosen and reasonably priced, in keeping with Peter's belief that antiques should circulate, rather than sit for years in shops.

Hageman Antiques also does business on a wholesale basis, importing containers of antiques directly from Europe. With Peter's contacts in Europe, he has been able to assemble an interesting and varied collection of European antiques which the antique shopper will find worth viewing.

Pierce County

Puyallup, the town of "generous people," offers you a generous tour.

EIGHT GIFTS OF PUYALLUP			
	Take yourself out to breakfast. You're going to need it.		
a.m.	Meeker Mansion	Best tour	Puya/Attraction
a.m.	Frontier Museum	Best western artifacts	Puya/Museum
p.m.	Ryan House	Best arts and crafts	Puya/Museum
p.m.	Van Lierop Bulb	Best bulb farm	Puya/Farm
For lunch and supper, choose from among these restaurants:			
	Sea Dragon	Best Chinese	Puya/Restaurant
	Anton's	Best for groups	Puya/Restaurant
	Balsano's	Best Italian	Puya/Restaurant

Farm

VAN LIEROP BULB FARM
13407 80th Street E
Puyallup, WA 98372
Tel. (206) 848-7272
Hrs: Feb. - June   Mon. - Sun.   9:00 a.m. - 5:00 p.m.
     Sept. 15 - Oct. Mon. - Sat.   10:00 a.m. - 4:30 p.m.

    The Van Lierop Bulb Farm is a tradition in the Puyallup Valley since 1934. Bulb growing in this area began in 1910 and in the 1920s Simon Van Lierop was sent to the United States by a Dutch bulb company to sell bulbs. During the depression the farm in the Puyallup Valley where he was employed was unable to pay him in wages so he was paid in bulbs. By 1934 he was able to send for his fiancee Beatrice, and they opened their own bulb farm. Today their oldest son Neil and his family continue the tradition of raising bulbs.
    In the spring the farm's flower shop is open and features farm fresh cut daffodils, tulips, and iris in their blooming seasons. They offer a special service in which they box daffodils or tulips for shipping across the United States. A multitude of spring bulb and garden flowers, unique gifts, and spring holiday selections are also available in the shop. The blooming spring gardens have over 150 varieties of crocus, daffodils, hyacinths, tulips, and a variety of minor bulbs in a home garden setting. All bulbs grown in the garden may be ordered and will be delivered in time for fall planting.

A visit to Van Lierop bulb farms in the spring is a delightful experience. The vast array of beautiful blooms is breathtaking. Customers are advised to order by June 15 to be sure of receiving their chosen selections. For those who wish it, a catalog is available by writing to the farm. Don't miss this wonderful place when you are in the Puyallup Valley.

Restaurant

ANTON'S
3207 E Main
Puyallup, WA 98372
Tel. (206) 845-7569
Visa, MasterCard and AMEX accepted.

Basil and Jim Anton have been the proprietors of Anton's since they founded the business in 1963. Before that they were in the restaurant business with their father in Tacoma, so they bring years of experience to their restaurant, and it certainly shows. They offer the finest quality food served in congenial surroundings by a well-trained, helpful staff.

Family groups are encouraged at Anton's and the prices are moderate. This is a very popular place with local business organizations who meet here regularly. There are very good facilities for handling large groups. The dining room overlooks the Puyallup River so you can enjoy a lovely view with your delicious food. There is a good selection of steak, seafood, and pasta with wine and beer available to round out your meal.

Anton's offers the best in service and high quality food at a moderate price in a pleasant atmosphere.

BALSANO'S ITALIAN RESTAURANT
127 15th Street, SE
Puyallup, WA 98372
Tel. (206) 845-4222
Hrs: Tue. - Thu.   11:00 a.m. - 9:00 p.m.
      Friday   11:00 a.m. - 10:00 p.m.
      Saturday   4:00 p.m. - 10:00 p.m.
      Sunday   4:00 p.m. - 9:00 p.m.
Closed on Christmas, Easter and Thanksgiving.
Visa and MasterCard are accepted.

Balsano's has just celebrated its third birthday and is becoming one of the most popular restaurants in Puyallup. Owners Tom and Rita Pantley and Ed and Clara Greer named their restaurant in honor of Tom's grandfather who was the last of the Balsano's. The restaurant is a family project and most of the recipes are from Calabria in Southern Italy, except the cream sauce dishes which originate in Northern Italy.

Veal lovers are in for a treat when they dine at Balsano's. The veal is cut on the premises and incorporated into dishes such as veal Saltimboca, veal sauteed in white wine and sage with spiced ham and cheese served on a bed of spinach, and veal Carciofi, veal with artichoke hearts and lemon. Another wonderful dish is scallops and prawns saute, fresh vegetables and a light white wine lemon sauce with fennel. There are also numerous pasta and chicken dishes and three specials each evening. The wines are predominantly Italian and reasonably priced.

With one day's notice, Tom will help you plan a family style dinner of five or six courses. Beginning in the fall, Monday evenings, they will be holding Italian cooking classes. Balsano's has a lot to offer the discriminating diner with fine Italian food in a pleasant family oriented atmosphere.

SEA DRAGON
15305 Meridian South
Puyallup, WA 98371
Tel. (206) 848-7222
Hrs: Sun. - Thu.   11:00 a.m. - 10:30 p.m.
     Fri. - Sat.   11:00 a.m. - 12:30 a.m.
Closed on Christmas Day and Thanksgiving Day.
Visa, MasterCard and AMEX are accepted.
and,
1106 E Main
Puyallup, WA 98373
Tel. (206) 848-4899

Peter Nee opened his first restaurant in Hong Kong eighteen years ago. He brought his expertise in Chinese cuisine to Puyallup ten years ago, opening a restaurant in the downtown area and expanding with the opening of the Meridian South restaurant five years ago. The interior is beautifully decorated with lovely oriental designs and etched glasswork above the booths. There is unique artwork decorating the walls and the atmosphere is serene and quiet.

The menu is Cantonese and Mandarin with family style dinners among the most popular offerings. The Cantonese dinner offers Won Ton Soup, barbecued pork and sweet and sour prawns. The seafood specials are also very popular. For those who love spicy food, the Four Seas dinner is a good choice. It offers Mandarin fried chicken, braised prawns with chili sauce and

Peking style pea pod beef. There are many appetizers, soups, chow meins and poultry, meat and seafood dishes.

Sea Dragon offers a wonderfully varied selection of delicious, well prepared Chinese food. This is a charming place to dine and after you have enjoyed your meal, take the time to listen to the live music provided for your entertainment five nights a week.

Steilacoom

The name comes from the Indian village, the word meaning "pink flower." An army post called Fort Steilacoom was established east of here in 1849. The town, one of the first on the Sound, began in 1851 and within two years was site of a barrel factory and salmon-packing plant. Its docks loaded lumber bound for California. The fort closed in 1869. The 700 acres of surplus land was given the state in 1874.

Western State Hospital, a facility for treatment of the mentally-ill, is now on grounds once used by the military post. About 4,900 people live in the town, which got its charter in 1853 to become Washington's first incorporated city.

Old orchards ring the town where Hudson Bay Company once contested grazing rights with early American farmers. This is the ferry landing for service to the off-shore islands which have been settled almost as long as the plateau above the little town.

Attractions

A small brick building on Main Avenue at Starlung Street was the **first jail** in Washington Territory. Constructed in 1858, it was the Pierce County Jail while the county seat remained here through 1881. A house across the street was built in 1855. The Catholic Church was a chapel at Fort Steilacoom moved to town after troops left the post in 1867.

Blair Drug and Hardware Living Museum, 1617 Lafayette, uses a drug store building erected in 1895 to tell the story of days gone by. The museum serves breakfast; old-fashioned sodas and sundaes are dispensed from a fountain fabricated in 1906. Open Monday through Saturday from 7:00 a.m. to 8:00 p.m. Sunday open 12:00 noon to 8:00 p.m. Telephone 588-9668.

Eagle Island, located in the Sound between Anderson and McNeil Islands, is now preserved as a state park, accessible only by boat. This day use area has beaches, buoys for mooring boats, and a trail system for exploring. It is a tiny island between two larger masses of land, untouched by the farming which changed the looks of surrounding islands.

McNeil Island, for years site of a federal prison, was one of the first places settled in this area. Ezra Meeker, his wife Eliza Jane and his brother Oliver started farming here in 1853.

The campus-like **Western State Hospital** is open for visitors. Some buildings from the old Fort Steilacoom are part of the hospital including a row of residences used by doctors. These small homes were constructed in 1860, and are a marked contrast to more ornate officer's quarters at military posts constructed in Washington around the turn of the century.

Restaurant

E. R. ROGERS
1702 Commercial Street
Steilacoom, WA 98388
Tel. (206) 582-0280
Hrs: Mon. - Sun.   5:30 p.m. - 11:00 p.m.
          Sunday brunch   10:00 a.m. - 2:00 p.m.
Available for private parties and weddings.

There isn't another restaurant in the greater Seattle-Tacoma area which has such a sweeping, unobstructed, panoramic view. Every table in the house has a breathtaking view of historic Puget Sound. This seventeen-room mansion, built in 1891, is a perfectly restored Victorian. When you walk into the outside dining area you feel like you're back in the late 1800's, waiting for the schooner captain to join you for dinner. Inside you find rich mahogany walls, tongue-and-groove ceilings, dimly lit hurricane lamp on each table, and a sparkling crystal chandelier overhead.

Apropos of the attention to detail in decor, the staff is waiting to attend to your every need. Great pride is taken; the fact that the employees choose to work here for many, many years is testimony to their enjoyment and dedication.

You are encouraged to take your time and relax. The owners, Gordon Robertson and Bruce Miller are enthusiastic and fun. You will always find one of them in attendance on the premises. They created the recipe for one of the wines served, Chardonnay Cuvee, produced and bottled by Kiona Vineyards in West Richland, Washington.

Daily, mouth-watering fish specials are verbally announced. A house specialty is succulent prime rib. The menu offered is broad in scope and delicious to the palate. There is a bit of mystery and intrigue to the place; go to the upstairs cocktail lounge and ask the bartender to show you the "protector," only visible in the tree-- at night. You could also enjoy the fine music--while viewing the "protector."

Sumner

Rhubarb and daffodils grow in the crossroads town of Sumner, northeast of Puyallup. The newer freeways, Highways 410 and 167, keep through traffic west of the town of 4,500. Indians had a village here, where in 1883 George H. Ryan platted a town and named it for Charles Sumner, a U.S. senator during the Civil War. Ryan's old home is now the town's public library.

Golf Course

TAPPS ISLAND GOLF
20818 Island Parkway East
Sumner, WA 98390
Tel. (206) 862-7011
Hrs: Mon. - Sun. Dawn to Dusk
Visa and MasterCard are accepted

Up, up into the air it soars. It was a perfect tee off. But wait, maybe it wasn't so perfect. As you watch the ball slowly glide to the earth, you just know it's headed for the sandtrap. Ahhh, it just missed the trap. You're safe for now. If this scenario sounded fun to you, then you ought to make your way to Tapps Island Golf Course and turn it into reality.

One of the most unique courses in the Northwest, Tapps Island Golf Course is sure to provide you with a morning or afternoon of sporting excitement as you golf your way through its treacherous nine holes. The smallest green is 5,000 square feet, while the largest is a whopping 9,000 square feet. Always lurking where they're not supposed to be are those nasty water and sandtraps. But hazards apart, some of the other features include a beautiful view of Mount Rainier, abundant wildlife, dry ground in winter, senior and junior golfing rates, men's and women's clubs, tournaments, special monthly events and much more.

For your dining pleasure, Tapps Island Golf Course is also home to a delightful coffee shop, serving breakfast and lunch. Of course, there's a full-service Pro Shop for equipment rentals, purchase and repair. So, enjoy a terrific game of golf, some delicious food and a quality Pro Shop. Don't dream about that hole-in-one, make it real.

Pierce County

Tacoma

Bright with stately buildings and landmark churches, Tacoma lies between the waters of Puget Sound and its own deep-water port on Commencement Bay. The Olympic Mountains can be seen in the west over a tree-fringed foreground. Snow-covered Mount Rainier rises to the east commanding attention from this city of factories, railroad yards, and docks around the meandering tidewaters of the Puyallup River. A commercial district of imposing buildings and neat residential areas marches over the plain above the industrial area. Washed clean with frequent rain in the winter, its gardens and yards lush, Tacoma's homes are neat in contrast to her utilitarian factories and docks.

Tacoma's citizens for years thought they would out-do Seattle as the center of business and culture on Puget Sound. Now both cities are hemmed in by their suburbs and can grow no more. Tacoma's population reached about 160,000 in recent years, one third that of Seattle. The name is said to be a derivative of the Indian name for Mount Rainier, Tahoma. It translates to "nourishing breast."

Indians, who in 1855 had their last skirmishes with the settlers who came here to mill lumber and ship it by schooner, were said to be less-than pleased with the resulting city.

The old town, started next to a waterfront sawmill, brewery and barrel factory, grew quickly after its founding in 1852. Northern Pacific Railroad, building its way north two decades later, created a new Tacoma. The developers surrounded a Puyallup Indian burial ground, located near the Northern Pacific Railroad Headquarters, on Pacific Avenue at South Seventh. During grading of Pacific Avenue in 1873 a landmark rock sacred to the Indians was covered to bring the street to completion. Pacific Avenue was laid out in 1872 to agree with the coming railroad's alignment rather than the grid of old Tacoma. New and old Tacoma officially consolidated in 1884.

Urban planners like to recall the city that could have been instead of the straight streets laid out off Pacific Avenue. Frederick Olmsted, the landscape designer who created Golden Gate Park in west San Francisco, reworked the developer's plat to create a town plan in which streets follow the contours of hills, public parks were every where and the city blocks looked more like melons than the squares and oblongs accepted by developers of that era and many since. The plan was killed, and now exists in the Washington State Historical Museum. Tacoma Land Company, successor to the financially-strapped Northern Pacific Railroad, put the downtown lots up for sale in 1874 with quite conventional street grids.

Tacoma's early industrial development came rapidly when a railroad connected the Wilkenson coal field east of the city with the docks. Steamers called to take on some of the cheapest coal on the West Coast, handled in a natural harbor deep enough to receive the largest vessels. Tacoma's development-minded business community purchased tide flats for industrial expansion and talked county voters into passing a bond issue to buy land and give it to the army as an inducement to get more purchasing from the military. The business district flourished in the 1900s; residential areas developed one after another. While other cities of the time emerged with street car transportation, Tacoma's growth seemed fit to the bus and auto. Pacific Highway stretching south to Fort Lewis became the ultimate in strip commercialism long before planners existed to decry the trend or impose zoning regulations.

Attractions

Point Defiance Park occupies a promontory with sweeping views of the Sound, the Port of Tacoma and the narrows to the south. Old Fort Nisqually, moved here in 1934, was a Hudson Bay Company post located near where the community of Dupont is now, seventeen miles south of Tacoma. The U.S. government eventually bought out the trading company's properties in Pierce County for $650,000 in an 1869 settlement. Open daily, 8:00 a.m. to dusk. Telephone 591-5300.

Never Never Land, a theme park built on childhood stories such as the Three Bears, Billy Goats Gruff and the Mother Goose tales, is operated at Point Defiance Park by the Metropolitan Park District. Open from Memorial Day through Labor Day, 10:00 a.m. to 7:00 p.m. daily. Call 591-5845 for information and off-season operating days.

The **Point Defiance Zoo**, located near Fort Nisqually and rated "world class" by many visitors, and the **Aquarium** on the shore of Commencement Bay beneath the point, are also operated by the Metropolitan Park District. There is a boat house with rentals including fishing gear. Open Daily 10:00 a.m. to 7:00 p.m. Telephone 591-5335.

Next to the aquarium is the **Washington State ferry dock** with regular service to Vashon Island (see King County listing for Vashon). The **Tacoma Yacht Club**, with an imposing club house built in 1893, adjoins the ferry landing with several places to view small craft in the harbor.

Ruston Way provides a drive between the port, old downtown and Point Defiance. A massive urban renewal project is converting old businesses and mills into a two-mile strip of footpaths, public piers and small shops and restaurants.

City Fire Station Five, 3301 Ruston Way, is also the berth of a fireboat equipped with technologically-advanced fire suppression equipment. The crew holds open house about the vessel each Sunday afternoon, conducting tours and demonstrating some of its gear. Open from 1:00 p.m. to 4:00 p.m. Sundays only.

A short drive north around Commencement Bay leads to Dash Point (see King County listing for state park) with its lighthouse and a view of the harbor and city.

University of Puget Sound, 1500 North Warner Street, offers its stately campus for several community cultural activities including performances of the Tacoma Symphony Orchestra. Call 756-3555 for the current schedule.

One of the grand bank buildings of yesteryear at Twelfth Street and Pacific Avenue is now **Tacoma Art Museum.** The standing exhibits are augmented by traveling shows traded with major museums. Open Monday through Saturday from 10:00 a.m. to 4:00 p.m. Sunday from 2:00 p.m. to 5:00 p.m. Telephone 272-4258.

Washington State Historical Museum, 315 North Stadium Way, is in an imposing four-story building. The Greek Revival building was erected in 1911, and added to in 1973. Collections include not only local history, but exhibits dealing with cultures touched by area commerce in the orient and Alaska. Open Tuesday through Saturday from 9:30 a.m. to 5:00 p.m. Sunday from 2:00 p.m. to 5:00 p.m. Telephone 593-2830.

Overlooking Commencement Bay and the city harbor from a bluff is **Stadium High School,** 111 North E Street, designed in 1891 to be a chateau-style hotel similar to those constructed by Canadian Pacific Railroad. The depression of 1893 halted work. The school district later picked up a bargain. Their remodel, completed in 1906, is said to be the grandest high school on the Pacific Coast. Stadium bowl, in a ravine next to the school, was designed by Frederick Heath, architect of the high school remodel. The bowl has seated 32,000 persons for events held in years past.

Two of the Northwest's premier department stores, The Bon-Frederick and Nelson, and Nordstrom, are anchors of the sprawling 150-shop **Tacoma Mall.** The giant indoor shopping center is west of I-5 between the

South 38th or South 48th Street exits. There are 1,500,000 square feet of retailing space inside the mall, about twice the area of most regional malls in the northwest. Open daily. Call 475-4565.

Tacoma Dome, located north of I-5 off Pacific Avenue, was constructed as an example of plywood and laminated wood strength and is the largest wooden-dome structure in the world. Evangelists, rock musicians and athletes play here. Tours are offered at 10:30 a.m. and 2:30 p.m. Monday through Friday.

Harbor cruises, three times a day from May through September, are offered at Tacoma's old McCormick Steamship dock in the port. Departures at 11:00 a.m., 1:00 p.m., and 3:00 p.m. The company also books dinner cruises to Gig Harbor at 6:30 p.m. daily during its season and will charter boats at other times of the year. For reservations and rates call 572-9858.

For further information contact the **Tacoma/Pierce County Visitor and Convention Bureau**, 735 Saint Helens Street, Tacoma WA 98401. Telephone 627-2145.

Accommodations

EXECUTIVE INN
5700 Pacific Highway E
Tacoma, WA 98424
Tel.   (509) 922-0080
         (800) 528-1234

Just a stone's throw from many of the Tacoma's attractions, the Executive Inn offers comfortable and convenient accommodations with top flight service.

You are just minutes from Tacoma Shopping Mall, Sea-Tac airport, the Tacoma Dome, beautiful golf courses, Puget Sound fishing and boating, just to name a few. Even closer is the lounge, where the live music has made it one of Tacoma's most popular night spots. The inn is attractively designed with 140 oversized guest rooms, including six suites. All rooms feature air conditioning, color with cable television and direct dial phones. The staff will even pick you up at the airport. To wind down, swim a few laps in the pool, work out in the weight room, or just relax in the sauna. The dining room is tastefully decorated and provides a wide range of entrees.

But cast no stones, gather no moss, just check into the Executive Inn your "Best Choice" for accommodations.

HOLIDAY INN / TACOMA, 1425 East Twenty-seventh Street, Tacoma, Washington. Fine hotel with 160 contemporary rooms, excellent meeting facilities, and quality restaurant and lounge. There's room service, a pool and jacuzzi.

THE LAKEWOOD MOTOR INN
6125 Motor Avenue SW
Tacoma, WA 98499
Tel. (206) 584-2212

Landscaped in lush evergreens and delicate gardens, The Lakewood offers visitors a tranquil and serene suburban setting just minutes south of downtown Tacoma.

The rooms are tastefully furnished with added touches such as pleated shades decorated in a colonial motif with mauve, green or blue. There's a heated outdoor pool and lounge area. Just across the street is a four star restaurant, The Lakewood Terrace, and on the other side of the street is the area's oldest and most fashionable shopping center. Sightseeing tours pick up from the inn and there is airport limousine service available.

For a place far enough away from the din of the city, but with good access to it, rest and relax at the Lakewood Motor Inn.

NENDELS MOTOR INN
8702 South Hosmer
Tacoma, WA 98444
Tel. (206) 535-3100
     (800) 547-0106
All major credit cards accepted.

Located off I-5 at exit 128 (headed north), and exit 129 (going south); Nendels Motor Inn offers moderately priced rooms for families and business travelers. Each of the 144 rooms are attractively furnished, include color television, with first-run, in-house movies, complimentary coffee and direct dial telephones. VCRs are available for rent from the front desk, with unlimited movies. The outdoor, heated swimming pool is open from spring through the early fall, depending upon the weather conditions.

Room service is available twenty-four hours a day and is provided by the restaurant located next door to Nendels. Room service can be charged. You are within walking distance of a small shopping area, and the Tacoma Mall (Tacoma's largest mall) is only minutes away, Mt Rainier National Park is one hour drive and the Tacoma Dome is only ten minutes.

Nendels is a consistently good choice, no matter what area of the Northwest you may be traveling to.

SHERATON TACOMA HOTEL
1320 Broadway Plaza
Tacoma, WA 98402
Tel. (206) 572-3200

The Sheraton Tacoma soars twenty-six stories above the central business district of Tacoma. It is ranked as the third largest convention facility in the state and has played host to hundreds of conventions and conferences, ranging from 10 to 800 people.

The Sheraton's rooms are spacious, well appointed and the staff is courteous and eager to serve you. On the top floor of the hotel is the award winning Rose Room, with breathtaking views of Commencement Bay and Mt. Rainier. The Rose Room is open for lunch and dinner and offers a wide variety of Pacific Northwest cuisine. The Wintergarden Cafe, located on the fourth level, serves breakfast, lunch, dinner and Sunday brunch in a more casual atmosphere. At day's end, the Music Room is a popular spot for cocktails while enjoying the peaceful music of a grand piano. For livelier entertainment there's Elliott's, another cocktail lounge on the fourth floor.

The Sheraton is certainly the most comfortable hotel in town and the charming decor and gracious service make it an inviting place to stay.

SHILO INN
7414 S Hosmer
Tacoma, WA 98408
Tel. (206) 475-4020
     (800) 222-2244

The Shilo Inn is located close to the Tacoma Dome, Tacoma Mall and Mt. Rainier recreation area. It offers "affordable excellence", a hallmark of the Oregon based chain of western hotels, motels and resorts.

The Shilo Inn offers its guests an indoor pool, spa, exercise room, steam and sauna rooms among other amenities. Guests enjoy such standard Shilo Inn extras as free Continental breakfast, satellite TV, free airport shuttle service, popcorn and fruit. Kitchenettes are available.

The Shilo Inns offer group rates and senior discounts. There is a restaurant/lounge just across the street from the Inn and a jogging park, golf course and movie theater are nearby. This is a pleasant place to stay during your visit to Tacoma.

Antiques

THE KEY ANTIQUES, 5485 Steilacoom Boulevard Southwest, Tacoma, Washington. Fine antiques and country primitives. Visa and MasterCard accepted.

MEMORY MALL
744 Broadway
Tacoma, WA 98402
Tel. (206) 272-6476
Hrs: Tue. - Wed.   10:00 a.m. - 5:00 p.m.
      Fri. - Sat.   10:00 a.m. - 5:00 p.m.
      Thursday   10:00 a.m. - 9:00 p.m.
      Sunday   1:00 p.m. - 4:00 p.m.
Visa and MasterCard are accepted.

Memory Mall is one of the largest antique and collectible shops in Pierce county with over fifty dealers displaying their wares. There is a vast variety of items on display, from vintage clothing to 1960's Beatles postcards, to jewelry and coins.

As you wander down the aisles you'll find one booth filled with Pacific Northwest Indian paintings and beadwork. At another you'll find fishing poles, decoys and lures. At yet another, an assortment of collectibles such as pocket watches, dolls, toys and glassware. Clothing from the 1950's, old leather shoes and purses are scattered throughout and the mall carries one of the largest selection of costume and fine jewelry in the Pacific Northwest.

The Mall stays open late on Thursdays since there is an auction nearby. So pack a lunch, plan to make the day an event and take a stroll down Memory Mall!

As a token of your appreciation:

	THANK HER WITH CLASS		
a.m.	Le Snak	Best European griddle	Tac/Rest.
a.m.	Rumors	Best apparel	Tac/Apparel
a.m.	Memory Mall	Best Jewelry	Tac/Mall
p.m.	The Bavarian	Best ambiance	Tac/Rest.
p.m.	McCausland's	Best garments	Tac/App
p.m.	Pacific Northwest	Best wine	Tac/Gift
p.m.	The Cliff House	Best dinner menu	Tac/Rest.

If you really mean it, say it. But say it with class. You'll find that the reasons for thanking her will increase.

Apparel

CHAMELIANI BOUTIQUE, 1135 Broadway, Tacoma, Washington. An exclusive boutique with American and European designer clothes.

JASMINKA
3820 N. 26th Street
Tacoma, WA 98407
Tel. (206) 752-8700
Hrs: Mon. - Sat. 10:00 a.m. - 6:00 p.m.
Closed Sunday and major holidays.
Visa and MasterCard are accepted.

People who enjoy discovering new and unique clothing stores will love what they find in Jasminka. It is a casual boutique located close to the University of Puget Sound in the Proctor district. Owner Rondi Boskovich received a degree in clothing and textile and takes pride in selecting only comfortable clothing in natural fibers.

Rondi has contemporary and sophisticated styles and accessories that are constantly changing and never carries more than a few items in each style. Her merchandise comes from all over the world, including Asia, South America, Africa and the United States. She has interesting handwoven and hand dyed textiles in bright colors. There is a large selection of accessories with interesting beads, belts and one of a kind collector jewelry.

Jasminka's prices are moderate and very competitive and this is a definite "Best Choice" in Tacoma for unique quality fashions.

McCAUSLAND'S AND LADY M
6450 S Sprague
Tacoma, WA 98466
Tel. (206) 473-7848
Hrs: Mon. - Sat. 10:00 a.m. - 6:00 p.m.
Visa, MasterCard, AMEX and Diner's card are accepted.

Men and women who know and appreciate fine quality garments will find McCausland's to be an outstanding clothier. The men's department, with its warm atmosphere of dark wood and brass, carries suits of the finest cloth with a traditionally European accent, Bally and Cole-Haan shoes and luggage, Fila sports and athletic clothing and shoes, sweaters of the finest cashmere and wool from Scotland, and exquisite ties from Italy and other areas of Europe. Alterations are free of charge at McCausland's and, upstairs barber services are available.

Lady M is adjacent to McCausland's and carries moderately to higher priced clothing and accessories. Lavender walls with pink trim lend a warm and feminine atmosphere and the store carries a variety of quality lines including Fila sportswear, dresses and cruise wear made from the finest lightweight wools, silks and cottons. Free alterations are available.

Whether you wish to stop in to watch a ball game on TV while reclining on one of the plush leather couches by a roaring fire, browse through the store, or purchase a quality item, McCausland's and Lady M welcomes you.

OSTLUND'S PENDLETON SHOP
2310 Mildred Street W
Tacoma, WA 98466
Tel. (206) 565-6666
Hrs: Mon. - Fri.   10:00 a.m. - 6:00 p.m.
      Saturday   10:00 a.m. - 5:00 p.m.
Evenings by appointment.
Visa, MasterCard and AMEX are accepted.

Pendleton no longer means only classic coats and skirts. They have expanded, and Ostlunds carries their entire line, from clothes to blankets to accessories. Proprietor Larry Ostlund opened this wonderful store in May, 1985 and offers his customers one of the largest selections of Pendleton goods in the Pacific Northwest.

There are several divisions in the women's line of clothing, ranging from casual weekend wear to the traditional line of classic skirts, blazers and sweaters. Surprisingly, Pendleton doesn't just mean gorgeous wools any more. The Country Sophisticates line of spring and summer fashions for women is primarily cottons and silk blends. For men there is the Lobo line of active and weekend wear, as well as the traditional sweaters and wools.

Ostlund's carries the Northwest's largest inventory of Pendleton blankets with colorful Indian throw blankets, bed blankets and stadium blankets. They offer excellent personalized service. They will special order items, gift wrap and do alterations free of charge, and they keep a file on every customer, which includes sizes and purchases. Pendleton means quality and so does Ostlund's.

RUMORS
2311 N 30th
Tacoma, WA 98403
Tel. (206) 572-9767
Hrs: Mon. - Sat. 10:00 a.m. - 6:00 p.m.
Visa, MasterCard and AMEX are accepted.

Nancy Sharma is the owner of Rumors, a popular women's boutique in Old Town Tacoma. Nancy brings a sophisticated sense of fashion, great drive and determination to her boutique.

Her clothes are casual but sophisticated, and feature gorgeous sweaters, skirts, and blouses that she buys only two or three of in a style and only one of a size. She avoids labels you'd find in the major department stores and offers quality items that can carry you through many years of wear.

Rumors offers very personalized service. Cards are kept on file for all customers so the staff can help them choose new pieces to complement their previous purchases. This boutique is the perfect place to find unique, one of a kind clothes and accessories that reflect the sophisticated, yet casual lifestyle of the Northwest.

Florist

GRASSIS FLOWERS & GIFTS, 938 Broadway Plaza, Tacoma, Washington. Superior floral designs, green and blooming plants, balloons and gifts. Visa and MasterCard accepted.

Gift Shop

COLORS
3803 North 26th Street
Tacoma, WA 98407
Tel. (206) 759-0077
Hrs: Mon. - Sat. 10:00 a.m. - 5:30 p.m.
Closed on major holidays.

Owner Karan Godman considers "Colors" a neighborhood gift store. A rainbow of delights would be closer. There is a friendly sophistication about this shop from the moment you enter. You are greeted by staff with a cup of coffee, helped in your selections, and gayly waved goodbye when you exit with your gift-wrapped purchase. Complimentary , of course.

This once was a local gas station. It now is open, bright and airy with natural pine woodwork, brick floors, skylights, antique doors and windows, and colors...colors everywhere.

Karan stocks a wide variety of merchandise and you will have no trouble finding a special birthday or wedding present. The craft items are beautifully made; ceramic pottery in brilliant purples, oranges and reds that are totally usable from microwave to dishwasher. Interestingly designed, colorful, locally crafted baskets which can be custom-ordered to match your decor. Jewelry you won't find anywhere else in this region. Dried flower arrangements, greeting cards, children's toys and kitchen gadgets. The gourmet food section includes delights like Duggan's salad dressing and dessert sauces, and Scandinavian cold-pack jams. The aroma of fresh Caravali coffee fills the shop and can be purchased in whole-bean or ground.

U.P.S. will ship your purchases anywhere. Colors is a special store in Tacoma. It's just a fun, warm, happy experience. Definitely a "Best Choice."

PACIFIC NORTHWEST SHOP
2702 N Proctor
Tacoma, WA 98407
Tel. (206) 752-2242
Hrs: Mon. - Sat.   10:00 a.m. - 6:00 p.m.
      Sunday   12:00 noon - 5:00 p.m.
Visa, MasterCard, AMEX, Diners Club cards are accepted.
Complimentary gift wrapping, mail order catalog available and phone orders are accepted.

This colorful and exciting shop sells everything from Pacific Northwest cheese to Mt. St. Helens "Volcano Glass." Awarded an exclusive contract to sell wares at the Washington State Pavilion, Expo 86, in Vancouver, BC, one is immediately attracted by the shop's huge neon sign stating that it's "a taste of the Pacific Northwest."

The deli area is stocked with locally made truffles, Chehalis mints, jams, alder smoked salmon, pasta and one of the largest selections of Northwest wines in the state. There are locally designed t-shirts, a large book section, toys, jewelry by Northwest artists, reasonably priced pottery, North Coast Indian prints and serigraphs of Northwest mountain scenes.

Right in the middle of the shop are huge boulders from a quarry near Mt. Rainier complete with a waterfall. Further into the shop you'll find a giant apple tree from Eastern Washington. Throughout the year it is covered with merchandise appropriate to the season. There is no doubt that this store and its merchandise are a wonderful "taste of the Pacific Northwest."

THE UNDERGROUND SHOP, 311 1/2 South Eleventh Street, Tacoma, Washington. An unusual little gift shop with a large selection of alternative greeting cards.

Golf Course

BROOKDALE GOLF COURSE
1802 Brookdale Road E
Tacoma, WA 98445
Tel. (206) 537-4400
     (206) 537-9990
Hrs: Dawn to dusk, all year

Whether you're here for the game of golf, or just want to tag along for the exercise, you'll love the course at Brookdale. It's set among towering fir trees with a slowly meandering creek and Mt. Rainier majestically visible to the east. Brookdale is one of the Northwest's largest courses and even if it rained torrentially the day before it's still playable. It has a course rating of 68.3 for men and 72 for women.

Brookdale is almost sixty years old and although it has been remodeled over the years, the clubhouse still retains its original stone fireplace and its character. Owner Chuck Brown and golf Pro Tom Parkhurst provide numerous amenities to make a day of golfing enjoyable. There's a fully stocked Pro shop and a restaurant that serves breakfast and lunch and can accommodate up to 100 people for banquets. There is a thirty acre driving range and an excellent fleet of golf carts.

Brookdale is a very popular and very attractive course that attracts people from all over the state. There are more than 150 golf tournaments held there yearly. The fees are very competitive and a day's golfing at Brookdale is memorable.

NORTH SHORE GOLF COURSE
4101 Northshore Boulevard NE
Tacoma, WA 98422
Tel. (206) 927-1375
Visa, MasterCard, AMEX and Discover are accepted.

The North Shore Golf Course offers large tournament greens, grass of exceptional quality and a very dry course year round. This is an area of Puget Sound glacial deposits and the terrain is sand and gravel so that rain water drains through quickly.

The eighteen hole course plays sixty-four hundred yards and has over fifty traps and five lakes which give it the reputation of being difficult, yet add a charisma which eludes most courses. The front nine holes are relatively flat and the back nine are hilly.

The pro shop is fully stocked with apparel, shoes and accessories and there are power carts available for rent. The clubhouse is open daily for breakfast, lunch and dinner and can handle banquets of up to 200 guests. North Shore has a large covered driving range and a teaching area. Video lessons and a room to view your swing are provided along with a staff of four PGA pros.

A day filled with golfing, shopping and fine dining, all await the lucky participants of:

TACOMA'S BEST

a.m.	Antique Sandwich	Best steamed eggs	Tac/Rest.
a.m.	North Shores Golf	Best golf	Tac/Golf
	How about some shopping after the game?		
a.m.	Ostlund's Pendleton	Best clothing variety	Tac/Apparel
a.m.	Colors	Best gifts	Tac/Gift
a.m.	Gourmet Pantry	Best cheeses	Tac/Deli
a.m.	Jasminka	Best international garb	Tac/Apparel
p.m.	Grazie Cafe	Best luncheon buffet	Tac/Rest.
	Now for that second game of golf.		
p.m.	Brookdale Golf	Best golf	Tac/Golf
p.m.	Stanley & Seafort's	Best steaks	Tac/Rest.
	For those who like to eat a late meal:		
	Lobster Shop South	Best lobster	Tac/Rest.
	Harbor Lights Rest.	Best steamed clams	Tac/Rest.
	Engine House #9	Best history	Tac/Rest.

This full day may get the best of you!

Restaurant

THE ANTIQUE SANDWICH COMPANY
5102 N Pearl Street
Tacoma, WA 98402
Tel. (206) 752-4069

    An institution in Tacoma, The Antique Sandwich Company has been pleasing residents and travelers alike for over fourteen years. This aptly named sandwich shop is housed in a beautifully restored building that was constructed shortly after the turn of the century.
    It's no wonder that after fourteen years The Sandwich Company knows just what it takes to please their customers. Here, amidst a delightful decor of rustic antiques, you'll enjoy the many different kinds of sandwiches and soups that are served daily for both lunch and dinner. For breakfast, any of

the locals will tell you this shop is the home to the best cinnamon rolls in town, not to mention the steamed eggs. But the clincher for the food served at The Sandwich Company has to lie in its pervasive freshness. Everything served here is wholesome, fresh and delicious, including the desserts that are honey sweetened.

The Sandwich Company also hosts occasional concerts and open mike singing. For more information about up and coming events just give them a ring. Overall, The Antique Sandwich Company is a place to enjoy healthy and delicious food in an ambiance of the past. When in Tacoma, make the "Best Choice" and visit this institution.

THE BAVARIAN
204 N. K Street
Tacoma, WA 98403
Tel. (206) 627-5010
Hrs: Lunch Mon. - Fri.   11:00 a.m. - 4:00 p.m.
         Dinner   5:00 p.m. - 9:00 p.m.
                    Saturday   3:00 p.m. - 10:00 p.m.
                    Sunday   4:00 p.m. - 8:00 p.m.
Closed major holidays
Visa, MasterCard, AMEX and Diner's Club are accepted.

The Bavarian is small, intimate and comfortable, with German music playing softly in the background. It reminds you of the kind of dining room you would find in a German guest house. Along with its old country atmosphere, it offers traditional German food that is consistently delicious.

For lunch there are such favorites as rouladen, a rolled veal, seasoned with spices and filled with ham, onions and pickles, schnitzels and sausage combinations. All entrees are served with soup or salad, German bread and a choice of potato. The dinner menu is extensive, with a full page of schnitzels, several rouladen dishes, combination plates and other German favorites. For those who prefer American food, there is also a tempting array of steaks, seafood, salads and sandwiches.

After dinner on Fridays and Saturdays, there is live 50s and 60s music upstairs for those who like to dance, or just listen. The Bavarian is the "Best Choice" in Tacoma for authentic, finely prepared German meals in pleasant and relaxing surroundings.

(See special invitation in the Appendix.)

THE CLIFF HOUSE
6300 Marine View Drive
Tacoma, WA 98422
Tel. (206) 927-0400

Hrs:	Dinner	Mon. - Thu.	5:00 p.m. - 10:00 p.m.
		Fri. - Sat.	5:00 p.m. - 11:00 p.m.
		Sunday	3:00 p.m. - 8:30 p.m.
	Lunch	Mon. - Fri.	11:30 a.m. - 2:00 p.m.
	Brunch	Sunday	10:00 a.m. - 2:00 p.m.

One of the most breath taking views of Puget Sound, Mt. Rainier and Mt. Saint Helens awaits you in the handsome dining room of the Cliff House.

The restaurant is handsomely appointed in Northwest Indian art and bespeaks the extensive renovation it underwent a few years ago. Downstairs you'll enjoy a comfortable lounge featuring a piano bar and small dance floor. Luncheon diners often enjoy light entrees such as, shrimp and crab rarebit, cold poached salmon or a fritata omelette. The dinner menu highlights include fresh Northwest fare from steaks to seafood. Popular at Cliff House is the house version of cioppino filled with prawns, lobsters, scallops, salmon, halibut, crab, and clams simmered in wine, garlic and tomatos - a fine kettle of fish.

Both the food and the scenery at Cliff House are enough to take your breath away.

ENGINE HOUSE #9
611 N Pine
Tacoma, WA 98406
Tel. (206) 272-3435
Hrs: Mon. - Sun. 11:00 a.m. - 2:00 a.m.
Credit cards not accepted, checks okay.

Engine House #9 was built in 1907 and remained an active firehouse until 1965. It was renovated in the early 1970's and has been a popular tavern and eatery ever since. Owners Dusty Trail and John Farrell's goal was to offer fabulous food, a conversational environment, quantity and quality at a reasonable price and they have succeeded admirably.

There are daily soups and specials, such as mushroom barley soup and an Irish French dip, clam chowder and grilled oysters, turkey Creole soup and linguini to name only a few. Their soft taco is huge with your choice of meat, lettuce, tomato, and loads of guacamole. The Caesar salad is served with a secret dressing and is excellent. For something a little different try bangers and onions - English style sausages smothered in fried onions and served with hot mustard. Be sure to leave room for dessert, whatever your meal selection. The chocolate mousse and cheesecake are delicious.

Engine House #9 has one of the best selections of beer in the Pacific Northwest, with beers from around the world featured. They also have a very nice selection of wines. The atmosphere of this neighborhood establishment is casual and friendly and towards evening it becomes just plain fun! It is a tavern eatery, so keep in mind you must be twenty-one to enter.

FUJIYA, 1125 Court "C", Tacoma, Washington. Traditional Japanese bill-of-fare with excellent sushi here. Visa and MasterCard accepted. Open for lunch and dinner, closed Sundays.

THE GOURMET PANTRY
110 Tacoma Avenue N
Tacoma WA 98403
Tel. (206) 627-2213
Hrs: Mon. - Fri.   9:00 a.m. - 8:30 p.m.
          Saturday   9:00 a.m. - 6:00 p.m.
Closed major holidays.
Visa, MasterCard and AMEX are accepted.

As a combination restaurant, deli and kitchen shop, the Gourmet Pantry wears many hats and handles. Owners Max and Evelyn Burton purchased the Pantry in 1983 from Jeff Smith, otherwise known as television's "Frugal Gourmet."

At lunch and dinner you'll enjoy a variety of homemade soups, as well as hearty sandwiches. Desserts such as carrot cake, four layer cheese cake and Black Forest torte are superb. The take out deli is the perfect place to come for the makings of a picnic. The international deli section has a variety of delectable delights such as French cheeses, English marmalade, and Danish cookies, jams and jellies. The kitchen shop is filled with quality functional gadgets. There's a great selection of glasses, pots, pan s and copperware.

Because there's so much that's so different, the Gourmet Pantry defies all labels.

GRAZIE CAFE
2301 N 30th
Tacoma WA 98402
Tel. (206) 627-0231
Hrs: Mon. - Thu.   11:30 a.m. - 10:00 p.m.
　　　Fri. - Sat.　　10:30 a.m. - 11:00 p.m.
　　　Sunday　　　9:30 a.m. - 9:00 p.m.
Visa, MasterCard and AMEX are accepted.

Champagne taste at reasonable prices. That's the key word at Grazie. It has only been since January 1986 that Robin Wong has taken over Grazie. Since them he has turned what was already a popular restaurant into one where the tables are really in demand, the reason being is the quality of the mostly Italian food here.

A 19th Century Victorian apartment building overlooking the water in Old Town Tacoma houses this tastefully decorated restaurant filled with antiques. The buffet features an elaborate spread of fifteen to twenty entrees including salads, fruit trays, meat trays and pasta. Look for the special dinner entrees, such as tomato based fetucinni or rolled scallops and veal stuffed with black currants and pine nuts.

Stop in on Saturdays for the Champagne luncheon buffet. Or enjoy your lunch with something from the wine list. When in Old Town, be on the lookout for the Victorian overlooking the water.

HARBOR LIGHTS RESTAURANT
2761 Ruston Way
Tacoma, WA 98402
Tel. (206) 752-8600
Hrs: Mon.-Thu.　11:00 a.m. -12:00 midnight
　　　Friday　　　11:00 a.m. - 1:00 a.m.
　　　Saturday　　12:00 noon - 1:00 a.m.
　　　Sunday　　　2:00 p.m. - 9:00 p.m.
Closed major holidays.
Visa, MasterCard and AMEX are accepted.

A family that has operated the same restaurant since 1919 knows what food stands the test of time.

La Moyne Hreha is a third generation family owner of a restaurant that features consistently good food instead of what is trendy. For lunch you can enjoy ample servings from the charcoal broiler, including steaks, veal and French dips. Check out the numerous seafood entrees, salads and sandwiches. At dinner time treat yourself to steamed clams, all four pounds of them. The extensive offering of seafood specialties include lobster thermidor, silver smelt and oyster dishes.

For quality that you can count on from one generation to the next, drop in at Harbor Lights Restaurant.

HAWTHORNE HOUSE, 410 E. 26th Street, Tacoma, Washington. Hawthorne House, one of the early structures in Tacoma, has been converted into a delightful restaurant and a country gift shop. Open 10 a.m. to 6 p.m. daily.

JUDICIAL ANNEX RESTAURANT, 311 South Eleventh Street, Tacoma, Washington. A casual restaurant with homemade soups, sandwiches, daily specials and a soda fountain. Open 8 a.m. - 6 p.m. weekdays. Visa and MasterCard accepted.

LIEU'S, 14102 Pacific Avenue, Tacoma, Washington. Cantonese and Mandarin cuisine and a casual atmosphere. Lunch and dinner. Closed Mondays. No credit cards, please.

THE LOBSTER SHOP SOUTH
4013 Ruston Way
Tacoma, WA 98402
Tel. (206) 759-2165

Hrs:	Lunch	Mon.-Fri.	11:30 a.m. - 2:30 p.m.
	Dinner	Mon.-Thu.	5:30 p.m. - 10:00 p.m.
		Friday	5:30 p.m. - 11:00 p.m.
		Saturday	5:00 p.m. - 11:00 p.m.
	Brunch	Sunday	9:30 a.m. - 1:00 p.m
	Dinner		4:00 p.m. - 9:00 p.m.

Visa, MasterCard AMEX, and Diner's Club cards are accepted.
and,

THE LOBSTER SHOP
6912 Soundview Drive NE
Dash Point, WA 98422
Tel. (206) 927-1513

Hrs:	Mon. - Thu.	5:30 p.m. - 10:00 p.m.
	Friday	5:30 p.m. - 11:00 p.m.
	Saturday	5:00 p.m. - 11:00 p.m.
	Sunday	4:30 p.m. - 9:30 p.m.

Visa, MasterCard AMEX accepted.

The first Lobster Shop in Dash Point transformed a little beachhouse into a quaint, warm and casual success. There is a lot of barn wood and knotty pine, it is totally unpretentious, its popularity grew so that The Lobster Shop South was opened shortly after. Although The Lobster Shop South has a more sophisticated ambiance, with large windows, multi-level seating and an outside deck, the food is still delicious.

Lunch at Lobster Shop South features a different daily fresh sheet with six to eight items. Dinner fare at both restaurants is primarily seafood from scallops to prawns. There is an excellent wine selection. Sundays at the Shop South are a treat with a buffet brunch which includes everything from traditional breakfast to smoked salmon, chicken Divan, oysters Rockefeller to homemade pastries.

Simplicity and consistency make The Lobster Shops a sure bet and a "Best Choice."

Pierce County

STANLEY AND SEAFORT'S SALOON AND GRILL
115 E 34th Street
Tacoma, WA 98404
Tel. (206) 473-7300
Hrs: Dinner   Mon. - Fri.   4:30 p.m. -11:00 p.m.
                    Sat. - Sun.   5:00 p.m. - 9:00 p.m.
     Lunch   Mon. - Fri.   11:00 a.m. - 2:00 p.m.
Visa, MasterCard and AMEX are accepted.

Feast your eyes on the view from the picture windows where you can scope out the city, land and harbor below. While you're at it, enjoy the fine dining that Stanley and Seafort's Saloon and Grill offer.

The lunch menu provides four fresh fish entrees daily and they always offer fresh salmon, sometimes flown in from Norway and New Zealand. Dinner focuses on fresh Northwest seafoods, but the steaks are about the best this country has to offer. It's Midwest beef, locker aged twenty-eight days and never frozen. For something with some zing to it try the charcoal-grilled breast of chicken Cajun style.

Step in this dining room, or step out on the deck; with this kind of view and this kind of food, you'll see why this is a "Best Choice" restaurant in Tacoma.

TOWRY'S Le SNACK CAFE ESPRESSO
322 Tacoma Avenue South
Tacoma, WA 98402
Tel. (206) 272-5937
Hrs: Tues. - Fri.   7:00 a.m. - 2:30 p.m.
                          Lunch starts at 11:00 a.m.
      Sat. - Sun.   8:00 a.m. - 2:30 p.m.
      Breakfast and Brunch all day.

This small, unpretentious eatery is a wonderful discovery. Towry's Le Snack Cafe Espresso is a European, bistro-style cafe owned and operated by Marcy and Dale Towry. Dale was trained in classic European style cooking and has been a cooking institution in the Northwest for over twenty years.

The Towrys purchased Le Snack in 1986; they totally renovated the small kitchen area and that enabled them to increase the selection of items offered.

Breakfast at Le Snack is not boring...they offer bacon and eggs, but use your flair for adventure and order one of the international egg dishes like: peasant potato pie, a delectable baked egg dish filled with bacon, onions, peppers, potatoes and Swiss cheese. Or, try Mititei, a Romanian, skinless sausage prepared by "LeChef". European griddle fare includes Pfannkuchen, a German oven-baked pancake, or, Eierkuchen, German egg cakes. Both dishes are served with fruit and whipped cream and are fantastic!

The brunch menu offers eggs Florentine or Italian birdsnest, a pasta cooked *al dente*, then made into a nest to hold the two poached eggs and Italian sausage. A fine marinara sauce with fresh grated parmesan then tops this creation.

Mediterranean cooking with a hint of Eastern Europe is highlighted on the luncheon menu. The house soup is Slovak Sauerkraut. Don't frown, it is a very popular dish. Try the Turos Csusza, a Hungarian dish of noodles tossed with bacon, green onions and cottage cheese. The chicken Grecque is Dale's own recipe of chicken breast meat sauteed with olives, onions, mushrooms and feta cheese and served with a rice pilaf.

For the lighter appetite, there are homemade soups and salads. Be sure to check the chalkboard for the daily specials. You will blow your diet completely when the pastry tray passes by...New York baked cheese cake, chocolate and lemon tortes, with a cup of espresso or Viennese coffee will complete your dining experience at Le Snack.

To reach this restaurant, take the city center exit off of I-5 and head north into downtown Tacoma to 11th Street. Turn left on 11th and watch for Tacoma Avenue South. A right turn on Tacoma Avenue to 4th and Tacoma. You're there. There's plenty of parking at the rear of the cafe.

Theater

PANTAGES CENTRE, 901 Broadway, Tacoma, Washington. A restored 1918 opera with live professional theater, dance and music. Free tours on Thursday from 1 - 3 p.m. Call 206 591-5894 for ticket information.

Tours

TACOMA HARBOR TOURS, 535 Dock Street, Tacoma, Washington. Puget Sound sightseeing and dinner cruises and charters.

SAN JUAN COUNTY

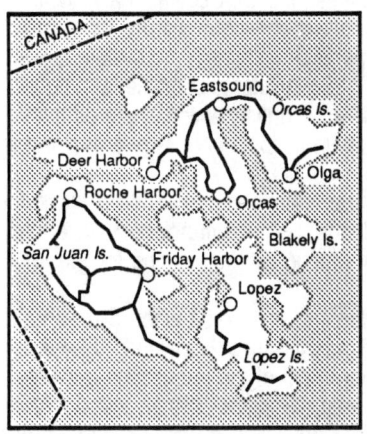

The rocky shores of these islands tell stories like a time warp. Fossilized remains of a fish which existed eighty million years ago have come from little Skipjack Island on Boundary Pass, almost in Canada. Washington State Ferries call daily at Lopez, Shaw, Orcas and San Juan Islands, but in fact this county contains 172 islands rated as habitable. Some are little more than a campsite amid firs and cedars, others have abandoned farmsteads where one can only speculate on the settler's story. Only ten islands, according to local residents, are actually inhabited on a year around basis. About 8,900 residents now inhabit the islands, a gain of 1,000 since the census of 1980.

Bicycle tour groups pedal flat roads, whiz down small hills and look up to 2,454-foot-high Mount Constitution on Orcas Island, a geologic testimony that these islands are tops of large chunks of the earth's crust, wrenched by movement on a fault beneath the surface. Limestone exposed on San Juan Island was developed in shallow water during recent times, while rocks on down the shoreline came from a deep ocean floor and show perhaps 200 million years of aging. Lopez Island, too, has rocks from an old ocean floor, although about fifty million years younger than those on San Juan. Beneath this island group, still pushing upward, is the plate connected to Vancouver Island.

This group of islands on the international border is a magnet for tourists and summer residents. The county has 375 miles of shoreline on saltwater as its main attraction. Trips to the outside world for the most part are by ferry boats plying routes between Vancouver Island and Anacortes on an island jutting out into the straits south of Bellingham. Rich in food, the fast-moving tidal currents support a menagerie of marine life. Most of the islands are heavily wooded. In the vast rain shadow of the Olympic Mountains to the south west and Vancouver Island to the north west the islands get about twenty-seven inches of rain a year. Vegetation tends toward madrone and oak mixed with firs rather than the Sitka Spruce, hemlock and fir of Washington's coastal forests.

Temperate weather makes the islands a pleasant place to live. Summer days are between seventy and ninety degrees, the nights in the fifties. Winter lows in January, the coolest month, are close to freezing. Constant temperature of the sea water moderates extremes. What rain hits here comes between November and April. The wettest months are December and January when about four and a half inches of rain falls each month. Farms, for the most part, are little better than subsistence operations although the climate is well-suited for orchards and specialty crops. Many residents combine farming with commercial fishing or a small business in an economy which is geared to take care of the waves of tourists debarking with almost every ferry arrival in the summer. The off-season is very slow.

The little bays and harbors on the main islands provide a place for boats to load for trips to the smaller islands. Some home owners have large boats or float planes which enable commuting without waiting for the inter-island ferry service.

Discovery of the island group dates to the 1790s when Spanish and English ships probed the Sound and waters off Vancouver Island. It fell to the 1841 American Wilkes expedition to map most of the larger land masses in what amounts to just 179 square miles of area. The homey names such as Yellow Island (off Shaw in San Juan Passage), Center Island (with an air strip and little else in Lopez Sound), or Dot Rock (a marine preserve on Decatur Island's east shore) indicate that settlers had to go about placing their own names on many little land masses as they took the islands from the Indians in a slow colonization that began in the late 1840s.

Looking down on the county from an airplane flying over Puget Sound from the south, you would see a large island on the left at the Canadian border marked by Haro Channel. San Juan Island has about one-third of its interior area under cultivation, with the tiny town of Friday Harbor tucked away on the north side in the arm of a forested point of land. Lopez Island, its roads for the most part on a north-south grid, would be dead ahead, a combination of timber, pastures and cultivated lands on a rather narrow axis. Looming beyond both San Juan and Lopes is the large mass of Orcas, a "U" shaped island with a long sound between its arms and Mount Constitution towering in the mountainous center of the eastern-most arm. Shaw, a small blob between Orcas and the two southern islands, is the smallest of the main group reached by public ferry service. Lesser islands ring the group on the north and pop up between passages creating the idea that you are seeing tops of a broken land now washed by the sea.

ATTRACTIONS

Shaw Island, with its little ferry dock on Harney Channel just a few hundred yards from Orcas, has eleven miles of public roads but is mostly private vacation homes. Residents discourage sightseers. About 150 people live on the island year around. The ferry concession and store are operated by a group of Franciscan nuns. There is only one public place to spend the night on Shaw, a county park on the island's south shore with few tent spaces.

There are ten marine parks in the entire island group. Information on each is available by calling 468-2251 on Lopez where the state maintains a coordination point for parks, or 378-2044 on San Juan. Some of these boat parks rate special mention:

Stuart Island Marine Park, ten miles northwest of Friday Harbor is the largest, and has one of the most sheltered harbors for private boats touring the region. There are some private farms and a lighthouse station on the western end of the island. A log school house, built around the turn of the century, stands next to the modern school serving the resident families.

In the Strait of Georgia off the east shore of Orcas is the state-owned **Clark Island**. This skinny island, with a group of rocks called The Sisters at its south tip, is a state marine park accessible by boat only. There are eight primitive camp sites with no water. Beautiful private beaches, spectacular views.

James Island State Park, another primitive camp area with thirteen tent sites, is east of Decatur Island on Rosario Strait. Besides a fine beach, the timbered hill which rises 272-feet above sea level provides hikers a view of ships passing the straits. Accessible by boat only.

One of the most popular small-boat camping spots in the county is **Jones Island** off the southwest tip of Orcas where the campground is almost on the beach. This state park island can be a base from which San Juan, Orcas and other larger islands are reached.

Several of the smaller islands have fascinating stories out of the past. **Sinclair Island**, a flat one on the right as the ferry heads out from Anacortes, was home-base for Larry Kelly, said to be a smuggler of the 1890s. His operation ran undocumented Chinese into the United States from Canada. Landing on private islands is still frowned on today. Many uninhabited islands are designated wildlife refuges where disturbing habitat could lead to a citation. Electrical power is supplied between many islands by undersea cables. Charts show the crossings and large white signs on shore mark them so boats can stay clear of danger when anchoring. Marinas have detailed charts for boaters, along with warnings on the narrow passages where tidal runoffs can be dangerous to small craft.

For further information, contact the **San Juan Island Chamber of Commerce**, 125 Spring Street, Friday Harbor WA 98250.

Lopez Island

San Juan residents nick name Lopez "the friendly island," and advise tourists to wave and smile a hello as they tour the place. Flat and full of many farms, this has become a favorite place for the growing number of bicycle tours which ride the ferries, explore by bicycle and camp along the way. The full-time population is about 1,400, many of them connected with farming operations. Sheep and other livestock are the primary output of the few farms.

Attractions

There is a mile of beach on **Spencer Spit**, a newly-developed state park on the east shore of the island. Clamming is said to be good most of the year, the beach shallow enough for wading, and the fishing good nearby. Twenty-eight developed campsites. Call for reservations during the summer season, 468-2251.

Bicycle tours of the island halt at the tiny **Agate Beach Park**, a day use area on the southern tip of the island. Close to the ferry on the north end is **Odlin Park**, operated by San Juan County, which has camp and picnic sites. Reservations are recommended for summer campers. Telephone 468-2217.

Accommodations

MAREAN'S BLUE FJORD CABINS
Route 1
Box 1450
Lopez Island, WA 98261
Tel. (206) 468-2749
No credit cards are accepted.
Personal checks are welcomed.

For those who seek seclusion in unspoiled surroundings, Marean's Blue Fjord Cabins offers a lovely, private respite. The Nordic chalet style dwellings are nestled among sixteen acres of cedar and fir groves which end at a "mini-fjord" known as Jasper Bay.

The cedar log construction and open beam ceilings of the gracious cabins fit naturally into the otherwise undisturbed setting, and the largest chalet affords a water view from living room or deck. All of the charming accommodations have kitchens, carpeting, television, radio and splendid forest views.

Other visitors to Blue Fjord include pods of Orca whales in Lopez Sound, bald eagles, sea otters and an array of water birds. A short walk to the rock and gravel beach places you in a quiet world of sea creatures, and a stroll along the logging roads may reveal a passing deer or other forest creature. Several good restaurants are on the island if you care to dine out. A visit within these unspoiled surroundings in such comfort will leave you feeling very spoiled indeed!

Campsite

HUMMEL HAVEN BICYCLE CAMP, Route Two, Box 3940, Lopez, Washington. A great home base from which to explore Lopez Island by bicycle. Several spacious and secluded campsites are nestled among forty acres of alder and cedar. Call for details about other amenities.

Restaurant

MACKAYE HARBOR INN, Route 1, Box 1940, Lopez Island, Washington. On the shore of beautiful MacKaye Harbor, this elegant inn has five rooms, superb breakfasts, and a fine restaurant (call for seasonal hours).

San Juan County

Orcas Island

The largest, and topographically the most interesting of the San Juan Islands, Orcas is able to swallow its thousands of visitors into resorts, campgrounds and parks so few feel crowded. There are 2,560 full-time residents on the island, many living in the quaint community of Eastsound. It is located at the island's narrowest point. Part of the beach and waters just east of the town are a commercial oyster bed. Westsound, a community west of the road coming north from the ferry landing, has most of the island's commercial fishing fleet. From the Victorian hotel building above the ferry landing, recently restored and operating year around, to the smallest community at the end of a county road, you will find old buildings still in use. Eastsound has many homes of note.

Orcas was not settled until 1859 when Hudson Bay Company detailed four hunters to live here and shoot deer for meat consumed at the large Victoria trading post. Deer Harbor was their home port. Farmers drifted to the island in later years, concentrating in the Crow Valley. Tree fruit became an export crop in the 1900s, but the market has been lost. Some berries grown here are still significant cash crops in off-island trade.

Attractions

Rosario Estates Resort, on the east shore of East Sound, was created as the private estate of Robert Moran. A shipbuilder, and one-time mayor of Seattle, Moran had a large stone house built in 1910 as his second home. The place uses ship's hardware for window fasteners, door pulls and cabinets, and sports a pipe organ in the mezzanine overlooking the main room. The restaurant and Vista Lounge give the public an opportunity to see much of Moran's building. Telephone 376-2222.

Moran State Park and Mount Constitution are one of the most-visited locations in the islands. The 3,325-acre park was given to the state by Robert Moran in 1921. Pinkish lava on Mount Constitution leaves no doubt of the volcanic past for this remnant of the North Cascades. A fifty-two foot high lookout tower atop the peak stands next to the Bellingham television station's transmitter tower. The view from here is unmatched in the state. The Civilian Conservation Corps built much of Moran's campgrounds and picnic areas in a rustic style of rock masonry and timber frames. Freshwater lakes provide swimming which is often warmer than the saltwater beaches, and boats can be rented for fishing. There are over 130 developed camp sites here.

West Beach Resort has the only public campground on the west shore of Orcas. There is a grassy campground for tents and recreation vehicles, moorage for boats, a small store and boat rentals.

Sucia Island State Park, in the island group about three miles due north of Orcas, is one of the state's boats-only parks which is easily accessible for day use in rental craft from Orcas. There are exceptional small harbors here for anchoring larger boats, nineteen tent sites ashore--carry your own water--and several rock formations of interest to geologists.

For information, contact **Orcas Island Chamber of Commerce,** Box 252, Eastsound WA 98245. Telephone 376-2273.

Deer Harbor

Orcas was not settled until 1859 when Hudson Bay Company detailed four hunters to live here and shoot deer for meat consumed at the large Victoria trading post. Deer Harbor was their home port. The tiny village of modern times has a sheltered harbor, and comes with Fawn Island as part of its bay.

Accommodations and Restaurant

DEER HARBOR, P. O. Box 142, Deer Harbor, Orcas Island, Washington. A lovely resort with comfortable cabins, lots of moorage, fuel and supplies, gift shop, restaurant, grocery store, laundry, indoor pool and hot tubs.

Eastsound

The collection of small shops and homes with the largest concentration of permanent residents is Eastsound, on East Sound, the long tongue of water reaching up into the mid-section of the land mass. This is the island's narrowest point. Part of the beach and waters just east of the town are a commercial oyster bed.

Attractions

Orcas Theater and Community Center, North Beach Road in Eastsound, presents performing arts all year. Call 376-5345 or 376-4873.

San Juan County

A clapboard-sided building on the Horseshoe Highway houses **Darvill's Rare Print Shop**. Fred Darvill moved the shop to his summer home in Eastsound in 1942, bringing with him a massive collection of prints from the past 200 years. The shop changed hands in 1971 and began year around operation in 1973. Open Monday through Saturday from 10:00 a.m. to 5:30 p.m. Telephone 376-2351.

Accommodations

BEACH HAVEN RESORT
Route 1 Box 12
Eastsound, WA 98245
Tel. (206) 376-2288
No credit cards. Personal checks are accepted.

The quiet relaxation and scenic grandeur of Beach Haven Resort has guests returning year after year to leisurely stroll the gentle slope of a large private pebble beach, perhaps spot a soaring bald eagle or passing Orca whale, or watch a seagull outlined against a fiery sunset.

Beach Haven has a dozen log cabins complete with kitchens and baths with showers, and range from one to three bedroom units plus a four bedroom, two bath vacation home. All are on the beach and most have woodburning stoves (firewood is free). Rowboats and buoys are available for rent and outstanding fishing is an easy boating distance away. There's good crabbing off the beach, horseshoe pits and a playground nearby. Cabins or lodge apartments may be rented (with a two day minimum) by the day or week.

For those with the courage to holiday without TVs and telephones, the off season is the premium time for Island peace and tranquility. The rates change to include a third night free with a two night reservation from October to April, excluding public holiday periods. Beach Haven Resort - escape from your world and enter theirs.

TURTLEBACK FARM INN, Route One, Box 650, Eastsound Washington. Meticulously restored and expanded, this turn-of-the-century farmhouse is set on eight acres in Orcas Island's beautiful Crow Valley. Seven guest rooms, private baths, charming parlor, dining room, and spacious deck.

Delicatessen

MURPHY'S CAFE AND DELI
P.O. Box 109
Post Office Building
Eastsound, WA 98245
Tel. (206) 376-2008
Hrs: Mon. - Sat. 9:00 a.m. - 4:00 p.m.
VISA, MasterCard, and personal checks (with proper ID) are accepted.

Discover a hidden treasure in Murphy's Cafe and Deli where the finding is well worth the search. Owner Frank Murphy has been cooking for over thirty years, the last twenty on Orcas Island.

Epicurean sleuths will divine three or four excellent homemade soups and chowders at Murphy's, including specialties such as crab bisque, tomato bisque and clam chowders with tantalizing "extras" such as crab. Very generous sandwiches can be purchased half or whole and contain only the best and freshest ingredients. You'll miss a good clue if you skip over Frank's Reuben, hot pastrami or cheddar crab melt! Entrees change daily and come with a salad bar. Murphy's also boasts Orcas Islands finest buffet bar, acclaimed by locals and visitors alike. Imported and domestic beers and wines are available. Complete your meal by letting your sweet-tooth radar-in to some homemade pie or pastries.

Have your next detective convention at Murphy's in a private banquet room that seats thirty-six and is available anytime but Wednesdays. It's no mystery to the bicyclists and bikers where to find a good box lunch to take to other areas of the island! Murphy's Cafe! Elementary my dear, elementary.

Resorts

ROSARIO RESORT AND SPA
Eastsound
Eastsound, WA 98254
Tel. (206) 376-2222
All major credit cards are accepted.

Sometimes they cruise in on yacht, and sometimes they drop in by sea plane and a few peddle in on bicycles. But it all started with a Seattle ship builder whose search for a place to rebuild his health came to a close at Rosario.

The mansion that Robert Moran built overlooking Cascade Bay has become a resort and spa offering today's visitors a chance to revitalize themselves in luxury and healthy living. Spa facilities include state of the art exercise equipment, indoor pool, massage cabanas and a salon featuring ocean body wraps, facials, salt glows, hair styling and many other pampering services rom which to choose. Most of the graciously appointed rooms overlook the panorama of blue water, green forests and distant islands. Fine dining, accompanied by grand piano music, is yours in the ornate Orcas Room. The Friday seafood buffet and Sunday Champagne brunch are renowned.

By the way, shipbuilder Moran's efforts paid off. He lived many years after building Rosario, eventually leaving behind a resort where others could live it up.

SMUGGLER'S VILLA RESORT
P. O. Box 79
Eastsound, WA 98245
Tel. (206) 376-2297
Visa and MasterCard are accepted.

Looking for a quiet hideout? Try Smuggler's Villa. Located on the north shore of Orcas Island, Smuggler's Villa offers the best of both worlds for those seeking a quiet hideaway with plenty of activities.

All of the condominiums at Smuggler's Villa are two bedroom units and are furnished with woodstoves, color TV, microwave ovens, washers, dryers and dishwashers. There are tennis, basketball and volleyball courts, an outdoor swimming pool and indoor sauna and hot tub on the premises. The private gravel beach is a fine spot for beachcombing and clamming. If you come by boat, moorage is right near your patio door. Smuggler's is next to the airport and only a mile away from town.

Conference facilities are also available, making Smuggler's Villa Resort a "Best Choice" for a fun hideaway in Washington.

Restaurant

LA FAMIGLIA RISTORANTE
Prune Alley and "A" Street
Eastsound, WA 98245
Tel. (206) 376-2335
Hrs: Mon. - Sun.   11:30 a.m.-2:30 p.m.
                   5:00 p.m.-9:00 p.m.
Closed Sunday during winter season.
Visa, MasterCard, Discover and AMEX are accepted.

When you live on an island, it's not easy to make due with what's on hand, but Raymond and Patty Brogi, have gone out of their way to feature a menu based upon the food of the waters and land near by.

La Famiglia started out eleven years ago as a small pizzeria, it has since evolved into a delightful Italian restaurant popular with Orcas Island natives and visitors alike. While much of their raw materials are local, the menu has Italian favorites such as chicken Cacciatore, Scallopine, Canelloni and Calzoni's. There is no shortage of vegetarian meals. There is also a wide selection of seafood, and hearty New York steaks. Cocktails are served, as are select coffees and the cheesecake is the most popular dessert.

So whether you want something with a strong Italian accent, or fresh from the waters of the Puget Sound, learn to pronounce "La Famiglia" and you'll get what you please.

Olga

Olga, a small village on Buck Bay, is an art colony with a collective handling the artists' marketing. Craftspeople work in several small cabins of what was once a resort. There is a store and deli, and a small public beach.

Attractions

Obstruction Pass State Park is a short drive beyond Olga. The pebbled beach is isolated, campsites are about a half-mile hike from the auto parking area.

Art Gallery

ORCAS ISLAND ARTWORKS AND CAFE OLGA, Star Route Box 155, Olga, Washington. A superb gallery devoted to island artists whose work includes fine art, functional art, wearable art, and special guest shows. Adjoining cafe offers home cooking with an international flair.

Restaurant

CAFE OLGA, Star Route, Box 155, Olga, WA. Home cooking with an international touch.

Orcas

A small village, served by the ferry service, nestled amidst hilly, forested terrain.

Attractions

For the acclaimed "finest view" in the Pacific Northwest, journey to the top of **Mount Constitution**. At 2,500 feet it is the highest spot in the San Juan archipelago. Uninterrupted views of all of San Juan, the Canadian Gulf Islands, Vancouver Island, Mount Rainier and Mount Baker await you. The steep six mile road that leads to Mount Constitution is not recommended for trailer or RV vehicles.

Moran State Park, near Mount Constitution, has 4,934 acres, full amenity camping facilities for 148, a number of hiking trails, warm water swimming and good fishing. Wildlife, such as black-tailed deer, river otter, muskrat and raccoon can regularly be seen; especially in the evening hours. Call 376-2326 for reservations.

Accommodations

ORCAS HOTEL
P. O. BOX 155
Orcas, WA 98280
Tel. (206) 376-4300
Visa, MasterCard and AMEX are accepted.

On a rocky knoll above the ferry landing, the Orcas Hotel dominates the view as your ferry arrives on Orcas Island. This beautiful hotel, a three story Victorian resort, was built between 1900 and 1904 and was restored to mint condition in 1985.

Twelve guest rooms are furnished with a collection of antiques and new, comfortable queen sized beds. The log cabin quilts were custom stitched by Orcas quilters with the colors carried through the wallpaper and decor which makes each room unique. With the exception of three third floor rooms which have private toilets and sinks, most rooms share the six bathrooms that are separate and down the hall.

The country-style dining room serves three meals a day all year. A farm breakfast will start your day right, and dinners feature fresh seafoods and shellfish in season. There is also tender and tasty prime rib and steaks, chicken, and at least six specials every day. There is a lovely cocktail lounge and live music is provided on Sundays and other appropriate occasions. For comfortable accommodations, Orcas Hotel is your "Best Choice."

Bed and Breakfast

WOODSONG BED AND BREAKFAST
P. O. Box 32
Orcas, WA 98280
Tel. (206) 376-2340
No credit cards are accepted.
Personal checks are welcome.

A beautifully restored schoolhouse, Woodsong Bed and Breakfast sits on four acres of woods and meadows and is less than 300 yards from the water. Located only two miles from the ferry dock, Woodsong has become quite popular among bicyclists, as well as guests from around the world and across the United States.

The two spacious and bright guest rooms are furnished with comfortable country antiques and fresh flowers. A huge room features a thirteen foot ceiling, woodburning stove, corner game area and organ. There is also a sun porch with hot tub. A Continental breakfast is served during the summer, with juice, freshly baked coffee cakes, breads or muffins, fresh fruit, and coffee or tea. The winter season has an added bonus of full breakfasts such as, apple pancakes with sausage or cheese and herb omelets with biscuits and wild blackberry jam.

Serving good conversation, delicious breakfasts and pleasant relaxation...and where hospitality is the lesson plan at the old schoolhouse, it's Woodsong Bed And Breakfast!

San Juan Island

Now a peaceful place with timbered hills and the largest farms in the county, this was the scene of international tension. The treaty of 1846 set the 49th parallel as the boundary between British claims to Canada and U.S. claims to the Oregon Territory. All of Vancouver Island, which extends far south of the 49th parallel went with Canada but the treaty did not resolve the channel boundary. Britain insisted on Rosario Strait which would have put all the islands in their jurisdiction. The U.S. wanted Haro Channel west of San Juan.

The Hudson Bay Company sheep farm on San Juan Island set the stage for another battle between American squatters and the crown's interest. When a company pig was shot in 1859, the troops were called out. Historians later designated this the "pig war." Both countries put garrisons here. It was not until an 1872 international arbitration that the county's namesake island was officially American territory.

The fuss involved an island fifteen miles long, seven miles across at its widest point; approximately 55.4 square miles of land.

Attractions

Lime Kiln State Park, a day use area on the western shore, is a favorite spot for whale watchers and those curious about shipping in Haro Channel on the international border. High grade lime was refined here for making Portland cement, and shipped by water in large quantities during earlier years before railroads made other quarries more economical for mining. On West Side Road, the park includes a lighthouse built in the 1880s.

English Camp, on West Valley Road, has a blockhouse and several restored buildings giving an idea of life here between 1860 and 1872 for the English garrison which came in response to the pig war and remained until the international arbitration was complete. Buildings are open daily from 9:00 a.m.

to 6:00 p.m. during the summer. National Park Service interpretive materials are available to aid in viewing this site.

American Camp, at the island's south end, has a partially-restored fort in what is an open grassland often hopping with rabbits that are the bane of island farmers. An exhibit center dealing with the boundary dispute is in American Camp, open daily from 8:00 a.m. to 4:30 p.m. One of the best beaches on the island is part of this park. Take Cattle Point Road south to reach the historic site and the beach. The visitor information center for both camps is in Friday Harbor, co-located with the county Chamber of Commerce office at 125 Spring Street. Telephone 378-2240.

Hotel de Haro at Roche Harbor was built in 1886 as a hotel for guests of the Roche Harbor Lime Company. The wood-frame three-story building looks like it came from a resort of another era.

The Mausoleum, a monument to the family of John S. McMillan of the lime company, is located in the woods not too far off. There is an interpretive pamphlet on symbols used in The Mausoleum which is available at the hotel desk.

San Juan County Park on Small Pox Bay provides campsites on the west shore. Popular with scuba divers and bicyclists, summer campers may want to arrive early or be ready to set up in close quarters in overflow areas.

Six miles west of Friday Harbor is a private campground called **Lakedale** on a small lake with trout, boats and swimming. There is a small store. The operators do not take reservations.

For information, contact the **San Juan Island Chamber of Commerce**, Box 98, Friday Harbor WA 98250.

San Juan Island

Friday Harbor

Friday Harbor, a village of 1,200 people living around a small bay of the same name, has most of its homes on a flat above the docks. The small business district is on the slope in between. The community is named for Friday, an Hawaiian herdsman who ran the Hudson Bay flock in the time of the boundary dispute. This is the county seat for San Juan County

Attractions

The Whale Museum, 62 First Street North, cooperates with charter boat skippers in tracking whales moving among all islands. Three pods, totaling seventy-seven killer or orca whales, are part of the resident population. Grey whales at times migrate close to shore for feeding. The Museum is open daily from 10:00 a.m. to 5:00 p.m. from Memorial Day through September. From October through May, open Wednesday through Monday, 11:00 a.m. to 4:00 p.m. Telephone 378-4710.

University of Washington **Friday Harbor Laboratories**, 620 University Road, has a long, squat laboratory building overlooking the ferry docks. Marine research in a 464-acre preserve has been carried out here since 1904. Open Wednesday and Saturday from 2:00 p.m. to 4:00 p.m. during the summer.

San Juan County Historical Museum is located on Price Street near Spring Street in Friday Harbor. Ask at the visitor information center about current schedules for the museum.

For further information, contact the **San Juan Island Chamber of Commerce**, 125 Spring Street, Friday Harbor WA 98250.

Accommodations

ELITE HOTEL, P. O. Box 151, Friday Harbor, WA. Clean, dormitory accommodations. Located in the heart of Friday Harbor, a stones throw from the ferry, an excellent site for travelers on a strict budget.

FRIDAY HARBOR MOTOR INN
410 Spring Street
P.O. Box 962
Friday Harbor, WA 98250
Tel. (206) 378-4351
      (800) 752-5752
All major credit cards are accepted.

Located in the heart of Friday Harbor, capitol city of the San Juan Islands, is the Friday Harbor Motor Inn. Offering seventy-two units, some with kitchen facilities, the Friday Harbor Motor Inn is a perfect retreat destination or stop over point on your tour of North America's great Inland Sea area.

Along with its island ambiance, the inn offers most of the amenities of the city, such as remote control color cable television and direct dial telephones in every room. The Friday Harbor Motor Inn also boasts a fine staff, starting with your hosts Tom and Donna Nawrocki. Their personalized service begins with pickup at the ferry dock a few block away or at the airport just a half mile distant. Speaking of transportation, the inn also has a big, red double decker English Country bus that leisurely travels the backroads of the island with loads of smiling tourists discovering the secrets of the interior and learning about the wealth of history that surrounds this island paradise.

Another special feature at Friday Harbor Motor Inn is the comfortable meeting space for board meetings, company retreats, business conferences and social gatherings. There is also complete catering service available for these events. Well, there you have it, the perfect spot for just about any occasion. Friday Harbor Motor Inn. Make them a part of your delightful visits to San Juan Island.

ISLAND LODGE AT FRIDAY HARBOR
1016 Guard Street
Friday Harbor, WA 98250
Tel. (206) 378-2000
Visa and MasterCard are accepted.

Don't forget to bring some bread for the ducks who live in the two ponds at Island Lodge. The ducks regularly adopt the guests and expect a token of "edible" respect in return. Then, after watching a spectacular sunset as it paints the islands in the sea, end your day at the Island Lodge with a relaxing soak in a hot tub, followed by a refreshing night snuggled under a down comforter.

Comfort, pleasure and convenience mark the Island Lodge. Located half a mile from the ferry landing, the lodge is far enough away to enjoy real solitude, but close enough to afford all that Friday Harbor has to offer. Each of the twenty rooms has been redesigned for your comfort. All include beautiful silk flower arrangements and singular artwork by local artists, in association with the Sunshine Gallery. There is nothing "institutionalized" about the Island Lodge.

Owners Jim and Nancy Smith call it "an ecological Disneyland," citing the great crabbing, fishing, eagles, Orca whales, sea otters, and much more that is available for your enjoyment...and all without a carnival atmosphere!

San Juan County

Bed and Breakfast

DUFFY HOUSE BED AND BREAKFAST
760 Pear Point Road
Friday Harbor, WA 98250
Tel. (206) 378-5604
Visa and MasterCard are accepted.

Duffy House Bed and Breakfast is nestled on a broad, sloping hillside surrounded by fruit trees, English style box vegetable gardens and a literal tapestry of flowers. The gracious Tudor home faces a fantastic view of Griffin Bay and the Olympic Mountains. Built in 1926 by skilled shipwrights, the Duffy House was recently restored to its original splendor by innkeeper Toddy Beeston with help from longtime friend Gary Bryant. Toddy was raised in Duffy House and, after a career in the "people business," decided to open a bed and breakfast in order to share her home and hospitality with others.

Located a short drive from downtown Friday Harbor, Duffy House offers the serenity and beauty of San Juan Island. Couple that with a spectacular view of pleasure craft navigating Griffin Bay on their way to Friday Harbor, the Northern San Juan Islands and the snow capped Olympic Mountains and you have part of the charm of Duffy House. With 600 feet of waterfront, guest have the opportunity to explore tide pools and enjoy the activities of water birds and an occasional sea lion.

Toddy's gracious hospitality, the amenities of the four guest rooms, beautifully restored in 1920s decor with down quilts and pillows on the beds, and her European style breakfasts has resulted in repeat guests. Her table setting is so lovely guests frequently take pictures. Breakfast consists of boiled eggs in egg cups, thin sliced smoked turkey, ham or salami, an assortment of cheeses or quiche, fresh fruit plate, banana bread, coffee cake or muffins, several juices, coffee and tea.

Visit Toddy at the Duffy House for a serene and restful experience. Check the progress of the vegetable garden, watch the local eagles and keep an eye out for the deer who regularly prune Toddy's shrubbery and flowers. Duffy House is a "Best Choice" you'll not want to miss!

OLYMPIC LIGHTS B & B, 4531 A Cattlepoint Road, Friday Harbor, WA. A wondrous getaway in a bright and beautifully furnished home overlooking the Straits of Juan de Fuca and the Olympic Mountain range. A great place to relax.

SAN JUAN INN BED AND BREAKFAST
50 Spring Street
Friday Harbor, WA 98250
Tel. (206) 378-2070
Visa and MasterCard are accepted.

The San Juan Inn was constructed in 1873 and has been serving guests continuously ever since. The Inn was purchased by Norm and Joan Schwinge in 1979, they have painstakingly restored the building to reflect its original nostalgic period, and furnished it accordingly.

Each of the ten rooms is adorned with brass or wicker beds, delicate wallpaper, lace curtains, and even handmade plump calico cat doorstops. The "Necessary Room," is a Victorian classic with a pink, claw foot tub, and a stained glass window and skylight. The parlor, an inviting room with a wood burning stove and beautiful view of the harbor, is a favorite gathering place for evening conversation and games. An old fashioned garden provides fresh roses for the rooms. There are also a Victorian settee and chairs located under an ornamental cherry tree that provides a perfect spot to read, picnic, or just relax before dinner.

A stay at the San Juan Inn Bed and Breakfast will turn back the clock to the romantic days of yesteryear with its promise of quaintness, charm and ultimate comfort.

San Juan County

For just the two of you:

	ROMANCE ON THE HIGH SEAS TOUR		
	Your "Best Choices" in lodging:		
	Island Lodge	Best friendly solitude	FriH/Accom.
	Duffy House B & B	Best serenity	FriH/B & B
	Fri. Harbor Motor Inn	Best location	FriH/Accom.
a.m.	Mojo's	Best breakfast	on Spring St.
a.m.	Wind 'n Sails	Best wind 'n sunshine sail	FriH/Nautical
	Dinnertime choices:		
p.m.	Downriggers	Best seafood delicacies	FriH/Rest.
p.m.	Gollywobbler Rest.	Best meal-on-the-deck	FriH/Rest.

Now if the whole family is along, including the kids, the same "Best Choices" hold true...just change the name to "Romancing the High Seas."

Jewelry

DAN LEVIN ORIGINALS, 50 First Street, Friday Harbor, San Juan Island, Washington. Fine jewelry designs in 14K and 18K gold by artists-goldsmiths Dan and Diane Levin.

Restaurant

DOWNRIGGERS
10 Front Street
Friday Harbor, WA 98250
Tel. (206) 378-2700
Hrs: Mon. - Sun.   11:00 a.m. - 2:00 a.m.
        Sunday Brunch   9:00 a.m. - 1:00 p.m.
All major credit cards are accepted.

While dining on the large deck on Downrigger's water side, you can enjoy the bustle of the sailboats and fishing fleet docked at Friday Marina Harbor, or watch the activity on the ferry landing just a few feet away. Water and island views, as well as the nautical decor, enhance your feeling of freedom from landlocked cares and worries.

Chef Richard Eriksen makes sure that your dining experience is just as pleasurable as the environment around you. Northwest seafood delicacies, never frozen, include Vancouver Island clams, Wescott Bay oysters, farmed on nearby San Juan Island, salmon, and bottom fish such as, cod, snapper and halibut. After enjoying any of the enticing appetizers, a generous salad bar beckons with cobb or wilted spinach salads. Beef, pasta, and game entrees enhance the menu, and the wine list includes a wide variety of Northwest wines. Top off your meal with Downrigger's specialty dessert, Banana Foster - vanilla ice cream topped with bananas sauteed in rum, banana liqueur and brown sugar.

Whether enjoying the full service lounge with big screen television or enjoying the special service and fine food in the restaurant, Downriggers' staff will only be satisfied if your experience results in your returning again and again.

GOLLYWOBBLER RESTAURANT
310 West Street
Friday Harbor, WA 98250
Tel. (206) 378-2753
Hrs: Summer		Mon. - Sun.		11:00 a.m. - 10:00 p.m
	Winter		Lunch Tue. - Sun.	11:00 a.m. - 3:00 p.m.
			Dinner Wed. - Sat.	5:00 p.m. - 9:00 p.m.
Visa, MasterCard, AMEX and Diner's Club are accepted.

The Gollywobbler Restaurant (named after the gollywobbler sail of old sailing vessels) sits on a bluff overlooking Friday Harbor Marina, the northern San Juan Islands and the Canadian Gulf Islands. This spectacular view always treats diners with the comings and goings of the fishing fleet, pleasure craft and Washington State ferries and sometimes glimpses of Orcas and Bald eagles enhance the meal! Owners Chuck and Lisa Turner have completely restored this lovely 1880s vintage house and added a modern commercial kitchen. Chuck credits chef Jim Koltai's seventeen years of experience and cooking creativity with much of the success of Gollywobbler.

A full luncheon menu is featured that includes popular sandwiches such as, Monte Cristo, seafood club, BLTAA, French Dip and soup de jour or clam chowder. The Harbor View salad with romaine lettuce, shrimp, mushrooms, tomato, Parmesan cheese, croutons with a Caesar style dressing is one of the salad choices. Fine salads and the very popular chicken Dijon, oriental medallions of beef, New York steak, chicken Marsala, pan fried oysters, scallops and more are among the dinner entrees. To complement your meal, a fine selection of Northwest wines and beers from local microbreweries are featured. Dessert poses a dilemma of choosing between the likes of chocolate decadence and homemade Marionberry pie. Sunday buffet brunch is held on the deck (weather permitting) and summer barbeques of baby back ribs are special fun.

The Gollywobbler Restaurant is a wonderful place to enjoy refreshment on the deck, a super lunch or a most memorable dinner while observing the activity and scenery that make the San Juan Islands such a pleasant place to visit.

Tours

WIND 'N SAILS
P. O. Box 337
Friday Harbor, WA 98250
Tel. (206) 378-5343
Hrs: Summer   8:00 a.m. - 6:00 p.m.
          Winter   9:00 a.m. - 5:30 p.m.

The San Juan and Canadian Gulf Islands are renowned as a playground for sailors. Now you can experience the fun of exploring secluded coves, island retreats, and marine parks that are accessible only by boat. Dine on fresh salmon, snapper, Dungeness crab and steamed clams caught by you or your hired crew. Enjoy the sun, the antics of sea lions, the multitude of sea birds and, if you are very lucky, watch the massive and graceful Orca whales.

All this is waiting for you at Wind 'N Sails, Friday Harbor's largest sailboat charter company with over twenty-five high performance sailboats available for your pleasure. You may choose from any number of charter packages. Owners Ray and Paola Rutledge even offer personalized sailing lessons. Also, two "chase boats" are on call to solve any problems you may have while on the water. If you decide to use one of the approved Wind 'n Sails skippers, your solitude is guaranteed, as the skipper is picked up at your moorage each night by one of the chase boats, allowing you to enjoy the privacy you desire and experience the thrill of sailing without the responsibility.

Daily and weekly rates are available, as well as off season charters. Contact Ray and Paola about your boating needs and they will be happy to help you escape into the adventure of your choice.

SAN JUAN KAYAK EXPEDITIONS, 3090-B Roche Harbor Road,, Friday Harbor, Washington. Provides reliable two-person sea kayaks and equipment for two to four day trips through the San Juan Islands, five-day trips to Canadian Gulf Islands, and winter expeditions to Mexico and Belize.

Roche Harbor

Restaurant and Accommodations

ROCHE HARBOR RESORT, Box 4001, Roche Harbor, Washington. A must during your San Juan Island! The resort has a historic luxury hotel, a fine restaurant and lounge, moorage for lots of large boats, full-service marina, pool, beautiful gardens, and more.

SKAGIT COUNTY

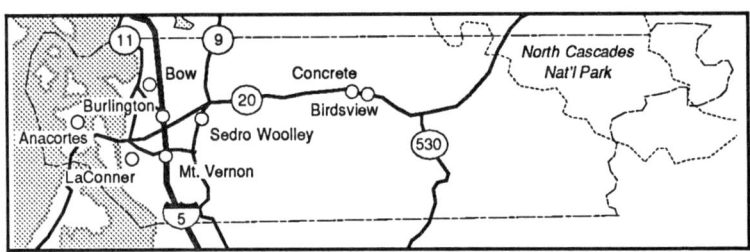

Long and narrow, Skagit County begins in Puget Sound with several islands, including the one on which Anacortes is located. A bucolic river valley extends eastward to the jumbled mass of the Cascade Mountains. Highway 20, the newly constructed and scenic route through North Cascades National Park, uses Skagit as its gateway. Much of the park land, a mountainous wilderness, is actually in Whatcom County, the northern neighbor to Skagit. About two-thirds of the 1,735 square miles of Skagit are either national forest or federal wilderness lands.

Skagit County was created by the territorial legislature in 1883, with the county seat established at Mount Vernon, a growing farm community on the meandering lower reaches of the Skagit Valley. Although early mariners charted the coast -- Fidalgo Island on which Anacortes lies is named for a Spanish explorer and was an 1842 fur-trader's camp--it was not until the 1860s that real settlement began. The 7,127 acre Swinomish Indian Reservation was created by treaty in 1873 as homesteaders put their mark on the lands.

Fidalgo Island, first with fish canneries, and in modern times Shell and Texaco oil refineries and water-related businesses, developed into a significant position in the local economy. Timber from private woodlands and the Mount Baker National Forest became an early source of income to complement that from the rich dairy farms which grew up in the valley. While dairying remains a significant part of the agriculture sector here, Skagit Valley has an increasing reputation for production of two specialty crops for home gardeners--flower bulbs and vegetable seeds are raised for export.

About half of Skagit's 66,000 residents live in rural homes or very small communities. Mount Vernon, with 13,600 people in its immediate area is the largest town. Anacortes with 9,500, Sedro-Woolley with 6,300 and Burlington with 3,800 residents are the other significant communities.

Growth in this county has been tempered by two significant environmental fights in recent history. A copper mine was proposed for the North Cascades, which are for the most part raw wilderness, accessible only on foot or with pack animals. The region became a 2,500 square mile National Park where recreation, not mining, is king. Guemes Island, a short ferry-boat ride from the Anacortes waterfront, was proposed for an aluminum plant. Environmentalists called it a recreation area and blocked the development which would have meant many new jobs in an area with many unemployed persons. Seattle City Light's Ross Dam, on Highway 20 over the north county line, figured in another North Cascades dispute. The utility wanted to raise the height of the dam to increase water storage for it's generators. This time Canadians protested saying the project would flood the valley on the international border.

The Skagit Valley east of the Sound gets progressively more precipitation, moving from about twenty-five inches in the western county to over forty-five inches in the mountains. January low temperatures are about thirty degrees. The valley lowlands get between six and nine inches of snowfall every year. Skagit's commercial tulip fields draw spring visitors, an art colony at little La Conner has become a year-around attraction, all complementing water and mountain recreation. Seattle City Light operates several hydroelectric plants in the upper valley which were built in the 1920s, creating lakes and fishing places with mountain views. Bicyclists prowl the flat roads of the valley where every road seems to have a new an picturesque farm.

North Cascades National Park

Canada and the United States jointly manage the northernmost area of this rugged collection of mountains. With a break for the corridor along Highway 20, the park and National Forest wilderness areas continue unbroken for fifty miles south to Lake Chelan. The park itself is joined by National Recreation Areas on Ross and Chelan Lakes. Passayten Wilderness is on the east and Glacier Peak Wilderness extends southward, all managed for recreational use and conservation of scenic resources.

Highway 20, completed about a decade ago, is one of only three roads which actually reach park lands. From Marblemount on the west, a gravel road winds southeastward to Cascade Pass trail head. From the head of Lake Chelan an old road twists northward toward Cascade Pass, carrying hikers on a park service bus. In British Columbia, a road winds south from Hope to the head of Ross Lake. Put another way, the steep mountain terrain is fit for foot travel and becomes easier if you arrange for pack animals to carry part of the outfit on extended treks over the 350 miles of trails inside the region.

Many park visitors simply drive the highway, pull over at viewpoints to see the distant peaks, and content themselves with short day hikes or easy car-camps at Newhalem and Diablo Lake campgrounds. One other viewing opportunity is from the west taking Highway 542 to Mount Baker, where a national forest trail leads close to Coleman Glacier. If you want to do more than brief hiking, write ahead and get information, including that from Seattle City Light which has a string of camps on the east shore of Lake Ross.

For information contact **Park Superintendent**, **North Cascades National Park**, Sedro-Woolley WA 98284; **Supervisor**, **Mount Baker National Forest**, Federal Office Building, Bellingham WA 98225; and Seattle City Light, 1015 Third Avenue, Seattle WA 98104.

ATTRACTIONS

Samish Bay, and the small towns of Bow, Blanchard and Edison on its edge are part of a sizable community with nearly 4,000 residents.

Where the Skagit splits into two forks at Rockport, a **state park** provides camping in a stand of old growth Douglas Fir trees. Bald eagles which winter on the river can be seen at viewing spots from here down stream to Concrete.

Sauk Mountain, a seven mile drive from here and a mile and a half hike, provides a panoramic view of the county all the way to the Sound and of the North Cascades peaks to the east.

For further information, contact the **Visitor Information Center for Skagit County**, 1231 Goldenrod Drive, Burlington WA 98233. Telephone 757-4514.

Anacortes

Fidalgo Island came of age in 1869 when its first store was opened by William Munks, but it was the boosterism of Amos Bowman which lifted the place to its present industrial and water-oriented development. Bowman tried to convince Canadian Pacific Railroad this was the place for its terminals and ferry connection to Vancouver Island. He built wharfs and a store. The post office opened in 1879 was called Anna Curtis after his wife. That was turned into a Spanish-sounding Anacortes to fit the Fidalgo Island name already existing.

Canneries, and several wood products mills turning out lumber, shingles and boxes established here, even if the Canadians kept their water terminal in Canada. Two oil refineries, processing crude brought in by tanker, now operate on a peninsula east of town. The Burlington Northern Railroad did reach Anacortes, but it stopped passenger service years ago and the depot is now an historic display area. The island has long-since been linked to the mainland by a causeway and bridge carrying Highway 20 to the Washington State Ferry docks where boats depart regularly for the San Juans and Victoria, B.C.

The city is triangular in layout, with rail tracks and highway approaching on one side, the waterfront facing the bay on the other and residential areas inland and in between.

Attractions

Several buildings on Commercial Avenue were constructed in the 1890s and remain in use today including the Moyer Building at Seventh, and the McNaught at Fifth.

A **mural** saluting the halibut fishermen of the 1930s is on the wall of the Post office at Sixth and Commercial Avenue. This work by Kenneth Callahan was winner in a Works Progress Administration competition.

There is a scale model coal-burning steam locomotive in residence at the **Anacortes Depot**, 611 R Avenue. The narrow gauge train was built by the Thomas Thompson family in their Anacortes backyard shop. Scheduled operations began in the summer of 1986. Check with the chamber of commerce for current operating hours of the Glorious Anacortes Railway.

The **Swinomish Indian community**, like several enterprising tribes in Washington, operate a perpetual bingo game. Their club house, at 1 Swinomish Channel Drive off March Point Road, is open at 5:00 p.m. seven nights a week with sessions beginning at 7:00 p.m., 7:30 p.m. and 10:30 p.m. There are even noon-time matinees Saturday and Sunday. Telephone 293-4687.

Deception Pass, where Highway 20 crosses a swift-moving tidal flow to Whidbey Island (see listing under Island County), is a scenic place. Indian people gave Skagit County a story totem, called **Maiden of Deception Pass** in the 1976 Bicentennial year. The cedar statue is on the site of a Samish village, Rosario Beach, about one mile north of Highway 20 on Rosario Road.

Rosario School, off Sharpe Road east of Rosario Road, was built as a two-story school in 1890. Worried parents had the second story removed in 1909, fearing a high wind would topple the building. Skagit Historical Society now owns the structure.

Anacortes Art Gallery, 414 Commercial Avenue, specializes in works of northwest artists. Open Tuesday through Saturday, 10:00 a.m. to 4:30 p.m. except during the month of January. Telephone 293-6656.

Skyline Marina on Burrows Bay south of town services many of the larger pleasure boats on the sound. A large repair facility takes vessels up to thirty-five tons in weight from the water for hull work. A planned community lies behind the marina with water cul de sacs providing moorage for local boats.

Guemes Island is a seven-minute ferry boat ride north of Anacortes. Several homes are on the island. There is a county park and beach on the point at the north end.

Above the Washington State Ferry docks at Shannon Point is **Sundquist Marine Laboratories**, a cooperative venture of several colleges and universities. Tours may be arranged by calling 293-6800.

For further information, contact the **Anacortes Chamber of Commerce**, 1319 Commercial Avenue, Anacortes WA 98221. Telephone 293-3822.

Accommodations

ANACORTES INN
3006 Commercial Avenue
Anacortes, WA 98221
Tel. (206) 293-3153
Major credit cards are accepted.

The Anacortes Inn is centrally located within minutes of several marinas and only ten minutes from the San Juan Island Ferry. It's within walking distance to fine restaurants and lounges in the downtown area.

The spacious, comfortable rooms face north and have beautiful views of the San Juan Islands, Fidalgo Bay, Mount Baker and the snow capped Cascades clear into Canada. The rooms are nicely furnished, with Charles Russell prints to add to the pleasant atmosphere. They have cable TV and direct dial phones. There is a large heated pool and complimentary coffee is available in the lobby.

Prices at the Anacortes Inn are reasonable, its comfort and location make it a "Best Choice" for accommodations in Anacortes.

DUTCH TREAT HOUSE
1221 31st Street
Anacortes, WA 98221
Tel. (206) 293-8154

As the name indicates, staying at this charming bed and breakfast is a treat. Hosts Bill and Mary O'Connor converted a large Dutch colonial home and began serving guests in January 1986. This is an excellent base for exploring the area. Visit the tidal rapids at Deception Pass, the Naval Air Station at Oak Harbor, the Skagit Valley tulip fields during the spring festival, the San Juan Islands and Victoria, B.C. or the Olympic Peninsula via the Keystone Ferry. Bill and Mary do everything they can to make your stay comfortable and pleasant.

There are four charming guest rooms available, each with appropriate country decor. They are all corner rooms and, therefore, very bright. The largest of the rooms with the best view of Mt. Baker is the most popular. Evenings are spent in the library, reading, playing cards, or sharing travel experiences with other national and international travelers. Delicious breakfasts await you, even if you're sailing on the 6:30 a.m. ferry. You might have quiche, souffle, waffles, or a Dutch Baby and fresh fruit in season. Before you leave, you'll want to find time to visit the back porch gift shop where you'll find lots of Mary's creations.

Bill and Mary will make your stay at Dutch Treat House a wonderful experience. As former travel agents, they have done extensive traveling themselves and love to meet new people and share experiences.

Skagit County

ISLANDS MOTEL AND LA PETITE RESTAURANT
3401 Commercial Avenue
Anacortes, WA 98221
Tel.   (206)   293-4644
Hrs: Restaurant
      Breakfast   Tue. - Sun.   7:00 a.m. - 10:00 a.m.
      Dinner   Tue. - Sun.   5:00 p.m. - 10:00 p.m.
Closed Monday

The Islands Motel and La Petite Restaurant offer a taste of Holland. Owner Fien Hulcher moved from Holland eight years ago and she, her daughter, Bela and son-in-law, David Poor operate the motel and restaurant to bring you the finest in accommodations and cuisine. The motel has been extensively renovated and remodeled and offers large, spacious rooms, most with a view of Guemes Channel, Fidalgo Bay or the Cascade Mountains, including Mt. Baker. Rooms are available to meet any needs, including family rooms with private bedroom. Fifteen units have fireplaces and many have private balconies from which to enjoy the view. A Dutch breakfast of a loaf of fresh baked bread, slice of ham, Dutch cheese, boiled egg, and coffee or tea is included in the room rate.

La Petite Restaurant offers some of the finest cuisine in Western Washington under the direction of chef David Poor. Appetizers change nightly and can include such choices as, peppered mackerel, steamed mussels or squid. Dinners vary with the season with six featured each night offering fish, shellfish, pork, chicken and specialty meats. David's Kipige Knoflook, breast of chicken with Parmesan pasta and garlic sauce is a favorite. There is a nice variety every night and the special sauces are wonderful. There is an extensive list of French and domestic wines. For dessert don't miss Advocaat, a Dutch custard with rum.

For fine accommodations and exquisite dining in the Skagit Valley stop at the Islands Motel and La Petite Restaurant - you'll be glad you did!

NANTUCKET INN
3402 Commercial Avenue
Anacortes, WA 98221
Tel. (206) 293-6007
Personal checks accepted with identification.
Reservations are recommended. A limited number of children are allowed. No smoking or pets, please.

Located on Fidalgo Island, in the town of Anacortes, Nantucket Inn is a lovely home built in 1925 by a local lumberman. The beauty of the home has been preserved including the original woodwork and gorgeous hardwood floors.

The ambiance of the inn is that of New England, which is reflected in the cozy living room with its fireplace and piano. The living room is a place where guests can spend the evening enjoying lively conversation, music and good company. You have a choice of six bedrooms, each individually decorated to be light and cheerful. Two rooms have their own bathroom while the others share one just down the hall.

Owner Sallie Lingwood has been running Nantucket Inn for the last seventeen years. She is an energetic person whose hobby is quilting. Her quilts are of museum quality and have won numerous awards. Sallie will be happy to direct you to scenic areas to enjoy a picnic, a stroll or a good book. Located nearby are several fine restaurants for breakfast, lunch and dinner. Ferries for a day of exploring the other islands are also close by.

Airline/Tour

WEST ISLE AIR, INCORPORATED
4000 Airport Road
Anacortes, WA 98221
Tel. (206) 293-4691
Hrs: Twenty-four hour service.
Visa, MasterCard and AMEX are accepted.

Get from Anacortes to the San Juan Islands in twelve minutes, as the eagle flies, instead of the half-day it takes by ferry, and enjoy the spectacular vistas at the same time with West Isle Air. Or plan a trip to Victoria, B.C. for the museums, shops, antiquity and international flavor. You'll arrive within only thirty minutes!

Owner-operator and chief pilot Gary Rovetto has a fleet of three and six passenger Cessnas, and can take people just about anywhere they want to go. Vancouver Island, Seattle, the Cascade Mountains, and San Juan Islands, not served by the ferry, are just a few of the beautiful destinations on the itinerary. Rates are as low as twenty-five dollars per person for about forty-five minutes of flight (at the time of this publication.)

To get the most spectacular perspective of this beautiful part of the country, see it from the air. West Isle Air can get you there!

Bed and Breakfast

BURROW'S BAY BED AND BREAKFAST, 4911 McBeth Drive, Anacortes, Washington. A lovely contemporary home overlooking Skyline Marina and the San Juan Islands. Large sitting room, separate bedroom, private entry, deck, private bath, fireplace, television, and continental breakfast plus lots of extras.

THE CHANNEL HOUSE
2902 Oakes Avenue
Anacortes, WA 98221
Tel. (206) 293-9382
Visa, MasterCard accepted

If you can't quite live like a king, you can still live it up like a Count at The Channel House. That's because this bed and breakfast inn was built, In 1902, to provide the Count Maroney of Italy a stately Victorian home on Puget Sound.

Just one and half miles from downtown Anacortes and less than a mile from the ferry terminal, the Channel House commands a breathtaking view of the Guemes Channel and the San Juan Islands, which is best enjoyed from the hot tub on the deck. The well-appointed guest rooms are furnished with such amenities as feather pillows and down comforters. You can expect evening coffee, tea and fresh baked cookies, as well as a home-cooked gourmet breakfast. Try the stuffed French toast or Washington apple pancakes.

Whether Anacortes is your destination, or a stopping off place, the Channel House will give you a memorable stay. You can "Count" on it.

OLD BROOK INN, 530 Old Brook Lane, Anacortes, Washington. The Inn has magnificent view of Fidalgo Bay, and is nestled amidst an ancient orchard with a babbling brook and a small lake. Two guest rooms, outstanding hospitality!

Skagit County

At the tip of Fidalgo Island, Anacortes is connected to the mainland by bridges and by daily ferry service. Do stop by the Chamber of Commerce to pick up a copy of their self-guided driving tour of Anacortes and Fidalgo Island.

\multicolumn{4}{c}{ANACORTES TOUR}			
a.m.	Anacortes Museum	Best history	Ana/Intro
a.m.	Chamber of Comm.	Best self-tour	Ana/Intro
p.m.	Boomer's Landing	Best views	Ana/Rest.
p.m.	continue the self-tour		
	For dinner try any one of these "Best Choices"		
p.m.	La Petite Restaurant	Best seafood	Ana/Acc.
p.m.	Slocum's	Best Cajun	Ana/Rest.
	Spending the night? Your choice: motel or bed & breakfast		
p.m.	Anacortes Inn	Best comfort	Ana/Acc.
p.m.	The Channel House	Best Victorian	Ana/B & B
p.m.	Dutch Treat House	Best charm	Ana/B & B
p.m.	Islands Motel	Best family-type	Ana/Acc.

Delicatessen

GER-A-DELI, 502 Commercial, Anacortes, Washington. A full-service delicatessen with everything made from scratch with quality ingredients. Service is quick and friendly.

Museum

ANACORTES MUSEUM
1305 Eighth Street
Anacortes, WA 98221
Tel. (206) 293-5198
Hrs: Thu. - Mon. 1:00 p.m. - 5:00 p.m.
Donations are happily accepted.

This wonderful museum will provide the entire family with a day of fun, excitement and a taste of rich heritage. There are three main galleries, as well as traveling exhibits several times a year.

The newest and possibly most publicized addition to the museum is Bobo the stuffed gorilla. Bobo was raised and lived for three years in

Anacortes before finding his permanent home at Woodland Park Zoo in Seattle. At that time he was the preeminent Northwest primate and has found fame again in his final home at Anacortes Museum.

Several intersting exhibits will fascinate you, from the turn of the century parlor, complete with a 1880s organ, vintage costumes, hearth, and a huge selection of 3-D slides. A complete replica of a cannery office displays fishing archives and labels. Also available is a Children's Art Gallery where classes are offered and displays of creative works can be viewed.

Restaurant

BOOMER'S LANDING
209 T Street
Anacortes, WA 98221
Tel. (206) 293-5108

Boomer's Landing offers fine dining and a beautiful and busy view. In addition to offering a fine view of the Cascades and Mt. Baker to the east, it overlooks the Guemes Channel, Guemes Island, and Fidalgo Bay to the west and north. As you enjoy your meal, you can watch a constant parade of boats and ships, ranging from sailboats and yachts to large oil tankers.

What really makes Boomer's Landing special, though, is not the view, but the food. Manager Dave Likely and his staff offer a variety of nice, reasonably priced lunches and dinners. For lunch there is plenty of seafood available, as well as salads and sandwiches. The "build your own sandwich" from the wide variety of ingredients available is very popular. Dinner features fresh local and exotic seafood, as well as chicken and steaks. There are nightly specials and the catch of the day. The Captain's Plate is a good choice for a chance to sample a variety of seafood. The desserts are homemade and wonderfully rich and delicious. Who can resist the Irresistible Mud Pie, Chocolate Decadence or the Butterfinger Moonlight - gran marnier, amaretto, and vanilla ice cream with butterfingers, a special Boomer's Landing creation.

The service at Boomer's Landing is excellent, and the wonderful food and unbeatable view make this a great place to dine.

SLOCUM'S
Skyline Way
Anacortes, WA 98221
Tel. (206) 293-0644
Hrs: Mon. - Thur.   5:00 p.m. - 9:00 p.m.
     Fri. - Sat.   5:00 p.m. - 10:00 p.m.
     Sunday Brunch   9:30 a.m. - 2:00 p.m.

If you love the freshest of local and exotic seafoods with the best of prime meats and Cajun spice, Slocum's is the place for you. Situated by a beautiful marina, Slocum's has become legendary for it's fine food, relaxing lounge and an eighteen feet wide brick fireplace which was built with over 68,000 bricks.

Owners Kelly Larkin and Joan Buchan are proud of their fine restaurant which serves such mouth watering entrees as Cajun sole, sole Florentine, rolled sole with Dungeness crab legs, or shrimp with stuffed flounder. Slocum's has weekly specials; one week you may find crab, another week prawns or oysters may be featured. At Slocum's you can enjoy a wonderful Sunday brunch, dinner buffets or Tuesday night crab feeds. There is a fine selection of Northwest wines including the local Fidalgo Island wine made by a completely chemical free process.

Slocum's is the place to go for a relaxing atmosphere and superb food making it a "Best Choice" in Western Washington.

Bow

Samish Bay, and the small towns of Bow, Blanchard and Edison on its edge are part of a sizable community with nearly 4,000 residents. William J. Brown, who homesteaded Bow in 1869, suggested the name after a large railroad station in London. The name of Bow went on the post office which was created when the railroad came through.

Attractions

This was the location, in 1900, of a commune named **"Equality."** It operated until 1904, then took out bankruptcy and disbanded.

On the large hill east of Blanchard is a cave in the talus slope of rock known locally as **"bat cave"** for its inhabitants. A rock fall in 1940 killed a local boy exploring the cave.

Bed and Breakfast

CHUCKANUT MANOR, 302 Chuckanut Drive, Bow, Washington. Famous for the Friday evening smorgasbord and Sunday champagne brunch, and five-course or à la carte dinners: two bedrooms and small living area perfect for small parties.

Restaurant

OYSTER BAR
240 Chuckanut Drive
Bow, WA 98232
Tel. (206) 766-6185
Hrs: Mon. - Sun. 5:00 p.m. - Closing
Visa and MasterCard are accepted.

The Oyster Bar opened in 1930 to sell fresh oysters from the Rock Point Oyster Company just a few miles away. Oysters can't be any fresher - "the oysters you eat today slept last night in Samish Bay!" In the intervening years the Oyster Bar has evolved into one of the premier restaurants in Western Washington. Owners Guy and Linda Colbert have fulfilled their dream of providing superior dining experiences for the sophisticated diner. Located high on a bluff with majestic firs framing Samish Bay and the San Juan Islands, the Oyster Bar is frequently graced with sunsets of dazzling reds, oranges and golds.

Be prepared for extraordinary taste delights beginning with appetizers such as, oysters sauteed with caviar and curry, mussels steamed in a saffron cream sauce or scallops grilled with pesto and red pepper sauce. Continue with soup de jour, crab bisque, wildgreens salad or Belgian endive salad with watercress, sliced apples, walnuts and Roquefort cheese tossed in a light vinaigrette dressing. For your entree, select from fresh oysters, swordfish, shrimp, chicken, salmon, lobster and steak. Among the more popular selections is salmon sauteed Cajun style, ragout of Maine lobster with morel mushrooms and three sauces or swordfish marinated and grilled with avocado butter. Desserts of light and airy raspberry souffle served with tart sauce or chocolate truffle terrine in a pool or pistachio sauce are equally special.

The hallmark of the Oyster Bar is creative food with the finest service possible. For elegant dining in an unmatched setting, your "Best Choice" is the Oyster Bar.

OYSTER CREEK INN
190 Chuckanut Drive
Bow, WA 98232
Tel. (206) 766-6179
Hrs: Mon. - Sun. 12:00 noon - 9:00 p.m.
Closed major holidays.
Visa, MasterCard and personal checks are accepted.

Owners Mick and Cheryl August have done everything possible to insure that their Oyster Creek Inn Restaurant offers everything that's best about the Northwest. The setting is typically Northwest, with tables in the restaurant and lounge overlooking Oyster Creek, framed by majestic firs, rhododendrons, and other natural foliage. Salmon spawn in Oyster Creek, otter play there, and deer walk by on the way to grazing meadows. The menu features selections that are local and seasonal, and the service and atmosphere couldn't be friendlier.

Lunch and dinner are served all day, and the dishes served are made with the freshest possible Northwest ingredients. If you fall in love with the dishes served, as often happens, ask Mick and Cheryl for the recipe; they are extremely generous in handing out their recipes. The oyster stew is the one most requested, but, it's difficult to perfectly replicate as the oyster stew from this Inn gets its oysters from just one mile away.

The sauteed Geoduck steak is a very popular Northwest offering. Of course steamed clams, poached fresh salmon, halibut, scallops and prawns are deliciously prepared by the Inn's chefs. There are sandwiches, such as smoked ham and cucumber and roast lamb with rhubarb chutney. Steaks, chicken, loin lamb chops and other meat selections are creatively prepared. There is a good selection of Northwest wines and beer and ale available to enhance your meal.

Whenever possible Mick and Cheryl use local cottage industry products in their cooking, such as the rhubarb chutney that accents the roast lamb. In the lounge you can buy many of these Northwest products and take a little bit of Oyster Creek Inn home with you to help you remember your visit to this Northwest restaurant.

RHODODENDRON CAFE
553 Chuckanut Drive
Bow, WA 98232
Tel. (206) 766-6667
Hrs: Mon. - Thu. 11:00 a.m.-9:00 p.m.
  Fri. - Sat. 11:00 a.m.-9:30 p.m.
  Sunday 10:00 a.m. - 9:00 p.m.
Closed Tuesdays, July 4th, Thanksgiving and December.
Visa, MasterCard are accepted.

What makes this Rhododendron bloom is variety - so much so that the catch phrase here is "happy eclectic." Where else can you order Tunisian or Cajun food and still enjoy old fashioned homemade ice cream for dessert?

Don and Carol Shank opened their restaurant in 1984, bringing experience from world-wide travels and years of working in fine Northwest restaurants. As the loyal following of locals can attest, Don and Carol will have something unique for you to try everytime you visit. You can expect fresh local seafood and exotic cuisine like Singapore saute - scallops sauteed in ginger, orange and white wine, Tuneiian eggah - sausage, potatoes, tomatoes, garlic and eggs and Spanakopita spinach and cheese baked in filo dough and served with hollandaise. Stew is served every night, but its seldom the same, constantly evolving under the creative input of the Shanks.

Classical or light jazz and quaint wall paper, give an elegant touch to the casual and comfortable atmosphere. The Rhododendron is where variety is really the spice of life.

Burlington

Once the center of an expanding railroad system, Burlington was platted by New York developers. Today this town of 3,800 people is a major crossroads for I-5 and Highway 20, its trade based on the rich livestock and specialty farms on the edge of the Skagit Valley.

For information contact the **Burlington Chamber of Commerce**, Box 552, Burlington WA 98233. Telephone 757-1121.

Accommodations

COCUSA MOTEL, 200 West Rio Vista, Burlington, Washington. Sixty-one air-conditioned units with cable television, coin laundry, and heated pool. Next door, a restaurant and six efficiency units.

Concrete

The Skagit River still meanders across a narrowing valley when it passes the little town of Concrete, 600 residents strong. Even smaller villages with names like Cape Horn and Birdsview, relate to river points, but Concrete tells it like it is. Cement factories were built here in 1905. Concrete is the business of the town, the huge limestone quarries nearby a steady source of jobs through 1968. Now, the community sells its history and old buildings, and acts as a starting point for people heading into the mountains or to the lakes created by Puget Power Co. reservoirs just a short drive from here.

Attractions

Old cement silos, east of town at the Baker river bridge, and west of town at Superior Avenue and Highway 20, mark the exit to Concrete. Plants were at both locations. Highway 20 now bypasses the old town.

Concrete's **Visitor Information Center** on the railroad tracks east of E Street has a walking map which identifies just about every building in town from offices of Lone Star Cement Company to where Puget Power captures migrating fish to take them above the Baker dams.

Long before the days of pre-stressed concrete beams, engineers in 1918 built the **Henry Thompson Bridge**. This span with arched concrete members poured in elaborate falsework and cured, was at the time the longest single-span attempted with concrete construction. On Dillard Avenue where it crosses Baker River northeast of town.

For more information, contact **Concrete Chamber of Commerce**, Box 12, Concrete WA 98237. Telephone 853-8181.

Restaurant

DEL CONTE'S TIMBERLINE RESTAURANT, 4286 Highway 20, Concrete, Washington. Outstanding meals in a decor so interesting you have to see it to appreciate it fully.

La Conner

Swinomish channel, a tidal river that separates Fidalgo Island from the delta country, provides the reflecting pool for this quaint town of 650 people.

Snow capped Mount Baker rises to the rear, mansions of merchant princes line the low tree-covered hill and a commercial district with wharfs that once shipped produce to a hungry Seattle now are shops and museums for area artisans. Swinomish Indian Community is across the bridge, its church predating other settlement in the area. John and Louisa Conner bought the trading post here in 1870. Their names were chosen, together, when residents wanted to distinguish the town from Swinomish, the name of the Indian reservation.

The fields around the town provide an example of early reclamation work, carried out in the 1880s. Rich fields were reclaimed from tidelands through extensive diking projects. Within a short time the steamer Fanny Lake was calling here regularly, taking produce of the Skagit Valley and passengers to Seattle.

Attractions

Skagit County Historical Museum, 501 Fourth Street, traces the heritage of the many people who live here and in the off-shore islands. There is a research and reference library and a gift shops selling publications related to area history. Open Wednesday through Sunday, 1:00 p.m. to 5:00 p.m. Telephone 466-3365.

Gaches Mansion, an 1891 home erected by a grain merchant, was restored by the non-profit Friends of LaConner Landmarks, offers tours each Friday through Sunday between 1:00 p.m. and 5:00 p.m. Telephone 466-4288.

Valley Museum of Northwest Art, on the second floor of the Gaches Mansion, Second and Calhoun streets, is dedicated to an awareness of regional art. Museum sponsors are gathering a permanent collection and invite three shows a year by Northwest painters. Telephone 466-4446 or 466-3033.

Salish Seas Aquarium, 610 First Street, has a salt-water tank filled with creatures of Puget Sound. Another "touch tank" lets visitors pick up some of the more durable marine animals. Workshops and trips, concentrated in winter months, are sponsored by the aquarium. From April through October open daily between 10:00 a.m. and 6:00 p.m. November through December, Monday and Wednesday afternoons 1:30 p.m. to 5:00 p.m., Thursday 11:00 a.m. to 9:00 p.m. and Friday through Sunday 10:00 a.m. to 5:00 p.m. January through March, Friday through Sunday from 11:00 a.m. to 5:00 p.m.

The **Pioneer Monument**, at the east side of town near Sullivan Slough, was proposed in 1925 and finally dedicated in 1936 during the annual picnic of the county's Pioneer Association. They decided so many people had contributed to launching the county that the monument ought to honor all without carving any name on the shaft. A copper box behind the plate holds a list of pioneers. The association still has picnics each August, the original members long-since dead.

Roozengaarde, show garden of Washington Bulb Company, is on Beaver Marsh Road north east of La Conner. Washington is now the largest bulb grower in the world. Cut flowers are on sale year around at the gardens. Open daily. Telephone 424-8531. Go west on McLean Road leaving I-5 at exit 226, then left to 1587 Beaver Marsh Road.

For information, contact the **La Conner Chamber of Commerce**, Box 644, La Conner Wa 98257. Telephone 466-3329.

Accommodations

THE HERON IN LACONNER
117 Maple Street
P. O. Box 716
LaConner, WA 98257
Tel. (206) 466-4626
MasterCard, VISA and personal checks are accepted.

This Victorian style country inn is located in the heart of LaConner and marks the entrance to a walking tour with the first of six antique stores just one block away. Its three decks overlook scenic farm fields, the Cascade Mountains, Mount Baker and Mount Rainier.

All eleven rooms are structurally unique and individualized with custom tiled private baths, phones and televisions. Some rooms have jacuzzi baths, others have wood burning fireplaces. The bridal suite has a fireplace and jacuzzi for two. The furnishings are antiques or antique in appearance, and the parlor, with its large stone fireplace sets the scene for conversation or quiet reading in wing back chairs, camel back couch and bookshelves full of literature. A conference/banquet room is provided for small meetings. Complimentary Continental breakfasts are provided with coffee, juices and fresh local pastries. Space is available for bicycle storage.

At the Heron in LaConner you can enjoy the lightness of a country inn, the elegance of the Victorian era, modern amenities and old fashioned hospitality.

LaCONNER COUNTRY INN
2nd and Morris Streets
P. O. Box 573
LaConner, WA 98257
Tel. (206) 466-3101

Enjoy the cozy and relaxing atmosphere in the parlor and library of this charming inn. The huge stone fireplace, crackling fire, soft couches, easy chairs and tables for games have made the parlor a favorite gathering place for the inn's guests. Hosts Rick and Reinhild Thompson opened the LaConner Country Inn in 1977 to meet the need for overnight accommodations in this historic town and have created a charming country atmosphere for a relaxing stay.

Each of the twenty-eight units is equipped in the tradition of country inns with large rooms, brass beds, lots of natural wood accents and a fireplace. There are rooms equipped with twin, queen or king-sized beds and a family suite that sleeps six. Children twelve and under share a room with their parents at no charge. A complimentary Continental breakfast is offered and Barkley's Restaurant is immediately adjacent to the inn and will provide room service, if desired. A conference center for small conferences and seminars is also available.

The LaConner Inn offers a charming country inn ambiance with excellent service and accommodations in this historic and very unique town.

Antiques

MORRIS STREET ANTIQUES
505 Morris Street
P. O. Box 1219
La Conner, WA 98257
Tel. (206) 466-4212
Hrs: Mon. - Sun. 11:00 a.m. - 5:00 p.m.
Closed Christmas and Thanksgiving.
Visa and MasterCard are accepted.

Morris Street Antiques owners, Don and Jo Ann Mulanax have done a beautiful job of restoring a turn of the century house, including one of the most inviting front porches you'll ever see, to create this lovely and charming shop. Don's background as a ship builder served him well when he added tastefully designed shelves throughout the house to display the antiques.

Choice porcelains and a large selection of depression glass adorn shelves throughout the shop. Don and Jo Ann are long time boaters, and have discovered some very unique nautical pieces. The furniture, pottery, and other beautiful items displayed in the shop are of excellent quality. Don has been a woodcarver all of his life and several examples of his work can be found at Morris Street Antiques, ranging from the dogwood blossoms that decorate the sign to the carousel animals in the shop.

There is something for everyone at Morris Street Antiques, and if you're looking for something special that's not currently among the offerings, Don and Jo Ann will do their best to find it for you. This shop offers a truly delightful shopping experience in warm and comfortable surroundings for the novice and connoisseur alike.

SOMETHING OF VALUE
212 Morris Street
P.O. Box 947
LaConner, WA 98257
Tel. (206) 466-4711
Hrs: Mon. - Sun. 10:00 a.m. - 5:00 p.m.

Something of Value is housed in a 1900's house that was restored to its original splendor by owner Pat Kniser. Pat opened her shop in 1986 and has been involved in the antique business for several years, taking advantage of frequent trips to Hong Kong to acquire oriental art objects and Chinese antiques. Marie Johnson, Pat's associate, makes purchasing trips to the East Coast, Europe and Nevada. Together they have assembled an impressive collection sure to please any shopper.

Something of Value carries mostly antiques, with a few new items that meet Pat's criteria for uniqueness and beauty. There are an astounding number of figurines displayed, including Royal Doulton, Hummel and Lladro. Oriental selections include plates, porcelain and Imari china. There are also new and old ivory Netsuke. There are antique French posters, fine European porcelain and crystal and antique jewelry.

Pat and Marie literally scour the world to acquire truly rare and unique pieces for Something of Value. When in La Conner, be sure to visit, browse, converse, enjoy yourself, and take home a unique and memorable treasure.

Art Galleries

EARTHENWORKS
First and Washington Street
P. O. Box 702
LaConner, WA 98257
Tel. (206) 466-4422
Hrs: Mon. - Sun. 11:00 a.m. - 5:00 p.m.
Closed Thanksgiving, Christmas and New Year's Day.
MasterCard, Visa, AMEX and Discover cards are accepted.

"There is nothing in the Earthenworks gallery that anybody <u>needs</u>, but there are a lot of things you'll want to enrich your environment!", according to owners Cynthia and Donald Hoskins. Large open galleries, tastefully displayed artwork and appropriate mood setting music come together for leisurely browsing at Earthenworks. Although the art is predominantly produced by Northwest artists, Cynthia and Donald travel the United States to find work by new artisans to bring to their customers.

There are large wall murals of exotic hardwoods produced by Dick Fichter, realistic detailed birds by local woodcarver Gene Boyd and beautiful, delicate watercolors of stylized birds by Lee Bogle. Sculptured, as well as functional pottery by such artisans as Sam Scott, Charles Talman, Matthew Patton and Don Salisbury are displayed. In addition, exquisitely carved jewel boxes, desk accessories, kitchen items and decorative basketry can be found here. Wearable art from about forty different designers from all over the U.S. adorn racks, including woven garments, silk batik and other one-of-a-kind or limited edition clothing.

Call for schedules of art and fashion shows at both' the LaConner and Port Townsend locations. Earthenworks is a Best Choice" gallery where your purchases are destined to be heirlooms!

LaCONNER GALLERY
714 First Street
P. O. Box 681
LaConner, WA 98257
Tel. (206) 466-3878
Hrs: Mon. - Sun. 10:30 a.m. - 5:30 p.m.
Closed Christmas, New Years and Thanksgiving
Mastercard, Visa and Discovery cards accepted.

The quality of LaConner Gallery beckons visitors to enter and enjoy a wonderful mixture of art forms. Owner Sharon Anderson, an artist herself, has created a particularly pleasing assemblage of art --ranging from a large selection of excellent paintings by professional artists, to lead crystal figurines, quartz crystal items, pewter fantasy pieces, wood carvings and soapstone sculpture.

Opened in 1977, as a small gallery, Sharon has expanded the LaConner Gallery to its present size with paintings hung literally from floor to ceiling. There is a complete turnover of art pieces every three months.

The LaConner Gallery is first and foremost an art gallery featuring framed, excellent quality paintings primarily created by Northwest artists using a variety of media, including oils, water colors, acrylics and hand-etched brass. Sharon offers a exciting collection of visionary pieces that allow you to see beyond the ordinary and to experience a bit of the metaphysical. The paintings include an impressive array of the flora, fauna and the natural beauty of Washington's mountains and seascapes. Sharon has quality art to fit every budget (including paintings by Dali and Picasso). You'd better plan to spend a good amount of time if you wish to see all the paintings displayed in the LaConner Gallery.

There is a full display of handcrafted items, including jewelry, hand-blown glass pieces made from Mt. St. Helens ash, hand-blown oil lamps, Presence Monastic hanging-crystal pieces made by an Oregon Monastery and Italian sterling silver chains. You'll even find some wonderful mythical pewter pieces mounted in semi-precious rock. Add the time to your schedule to investigate all that is within.

Quality doesn't just apply to the artwork within--it also extends to the quiet, helpful service provided. The staff serves as your information source and are all more than willing to spend time answering your questions and providing details regarding the Gallery's holdings. Enjoy the special blend of products and reap the benefits of a wonderful symbiosis between the artists and the gallery.

Bed & Breakfast

KATY'S INN BED AND BREAKFAST
503 S 3rd, Box 304
La Conner, WA 98257
Tel. (206) 466-3366
Hrs: Year round
No credit cards accepted, personal checks okay

Originally built in 1876 as a private residence for a sea captain, Captain John Peck, Katy's Inn is one of the oldest buildings in historic LaConner.

Located on the hill just two blocks from downtown, the inn commands an excellent view of the town and the busy and beautiful Swinomish Channel.

Dale and Vivian Rancourt are the third owners of the house and have done a wonderful job of restoring it to the splendor of its past. The inn is named after Vivian's mother, Katy. Not only did Katy personally test and approve each aspect of the Inn, but she made the quilts that warm today's guests. Many of the antique furnishings in the inn were Katy's and it is a lasting tribute to the memory of a warm and loving mother. There are four guest rooms available, each with a door to the veranda with its excellent view. When weather permits, the tasty breakfast, served elegantly with crystal and linens, that starts your day is served on the veranda.

Dale and Vivian do everything in their power to make your stay with them enjoyable. The warm and friendly atmosphere and the charming decor make a stay at Katy's Inn a pleasant and relaxing experience.

RAINBOW INN BED AND BREAKFAST
1075 Chilberg Road
La Conner, WA 98257
Tel. (206) 466-4578

Completely restored and opened in the fall of 1985 by innkeeper Marlene Dulin, this charming bed and breakfast inn is located only a half mile east of LaConner in a turn of the century farmhouse. It is a favorite retreat for couples and small business groups alike. Marlene also caters dinners, lunches and parties.

The Rainbow Inn offers eight rooms with central heating and cooling, including five with private baths and some with claw-footed tubs. Each room is lovely and furnished with charming period furniture and antique patterned wallpaper. The primary gathering place for guests is the parlor, with it's unique wood burning, ceramic fireplace. Also popular is the hot tub on the back deck, with a view of snow capped Mount Baker in the distance. Marlene provides a full course gourmet breakfast, featuring fresh fruit, omelettes or crepes and freshly baked pastries.

The Rainbow Inn is an excellent base from which to explore the Skagit Valley. It's setting in the heart of pastoral farming country and its warm hospitality, make it a "Best Choice" for a relaxing get away.

Books

SKAGIT BAY BOOKS, 612 South First, LaConner, Washington. Skagit Bay Books is one of LaConner's treasures. A fine selection of Northwest and marine books, children's books, best sellers, and more.

Gift Shop

THE WOOD MERCHANT, 707 South First, LaConner, Washington. Seventy Northwest woodworkers produce a enormous selection of handmade wooden gifts for you to buy here.

THE STALL IMPORTS
712 First Street
La Conner, WA 98257
Tel. (206) 466-3162
Hrs: Mon. - Sun. 10:30 a.m. - 5:00 p.m.
Closed Christmas and Thanksgiving
Visa and MasterCard are accepted.

People travel to La Conner from all over the Northwest to shop in the unique specialty shops. One of the more unique and fun shops is The Stall Imports, owned by June Flora and her daughter Kay Trelstad. They specialize in products from Mexico, South America and India. The shop has been located in its present waterfront location, with lots of space, since the fall of 1986.
Plan to spend plenty of time when you visit The Stall Imports so you won't miss any of the special merchandise and will have time to talk to June or Kay about the many things that will catch your eye. Both women love to take the time to talk to their customers. You will find luxurious sweaters of cotton and wool from Ecuador, Peru and Mexico. There are pictures, masks and tuck-woven Peruvian wall hangings to enhance your home. There is also leather, jewelry and wonderful pottery. One corner of the shop is devoted to Christmas items year round and has a wide variety of nativity scenes from around the world.
There is something for everyone and browsing is a fascinating experience at The Stall Imports. This is a delightful shop with charming and helpful owners and shouldn't be missed when you're visiting La Conner.

Restaurant

AT'S A PIZZA
201 Morris Street
La Conner, WA 98257
Tel. (206) 466-4406 or 466-4407
Hrs: Mon. - Thur. 11:00 a.m. -10:00 p.m.
      Fri - Sat. 11:00 a.m. - Midnight
      Daily Special 11:00 a.m. - 4:00 p.m.

Looking for a comfortable family restaurant in which to enjoy excellent homemade Italian food at moderate prices? You've found it--and more--in At's A Pizza at the corner of Second and Morris in La Conner. Owner Judy Iverson, daughters Cherri Gregory and Julie, and staff are ready to serve you some "standards" with their special touch as well as some new creations to tempt your appetite. At's A Pizza specializes in homemade clam chowder, chili, spaghetti, lasagna, grinders, cold sandwiches, taco salad and more!

The New York style pizzas are excellent and come in four sizes, with the smallest measuring 14 inches in diameter and the largest 18 inches in diameter. Order one of the specials or design your own from a substantial list of ingredients. For the adventurous, try the Barbeque Pizza - a creation utilizing barbeque sauce, roast beef, mozzarella cheese and other favorite toppings.

Grinders, served hot on hogie rolls, contain selected meats, mozzarella cheese, and homemade "Italian" sauce. Be hungry before you attempt the Lu Ming Sandwich, a 10 inch hogie roll creation containing roast beef, onion, and mushrooms "sauteed" in a special sauce. For a lighter meal try the At's A Rolls - homemade pizza dough, sauce, mozzarella cheese, two toppings of your choice, folded over, baked and topped with Parmesan cheese. Another invention of At's A Pizza is a baked garlic roll made of pizza dough brushed with garlic oil and sprinkled with Parmesan cheese and basil.

While adults enjoy draft or bottled beer or a fine Northwest wine, the kids can have fun in the video room that is upstairs and out-of-hearing range. If a video game record score is broken, a free pizza is won!

Visit At's A Pizza and enjoy excellent food in a relaxing atmosphere. Judy, Cherri, and staff want you to enjoy their hospitality and leave happy, full and eager to return. Visa, MasterCard, personal check with ID accepted. Free delivery within four miles.

BARKLEY'S OF LA CONNER
2nd and Washington
P. O. Box 498
LaConner, WA 98257
Tel. (206) 466-4261
Hrs: Lunch   Mon. - Sat.   11:30 a.m. - 3:00 p.m.
      Dinner   Mon. - Sun.   5:00 p.m. - Closing
      Brunch   Sunday   10:00 a.m. - 3:00 p.m.
All major credit cards are accepted.

Michael Hood, proprietor and chef at Barkley's of LaConner brings "the bounty of the Skagit Valley and Puget Sound" to locals and visitors alike. Sous Chef Ben Elder and waitress Jean Bartlett use their special talents to help create the ambiance of casual elegance in which to enjoy fine dining.

Both dinner and lunch menus feature seafood and pasta, including daily specials that reflect seasonal items. If it isn't fresh, it isn't found at Barkley's. In season there are such local delicacies as Pacific pink scallops, Whidbey Island mussels, Manila clams from local beaches, salmon, sturgeon and more. Seafood is deliciously and imaginatively presented, as are the many non seafood items also available. Sunday Brunch ranges from standard country breakfasts to such items as eggs Fellini, Fettucini Carbonara, or Italian Sausage Canneloni and champagne to complement your selection. For the kids, Michael has created "Green Eggs and Ham."

The excellent food and comfortable elegance offered by Barkley's make this a definite "Best Choice" in Skagit county.

BLACK SWAN
505 S. First
P. O. Box 476
LaConner, WA 98257
Tel. (206) 466-3040
Hrs: Seasonal
Major credit cards accepted
Reservations suggested

Black Swan proprietor and chef Martin Hahn has successfully captured the charm of the little provincial restaurants found throughout Europe, but rarely in the United States. He presents extraordinary meals featuring fresh Northwest ingredients with a Mediterranean flair. Martin and his staff take pride in the care paid to the presentation of fine food and service.

The menu at the Black Swan changes to reflect seasonal fare, with an emphasis on fresh seafood. There is also local game, local lamb, beef and veal during the winter. Martin is particularly well known for his innovative combinations of fresh local ingredients, including colorful and tasty salads of edible flowers and foraged greens. To accompany your meal, the Black Swan wine list offers between 50 and 100 labels, with an emphasis on Northwest and provincial European wines. Delicious desserts, homemade gelato and espresso are served to complete your meal.

The atmosphere at the Black Swan is casual and comfortable and the food is unparalleled. If you haven't time for a full dinner, treat yourself to the more simple cafe menu, espresso, or wine offered in the Cafe Pojante, newly opened on the first floor. Any dining experience at the Black Swan will be truly memorable.

CALICO CUPBOARD
720 S 1st Street
La Conner, WA 98257
Tel. (206) 466-4451
Hrs: Mon. - Fri. 7:00 a.m. - 5:00 p.m.
     Sat. - Sun. 8:00 a.m. - 5:00 p.m.
Closed Christmas and Thanksgiving
No credit cards accepted, personal checks okay

Linda Freed opened the Calico Cupboard restaurant and bakery in 1981 and has developed a strong following of customers who appreciate her emphasis on healthy foods made from the highest quality ingredients. All the bakery products are made on the premises from freshly milled, organically grown whole grain and unbleached flours, honey and other natural ingredients without additives or preservatives.

Among the choices offered for breakfast at the Calico Cupboard are special omelettes, such as vegetarian or shrimp. Breakfasts are accented with fresh toast or pastries from the bakery. For lunch there is a selection of several soups, hearty sandwiches served on freshly baked breads, salads, and of course, wonderful baked goods. Afternoon tea is served from 2:30 p.m. to 5:00 p.m. and is the perfect time to sample one of the luscious pastries offered by the bakery.

Calico Cupboard is a full scale bakery creating delicacies from wedding cakes to cookies. Everything is available to take out, including lunches. You'll enjoy dining in the pleasant atmosphere with old fashioned service and wholesome, delicious food. When you leave, pick up a Calico Cupboard T-shirt which reads on the back, "The Sweetest Buns in Town--Naturally!"

Seafoods

PRIZE CATCH SEAFOODS CO.
109 N 1st Street
P. O. Box 273
LaConner, WA 98257
Tel. (206) 466-4707
 (800) 843-5574 outside of WA
Hrs: Mon. - Sun. 10:30 a.m. - 5:30 p.m.
Closed Thanksgiving and Christmas.
Visa and MasterCard are accepted.

When entering LaConner the right turn to take is a right at Morris and First to the Lime Dock and the Prize Catch Seafoods Company! Owners Norm and Milet Hopping purchased their "smoked seafoods boutique" late in 1985 and since then have perfected brine recipes to provide for smoked seafoods that are low in sodium and totally nitrate free. There are even NO sodium products for those people with salt restrictions.

The smoked salmon, halibut, cod, and oysters are the finest tasting seafoods available. Norm even applies his special "New England recipes" to produce an old-fashioned, thick-cut smoked bacon. Suppliers to gourmet restaurants and grocery stores in Western Washington and Hawaii...you too can enjoy these specialties by either stopping in, or phoning to place your product order. Wherever the big brown UPS trucks travel...it's delivered.

Local, fresh catch-of-the-day is kept in refrigerated cases at Prize Catch. A tank of Dungeness crabs awaits your order. Norm will tell you how best to prepare them, or he will steam them for you. Once you've visited and experienced Prize Catch you will become one of their growing list of "regulars."

(See special invitation in the Appendix.)

Seeds

TILLINGHAST SEED COMPANY
623 Morris Street
LaConner, WA 98257
Tel. (206) 466-3329
Hrs: Mon. - Sat.   9:00 a.m. - 5:30 p.m.
            Sunday   11:00 a.m. - 6:00 p.m.
Closed Christmas and Thanksgiving
Visa and MasterCard are accepted

Tillinghast Seed Company, founded in 1885, is in the second century of serving their customers Their 1987 Seed Catalog is the 102nd issue! The business remained in the Tillinghast family until it was purchased by Arberta Lammers and Brian Scheuch in 1980. They still occupy the original clapboard building with its covered porch and plank floors. They sell seeds and bulbs, but Arberta and Brian have expanded to create a unique country store offering much more.

There is a flower shop, kitchen shop, gourmet coffee and candy shop, basket shop, and a year-round Christmas shop. The store also has a wildlife gallery featuring the work of internationally known La Conner artist, David Hagerbaumer. The seeds and bulbs offered by Tillinghast Seed Company are available throughout the world by catalog. They carry a large assortment of plants and seeds that have proven successful in the maritime climate of the Pacific Northwest.

Arberta, Brian, and their staff enjoy serving their customers, some of whom are third and fourth generation customers. As Arberta says, "There is something special about the feel of this old building, it has its own sense of personality." Visit the Tillinghast Seed Company and experience the long history of service to the "growing" community.

Mount Vernon

Bricks rich with age, the old Skagit County courthouse building stands alongside a modern structure where the county government serves. Inside the new building is a twenty-four by thirty-six foot American flag which was flown from atop a 174-foot high cedar tree when Independence Day was celebrated at Mount Vernon in 1877. There's a lot that connects with that 1877 platting of a town on a big bend of the Skagit River, and a lot which connects to the 13,600 people who make a modern city their home. When it began, reclamation was important, marshes and floodways were turned into pastures for growing numbers of dairy cattle.

Milk and cheese remain important, but the specialized bulb and seed farming has proven a better use for many of these fertile fields. The traditional downtown commercial area faces changes too, with a new shopping mall at College Way and Riverside Drive.

Attractions

Washington Cheese Company, 900 East College Way, has observation windows from which you can watch the cheese processed from beginning to completed product. Samples are available. Open Monday thru Saturday. Telephone 424-3510.

West Shores Acres, on Downey Road has a one and a half acre flowering bulb display garden which surrounds a 1912 Victorian farmhouse. Mon. thru Sun. tours available. Call 466-3158 for further information.

For further information, contact the **Mount Vernon Chamber of Commerce,** Box 1007, Mount Vernon WA 98273. Telephone 336-9555.

Accommodations

BEST WESTERN MOTOR INN
300 W College Way
Mt. Vernon, WA 98273
Tel. (206) 424-4287
All major credit cards are accepted.

Best Western Motor Inn offers the best of both worlds...Puget Sound and the Skagit Valley, and the Cascade Mountains. As soon as you arrive, you'll receive a list of "seventy-six things to do", and the well informed staff have extensive knowledge of the happenings in the area.

Clean, comfortable accommodations and excellent service are provided by Best Western. Sixty-six units feature queen beds, satellite TV which includes Showtime, A&E, and in-room coffee. The mini suites sleep up to four people and include a kitchenette, queen bed, living room area and queen sleeper sofas. Some units have mini refrigerators.

There is a pool and courtyard, in season, and a hot tub to soothe tired bodies. When you receive your list of seventy-six things to do, add one more and make it seventy-seven...spending a restful night at Best Western Motor Inn!

(See special invitation in the Appendix.)

THE DOWNEY HOUSE BED AND BREAKFAST
1880 Chilberg Road
Mount Vernon, WA 98273
Tel. (206) 466-3207

The Downey House, built in the early 1900's by Peter Downey for his son Art, was originally located three miles north of its present site. In 1965 Jim and Kay Frey acquired the house and had it moved to Pleasant Ridge, which overlooks stately Mount Baker, the nearby Skagit River, and the tulip fields that bring visitors from miles around each spring.

In April of 1985, after seven and a half months of remodeling, The Downey House was opened as a bed and breakfast. The character of past generations has been beautifully recreated through restorations and antique furnishings. Special features were added, including a masonry wood stove and oven, and a hot tub. The stairway and hallway leading to the four individual guest rooms is accented with enlargements of old photographs of the region. Kay and Jim enjoy providing the history of the photos and pointing out the friendship between the Downeys and their ancestors.

The old dining room table is a frequent gathering place for guests and hosts. It is here that Kay serves her wonderful wild blackberry pie (a la mode, of course) with lots of fresh hot coffee and pleasant conversation.

A real country breakfast is served--homemade and plentiful, and can include crêpes topped with fresh blueberry topping, peaches or seasonal fresh fruit, swedish potato sausage, omelets and hash browns, or quiche. The Downey House has been the setting for weddings and family reunions and has served as a "think tank" for executives planning business strategies. It's a favorite stopping place for vacationers headed for Puget Sound.

Let Jim and Kay provide you with outstanding food, warmth, and old fashioned hospitality at the Downey House Bed and Breakfast in the quiet, rural setting of Pleasant Ridge. You'll depart relaxed--refreshed--and have two new friends.

(See special invitation in Appendix.)

Cheese

WASHINGTON CHEESE
900 E College Way
Mt. Vernon, WA 98273
Tel. (206) 424-3510
Hrs: Mon. - Sat. 9:30 a.m. - 5:30 p.m.
Closed Sundays, Thanksgiving, Christmas and New Year's Day.
Visa and MasterCard are accepted.

Washington Cheese was founded in 1977 by more than 100 Northwest dairy farmers and has complete control of the cheese making process from the farm to the supermarket. This control insures the highest quality cheese products possible. Washington Cheese is one of the few natural cheese plants fully accredited by the U.S. Department of Agriculture. The flavorful mixture of Holstein, Guernsey and Jersey milks from dairy farms in the surrounding area leads to the superior flavor of the cheeses.

From the Washington Cheese viewing rooms overlooking the huge vats where 300,000 pounds of fresh milk are converted into 30,000 pounds of delicious natural cheese, you can watch the entire process. You can then proceed to the retail shop where you sample the results and pick your favorites to take home. There are a number of cheddars and jacks available, including a unique salmon cheddar containing locally caught fish.

A visit to Washington Cheese is educational, fun and tasty, you won't want to leave without "buying a chunk of Washington!"

Gift Shop

PLEASANT RIDGE POTTERY
1937 Chilberg Road
Mount Vernon, WA 98273
Tel. (206) 466-4592
Hrs: Fri. - Sat. 10:00 a.m. - 5:00 p.m.
Rest of the week by appointment or chance
Mastercard and Visa accepted

In 1984 owner Kit Muehlman and manager Marguerite Goff moved their pottery activities from the living and laundry rooms, respectively, into their current location just four miles east of LaConner and six miles west of Conway (I-5 exit 221).

Pleasant Ridge Pottery occupies a building designed and built by Kit and her husband, Dan to house the potter's studios, as well as, a display gallery.

The whole building is open to the public. You can watch Kit and Marguerite at work, "throwing" the raw clay on a potter's wheel, the glazing and kiln drying. You appreciate the items you take home more when you've learned the many steps required to produce the finished product.

Kit specializes in functional stoneware, porcelain lamps, bowls, and casseroles; producing only a limited number of each creation. Since her own children were born, Kit has been making beautiful children's lamps decorated with rocking horses and gingerbread men. She mixes all of her own glazes.

Marguerite has a fine arts degree and specializes in sculpting. She especially enjoys the excitement of forming the clay on the potter's wheel and making original pots. She will do custom work, with variations on a theme, to suit your decor.

The attached gallery presents pottery, Skagit County weaving, Windsor chairs (made by Kit's husband, Dan), handmade baskets, paintings, dried flowers and silk screened pillows. Visit anytime--call ahead on weekdays.

Restaurant

CAFE EUROPA, 516 South First, Mount Vernon, Washington. Fresh homemade soups, European desserts, breads, espresso coffees, and items from the charbroiler await you at the Cafe Europa. The food, service and ambience should not be missed.

FARMHOUSE INN
1376 LaConner-Whitney Road
Mt. Vernon, WA 98273
Tel. (206) 466-4411
Hrs: Mon. - Thu.   7:00 a.m. - 1:00 a.m.
     Fri. - Sat.   7:00 a.m. - 2:00 a.m.
     Sunday   7:00 a.m. - 12:00 midnight

If you enjoy good country-style home cooking, you'll love dining at the Farmhouse Inn, a favorite with the locals from Mount Vernon, Burlington, Anacortes and LaConner, and only 7 miles west of the I-5 Exit 230 on SR20. Owners Tore and Dianna Dybfest, began serving guests in June, 1980 in their attractive restaurant decorated with implements from early farming days. Enjoy viewing the full-size sculpture of an Irish farmer and his plowhorse.

The baked goods served at the Farmhouse Inn are the result of three dedicated bakers who spend their nights baking at least ten different fresh pies, cornbread, blueberry muffins, carrot cakes and cheesecakes for your eating pleasure.

Along with standard breakfast fare, the Farmhouse Inn breakfast menu features Norwegian waffles, Swedish pancakes, Hangtown Fry (fresh oyster, bacon and cheese omelette), Eggs Benedict, and steak and eggs. Side orders include farmhouse sugar-cured bacon, smoked ham or sausage, and buckwheat pancakes.

For lunch the menu offers a number of sandwiches and burgers to consider, sundaes, ice cream, milk shakes, or banana splits. The Farmhouse Inn provides special fare for children under twelve, and for seniors. On weekdays a Sandwich Buffet is offered. Select your luncheon from a choice of salads, croissants, breads, beans, roasted turkey and roast beef, corned beef and soup. Be sure to try the Scandinavian Country Soup.

The dinner menu favorite is the fresh roasted turkey with all the trimmings including homemade cornbread with honey butter. The Veal Cordon Bleu is made from scratch and tastes outstanding. Excellent steaks are available for the "meat and potatoes" eater. Fresh from the Puget Sound are grilled oysters, batter-dipped cod, clam strips, beer batter dipped prawns and a Seafood Harvest plate with assorted variety for those that have a hard time making one choice. For the light eater, the Farmhouse Inn offers several nice salads.

The full service lounge features live music Friday and Saturday nights (country and western, 50's and 60's soft rock, and top 40's). There's even a dance floor for those wishing to "cut a rug" with their favorite person.

Tore and Dianna want to be your hosts for home cooking and courteous service in a real "down-home" atmosphere. Gather your family, visit the Farmhouse Inn and enjoy!

WILDFLOWERS
2001 East College Way
Mount Vernon, WA 98273
Tel. (206) 424-9724
Hrs: Lunch Mon. - Sun 11:30 a.m. - 2:30 p.m.
     Dinner   5:00 p.m. - 9:00 p.m.

Mick and Cheryl August have established their Wildflowers restaurant in a house that they renovated. It is beautifully appointed, with flowers everywhere. They have created elegant surroundings while maintaining a casual atmosphere. Be prepared to be pampered as you enjoy "American fare with a flair." The staff is gracious and you will feel as if you are a guest in their home, one of the charming benefits of this small restaurant.

The general format is American bar and grill. Lunches include a choice of soup or house salad and hot cheese bread. Among lunch favorites are grilled breast of chicken with curry butter and peach chutney or grilled, sliced sirloin steak with sauteed onions and chili butter. Dinners are culinary happenings, from the appetizers through outstanding desserts. The signature dish is the Greek style roast lamb marinated in garlic and mustard. Others choices include filet of salmon with lemon-vermouth glaze, a small beef tenderloin steak with crab and bernaise sauce and much more. All are delicious and moderately priced. There is an extensive wine list and rare cordials, brandies and aperitifs gathered from around the world.

For elegant dining with personalized service and outstanding food, be sure to visit Wildflowers.

Sedro-Woolley

Local folks make a big thing of the hyphen in the name of their town, which traces its linage to a development-minded gentleman named Mortimer Cook. He came here after launching Santa Barbara, California on a course of development. The 1886 construction of a store was followed by a shingle mill, and designation of the town as "Sedro," a misspelling of the Spanish *cedro* for cedar run through the shingle mill.

The Great Northern and Northern Pacific Railroads established a junction north of Sedro in 1889. P. A. Woolley named a town site at the junction after himself. The next year the two towns incorporated as one, placing the hyphen in the official name. Map makers and about everyone but the Skagit County Historical Society have long-since dropped the hyphen.

Cook shipped his singles by riverboat to the local trade on Puget Sound. Woolley milled western red cedar too, sending shingles east by the train load. Today this little logging community boasts of steelhead fishing in the Skagit river instead of log rafts and boats. North Cascades National Park has its headquarters here, and Highway 20 winds its way east over two mountain passes carrying tourists instead of wood.

Attractions

Lake Whatcom Railway, SR 9 at Wickersham, provides a scenic one and a half hour train trip through the countryside. Steam-powered trains depart on Tuesday and Saturday, at noon, June thru early-September. Call 595-2218 for further info.

Pacific Northwest Float Trips, departing from the Country Store at the junction of SR 20 and 530, offers whitewater rafting, bald eagle sightseeing, fishing and gold-panning trips on the Northwest rivers, including

Toutle Rapids. Write to P. O. Box 736, Sedro-Woolley for information, or call 855-0535.

For further information, contact the Sedro-Woolley Chamber of Commerce, 714 Metcalf Street, Sedro-Woolley WA 98284. Telephone 855-0770.

Art Gallery

LEE MANN GALLERY
2128 Bassett Road
Sedro Wooley, WA 98284
Tel. (206) 856-0581
Hrs: Mon. - Sat. 9:00 a.m. - 5:00 p.m.
Visa, MasterCard and AMEX are accepted.

If there are aspects of the Northwest mountains, lakes, oceans or wildlife that have piqued your interest or captured your emotions, this is the place to find outstanding photographs of them. Lee Mann has captured many facets of the Northwest in all their beauty, and his work is marketed throughout Western Washington and elsewhere. The best selection of his work, encompassing the Northwest experience from ocean to mountains, is to be found right here at the Lee Mann Gallery.

Lee's work on environmental education projects that resulted in his producing slide shows and film strips about the Northwest led him into his present vocation. His love of nature, broad knowledge of the life cycles and habits of animals and immense patience have led to his producing the largest selection of nature photographs of the Northwest.

Visit the Lee Mann Gallery and select photographs that you'll enjoy for years to come.

Outdoor trip-planners

KM RANCH, 946 Cockreham Road, Sedro Woolley, Washington. Daytime horseback rides, overnight camping trips, hiker's pack trips, custom fishing and hunting trips.

SKAMANIA COUNTY

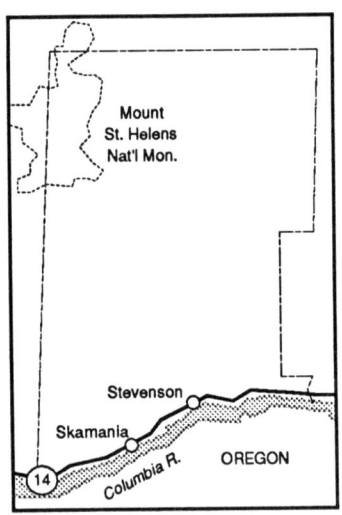

Cascade Mountain forests, broken by lava beds and the huge mass of Mount Saint Helens, occupy most of this 1,672 square-mile county which fronts on the Columbia River and runs north to Lewis County. Most of the 8,000 residents live in small communities along the Columbia River where the famed Columbia River Gorge frames vistas of rock, water and tall mountains. The giant forest fire of 1902, called the Yacolt burn, killed timber from Clark County in the west almost to Stevenson, Skamania's county seat. Now the second growth forest is yielding timber which sustains much of the local economy.

Skamania takes its name from an Indian word for "swift waters." Before Bonneville Dam flooded the two-and-a half miles of rapids in which the river dropped almost seventy feet, there was indeed swift water here. These rapids caused botanist David Douglas in 1825 to name the mountain range "Cascades." The Pacific Crest Trail, following the Cascade Mountain crests, winds from north to south through eastern Skamania County reaching the river near the small town of Cook. The county was created in 1854.

Among the geologic wonders of the gorge is the Great Bonneville Landslide which is dated to the year 1,205 and for a time dammed the entire Columbia River's flow. Red bluffs above the river show the rock face left after the giant slide, and Greenleaf Falls cascades 300 feet over the jumbled surface of the landslide each spring, then dries up as water becomes scarce on the hillside above. The slide area is just upstream and above the present town of North Bonneville.

ATTRACTIONS

Much of the **Mount Saint Helens National Volcanic Monument** (see listing under Clark County) is in Skamania. A system of scenic forest roads up the Wind River takes travelers deep into the forest with connecting roads to the east side of the mountain and then to the closest viewpoints of the crater reached by car. They overlook **Spirit Lake**.

Beacon Rock is the world's second largest free-standing monolith, the Rock of Gibraltar is the first. Thirty-five miles east of Vancouver on Highway 14, Beacon Rock is a state park, and very climbable. A fenced trail leads to the top, 848 feet above the Columbia River. Campsites, swimming, fishing and other facilities are available at the park along with views of the famed Columbia River Gorge.

North Bonneville, with about 400 residents, is the ultimate in planned communities. The resort-like town was created in 1978 to replace the old town wiped out by construction of the second powerhouse at Bonneville Dam. The half-century old dam has extensive visitor facilities. Construction began here in 1933, with work completed in September, 1937.

Hamilton Island, located almost at Bonneville Dam on the Columbia River, provides an interpretation of Indian and pioneer days, plus a demonstration of the fishing wheel used to take thousands of tons of salmon from the river before the states of Oregon and Washington outlawed them. Among the exhibits, an Indian village, pioneer cemetery, and the first portage railroad for Columbia River boats.

Bridge of the Gods, a bridge over the Columbia River completed in 1926 takes its name from the rock arch described in an Indian legend. U.S. Army Engineers maintain an information kiosk here to assist visitors looking at Hamilton Island and the Bonneville dam and power houses.

Steamboat excursions on the Columbia operate each summer out of Stevenson. With 1,200 residents, this is the county's largest town and county seat. The docks are two blocks from the center of town. Current steamboat excursions from Stevenson to Bonneville Dam operate daily from mid-June through the end of September. Call (503) 427-5141 for departure times. The stern-wheeler spends its winter months plying the Willamette River out of Portland.

Stevenson is a neat residential community with an old-fashioned town square, and a 1903 courthouse building at the top of a hill. A rock marked "H. B. Co. 1811" is believed to have marked early boundaries of the fur company's franchise. The rock became part of the Stevenson high school campus in the 1930s.

Skamania County Historical Museum, on Vancouver Street in Stevenson, traces events from days when the Cascades of the Columbia made this a portage location for travelers. Open Monday through Saturday from 12:00 noon to 5:00 p.m., and Sundays from 1:00 p.m. to 6:00 p.m. Telephone (509) 427-5141, extension 218.

Carson, a tiny community just north of Highway 14 three miles upstream from Stevenson, is an old hot springs resort which has enjoyed a resurgence in popularity in recent years. **Saint Martin's Hot Mineral Spring Hotel** with its four-story frame construction, welcomes guests as it did in the days when guests came upstream from Portland and Vancouver by steamboat. For hotel information call (509) 427-8292. Margaret Saint Martin developed the 122-degree mineral springs as a resort in 1888.

Wind River Tree Nursery, ten miles north of Carson on the Wind River Highway, is the source of millions of seedling trees planted each year by the U.S. Forest Service. One of the largest nurseries in the world, this facility also includes an arboretum. Visitors are welcome. One of the most interesting times is in late January when lifting and packaging of seedlings begins. Trees are shipped to reforest logging sites all over the Pacific Northwest.

For further information, contact the Skamania County Chamber of Commerce, Box 759, Stevenson WA 98648. Telephone (509) 427-8911.

SNOHOMISH COUNTY

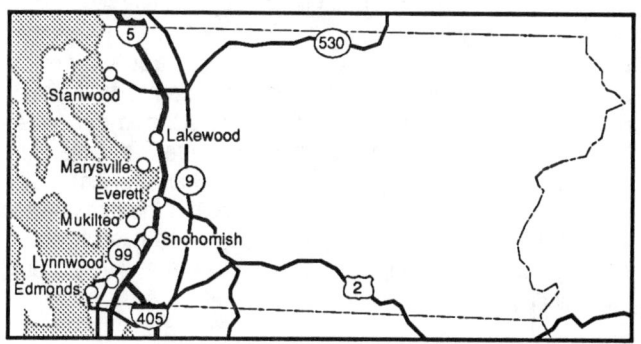

Snohomish is almost a twin to King County in area and orientation, lying just north of Washington's most populous county. Snohomish too stretches from the waters of Puget Sound to the crest of the Cascade Mountains, taking in 2,098 square miles. About half of the land is in federal ownership under two National Forests. Glacier Peak, a 10,568 foot land mark, is the highest point in the county. The Glacier Peak Wilderness Area surrounds the mountain itself and connects to North Cascades National Park trails (see listing under Skagit County).

This is also a county with most of its 340,000 residents living near the Sound or in one of the three valleys formed by streams draining the Cascades to the east. From the south these are the Skykomish River which provides a route for Highway 2 east through Stevens Pass; and the Stillaguamish River which has one fork twisting south and eastward to Sloan Peak and another to the north carrying Highway 530 to Darrington where other major tributaries reach further into the timbered mountains.

Everett has a long history of industrial development. Puget Sound Reduction Company built a metal recovery plant in 1893. Ores with such diverse yields as lead and silver were shipped in to the plant. Lumber mills developed on the waterfront. The area figured in Washington's labor unrest early in this century, including a 1916 shooting when Industrial Workers of the World attempted to come ashore on an Everett wharf filled with police and vigilantes. Boeing picked Everett for one of its aircraft plants during World War II, and many of the county's residents continue to work for Boeing and its subcontractors today.

The county, the river and the town of Snohomish all take their name from the Indians who lived over much of the area from the Sound east into the Cascade foothills. Actual meaning of the word is obscure, apparently simply a term for "people" applied by the tribes. There were distinct upriver villages and those on the Sound which were linked with harvest of salmon. The entire tribe is now consolidated on the Tulalip Reservation, an 8,930 acre preserve created by treaty in 1855. It was 1861 that the county was officially created during a territorial reorganization.

Modern Snohomish County has found itself with some curious political problems as residential areas mushroomed out from the Seattle Metropolitan area after World War II. Well over half of its residents live in rural areas under county jurisdiction, many in subdivisions where there is a demand for urban-type services. In 1979, county voters adopted a charter which created the strong county-executive type of government in place of the three-person county commission which had roots in territorial days. The executive is in charge of all county services, carrying out ordinances set by a county council made up of delegates elected from districts.

ATTRACTIONS

Lake Stevens, eight miles east of Everett, is the name of the largest lake in the county and of a town of the same name. This deep lake has land-locked salmon and other game fish. The rural setting, with its large lake, is site of a Hewlett Packard electronics plant and the home of about 2,400 people within city limits. Once the site of the giant Rucker Brothers lumber mill from 1906 to 1925, the community grew slowly and incorporated in 1960. For information, contact **Lake Stevens Chamber of Commerce**, C-60002 Suite 219, Lake Stevens WA 98258. Telephone 334-0433.

Stevens Pass, on Highway 2 forty miles east of Everett, is one of Western Washington's most popular ski area. The pass honors the Great Northern Railroad's chief engineer who drilled a tunnel beneath the 4,061-foot summit. The highway provides summer travelers with stops at the interesting communities of Gold Bar and Index, and is a route into camps and fishing streams on the Snoqualmie National Forest.

The **South Fork** of the Stillaguamish River, between Granite Falls and Arlington, is popular with **kayackers**. Fifteen miles of river, rated moderate in difficulty, are close to a good highway and end where the North Fork Stillaguamish joins for its meandering trip across a broad valley to the sound.

Snohomish County's forests and mountains draw **hikers** and fishermen by the hundreds to U.S. Forest Service camps and trails. About forty percent of the land is designated wilderness where recreation use is of primary importance. For information contact the **Supervisor's office**, 1022 First

Avenue, Seattle WA 98104, telephone 442-0170; or **Darrington Ranger Station**, Darrington WA 98241, telephone 436-1155.

Arlington, a town of 3,300 three miles east of I-5, is the gateway to Cascade recreation areas. Highway 530 leads east to Darrington, then a north branch joins Highway 20 into the North Cascades National Park.

Granite Falls, on Highway 92, is the start of a 101-mile highway loop through the Mount Baker National Forest. There is a local historical **museum**. On up the highway is **Monte Cristo**, now a ghost town. It was once linked by railroad to Everett, where the reduction plant processed ore yielding gold, silver, copper and other minerals.

For further information, contact the **Snohomish County Visitor Information Center**, Box 2211, Lynnwood WA 98036. Telephone 745-4138.

Edmonds

On Puget Sound just north of the King County line, Edmonds has about 27,700 residents and a large marina. The name is a misspelling. Edmond's first postmaster wanted to honor George F. Edmunds, a U.S. Senator from Vermont, but he evidently turned in the incorrect spelling to the U.S. Postal Service. Legend has it that when logger George Brackett petitioned to establish the town of Edmonds in 1890, he added the names of his two oxen to the list to achieve the requisite number of applicants for the petition.

The Edmonds waterfront is an important ferryboat terminal. Service from here to the Kitsap Peninsula and the floating bridge beyond connecting to the Olympic Peninsula is used by many residents in the northern part of Seattle metropolitan area.

Edmonds is more than a small city in the political life of Snohomish County. It is also Edmonds School District 15, the fifth largest in the state with an enrollment of 17,000 students and a faculty of 1,500. The district serves the suburban area on the King County line in which 100,000 people live in rural subdivisions and four smaller incorporated cities besides Edmonds.

Attractions

The **public fishing pier**, right next to downtown, gives access to year-around saltwater fishing. Nearby is a major marina for the area, with moorage for 700 boats.

Edmonds Underwater State Park is on the north side of the ferry dock. SCUBA divers say this is the most popular diving location in the Pacific Northwest. Among the attractions are three old dry dock barges now resting on the bottom and home for marine life.

For further information, contact the **Edmonds Chamber of Commerce**, Box 146, Edmonds WA 98020. Telephone 776-6711.

Bed and Breakfast

THE MAINSTAY
729 Main Street
Edmonds, WA 98020
Tel. (206) 775-2717

Set your sails for the Mainstay if you'd like to spend a night in a Victorian home that has been occupied by just two families since the first of this century.

Today the Mainstay is an elegant bed and breakfast inn that retains the charms of the 1880s, which was when it was built by an eastern lumber company magnate. It commands a superb view of Puget Sound and you can watch the ships pass on their way to the straits of Juan De Fuca.

Hosts Rich and Cheryl Hansen, only the second family to have owned this home since 1904, have filled the home with gracious antique furniture, and decorated it with artworks from both the old world and the new. Expect special touches like fresh flowers and a wrapped chocolate on your pillow. Curl up and relax next to the parlor fire. You're advised to wake up hungry to best enjoy Richard's gourmet fare. Although European in tradition, this breakfast is not continental. It's a generous and multiple course meal featuring favorites like mouth-watering quiche, home-baked bread and poached pear Zinfandel.

An added bonus is that the Mainstay's location is just a few blocks from downtown shopping and the ferry terminal. The Mainstay cannot accommodate children or pets and requests that guests not smoke. So even if your trip has been rough, the Mainstay will make your rest smooth sailing.

Delicatessen

PETOSA'S FAMILY GROCER
50 Fifth Avenue, South
Edmonds, WA 98020
Tel. (206) 774-5244
Hrs: Mon. - Sat.   9:00 a.m. - 9:00 p.m.
     Sunday   9:00 a.m. - 8:00 p.m.
     Closed Christmas day

Tom and Betty Jo Petosa started a grocery in the Greenwood area of Seattle years ago and expanded to Edmonds, with a second store in March of 1986.

They specialize in quality fresh produce and meats, along with a full-service deli. The deli specializes in homemade fare like grandma used to bake. Try the bread pudding, custards and delectable desserts. French pastries made here literally melt in your mouth. Sandwiches, light salads and broasted chicken. You will find a superb selection of wines to go with the fare.

This is a family run business; pride is taken in serving you the very best.

A fun day, a picnic, good company and a superb choice of creative cooking to add the appropriate flourish as the grand finale´.

\	A PICNIC TOUR OF EDMONDS		
a.m.	Basketta's Shop	Best picnic baskets	Edm/Gift
a.m.	Petosa's Grocer	Best picnic goodies	Edm/Deli
a.m.	C-Fresh Sea Food	Best fresh, fresh seafood	Edm/Sea.
p.m.	Sierra Park	Best trails and nature	Edm/C of C
	Now, your mood determines the "Best Choice" for dinner:		
p.m.	Bel Piemonte	Best No. Italian cuisine	Edm/Rest.
p.m.	Clark's on Edm. Bay	Best seafood, beef & pasta	Edm/Rest.
p.m.	L'Escargot	Best French cuisine	Edm/Rest.
p.m.	Quintana Roo	Best chili w/soul	Edm/Rest.
p.m.	Sailor's Restaurant	Best dinner w/entertain.	Edm/Rest.
p.m.	Seattle Style Rest.	Best mesquite char-broil	Edm/Rest.

Florist

THE WEED LADY
122 Fourth Avenue South
Edmonds, WA 98020
Tel. (206) 775-3800
Hrs: Tues.-Sat. 10:30 a.m.-5:30 p.m.

When you gather wild flowers, dry them, and sell them, you're just asking for a nick-name. To neighborhood kids who watched Joan Searle begin her dried flower business, back in the 1960s, she became the "Weed Lady."

Today, Joan's arrangements and crafts are popular for celebrations of every kind. Step in to the old house, you'll not only feast your eyes on a kaleidoscope of dried flowers, but be greeted by fragrant potpourris filling the air. Go around back and admire the flower and herb garden where fresh cut flowers are often used for weddings and an annual herbal luncheon is held in the summer. The staff will help you choose your own decorations from the dried materials available, or if you don't have time to make your own, take one of the already creatively fashioned wreaths or arrangements.

Although times have changed, and the business has grown like a weed, Joan still does all her own pickings in the wild. Other country gifts and Northwest Artisans all add up to The Weed Lady shop being a memorable experience.

(See special invitation in the Appendix.)

Gift Shops

BASKETTA'S RETAIL SHOP
300 Admiral Way #104
Edmonds, WA 98020
Tel. (206) 776-1445
Hrs: Mon. - Sun. 10:00 a.m. - 9:00 p.m.
and,
201 5th Avenue S Suite L
Edmonds, WA 98020
Tel. (206) 776-1002

If what you need is a real basket case, don't sweat it. Instead, head to Basketta where you'll find jazzy sweatshirts, original greeting cards, and decorative baskets from around the world.

Owner Joanne Phillips has traveled to Hong Kong, Thailand, Singapore and Taiwan in search of distinctive and functional baskets. You'll see the product of her efforts lining the walls and hanging from the ceiling. Basketta also features baskets from west coast Indian tribes, as well as popular pine needle baskets from local Edmonds artists. Wicker creations come in many forms, including wall hangings, plant holders, baby carriers and furniture pieces. Along with the baskets, Basketta is well known for its original cards and appliqued sweatshirts. Especially for the skipper and first mate is a pair of sweatshirts. One says, "Don't yell at me." The other says "I'm not yelling."

So whether you need a sweatshirt, or something in which to pack a picnic. Make a stop at Basketta's, your "Best Choice" for fun, baskets and unique gifts.

THE WOODEN SPOON, 319 Main Street, Edmonds, Washington. Owner Cheryl Larabee describes her store as "sophisticated country." You'll find a wide array of kitchen collectibles, linens, gourmet items and gifts.

Restaurant

BEL PIEMONTE NORTHERN ITALIAN RESTAURANT
P. O. Box 42
Edmonds, WA 98020
Tel. (206) 771-7950
Hrs: Tue. - Sat. 5:30 p.m. - 10:30 p.m.
Closed Christmas.
MasterCard and Visa are accepted.
Reservations are advised.

If it's pizza you want, you had better go elsewhere. This Italian restaurant caters to the refined cuisine of northern Italy and serves it in European style.

Don't expect to find many of the offerings most Americans have grown to expect in Italian restaurants. The food at Bel Piemonte is more varied, abundant and satisfying than the Italian food with which we've grown familiar. The small and intimate restaurant lends itself to personal service by owners Giuseppe and Linda Surbone who prepare and serve your dinners with charm and pleasure. Linda spent five years learning northern Italian cooking in Turin to assure you of authentic and delicious dining. Everything is prepared from scratch including elegant desserts like the profiterole - cream puffs with ice cream and chocolate sauce. In European style, the menu begins with appetizers and progresses through the first of several courses.

This is a great way to really learn about this kind of food, but if you're in a hurry, you're out of luck. With food like this - Italian food with a difference - who's in any hurry?

CLARK'S ON EDMONDS BAY
51 W Dayton
Edmonds, WA 98020
Tel. (206) 774-5811
Hrs: Lunch Mon. - Sat. 11:30 a.m. - 3:00 p.m.
     Dinner Sun. - Thu. 4:00 p.m. - 10:00 p.m.
            Fri. - Sat.   4:00 p.m. - 11:00 p.m.
     Brunch Sunday   10:00 a.m. - 3:00 p.m.

It's great to dine right on the water. At Clark's On Edmonds Bay you would have to roll up your pants to get a closer view of the bay. The third floor dining room gives you the feeling of being afloat on the sea.

Enjoy the sunsets over Puget Sound and the Olympic Peninsula while savoring some of the best seafood meals Edmonds has to offer. The restaurant is owned and operated by Clark and Kim Covey. Although known for its seafood, Clark's serves excellent choice aged beef and pasta dishes. Appetizers run the gourmet gamut of escargot, Dungeness crab, calamari and fresh local oysters on the half shell. The wine list includes French imports and features a superb selection of Northwest vintages.

Remember, when the name says "Clark's On Edmond's Bay," you won't have to get your feet wet in order to enjoy the freshest seafood and view that Edmond's has to offer!

COURTYARD THEATRE AND RESTAURANT
238th and Highway 99
Edmonds, WA 98020
Tel. (206) 771-3341
Hrs: Restaurant open Mon.-Sat. for lunch and dinner and open for Sunday Brunch.
     Box office: Mon. -Wed. 10:00 a.m. - 6:00 p.m.
                 Thurs-Sat. 10:00 a.m. - 7:00 p.m.
     Shows: Wed.- Sat. 8:00 p.m.

Want a break from the usual? Try the only dinner theater in greater Seattle, which also serves as a mini shopping center. Stroll along a cobblestone lane, view the old world atrium, poke around a few shops, relax in a plush burgundy chair set between wrought iron dividers, where you can delight in the magnificent view of the Cascade mountains to the east.

Every seat in the house has a good view of the stage. The stage is designed with Elizabethan flair, giving you the chance to enjoy good theater as Shakespeares's patrons once did.

So if the whole world is a stage, why not have one as part of a small shopping center? You can enjoy the play and eat your dinner too!

L'ESCARGOT
419 Main Street
Edmonds, WA 98020
Tel. (206) 778-9888
Hrs: Tue. - Sat.   5:30 p.m. - 10:30 p.m.
       Sun. - Mon. Banquets only, luncheon groups up to eighty people.
Reservations requested.

Owner/chef Jean Ibarbide worked in his parents' hotel in Barretz, France in Basque country. From this beginning, he continued refining his culinary skills and has cooked for Queen Elizabeth, as well as Prince and Princess Narechem of Russia. In 1957, Jean won eight gold medals in Brussels, Belgium at the Culinary Olympics.

At L'Escargot, Jean has taken his skills and blended them with those of his wife, who created an elegant, intimate interior with exquisite crystal chandeliers. Chef Jean serves a variety of fantastic meals from fresh rock lobster to French dinners that are an epicurean's dream.

Jean and his wife invite you to indulge in a palate pleasing, relaxing evening at L'Escargot, an unforgettable "Best Choice" in Edmonds, Washington.

QUINTANA ROO
303 Dayton Street
Edmonds, WA 98020
Tel. (206) 778-9096
Hrs: Mon. - Fri.   11:30 a.m. - 10:00 p.m.
       Sat. & Sun. 12:00 noon - 10:00 p.m.

You know what they say, "when you're hot, you're hot--" especially if you're a chili champion like Quintana Roo owners Chris and Eileen Matt.

Chris and Eileen have twice won the Washington Chili Championship and have competed against the world's best at the World Championship Chili Cook-off down in Terlingua, Texas. Their chili is made with filet mignon, special sauces, but no beans. So if you ask around for the best Mexican food in Edmonds, you'll probably get directions leading you a little off the beaten track, but just two blocks south of Main Street on Dayton Street to Quintana Roo.

When you find this restaurant, with its outdoor patio, you can enjoy the chili, or another house favorite, the gordo burrito. Gordo means "fat" and true to its name this one weighs in at two pounds and is smothered in meat, beans, rice, avocado, tomatoes, cheese and a choice of sauces; the range is mildly spicy to smoking hot. Cool off your palate with one of the eight Mexican beers, or fight back with a shot of tequila.

When someone tells you this is good Mexican food, they're not full of beans. It's the truth. It's just the chili that doesn't have the beans!

SAILOR'S RESTAURANT
Atop Harbor Square
190 W Dayton
Edmonds, WA 98020
Tel. (206) 771-5331
Hrs: Mon. - Sun. 7:00 a.m. - 10:00 p.m.
Visa, MasterCard, Diner's Club and AMEX are accepted.

The combined talents from Jim Hill's seventeen years in the meat business and wife Shirlee's penchant for cooking great food has caused the success of Sailor's Restaurant since 1979.

Only the highest quality ingredients, and remember Jim knows his stuff, from the meats to the fresh seafood are used. Shirlee's huge omelettes, affectionately referred to as "yellow footballs", will start your day. Specials change weekly providing you with tempting choices of fish and seafood.

Relax and enjoy your meal while you take in the panoramic view of sailboats, windsurfers, ferry boats, trains and trolley cars. The decor is elegant with oak, brass, mirrors and plants providing a welcome ambiance. After dinner, listen to live entertainment on Thursday through Sunday nights.

(See special invitation in the Appendix.)

SEATTLE STYLE RESTAURANT
in Dawson City
238th & Highway 99
Edmonds, WA 98020
Tel. (206) 775-3103
Hrs: Mon. - Sat.　lunch　　11:30 a.m. - 3:00 p.m.
　　　Sun. - Thurs. dinner　5:00 p.m. - 9:00 p.m.
　　　Fri. - Sat.　dinner　　5:00 p.m. - 10:00 p.m.

    A special restaurant, opened four years ago by partners Mike Riley, Joe Shanks and Bill Shanks. The name of the restaurant comes from the type of clam chowder they serve--Seattle style. Their vision is that this chowder should achieve national recognition just as Manhattan chowder has received. It is worthy of such acclaim.
    The aim is to provide the highest quality possible in a neighborhood setting. They serve "bled" ling cod, which is cod that has been caught individually, rather than by the large trawlers, prepared on site and shipped directly to Edmonds. They specialize in swordfish, halibut and salmon--charbroiled with mesquite, rubbed with garlic and seared on the open flames many pasta dishes with seafood are also available. Additional seafoods such as mussels, clams, oysters, prawns, scallops, shrimp, etc. are also house specialties.
    There are twelve kids in the Shank's family--restauranting is the family forte. They help to provide the comfortable, casual and relaxing atmosphere--so you can enjoy the delectable seafood served.

Recreational Vehicle Repair

J - S RV REPAIR
22214 Highway 99 North
Edmonds, WA 98020
Tel. (206) 778-5935
Hrs: Mon. - Fri. 8:00 a.m. - 5:00 p.m.
Closed all major holidays

    Looking for a reliable repair shop for your RV, trailer or camper? This is it! No employee has less than ten years of experience. Owners Wally and Dick have a policy which states, "If you can't do it right, then don't do it at all."
    They specialize as the only shop, in western Washington, which recharges refrigerators. Other services include: repair of air conditioning, generators, appliances, and refurbishing of interiors and exteriors. In short-

-they do all repairs except oil changes and grease jobs. Estimates for insurance and collision repairs gladly tendered and performed.

Easy to get to: take 220th Street S.W. exit off I-5 when going north from Seattle.

It happens to the best of us...so just make the best of the situation and enjoy your day while the camper/RV is in good hands for its needed cure.

BEST LAID PLANS...HOW TO ENJOY THE DAY IN EDMONDS WHEN THE FAMILY'S WHEELS WON'T			
a.m.	J-S RV Repair	Best vehicle repairs	Edm/RV
a.m.	The Weed Lady	Best dried flowers	Edm/Florist
a.m.	Monarch Trading	Best idea for sleep	Edm/Wool
a.m.	Spin-A-Yarn	Best knitting supplies	Edm/Textiles
p.m.	C-Fresh Sea Food	Best view and brew	Edm/Sea.
Now, go pick up you wheels and enjoy the rest of your day.			

Seafood

C-FRESH SEA FOOD
300 Admiral Way #101
Edmonds, WA 98020
Tel. (206) 771-4248
Hrs: Mon.-Sat.   10:00 a.m. - 6:00 p.m.
      Sunday   12:00 noon - 6:00 p.m.

You know your fish is fresh when you can watch the boats come in to drop off the day's catch. Bud and Dorothy Christensen's customers at C-Fresh enjoy looking out over the water, from the shop, where they often see the gill netters returning to port. Here you can pick out the fixings for the perfect seafood dinner, or sit out at the picnic tables to enjoy a crab cocktail complemented with a little beer or wine.

The Christensen's have been operating from the same waterfront location for twenty-six years and buying fish the same way--directly from the fishermen operating out of the Port of Edmonds, or through a buyer in Alaska who puts fresh salmon on a plane to them. Live Dungeness and king crab is flown directly from Wrangell and other Alaska ports. New agreements with west coast fishermen provide the shop, and its customers, with live fresh crab year round.

If you make a catch on a charter boat, Bud and Dorothy can pack it for you and send it anywhere in North America. With seafood this fresh, it's easy to get hooked on a place like this.

Textiles

SPIN-A-YARN
526 Main Street
Edmonds, WA 98020
Tel. (206) 775-0909
Hrs: Mon. - Sat. 10:00 a.m. -5:00 p.m.

You want something like those knits in the fancy fashion magazines? Right? But your pocket book says "department store prices...can't afford it." At Spin-A-Yarn you can find the inspiration, instruction and yarns for creating your own original.

Spin-A-Yarn provides the yarns and shows you the intricacies of knitting techniques. The teaching comes free. You just supply the labor. The result is an affordable sweater. Browse the selections of yarn that come from England, France, Italy and Japan, from basic solid wools to multi-colored blends, wool twisted with metallics, cotton, silk, Cashmere, even leather. There's also mesh backing and yarn for latch work rugs, with which you can create a Persian design or an unusual souvenir of your trip to Edmonds.

So wear that classy knit. Let 'em think you bought it in Paris--even if it's a a tall tale, you can or spin-a-good yarn.

MONARCH TRADING COMPANY
170 W Dayton
Edmonds, WA 98020
Tel. (206) 774-8911
Hrs: Mon. - Sat. 10:00 a.m - 6:00 p.m.
and,
#180 Bellevue Square
Bellevue, WA 98004
Tel. (206) 453-0922

If counting sheep doesn't put you to sleep at night...one sheep product, provided by Monarch Trading Company, is guaranteed to give you a better night's snooze.

This New Zealand firm is so sure that one of its two inch thick lambs wool mattress pads will improve your sleep they'll guarantee it in writing. This is just one of the products with which New Zealander A. W. Mason stocks his shop in Edmonds' Harbor Square. Nearly all of his luxury suede and wool products come from his homeland, a place where 70 million sheep outnumber the people twenty times over. And it was there that a reputation for fine sheep products grew, partly because they perfected a tanning process which makes their wool washable. But it is sometime difficult to convince customers that the plush lambskin rugs are both durable for walking on and machine washable! Customers have a pick of colors and shapes in these rugs. Monarch also features the finest, softest, most pliable suedes and leathers in a classy range of men's and women's outerwear and clothing.

So whether you're looking for a good night sleep, or a washable wool rug, Monarch Trading Company has it.....and, they ba-a-a-a-a-ack their product!

Not into putting out a lot of energy to see Edmonds? Really feeling laid back? Here's the tour for you.....

ROCKING CHAIR TOUR OF EDMONDS		
a.m. The Mainstay	Best pampered guests	Edm/B & B
a.m. Public fishing pier	Best people/boat watching	Edm/Attrac.
a.m. Underwater Park	Best scuba watching	Edm/Attrac.
p.m. Courtyard Restaurant	Best lunch	Edm/Rest.
p.m. Dawson	Best quaint shops	Edm/Rest.
p.m. Courtyard Theater	Best dinner theater	Edm/Rest.

Do note that the last three entries, in this tour, are all located under the same roof!

Everett

The largest city in Snohomish County, Everett is a creation of John D. Rockefeller and a group of East Coast developers. The city they laid out in 1891 now has over 55,000 residents. First growth came amid speculation that Great Northern Railroad would locate its saltwater terminal here. Ore from the Monte Cristo mines was pouring into the reduction plant. Speculators with interests in the mines backed the land company marketing the town. Everett grew so rapidly with its superior harbor facilities that the county seat moved here in 1896. The name Everett comes from Everett Colby, son of Charles L. Colby, a principal in Rockefeller's Everett Land Company.

Names of the early developers are on the downtown streets, where several buildings constructed in those booming times, now restored, are still in commercial use. The sprawling Boeing plant which is an outgrowth of company dispersion in World War II, now makes two of the largest aircraft, the 747 jumbo jet and the newer 767. Both are assembled at Everett from parts fabricated in several locations.

Attractions

The **Everett Public Market**, 2804 Grand Street, has nearly sixty shops including an antique mall with over thirty dealers. Open Monday through Saturday from 10:00 a.m. to 5:30 p.m., Sundays from 12:00 noon to 5:00 p.m. When the building was constructed in 1908 it was for a livery stable. Aircraft wings were fabricated here during World War II and it later served as a warehouse until its 1983 conversion to a market. Telephone 252-1089.

Jetty Island, a city park, uses what was in 1895 the training dike to reshape the flow of water from Snohomish River to create a large harbor. Now warm water swimming and miles of sandy beaches are part of this island. It is also the winter home for migrating sea lions. Each summer from July through September, the city offers free ferry boat service and a series of events. Boats leave Marina Village every half hour, Wednesday through Sunday from 11:00 a.m. to 7:00 p.m. Telephone 252-1631.

Legion Park, on Alverson Boulevard, is a recreation area featuring the **Everett Area Arboretum**, with a collection of native and exotic plants. Also at the park is the **Snohomish County Museum**.

Forest Park, on East Mukilteo Boulevard off 41st Street, has a popular animal farm operating each summer. Loaned or donated farm animals are popular with children. There are pony rides for an hour each morning at 10:00 a.m. and each afternoon at 1:00 p.m. There's also a heated pool and various other outdoor recreational facilities. Open daily, 9:00 a.m. to 5:00 p.m., May through the first week of September. Call 259-0311.

Everett Mall, with over 100 shops and four anchor department stores, is located at Exit 189 on I-5, then west to Everett Mall way. Open Monday through Friday, 10:00 a.m. to 9:00 p.m., Saturday 10:00 a.m. to 6:00 p.m., and Sunday 12:00 noon to 5:00 p.m. Telephone 355-1771.

For people used to seeing small riverfront boat launching ramps, the **Port of Everett** has a thirteen-lane facility, one of the largest and busiest small-boat launching sites on the coast. The marina is large, too, and has a Victorian-style market place of shops and restaurants.

Grand Avenue Park on the waterfront between 16th and 19th streets, has a small granite marker on the spot that George Vancouver, the explorer, is thought to have landed in 1792. Vancouver was the first to chart Port Gardner, the bay which is Everett's busy anchorage.

Boeing 747-767 Division offers a ninety minute tour which includes a slide and film presentation along with a visit to the assembly plant. No one under twelve permitted. Tours Monday thru Friday. Call 342-4801 for further information.

For further information, contact **Everett Area Chamber of Commerce**, 2532 Wetmore Avenue, Everett WA 98206. Telephone 252-5106.

Accommodations

APPLE INN
8421 Evergreen Way
Everett, WA 98204
Tel. (206) 347-1100
Call collect for reservations.

After a long drive, you need a place to unwind, not too far from good food, but close to the heart of the Everett industrial area. Who could resist that. And the Apple Inn is a tempting place as its accommodations are so pleasing.
Manager Tom Dupar and his staff work hard to provide the considerate, efficient service that weary travelers appreciate. For the moderate rates charged you will enjoy cable TV, a queen size bed, 24 hour switchboard and message service, free local calls and a complimentary Continental breakfast. There are no less than twenty fine restaurants within ten minutes of Apple Inn and several within one block. A twenty-four hour coffee shop is adjacent to the motel.
Located one mile west of Interstate 5, exit 189, and one block south of SR 526 are the inviting accommodations of the Apple Inn. You'll applepreciate your stay.

HOLIDAY INN OF EVERETT
101 128th Street, S. E.
Everett, WA 98208
Tel. (206) 745-2555
Reservations: 1-800-HOLIDAY

The Holiday Inn of Everett has undergone many additions and changes since it was originally built in 1969. The Convention Center and Holidome are just a couple of the more recent improvements added to serve the business and vacation traveler. The Holidome Center for family activities has an indoor pool, jacuzzi and game room (which includes ping pong and video games). Also located in the Holidome is Spinnaker's Galley, which serves breakfast, lunch and dinner (open from 6:30 a.m. to 10:30 p.m.) and a lanai, which is used for Sunday brunch (9:30 a.m. to 2:00 p.m.). Parents can enjoy a quiet meal, snack or coffee in Spinnaker's Galley while watching their children enjoy the pool! You can enjoy either live or prerecorded entertainment in the newly remodeled Distillery Lounge. Holiday Inn patrons can take advantage of the indoor tennis court, located a few blocks away, or the golf course, only a few miles away.

Located just minutes away from Boeing, the GTE Training Center and Canyon Park Technology Corridor, the Holiday Inn serves many businesses. The Convention Center accommodates groups up to six hundred for receptions and three hundred and fifty for dinner. There are different sized meeting rooms to suit your needs.

As there is easy access to I-5 and less than ten miles from I-405 and I-5 interchanges, the Holiday Inn is a convenient meeting place for corporations. The Everett Mall and Alderwood Mall are just minutes away. The Holiday Inn provides complimentary transportation to shopping and Paine Field (for the Boeing Tour Center).

The Holiday Inn of Everett features non-smoking rooms (even a non-smoking floor), suites and handicapped rooms. All rooms have complimentary TV with CNN, EXPN, SHO and standard TV programming, as well as, Satellite Cinema which shows current movies for a small charge.

When making your reservations be sure to ask about the Great Rates Program with savings of twenty to fifty percent. The Travel Venture Club for senior citizens, and the Priority Club in which you can receive exciting awards and special guest privileges. Consider staying at the Holiday Inn of Everett on your next trip to western Washington.

Snohomish County

MARINA VILLAGE INN
1728 West Marine View Drive
Everett, WA 98201
Tel. (206) 259-4040

Sometimes when you're far from your home, what you desire most is a tranquil place full of personal comfort. For those times, introduce yourself to a most unusual inn on Port Gardener Bay. Here, amongst great bay windows, spectacular views and the sounds of the sea, you won't find the hustle of a big city hotel. Instead, the only thing you'll find is serenity.

Relax in a room that has been designed to be your own luxurious retreat. The artwork, the colors, and the furnishings have all been selected with care that is beyond reproach. A personal retreat should be filled to the brim with tender surprises. With this in mind, you'll find in your room such things as a wet bar, a refrigerator, a telephone in the bath, a large dressing room, a brightly lighted make-up mirror over hand made pottery sinks, king size or two double beds, a built in pants presser, thirty channels of television, free overnight moorage and, in some rooms, an invigorating whirlpool bath.

This perfect place for privacy, comfort and relaxation, is surrounded by all the attractions of the Northwest's largest marina and a waterfront village full of restaurants and shops. At Marina Village Inn they specialize in pampering you with the luxuries you deserve. The next time you're away from home and are looking for a personal retreat, remember this enchanting, tranquil inn.

NENDELS MOTOR INN
2800 Pacific Avenue
Everett, WA 98201
Tel. (206) 258-4141
     (800) 547-0106

Easy access from I-5 and its central location to Puget Sound and the North Cascades makes Nendels Motor Inn a perfect base from which to explore Western Washington.

Nendels boasts 135 spacious and beautifully decorated guest rooms equipped with comfortable king and queen sized beds, color TV, in-room movies, air conditioning and telephones. Non-smoking rooms are available on each floor. Among the amenities are a seasonal outdoor pool, jacuzzi and an indoor exercise room with a Universal gym and exercise bike. Nendels provides transportation to local shopping malls, Paine Field (Boeing Tour) or the train terminal. Meeting and banquet facilities for groups of 8 to 200 are provided with catering and audio-visual equipment available.

Victor's Restaurant adjoins Nendels and offers full breakfast, lunch and dinner menus featuring American cuisine. Breakfasts range from Continental breakfast to pancakes, waffles and filling three egg omelets. Salads and sandwiches anchor the luncheon menu with an excellent selection of entrees with such favorites as Pacific salmon, top sirloin, linguini with clams and Penne Bolognese. Dinner begins with several appetizers with exceptional presentations of salads, pasta, seafood, poultry and beef.

Call Nendels Motor Inn in Everett and make arrangements for your next business meeting or leisure stop. Ask about weekend getaways or Seahawk packages which include room, game tickets and Sunday brunch.

NORTHWEST MOTOR INN
9602 19th Avenue, S. E.
Everett, WA 98204
Tel. (206) 337-9090

Whether you're spending one night or several weeks in the Everett area, the Northwest Motor Inn is what you would expect of a great motel--plus a little extra. Management is highly professional, the property is immaculate and security is excellent. It's no accident that 85% of the clientele is return business, or referred business.

The inn offers 120 rooms, king size and queen size beds, or, if you prefer, water beds are available. The usual amenities are provided: a swimming pool, hot pool, conference rooms, guest laundry, complimentary coffee bar, and direct dial telephones. There are 26 fully equipped kitchen units that offer the option of preparing your own meals. You can also dine out at one of the several fine restaurants in the Everett area.

This motor inn is minutes from the Boeing plant. You are just twenty minutes from Seattle when staying here. The Canadian border is one hour and twenty minutes to the north.

Located at the northbound exit of Interstate 5, exit 189--just across from the Everett Mall. The Northwest Motor Inn is a real find and real value for the business or vacation traveler. Moderately priced.

Snohomish County

There's much to admire in those gifted few who can work the raw materials of this country into creations that bless our lives. Here's a tour that highlights these artisans skills.

\multicolumn{4}{c}{FROM EVERETT, WASHINGTON WITH LOVE}			
a.m.	M & M Rings & Crafts	Best goldsmiths	Ever/Jewelry
a.m.	Larry Carter	Best woodcarver	Ever/Wood
a.m.	Flo's Bunka Embroid.	Best original needlework	Ever/Textile
a.m.	Old Town Antiques	Best old-world crafts	Ever/Antique
a.m.	City Floral	Best floral designs	Ever/Florist
p.m.	Joe's Off Broadway	Best-flair lunches	Ever/Rest.
p.m.	Salvatore's Antique	Best rare collectibles	Ever/Antique
p.m.	H & L Sporting Goods	Best outdoor gear	Ever/Sport
p.m.	Legion Park	Best 3-for-one-tour	Ever/Attract.
\multicolumn{4}{c}{"Best Choices" for those gifted in the culinary arts:}			
p.m.	Bacchus By The Bay	Best gourmet meals	Ever/Rest.
p.m.	Joe's Off Broadway	Best combo meals	Ever/Rest.
p.m.	Klondike Kate's	Best hearty meals	Ever/Rest.
p.m.	Pelican Pete's	Best fresh foods variety	Ever/Rest.
p.m.	Spinnikar's Galley	Best family restaurant	Ever/Accom.
p.m.	Victor's Restaurant	Best American cuisine	Ever/Accom.

EVERETT PACIFIC HOTEL
3105 Pine Street
Everett, WA 98201
Tel.   (206) 339-3333
         (800) 833-8001 USA
         (800) 854-1600 CANADA

It's hard to feel at home at a large full-service hotel and convention center, but the friendliness and service of the staff at the Everett Pacific Hotel provides the real "homey setting" for its guests.

The Everett boasts 250 rooms and meeting facilities for groups from twenty to 1,100. Banquets can be served to groups as large as 600. But there's also amenities for individual guests and families, like the fitness center and licensed child activity center that operates on the weekends. Enjoy the spacious well-appointed rooms, plunge into the heated swimming pool, or revitalize yourself in the jacuzzi and sauna. Dining can be provided, by room service, or at either of the two in-house restaurants. The Courtyard serves breakfast and lunch, while the J. J. Hill provides an elegant atmosphere for intimate dinners.

It may not be home, but it is a place you can feel at home in...The Everett Pacific Hotel.

Antiques

OLD TOWN ANTIQUES MALL
Everett Public Market
Everett, WA 98201
Tel. (206) 252-1089
Hrs: Mon. - Sat.   10:00 a.m. - 5:00 p.m.
         Sunday   12:00 noon- 5:00 p.m.

Step back into the past at the Everett Public Market where you'll find historic pieces in a historic building! The Old Town Antique Mall, owned by Barry Hollander and managed by Linda Fields, occupies the entire top floor of the Public Market (that's 15,000 square feet). The Old Town Antique Mall is the home for twenty-six dealers today, and is expanding continuously!

You will find dealers specializing in furniture, glass, vintage clothing (including a rare red Edwardian party dress), country primitive items, granite ware and much, much more. The individual dealers travel throughout the country seeking unique and authentic items for their shops. You benefit by being able to see it all at this one location. There aren't many places where you could find such a fine overall selection. If it's collectible, it's probably here!

Browsing is a favorite pastime of visitors to the Antique Mall. Where else will you find an ironing board that also serves as a ladder and stool? Or, find a large collection of antique jewelry, clothing, furniture, collectibles, or whatever?

Here at the Old Town Antique Mall you can get a feel of what life was like before plastics, transistors, and integrated circuits. A visit to this shop would be a definite "best choice" on your trip to the Everett Public Market.

Attractions

BOEING TOUR CENTER, Eighty-fourth Street, S.E., Everett, Washington. Learn the history of the Boeing Commercial Airplane Company, see how the planes are built. Call for tour- time information.

Florist

CITY FLORAL
2715 Colby
Everett, WA 98201
Tel. (206) 259-8171
Hrs: Mon.-Sat 8:30 a.m.- 5:30 p.m.
and,
1402 Everett Mall Way
Everett, WA 98208
Tel. (206) 353-8800
Hrs: Mon.-Fri.   9:30 a.m.-9:00 p.m.
      Saturday   9:30 a.m.-6:00 p.m.
      Sunday   12:00 noon-6:00 p.m.
Visa, MasterCard, AMEX and Discover cards accepted.

If it's quality floral service you want..quality you can bank on... look for the florist in the old bank building on Colby. That's City Floral, which has been a blooming business in Everett since 1904. Owner Ralph Quass moved into the building in 1974 to take advantage of the larger floor place. That same year he opened up a second location in the Everett Mall, in a large open area, to create the atmosphere of a European flower market with its buckets of cut flowers.

One of the things that makes City Floral different is that it has a long established policy of shipping directly from California, thereby ensuring freshness and longer life of the blooms and floral designs. The emphasis at City Floral has been on living plants and live flowers; but you can also get a mylar balloon, stuffed animal, coffee mug or vase with your order. Because City Floral subscribes to six wire services you can send flowers virtually anywhere.

So when you want to "say it with flowers," call City Floral for the quality you can bank on; because they do business with "interest."

Jewelry

M & M RINGS AND CRAFTS
2804 Grand Avenue
Everett, WA 98201
Tel. (206) 259-5466
Hrs: Mon. - Sat. 10:00 a.m. - 5:30 p.m.
 Sunday 12:00 noon - 5:00 p.m.
Visa and MasterCard are accepted.

 Macel Anderson and Monty Pearson excel in designing and hand crafting jewelry made with semi-precious stones. Macel's one of a kind necklaces come in a variety of color combinations to enhance your wardrobe. Monty's pieces are made from individual wax castings, and he creates custom pieces from stones selected from the shop's large inventory, or from stones provided by his clients.
 Your knowledge of larimar, imperial jaspar, sugalite, chryscolla, or snowflake obsidian will save you money if you are able to identify the Mystery Gem of the Day, you will receive twenty-five percent off any purchase of ten dollars, or more.
 A spectrum of other crafts can be found at the store, from handcrafted refrigerator magnets to sterling silver bolo ties. Visiting M & M Rings and Crafts is an enriching experience for everyone, young or old.

Restaurant

BACCHUS BY THE BAY
Everett Marine Village
1728 W Marine View Drive
Everett, WA 98201
Tel. (206) 258-6254
Hrs: Mon. - Sun. 6:00 a.m.-12:00 midnight
Visa and MasterCard are accepted.

 With 180 wines on the wine list to choose from, its no wonder that this restaurant renown for its libations and its complementing fine food. Named after the Roman god of wine and merry making, Bacchus by the Bay does its utmost to live up to its name. They offer the finest dining and waterfront view in Everett.
 Owner Al "Guido" Frederickson, is an expert gourmet chef who collaborates with executive chef Rick Scampi to prepare and properly serve some of the finest meals available on the west coast. The atmosphere is

comfortable, casual and stimulating with the emphasis on fine food and drink at reasonable prices.

You can start your day with breakfast omelettes that range from the standard to the more exotic like crab and caviar or smoked salmon. A lunch salad offering includes breast of turkey, pasta or crab Louie. Try the luncheon steak for a stick to your ribs meal. For dinner Guido sets out the linen and candles. Begin with hors d' oeuvres such as, escargots, pate´ or steamers. Dine on rack of lamb, veal scaloppine or Cajun bouillabaisse.

This is the place, Bacchus By The Bay, to eat, drink and be merry.

JOE'S OFF BROADWAY RESTAURANT
2008 Hewitt Avenue
Everett, WA 98201
Tel. (206) 252-4848
Hrs: Mon.-Sat. 6:00 a.m.-10:00 p.m.
     Sunday   8:00 a.m.- 8:00 p.m.

When a restaurant measures its meals in mileage, you know it's a place where the portions go a long way. At Joe's Off Broadway you can get a 150 mile breakfast or a 300 mile breakfast, both guaranteed to to get you those distances. And breakfasts are served all day long.

Owner Joe Lange has created that special restaurant you'll remember. Like, remember the old fashioned soda fountain, the juke box music, a large variety of good food, and an all you can eat buffet? Well it's here. If you are in the neighborhood between 3:00 p.m. and 6:00 p.m. take advantage of the early bird dinners; all the fixings, at a reduced rate. Regular dinners offer combination specials where you can mix and match entrees like salmon steak, scallops, lobster, stuffed crab, steak or chicken.

So if you are going for the mileage, top off your tank at Joe's.

KLONDIKE KATE'S
3120 Hewitt Avenue
Everett, WA 98201
Tel. (206) 258-4599
Hrs: Mon. - Fri. 11:00 a.m.- 12:00 midnight
     Saturday   5:00 p.m. - 1:00 a.m.
     Sunday   4:00 p.m.- 8:00 p.m.
Visa, MasterCard, Diner's Card and AMEX are accepted.

Klondike Kate's is the most recent in a long series of businesses that have occupied this beautiful building since it opened in 1892. Today the building is the colorful setting for this restaurant known for fine dining and good music. The well-preserved ambiance is created in part by the ornate walls of the restaurant and bar. Peruse the early photographs, especially the one of Teddy Roosevelt, who campaigned near the steps of the building 1903.

Start your luncheon with appetizers, or one of the tasty soups. From there, your options range to chilled salads, sandwiches, burgers and then there's the Rich & Hearty Stew. And it is just that. Dinnertime at the Klondike's, offers boneless breast of chicken, and seafood selections. You can have scallops, scampi, oysters, crab and sole. Join the happy hour between 4:00 and 7:00 p.m., upstairs, where you can enjoy reduced prices, complimentary nibbles and piano music. Following happy hour the music changes for dancing.

Even Teddy would have charged up the stairs for this action.

PELICAN PETE'S FINE FOOD
1722 W Marine View Drive
Everett, WA 98201
Tel. (206) 252-3155
Hrs: Mon. - Tue.   11:00 a.m. - 12:00 midnight
      Wed. - Sat.   11:00 a.m. - 2:00 a.m.
      Sunday   10:00 a.m. - 1:30 a.m.
All major credit cards are accepted.

Dine next to a hanging planter that used to be a racing shell and enjoy the view of Mt. Baker towering over the second largest marina on the West Coast, moorings for 2,200 yachts. During the summer, have lunch outdoors right along the water's edge.

Patterned after a casual European style cafe, Pelican Pete's offers a wide spectrum of homemade gastronomical delights from Maui style ribs and freshly made pasta, to prime rib. Be sure to ask for the "Fresh Sheet," which lists that day's pasta, seafood and beef specials. For dessert, treat yourself to the famous "Mile High" Mud Pie.

Wednesday nights are special at Pelican Pete's. Starting at 9:30, famous comedy acts are presented for your enjoyment. These are acts that have been featured on such national television shows as The Tonight Show, The David Letterman Show, and Merv Griffin; come prepared to laugh!

Textiles

FLO'S BUNKA EMBROIDERY
Everett Public Market
2804 Grand Avenue
Everett, WA 98201
Tel. (206) 252-3838
Hrs: Mon. - Sat. 9:00 a.m. - 5:30 p.m.

You must see Japanese bunka (pronounced boon caw) embroidery to appreciate the beauty created by "painting with yarn"! A visit to Flo Fanning's Japanese Bunka Embroidery at the Everett Public Market will not only allow you to see this art form, but you'll also have the opportunity to learn about and learn how to do bunka embroidery. Flo was introduced to this art form in the mid 1970's. She has since created more than three hundred pictures. She has a teacher's certification and is one of the few semi-masters in the United States.

Bunka embroidery originated when the punch needle was introduced to Japan about fifty years ago. After several years of development, bunka embroidery is now part of the needle craft art. Special four-ply rayon thread is separated into stretchy strands that are introduced into rayon fabric using the punch needle. The art is easy to learn as only two stitches are used: straight and fluffy. Pictures are created from the back to the front with texture and depth created by layering.

Flo is particularly expert in blending colors to create what can only be described as paintings with yarn. She is more than willing to share her techniques with you. Ten classes per week are taught in her shop or at the senior citizen centers. Private lessons can be arranged.

Flo carries a large selection of kits and supplies and will arrange for them to be shipped to your home if you wish. You'll find several beautiful bunka embroidery pictures for sale at Flo's Bunka Embroidery. The pictures make outstanding gifts and will definitely be conversation pieces in your home.

Woodcarver

LARRY CARTER, WOODCARVER
Everett Public Market
2804 Grand Avenue
Everett, WA 98201
Tel. (206) 259-5045
Hrs: Mon. - Sat. 10:00 a.m. - 5:00 p.m.
Or by appointment.

Lions, and tigers and bears! Oh my! Horses, pigs, goats, giraffes, zebra, dogs and cats! Oh boy! You can find any of these wonderful creatures in Larry Carter's woodcarving shop at the Everett Public Market. Eight years ago Larry began whittling as a hobby, and that hobby became his profession about three years ago.

The main attractions are carousel animals, either authentic reproductions of classic carousel animals or whimsical beasties derived from real animals modified with a healthy dose of imagination. You'll find several humorous characters lounging and/or lurking on his work benches and shelves. His animals are also exhibited at art and craft shows and regional shopping malls.

When you visit Larry's shop you'll undoubtedly find one or more of his carousel creatures in the process of creation. It takes approximately one month to complete an animal. Larry uses his jack knife on projects both large and small.

Larry teaches carving classes mornings and evenings in his shop, and at the senior citizen centers. Call for times on the classes where you'll learn what materials to use, how to select and maintain tools, and how to proceed with carving art objects.

Take a trip back to your childhood while at the Everett Public Market. You're guaranteed a fun experience and a memorable time.

Sporting Goods

H&L SPORTING GOODS
2806 Colby
Everett, WA 98201
Tel. (206) 259-5515
Hrs: Mon.-Sat. 10:00 a.m.-5:30 p.m.
MasterCard and Visa accepted.

Here is a place that's teeming with everything to outfit your team: jerseys, sweats, hats, shoes of all descriptions.

As a major supplier of team oriented sportswear for forty-two years, H&L Sporting Goods is the place to go to get outfitted with something brandishing the name of your favorite team. Wintertime and you'll find the store fully stocked for winter sports; including plenty of soft goods in ski wear, but also basketball and raquetball.

H&L is particularly well known for its fleece goods and they carry the largest selection of sweat suits in western Washington. The shoe department focuses on specialty shoes for serious athletes, including basketball, cleated shoes for football, baseball and soccer.

So if you want to be a good sport, and look like one, try something on for size at H&L Sporting goods.

Lakewood

Lakewood is a flag stop on the Great Northern Railroad a few miles north of Marysville. The county road from I-5 leads west through Lakewood to Warm Beach, a clamming area on Port Susan. Several small lakes lie in the timbered area to the west of Lakewood.

Attractions

Wenberg State Park, about half way between Lakewood and Warm Beach, provides a base for exploring the area. There are seventy five campsites including ten with full hookups for recreational vehicles. Lake Goodwin, next to the park, is known for its trout. Other lakes worth checking out are **Martha** and **Showcraft**.

Golf Course

MEADOW PARK GOLF COURSE
7108 Lakewood Drive W
Lakewood, WA 98467
Tel. (206) 473-3033
Visa and MasterCard are accepted.

An eighteen hole course with a PNGA rating of sixty-five for men and sixty-nine for women, Meadow Park Golf Course is fairly level and does not present a great deal of difficulty for the golfer. The course has excellent drainage so that even after a rain shower or during the winter months, players may comfortably use the course.

The pro shop carries a full line of equipment including bags, clothing and shoes, and power or pull carts are available. There are lockers on the premises, as well as showers and a driving range.

Swing by the "nineteenth hole" after the match for a meal in the restaurant or a cocktail in the lounge, which has a great view of the course. During the summer you may enjoy outside dining on the patio and banquet facilities are available for up to one hundred people. Reservations are required one week in advance for weekend play , so please call resident pro Lynn Rautio for reservations, lesson information or tee time.

Restaurant

LAKEWOOD TERRACE
6114 Motor SW
Lakewood, WA 98464
Tel. (206) 588-5215
Hrs: Coffee Shop: Mon. - Sat. 7:00 a.m. - 8:00 p.m.
                   Sunday   8:00 a.m. - 2:00 p.m.
      Dining Room: Mon. - Sat. 11:30 a.m. - 2:00 p.m.
                                5:00 p.m. - 10:00 p.m.
                   Sunday   10:00 a.m. - 2:00 p.m.
                                3:00 p.m. - 9:00 p.m.
      Lounge: Mon. - Sat. 11:00 a.m. - 1:30 a.m.
                   Sunday   2:00 noon - 12:00 mid.
Visa, MasterCard, AMEX and Diner's Club are accepted.

Lakewood Terrace opened in 1937 and has since been a popular dining spot in this area. The decor features Northwest artwork, pleasing colors and there is a cozy fireplace to enhance the warm ambiance in the winter. A coffee shop provides an excellent variety of delicious food for breakfast, lunch, and dinner, everything from eggs Benedict to burgers, sandwiches and salads.

The dining room features continental cuisine during lunch with three daily specials, such as sole with capers or blackened red snapper. For dinner there are choices such as French lamb chops, chicken Cordon Bleu, seafood fettucini, veal scallopini and Chateaubriand for two. There are three nightly specials and Sunday brunch offers a choice of eighteen different entrees. An extensive wine list exists with many Northwest wines offered.

Emphasis at Lakewood Terrace is on good, fresh, high quality food and excellent service. This restaurant is a tradition in the Tacoma area where you can be certain you'll find the best in fine dining.

Lynnwood

Suburban residents in the south county flock to this small city of 23,000 on Highway 99, drawn by an estimated 500 specialty stores scattered about in shopping centers and strip malls.

Attractions

Schriber Lake, a small park with a pond and a peat bog, is eighteen acres in the commercial center of Lynnwood. There is a half-mile pathway with nature trail signs identifying the native plants and trees. It extends into the pond itself as a floating walk way.

Lynn-Swim Recreation Center features an indoor-outdoor swimming pool.

For further information, contact the **Snohomish County Visitor Information Center**, Box 2211, Lynnwood WA 98036. Telephone 745-4138.

Accommodations

SILVER CLOUD INNS, 29332 Thirty-sixth Avenue West, Lynnwood, Washington. Moderate prices, immaculate rooms, queen-sized beds, free local calls, jacuzzi, free laundry, valet service, complimentary coffee bar, and more.

Restaurant

VILLA GIULIO RISTORANTE ITALIANO
19721 64th Avenue West
Lynnwood, WA 98036
Tel. (206) 774-2186
Hrs: Tue. - Fri.   11:00 a.m.-2:00 p.m.
                    5:00 p.m.-10:00 p.m.
      Sat.-Sun.   5:00 p.m.-10:00 p.m.

Upon entering Villa Giulio Ristorante Italiano you will see a beautiful Italian flag on the wall. The tone of Italian atmosphere is set with white walls, lattice work, green tablecloths, and red carpet. Owner Giulo Pellegrini's wife, Janie, has created a lush, romantic atmosphere with a splendid array of green plants.

Before opening the restaurant in November 1985, Guilo had been cooking for twenty-one years and owned other restaurants for more than fifteen years. He prides himself in making everything from scratch. The pasta, desserts, and spumoni are freshly made on the premises. You can watch pizza dough being tossed, too. Family recipes are used as are the spices his mother sends from Italy.

Select a delicious appetizer such as calamari or mussels cooked in basil, garlic, and wine sauce. The main courses include fresh seafood, chicken, or veal. A fine collection of wine is offered. The staff will spoil you with superb service. Bring your family and enjoy the food and moderate prices.

Marysville

The Snohomish River delta provides a pastoral setting for Marysville, a town of 7,100 people. Stimpson Logging Company built a mill here in 1887. The town was incorporated in 1891 and soon became a major shingle and lumber milling point.

Everett, with its better harbor, took over the lumber trade early in this century and Marysville became a major trade center for surrounding farms. Now, the town bills itself as the "strawberry capital" and points to the large export crop of berries raised each spring.

Average rainfall is about thirty-nine inches a year, the low temperatures average a degree or two above freezing in January and hit the mid-seventies in the warmest months of August and September.

Attractions

The Snohomish Indian people operate a major **salmon hatchery** a few miles north of Marysville, on Waterworks Road, part of their Tulalip Reservation. As one of the primary salmon-fishing tribes on the Sound, the Snohomish also rear eggs taken on the Stillaguamish River in cooperation with the Stillaguamish people. The hatchery is open for viewing.

Marysville Historical Society, Box 41, Marysville WA 98270, has a twenty-page booklet with a brief sketch of the history for several locations in town. Call 334-4919 or 659-3557 for information on society activities.

For further information, contact the **Marysville Chamber of Commerce**, Box 151 Marysville WA 98270. Telephone 659-7700.

Pottery

MELINNA MALAN-NICELY STUDIO POTTER, 5620 Sixty-first Drive, Northeast, Marysville, Washington. Features while stoneware clay pots, functional dinnerware and baking dishes using underglaze slip decorations of floral designs.

Mukilteo

Most Seattle residents probably think of the town with the funny name as the Whidbey Island ferry terminal and pass right on through. The name Mukilteo comes from an Indian word for "good camping ground," which is what some 5,100 people have decided in modern times, living here on Elliott Point in a relaxed community. The post office was created in 1862.

Attractions

Mukilteo Lighthouse, a trim concrete building with white walls and red roof, was built in 1905. The light can be toured by contacting the local Coast Guard station.

The **Washington State Ferry** dock is a busy place, with frequent service to Whidbey Island and Clinton. Telephone 542-7052. A **public fishing pier** is near the dock, there are boat rentals, and a small state park with boat launching ramp. A lighthouse built in 190 is open to visitors.

For further information, write **Mukilteo Business Association**, Box 545, Mukilteo WA 98275.

Restaurant

MUKILTEO CHOP AND OYSTER HOUSE
8330 53rd Avenue W
Mukilteo, WA 98275
Tel. (206) 353-6733
Hrs: Lunch   Tue. - Fri.   11:00 a.m. - 2:00 p.m.
          Dinner Sun. - Thu. 5:00 p.m. - 10:00 p.m.
                     Fri. - Sat.   5:00 p.m. - 11:00 p.m.

Although Mukilteo Chop and Oyster House has an impeccable reputation for fine dining, the two story brick mansion which houses the restaurant has a colorful past. When it was built in the 1930s, it appeared to be a respectable family house, but it concealed an illegal still in the basement. The door to this illegal lower level was cunningly concealed inside the boiler in the basement. There was even a secret tunnel leading out to the cliffs on Possession Sound. By the 1950's the house had undergone a conversion to a restaurant and complete respectability.

There are upstairs and downstairs dining rooms with huge picture windows that look out on views of towering firs framing Puget Sound and Whidbey Island. The Mukilteo Chop and Oysters has a complete selection of steak, seafood and specializes in local oysters. Owner and Chef Craig Erickson takes pride in his establishment and serves only the best and freshest cuisine, delightfully and originally prepared.

The setting of Mukilteo Chop and Oysters is picture perfect, with the lovely grounds surrounding the house and the unsurpassed views. This combined with the superlative food make this a "Best Choice" for dining in this area.

Snohomish

Created as a ferry crossing on the military road connecting Fort Steilacoom with Bellingham, Snohomish is an old community in a part of the state which was settled a quarter-century later. About 5,300 people now live in this historic town with a bustling collection of antique and specialty shops on First Street at the river's edge.

A Victorian-era flavor is reflected in its many homes and commercial buildings. North of 2nd Street are substantial residential dwellings;

restoration work has also been completed on many 19th century buildings along 1st Street and the riverbank.

There was one store here in 1860, two by 1864, but the town site was not laid out until 1871. That was ten years after the legislature had designated Snohomish as county seat for the namesake county. In 1896 the courthouse would move to Everett in one of those political tussles between towns which punctuated early history of Western Washington. Snohomish residents turned the vacated courthouse into a high school.

Attractions

Blackman Museum, 118 Avenue B, was built in 1878 as home of one of the early lumbermen. Interior furnishings reflect the Victorian era and the hall wallpaper is said to be 105 years old. Open Saturday and Sunday, 12:00 noon to 4:00 p.m. Telephone 568-2526.

Star Center Mall, 829 Second Street, is one of twenty antique stores clustered between the railroad tracks and Avenue D south of Second Street. Like other antique malls developed in Washington, this one has several specialized dealer shops under one roof offering items as varied as art deco figurines and old radio equipment. This is the original antique mall in the state, and at last count had 110 dealers operating. Open daily, 10:00 a.m. to 5:00 p.m. and Saturdays until 8:00 p.m. Call 568-2131.

One of the West Coast's few remaining **old-growth sawmills** is across the river. Seattle-Snohomish Mill Company has a carriage and head saw which can handle a log fifty-five feet long and six feet in diameter. Special timbers such as boat keels are custom-cut at the mill. Operations can be viewed from First Street looking over the water to the plant.

Silverbow Honey Country, 1220 13th Street, has been in the honey processing business for forty years. There are retail and wholesale sales. Plant tours by appointment; call 568-2191 and ask for the manager.

A brochure providing an historic building and home **tour** is available, and a driving tour, from the Chamber of Commerce offices in the Waltz Building on Avenue B, just adjacent to the Blackman Historic Museum.

For further information, contact **Snohomish Chamber of Commerce**, 116 Avenue B, Snohomish WA 98290. Telephone 568-2526.

Bed and Breakfast

COUNTRYMAN BED AND BREAKFAST
119 Cedar Street
Snohomish, WA 98290
Tel. (206) 568-9622

Countryman Bed and Breakfast will stay in your memories long after you have visited. Sandy and Larry Countryman will be your hosts in this twenty-eight room, 19th century Queen Ann Victorian mansion which is listed in the National Historic Register. Originally a doctor's office and residence, it has been completely restored to its current use as a bed and breakfast inn and gallery.
   The guest's bedrooms are spacious with authentic period furniture and decor. The parlor boasts an art gallery of original and collector paintings, etchings and engravings.
   The Countrymans are Snohomish's unofficial tour guides. Their tour featuring Victorian architecture with town and family histories is a major attraction.
   Included in the rates are the tour, family style breakfasts which include blueberry muffins, hash browns, eggs fixed to your liking and other delicious, traditional fare; and a package of prints by your host and artist Larry Countryman.
   Countryman's is located a block from an estimated 150 antique shops in what has become known as the antique capital of the Northwest.

Antiques

ANOTHER ANTIQUE STORE, 924 First Street, Snohomish, Washington. The oldest antique store in Snohomish, Another Antique Store features fine quality American Walnut and Oak furniture.

FIRST BANK ANTIQUES, 1001 First Street, Snohomish, Washington. You'll find some of the finest antique furniture anywhere at First Bank Antiques. Furniture restoring and repairing available; dealers are welcome.

RICK'S ANTIQUES, 916 First Street, Snohomish, Washington. At Rick's, you'll find some of the finest quality furniture anywhere.

Snohomish County

SALVATORE'S ANTIQUE MALL
102 Avenue D
Snohomish, WA 98290
Tel. (206) 568-5655
Hrs: Mon. - Sat. 10:00 a.m. - 5:00 p.m.
      Sunday 12:00 noon - 5:30 p.m.
Visa and MasterCard are accepted.

For those who love to stroll down memory lane among spectacular collections of antique furniture and rare collectibles, Salvatore's Antique Mall was created just for you!

Containing high quality furniture, this is a browser's paradise just bursting with merchandise where dealers display everything from glassware and Oriental items to railroad collectibles.

SNOHOMISH STAR CENTER MALL, 829 South Second Street, Snohomish, Washington. The mall's five shopping levels and 110 dealers display a seemingly-endless array of quality antiques and collectibles.

Art Gallery

GOLDEN GALLERY OF FINE ART, 1024 First Street, Snohomish, Washington. Fine original painting, limited edition prints, and bronze and wood sculpture.

Gift Shop

JOYWORKS
1002 1st Street
Snohomish, WA 98290
Tel. (206) 568-5050
Hrs: Mon. - Sat. 10:00 a.m. - 5:30 p.m.
      Sunday 12:30 p.m. - 5:00 p.m.
Closed Easter, July 4th, Thanksgiving and Christmas.
MasterCard and Visa are accepted.

Visit Joyworks for gifts fanciful or functional, warm and wonderful, unique or unusual!!! Owner Clarice Johnson opened Joyworks in 1983 in one of the stately historic buildings in downtown Snohomish. Since then, Clarice and her colleagues, Cassie, Luanne, Kay and Colleen have been creating an atmosphere of casual fun as they enjoy customers discovering the wonders gathered at Joyworks.

There are many handcrafted items at Joyworks and wreaths. Choose from beautiful arrangements created from dried weeds and flowers sometimes gathered in Washington, or from silk flowers so real looking you'll have to touch them to be sure they are silk.

The unusual country gifts at Joyworks represent treasures found on Clarice's buying trips all over the United States. In one corner you'll find gift cards, including Victorian reproductions, lots of wood and tin items, linens, laces, potpourri, candles and afghans, hats, wreaths, ribbons and children's books. The kitchen area is bursting with gifts including functional pottery, miniature cookie cutters, and lots, lots, more. The craft section includes paints, stencils, bastetry materials, flowers, and supplies for creative projects. A cheery Christmas corner is only a hint of the wonderful and unusual decorations and gifts filling the shop for every special holiday.

In addition to providing gifts, Clarice and her crew are happy to design special-order flower arrangements, and classes on decorating, wreathmaking, and basketweaving. At Joyworks, you are guaranteed a fun time and successful shopping!!!

Golf Course

SNOHOMISH PUBLIC GOLF COURSE
7806 147th Avenue SE
Snohomish, WA 98290
Tel. (206) 568-2676
Hrs: Golf Year Around

In 1966 Gordon and Dave Richards purchased a farm on Dutch Hill just outside Snohomish. They converted the beautifully rolling hills into the Snohomish Public Golf Course that opened in April, 1967. The evergreens planted in the the late sixties have now matured and have mastered the art of eating errant golf balls.

The Richard's hired Duane Jacobson to run the golf shop and his wife to manage the restaurant. Duane's son, Fred, was eleven at the time. Today, Fred is grown-up and is the golf pro at the club. The restaurant owner is Rose Snyder, who used to work for Fred's mother. She's considered to be one of the best golf course cooks anywhere and prepares all her meals from scratch. The continuity provided by these hospitable individuals is reflected in the quality of the course and its service.

The Snohomish Public Golf Course is extremely popular with beginning and expert golfers. The course plays 6315 yards from the regular tees, 6779 yards from the championship tees, and 5980 yards for the ladies with the a par of 74 and 72 for men. Golf carts are available for rental, although the course is a good walking course. Number 16, a long par 4, is especially difficult, while number 13, which plays over a pond in the woods, is the most scenic. There's an excellent pro shop, a driving range, and outstanding instruction available by appointment. The course hosts between 100 and 120 tournaments each year. With ample parking, several avid golfers park their RVs in the lot and golf to their hearts content.

The Snohomish Public Golf Course is eight miles from I-5. Take the Wenatchee exit and follow the signs. Since it's considered to be one of the best public golf courses in Western Washington and is very popular, it's a good idea to make reservations.

Honey

SILVERBOW HONEY COMPANY, INC.
1220 Thirteenth Street
Snohomish, WA 98290
Tel. (206) 568-2191
Hrs: Mon. - Fri.   8:00 a.m. - 5:00 p.m.
          April - September
          Saturday   9:00 a.m. - 3:00 p.m.
Closed on major holidays.
Visa and MasterCard are accepted.

Millions of honey bees travel billions of miles to produce the many flavorful and nutritious honeys marketed by Silverbow Honey Company. The industrious bees work the year round producing honey from California, Oregon and Washington to the clover country of the Dakotas. Professional beekeepers work with hives at night when the bees are resting, moving the hives between orchards on eighteen-wheelers as the season progresses. The result: lovers of fresh honey have over thirty different flavors of honey to enjoy!

The Silverbow Honey Company's retail store serves all facets of the bee business, including everything necessary to establish hives and raise honey, whether it be a hobby or commercial enterprise. The store stocks clever gifts such as stuffed bees and bears as well as honey cookbooks and beekeeping books. To learn more about bees, beekeeping and the production of honey, take a tour of the Silverbow Honey plant. Special appointments can be arranged for groups of eight or more.

Buzz into Silverbow Honey to learn more about nature's sweetener, and by all means honey lovers, stop by the popular tasting area and sample some of the thirty different flavors. You'll bee delighted!

Ice Cream parlor

SNOHOMISH VALLEY ICE CREAM COMPANY
902 1st Street
Snohomish, Wa 98290
Tel. (206) 568-1133
Hrs: Memorial Day to Labor Day
    11:00 a.m. - 9:00 p.m.   Mon. - Sat.
    12:00 noon - 9:00 p.m.   Sunday
  Winter:
    11:00 a.m. - 5:30 p.m.   Mon. - Sat.
    12:00 noon - 5:00 p.m.   Sunday
No credit cards, personal checks are accepted.

For eighty-two years the Old Pharmacy Building dispensed all sorts of wondrous and magical portions to cure what ailed the inhabitants of the Snohomish area. Today, the tradition continues as Scott McElhose and his staff take over the responsibility of curing sweet tooth attacks!!!

The soda fountain portion of the Snohomish Valley Ice Cream Company stocks thirty-five flavors of VitaRich ice cream, which are generously dispensed in homemade waffle cones or used in old-fashioned floats, shakes, malts, and banana splits.

Another section of the building is devoted to freshly-prepared and sinfully delicious caramel corn. Chocoholics can be treated in yet another area, where chocolate truffles, almond cluster, pecan cluster and other scientifically designed compositions are dispensed. Easily portable configurations to provide sugar fixes include candies, gumdrops and jawbreakers of various sizes to suit other patients.

Scott has searched the world for the special products for his shelves. Local preserves and coffees are also available, as are quite lovely and functional tins and gift boxes in which to disguise the real nature of your purchase.

Pottery

MELINNA MALAN-NICELY STUDIO POTTER, 5620 61st Drive, N.E., Marysville, WA. Telephone 653-5925. By appointment only. Featuring white stoneware clay pots, functional dinnerware and baking dishes using underglaze slip decoration with lots of Iris.

Restaurant

CABBAGE PATCH RESTAURANT AND INN
111 Avenue A
Snohomish, WA 98290
Tel. (206) 568-9091

    The Cabbage Patch Restaurant is located in an old house that was built around the turn of the century. Customers have a choice of three seating areas. There is the original parlor, a large glass-walled garden room with a beautiful English Rosette window, and upstairs is the bar room, featuring an authentic oak bar and a player piano wired to control buttons at the bar.
    Owner Sandra McCutchins presides over a staff of cooks, each with her own specialty. Linda prepares the evening sea food and succulent prime rib; Shirley provides lunches of homemade soups and salads, including the house specialty, Cabbage Patch Soup; and Kris produces homemade desserts, featuring pie and their most popular dessert, blackberry cobbler. Sandra also operates the Cabbage Patch Inn, which is a bed and breakfast place right next door to the restaurant.
    The Cabbage Patch Restaurant and Inn are located in the heart of the Snohomish historical district. It is just a few blocks to downtown Snohomish which is known as the "Antique Capital of the Northwest." Both the restaurant and the inn offer charming surroundings in refurbished turn of the century houses and warm and gracious hospitality.

THE COLLECTOR'S CHOICE RESTAURANT
Star Center Mall
120 Glen
Snohomish, WA 98290
Tel. (206) 568-1277
Hrs: Mon. - Fri.   7:30 a.m. - 8:00 p.m.
        Sat. - Sun.   8:00 a.m. - 8:00 p.m.
Visa and MasterCard are accepted.

    John and Donna Hager were operating a small antique space when they noted the need for a place for antique shoppers to get a cup of coffee and a bite to eat. The Collector's Choice was opened as a small restaurant in 1983 and has expanded in size, menu and reputation. They now meet the needs of local business and professional people, as well as provide fine dining for Snohomish residents, antique shoppers and vacationers.
    This is a popular breakfast place with choices such as omelettes, fresh fruit, cottage fried potatoes, and homemade biscuits and muffins. Coffee is

freshly ground and there are mini-breakfasts for the light eater. Three different casseroles are featured on the lunch menu, along with sandwiches, hamburgers, quiche, homemade soup and salads, including a salad bar. Dinners are excellent, from the delightful appetizers to the sinfully delicious desserts. There are daily specials, as well as steaks, chicken, fettucini and seafood selections. The homemade desserts are the perfect finish with blackberry pie a special favorite.

This is a pleasant place to enjoy fine food and outstanding service. John and Donna love serving people and make them feel comfortable and at home. Whether shopping for antiques at the Star Center Mall or just visiting Snohomish, The Collector's Choice Restaurant is a "Best Choice" for dining. Also visit The Collector's Choice II in Centralia Square, downtown Centralia.

RIVER'S EDGE CAFE
1011 First Street
Snohomish, WA 98290
Tel. (206) 568-1283
Hrs: Mon. - Sun.   6:00 a.m. - 8:00 p.m.
          Summer hours are extended to 10:00 p.m.
Visa and MasterCard accepted.

The River's Edge Cafe occupies a historic building overlooking the Snohomish River and the decks look out on spectacular Mount Rainier.

Throughout the cafe are antiques, memorabilia and photographs, all from the heritage of Suzy and Jim Ryan, owners. One wall of the restaurant still displays the advertisement for Bellingham Coal, painted on what was once an exterior wall. Quilts adorning the walls of the dining room were handmade by Suzy's mother and grandmother. Suzy and Jim enjoy sharing the history of the building and its collection with visitors, if you ask. You'll even find some books for browsing while you enjoy a leisurely meal at River's Edge Cafe.

Breakfast is served all day, and includes specials such as homemade biscuits and gravy, huge four-egg omelets and "build-your-own" omelets, in which you select the ingredients of your choice. The Chef's Special is generous enough to split and serve to two!!!(And it's okay with the management to do so.)

The lunch and dinner menus include homemade soups, fresh salads, steaks, burgers, seafood, chicken, and a variety of sandwiches. The River's Edge Burger, to which you can add sliced avocado, cheeses, mushrooms and bacon is one of the best burgers you'll find anywhere! There is also a Mexican menu with several entrees like: taco salad, Mexican versions of the burger, and some combination meals.

Try the River's Edge once and you'll be back.

Sport

HARVEY AIRFIELD
9900 Airport Way
Snohomish, WA 98290
Tel. (206) 568-1541
    (800) 821-8064 Bellevue
    (800) 259-2944 Everett
Hrs: Airfield
    Summer 6:00 a.m. - 10:00 p.m.
    Winter Daylight hours
  Restaurant
    Summer 6:00 a.m. - 9:00 p.m.
    Winter 6:00 a.m. - 8:00 p.m.
Closed Christmas and Thanksgiving.
Mastercard and Visa are accepted.

    Appreciate the diverse beauty of Western Washington from the sky! At Harvey Airfield, just south of downtown Snohomish, one to three people can enjoy a one hour plane ride for only $56 plus tax (at the time of this publication.)

    As you fly over vast expanse of lower Puget Sound, you'll gasp at the rugged spires of the Cascades and the green velvet slopes of Western Washington. All services of a private airport are provided at Harvey Airfield, including training for private and commercial pilots' licenses. Harvey's Airport Restaurant serves down to earth breakfasts, lunches feature take-off low calorie plates, plane good sandwiches, hamburger heaven, full-load departures, pre-flight appetizers, and salads with a leading edge. If you aren't flying the straight and narrow, indulge in the homemade pie in the sky. In the evening, park your sopwith camel and dine first class on Harvey's well presented dinners including seafood, poultry, pasta, steaks, and combination dinners.

    As you dine, your free entertainment is the airshow of the arrivals and departures. Over 300 planes call Harvey's home, including some older planes and genuine airborne antiques. Hot air balloons launch mornings and evenings from the airfield and skydivers can drop in at anytime. Part of your Snohomish visit should include some flying and dining; you'll love both and undoubtedly book a return trip!!!

(See special invitation in the Appendix.)

Tour

SNOHOMISH RIVER QUEEN
1001 1st Street
Snohomish, WA 98290
Tel. (206) 568-7609 or leave message.
Hrs: Open to charters until noon and after 5:00 p.m.
Public Cruises
    12:00 p.m., 1:00 p.m., 2:00 p.m. and 3:00 p.m.
Visa and MasterCard are accepted for charters only.

Step into the past as you step aboard the Snohomish River Queen, one of the charming reminders of how historic Snohomish evolved through the trade generated by the Northwest river boats.

The River Queen was built by Elbert "Cap" Davis as a sea-going boat, and he and his wife lived on the vessel for twenty years. When Larry McGee and his partners Corey and Candy Prentice bought the 55-foot craft, they renovated the boat into a luxurious version of the old Northwest river boats. "Cap", now in his eighties, has been actively involved in the reconstruction of his beloved Queen and will remain skipper for some of the cruises.

The interior of the Snohomish River Queen's decor has lots of brass, oak and plush carpets. The Queen boasts a large main cabin, lounge and dining area and concession/bar area. The boat is licensed for 49 passengers, who can enjoy great visibility from within all the salons and on the decks. A modern sound system functions for the historic narratives on the scheduled cruises and provides music on charter cruises. Live music is available for special occasions. The Queen and her crew are Coast Guard certified and all safety equipment is in place.

Be at the dock behind the Silver King Restaurant, at the middle of First Street, and cruise the Snohomish River in ultimate comfort! The meandering river passes through rich farm land, under historic railroad bridges and finally through Everett into Possession Sound. The wild blue heron and other river wildlife is abundant. Book the River Queen for tours, weddings, anniversaries, group parties....or just plain fun.

Stanwood

This was marshy land when settlers began work near the mouth of the Stillaguamish River in 1866. Water was drained, pastures and croplands created. Many of Stanwood's 1,700 residents are Scandinavians, descendants of the hard-working farmers who brought the land into production. Now the business district has a Scandinavian decor, specialty shops and a bakery which draws comment from many visitors.

Attractions

Camano Island (see listing under Island County) is just over the causeway on Highway 532. There is a large state park and other recreation facilities.

For further information, write **Stanwood Chamber of Commerce**, Stanwood WA 98292.

Golf Course

KAYAK POINT GOLF COURSE
15711 Marine Drive
Stanwood, WA 98292
Tel. (206) 652-9676
Hrs: Year round golfing.

One will travel far to find a more beautiful or challenging golf course than Kayak Point Golf Course located eight miles south of Stanwood. To get to this course, take I-5 Exit 199, Marysville and drive thirteen and a half miles on scenic Marine Drive until you come to the course entrance. Literally carved out of the forest, Kayak Point provides a sloping terrain and abundance of trees. The course is a superb challenge for the most seasoned golfer. As resident pro Elwin Fanning says, "You get a little bit of everything..uphill lies,..downhill lies..sidehill lies...the kind of shots you don't encounter on most public courses. No two holes are alike."

Kayak was named the "fourth best course in the Pacific Northwest" by *Northwest Golfer* magazine. The fairways are all tree lined; shots made over bunkers to large tiered greens demand extreme accuracy for birdie attempts. On the 14th tee, you must select which of the two fairways to hit. The course regularly plays at a bit over 6,000 yards (5,400 for women) and can be extended to 6,700 for championship play. The course covers 250 acres of a 650 acre county park on Puget Sound and offers many views of the Sound, the Olympic Mountains and Camano Island. Deer and other wildlife are often spotted on the course.

Play Kayak Point Golf Course for challenging golf and fantastic scenery! The course boasts a modern clubhouse with pro shop, food service and driving range. Use of the course's rental carts is recommended.

Tulalip

Gift Shop

LYNCH'S TRADING PORT
2624 Tulalip Highway
Tulalip, WA 98270
Tel. (206) 653-2929

    Remember those Indian trading posts you see in the old western movies? Well, Lynch's Trading Port is not exactly like the ones you saw in the movies because it is authentically Indian. Owned by Nana Lynch, this attractive and delightfully arranged store is on the Tulalip Indian Reservation adjacent to Marysville, just a few miles off I-5.

    The shop features Indian arts and crafts: wood carvings, basketry, moccasins, silver and turquoise jewelry and other fascinating items. Have you ever wondered where you could get a genuine feathered Indian headdress, you can find one in this store along with dance and war masks. There are also exotically, colored porcupine quill earrings. In addition to Indian wares, there is an antique shop with individual rooms furnished with such rare finds as a 100 year old walnut bellows organ and beautiful displays of china and crystal.

    Be sure to visit this "Best Choice" in Western Washington and appreciate the Indian heritage Nana will share with you.

THURSTON COUNTY

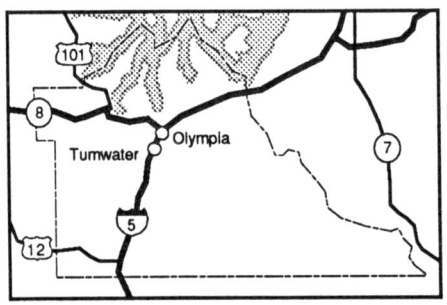

Small as far as Washington Counties go, this area at the south of Puget Sound is rich in history. The 727-square mile county has about 125,000 residents. Olympia, the capital city with 28,000 and Lacey, an outpost on the plain east of Olympia with 14,000 people, are the only large communities. Next to the capital city, Tumwater, home of the massive Olympia Brewing Company plant, is probably the best known town.

It was to Tumwater, "tum wa ta" in Chinook jargon, that Indians came for hundreds of years. Here the falls of the Deschutes River provided a place to catch the salmon migrating up stream. Settlers from a wagon train of 1845 came here against advice of the Hudson Bay Company. Michael Simmons had a grist mill going on the west bank at the middle falls in 1846 and the next year a water-powered sawmill jointed the upstream development. Closer to the Sound, Olympia was settled as Smithfield in 1846, renamed Olympia in 1849. When Oregon's legislature created the county in 1852, it chose Thurston for a name, honoring Samuel R. Thurston, the first delegate Oregon Territory sent to Congress.

Congress split Washington Territory from Oregon Territory in March, 1853. Olympia was designated territorial capital in the same year, giving Thurston County importance far beyond its population or the wealth of its timbered hills, fertile fields and glacier-scarred plains. The Nisqually River, draining the flanks of Mount Rainier and entering Puget Sound a few miles east of Olympia, is the county's eastern boundary. Lewis County lies to the south, Grays Harbor to the west and the waters of the sound make the northern limits of the capital county.

ATTRACTIONS

Nisqually National Wildlife Refuge, was established to protect the local environment, as well as the plant and animal life that is dependent upon it. There is a combination of salt/fresh water marshes, tideflats, forests, grasslands, swamps and streams that provide habitats for a variety of mammals, birds and reptiles. Accessible only by foot trails that vary in length from one half to five miles. There's a birdwatching platform, photo blind, interpretive literature and fishing facilities available. Open daily. Phone 753-9467 for further information.

Millersylvania State Park, ten miles south of Olympia, is one of Washington's grand old parks. Set under a forest of old growth fir, with swimming facilities and boat launching on Deep lake, most of the park buildings were constructed in the 1930s by the Civilian Conservation Corps. There are over 180 camp sites including several with full hookups for recreational vehicles in this 720 acre park.

Bush Prairie, just south of the turn off from Highway 99 for Millersylvania Park, is one of many settlements by pioneers who came in the first Oregon Trail wagon trains. It is named for George W. Bush, a black freeman, who developed a farm here contrary to Oregon Territory laws forbidding Negroes property ownership. Congress passed a special law giving Bush title to the claim.

Tenino, a crossroads town of 1,300, was built when the railroad came through from the south in the 1870s. Some say the name was taken from the work locomotive number 1090 (ten-nine-oh), others point out the name existed before the railroad. Tenino is the Chinook jargon word for "fork in the trail."

During the Great Depression Tenino's bank made national news by issuing wooden money, which turned an $11,000 profit as collectors sought the temporary coins printed on veneer. The bank, 213 Sussex, is now an antique store. Sandstone from Tenino quarries built many structures, including the first jetties at Grays Harbor which received 375,000 cubic yards via railroad.

The mounded deposits of massive glaciers which spread southward and then withdrew between the Cascades and Willapa Hills provide geologists with speculation. Some of the most noticeable bumps, called Tenino Mounds, are between Tenino and I-5.

Grand Mound, a community twenty-five miles south of Olympia and five miles west of I-5 on Highway 12, has the largest mound of them all. It rises 125 feet above the prairie. Geologic evidence indicates the massive glacier flowed down out of British Columbia filling Puget Sound with ice that eventually drained through a path which is now the Chehalis River. Scientists debate theories on how the mounded deposits of glacial material were formed.

Puget Sound's underwater reefs provide the attraction at **Tolmie State Recreation Area**, on the Sound eight miles north of Olympia. This popular day use area has picnic tables, and cold water showers. Views of the Sound and its mountain backdrop are nice.

Evergreen State College, three miles northwest of Olympia, is the first four-year college to be started in the state in the twentieth century. A 1967 study picked the site, the state commissioned master planners and architects to create a campus which continues to grow.

For further information, contact the **Olympia Chamber of Commerce**, 1000 Olympia Street, Olympia WA 98507. Telephone 357-3362.

Olympia

The classic dome of Washington's Capitol can be seen above the green fir trees as you approach the small city of Olympia from any direction. About 25,000 people live here, plus several hundred more when the legislature is in session. It is a far cry from the collection of wooden buildings that sprang up after Governor Isaac L. Stevens brought the territory's first legislature into session here in 1854. Design of the state's campus-like complex of capitol and office buildings began in 1893, six years before statehood. The land mark Legislative Building, as it was officially designated, was completed in 1928. A lake, complete with fish ladder for the migrating salmon, came in 1950 turning the Deschutes River into part of the capital landscaping.

Down by Budd Inlet, Olympia's manufacturing developed over the years. From knitting mills to processing plants for the tiny Olympia oyster, these businesses could take their choice in shipping by land or water. Deep-draft vessels can call in Budd Inlet, which at low tide is surrounded by acres of mud flats. Thurston County has operated a port here since 1926.

Attractions

Washington's first legislative hall was on Capitol Way between State and Olympia Avenues almost at the harbor, the site now marked by a bronze plate. The present capital campus developed to the south. The best way to see the **Capitol buildings** is to drive in from Capitol Way, which splits the area and extends from the port southward.

It took six years to construct the **Legislative Building** at Wilder and White Streets, which most people simply call "The Capitol." A square of concrete, 130-feet on a side, supports the four piers upon which the stone dome rests. It is 287 feet from the ground to the top of the dome. Legislative chambers are in wings at each side. Also impressive is the state reception room.

Closest to Capitol Lake, and almost west of the Legislative Building, was the Governor's Mansion, oldest building remaining in the governmental group. Built in 1908 in the Georgian Revival style, by 1980 the mansion was slated for demolition to make way for an office building.

Thurston County Courthouse, 1110 Capitol Way, was built in 1930. Like many public buildings of its day, the exterior is of block construction with ornamentation added that is now called art deco. The sandstone used here was quarried at Tenino, a small crossroads community southeast of Olympia.

Thurston County's **original courthouse**, located on Legion Way opposite Sylvester Park, may be one of the most interesting buildings in town. Towers sprouted from the roof in a Romanesque style. Built in 1891, this building has done duty as a city hall and state capitol, and is now offices for the Board of Education. An earthquake in 1949 damaged turrets, causing their removal. The central tower seen in old photos was destroyed by a 1928 fire.

The **State Capitol Museum**, 211 21st Avenue West, was built in the 1920s as a private dwelling. A banker gave it to the state in 1939. Residential furnishings remain on the first floor and the state's history unfolds in exhibits on the second floor.

All of the above attractions are collectively known as **The Capitol Group**. In totality it includes the buildings for the legislative, judicial, insurance, labor and industries, Social Security and public lands, transportation, and general administrative offices. The Legislative Building's guided **tours** are offered Monday thru Friday, when legislature is in session; call 586-8687. A tour of the **Governor's Mansion** is on Wednesday; phone 586-8687 to reserve space for the tour. Self-guiding tours of the **Greenhouse Conservatory** are available daily. Call 753-5590.

One of Olympia's oldest residences, **Bigelow House** at 918 Glass Avenue, was constructed in 1854. Pioneer lawyer Daniel Bigelow is believed to have used a pattern book in picking the design of the cottage.

Mima Mounds Natural Area Preserve, 445 acres, an interpretive center details the natural history of the area and presents various theories on the mounds' origin. Self-guiding trails traverse the forests and open prairie. Open daily 9:00 a.m. to 9:00 p.m. Call 753-2449 for further information.

For further information, contact the **Olympia Chamber of Commerce**, 1000 Plum Street, Olympia WA 98507. Telephone 357-3362.

Accommodations

THE GOVERNOR HOUSE
HOTEL AND CONFERENCE CENTER
621 South Capitol Way
Olympia, WA 98501
Tel: (206) 352-7700
 (800) 356-5335
All major credit cards are accepted.

Olympia, capitol city of Washington, is a place of much business and sightseeing. Many travelers find themselves there every year enjoying the many attractions Olympia has to offer. Experienced travelers of the area already know where the finest hotel in town is. But for those vacationers and business people seeking this establishment, it will only take a few minutes, because of its location, to discover The Governor House, the best downtown accommodation in Olympia.

The Governor House, only steps away from the bustling activity of the town's center, plays gracious host to both vacationers and those on official business alike. From this convenient location, you can enjoy the rich history and sights of Washington's capitol, as well as conduct your business without having to be shuttled into the area. This modern hotel offers street access to the multiple story building in which it is housed. The interior is bright, airy and decorated in a variety of subtle, relaxing colors. All rooms, exuding an air of luxury and comfort, are plushly furnished and come equipped with all the amenities you would expect of a fine hotel.

So, whether you're an experienced traveler or not, on business or pleasure, you'll most assuredly enjoy The Governor House, an institution in Olympia. Visit, relax and savor this fine hotel.

THE VANCE TYEE MOTOR INN
500 Tyee Drive
Olympia, WA 98502
Tel. (206) 352-0511

Capitol Idea - stay in a full-service motor inn just ten minutes from the Washington Capitol and governor's mansion.

For years the Vance Tyee Motor Inn has been pleasing guests with good service and comfortable accommodations. A major remodeling begun in the summer of 1987 was to make the inn even better. Enjoy sitting back in massive and attractively decorated lobby, dine in the expanded dining room. From your table enjoy the sunny southern exposure over looking the grounds and pool. There's live music Tuesday through Saturday evenings, usually top Forty selections. For a little excitement, warm up to a few sets of tennis on the courts. The Tumwater Valley Golf Course is just five minutes away. Pamper yourself in the tanning salon or beauty salon.

So capitalize on this "Best Choice" by making it your choice for accommodations.

Bed and Breakfast

HARBINGER INN
1136 East Bay Drive
Olympia, WA 98506
Tel. (206) 754-0389
Visa, MasterCard and AMEX are accepted.
Off street parking. Adequate provision for smokers.

The newly and painstakingly restored Harbinger Inn is your "Best Choice" for Bed and Breakfast Inns in Olympia. Now owned by Emma and David Mathes, this lovely house built in 1910 has regained its original charm.

Complete rewiring, reroofing, and stripping of the beautiful woodworking has brought the house up to modern standards while keeping the ambiance of days gone by. While stripping years of built up paint, the Mathes found stencils of tulips, swans, grass pods and windmills. Interesting features such as a waterfall on the back hillside, originally used as the source of water for several houses including Harbinger, and a mysterious street to basement tunnel have been preserved.

There are four second floor guest rooms with panoramic views of the waterfront and the mountains. Restoration of the walls, floors and woodwork in the guests rooms and turn of the century furniture give the rooms romantic grandeur. Each evening before retiring, guests leave a request for either

Continental or full breakfast to be served in their room or in the dining room. Emma serves only homemade and delicious meals.

The Mathes are happy to help you plan your day's activities with options such as, boating, bicycling and point you toward interesting areas to explore.

Bakery

WAGNER'S EUROPEAN BAKERY AND CAFE
1013 Capitol Way
Olympia, WA 98501
Tel. (206) 357-7268
Hrs: Mon. - Fri.   7:00 a.m. - 6:00 p.m.
          Saturday   7:30 a.m. - 5:00 p.m.
Closed Sunday, Christmas, New Year's and Thanksgiving.

Rudy Wagner moved to Olympia in 1957 from his homeland of Germany and set out to learn the bakery business. He worked in a small bakery to learn the basics, then opened his own shop twenty-six years ago. Rudy was successful from the start, expanding and moving to his present location six years later. The bakery and cafe are warm, cheerful and always busy in the morning and at lunch time.

Wagner's specializes in European pastries, using only the best ingredients available. Rudy discovered that American's taste in baked good differs somewhat from European's and combining the two preferences has created truly outstanding selections sure to please everyone. The Schwarzwälder which is similar to Black Forest cake is an overwhelming favorite, as are the fresh strawberry and raspberry mousse. The cafe sells only bakery items in the morning, but offers two different soups and sandwiches served on a variety of fresh baked bread as well as homemade salads for lunch.

Be sure you take the time to stop by Wagner's European Bakery and Cafe to sample some of the best baking in Olympia. The delicious selections, warm atmosphere and top-notch service combined with reasonable prices are sure to please.

Thurston County

"Best Choices" in beds, books, boxes of goodies, baked goods, black olives, breast of chicken, bay shrimp, blackened Cajun cookery, banana cream or blackberry yogurt, Bohemian coffee, beers–domestic and imported, burgers, bleu cheese spread and Black Forest cake!

B-B-B-BEING THERE		
Harbinger Inn	Best B & B	Oly/B & B
Vance Tyee Motor Inn	Best service	Oly/Accom.
The Bookmark	Best books	Oly/Books
Drees	Best giftware	Oly/Gift
Ben Moore's Restaurant	Best casual elegance	Oly/Rest.
The Bristol House	Best Cajun and French	Oly/Rest.
Carnegie's	Best Mediterranean	Oly/Rest.
The Chattery Down	Best wholesome Am.	Oly/Rest.
Crackers	Best drunken prawns	Oly/Rest.
Especially Yogurt	Best lunch and yogurt	Oly/Ice
Gardner's Restaurant	Best Italian & Continental	Oly/Rest.
La Petite Maison	Best Pacific N.W. cuisine	Oly/Rest.
The Spar	Best burgers and malts	Oly/Rest.
The Trails	Best prime rib	Oly/Rest.
The Urban Onion	Best bread, beef & beer	Oly/Rest.
Wagner's European Bakery	Best European pastries	Oly/Bakery

Books

THE BOOKMARK
511 South Sound Center
Olympia, WA 98503
Tel. (206) 491-2821
Hrs:　Mon. - Fri.　　10:00 a.m. - 9:00 p.m.
　　　　Saturday　　　10:00 a.m. - 6:00 p.m.
　　　　Sunday　　　　12:00 noon - 5:00 p.m.
Most major credit cards are accepted.

　　　The Bookmark is a well established bookstore owned and operated by Lilo Peter. It has been in the South Sound Center Mall since the late 1960's. Lilo considers her store a general bookstore, but does specialize in science fiction and juvenile books and has a large section dedicated entirely to books on the Northwest, including travel books, maps and magazines.

What really sets the Bookmark apart from other bookstores is the wonderful personal service. A friendly and helpful staff will do everything possible to help find the book you need. If you're travelling through the area and the book you want is not in stock, they will locate and ship it anywhere for you. They have customers from as far away as Wisconsin, Florida and Alaska.

Lilo is continually hunting for unusual books to stock on every subject from the arts to mysteries. She tries to carry books that are not available anywhere else in the area. Her drive and dedication to excellence have made The Bookmark a "Best Choice" for literary shopping in Olympia.

Delicatessen

BAYVIEW MARKETPLACE DELI AND BAKERY
516 West 4th Avenue
Olympia, WA 98506
Tel. (206) 352-4901
Hrs: Mon. - Sun. Opened 24 hours a day.
Closed on Christmas Day.

On Budd Inlet off the Bay of Puget Sound in Bayview, is a wonderful and welcome addition to downtown Olympia, the Bayview Marketplace Deli and Bakery. The deli is open twenty-four hours a day for sandwiches, salads and ice cream. Upstair is view seating available and a solarium is being added on the west side overlooking the water.

Bayview Deli serves breakfast from 6:00 a.m. to 10:00 a.m. You may get anything from croissant sandwiches to their most popular breakfast, country biscuits and gravy. Lunch begins at 10:00 a.m. and is served until 3:00 p.m. For lunch choose from smoked and fried chicken, pork barbecued ribs or any number of sandwiches and salads. Dinner hours are from 3:00 p.m. to 8:00 p.m. in this casual serve yourself atmosphere. Entrees range from scallops to fettucini and there is a full salad bar for both lunch and dinner. You can also call in advance and order exceptionally well prepared box lunches for meetings or seminars or stop by on your way home for a fresh made to order pizza.

Bayview is also known in the area for its quality catering service and has won the Olympia Deli and Catering Award for several years in a row. They handle many legislative functions and specialize in French, Greek and Italian cuisine. Whether you want catering service for a large group, something to take along for a picnic, or a delicious, quick meal in attractive surroundings with a nice view, Bayview Marketplace Deli and Bakery is the place to find what you need.

Gift Shops

DREES
524 Washington Street
Olympia, WA 98501
Tel. (206) 357-7177
Hrs: Mon. - Sat.   10:00 a.m. - 6:00 p.m.
     Sunday   12:00 noon - 5:00 p.m.
Closed Sundays from Sept. - June

Ruthann Panowicz, the proprietor of Drees, a charming gift shop, brings a lot of experience and knowledge to her business. She is very selective in what she carries and offers a wide range of items from which to choose. She is more than happy to help her customers make their selections and answer any and all questions.

There is a lot to be found in this shop. There is a section of gourmet foods, featuring Northwest products, perfect for making up gift boxes. There are decorative accessories for the home, antiques, gourmet cookware, paper products, linens and children's toys. There is a bridal registry service. Seasonal decorations are carried too, and a Christmas open house is a yearly feature.

Drees has gifts to suit everyone's taste and budget. Ruthann is so helpful and knowledgeable that you will come away very satisfied with your delightful shopping experience.

ARCHIBALD SISTERS, 113 West Fifth Street, Olympia, Washington. Quality soaps, lotions, cards, jewelry, clothing, and accessories.

Ice Cream

HOFFNAGLE'S ICE CREAM
4443 Martin Way
Olympia, WA 98506
Tel. (206) 456-3336
Hrs: Sun. - Thur. 11:00 a.m. - 10:00 p.m.
     Fri. - Sat. 11:00 a.m. - 12:00 midnight
and,
Off I-5 at Harrison
Centralia, WA
Tel. (206) 736-3336

2900 78th Avenue SE at 29th
Mercer Island, WA 980040
Tel. (206) 236-1728

If you want to know about the legend of Hubert Hoffnagle, you'll just have to ask when you get there and enjoy some legendary ice cream. What's in a name, anyway?

Indulge in one of over forty-three flavors of ice cream from Hawaiian delight, made with fresh papaya, to peach, or their flagship flavor, Madagascar vanilla. For special occasions you'll want to try one of their novelty cakes or pies handcrafted by their decorators. Co-creators and developers Tom Moyer and Les Kandel are proud of how much customers enjoy their ice cream and are equally proud that they have won several local awards for desserts. The Lacey and Centralia emporiums offer an old fashion miniature golf course right next to their store. Each shop is bright, colorful and decorated with neon artwork.

When you finally leave, your palate will know what really good ice cream is, and you will know how to ask for a great ice cream by name.

Restaurants

BEN MOORE'S RESTAURANT
112 W 4th
Olympia, WA 98501
Tel. (206) 357-7527
Hrs: Monday 9:00 a.m. - 8:00 p.m.
     Tue. - Thu. 9:00 a.m. - 9:00 p.m.
     Fri. - Sat. 9:00 a.m. - 10:00 p.m.
Bar Mon. - Sun. 11:00 a.m. - 2:00 a.m.
Closed Sundays.
AMEX, Visa and MasterCard are accepted.

Ben Moore's Restaurant, a dining establishment for over fifty years, has been owned by Michael Murphy since 1983. Here, after a few touches of his own, Michael has created a refuge where the weary traveler is given the opportunity to dine in a style that can't be found elsewhere. It's a charming, intimate and relaxed restaurant that will awaken even your most fatigued senses.

Ideally located in downtown Olympia, Ben Moore's is a beautiful place to unwind from the strain of the road. Here, amidst an ambiance of casual elegance, you'll be able to choose from a number of delicious dishes for breakfast, lunch or dinner. A variety of filling omelets, thick steaks and several types of fresh seafood, all await your approval. A favorite is the piranhas' omelet; an omelet filled with feta cheese, sausage and black olives. You'll attack it as eagerly as the fish it's named after.

If you've got a special event on the horizon, Ben Moore's restaurant also features a banquet service, as well as full service outside catering. This Triple A rated restaurant will make any event a well remembered one. So you see, you need not be a weary traveler to enjoy a fine dining experience. But if you are, and have sore, road strained muscles, Ben Moore's restaurant will mend them.

THE BRISTOL HOUSE
2401 Bristol Court SW
Olympia, WA 98302
Tel. (206) 352-9494
Hrs: Mon. - Wed.   7:00 a.m. - 3:00 p.m.
      Thu. - Fri.   7:00 a.m. - 10:00 p.m.
      Saturday   5:00 p.m. - 10:00 p.m.
      Sunday   8:00 a.m. - 2:00 p.m.

Bristol House owners P. H. Schmidt and Adolph Schmidt, who is also the chef, are committed to producing the best meals possible for breakfast lunch and dinner. Everything is freshly prepared and baked on the premises, Adolph bakes every day using only the finest ingredients.

The results of Adolph's care and concern for the pleasure of his patrons are outstanding and the food is unfailingly excellent. Breakfasts feature eggs done to order and fresh baked goods. There are three specials for lunch every day, in addition to the regular menu. The Cajun dishes are a speciality and are excellent. Dinner each night features four specials. There is fresh fish everyday and Cajun specialties as well as more classic French cuisine.

Bristol House is one of the best restaurants in town. They can accommodate groups for parties and if they are asked in advance, they will do a cooking demonstration and let your party tour their cooking facilities. This is a wonderful place for any meal of the day, where you can be sure you will get only carefully prepared meals of the highest quality.

CARNEGIE'S
302 E 7th
Olympia, WA 98501
Tel. (206) 357-5550

Hrs:	Lunch	Mon. - Fri.	11:30 a.m. - 2:00 p.m.
	Dinner	Mon. - Sat.	5:30 p.m. - 10:00 p.m.
		Sunday	4:00 p.m. - 9:00 p.m.
	Lounge	Mon. - Sun.	11:30 a.m. - Closing

Closed Christmas Day, Thanksgiving, and New Year's Day.
Visa, MasterCard, AMEX and Discover are accepted.

Industrialist Andrew Carnegie built 2,509 libraries throughout the world in the early 1900s, including Olympia's Carnegie Library which was built in 1914. The building is on the State and National Historic Register. In 1978 it was purchased by John and Susan Senner and renovated to its original appearance. When the restoration was completed in 1980, John and Susan opened their restaurant. This is their fourth successful restaurant in renovated historical locations. They have remodeled the old Northern Hotel in Missoula, Montana; a granary in Billings, Montana, and an old railroad depot in LaCrosse, Wisconsin.

Carnegie's is a charming restaurant, with more than 8,000 books on the shelves. There are three wood burning fireplaces and various oil paintings from the Carnegie Library in Everett, which decorate the walls. The distinctive decor is more than matched by the cuisine offered by Chef Scott, a Sous Chef from the East Coast, and Chef Hal who has Cajun roots. For lunch there is a selection of soups, salads, hamburgers, sandwiches and several chicken and seafood entrees. Each night for dinner there are three fresh fish specials, as well as the regular menu selections which include stuffed curried chicken, Greek style prawns and veal Jacqueline, all of which are extremely tasty and very popular.

In place is a nice wine list featuring Northwest wines and many wines available by the glass. Relax in the pleasant ambiance after dinner with an espresso and one of the delectable desserts. Carnegie's is a worthwhile dining experience in unusual surroundings. The wonderful food and the friendly and competent service are sure to please you.

THE CHATTERY DOWN AT BUCK'S FIFTH AVENUE
209 E 5th Avenue
Olympia, WA 98501
Tel. (206) 786-5006
Hrs: Mon. - Sat. 8:00 a.m. - 5:30 p.m.
Visa, MasterCard and AMEX are accepted.

If you're in downtown Olympia you've probably already run across it, but if you haven't, you'll definitely want to do so. It's The Chattery Down, a place to enjoy a good meal and terrific shopping at the same time.

The Chattery Down, with its early 20th century exterior, fits perfectly into the revitalized area of downtown Olympia. It's a collection of charming boutique shops and a super eatery. So, while you're shopping you can also partake of a wholesome meal, or perhaps you'd like to eat before shopping. Whatever you decide, you'll enjoy homemade muffins, sandwiches, soups and other delightful entrees served. Before you begin or end your shopping spree, don't forget to try one of the many fabulous desserts made as you watch.

The Chattery Down is the perfect place to visit for breakfast or lunch. There, you can shop to your heart's content and satisfy your tastebuds at the same time. Stop by, have a spot of tea or a glass of wine. Visit this quaint collection of shops in Olympia. You'll be glad you did.

CRACKERS
317 E Fourth Avenue
Olympia, WA 98501
Tel. (206) 352-1900
Hrs: Sun. - Thu. 7:00 a.m. - 12:00 midnight
Fri. - Sat. 7:00 a.m. - 3:00 a.m.
Closed on Christmas Day and Thanksgiving Day.
Visa, MasterCard and AMEX are accepted.

Crackers, located in the Ward Building, is named in honor of the Marx Brothers and is a favorite gathering place for local legislators, theater people, the press and Seattle Portland commuters. The decor features cedar, oak and inlaid walnut, with the windows overlooking Fourth Avenue and the Ward Building's atrium. The ambiance is informal, what one might term "casual class." Background music is eclectic, ranging from Tommy Dorsey and Glenn Miller to fifties and sixties rock 'n roll to classical.

This restaurant has an extensive menu and most items are available any time of day. Breakfast features delicious omelettes and standard breakfast selections, as well as a unique "cheese steak", shredded rib eye combined with vegetables, cheese and Italian sauce. All soups and salads are homemade and there is a good selection of hamburgers and sandwiches. The dinner menu features some very special entrees, such as drunken prawns, Amoretto, New York Mafia beef, Crackers Clackers-a breast of chicken pounded then wrapped around cream cheese, bay shrimp, crab, shallots and chives, topped with honey mustard sauce. In addition to the regular menu, specials are offered nightly.

Crackers was the first wine bar in Olympia and they highlight Washington and Oregon wines. All wines are available by the glass. This establishment has recently expanded next door into the oldest wood structure in Olympia, built in 1898. The new lounge offers many different types of entertainment including jazz, blues, swing, sixties and seventies music and comedy acts. When in Olympia, have a delicious dinner at Crackers, and then enjoy quality entertainment in their lounge and see for yourself why this is one of the city's most popular places.

"DIRTY DAVE'S" GAY 90'S PIZZA PARLOR
3939 Martin Way
Olympia, WA 98501
Tel. (206) 456-1560
Hrs: Mon. - Thu.   11:00 a.m. - 11:00 p.m.
 Fri. - Sat.   11:00 a.m. - 12:00 midnight
 Sunday   12:00 noon - 11:00 p.m.
Closed on Christmas, New Year's, Easter, and Father's Day.
Visa and MasterCard are accepted.

"Dirty Dave's" offers more than just pizza, it offers fun. This is a very family oriented place. There are video games galore to amuse the kids while mom and dad enjoy twenty-five cent glass of beer. Dave started in the pizza business in 1963 in Southern California, moving to Olympia and opening "Dirty Dave's" in 1971. He is ably assisted by his family and business has been booming every since he opened.

Dave's prices are very reasonable and the pizza is great. The secret behind Dave's success is the wonderful family recipes he uses for pizza and his insistence on freshness and high quality. The "Gay 90's Special" has been a favorite pizza among customers for twenty-six years; the secret is the roasted cashew nuts. In addition to pizza, the menu includes submarine sandwiches, fresh steamed clams, spaghetti, ravioli, and lasagna dinners which include salad and garlic bread. There are daily luncheon specials.

When you visit "Dirty Dave's," you might find someone playing the piano to entertain the crowd. If you play, don't be shy, you can have a turn. Take some time and read the signs and posters on the walls; it would take at least a week to read all of them. Stop by and see why "Dirty Dave's" Gay 90's Pizza Parlor is one of Olympia's favorite family spots for good food and fun.

GARDNER'S RESTAURANT
111 W Thurston Avenue
Olympia, WA 98501
Tel. (206) 786-8466
Hrs: Tue. - Thu.   11:00 a.m. - 9:00 p.m.
      Fri. - Sat.   11:00 a.m. - 9:30 p.m.
Closed Sunday and Monday.
Reservations required. No smoking allowed.

Gene Gardner and his wife Libet, proprietors of Gardner's Restaurant, bring many years of experience to this charming restaurant. Their expertise has created one of those rare restaurants where everything comes together perfectly to provide a totally enjoyable dining experience.

The Gardners are totally committed to using only the freshest and best ingredients the Northwest has to offer. The produce couldn't be fresher, it comes from the Olympia Farmer's Market which is just across the street from the restaurant. Fresh seafood is a specialty here, along with freshly made pasta. Everything is prepared with the Northwest approach of lighter sauces that let the fresh flavors through. The menu is Italian and Continental and everything is consistently excellent.

Gardner's Restaurant is small and intimate, only eleven tables making reservations a must. The service is excellent, with warm personal attention that doesn't overwhelm you, but adds greatly to your total dining experience. The fantastic food and excellent service combine to make this a most memorable place to dine.

LE PETITE MAISON
2005 Ascension
Olympia, WA 98502
Tel. (206) 943-8812
Hrs: Lunch   Mon. - Fri.   11:30 a.m. - 2:00 p.m.
      Dinner   Tue. - Sat.   5:30 p.m. - 9:00 p.m.
Closed Sunday

The owner of Le Petite Maison, Jeff Philpot, and his able staff bring you the freshest, most delicious food possible at this delightful, small and intimate restaurant. The emphasis here is on what's fresh and the seasonal specials are wonderful. This is Pacific Northwest Cuisine at its best.

The menu changes daily and the choices depend on what's the best fresh fish and seafood available that day. Someone goes daily to Westport to pick out the freshest fish and seafood possible. There might be red rock crab, mussels, squid or Olympia oysters, famous throughout the Northwest. In the spring there will be fresh picked chantrelles and morel mushrooms. In the fall try such specialties as pheasant or venison. The desserts available to round out your meal are fantastic. A specialty is a triple chocolate cake, made without flour, using ground hazelnuts or almonds, truly a spectacular treat. There is a very good selection of wines, including of course Northwest wines, to complement your meal.

The distinctively different menu and the high standards offered by Le Petite Maison along with the warm, personalized service make this a restaurant you shouldn't miss when in Olympia.

THE SPAR CAFE, BAR AND CARDROOM
114 E 4th Avenue
Olympia, WA 98501
Tel. (206) 357-6444
Hrs: Restaurant Mon. - Sun. 6:00 a.m. - 9:00 p.m.
      Lounge Mon. - Sun 11:00 a.m. - 2:00 a.m.
Closed Christmas and Thanksgiving.
Visa and MasterCard are accepted.

The Spar is a link to the past. It was built in 1935 as a recreation center for the local male population, with pool and card tables. When prohibition ended in 1939, a bar was added. The present owner is Alan McWain whose father purchased The Spar in 1945. In bygone days it was frequented by millworkers, longshoremen, shoppers and merchants. The decor is reminiscent of the building's past, the ceilings are high and the large lunch counter has the original mahogany stools. Photos from the 1930s and 1940s decorate the walls.

Breakfast offers cereal, eggs, meat, strawberry waffles thirteen different omelettes and daily specials. For lunch and dinner there are daily fresh fish specials such as, grilled halibut or small yearling oysters, as well as the regular menu. Dinner entrees come with a salad and homemade beef barley or French onion soup. The burgers and fries are great, and the milkshakes are hand dipped, just like in the good old days.

Try The Spar when you are in Olympia for an unusual dining experience and a taste of the past.

THE TRAILS
7842 Trails End Drive, SE
Olympia, WA 98501
Tel. (206) 753-8720
Visa, MasterCard, AMEX, and Diner's Club are accepted.

The Trails, so named because it is very near the end of the Oregon Trail, is a rather unique place. It is a restaurant, lounge and an indoor horse arena. The arena is located directly below the restaurant and every weekend you can enjoy different types of horse shows as you dine. There are several rodeos during the year and one or two circuses and dog shows. On week nights, stop in for dinner and watch cattle roping, cutting or mounted drill practices.

Food offered by The Trails is excellent, there is a touch of the "Old West", with twentieth century flair. The menu includes numerous barbecue selections, steaks, seafood and salads. Mesquite top sirloin and roast prime rib are both served with fries or beans and are local favorites. At lunch time those in a hurry may order The Saddlebag, prime rib sliced on a French roll with the house bleu cheese spread and soup or salad. They guarantee that they'll serve in ten minutes or less or it's on the house! A good selection of everything exists from light lunches to burgers and fries.

The lounge provides live entertainment Wednesday through Saturday with danceable top forties music. Whether you come to The Trails to dance, to enjoy the equine entertainment, or to partake of their delicious, hearty food, you'll have fun at this unique spot.

THE URBAN ONION
117 E Legion Way
Olympia, WA 98502
Hrs: Mon. - Thurs. 7:00 a.m. - 11:00 p.m.
       Fri. - Sat. 7:00 a.m. - 12:00 midnight
Closed Sunday

The Urban Onion is a delightful restaurant located in the Olympian Hotel. Owners Jim and Debbie Mead produce the best food possible working with entirely fresh ingredients and using no preservatives. They offer a good selection of fresh, wholesome food for breakfast, lunch and dinner.

For breakfast, the ten grain pancake is a treat. One of the most popular lunch selections is the haystack, an open faced sandwich served on herb-onion bread baked fresh daily at the restaurant in forty-eight ounce juice cans. The bread is served with soup for lunch too. There are several salads to choose from, including the popular taco salad with freshly made guacamole. For dinner there are entrees of grain fed beef, home made pasta, and home made sausage among others. They offer some of the best pasta in town. Both beer and wine are available.

The prices at The Urban Onion are moderate, and for any meal of the day, this is a good place to dine.

Yogurt Parlor

ESPECIALLY YOGURT
101 N. Capitol Way
Olympia, WA 98501
Tel. (206) 754-6480
Hrs: Mon. - Thu.   7:00 a.m. - 10:00 p.m.
      Fri. - Sat.   7:00 a.m. - 12:00 midnight
      Sunday   12:00 noon - 10:00 p.m.

Especially Yogurt is a family run business that offers much more than just yogurt. Owner Paul Delashaw and his parents bring their customers delicious breakfasts and lunches, as well as an unbelievable number of different kinds of yogurt.

Breakfasts feature fresh baked muffins and quiche. They make forty-six kinds of muffins and six different ones are offered each day. For lunch the croissant sandwich is excellent and features home baked croissants. Then, of course, there is the yogurt. Wonderful, creamy tasting, delicious yogurt in a myriad of flavors, the best part is, it's good for you. It just tastes creamy, their yogurt is mostly two percent fat content, and some of it is non fat. The flavors include the standard vanilla, chocolate and strawberry and such exotic delights as banana creme (one of their biggest successes) kahlua, mint chocolate, kiwi, blackberry and peanut butter to name just a few. Of course, you can have a taste before you decide which one to try.

Especially Yogurt will set aside space to accommodate parties if notified in advance. This is a place to have a good time in clean, congenial surroundings, with the best yogurt in town.

Tumwater

The giant brewhouse of Olympia Brewing Company stands watch over the Washington terminal of the Oregon Trail. From here the settlers scattered to farm the islands and prairies of the Puget Sound country. There have been white inhabitants here continuously since 1845. Indian artifacts indicate settlement and perhaps a permanent village for five centuries before. Modern

Tumwater is home to about 7,000 people. It's trim residential community is small in size when compared with the massive brewery buildings.

Pioneers used the water falls to gain the needed elevation for water-powered mills which ground grain and cut lumber. It fell to Leopold E. Schmidt, who learned brewing in Germany, to pick this as site of a major brewery. Tasting water from an artesian well, Schmidt moved from Montana to start Capital Brewing Company in 1896. The first beer flowed in the same year. Olympia Brewing Company purchased the holdings and designed the new plant which overlooks Deschutes River waters backed up by the 1949 dam which created Capitol Lake in Olympia.

Attractions

The **Olympia Brewing Company** welcomes visitors for plant tours and a sampling of the beers produced here. The hours, daily 8:00 a.m. to 4:30 p.m., are even listed in large letters and numbers on the side of the brewhouse visible from I-5. Plant tours take about an hour, and in the summer visitors may want to bring a sweater as they stroll through vast rooms kept at temperatures just above freezing. For information, write the brewery at Box 947, Olympia WA 98507.

Local historic buildings and collectibles of that era are open for your viewing at the **Henderson House**, 602 Des Chutes Way, open daily, and the **Crosby House** at Grant and Des Chutes Way, open Thursday and Sunday afternoons. Call 753-8583 for further information.

For further information, contact the **Olympia Chamber of Commerce**, 1000 Olympia Street, Olympia WA 98507. Telephone 357-3362.

Accommodations

TYEE HOTEL
500 Tyee Drive
Tumwater, WA 98502
Tel. (206) 623-8030

The Tyee, located at the southern end of Puget Sound, has twenty lovely acres which help to make it a delightful place to stay. This is a perfect place for families, it has an outdoor pool, tennis and basketball courts and lovely gardens in which to enjoy a stroll or a picnic. The inn is located within easy driving distance of Washington's beaches and is not far from the state capitol in Olympia.

Thurston County

There is a delightfully unhurried ambiance at the Tyee. Picnics are provided for guests who wish to stroll and enjoy the grounds and clam bakes can be arranged for group visits. The Coffee House serves wonderful muffins, as well as a full breakfast. The roomy dining room, Chantrell's, offers first class cuisine and service. The inn has meeting rooms which are able to accommodate large groups of people.

The Tyee is a pleasant and relaxing place to stay during your visit to the Tumwater area.

WAHKIAKUM COUNTY

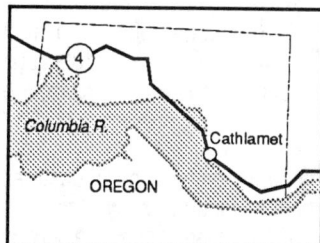

Tiny, sandwiched between the lower Columbia River's island-filled channel on the south and Pacific County on the north and west, Wahkiakum contains just 261 square miles. Its 3,800 residents depend on logging from the timbered hills inland, farming fields cleared of trees, and seasonal fishing. Highway 4, which follows the river bank westward from Kelso, makes no attempt to traverse the wild country between Skamokawa and the county line at Grays Bay. The former salmon canning village of Altoona, which boomed from 1870 through 1900, was not reached by road until 1952. Today less than 4,000 people live in the entire county, and Cathlamet, the county seat, had 635 residents at the last official census.

The county takes its name from the Wahkiakum Indian tribe which lived here for years in villages near the river shore. Capt. George Vancouver's 1792 expedition mapped some of the county shoreline, discovering that the main channel-- now called Miller Sands channel--hugs the north shore to the bend at Skamokawa, then heads for the Oregon side looping around Puget Island. Shipmates named the large island for Peter Puget, Vancouver's second lieutenant, who also has Washington's Puget Sound named for him. Lewis and Clark camped in Wahkiakum's villages in 1805 and by the 1850s settlers working down river from Fort Vancouver had homesteads scattered at some landings. Commercial salmon fishing, dependant on canning for preservation of fish, provided the county's single economic boom and left behind a legacy of buildings which draw modern visitors to this sparsely-populated north shore.

ATTRACTIONS

Puget Island, connected to the mainland with a ferry crossing just upstream from Cathlamet, is one of the largest channel islands in the lower Columbia. Five miles long and two miles wide, much of the farm land was reclaimed in federal projects which built dikes on the shoreline. A group of Norwegian emigrants for years farmed peppermint in the rich loam left by major river floods. Roads rim all but the northern downstream tip, making it an easy tour by foot, bike or car. On the southern downstream tip is **Puget Island Light**, a critical marker for pilots who must take vessels through a tight turn in the channel.

Skamokawa, where the river-side highway heads inland, has about 500 residents. It serves small boats traveling on the Columbia and motorists passing on Highway 4. The remnants of what was dubbed **"Little Venice"** can be seen in the slough which is the mouth of Skamokawa Creek--several commercial buildings were built on floats. A national historic district preserves the community's remaining buildings. **Redman Hall,** built in 1894, and the local tavern, where a collection of photographs document the town, are among attractions.

Grays River Valley is an area of dairy farms, all of them on pastures hewn from the massive forest which greeted homesteaders. Many of the hills above the valley were logged in the 1920s and are now nearing age for a second timber harvest.

Two and a half miles from Rosburg, on a county road, is a **covered bridge** over Grays River. Built in 1905 as an open span, the county elected to put a bridge house over it in 1908. This is believed to be the only covered bridge in the state which still takes regular vehicular traffic.

South from Rosburg is the road to the former cannery site at Altoona. This is one of many roads which attract **bicycle riders** because of its slight grades and scenic views of the river and the small bay.

For further information, contact the **Tourist Regional Information Program,** Box 128, Longview WA 98632. Telephone 577-3321.

Cathlamet

Cathlamet in Chinook jargon relates to the rocks. The name was applied to this stretch of river and the Indian tribe which had a village here and lived in cedar long houses similar to those of the fishing Indians on Puget Sound. Historians say smallpox hit the village hard in 1825; the village was so decimated by the disease that those that didn't die...fled the area.
The first commercial cannery in Washington was built here by the Hume brothers. Today, Cathlamet is a picturesque riverside settlement. It connects with rural Puget Island via a bridge, and is locally known as "Little Norway" for its largely Scandinavian population.
The irregular shore of the Columbia River charts the twisting course of Main Street, which lies at the base of a steep hill. The early business community is located on Main Street. Commercial enterprises, after the close of the salmon cannery, included a cheese factory and a specialty lumber mill turning out packing boxes made of spruce.

Attractions

A wharf repair job in 1987 is to make Cathlamet again a port of call for river steamers. Several **tour boats** now travel the Columbia between Astoria and the Portland area. The town owns the dock being refurbished.

The **Wahkiakum County Historical Museum** includes Indian, logging and pioneer life exhibits. Open Tuesday thru Sunday during May to October, and Thursday thru Sunday during the rest of the year. Phone 795-3954.

The **John Fitzpatrick House**, built about 1860, in later days became the home of Wahkiakum's most distinguished citizen, former U.S. Representative Julia Butler Hansen.

Community Congregational Church shows some of the New England architectural influence which was present in Cathlamet's early construction. It is on Alley Street, set on a rocky rise above town. The church was built in 1895.

The **White-tailed Deer National Wildlife Refuge** is 4,400 acres on the mainland, and several of the nearby islands; located just below Cathlamet the wildlife can often be viewed from Steamboat Slough Road, especially in the morning and evening when the deer are feeding in the pastures. Motorists are cautioned to watch out for the animals, in or near the roadways, at all times.

For further information, contact the Tourist Regional Information Program, Box 128, Longview WA 98632. Telephone 577-3321.

Bed and Breakfast

**THE GALLERY BED AND BREAKFAST
AT LITTLE CAPE HORN**
4 Little Cape Horn
Cathlamet, WA 98612
Tel. (206) 425-7395

The Gallery at Little Cape Horn, on Ocean Beach Highway between mile markers forty-one and forty-two, offers a charming out of the way place to relax. Hosts Eric and Carolyn Feasey's unique home is surrounded with beauty. Picture windows frame a majestic view of the Columbia River. Seals frolic, gulls soar, tugboat captains wave or blink lights as they chug by, ships glide quietly by, there is always something to watch. At night, after the magnificent glowing sunset has faded, stars sparkle in the clear dark night skies.

After a comfortable night in spacious accommodations, you will be served a special breakfast, prepared by your hosts while you stroll the beach or browse in the Gallery Gift shop for a memento of your visit.

This is a truly memorable place to stay and highly recommended for a delightfully quiet and relaxing time.

WHATCOM COUNTY

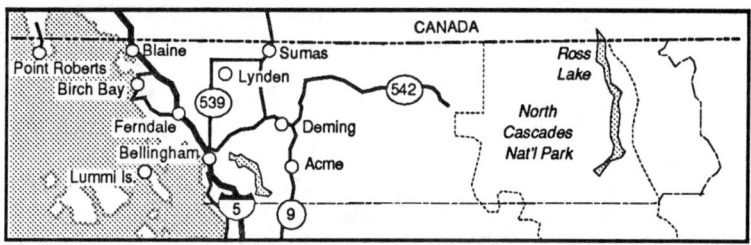

The farthest north county on Washington's coast, Whatcom is named for an Indian chief. Its 2,125 square miles include Point Roberts, attached to the Canadian mainland but part of the United States as a result of the treaty of 1846 setting the Forty-ninth parallel as the international boundary. From sea level on the Sound, Whatcom rises dramatically to its highest point, 10,778 foot high Mount Baker, at mid-county. To the east are the North Cascades, a forty-mile wide mountain group impenetrable except to foot or pack train travelers following narrow trails.

There are about 116,000 residents in the county, nearly half of them living in the industrial center of Bellingham with its deep-water port and oil refineries to the north. The population has grown at a rate of about 1,600 persons a year in the past four years, over half of the gain coming from in-migration of adults. Intalco Aluminum's reduction plant is the county's largest employer with 1,200 on the payroll. While Georgia Pacific Corporation and Mount Baker Plywood represent the traditional forest-products base of the economy, the newer Mobil and ARCO oil refineries are pushing the timber industry for places among the largest employers.

Bellingham Bay was charted by Spaniards in 1791 and has been home of the Lummi Indians for centuries. The first settlers opened at sawmill at Whatcom Falls in December 1852. A Hudson Bay employee, William Pattle, discovered coal in 1851 west of the future town site. Coaling of steamers became a big business within a decade. Farmers on the coastal plain work with about thirty-four inches of rain a year.

ATTRACTIONS

Lummi Indian Reservation and **Lummi Island** are across the bay from Bellingham. The reservation has a history dating to an 1855 treaty. It welcomes visitors. Follow Lummi Shore Road. The island developed as a resort. Indians say that a great battle was fought with invading tribes from the north on Gooseberry Point, near where the peninsula and island form a narrow channel.

Demming, a small community on Highway 542, stages a competition for professional loggers during a two day festival the second weekend in June.

Whatcom County operates a resort at **Silver Lake Park**, on a county road north of Maple Falls. The 411 acre park was logged over, then homesteaded and finally developed as a commercial resort before the county took it over. In addition to facilities you would expect at a public park, Silver Lake has six cabins for year around rental. This is a horse-oriented park with stables and the terminus for a horse trail being developed to reach Glacier on Highway 542. Telephone (206) 599-2776.

Larrabee State Park, on Highway 11 seven miles south of Bellingham, combines 3,600 feet of shoreline on Samish Bay with an extensive reserve of hiking trails to the east. This is Washington's first state park. Land was donated by the Larrabee family from a twenty acre holding in 1910. The state put itself into the park business here in 1923, and now owns a total of 1,886 acres extending from shore up the slopes of Chuckanut Mountain. Campsites, boat launching, picnic areas, and two fresh water lakes plus a view point from which you can see the Olympic Mountains, the San Juan Islands and ships heading to or from Bellingham's harbor.

Much of Whatcom County's low lands get about ten inches of snow each year, which often melts soon after falling. In the back country, snow stays for the season, creating several cross-country ski areas. **Whatcom County Parks**, 3373 Mount Baker Highway, Bellingham WA 98226, has a directory of over twenty trails. One group is in the North Fork, Nooksack River basin, the other in the Baker Lake area.

Mount Baker, the highest peak in this part of the Cascades, is accessible from two roads leading east from the community of Glacier on Highway 542. Glacier Creek road leads to a trail head on the west slopes where day hikes or camping trips originate. The Austin Pass extension of Highway 542 continues east to the downhill ski area located between Baker and its eastern cousin, **Mount Shuksan**. This is the trail head for two routes into **North Cascade National Park** (see listing under Skagit County).

Mount Baker Ski Area at Heather Meadows has six chair lifts and rope tows for beginners. The area is known for expert and intermediate runs. During the season, tows operate Friday, Saturday, Sunday and most holidays.

Groomed cross-country ski trails are part of the operation and some U.S. Forest Service logging roads in the area are also marked for ski touring.

Salmon Ridge, also on Mount Baker highway, has twenty-five kilometers of groomed cross country trails over a wide variety of terrain. It, too, operates on a Friday, Saturday, Sunday and holiday schedule each winter.

For further information, contact the **Whatcom Chamber of Commerce and Industry**, Box 958, Bellingham WA 98227. Telephone 734-1330.

Acme

This is a flag stop on the railroad. The village was named in 1887 by Samuel Parks. It is said the name came from the Acme hymnbook he carried with him. The South Fork Nooksack River flows through a broad valley north of Acme. A marshy area northwest of town, on the divide between the South and North forks, has extensive peat bogs and is known for its diverse wildlife habitat.

Bellingham

Discovered in 1792 by the English explorer Captain George Vancouver; Bellingham overlooks the sheltered cove of Bellingham Bay to the 172 picturesque islands of the San Juan archipelago, the Olympics and Cascades.

Now a city of 46,000, Bellingham had its roots in a small sawmill constructed in 1852 at the falls on Whatcom Creek by Henry Roeder and Russell V. Peabody. A party of Alaskan Indians in May 1855 attacked the community; which by then had sprawled over several miles of water front. The government responded by establishing Fort Bellingham the next summer. A blockhouse remains on the site of the encampment. Four small boom towns emerged from these beginnings, probably spurred on by the early discovery of coal east of here which could easily be hauled by wagon to service ships seeking fuel.

Whatcom, northern-most town site, started in 1852. Bellingham and Fairhaven were launched in 1853 and Sehome in 1854. Sehome later changed its name to new Whatcom, since it was just to the south of the original Whatcom. An 1890 consolidation joined Bellingham and Fairhaven as Fairhaven. Finally in 1903 all three consolidated as Bellingham. The result is the discovery of several old commercial centers at varied locations in the rather large limits of modern Bellingham.

A network of electric street car lines radiated out to give linear commercial centers in residential areas. The street cars stopped running in 1938. Bellingham is now truck and car oriented, the wholesale distribution center for all of the northwest corner of the state.

Attractions

A scenic driving tour is afforded by Chuckanut Drive. SR 11 winds along the shoreline of Samish Bay and offers magnificent view of the Puget Sound. At the intersection with Hawthorn Road is **Fairhaven Park** where a large rose garden is in bloom from mid-June through September.

Maritime Heritage Center, 1600 C Street is the interpretive educational facility that depicts salmon spawning, hatching and rearing in ponds and channels. The center is open Monday thru Friday. Whale watch/search excursions and dinner cruises to the San Juan Islands are offered from May to September. Call 676-6873 for further information.

Western Washington University occupies a hillside site which overlooks Bellingham proper. Founded in 1893 as a state normal school; today the campus covers 180 acres and has sixty-nine permanent buildings.

Sehome Hill Arboretum, is reached by a footpath from the campus of Western Washington University. A collection of native plants and trees are collected and displayed as they existed before the loggers and farmers cleared the land. Since 1969, paths through the diverse forest have let people study nature at work, with plantings augmenting species not present when the project began.

Western's Outdoor Museum consists of art work designed for exterior display, within the campus at the university. Initiated in the early 60s as a compliment to the buildings and ambiance of the campus; the walking art tour is fully explained in a booklet you can obtain at the Visitor's Center at WWU.

Georgia-Pacific Corporation, 300 West Laurel Street, offers a one and a half hour tour about how logs are chipped, pulped, bleached, dried and made into paper and tissue products. Open Monday thru Friday, June thru August. Do wear good walking shoes, no open-toed sandals, cameras, sketches or children under twelve. Call 733-4410 for information.

The Bellingham Parks and Recreation Department can provide a **facilities guide/map** which enumerates the park lands and public facilities available for your enjoyment. Listed are fifty alternatives for meeting your baseball, boat docking, equestrian trail riding, hiking, swimming, tennis, camping, outdoor cooking and picnic needs.

Special note is taken by the county residents during May. It's anticipation of the **Ski to Sea Festival** takes five days over Memorial Weekend and is an eighty-five mile relay race from Mount Baker ski area west to Bellingham Bay with competition in skiing, running, bicycling, canoeing and sailing.

Eldridge Avenue, one of the town's older residential areas, has a **map for walking tours**. Thomas Roeder, a partner in the first saw mill, homesteaded on what is now the avenue in 1852. The oldest home now standing is an 1870 frame house known as carpenter Gothic. Ask for the brochure at the museum or tourist information centers.

The old commercial district at the south of Bellingham markets itself as **Fairhaven,** an historic village. Structures date from 1890 in the area between McKenzie and Mill avenues, 10th and 12th streets. In 1891 the railroad tracks were on 9th street and continued north to British Columbia. An **information gazebo** at 12th Street and Harris Avenue has copies of a walking tour brochure for this district which grew rapidly then was bypassed by commerce for a time.

Whatcom Museum of History and Art, 121 Prospect Street, is still Bellingham's major landmark. The brick building was constructed in 1892 as a city hall. In use as a museum since 1940, the building was restored over ten years ending in 1965. Exhibits change every month, with logging tools, maritime history, and Indian culture getting wide display. Open Tuesday through Sunday from 12:00 noon to 5:00 p.m. Telephone (206) 676-6981.

For further information, contact the **Bellingham-Whatcom County Visitors and Convention Bureau**, Box 340, Bellingham WA 98227. Telephone (206) 671-3990.

Accommodations

BEST WESTERN HERITAGE INN
151 E McLeod Road
Bellingham, WA 98226
Tel.   (206) 647-1912
       (800) 528-1234

Make your reservations to stay in the Best Western Heritage Inn and then be prepared for some pleasant surprises! When you take I-5 exit 256 and begin looking for the motel, don't look for the standard boxy motel, instead feast your eyes on two colonial style buildings in the very heart of shopping and fine dining.

The Heritage Inn has sixty-one rooms which allows manager Chuck Valley and his staff to give quality, personal service to each and every guest. The inn has that homey feeling you really appreciate after a long day on the road. All of the rooms are stylishly furnished with special Bassett furniture from New York. Three suites include kitchenettes and six executive rooms are perfect for the business traveler. The executive rooms are a comfortable setting for meetings during the day, with wet bars, refrigerators and microwave ovens for evening social engagements. Continental breakfast is provided for all guests and each room has coffee and tea. All units are air conditioned with HBO and ESPN available on color TVs. There is an outdoor pool and a jacuzzi for your relaxation.

Conveniently located with easy access to Mt. Baker ski area, beaches, a shopping mall across the street, Western Washington University, theaters and several restaurants. The Heritage Inn is your "Best Choice" for accommodations in Bellingham.

THE COACHMAN INN
120 Samish Way
Bellingham, WA 98225
Tel.   (206) 671-9000
       (800) 732-1225
All major credit cards are accepted.

A soak in the hot tub at the Coachman Inn is the perfect end to a long day of skiing. The Inn is located just one hour from the Mount Baker ski area and one and a half hours from either the Seattle or Vancouver, B.C. ski areas. It is also convenient for non skiers who wish to spend time enjoying Puget Sound, the Nooksack or Skagit rivers or the North Cascade trails. The

Coachman Inn has sixty units, all of which have been completely redecorated with new beds, furniture, drapes, and paint.

The lobby is the hub of activity at The Coachman Inn. There are comfortable couches for conversation while you enjoy the snacks and beverages available. A delicious Continental breakfast is served every morning. The friendly staff will be happy to help you plan side trips to shopping, dining, fresh and salt water activities, mountain hikes or a trip to the winery.

Make The Coachman Inn your headquarters when exploring Whatcom and Skagit counties or when just passing through. The service, relaxation, and comfort offered by The Coachman Inn can't be topped!

THE NORTH GARDEN INN
1014 N Garden Street
Bellingham, WA 98225
Tel. (206) 671-7828
Visa and MasterCard accepted.

Frank and Barbara DeFreytas preside over The North Garden Inn which occupies the Victorian mansion which was built in 1896 by Robert I. Morse and is on the National Historic Register. The Inn is located on a hill overlooking Bellingham Bay and several rooms have a wonderful view of the bay, marina, Lummi Islands and the San Juan Islands. West facing rooms have a view of the gorgeous sunsets famous in the Northwest. The Inn is very conveniently located near Western Washington University and downtown Bellingham. Frank and Barb are very involved in the arts and culture of Bellingham and the area and are delighted to recommend many activities to enjoy during your visit.

The Inn offers ten guest rooms and five full baths. Each of the rooms has a musical name, the Adagio Suite features a queen size bed and private bath; the Rhapsody Room boasts a fantastic view, and so on. There are accommodations to fit most needs. The living room, dining room, and sitting rooms on the second and third floor are a meeting place for guests to enjoy conversation and sometimes music, there are two grand pianos available. Barb serves a delicious continental breakfast which includes fresh breads, muffins, or pastries made from flour ground at the Inn, fruit, juice, assorted cereal, coffee and tea.

Frank and Barbara are warm and gracious people who enjoy sharing their home. They enjoy meeting and talking with new people and sharing experiences. They will do everything they can to make your stay in the delightful North Garden Inn a memorable experience.

THE PARK MOTEL
101 N Samish Way
Bellingham, WA 98225
Tel. (206) 733-8280
All major credit cards are accepted.

The Park Motel is conveniently located just off I-5 in Bellingham, near Western Washington University and close to the downtown area and shopping centers. It is a good spot for business travellers and tourists alike. The Park Motel is an ideal place to make your headquarters when exploring the San Juan Islands, Canada or the North Cascades and Mt. Baker. There are fifty-six distinctively decorated, spacious guest rooms with queen sized beds, cable television with movies and sports, individual temperature controls, and a large spa and sauna. A complimentary Continental breakfast in the morning and snacks and beverages during the rest of the day are available in the lobby.

In addition to the comfortable guest rooms, there are some very special features available at The Park Motel, such as a deluxe furnished apartment. The apartment sleeps seven and has a full kitchen and laundry facilities. For that special occasion, try one of the luxurious suites with in-room Continental breakfast, complimentary champagne, and a private spa. Upon request The Park Motel will recreate a particular era with period music and decorations. Free shuttle service to the airport is also offered.

The Park Motel can also arrange seminars, business meetings or social functions, complete with audio-visual equipment and catered meals. Whether you are in Bellingham on business or for pleasure, you'll find your needs expertly met by the friendly, helpful staff at The Park Motel.

Antiques

ALADDIN'S LAMP ANTIQUE MALL
1318 Bay Street
Bellingham, WA 98225
Tel. (206) 647-0066
Hrs: Mon. - Sat.   10:00 a.m. - 7:00 p.m.
      Sunday   12:00 noon - 5:00 p.m.
Closed Christmas, New Year's, Easter and Thanksgiving.
Visa and MasterCard are accepted.

In one of Bellingham's charming old brick buildings is Aladdin's Lamp Antique Mall which offers a chance to step into the past as you browse through the countless items displayed by more than twenty-five dealers. Owner Walter Robinson and associates Steve Stimson and Pat Halvorson go out of their way to provide information on the selection to be found here. All of the merchandise you'll see is priced reasonably, based on availability. Quality antique furniture is one of the specialties here and the staff repairs and restores furniture, including re-caning chairs.

In the collector's mall there is a large selection of old and new comics, lots of records and outstanding vintage, Victorian to the present, clothing. There are Americana paper items, tools, toys, glassware and furniture dating from all eras. There is a significant collection of movie posters to delight any movie fan. The second floor has local artists' studios and a gallery to display their works. You will also find a selection of antique prints in the gallery.

Take a break from browsing and have a meal, snack or espresso coffee at Alladin's Cafe located at the back of the mall. They offer great homemade soups, salads, sandwiches and desserts for you to enjoy. There is something to appeal to nearly everyone at one of the Northwest's biggest and best malls, Aladdin's Lamp Antique Mall, and many antiques you may not see elsewhere. You'll want to visit more than once since new selections are added daily.

BELLINGHAM ANTIQUE MALL, 202 West Holly Street, Bellingham, Washington. Twenty-five dealers offer fine oak and Victorian furniture, timepieces, glassware and china, estate jewelry, and much more. Park free at Parkade across from the mall.

A DAY OF BEAUTY

a.m.	North Garden Inn	Best memorable stay	Belli/B & B
a.m.	The Bagelry	Best hot-from-the-oven	Belli/Rest.
a.m.	Jody Bergsma Gallery	Best "Little People" art	Belli/Art
a.m.	Gallery West	Best diversified art	Belli/Art
a.m.	The Glasserie	Best brilliant glass	Belli/Gift
p.m.	New Peking Rest.	Best Szechwan	Belli/Rest.
p.m.	Village Books	Best selection	Belli/Book
p.m.	Cookie Cafe	Best chocolate chip	Belli/Bakery
p.m.	WWU Outdoor Mus.	Best exhibit	Belli/Intro
p.m.	Sehome Hill Arbor.	Best view	Belli/Intro

This tour was envisioned as a gift to your senses. Hot-from-the-oven bagels 'n cream cheese, tours of the local art galleries, a spicy luncheon, then pick up a good book, grab a sack of fresh cookies and adjourn to a walking tour of the WWU campus art exhibits and complete your day at the top of the hill, secure in Mother Natures embrace, at the Arboretum. Find yourself a sunny spot, enjoy the book, the munchies and the sunset!

JODY BERGSMA GALLERY
1344 King Street
Bellingham, WA 98226
Tel. (206) 733-1101
Hrs. Mon. - Sat. 9:00 a.m. - 6:00 p.m.
      Sunday   12:00 noon - 5:00 p.m.

Jody Bergsma is an artist known nationally for her watercolors of "Little People" with large expressive eyes. The gallery in Bellingham features the nearly 300 individual "Little People" prints, as well as her abstract watercolors. In addition her brother Mark, an outstanding photographer, and her sister Shawn, who does calligraphy, are also featured.

The gallery display is complete with a collection of "Little People" paintings Jody did as a teenager. She began selling when she was thirteen and had created and sold over 10,000 originals by the time she completed school.

A tour of this 7,000 square foot gallery will quickly capture your imagination as you follow the career of a young girl who is now one of the Pacific Northwest's most successful artists.

After you've had a chance to browse through the gallery, be sure to make time for a stop at the coffee shop to try some fine gourmet coffee and popular homemade pastries.

GALLERY WEST
1300 12th Street
Bellingham, WA 98225
Tel. (206) 734-8414
Hrs: Mon. - Thu. 10:00 a.m. - 5:30 p.m.
      Friday   10:00 a.m. - 8:00 p.m.
      Saturday   10:00 a.m. - 5:30 p.m.
      Sunday   12:00 noon - 4:00 p.m.
Extended hours during summer and Christmas season.
Closed major holidays.
Visa, MasterCard, and AMEX are accepted.

If you appreciate fine art and handmade craftsmanship of high quality, be sure to visit Gallery West to see the impressive collection of unique jewelry, pottery, woodcarving, weaving, handblown glass and baskets. Owner Dave Lucas and manager Karolyn Duffy have arranged nicely displayed exhibits in this spacious gallery. You will find many one of a kind pieces that Dave has found on his buying expeditions.

Before buying Gallery West in 1974, Dave, who has an art degree from Western Washington University, used to exhibit his pottery and sculpture in the gallery. Now he concentrates his efforts and talents on finding and presenting arts and crafts that will delight his customers. Among the many fine works exhibited are Ran Jack's exquisite carved wooden birds, Mark Matsui porcelains, woven blankets by Jan Witcroft and a large selection of outstanding inlaid wooden boxes by Robert McKeown. There are Tom Wood pastels featuring Northwest landscapes and limited edition prints of the Northwest and Alaska by Rie Munoz. There is also an exclusive gallery of Lee Mann photography on the second floor.

Dave's staff is experienced and will offer any help you need. They are happy to answer questions and offer suggestions. They will professionally frame any poster art pieces you select from the large number available. If you are looking for a unique gift, for the perfect unusual and beautiful accessory for your home, or if you just love to look at wonderful art work and handcrafts of the highest quality, you'll find a visit to Gallery West very rewarding.

MATTER DANZ GALLERY, 209 Prospect, Bellingham, Washington. View fine art and take advantage of professional art services. Call to obtain schedule of events.

Bed and Breakfast

HERON REACH
1601 4th Street
Bellingham, WA 98225
Tel. (206) 671-2811
No credit cards accepted, personal checks okay.
Deposit required with reservations.

If gorgeous sunsets over the San Juan Islands, classical music and quiet conversations appeal to you, then you'll love the evenings at Heron Reach bed and breakfast. Sharon Hockenson began sharing her home, hospitality, and spectacular sunsets with guests in December, 1984. Heron Reach is located on the edge of a quiet residential area, and the peace and tranquility are delightful.

There are two private guest rooms available, each tastefully decorated with antiques and each with its own distinct personality. Sharon provides a full breakfast with emphasis on healthful, nutritious food. You'll enjoy her homemade granola, blueberry muffins, and baked stuffed apple - filled with almond butter, brown sugar, nuts, raisins, or whatever strikes her fancy. In addition to fresh fruits and juices, there is coffee and regular or herbal tea.

Heron Reach is just a few minutes walk from historic Old Fairhaven. Also just a few minutes away is the Port of Bellingham Marina Park for picnics, walks, and sea gazing. Sharon even has limited space to park your boat or trailer and is only a few blocks away from a public boat ramp. Plan a stay at Heron Reach, you'll be close to many points of interest in the Bellingham area The accommodations and hospitality are unbeatable.

RIVER VALLEY BED AND BREAKFAST, 2010 Valley Highway 9, P. O. Box 158, Acme, WA. Turn-of-the-century home, five guest rooms, full country breakfast at this B & B.

So now you're here in Bellingham. You've been looking forward to all the great outdoor activities, the recreation, breathing clean air; you've walked those few extra miles to get in shape, lost a few pounds so the clothes fit great...Go Get-Em!

THE GREAT OUTDOORS TOUR

	"Best Choices" for basic camping, or plush camping sites:		
a.m.	Heron Reach	Best views and walks	Belli/B & B
a.m.	Sudden Valley	Best large-scale facility	Belli/Acc
	Now for obtaining the basic equipment:		
a.m.	Base Camp, Inc.	Best outfitters	Belli/Sport
a.m.	Brentley Softpacks	Best packing	Belli/Sport
a.m.	Fairhaven Boatworks	Best wind surfing gear	Belli/Sport
p.m.	Fisherman's Cove	Best appros lunch	Belli/Rest.
	You're all set now...if you wanted others to "do the driving," or were interested in skiing and hiking:		
p.m.	Island Mariner Corp.	Best cutter cruise	Belli/Tours
p.m.	San Juan Sailing	Best sailing choices	Belli/Tours
p.m.	Mount Baker Ski	Best slopes	Belli/Resort
p.m.	Fairhaven Restaurant	Best seafood dinner	Belli/Rest.

SCHNAUZER CROSSING BED AND BREAKFAST
4421 Lakeway Drive
Bellingham, WA 98225
Tel. (206) 733-0055

Schnauzer Crossing Bed and Breakfast is a destination inn on Lake Whatcom where you can pedal, paddle or watch others in these endeavors, and enjoy the pleasing accommodations located under a canopy of tall evergreens.

It's also the home of Donna and Monty McAllister, innkeepers who like to treat their guests right. They'll lend you one of their bicycles and steer you right for a good ride, or if you like, you can borrow the canoe, or the small sail boat to test the waters on Lake Whatcom. Maybe a good set of tennis would be your pleasure, take advantage of the private court.

Unwind and enjoy the view from the patio deck outside and the comfortable living room with its floor to ceiling French doors. You'll look forward to breakfast when Donna brings out the china, crystal and silver and serves her quiche, freshly sliced fruit and muffins. If you are traveling with pets, Schnauzer Crossing even provides an outdoor kennel.

To find Schnauzer Crossing, take exit 253 off of I-5 and follow Lakeway Drive about three and half miles and watch for the Schnauzer Crossing sign at the end of the drive way.

SPRINGCREST FARM BED AND BREAKFAST
6058 Everson-Goshen Road
Bellingham, WA 98221
Tel. (206) 966-7272

Springcrest Farm, located in the beautiful Nooksack Valley about ten miles from Bellingham, has been a working farm since 1891 when it was first homesteaded. Less than half of the farms 113 acres is cleared for buildings and pastures and the rest remains wooded, providing natures trails and a habitat for wildlife of the area. From the farm's elevated slopes, with a sunny southern exposure, you can see the snow-capped mountains of the Coast Range clear into Canada. The farm is a dairy farm with one of the few remaining herds of Jerseys in this part of the country.

Hosts George and Kaye Haggith provide two guest bedrooms, each furnished with authentic homestead era furniture, including cherrywood "sleighbed" headboards and footboards. Rooms have private entrances and separate refrigerators. As you would expect, the breakfast served to guests is a real farm style breakfast with the richest milk and cream you've every tasted, eggs, meats, fresh fruits and berries in season, homemade breads and wonderful homemade coffee cake. There is lots to do in the area, walking in the woods, fishing at a lake one quarter mile away, or golfing at one of the seven golf courses within twelve miles of the farm.

Springcrest Farm is only one hour from Vancouver, B.C. and Mt. Baker and two hours from Seattle. It's about one hour from the B.C. ferry at Tsawwassen which goes to Vancouver Island. The farm cannot accommodate pets, and the hosts request that guests not smoke. Springcrest Farm offers a pleasant and relaxing stay in the country, with the convenience of urban Bellingham and a variety of vacation activities nearby.

A easy, informal, lazy-day tour of Bellingham. No rush, no fuss; just meander.

	WALKING IN CIRCLES THROUGH BELLINGHAM		
a.m.	Tony's Coffees	Best eye opener	Belli/Coffee
a.m.	Aladdin's Lamp Ant.	Best antique mall	Belli/Ant
a.m.	The Greenhouse	Best home goodies	Belli/Kitchen
a.m.	Paper Dreams	Best stationery	Belli/Stat.
p.m.	Pacific Cafe	Best lunch	Belli/Rest.
p.m.	Oberg's Red Top	Best drive-in flowers	Belli/Florist
p.m.	Original in Gold	Best creativity	Belli/Jeweler
p.m.	Coachman Inn	Best hot tub	Belli/Accom.
	Now for supper choices that will liven you up:		
p.m.	Oriental Star	Best Vietnamese	Belli/Rest.
p.m.	Dos Padres	Best gourmet Mexican	Belli/Rest.

Bakery

COOKIE CAFE
1307 Cornwall Avenue,
Bellingham, WA 98225
Tel.   (206) 671-8550
Hrs: Mon.-Sat.   7:00 a.m. - 5:30 p.m.
          Sunday   9:00 a.m. - 4:00 p.m.

If you're not happy with how the cookie crumbles, try a chewy chocolate chip, one of the favorites at the Cookie Cafe. Ever since its opening in 1980, The Cookie Cafe has become a Bellingham institution for sweet tooths--all because owner Stephanie Costello loves to bake and couldn't find a good cup of coffee.

So now in an atmosphere bathed in classical music, quiet conversation or easy contemplation a loyal clientele enjoys a range of goodies that includes cookies, muffins, Danish pastries and croissants. What makes these treats even better is to follow each bite with a sip of fine coffee or espresso. Other cookie favorites include fudge chocolate chip, snickerdoodles, oatmeal raison and molasses ginger.

So treat yourself by finding out what's cooking at the Cookie Cafe, your "Best Choice" for goodies.

Books

VILLAGE BOOKS
1210 11th Street
Bellingham, WA 98225
Tel.   (206)   671-2626
         (800)   392-BOOK in WA
Hrs: Mon. - Sat.   10:00 a.m. - 10:00 p.m.
         Sunday   10:00 a.m. - 6:00 p.m.
Closed Christmas, New Year's Day and Thanksgiving.
Visa, MasterCard, and Discover cards are accepted.

Owners Chuck and Dee Robinson, who founded Village Books in 1980, describe their shop as "the bookshop designed for browsing." They have developed one of the largest bookstores in the state with strong sections of children's books, modern fiction, women's studies, and political science. Their staff, all readers themselves, are knowledgeable and will help you find good books for your educational and recreational reading. They even provide a toll free number statewide to be able to answer readers' questions and help them find particular books. If they don't have the book you need, they have one of the best systems available to help you find what you seek.

Village Books sponsors a reading series where noted professionals read poetry and literature in the store. They also have a rental library where you can rent hard cover fiction and best sellers for a few dollars. You are able to read current hits at a fraction of the cost and, if you decide you want the book for your personal library, your rental applies toward the purchase.

When they expanded in 1985, Chuck and Dee added the Colophon Cafe, owned by Ray and Taimi Dunn. Located within the bookstore, the Colophon offers coffee, espresso, unusual soups - African Peanut, Curried Banana, etc., as well as ice cream treats. Their hours are the same as the bookstore. For the serious book lover or the occasional browser, Village Books is the place to go. Be sure to stop there when you're in the Old Fairhaven District in Bellingham, you'll enjoy your visit.

Coffees

TONY'S COFFEES AND TEAS
1101 Harris Avenue
Bellingham, WA 98225
Tel. (206) 733-6319
Hrs: Mon. - Sun. 7:30 a.m. - 11:00 p.m.
Closed Christmas, Thanksgiving, and New Years.
MasterCard and Visa are accepted.

The rich aroma of freshly roasted coffee greets you as you enter Tony's Coffees and Teas, located in the Terminal Building which has been restored to its 1889 appearance. The shop has been in operation since 1971 and was recently acquired by Bob and Marcy Elliott. There is a wonderful selection of the finest coffees, teas, spices and cheeses available, as well as a coffee house which serves freshly brewed coffee and tea.

Upstairs at Tony's are large burlap sacks of green coffee beans from all over the world. Coffee is roasted on the premises daily. At least twenty different kinds and a half dozen blends, including the very popular Tony's blend are always fresh. The roasts include full city, espresso, Viennese and French. There are a full range of coffee making accessories available. If tea is your drink, you'll appreciate the forty different green and black teas and about twenty-five herbal teas available in bulk. Gourmet cooks can select from the more than sixty-five different fresh spices from all over the world. The specialty cheeses stocked include double Gloucester, Halvah, and the Northwest's own Cougar Gold. Tony's staff is very helpful and happy to answer any questions.

Tony's coffee house serves fine coffee and tea drinks along with various pastries, soups, salads and sandwiches. They have a wide range of espresso and specialty drinks, with or without caffeine. Tony's Coffees and Teas is the place to shop for the richest and best coffees, teas, spices and cheeses in Bellingham.

Florist

OBERG'S RED TOP FLORIST
1220 Lakeway Drive
Bellingham, WA 98226
Tel. (206) 734-8454
Hrs: Mon. - Fri. 9:00 a.m. - 8:00 p.m.
    Saturday 9:00 a.m. - 5:30 p.m.
Closed Sundays and major holidays
Visa, MasterCard, AMEX, and Discover cards are accepted.
Wire services - FTD and Teleflora.

Owners Janice and Michael Oberg have converted a former Wendy's drive-in into a really unique flower shop. You can use the drive-through facility to pick up flowers. First you read the selection available, place your order over the speaker, and drive to the window to pick up your flowers. Many people take advantage of this by calling ahead and then picking up their order at the window without having to leave the car. It's perfect for people in a hurry, and especially good for people with small children in the car.

The spaciousness of the old drive-in is perfect for the Oberg's flower shop. The five large windows show off the flower and gift displays and there is ample room inside for the many lovely flowers, plants, and gifts they stock. There is always enough parking for customers, too, even on the busiest days. Oberg's has a large selection of silk flowers, arrangements and do lots of custom silk designs. They also have dried flowers and lovely European gardens. Balloon bouquets are another specialty, and of course, they do wonderfully beautiful fresh flower arrangements for any occasion.

Whether you use the convenient drive through service, or take the time to come in and browse through the lovely displays, you'll find what you want at Oberg's Red Top Florist.

Gifts

PAPER DREAMS
1206 11th Street
Bellingham, WA 98225
Tel. (206) 676-8676
Hrs: Mon. - Thu. & Sat.   10:00 a.m. - 9:00 p.m.
          Friday   10:00 a.m. - 9:30 p.m.
          Sunday   12:00 noon - 5:00 p.m.
Closed Christmas, New Years, Thanksgiving and Easter.
Visa, MasterCard, and Discover cards are accepted.

Paper Dreams has an impressive selection of paper and gift items. Since Chuck and Dee Robinson opened the store in 1982 they, and manager JoAnn Hanesworth, have seen it grow and prosper. The old brick walls and high ceilings of their shop are perfect for Paper Dreams and give it an open and airy feeling that make it an ideal place to browse and enjoy the many delightful and whimsical offerings.

As the name indicates, Paper Dreams has anything you might ever want or need in paper, from stationery and envelopes by the box or by the pound to an incredible selection of greeting cards. You will find much more than just paper creations, though. There is a Northwest gift section that has wonderful products from cottage industries and Northwest artisans. There is a Christmas section all year long, and one of the largest selection of calendars in the state, more than 375 varieties. There are also posters, T-shirts, magnets, windsocks, kites, and much more.

In addition to the already tremendous selection of gifts and paper products from which to choose, there is fudge - wonderful, scrumptious, rich, delicious fudge. Paper Dreams makes its own "Dream Fudge", cream and butter fudge, in many flavors, such as Oreo Cookie Fudge, Strawberries and Cream Fudge, and Peanut Butter and Chocolate fudge, to name just a few. It's available by the piece or by the pound, and you will want to end your Paper Dreams shopping experience with this terrific treat.

Glassware

THE GLASSERIE
1306 11th Street
Bellingham, WA 98225
Tel. (206) 734-3638
Hrs: Mon. - Thu.   10:00 a.m. - 6:00 p.m.
      Friday   10:00 a.m. - 9:00 p.m.
      Saturday   10:00 a.m. - 6:00 p.m.
      Sunday   12:00 noon - 5:00 p.m.
Closed major holidays.
Visa and MasterCard are accepted.

    The beauty and brilliance of fine glasswork lure you on as you enter The Glasserie. You will be enchanted by the shine and shimmer of the fine glass pieces displayed by owners Deena Matlack and Bruce Walker. Deena's love of fine glass objects dates back to when she created commissioned stained glass pieces. The Glasserie is a wonderful gallery where the emphasis is on one of a kind hand blown original glass created and signed by famous international artists for the serious collector.

    There are several museum quality art pieces by Orient and Flume, Steven Correia, and others with national and international reputations. There are also pieces of interest to those who don't collect, but appreciate fine work. There is a wide selection of handcrafted jewelry and also from nationally known artists.. There are many different pieces made from Mt. St. Helen's ash glass and intricately colored paper weights. The second level has a display of Oriental work with some unusual pieces from China and Japan. In the rear of the gallery is the custom glass studio.

    You will be overwhelmed and enchanted by the style and beauty of the collection of glass art offered at The Glasserie. Whether you are a serious collector, looking for a special gift or an accent for your home, or just want to browse in a fantastic wonderland of color and brilliance, you'll be delighted with The Glasserie.

Jewelry

ORIGINALS IN GOLD
1303 Cornwall
Bellingham, WA 98225
Tel. (206) 734-7891
Hrs: Mon. - Thu.   9:30 a.m. - 6:00 p.m.
     Fri. - Sat.   9:30 a.m. - 9:00 p.m.
Closed during major holidays.
Major credit cards are accepted.

July 4, 1974 was an important day for Sharon Jones, and the beginning of what is now Originals In Gold. On that day Sharon left her former profession of nursing to devote her time to designing jewelry. After three years as a street artist in San Francisco, Sharon and her family moved to Bellingham and opened Originals In Gold. In the years that have followed, Sharon has gathered a fine staff of talented, creative jewelers. The quality of their work has made Originals In Gold so successful that the store has recently moved to a beautiful new location with ample room to create and display their work.

Custom designed jewelry is Sharon's specialty and she guarantees her customers will be happy with the final piece. In creating a design, Sharon or a member of her staff works closely with you so the design will meet your needs and expectations. Originals In Gold has a large inventory of diamonds, precious gems and colored stones. You will find fresh water pearls, emeralds, tourmalines, garnets and different colored sapphires, which can be incorporated into distinctive jewelry designs that are sure to please. Also, Originals In Gold is one of the few jewelry stores able to work in platinum.

In addition to custom designed jewelry, you will also find a stock of high quality ready made jewelry items. There are some lovely silver pieces with added ivory or other combinations of metals by Northwest artisans. A visit to this creative shop is an experience not to be missed. Whether you are seeking an originally designed piece of fine jewelry or something from the stock of ready made creations, you will find something of distinction to suit you at Originals in Gold.

Kitchenware

THE GREENHOUSE
1235 Cornwall
Bellingham, WA 98225
Tel. (206) 676-1161
Hrs: Mon. - Thu. & Sat. 9:30 a.m. - 6:00 p.m.
     Friday   9:30 a.m. - 9:00 p.m.
     Sunday   12:00 noon - 5:00 p.m.
Closed major holidays
Visa, MasterCard, and AMEX accepted.

    When The Greenhouse began fifteen years ago it was a small plant store. Today it is a beautiful store with 6,000 square feet of retail space and the only plants you see are for decorative purposes and not for sale. Owners Chris Foss and Foster Rose have built The Greenhouse into an impressive store that offers something for every room in the house.
    The Greenhouse offers so much it's hard to know where to begin. The housewares section offers crystal stemware and decanters, glassware, a huge selection of unique kitchen gadgets, some of the finest pots and pans and cooking accessories you'll ever see. The children's department has a wonderful selection of furniture and accessories, and yet another department has everything you need for your home office, including desks, chairs, computer tables and accessories. There is imported European and American living room furniture and a large selection of closet storage solutions which will delight those who need help organizing their closets.
    Chris and Foster have brought The Greenhouse from humble beginnings to the largest retailer of its type north of Seattle. They offer fine quality products for every room of your house at outstanding prices. You'll find what you want for your home at The Greenhouse.

Pottery

    GOOD EARTH POTTERY, 1000 Harris, Bellingham, Washington. Whether you're looking for functional or decorative pieces--or a new ceramic sink, you'll find absolutely beautiful pottery produced and sold here.

INDIAN STREET POTTERY
1309 Indian Street
Bellingham, WA 98225
Tel. (206) 733-3432
Hrs: Wed. - Sat. 11:00 a.m. - 5:00 p.m.
Visa and MasterCard are accepted.

Artistic and creative pottery adorns the walls and shelves of the gallery at Indian Street Pottery. Eugene and Ene Lewis, owners and artisans, are educated in ceramics and both like to throw pottery together.

Eugene has done graduate work in both ceramics and painting. He combines these disciplines to turn out eye-catching and provocative pottery with dramatic glazes. He likes to employ low-fire work in which the pieces are put into wood shavings directly from the oven creating interesting patterns and special effects. Ene specializes in two dimensional creations, with painting as a component of the final product. She also creates detailed oil lamps and Humpty Dumpty jars from clay. Both artisans produce lovely functional porcelain vases and bowls with abstract floral designs. If you prefer, Eugene and Ene will design and create custom place settings for you in either stoneware or porcelain.

For functional and decorative handcrafted pottery in all price ranges, visit Indian Street Pottery. It's easy to find near Indian Street and Holly off I-5 at Exit 253.

(See special invitation in the Appendix.)

Resort

MOUNT BAKER SKI AREA
1017 Iowa Street
Bellingham, WA 98226
Tel. 206 734-6771
Hrs: Fri. - Sun. 8:30 a.m. - 3:30 p.m.
All holidays during ski season.
Summer food services available on weekends.

The year was 1930, everything, it seemed, was on the skids. But at Mount Baker, that's just the way they wanted it with the opening for the ski area and operation of a new rope tow.

Beginning with the construction of a luxury hotel on the meadows below Mount Baker back in 1918, the resort was simply the place to enjoy breath taking views and clean mountain air. That changed with the introduction of skiing. Today, the resort offers, off-season hiking and six double chair lifts providing short lift lines and a variety of terrain to suit all ability levels during the long ski season. While skiing you'll enjoy outstanding views of Mount Baker and Mount Shuksan. The day lodge has three areas for hunger attacks, including a sandwich deli, The Diner, and the tap room for beer, wine, pizza and snacks

To find Mt. Baker Ski Area, go fifty-six miles out of Bellingham via SR 542 to the Mount Baker Ski area your "Best Choice" for skiing fun.

SUDDEN VALLEY
2145 Lake Whatcom Boulevard
Bellingham, WA 98226
Tel. (206) 734-6430
Visa, MasterCard and AMEX are accepted.

Sudden Valley is a treasure you must explore. Located eight miles from Bellingham, Sudden Valley occupies 1,200 acres of pristine woodlands with a large expanse of waterfront on Lake Whatcom and its own private lake, Lake Louise. Sudden Valley is the permanent home for 2,000 residents and can be your home for a day, a week or a lifetime.

The accommodations for vacation or convention guests vary from the Sudden Valley Campground, with eighty-nine sites, to fully equipped condos ranging from studios to three bedroom units. Special packages and group rates are available.

Water sports include fishing, water skiing, sail boarding and swimming in Lake Whatcom. Lake Louise features swimming or rental canoes and paddle boats. Both wet and dry moorage is available. Sudden Valley boasts no less than four swimming pools.

Landlubbers can focus on hiking through the forests and observing wildlife or activities such as tennis or golf. There are seven tennis courts and an eighteen hole PGA championship course which serves as the site for a variety of tournaments including the Washington State Open and the Washington State Amateur. The Clubhouse features a full service pro shop.

The resort was originally the ranch of Glen Corning. The ranch house has become the adult center, and three barns now serve as dance and meeting halls, a children's play yard, arts and crafts areas, basketball court and a theater. The Clubhouse also features a restaurant for fine dining with everything from seafood to prime rib available nightly. The lounge has a full service bar and live entertainment on weekends.

If driving from the south, take I-5 exit 240 east and follow the signs. If driving from the north, take I-5 exit 253 east on Lakeway Drive. Turn south on

Lake Whatcom Boulevard and watch for the signs to reach this "Best Choice" resort, Sudden Valley.

Restaurants

THE BAGELRY, INC.
1319 Railroad Avenue
Bellingham, WA 98225
Tel. (206) 676-5288
Hrs: Mon. - Fri. 7:00 a.m. - 5:00 p.m.
     Saturday   8:00 a.m. - 5:00 p.m.
     Sunday   9:00 a.m. - 4:00 p.m.
Closed major holidays

Ken and Marguerite Ryan keep the oven hot all day at the Bagelry to make sure that all of the varieties of bagels they serve are fresh. Usually the bagel you are served is less than an hour old, and that's really fresh! The Ryans are from New York with experience in the bagel and restaurant business. The bakery manager, John Vuolo, and bakers Angela Salgado and Nicole Hurtubise have been with the Bagelry since it opened and together this crew provides outstanding bagels for their retail customers and the same high quality bagels to area stores and restaurants.

Everything served at The Bagelry uses the highest quality and freshest ingredients available. All the meats served in the bagel sandwiches are cooked on the premises. The Bagelry prepares the superb soups offered daily. There is an excellent selection of delicious cream cheese spreads made fresh daily, including scallion, cinnamon, vegie spread, strawberry and more. There is a breakfast special of two eggs, buttered bagel and coffee and a selection of several omelettes.

The Bagelry is a family run business with a casual atmosphere, where the welcome mat is always out with fast and friendly service.

THE CLIFF HOUSE, 331 North State Street, Bellingham, Washington. One of Bellingham's best views accents your meal at this fine restaurant. Outdoor dining in season.

DOS PADRES

1111 Harris
Bellingham, WA 98225
Tel. (206) 733-9900
Hrs: Sun. - Thu.   7:30 a.m. - 10:00 p.m.
       Fri. - Sat.   7:30 a.m. - 11:00 p.m.
Lounge open until 12:00 midnight
Closed Christmas Eve, Christmas, and Thanksgiving
Visa and MasterCard are accepted.

Dos Padres offers fine family dining in a family operated business. Rose and Bill Martinez and their family are well into their second decade of serving customers their delicious gourmet Mexican food. They take pride in offering only the best food and <u>everything</u> is made from scratch. An extensive breakfast menu has recently been added with a full range of country style breakfasts, as well as some Mexican specialties such as a Mexican omelette, chorizo and eggs, and Huevos Rancheros.

There is a tremendous selection of dishes available for lunch and dinner. The homemade soups, barbeque ribs and hamburgers are only a few of the American choices available. Mexican specialties include such delights as enchiladas verdes, a dish from the central Highlands of Mexico which features chicken or cheese enchiladas served with a subtle green tomatillo sauce, a hint of fresh cilantro and baked with sour cream. Another great selection is chilaquelles con pollo verde which features broken corn tortillas toasted and simmered in tomatillo green sauce with chicken and sour cream. Fish lovers won't want to miss Ruben's Ensenada ceviche cocktail of fresh rock fish marinated in lemon-lime juice, cilantro and garlic.

Rose's Cantina offers a good selection of cocktails, beer, and wine, including Sangria by the glass and liter. For service and high quality, delicious Mexican food, you can't do better than Dos Padres.

IL FIASCO, 1308 Railroad, Bellingham, Washington. One of the most popular restaurants in Whatcom Country. Visit and enjoy fine Italian food in a warm, comfortable atmosphere.

FAIRHAVEN RESTAURANT
1114 Harris
Bellingham, WA 98225
Tel. (206) 676-1520
Hrs: Lunch   Mon. - Fri.   11:30 a.m. - 2:30 p.m.
      Dinner   Mon. - Sun.   5:30 p.m. - 10:00 p.m.
Closed major holidays
All major credit cards are accepted.

    Since Joe McConkey, owner and chef, bought the Fairhaven Restaurant, it has become one of the finest dining establishments in Western Washington. The atmosphere, however, remains friendly and unpretentious. This is a place where you will feel at home whether you're wearing jeans or a three piece suit. Joe learned much of his cooking expertise from his grandmother, who was a chef for many years. The restaurant offers plentiful seating, including a banquet room that seats fifty.
    The extensive seafood selection at the Fairhaven couldn't be fresher. There is a special holding tank where mussels, clams, and oysters are kept alive in seawater until prepared. There are dishes which feature steak, veal and chicken as well. Try one of the Fairhaven originals such as salmon Joseph, cod Margaret-Elizabeth or veal Gran Marnier. Joe will even provide you with any of his recipes upon request. There is a fine wine cellar, presided over by wine steward Norman Wassen. You can choose from over 225 labels with several premium wines available by the glass.
    When you dine at the Fairhaven Restaurant you'll appreciate the cooking style that doesn't overwhelm the natural flavor of the fresh ingredients with heavy sauces. Joe makes everything from scratch and it's all delicious. This is a definite "Best Choice" when dining in Whatcom County.

FISHERMAN'S COVE
Lummi View Drive
Bellingham, WA 98226
Tel. (206) 758-2446
Hrs: Mon. - Sun.   9:00 a.m. - 3:00 p.m.
        Mon. - Sun.   8:00 a.m. - 9:00 p.m.

    Gooseberry Point overlooks Hale Passage, Lummi Bay, Lummi Island, and portions of the San Juan and Canadian Gulf Islands. It is a half hour from Bellingham and is a perfect site for viewing the wonderful Puget Sound sunsets. Salmon fishing is great here and it is also the terminal for the Lummi Island ferry. No matter what reason brings you to Gooseberry Point, be sure you visit the Fisherman's Cove restaurant while you are here. There is a boathouse providing boat and motor sales and a gift shop, as well as the restaurant.

The Jones family built the restaurant in 1945 and continue to operate it, although it was purchased as a Lummi Tribe enterprise in 1986. Chef Bill Scrimsher has been supervising breakfast, lunch and dinner at Fisherman's Cove ever since the restaurant was built. He and his staff bring you some of the best and freshest seafood you'll ever enjoy. The Fisherman's Cove Seafood Dinner of crab cocktail, oysters, prawns, salmon, white fish and scallops is an outstanding way to taste a good selection of different seafoods. Of course there is chicken and steak available too, and a good selection of soups and sandwiches for lunch.

The gift shop features Indian art from local artisans of the Queen Charlotte Island area. Among the selections are lovely jewelry and carvings. If you are a boater, you can obtain fuel, propane, parts, accessories and service at the boathouse. The convenience store has everything you need to stock your craft. Fisherman's Cove is well worth a visit to enjoy this wonderful area.

LA CASA VIEJA, 2030 King Street, Bellingham, Washington. Fine Mexican fare in a family atmosphere. Patio dining available in good weather.

M'SIEURS, 130 East Champion, Bellingham, Washington. Simple and elegant food, casually-elegant atmosphere. Northwest ingredients prepared to order in French or Italian style.

NEW PEKING RESTAURANT
1208 E Maple Street
Bellingham, WA 98225
Tel. (206) 734-5272
Hrs: Mon. & Wed. - Sat.   11:30 a.m. - 10:00 p.m.
      Sunday   4:00 p.m. - 10:00 p.m.
Closed Tuesdays, Christmas and Thanksgiving.
Visa and MasterCard are accepted.

Sam and Jessica Chang serve wonderful hot, spicy food in their New Peking Restaurant. Sam learned Mandarin, Szechwan, and Hunan cooking in a three year cooking school in Taiwan and expanded on his experience in Japan and Bellevue before opening his restaurant in March, 1986. He is assisted by his brothers Alven and Steven who are assistant cooks.

The daily lunch special includes soup, appetizer, fried rice, fortune cookie, Chinese tea, and a choice of one of twelve tasty entrees. You get to choose the degree of "hot and spicy" when you choose a spicy entree. For dinner Sam and Jessica offer an unbelievable eighty-six different meals on the menu, plus complete dinners for two or more that let you try several of their specialties. Among the favorites are sizzling rice soup, moo shu pork, braised shrimp in chili sauce, hot and spicy shrimp in Szechwan sauce, lemon chicken, and seafood paradise. Sam will be happy to prepare Peking Duck if he has two days advance notice.

The New Peking Restaurant offers an unbeatable selection of delicious Chinese food. There is something for every taste here, well prepared and served in pleasant and congenial surroundings.

ORIENTAL STAR VIETNAMESE RESTAURANT
4 Prospect Street
Bellingham, WA 98225
Tel. (206) 671-5503
Hrs: Lunch Tue. - Sat.   11:30 a.m. - 2:30 p.m.
         Dinner   5:00 p.m. - 9:00 p.m.
Closed Sunday and Monday
Visa, MasterCard, and AMEX are accepted.

When Du Tri Khuu came to the United States from Vietnam in 1975, he found a job working in a French restaurant in Des Moines, Seattle. He advanced rapidly, learning everything he could about the restaurant business. In 1982 he realized a long held dream and opened the Oriental Star Vietnamese Restaurant in the heart of downtown Bellingham. His hard work has paid off and the Oriental Star has earned a reputation for presenting outstanding meals with superb personalized service. The Oriental Star has been recognized by *Pacific Northwest* magazine listing of fine dining and by local newspapers.

The Oriental Star serves Vietnamese food which is a unique blend of French and Chinese cuisines. There are several lunch specials served daily, as well as sixty-four different dishes available for evening dining, many of them Du's own creations. Some of the most popular dishes are, Ga Xoa Sa - Lemon Grass Chicken, Vit Xoa Gung - ginger duck, Vit Nau Cam - Duck a´ la orange, fresh snapper and clams in curry sauce, French bouillabaisse or Oriental prawns and many more.

Be sure to dine at the Oriental Star Vietnamese Restaurant when in Bellingham. You will enjoy the different and interesting taste treats Du has created for you.

PACIFIC CAFE
Mt. Baker Theater Building
100 N Commercial Street
Bellingham, WA 98225
Tel. (206) 647-0800
Hrs: Lunch   Tue. - Sat.   11:30 a.m. - 2:00 p.m.
      Dinner Tue. - Sat.   5:30 p.m. - Closing
      Brunch Sunday   9:30 a.m. - 2:00 p.m.
Closed July 4, Thanksgiving, Christmas and New Year's.
Visa, MasterCard, and AMEX are accepted.

Robert Fong, owner of Pacific Cafe, has traveled extensively and sampled the cuisine of many countries. He and his partners Wayne Kent, Danish baker, and Gordon Ho, Chef, have created an international menu of culinary excellence at the Pacific Cafe. They are conveniently located in downtown Bellingham, and the restaurant is very popular, so reservations are recommended for dinner.

The main emphasis at the Pacific Cafe is on fresh seafood, including fresh cooked Dungeness crab, a Northwest delicacy. Fresh Hawaiian fish are popular and the menu changes with the seasons ensuring a variety of fresh fish offerings throughout the year. The menu is truly international with such dishes as shrimp Szechuan, Punjabi shrimp curry, Singapore chili crab, and linguine Parmesan. The chefs at Pacific Cafe delight in serving exotic and different dishes from around the world.

There is a good selection of French and Northwest wines to complement any meal. Wayne produces outstanding Danish pastries with which to end your fine lunch or dinner, and he'll even share his recipes with you. Dining at the Pacific Cafe will be educational, as well as delicious, since both cooks also wait on tables and love to chat with their customers about the wonderful international cuisine they produce.

Sport

BASE CAMP, INC.
901 W Holly Street
Bellingham, WA 98225
Tel. (206) 733-5461
Hrs: Mon. - Sat. 10:00 a.m. - 6:00 p.m.
Closed major holidays.
Visa, MasterCard, AMEX and Discover cards are accepted.

If your interest lies in the outdoors and outdoor pursuits, Base Camp, Inc. is for you. Whether you're interested in cross country skiing, climbing, hiking, backpacking, or canoeing, they will sell you the equipment you need and offer expert help in locating areas and activities that meet your interests and abilities. Owners Frank and Carol Schultz opened Base Camp in 1972 after years of helping friends acquire equipment and knowledge to enjoy the outdoor activities available in the Pacific Northwest.

During the winter, Base Camp specializes in cross country skiing. Frank has participated extensively in Nordic skiing as both a coach and a racer. Under his supervision Base Camp offers classes and day trips for those learning about this delightful sport. They also arrange ski vacations to Canada and carry a large selection of quality merchandise for sale and rental. There is information and equipment for hiking, climbing and canoeing, as well as backpacking, cross country skiing and mountaineering.

Base Camp offers a comprehensive selection of equipment for both winter and summer outdoor activities. They have the largest selection of trail maps and guides in Whatcom County and are delighted to share their experiences with you and answer any questions and are always current on trail conditions for hikers. Let Frank and Carol help you fully enjoy your outdoor experiences in the beautiful Pacific Northwest.

BRENTLEY SOFTPACKS
1208 10th Street
P. O. Box 4000
Bellingham, WA 98227
Tel. (206) 733-5608
Hrs: Mon. - Sat. 10:00 a.m. - 6:00 p.m.
Closed Sundays, Christmas, and New Year's Day.
Visa and MasterCard are accepted.

Whatever your carrying needs may be, for personal or business use, books, clothes, camera equipment, musical instruments, while bicycling or skiing, for hiking or travel purposes, Brentley Softpacks is the place to shop.

You'll find a wide selection of bags and packs made with the highest quality materials available and constructed to insure the product's life time guarantee. This includes multiple stitching and binding of all seams so there are no raw edges of fabric to fray.

Brent Harris has been designing and manufacturing softgoods and internal frame backpacks professionally for eleven years, with most of his teen years spent dabbling in the art as well. His experience as a mountaineer and Nordic ski instructor have given him good knowledge of the requirements for back country activities, his packs and bags reflect this.

When Brent's wife, Rose Drapeau-Harris, became involved in the business in 1984, she provided the impetus to expand their product lines to include an impressive variety of town use bags, purses, organizers, kid packs, and diaper bags.

Brent's highly acclaimed reputation for his custom designing skills has brought the business some unusual projects, as well as work from throughout the West and Midwest.

Brentley Softpacks' retail store in the historic Old Fairhaven District of Bellingham will be increasing in size by 700 square feet this year, along with the printing of their anxiously awaited mail order catalog by summer's end.

For the highest quality softpacks, personal service and competitive prices, there is no better place than Brentley Softpacks; backpacks and softgoods for wilderness, town and travel.

FAIRHAVEN BOATWORKS
AND WASHINGTON WIND SPORTS
501 Harris
Bellingham, WA 98225
Tel. Fairhaven Boatworks   (206)   647-2469
      Washington Wind Sports   (206)   676-1146
Hrs: Winter   Tue. - Sun.   10:00 a.m. - 6:00 p.m.
      Summer   10:00 a.m. - 10:00 p.m.

Just down the hill from the Old Fairhaven District you can enjoy wonderful water sports in inexpensive ways. Water sports, sailing, fishing, crabbing, or windsurfing, offer a wonderful way to enjoy the special recreation opportunities of the Pacific Northwest. Fairhaven Boatworks, owned by Tip Johnson, and Washington Wind Sports, owned by Nygren are ready, willing, and eager to help you enjoy all kinds of water sports.

Fairhaven Boatworks has a rental fleet of rowing dories, kayaks, shells, small sailboats and powered fishing skiffs. Sailing lessons are available for those new to the sport and, of course, safety gear is provided. You can get on the water in Bellingham Bay, nearby, or rent a car top carrier to carry your boat to a place of your choosing. Tip also rents fishing gear and crab pots for luring and catching that wonderful delicacy, the Dungeness Crab.

If boating doesn't get you close enough to nature and you want to enjoy the water even more, then Washington Wind Sports is the place for you. Pete carries a full line of wind surfing gear, you'll find anything and everything you need for the sport. Rental gear is available as are lessons on both Lake Padden and Lake Whatcom. Bellingham is an excellent sailing location with plenty of "good air" off Post Point. In addition to sailboards, Pete has rowing shells and quality accessories for sale. Whether you prefer your water experience from a boat or from a board, you'll find what you need at Fairhaven Boatworks and Washington Wind Sports.

Sailing

ISLAND MARINER CORPORATION
#5 Harbor Esplanade
Bellingham, WA 98225
Tel. (206) 734-8866
Hrs: Summer: Mon. - Sun. 9:00 a.m. - 5:00 p.m.
Call for winter hours, always call ahead.

The best way to explore the 172 San Juan Islands is aboard the eighty-three foot former Coast Guard cutter *Rosario Princess*. Owner and Skipper

Terry Buzzard has delighted thousands of people with his tours since the *Rosario Princess* was luxuriously refitted for touring Puget Sound in 1962. Both the Captain and the vessel are fully licensed and the ship has everything for passenger safety and comfort, including a full galley to provide delicious meals.

From May through September the *Princess* cruises the Islands on whale watch and nature watch outings. Naturalist and historian David Seymour, Director of the Maritime Heritage Center and an expert on Orca whales, is on board to identify the whales and provide information. Between Terry and David, the *Princess* has a very high success rate in locating at least one of the three Orca pods that live in the waters around the San Juan Islands. You can also cruise to the lavish Rosario Resort on Orcas Island on Friday for their seafood buffet, or on Sunday for their famous brunch.

Another cruise offered by Terry and his *Princess* is a sunset cruise on Bellingham Bay featuring the finest local foods served as delectable hor d'oeuvres. On board you have plenty of room to roam in the invigorating fresh sea air on the top or front deck and to relax in plush comfort in the enclosed main deck. Cruise aboard the *Rosario Princess* for a delightful taste of the nautical life in the Pacific Northwest.

SAN JUAN SAILING
#1 Harbor Esplanade
Bellingham, WA 98225
Tel. (206) 671-4300
Hrs: Mon. - Sat. 9:30 a.m. - 5:30 p.m.
Closed Sundays, Christmas, Thanksgiving
No credit cards accepted, personal checks okay.

Roger and Marlene Van Dyken moved to the Northwest in 1972 and discovered the joys of sailing in the waters off Western Washington. They established San Juan Sailing in 1982 to share their love of the sport with others, since much of the beauty of the area can only be appreciated from the water. Whether you want to sail for an evening or a week, either with a skipper or piloting her yourself, while enjoying whale watching, fishing for salmon or ling cod, retrieving crab pots full of Dungeness and rock crabs, or just relaxing in your cruise, San Juan Sailing will meet your needs.

San Juan Sailing's charter fleet has fourteen boats ranging in size from twenty-six to forty feet in length. All are superb sailing craft, fully outfitted for comfortable and safe sailing. If you don't sail, San Juan Sailing offers outstanding training, including a "Learn-'n-Cruise" week. They are fully accredited by the American Sailing Association and offer certification in a number of areas. If you are in the market for your own boat, Roger and Marlene will help you find the one that is perfect for your needs.

To get a feel for the enjoyment and relaxation that sailing offers, join one of the Sunset Sails that San Juan Sailing offers every Friday. Just bring your picnic lunch and enjoy the experience. The Western Washington sailing experience will capture your heart and imagination as it has thousands before you.

Birch Bay

This community on the larger Boundary Bay has its own harbor which is port of call for many small boat owners touring the San Juans and the Inland Passage in Canadian waters. Drayton Harbor, the more protected moorage, is a major commercial fishing port. The rural and unincorporated Birch Bay district has about 2,300 population.

Some of the state's richest farm lands were cleared from the forests by pioneers working south of Blaine toward Birch Bay. Crops as varied as cut flowers and daffodils developed along with a dairy industry blessed with a climate which keeps pastures green most of the year without irrigation. Birch Bay itself is a collection of summer homes served by small shops and restaurants.

Attractions

Birch Bay State Park, at the foot of Bay Road, has 167 campsites in a forested area and about 140 picnic spots on the beach. Park use is popular during the summer with reservations recommended. Telephone (206) 371-2800.

In addition **private campsites** are available at the Baywood Park, Edgewater Resort, Birch Bay Trailer Park and the Plaza Park.

Pacific Waterslides, Birch Bay – Lynden Road, is a commercial waterslide park with four twisting chutes sending riders to a big splash pond. Open daily during the summer months. Telephone (206) 371-7500.

For further information, contact the **Birch Bay Chamber of Commerce**, 4897 Lynden Road, Birch Bay WA 98230, telephone (206) 371-7633.

Candy

THE C SHOP
4825 Alderson
Birch Bay, WA 98230
Tel. (206) 371-2070
Hrs: Sandwich Shop   Mon. - Sun.   11:00 a.m. - 10:00 p.m.
     Candy Shop   Mon. - Sun.   1:00 p.m. - 10:00 p.m.

As you stand on the porch of this turn of the century building and look into the center part, you will see candy being made on vintage candy equipment. You can stand close enough to the candy maker to carry on a delightful conversation. To your right you will see the candy shop and you may wish to join the crush of people in it and treat yourself to your favorite candy or to a C Shop original such as a "Dream" or a Peanut butter Yumm. You may wish to walk to the left into the sandwich shop to spend a quiet, idle hour or two reading and enjoying good coffee or to indulge yourself to a sandwich made with whole wheat bread that was ground from grain fresh that morning at The C Shop.

Established in 1970 by Pat and Pat Alesse, The C Shop has been a pleasant addition for those who come to enjoy Birch Bay for its relaxed atmosphere, safe warm water swimming, miles of sandy tideflats, and gorgeous sunsets.

Gift Shop

LANDLUBBER GIFT SHOP, 8036 Birch Bay Drive, Birch Bay, WA. Creative gifts, country items and nautical-theme items. Espresso bar on premises.

Resort

EDGEWATER RESORT, 7954 Birch Bay Drive, Birch Bay, Washington. Thirty-three two-bedroom cottages on the bay, trailer park and grocery store.

Blaine

Blaine, on the Boundary Bay, is the border city through which I-5 traffic passes to and from British Columbia. It has about 2,300 residents. Large salmon runs, which appear to be returning after lean years in the early

Whatcom County

1980s, were the basis for commercial ocean trollers working out of Blaine and other small ports.

Blaine sits on the site of an Indian village. It is named after James G. Blaine, a candidate for president in 1885. There was a tent colony here in 1858. Miners from California took ship to Drayton Harbor, then walked to Fraser River gold fields. It was not until 1884 that a town site was platted. It grew to nearly 2,300 acres in size.

Attractions

The **Peace Arch**, put up in 1920 as part of a twenty-one acre park at the boarder, is the site of an annual observance of friendship between the United States and Canada. Sixty-seven feet tall, the white arch is located between the north and south lanes of I-5. Volunteers built the park so one half of the arch touches each country. The history of the border treaties is included in exhibits. Open from April through October 15 from 6:30 a.m. to dusk. Between October 16 and March 31 hours are 8:00 a.m. to dusk. Telephone (206) 332-8221. From Blaine enter by going north on Second Street. From Canada, use "O" Avenue south to park headquarters.

Semiahmoo Spit extends northward to make the separation of Blaine's Drayton Harbor from Boundary Bay. A county park, large **resort** and marina are being developed on the spit for opening in the summer of 1987. The new park uses bunk houses from the old Alaska Packer's Association cannery for its **exhibits** and is open Wednesday through Sunday from 1:00 p.m. to 5:00 p.m. Call (206) 332-4777 for park information. Resort promoters have offered weekend ferry service between here and Seattle, check for current schedules. Telephone (206) 371-2000.

The **Andrew Danielson Library** in Blaine specialized in a collection of Icelandic literature, and by 1940 had amassed a collection of 1,000 titles.

Accommodations

THE INN AT SEMIAHMOO, 9565 Semiahmoo, 9565 Semiahmoo Parkway, Blaine, Washington. One of the newest luxury resort hotels in the Northwest. Enjoy the Arnold-Palmer designed golf course, tennis, sailing, health club and marina.

JACOBS LANDING RENTALS
7824 Birch Bay Drive
Blaine, WA 98230
Tel.   (206) 371-7633
        (206) 371-2569
Visa, MasterCard, Discover Card and AMEX are accepted.

Getting wet in the Pacific Northwest can be a chilling experience. But the beach at the Jacobs Landing Rentals is said to be the warmest beach on the entire northwest coast.

That's not all you'll find at these beach front condominiums where the living is easy and designed for luxury at reasonable cost. Each of the spacious one, two or three bedroom units include a living room, dining area, fireplace, and all-convenience kitchen. All you need to bring is your food and clothing for a fine time. Be sure to pack your swim suit so you'll enjoy the indoor heated pool, or the jacuzzi. You have your choice of tennis or racquetball. When it's time to wind down, you can enjoy solitude on your private deck, or good company in the lounge.

So if you are tired of experiencing the big chill each year, warm up to Jacobs Landing on Birch Bay.

Apparel

BLAIR GRAPHICS, 810 Peace Portal Drive, Blaine, Washington. Custom T-shirts, sweat shirts, baseball caps, area souvenirs, tax and duty-free items, and fine art by local artists.

Bed and Breakfast

VICTORIAN ROSE BED AND BREAKFAST, 1274 Harrison Avenue, Blaine, Washington. The Victorian Rose, a 1905 Queen Anne-style cottage, offers quiet atmosphere and the excellent hospitality of innkeepers Marv and Geri Maddux. Full breakfast with fresh-baked muffins and locally-grown goodies.

Florist

AMUNDSON'S BLAINE FLORAL AND GIFTS
830 Peace Portal Drive
P. O. Box 1715
Blaine, WA 98230
Tel. (206) 332-6700
Hrs: Mon. - Sat.   9:00 a.m. - 5:30 p.m.
         Sunday   12:00 noon - 5:00 p.m.
Closed major holidays.

   Amundson's Blaine Floral and Gifts is a family run business. Sue and Harvey St. Clair bought the shop from an uncle, the original owner, and they are assisted by daughters Betsy and Amee and son Andrew and son-in-law, Troy. What started as a small flower shop some years ago has evolved into a large shop offering flowers, gifts, garden supplies and a nursery. The minute you enter the shop you know you are not in a typical florist shop. The shop is huge, with a tremendous diversity of merchandise for your browsing pleasure.
   There are lovely floral bouquets and arrangements, green and blooming plants, superbly designed European gardens, and beautiful silk flowers and arrangements. At the back of the store is the Cottage Room which is a complete crafts shop with Christmas items available year around. There is an amazing assortment of baskets, ribbons of all sizes, colors and patterns, Bradley Porcelain Dolls and plush stuffed animals by Gund, Kamar, and Dakin. Sue and Harvey are distributors of Jodi Bergsma's prints. There is a lovely section of oriental giftware and, of course, everything you need for gardening is available, along with bushes, trees, shrubs, and bedding plants in season.
   Let Sue, Harvey, Betsy, Amee, Andrew and Troy show you why Amundson's Blaine Floral and Gifts is one of the most unusual flower shops you'll ever visit. Plan to spend time browsing and enjoy the friendly service and quality products provided in this wonderfully creative shop.

Gift Shop

   BLAIR GRAPHICS, 810 Peace Portal Drive, Blaine, WA. Offering custom T-shirts, sweat shirts, baseball caps, area souvenirs, fine art pieces by local artists and tax/duty free items.

FORGET-ME-NOT GIFT SHOP
245 "H" Street
P.O. Box 3229
Blaine, WA 98230
Tel. (206) 332-5559
Hrs: Mon. - Sat. 10:00 - 5:30
Visa, MasterCard and AMEX are accepted.

Theo Hull and Norma Jean Bakarich, sisters who grew up in Blaine, returned there in 1979 and opened the Forget-Me-Not Gift Shop. They have recently remodeled the store and offer some of the nicest quality gifts you'll find anywhere. There's something for everyone at prices that fit every pocketbook.

Theo and Norma Jean have a delightful collection of musical gifts, including music boxes, musical picture frames, and even musical key chains. Among the favorite items in the shop are the beautiful David Winter Cottages, exquisite miniature sculptures of England's rich and quaint architectural heritage. There are beautiful oil lamps, paper weights, ornaments and vases made from Mt. St. Helen's ash glass. The vases and glass gifts have been selected for uniqueness and beauty and are a lovely accent to any home. The "Blaine or Washington Raindrops" glass ornaments made by Don Douglass are lovely and you'll want to own one. There is a selection of fine wood items, including Myrtlewood pieces and walnut desk accessories by Lasercraft. For the charm of the country look, there are wall hangings and decorator items for every room in the house.

Browsing in the Forget-Me-Not Gift Shop is a delightful experience. The selection of unique and charming gifts will captivate you, and the friendly service and atmosphere will make your shopping expedition memorable.

Resort

INN AT SEMIAHMOO, 9565 Semiahmoo Parkway, Blaine, WA. The newest luxury resort hotel in the Pacific Northwest. Enjoy the Arnold Palmer-designed golf course, tennis, sailing, health club and marina.

Deming

Accommodations

LOGS AT CANYON CREEK, 9002 Mount Baker Highway, Deming, Washington. Modern log cabins with stone fireplaces, two bedrooms, bath with shower, and fully-equipped electric kitchen. A beautiful wilderness setting.

Restaurant

CAROL'S COFFEE CUP
5415 Mount Baker Highway
Deming, WA 98244
Tel. (206) 592-5641
Hrs: Mon. - Sun. 5:30 a.m. to 8:30 p.m.
Closed Christmas, New Years and Thanksgiving.
Major credit cards and in-state personal checks are accepted.

A place where pancakes come a foot in diameter and cinnamon rolls reach a height of four inches is a place that measures up to your healthy appetite. That's Carol's Coffee Cup where the servings are generous enough for local loggers and the tastes are refined to please visiting dignitaries.

Carol's is a few miles east of tiny Deming, but that hasn't stopped a world wide clientele from frequenting this coffee shop that offers both hearty breakfasts and hefty lunches. Dinners range from steaks, hot beef sandwiches to the favored roast turkey dinner. If you drop in on the weekends, you'll enjoy fish and chips made from fresh fish.

This is a "Best Choice" for generous portions, friendly service in an old fashioned cafe atmosphere.

(See special invitation in the Appendix.)

INNISFREE RESTAURANT, 9393 Mount Baker Highway, Deming, Washington. Committed to the freshest ingredients, the restaurant grows its own produce or buys from other small, local organic growers. Meals are outstanding; service and setting is superb.

Tavern

THE DEMING TAVERN
P.O. Box 267
Deming, WA
Next to the Deming Post Office.
Tel. (206) 592-5282
Hrs: Mon.-Fri. 12:00 noon - 12:00 midnight
     Sat. - Sun. 12:00 noon - 2:00 a.m.
Closed Easter, Thanksgiving, Christmas Eve and Christmas Day.

If the best things in life are free, you might get one of the best steaks of your life at the Deming Tavern. You say, "what's the catch?"
Oh nothing much, just eat the entire steak and the dinner it comes with in thirty minutes. But be warned, its called the Paul Bunyan, weighs seventy-two ounces and comes with salad, spaghetti, baked potato and toast. So far, in its sixty years of service, no one has eaten the Deming Tavern out of business. The restaurant has built a reputation for juicy steaks and an ambiance that appeals to loggers, farmers, suburbanites and assorted professionals. As a matter of fact, it has also become a favorite for visiting diplomats who want to experience real Americana.
Owner Kirk Lyon says the Deming Tavern is truly "the hub of the world. So whether you are just a cog, or a big wheel, the Deming Tavern is a "Best Choice" for hearty appetites.

Wine

MOUNT BAKER VINEYARDS
4298 Mount Baker Highway
Deming, WA 98244
Tel. (206) 592-2300
Hrs: Wed. - Sunday 11:00 a.m. - 5:00 p.m.
Open weekends only January-March. Closed Christmas
and Thanksgiving
Visa and MasterCard are accepted.

When the Greek wine god Dionysious taught the world to make wine, the world would have to wait to taste wine produced with classic wine making techniques and modern equipment from grapes grown in the Noosack Valley.
The Mount Baker Vineyards, just west of Deming, is the place for sampling vintage wine and a perennial view. It is one of the few true vineyard wineries in the state. In a large airy tasting room you'll sample such varietal

wines as Gewurztraminer and Chardonnay. Madeline Angevine, a delicate refreshing wine with distinct aroma and flavor has really made a mark on dinner tables and fine restaurants. Ten years of research and evaluation of over 100 wild cherry plum trees of the region has resulted in the winery's popular plum wine.

If you agree that this is wine fit for a god, you can take home a bottle, or case of your favorite variety from this "Best Choice" winery - Mount Baker Vineyards.

Ferndale

Ferndale began in 1872 as the site of a school house situated amid ferns under a grove of trees. Today it has about 4,400 residents and is one of the fastest growing communities in Whatcom County.

For years lumbering, fishing and agricultural pursuits were the industry in this quaint town. Today agriculture continues to be important, but so too are the Arco and Mobil Oil Refineries and the Intalco Aluminum Corporation; who have found an advantage in Ferndale's close proximity to the deep waters of the Georgia Strait.

Intalco has located its reduction plant next to Mobil, bringing in bauxite by the shipload for processing with hydropower generated from the water coming off the Cascades. All three plants are west of town on Mountain View Road, allowing the old farm community to retain its charm on the banks of the Nooksack River.

Attractions

Tennant Lake Natural History Interpretive Center offers displays of the seasons, a nature walk and a boardwalk trail around the bog. The Center is open Friday, Saturday and Sunday; the grounds are open daily. Phone 733-2900.

Hovander Homestead, built in 1903, is a restored home which is now part of a large 500 acre park that encompasses a barn, milkhouse, children's farm zoo, gardens and picnic sites. Stroll along the Nooksack River trails; it's all adjacent to the Tennant Lake Natural History Interpretive Center.

The home and barns are furnished as they might have been in the early 1900s. The grounds are open daily; the home is open from Wednesday to Sunday, Memorial Day to Labor Day. Phone 384-3444.

During mid-July the Hovander Homestead is host to the **Annual Folkdance Festival & Arts and Crafts Fair.**

Pioneer Park, on First Avenue two blocks south of Main Street, is a collection of log cabins and other buildings of the pioneers. Each was disassembled and moved, then restored in the park where the Old Settler's Association has met annually since 1895. Now under care of the city, the park was created in 1901. The association began moving old buildings here for preservation in the 1930s and now has seven structures on display. Open daily.

Bed and Breakfast

ANDERSON HOUSE BED AND BREAKFAST
2140 Main Street
P. O. Box 1547
Ferndale, WA 98248
Tel. (206) 384-3450
MasterCard, Visa and personal checks are accepted.

"The best croquet in the county" is only one in a litany of compelling reasons to visit Anderson House Bed & Breakfast. The beautifully restored 1897 home overlooks such panoramas as Mt. Baker, Ferndale and the San Juan Islands, and is only minutes away from downtown Vancouver, BC.

Amenities include elegant touches like "a nice glass of sherry" in the evenings and, in the summer, the six beautifully appointed guest rooms are regularly decorated with roses from owners Dave and Kelly Anderson's rose garden. To top it off, within a few blocks is a cross-cultural selection of no less than six restaurants ready for your culinary exploration.

Get your vacation off to a great start. Visit Anderson House Bed and Breakfast and let Dave and Kelly spoil you!

Lummi Island

Accommodations

THE WILLOWS INN, 2579 West Shore, Lummi Island, Washington. Beautifully-restored country inn : four guest rooms, three baths, water views, beach access.

Lynden

Nooksack River provides the setting for this farming community first visited by prospectors on their way north to the Fraser River gold fields. A cabin appeared in 1860, its occupants Phoebe and Holden Judson. She named the town for a line in a poem by Thomas Campbell, changing the poet's linden tree to a lynden because she liked the way the word looked in written form. About 4,400 people live here today, far less than the 1900s when an estimated 110 mills in the area were turning out shingles.

Modern Lynden is at the heart of northern Whatcom's farm area. Dutch settlers put a stamp on the town. Darigold, the dairymen's cooperative, runs the largest powdered milk plant in the country here. Poultry production has been a part of the local farm scene for decades. Commercial bulb growers turn fields into a pallet of colors each spring, now part of the annual Dutch Tulip Celebration. Farmers credit the long daylight hours during warm summer months with helping to produce specialty crops such as berries which have a wide reputation.

Attractions

Pioneer Museum, 217 West Front Street, has a collection of equipment and autos from early in this century, plus some buggies and rolling stock of earlier eras. Open Monday through Saturday from June through September, and the balance of the year from Thursday through Saturday, 8:00 a.m. to 4:30 p.m. Telephone (206) 354-3675.

Berthusen Park, on Badger Road off Highway 539 west of Lynden, is an old homestead with an exhibit barn. This is the site, each August, of an antique tractor and machinery show. Some of the equipment may remain here on display during the rest of the year. Also on display at Hans Berthusen's barn are old boats and sleds. He built the barn in 1913. Open Thursday through Saturday from 8:00 a.m. to dusk. Telephone (206) 354-3754.

Edaleen Dairy Products, 9593 Guide Meridian, is open to public visits from 8:00 a.m. to 6:00 p.m. daily. Special times include milking at 8:00 a.m., ice cream processing Monday through Thursday after 2:00 p.m.

The **Peter Van Dyk Farm**, 1450 Van Dyk Road, is open to the public. Call 354-2052 to make arrangements.

For further information, contact the **Lynden Chamber of Commerce**, Box 647, Lynden WA 98264. Telephone (206) 354-5995.

Art Gallery

EARTH, WIND AND RAIN GALLERY
Delft Square
444 Front Street #104
Lynden, WA 98264
Tel. (206) 354-3451
Hrs: Mon. - Sat. 9:00 a.m. - 5:30 p.m.
Visa and MasterCard are accepted

The Earth, Wind and Rain Gallery is located on the lower level of the beautifully renovated Delft Building in downtown Lynden. This is an excellent place to find the work of Northwest artisans. Before opening their gallery in 1983, owners Bette and Brian Vander Haak visited numerous galleries from Bellingham to San Francisco to help them find and display the best art from Northwest artists.

The gallery displays many original and limited edition prints, all tending toward natural scenes with some "mild" abstract pieces interspersed. There is nearly every media represented, including oils, water colors, hand colored prints, lithographs and pen and ink. The pottery featured by the gallery is predominantly functional, with some tending to the more whimsical. A delicate oriental flair is represented by other pieces. Bette and Brian are always adding new potters for variety. There is work by local woodworkers, cards made by local artists and even hand-dipped candles.

Bette and Brian sponsor art competitions and shows on several occasions throughout the year. They also offer framing at reasonable prices. The Earth, Wind and Rain Gallery is the place to go for unique and original Northwest art.

Attraction

LYNDEN DUTCH VILLAGE
655 Front Street
Lynden, WA 98264
Tel. (206) 354-4440
Call for hours.

The huge windmill dominating the Lynden skyline beckons visitors to the new Lynden Dutch Village. Stepping into the village is like stepping into

Holland. Owners Jim and Carolyn spent considerable time in Holland photographing and studying Dutch architecture to make their village as authentic as possible. There are fine retail shops opening onto a canal. The canal can be crossed by any one of three authentic bridges. All of the merchants in the shops wear Dutch costumes to enhance the illusion that you are visiting Holland.

There is a theater-auditorium which features daily shows, including Dutch dancing. The retail shops include a large antique mall, Amsterdam sidewalk cafe and old time photo studio among others. The windmill, which is over seventy feet tall, contains an eight room bed and breakfast. Four of the rooms are within the windmill and take advantage of the marvelous view.

For a wonderful taste of Holland a visit to the Lynden Dutch Village is a must. As you browse at leisure through the many delightful shops and soak up the Old World atmosphere, you'll agree that this is a "Best Choice" for enjoyment.

Bed and Breakfast

LE COCQ HOUSE BED AND BREAKFAST
719 W Edson Street
Lynden, WA 98264
Tel. (206) 354-3032
Visa, MasterCard and personal checks are accepted.

The LeCocq House Bed and Breakfast is located in the predominantly Dutch village of Lynden. It sits on a half acre of landscaped grounds, in the midst of manicured lawns and well kept homes and is less than a ten minute walk from the heart of the shopping district. Innkeepers Bonnie and Bob Sunday thoroughly spoil their guests with their hospitality and hearty country style breakfast which sometimes features their famous Dutch Baby, a baked pancake with strawberries and whipped cream.

LeCocq House offers four rooms for guests and evenings can be spent in the comfortable den where there is conversation, games, television and a large selection of books. The Rustic Pine room holds one to four people and shares a bath, the Rose Room has room for two people and the adjoining Rosebud Room one, with shared bath, the Sunrise room accommodates one or two people and has a private bath and the Queen Room, with a queen-sized bed and private bath is perfect for one or two people.

For a serene, relaxing, cozy stay with great hospitality and super food located in the heart of Western Washington, don't miss the LeCocq House Bed and Breakfast.

Bakery

LYNDEN DUTCH BAKERY
421 W. Front Street
Lynden, WA 98264
Tel.   (206)   354-3911
Hrs: Monday   8:30 a.m. - 4:00 p.m.
          Tue. - Sat.   8:00 a.m. - 6:00 p.m.
No credit cards accepted

Before establishing the Lynden Dutch Bakery, owners Jim and Carolyn Wynstra spent time in Holland studying the architecture in order to bring a real taste of Holland to Lynden. The authentic facade of the building includes the hooks to raise furniture to the upper floors, as found in Holland. Since opening the bakery in 1986 the Wynstras have developed quite a following of those eager for their fabulous bakery items.

The aroma of fresh baked pastries and breads greets you even before you enter the bakery. Everything is baked fresh daily and the display cases are full of tarts, cream puffs and other tempting goodies. A specialty is "shingle bolts", although you may think of them as maple bars. They come in three sizes, and when you visit, be sure to ask for the story behind them. Among the special cakes offered is the wonderful Dutch Mocha Cake, a sponge cake with cream filling and mocha frosting. Each day a different variety of bread is featured, including Swedish Rye, Old World Rye, Seven Grain and more. They are all delicious and you'll want to visit daily so you can try them all.

The Lynden Bakery will tempt you as you walk by. Give in to temptation and sample any of their wonderful pastries, cakes and breads. You won't be sorry!

Whatcom County

Whether you decide to rough it at the campground or stay at one of the village's bed and breakfast inns, this Dutch date will make you want to tap dance. Wooden shoes aren't recommended.

A DUTCH DATE			
	KOA Campground	Best Camping	Lyn/Camp
a.m.	Dutch Mothers Rest.	Best breakfast	Lyn/Restaurant
a.m.	Dutch Village	Best shopping	Lyn/Attraction
p.m.	Lunch Bucket	Best lunch	Lyn/Restaurant
p.m.	Dutch Bakery	Best baked goods	Lyn/Bakery
p.m.	Earth, Wind And Rain	Best art	Lyn/Art

Campsite

LYNDEN KOA CAMPGROUND
8717 Line Road
Lynden, WA 98264
Tel. (206) 354-4772
Hrs: Full service March I to November I.
Limited service remainder of the year.
Visa and MasterCard are accepted.

Just outside of Lynden in a beautiful pastoral setting with lots of trees is the Lynden KOA Campground. Owners Dan, Shirley and Marty Martin, have dedicated themselves to making camper's visits pleasant, relaxing and memorable. Many guests stay weeks or months to take full advantage of the setting and the service.

The campground has more than 100 sites for RVs, as well as a tent camping area. There are some lovely, quiet wooded sites. There are two lakes stocked with trout and paddle boats are available for rent to leisurely explore the lakes. Swimming is restricted to the large swimming pool. There is an eighteen hole miniature golf course and a fine eighteen hole golf course is only a few miles away. There is a lodge with a well stocked convenience store and a gift shop featuring handmade country crafts. The Basement Deli offers tasty food for breakfast and lunch, including homemade pies and cakes and an ice cream parlor.

The Lynden KOA Campground is a good headquarters for exploring Whatcom and Skagit counties or even Canada which is just five miles away.

Shirley, Dan, and Marty will do their best to make your stay as memorable and relaxing as possible.

Gift Shop

LANDLUBBER GIFT SHOP, 1812 Eighteenth Street, Lynden, Washington. The shop features folk art, antiques, painted country furniture, country baskets, rag rugs, country lamps, throws and pillows, plus an espresso bar and more.

Restaurant

DUTCH MOTHERS RESTAURANT
405 Front Street
Lynden, WA 98264
Tel.   (206)   354-2174
Hrs: Mon. - Thu.   6:30 a.m. - 9:00 p.m.
       Fri. - Sat.   6:30 a.m. - 10:00 p.m.

Five years ago Lynden natives Jim and Carolyn Wynstra opened the Dutch Mothers Restaurant to emphasize the Dutch heritage of their home town. The Bloemen Kamer - flower room features a cheery atmosphere highlighted by plants and flowers beneath a skylight. The Theologie Kamer - theology room features pictures of early Dutch reformed pastors of Lynden and Dutch masters prints. The Borderij - farm room is furnished in rough a barn board motif and features scenes from the local community and Holland.

Chef Dini Mollink was in the restaurant business in Holland before coming to Dutch Mothers a few years ago. She produces fabulous Dutch dinners and buffets featuring such selections as Hutspot Met Worst and Krenten Bollen Met Erwten Soep - homemade raisin bun with ham and Dutch cheese and pea soup. In addition to the Dutch choices there are seafood, burgers, deli sandwiches and salads.

You can anticipate generous and delicious fare at the Dutch Mothers Restaurant for breakfast, lunch and dinner. This is a wonderful place to savor the flavor of Dutch tradition in a quiet, unhurried atmosphere.

Whatcom County

THE LUNCH BUCKET
880 E Pole Road
Lynden, WA 98264
Tel. (206) 354-3360
Hrs: Mon. - Fri.   6:00 a.m. - 8:00 p.m.
　　　Sat. - Sun.   6:30 a.m. - 8:00 p.m.
Closed Thanksgiving and Christmas
Visa and MasterCard accepted.

　　　The Lunch Bucket is located a few miles south of Lynden at the corner of Hanegan and Pole Roads and offers family dining for breakfast, lunch and dinner. Owned by Marinus Lagerwey and managed by Joyce Budde, The Lunch Bucket's charming surroundings were creatively done using weather seasoned old barn wood. Joyce and her staff provide delicious fare and friendly service.
　　　Breakfasts range from the hearty Country Breakfast - eggs, ham, bacon, or sausage, hash browns, toast or biscuit to three egg omelettes. Create your own meal from the list of side orders. The lunch selections includes a full menu of soups, salads, deli sandwiches, burgers and chicken. There is a children's menu for the peanut-butter and jelly set. Dinner offers a good variety, including chicken, roast beef, veal and seafood. They have fountain selections to top off your meal or enjoy a piece of extraordinarily delicious home made pie.
　　　The food at The Lunch Bucket is well prepared and hearty, with generous portions. The friendly service and delicious meals make this a fine choice for family dining.

VILLA GIULIO RISTORANTE ITALIANO
19721-64th Avenue West
Lynnwood, WA. 98036
Tel. (206) 774-2186
Hrs: Tues.-Fri.   11:00 a.m.-2:00 p.m.
　　　　　　　　5:00 p.m.-10:00 p.m.
　　　Sat.-Sun.   5:00 p.m.-10:00 p.m.

　　　Upon entering Villa Giulio Ristorante Italiano you will see a beautiful Italian flag on the wall. The tone of Italian atmosphere is set with white walls, lattice work, green tablecloths, and red carpet. Owner Giulo Pellegrini's wife, Janie, has created a lush, romantic atmosphere with a splendid array of green plants.
　　　Before opening the restaurant in November 1985, Guilo had been cooking for 21 years and owned other restaurants for more than 15 years. He prides himself in making everything from scratch. The pasta, desserts, and

spumoni are freshly made on the premises. You can watch pizza dough being tossed, too. Family recipes are used as are the spices his mother sends from Italy.

Select a delicious appetizer such as calamari or mussels cooked in basil, garlic, and wine sauce. The main courses include fresh seafood, chicken, or veal. A fine collection of wine is offered. The staff will spoil you with superb service. Bring your family and enjoy the food and moderate prices.

Point Roberts

This 149-square mile peninsula bulges with summer visitors each year, swelling the permanent population of 1,500 to an estimated 3,900 who flock to vacation homes and camp grounds. The point was charted in 1791. By the stroke of a treaty-maker's pen, the international boundary cut across the peninsula in 1846 leaving the south area to Oregon Territory, the north to Canada's British Columbia.

To reach the point, cross the international border taking Highway 99 north, then turn west following signs to Ladner and Tsawwassen. The road continues south back over the border on Point Roberts.

Attractions

On the west shore of the Strait of Georgia is **boundary marker number one** for the line which runs on maps and the ground from here east separating Canada and the United States. To the west, the boundary was set by international arbitration to separate the San Juan Islands from Canada's Vancouver Island (see San Juan County listing). **Monument Park** is at Roosevelt Road and Marine Drive.

Lighthouse Marine Park, at the tip of the point, includes the only surviving surveyor's monument from an earlier American survey of Washington and Idaho's northern limits. The lighthouse built in 1910 was declared surplus in 1971 and turned into a county park for day use. There are some places for overnight parking of recreational vehicles. Fishermen trolling off the point have taken record salmon. Telephone (604) 945-4911.

A small marina with boat sales and moorage, is located at the foot of Tyee Drive, the road leading south from the border crossing station. There is a U.S. Customs office for first entry of vessels coming to U.S. waters. Telephone (206) 945-2255.

Sumas

North of Lynden is Sumas, the alternate international border crossing and a town of 700 which like Lynden is a trade area for surrounding farms. The Indian trail which led from Birch Bay through Lynden went north through Sumas Valley and was the route of those 1858 miners going to Fraser River gold fields.

Restaurant

LONE JACK SALOON
115 1st Street
Sumas, WA 98295
Tel. (206) 988-0403
Hrs: Mon. - Sun. 10:00 a.m. - 2:00 a.m.
MasterCard and Visa are accepted.

In the old boom days of the Whatcom County gold rush a man named Jack built an opera house the best sophisticated money could buy.

Sophistication was short lived, but the opera house turned saloon remains to serve as the best place to whoop it up in Sumas. On weekend nights the Lone Jack is full to the rafters. It seats more than 400 for dinner, that's just two thirds of the entire population of the town. The Lone Jack is basically a "steak and potatoes" house with superb charbroiled steaks and prime rib at reasonable prices. The menu offers seafood including steak and lobster, as well as chicken and pork dishes.

In short, the Lone Jack Saloon serves great meals in an atmosphere best described as a "happening." The mixture of guests and the saloon makes for pleasant and memorial evenings. Yahoo!

APPENDIX

You are cordially invited to The Pleasant Beach Grill and Oyster House, 4738 Lynwood Center Road, Bainbridge, WA to receive a complimentary entree worth $9.95 with the purchase of another entree.

You are cordially invited to Days Gone Bye Antique Mall, 2209 N.E. Bel-Red Road, Bellevue, WA. to receive a free bottle of furniture polish.

You are cordially invited to BIRTHDAYS!, 15171 NE 24th, Bellevue, WA to receive 10% off any purchase of $20.00 or more. Sorry, not valid on wines or sale items.

You are cordially invited to.NGELO'S RISTORANTE, 1830 130th Avenue, N.E. Bellevue Receive one free dessert for parties up to four. Not valid with any other promotion. Valid through 1989.

You are cordially invited to.NEPTUNE'S, Crossroads Mall, 15600 N. E. 8th, Bellevue. Present coupon for a 10% discount on any product in the store. (Valid through 1989)

You are cordially invited to The Pumphouse, 11802 NE 8th, Bellevue, WA to receive a free non-alcoholic beverage with your purchase of a meal. Offer good thru 1989.

You are cordially invited to Indian Street Pottery, 1309 Bellingham, WA to receive 10% off your purchase with this coupon. Offer valid through 1989.

You are cordially invited to Remlinger Farms, P. O. Box 177, Carnation, WA for a free package of soup or popcorn with any $5.00 purchase. Offer good through 1989.

You are cordially invited to The Female Connection, 60 NW Boistford Plaza, Chehalis, WA to receive 10% off anything in the store. Offer good through June 14, 1989, not valid with any other offer.

You are cordially invited to Carol's Coffee Cup, 4415 Mount Baker Highway, Deming, WA to receive free coffee with any meal.

You are cordially invited to The Weed Lady, 122 Fourth Street South, Edmonds, WA to recieve one free bunch of wild baby's breath.

You are cordially invited to Sailor's Restaurant, 190 W Dayton, Edmonds, WA to recieve $5 off dinner for two from the weekly fresh features.

You are cordially invited to Golfun, 31531 First Avenue South, Federal Way, WA for one free round of Golfun for one paid round. Offer valid through 1988.

You are cordially invited to the Front Street Workout and Nautilus, 485 Front Street N, Issaquah, WA to receive 3 free aerobic and/or Nautilus workouts. Valid through January 1, 1988.

You are cordially invited to Prize Catch, 109 North First Street, LaConner, WA to receive one free package of smoked oysters with each gift carton purchased.

You are cordially invited to Best Western Motor Inn, 300 W College Way, Mt. Vernon, WA to receive 10% off the cost of a room. Offer valid through 1989.

You are cordially invited to.The Downey House Bed & Breakfast, 1880 Chilberg Road, Mount Vernon, to receive a 10% discount for a two-night stay November through January. (Valid thru 1989)

You are cordially invited to.THE BRITISH PANTRY, LTD., 8125 161st Avenue, N.E., Redmond. Receive a free cup of tea while you browse or dine. Valid thru 1989.

You are cordially invited to.REVEL CAFE, 2424 148th Avenue N.E., Redmond. Receive one menu item free with the purchase of one item of equal or greater value. (Valid thru 1989)

You are cordially invited to Dunville Gallery, 9025 35th Avenue SW, located in West Seattle, to receive a 10% discount off of any purchase. Not valid on sale price merchandise. Offer good thru 1988.

You are invited to The Pike Place Bakery, 1501 Pike Place, Seattle, WA or Cake Master Bakery, Renton Center, Renton, WA to enjoy a free Texas cinnamon roll. Offer good thru 1989.

You are cordially invited to Old World Fudge, 1530 Post Alley, Seattle, WA or 197 Gilman Boulevard, Issaquah, WA to receive one quarter pound of fudge free with the purchase of any one pound of fudge.

You are cordially invited to The Shy Giant, 1500 Pike Place Market #16, Seattle, WA to receive a complimentary frozen yogurt or dessert.

You are cordially invited to Sur La Table, 84 Pine Street, Seattle, WA to receive a $1 discount on your purchase of a string bag. Offer good through 1989.

You are cordially invited to.Tubs, 50th & Roosevelt Way N.E., Seattle, to receive $3.00 off when you bring a friend.

You are cordially invited to Harveys Airfield, 9900 Airport Way, Snohomish, WA to enjoy a complimentary appetizer with dinner after 5:00 p.m. Valid through 1989.

You are cordially invited to Mt. Si Golf Course, 9010 Meadowbrood-North Bend Road Southeast, Snoqualmie, WA to golf two eighteen hole games for the price of one. Not valid during tournaments, weekends or holidays. Offer good thru 1989.

You are cordially invited to The Bavarian Restaurant, 204 N K Street, Tacoma, WA to receive a second entree of equal or greater value at 50% off when you purchase a first entree. Offer valid through August, 1988.

You are cordially invited to.The Frazzled Duck, 14473 Woodinville-Redmond Road, Woodinville, to receive $5.00 off any purchase of $15.00 or more. Valid thru 1989.

INDEX

3 CRABS REST...................................17
A CHILD'S PLACE 198
A COOK'S TOUR............................285
ACRES OF CLAMS. 296
ADVENTURE UNLIMITED............236
AFFAIRS OF THE HEART. 32
AIRY GREETINGS..........................181
AL'S BROADWAY DELI 28
ALADDIN'S ANT. MALL 584
ALDERBROOK INN........................383
ALDRICH'S......................................106
ALEX. MCCALLUM TOPPIN........178
ALPENTAL SKI ACRES SNO......191
AMERICAN HEARTH B&B...........410
AMUNDSON'S GIFTS 614
ANACORTES INN 472
ANACORTES MUSEUM................477
ANDERSON HOUSE B & B.........619
ANDY'S TUKWILA STATION 207
ANGELO'S RISTORANTE 136
ANGELO'S RISTORANTE 153
ANGLOMANIA.................................170
ANOTHER ANTIQUE......................541
ANTIQUE BROKERS INT............226
ANTIQUE CONNECTION..............178
ANTIQUE FINDERS 227
ANTIQUE SANDWICH CO. 436
ANTIQUES GALLERY...................227
ANTON'S..418
APPLE A DAY SANDWICH.........46
APPLE INN......................................216
APPLE INN......................................522
ARCHIBALD SISTERS..................561
AREAWAY ANTIQUES, LTD. 228
ARLENE'S MADE-IN-WASH..........7
ARTHURS..80
ARTIST PALETTE GALL. 410
AT'S A PIZZA................................492
ATHLETIC SUPPLY CO. 312
AU GAVROCHE..............................252

AULD HOLLAND INN.....................93
AUSTRIAN DESIGN.......................127
B. J. SQUIDLEY'S.........................395
BACCHUS BY THE BAY............529
BAGELRY, INC. 600
BAINLERIDGE BAKERS..............359
BAKERY COTTAGE REST..........79
BALSANO'S ITALIAN REST.....418
BARKLEY'S OF LaCONNER......493
BASE CAMP, INC........................606
BASKETTA'S RETAIL SHOP....512
BAVARIAN......................................437
BAY AVENUE FISH HOUSE......395
BAYVIEW INN................................349
BAYVIEW MARKETPLACE........560
BEACH BASKET GIFT SHOP...412
BEACH HAVEN RES....................452
BEECH TREE MANOR 217
BEL PIEMONTE REST.................513
BELLEVUE HILTON.......................118
BELLEVUE HOLIDAY INN 119
BELLEVUE RED LION INN........119
BELLINGHAM ANT. MALL..........585
BEN MOORE'S REST...................562
BERRY PATCH...............................360
BEST OF ALL WORLDS............270
BEST REGARDS 271
BEST WEST EXEC. INN............216
BEST WEST WESTGATE 349
BEST WEST. HERIT. INN..........582
BEST WEST. MOTOR INN........497
BIG PEOPLE TOYS......................313
BIRTHDAYS!...................................135
BLACK SWAN................................493
BLAIR GRAPHICS..........................613
BLAIR GRAPHICS,.......................614
BLUE PARROT 271
BOARDING HOUSE......................172
BOAT SHED...................................351
BOB ALSIN ANTIQUES 228
BOB'S BAKERY..............................326
BOEHMS CHOCOLATES.............169

633

BOEING TOUR CENTER 527	CASA DEL SOL............................328
BOMBAY HOUSE 346	CASCADE MOUNTAIN INN........387
BOOK N' BRUSH..........................373	CASONI'S.......................................17
BOOKMARK..................................559	CEDARBROOK HERB FARM......14
BOOMER'S LANDING....................478	CEDARS GOLF CLUB...................23
BOONDOCKS ON COWLITZ........48	CEDARYM B&B.............................196
BOONDOCKS REST. 48	CENTRALIA SQUARE..................369
BOUTIQUE EUROPA....................369	CHAMBERED NAUTILUS...........256
BOWS N' CALICOS 199	CHAMELIANI BOUTIQUE...........430
BRADY'S OYSTER FARM............54	CHAMPION DISPLAY/COST....295
BREAKERS...................................392	CHANNEL HOUSE.......................476
BRENTLEY SOFTPACKS..........607	CHAR'S COVE................................94
BRISTOL HOUSE.........................563	CHATEAU FLORAL......................332
BRITISH PANTRY, LTD. 200	CHATEAU STE. MICHELLE.......341
BROADWAY GALLERY.................45	CHATTERY DOWN 565
BROOKDALE GOLF......................434	CHAUTAUQUA LODGE 393
BROWSERY 318..............................8	CHELSEA STATION B&B INN..257
BUD'S PLACE IN REDMOND 201	CHEZ DOMINIQUE CAFE...........253
BUFFY BUS...................................184	CHIN'S PALACE 336
BUGSY'S..325	CHINA BLUE 101
BURROW'S BAY B & B................476	CHUCKANUT MANOR. 480
C SHOP..611	CITY FLORAL................................528
C'EST CHEESE............................189	CITY PICNICS..............................296
C-FRESH SEA FOOD...................518	CLAM-ITY JANE'S..........................81
CABBAGE PATCH REST/INN.546	CLARK'S ON EDMONDS BAY..514
CAFE EUROPA.............................500	CLIFF HOUSE...............................438
CAFE OLGA..................................456	CLIFF HOUSE...............................600
CALICO CRAFTS..........................373	CLIFFORDS REST. 149
CALICO CUPBOARD 494	CLOVER GOLF.............................353
CAMLIN HTL..................................217	CLUB GREEN MEADOWS 30
CANTERBURY INN 66	COACHMAN INN 582
CAPITOL HILL ANTIQUES.........229	COCUSA MOTEL..........................483
CAPTAIN WHIDBEY INN 87	COFFEEVILLE, U.S.A...................28
CAPTAIN'S NAUTICAL SUP...294	COHASSETT STUDIO GALL....78
CARGO HOLD...............................356	COLLECTOR'S CHOICE II RS...370
CARNATION FARMS 154	COLLECTOR'S CHOICE REST.546
CARNATION GOLF COURSE.....156	COLLECTOR'S GIFT GALL.........30
CARNEGIE'S.................................564	COLLEGE INN 259
CAROL'S COFFEE CUP 616	COLOMBIA WINERY....................145
CAROLYN HARTNESS ART......236	COLONIAL CAFE............................81
CAROLYN STALEY PRINTS....237	COLORS...433
CARRIAGE HOUSE GALL..........229	CONNOISSEUR ANTIQUES.......230

634

COOKIE CAFE	590	DESSERTS, ETC.	167
COPACABANA	298	DEUX AMIS	272
COTTAGE BAKERY/DELI,	394	DIAMOND LIL'S	208
COTTAGE.	412	DIAMOND LIL'S.	172
COUGAR CERAMICS	40	DICK'S FOOD CENTER	71
COUGAR STORE	40	"DIRTY DAVE'S" PIZZA	566
COUGAR-YALE CHAMBER	39	DISCOVERY INN	67
COUNTRY GALLERY	159	DISTINCTIVE DESIGNS	128
COUNTRY KITCHEN STORE	132	DOMANI	138
COUNTRY STORE/FARM	326	DOS PADRES	601
COUNTRY STYLE GIFT SHP.	30	DOUPES GAZEBO ROOM,	391
COUNTRY TOUCH	412	DOWNEY HOUSE B & B	498
COUNTRY VILLAGE	150	DOWNRIGGERS	464
COUNTRYMAN B & B	541	DOWNSTREAM RIVER RUN.	148
COUPEVILLE INN	88	DREES	561
COURTYARD THEAT/REST	514	DRIFTWOOD GIFT SHOP	60
COVE GALLERY	58	DUFFY HOUSE B&B	462
CRACKERJACK CRAFTS	238	DUFFY'S	56
CRACKERS	565	DUGAN'S PIZZA	72
CRAIG'S ICE CREAM	283	DUNGENESS GOLF/REST	15
CRANE GALLERY	238	DUNVILLE GALLERY	239
CREEKSIDE REST	337	DUTCH MOTHERS REST.	625
CROSSING	31	DUTCH TREAT HOUSE	473
CROSSROADS FLORIST	126	DUTCH'S TOKE POINT REST.	400
CRUMPET SHOP	253	DYLAN'S REST..	31
CRUMPET SHOP	266	E. R. ROGERS	421
CRYSTAL MEATS	290	EARTH, WIND & RAIN GALL	621
CRYSTAL MOUNTAIN RES	407	EARTHENWORKS	488
CULPEPPERS	264	EBRU	138
CURRENT	267	EDGEWATER INN MOTEL	393
CUTTY SARK OF BELLEVUE	134	EDGEWATER RESORT	611
D'ANDREA	157	EGBERT'S	273
DAHL HOUSE B&B	372	EL PUERCO LLORON	298
DAN LEVIN ORIGINALS	464	ELEVATED ICE CREAM	106
DAS KRAUT HAUS	137	ELITE HTL	460
DAVID WEATHERFORD	230	ELLE SACS/KILIMANJARO	129
DAVIDSON GALLERIES	239	ELMER FUDGE	124
DAYS GONE BYE ANTIQUES	121	ELMER FUDGE	262
DEE'S CAFE	82	EMMETT WATSON OYSTER	299
DEER HARBOR	451	END OF THE RAINBOW	187
DEL CONTE'S TIMBERLINE	388	ENGINE HOUSE #9	438
DEMING TAVERN	617	ENOTECA	300

ESPECIALLY YOGURT	570
EVERETT PACIFIC HOTEL	526
EXCLUSIVELY NORTHWEST	273
EXECUTIVE INN	426
FAIRHAVEN BOATWORKS	608
FAIRHAVEN REST.	602
FAMOUS KIRKLAND FISH	182
FARMHOUSE INN	500
FEED STORE	173
FEMALE CONNECTION	372
FERRYMAN'S INN	368
FILL YER BELLY DELI	197
FINDERS	190
FINE IMPRESSIONS GALL.	240
FIREWORKS CERAMIC GAL	274
FIRST BANK ANTIQUES	541
FISHERMAN'S COVE	602
FISHERMAN'S REST.	300
FLO'S BUNKA EMBROID.	532
FLOWER STOP	198
FLOWERS, ETC.	47
FLURY/CO.	241
FOLK ART GALL/LA TIENDA	241
FORGET-ME-NOT GIFT	615
FOUNTAIN CAFE	107
FOUR SEASONS OLYMPIC	218
FOX PAW	361
FRAME IT ON BROADWAY	242
FRANCINE SEDERS GALL.	242
FRANCO'S HIDDEN HARBOR	301
FRANKLIN HOUSE GALLERY	102
FRAZZLED DUCK	334
FRENCH CREEK CELLARS	204
FRIDAY HARBOR INN	460
FRONT ST. WORKOUT	171
FRONT STREET CAFE	357
FUJIYA	439
GAINES HALLIDAY ANT.	231
GALLERY B & B	575
GALLERY MARJULI'	69
GALLERY WEST	586
GARDEN PATCH	125
GARDNER'S REST.	567
GASLIGHT INN	257
GENIE'S B&B	258
GEORGE'S BAKERY	192
GER-A-DELI	477
GIFT GALLERY	274
GIFT HAUS	55
GILMAN VILLAGE BOOKS	168
GLASS DESIGN GROUP	199
GLASS RAINBOWS	375
GLASSERIE	595
GLASSHOUSE ART GLASS	280
GLENACRES INN B&B	78
GOLD CREEK FISH FARM	330
GOLD MOUNTAIN GOLF	352
GOLDEN AGE COLLECT.	265
GOLDEN EGG SKI/SPORT	339
GOLDEN GALLERY OF ART	542
GOLDEN HORN	268
GOLDEN PHEASANT	174
GOLDWORKS	172
GOLFUN	164
GOLLYWOBBLER REST.	465
GOOD EARTH POTTERY	597
GOODY'S BY GOLLY	27
GOURMET PANTRY	439
GOVERNOR HOUSE	556
GRAND CENTRAL MERC.	288
GRAPE CHOICE	185
GRASS ROOTS	170
GRASSIS FLOWERS & GIFTS	432
GRAZIE CAFE	440
GREAT WINDS KITE SHOP	289
GRECIAN CORNER	302
GREEN EYE SHADE	105
GREENERY	10
GREENHOUSE	597
GREETINGS	275
GRT. N.W. TRADING	43
GUIDO'S PIZZERIA	296
H&L SPORTING GOODS	534
HAGEMAN ANTIQUES	231

HAGEMAN ANTIQUES	416
HALF SHELL	107
HANSON HOUSE B&B	258
HARBINGER INN	557
HARBOR LANDING REST	72
HARBOR LIGHTS REST	440
HARBOUR HOUSE	7
HARRY O'S	174
HARVEY AIRFIELD	548
HASTINGS HOUSE INN	102
HAUS OF ANTIQUES/TEA	165
HAVILAND WINERY	342
HAWTHORNE HOUSE	441
HEARTS/HOMESPUN	357
HEARTSTRINGS	374
HEIDI'S INN	390
HENRI'S	49
HERBFARM	161
HERITAGE HOUSE	102
HERMIE'S ORIG./ARTISTIC	391
HERON IN LACONNER	485
HERON REACH	587
HIGHLANDER REST.	43
HILTON SEA-TAC	218
HOFFNAGLE'S ICE CREAM	562
HOLIDAY INN / TACOMA	427
HOLIDAY INN OF EVERETT	523
HOLLY HAUS	357
HOLLY'S FINE FLOWERS	104
HONEY CHURCH ARTIQUES	243
HOODSPORT WINERY	382
HOUSE OF VAGABONDS	27
HUMMEL HAVEN BIKE CAMP	449
HYATT SEATTLE	219
IL FIASCO	601
INDIAN STREET POTTERY	598
INN AT SEMIAHMOO	612
INN AT SEMIAHMOO	615
INN DEERING/APARTMENT	103
INNISFREE REST	616
INSIDE STUFF/LAND. REST.	8
IS. INN B&B	325
IS. LODGE/FRIDAY HAR	461
ISLAND MARINER CORP.	608
ISLANDER	77
ISLANDS MOTEL/REST.	474
ISSAQUAH GALLERY	166
IVAR'S CAPTAIN TABLE	302
IVAR'S SALMON HOUSE	303
IZUMI	182
J-S RV REPAIR	517
J. F. HENRY	275
J. M. BIBBS	169
JACOBS LANDING RENT	613
JAMES HOUSE	103
JANSEN FLOWERS/GIFTS	47
JASMINKA	430
JODY BERGSMA GALLERY	586
JOE'S OFF BRDWY. REST	530
JOHN WAYNE MARINA	16
JOYWORKS	542
JUDICIAL ANNEX REST.	441
JUICY FRUITS	68
KAGEDO	232
KASHMIR CUSTOM JEWEL	334
KATY'S INN B & B	489
KAYAK POINT GOLF	550
KEEG'S	268
KEITH'S H'MESTEAD STEAK	193
KEL'S FLOWERS/GIFTS	29
KENMORE AIR HARBOR	313
KENNETH BEHM GALLERIES	123
KEY ANTIQUES	429
KIDDER GAL./AMERIND ART	243
KIKUYA	202
KIMZEY MILLER GALLERY	244
KING'S MOTEL	158
KITCHEN 'N THINGS	286
KITCHEN CUPBOARD	170
KLONDIKE KATE'S	530
KM RANCH.	503
KRESTINE KETCH	411
L'ESCARGOT	515
L. CRESCENT LOG CABIN RES.	9

LA CANTINA - WINE MERCH. ...315	LOWELL'S REST./BAR...............303
LA CANTINA WINE MERCH. 146	LUEPKE FLORIST.......................29
LA CASA VIEJA 603	LUNCH BUCKET 626
LA FAMIGLIA RISTORANTE.....455	LYNCH'S TRADING PORT.........551
LA FONDA MEXICAN REST.......108	LYNDEN DUTCH BAKERY.........623
LA PUSH OCEAN PARK RES. 5	LYNDEN DUTCH VILLAGE.........621
LaCONNER COUNTRY INN.......486	LYNDEN KOA CAMP. 624
LaCONNER GALLERY 488	LYNN MC ALLISTER GAL..........246
LAKESHORE GALLERY...............180	LYTLE HOUSE 63
LAKEWOOD MOTOR INN..........427	M & M RINGS & CRAFTS............529
LAKEWOOD TERRACE................535	M'SIEURS....................................603
LANDING REST 41	M. L. MALLARD LTD. 364
LANDLUBBER GIFT SHOP.........611	MACKAYE HARBOR INN..........449
LANDLUBBER GIFT SHOP.........625	MADE IN WASHINGTON.............276
LARRY CARTER, WOOD............533	MAGNANO FOOD........................291
LE COCQ HOUSE B & B 622	MAINSTAY 510
LE CURTYARD.............................337	MAMA'S MEXICAN KITCHEN....304
LE PETITE MAISON....................567	MANDARIN GARDEN...................175
LE SOMMELIER 315	MANRESA CASTLE......................99
LEE MANN GALLERY..................503	MAPLE VALLEY B&B..................186
LEGACY..244	MAREAN'S BLUE FJORD CA...449
LEGENDS 245	MARGEO'S...................................122
LER MONDS OF RENTON..........208	MARIE'S WILD/WOOLY..............358
LES THERIAULTS........................232	MARINA VILLAGE INN.................524
LIDO'S REST./INN........................109	MARJA'S BOOKS.........................70
LIEU'S...441	MARKET GRAPHICS...................246
LIL JON...139	MARKET SPICE 283
LIL' IODINE'S 71	MARVEL ON MADISON 233
LISA HARRIS GALLERY..............245	MARY KAISER DESIGN CO 105
LITTLE HOUSE.............................326	MARY McCRANK'S 376
LIZZIE'S VICTORIAN INN............103	MATTER DANZ GALLERY..........587
LOBSTER SHOP...........................442	MAYFLOWER PARK HTL 219
LOBSTER SHOP SOUTH...........442	MCBECKLANDS WOMEN'S.......409
LOG CASTLE B&B 90	McCAUSLAND'S/LADY M..........431
LOGAN LOFT................................260	MEADOW PARK GOLF.................535
LOGS AT CANYON CREEK........616	MEANY TOWER HTL....................220
LOLA'S ANTIQUES 45	MELINNA MALANSTUDIO............545
LONE JACK SALOON..................628	MEMORY LANE.............................64
LONE LAKE COTT./BR'KF'ST ...90	MEMORY MALL............................429
LONGVIEW FLORAL 47	MERCER IS. HIDEAWAY..............189
LOST MT. WINERY.........................18	METSKER MAPS 261
LOUIE'S...267	MICHELE LeROUX ANTIQUES...165

MIKE'S PLACE	91
MILTON YORK REST	394
MINGLEMENT	327
MISFIT REST	73
MISTY'S	56
MOLBAK'S	333
MONARCH TRADING CO	519
MORRIS STREET ANT	486
MOUNT BAKER SKI AREA	598
MOUNT BAKER VINEYARD	617
MR. PEEPERS GIFT SHOP	276
MT. SI GOLF COURSE	318
MT. ST. HELENS PARK/GIFTS	38
MUKILTEO CHOP/OYSTERS	539
MURPHY'S CAFE/DELI	453
N. B. NICHOLS/CO.	233
NANCY TEAGUE GALLERY	247
NANCY TEAGUE GALLERY	247
NANTUCKET INN	475
NELSON CRAB INC	401
NENDELS INN	320
NENDELS MOTOR INN	427
NENDELS MOTOR INN	524
NENDELS SEA/TAC	221
NEPTUNE'S	140
NEPTUNE'S CHARTER/GIFT	82
NEUHARTH WINERY	18
NEVILLE'S SHORELINE	413
NEW PEKING REST.	603
NEW WEST PROSPECTING	340
NEWAUKUM VALLEY GOLF	375
NINETY-SIX-3-PCE DUCKS	281
NONPAREIL	277
NORDIC HERITAGE MUSEUM	293
NORDIC INN	53
NORMAN BROOK FARM MILK	318
NORTH GARDEN INN	583
NORTH SHORE GOLF	435
NORTHWEST ART/FRAME	248
NORTHWEST MOTOR INN	415
NORTHWEST MOTOR INN	525
NORWAY KNITS	289
OAK TABLE CAFE	17
OBERG'S RED FLORIST	593
OCEAN CREST INN	65
OCEAN FRONT INN	70
OCEAN SHORES BUREAU	74
OCEAN SHORES INN	67
OGLE'S B&B	353
OLD BROOK INN	476
OLD GLENCOVE HTL	411
OLD HOUSE B&B INN	75
OLD TOWN ANT. MALL	527
OLD WINERY	32
OLD WORLD FUDGE	263
OLDE CENTRAL ANTIQUEs	353
OLYMPIC GAME FARM	13
OLYMPIC LIGHTS B & B	462
OMAR THE WOODCARVER	176
OPAL'S CHATTERBOX	28
ORCAS ART/CAFE OLGA	456
ORCAS HTL	457
ORIENT. STAR VIET. REST	604
ORIGINALS IN GOLD	596
OSTLUND'S PENDLETON SH	431
OWEN'S ANTIQUES	324
OYSTER BAR	480
OYSTER CREEK INN	481
PACIFIC CAFE	605
PACIFIC NORTHWEST SHOP	433
PACIFIC PLAZA HTL	221
PALACE HTL	99
PANACHE	277
PANTAGES CENTRE	444
PAPER DREAMS	594
PAPER MOON CARD SHOP	312
PAPILLON	122
PARK MOTEL	584
PARKER'S REST.	304
PELAYO ANTIQUES	234
PELICAN PETE'S FOOD	531
PELICAN'S WHARF	183
PENINSULA GOLF CLUB	9
PERGOLA WEST GIFT SHOP	278

PERIOD. FURNISHINGS 269	RIVER VALLEY B & B 588
PERIPHERY 355	RIVER'S EDGE CAFE 547
PETERSEN'S B&B 123	ROADHOUSE INN 379
PETITE BOULANGERIE 167	ROCHE HARBOR RES. 467
PETOSA'S FAMILY GROC. 511	ROOF HOUSE 76
PICTURE ATTIC 394	ROSARIO RES./SPA 453
PIKE PLACE BAKERY 254	ROY'S WESTERN BUFFET 57
PIKE PLACE FISH 305	RUMORS 432
PIKE PLACE MARK. CREAM 291	RUSSELL'S BACK ALLEY 111
PILLARS BY THE SEA 89	RUTH E'S 203
PIONEER MAPS 133	SABRINA'S BISTRO 204
PLEASANT BEACH GRILL 347	SAILBOATS UNLIMITED W. 310
PLEASANT RIDGE POT. 499	SAILOR'S REST. 516
POINT BROWN RES. CONDOS .. 68	SALEH AL LAGO 306
POMEROY LIVING HIST. FARM .. 33	SALISH LODGE 317
PORT TOWNSEND BAY CO 110	SALTWATER CAFE 362
POULSBO'S EVERGREEN MT .. 355	SALTY'S ON ALKI 306
PRINTLAND 249	SALVATORE'S ANT. MALL 542
PRIZE CATCH SEA. CO. 495	SAN CARLOS REST. 362
PT CHATHAM PACKING CO 262	SAN JUAN INN B&B 463
PT TOWNSEND ANTIQUES 101	SAN JUAN KAYAK EXP. 466
PUMPHOUSE 141	SAN JUAN SAILING 609
PUTNAM ANTIQUE MALL 330	SANCTUARY REST. 386
QUINTANA ROO 515	SANDPIPER BEACH RES 75
RAFFLES OYSTERS BAY. 350	SANDPIPER REST. 359
RAINBOW INN B & B 490	SARATOGA TRUNK 141
RED BARN ANTIQUES 147	SATSUMA JAPANESE REST. .. 153
RED LION INN 222	SCANDELL'S ICE CREAM 131
RED LION INN AT QUAY 25	SCANDIA GARDENS 358
RED RANCH INN 11	SCANDINAVIAN GIFT SHOP ... 278
REDMOND MOTOR INN 195	SCANDINAVIAN SPECIALTY .. 292
REMLINGER FARMS 155	SCARBOROUGH FAYRE 13
RENTON CENTER SEAF'DS 207	SCHNAUZER B & B 589
RES. AT PORT LUDLOW 96	SEA DRAGON 419
RES. OF THE MOUNTAINS 378	SEA STAR REST. 61
RESIDENCE INN - SEATT. S 222	SEA-FUN GALLERY 390
RESIDENCE INN SEA. EAST 120	SEA. EAST AUTO/TRUCK 194
REVEL CAFE 202	SEASON'S 61
RHODODENDRON CAFE 482	SEASONS MOTEL 378
RICK'S ANTIQUES 541	SEATTLE GARDEN CENTER ... 269
RIFFLESTEINS 209	SEATTLE KNIFE SUPPLY 287
RILEY'S 188	SEATTLE MARRIOTT HTL 223

Name	Page
SEATTLE STYLE REST	517
SHAFER MANSION	260
SHELBURNE INN HTL	397
SHERATON TACOMA HTL	428
SHILO INN	428
SHILO INN HAZEL DELL	26
SHOALWATER REST.	397
SHUMWAY MANSION	180
SHY GIANT	284
SIDNEY ART GALLERY	353
SIDNEY'S	58
SILVER BAY HERB FARM	351
SILVER CLOUD INNS	177
SILVER CLOUD INNS	196
SILVER CLOUD INNS	321
SILVER CLOUD INNS	536
SILVER WILLOW	179
SILVERBOW HONEY CO.	544
SIMPSON AVENUE DELI	54
SINGER GALLERIES	234
SIRRAH COLLECTIBLES	13
SKAGIT BAY BOOKS	490
SKIFF POINT GUEST HSE	346
SKIPPER'S GALLEY	307
SLOCUM'S	479
SMUGGLER'S VILLA RES.	454
SNOHOMISH ICE CREAM	545
SNOHOMISH PUBLIC GOLF	543
SNOHOMISH RIVER QUEEN	549
SNOHOMISH STAR MALL	542
SNOQUALMIE FALLS GOLF	162
SNOQUALMIE WINERY	319
SNOW GOOSE	249
SOFIE'S FLORAL/GIFTS	15
SOLSTICE/WATERFRONT	284
SOMETHING KNITTED	166
SOMETHING OF VALUE	487
SORRENTO HTL	224
SOU'WESTER LODGE	398
SOUND FOOD	329
SPAR CAFE, BAR & CARD	568
SPICY MAMA'S REST/LGE.	31
SPIN-A-YARN	519
SPRINGCREST FARM B & B	589
ST. CHARLES PLACE ANT.	206
STALL IMPORTS	491
STANLEY/SEAFORT'S SAL	443
STARBUCKS COFFEE	264
STARRETT HOUSE INN	100
STATON HILLS WINERY	316
STEVEN'S PASS	185
STIMSON GREEN MANSION	255
STONE PRESS GALLERY	250
STONINGTON GALLERY	250
STOUFFER MADISON HTL	224
STREAMLINER DINER	363
STUDIO FORE	130
STUDIO OUTPOST	400
SUDDEN VALLEY	599
SUNLAND GOLF CLUB	16
SUNNY FARMS COUNTRY ST	14
SUR LA TABLE	287
SWALLOWS NEST	323
SWAN INN	325
SWEET ADDITION	171
T & N ASIA GALLERY	251
TACK SHACK INC.	341
TACOMA HARBOR TOURS	444
TAPPS IS. GOLF	422
TEDDY'S ON ROOSEVELT	314
TEXAS SMOKEHOUSE BBQ	338
THAI KITCHEN	142
THEO'S REST./LOUNGE	31
THREE GIRLS BAKERY	255
THREE SISTERS DELI	360
THUNDERBIRD MOTOR INN	42
TIDE CREATIONS GIFT SHOP	71
TIDES TAVERN	413
TILLINGHAST SEED CO	496
TIMELESS TRAVELER	235
TONY'S COFFEES & TEAS	592
TOP CAT/SEAWAY GIFTS	59
TORERO'SMEXICAN REST	142
TOTEM POLE	31

TOWRY'S Le SNACK CAFE	443
TRADITIONAL PICNICS	279
TRAILS	569
TRIVIA/MORE.	170
TUBS	311
TUDOR INN	7
TURNING POINT	408
TURTLEBACK FARM INN	452
TWELVE BASKETS REST.	143
TWETEN'S LIGHTHOUSE	354
TYEE GOLF COURSE	281
TYEE HOTEL	571
UNDERGROUND SHOP	434
URBAN ONION	569
UWAJIMAYA	293
VAN LIEROP BULB FARM	417
VANCE HTL	225
VANCE TYEE MOTOR INN	557
VANCOUVER FOOD CENTER	29
VELVET GOOSE	160
VICTORIAN ROSE B & B	613
VILLA GIULIO RIST. ITAL	537
VILLA GIULIO RIST. ITAL	626
VILLAGE BOOKS	591
VILLAGE SHOPPE	160
VILLAGE THEATER	169
VINCE'S ITALIAN REST.	308
VISTA COMICS	46
W.B. SCOTTS	413
WAGNER'S EURO. BAKERY	558
WANG'S GARDEN REST	144
WASHINGTON CHEESE	499
WATER ST. DELI/REST	104
WATER STREET DELI-REST	109
WAYSIDE	279
WE HATS	282
WEBSTERS REAL FOOD	309
WEDGWOOD BROILER	309
WEED LADY	512
WEST COAST SEA TAC HTL	225
WEST ISLE AIR, INC.	475
WEST SEATTLE COINS	235
WESTGATE SUITES	350
WILD WINGS GALLERY	251
WILDFLOWER INN	167
WILDFLOWERS	501
WILLOWS INN	619
WIND 'N SAILS	466
WINE SELLER	112
WINNER'S CIRCLE	163
WINNER'S CIRCLE	176
WOOD MERCHANT	491
WOODBOX/GALLERY	7
WOODEN HORSE ANTIQUES	12
WOODEN SPOON	513
WOODINVILLE POTTERY	335
WOODSONG B&B	457
YE OLDE CURIOSITY SHOP	280
YUNG YA	310

ABOUT THE AUTHOR

Eric Larson, a lifelong resident of Washington, of Swedish descent, was raised in Issaquah and graduated from Washington State University.

As such, it's natural that the great outdoors and its recreational offerings have beckoned Eric since early childhood. Washington provides the environs for him to explore windsurfing, camping, hiking and skiing. Great loves, and great pride in his home state brought his skills to bear in bringing this book to fruition.

On a more personal level, his greatest loves and pride would best be exampled in his wife, Kelly and their new baby son, Stefan Andrew.

A young man of vision, formed by his heritage and environs, now moving onward to yet another book...about Washington, of course!

A LETTER TO THE READER:

The staff of Gable & Gray want to take this time to thank you for purchasing this book. We hope the book contributed substantially to your enjoyment of the area.

In our never ending quest to better our product, we ask you, the visitor, to help us....if in your travels you encounter a service or business establishment you feel should be a "Best Choice" then please take the time to drop us a note about them.

If your "Best Choice" is interviewed and selected for our next edition, we will ship you one of our books as our way of saying, "Thank You." Simply choose the book from the list at the front of this book and denote it in your letter.

NOTES:

NOTES:

NOTES:

NOTES: